CAMPUS
TRADITIONS

CAMPUS

Folklore from the Old-Time College to the Modern Mega-University

TRADITIONS

Simon J. Bronner

UNIVERSITY PRESS OF MISSISSIPPI

JACKSON

www.upress.state.ms.us

The University Press of Mississippi is a member of the Association of
American University Presses.

Copyright © 2012 by University Press of Mississippi
All rights reserved
Manufactured in the United States of America

First printing 2012

∞

Library of Congress Cataloging-in-Publication Data

Bronner, Simon J.
Campus traditions : folklore from the old-time college to the modern
mega-university / Simon J. Bronner.
p. cm.
Includes bibliographical references and index.
ISBN 978-1-61703-615-6 (cloth : alk. paper) —
ISBN 978-1-61703-616-3 (pbk. : alk. paper) —
ISBN 978-1-61703-617-0 (ebook)
1. College students—United States. 2. College students—United States—
Social life and customs. 3. College environment—United States.
4. Folklore—United States. I. Title.
LA229.B655 2012
378.1'980973—dc23   2012009070

British Library Cataloging-in-Publication Data available

For Wolfgang Mieder, Proverbial Big Man on Campus

CONTENTS

FIGURES

(All photographs are from author's collection, unless otherwise indicated)

PROLOGUE

"Here's the Syllabus"

BY THE TIME STUDENTS GRADUATE FROM COLLEGE, THEY ACCUMULATE plenty of courses but are not given enough credit for the traditions they bear. Sure, students are usually in college only a few years, and the locations of their education vary widely, but I argue that undergraduates in their hallowed halls, more than in any other place of their scholastic experience, embrace distinctive traditions because campuses constitute transitional spaces and times, precariously between childhood and adulthood, parental and societal authority, home and corporation, and play and work. One might falsely presume that the business of obtaining a degree precludes the handing-down work of tradition, but in fact, I find that campuses are hotbeds of expressive traditions fitting under the rubric of folklore, and even more so, rather than less, as universities have become engines of mass society.

The idea of tradition on campus refers inevitably to connection—to the past, to people, to place—whether this idea comes through in customs known to have been repeatedly enacted or to cultural practices designed to spread across space and maybe recur in the future. In both these cases, collegiate denizens recognize the feature of tradition allowing participants to socialize and feel a part of something larger than themselves. Tradition evokes a feeling of groupness, usually implying cultural work of participants' own making and less than official or corporate involvement. Sure, college authorities often have a hand in organizing campus events, but many, if not most, traditions embraced by students suggest their appropriation of customs or narratives for their own purposes. Often students intend to foster smaller identities within the corporate whole outside of the job of coursework, and even to subvert, transgress, or at least question the organizational control over students. Other consequences of their campus traditions might not be as evident to them— ritualizing coming-of-age, simultaneously separating from and longing for childhood and home left behind, adjusting to place, anticipating an uncertain future, realizing sexual and emotional profiles—but they are important in comprehending the repeated urge to folklorize college campuses by every generation of students.

In this book, I trace historical changes in the traditions of college students, especially as the predominant context has shifted from what I call the "old-time college" marked by its emphasis on its "we-ness" in size and sense of community to mass society's "mega-university," an organizational behemoth that extends beyond the central campus to multiple branches and offshoots throughout a wide region, and sometimes the globe. With the common association people make of folklore to small groups, one might assume that the mega-university has dissolved collegiate traditions and displaced the old-time college, but I find the opposite. Student needs for social belonging in large university centers and a fear of losing personal control have given rise to distinctive forms of lore in the sprawl of the skyscraper mega-university and a striving for retaining the pastoral "campus feel" of the old-time college. What the two types of institutions share in common is a need for social and psychological adaptation for students in transition between one stage and another, usually regarded as the most significant of their lives. In the moderate-size campuses between the two poles, students also share this adaptation and often a balancing act of small college feel with large-scale aspirations. The folkloric material students spout, and sprout, in response to these needs is varied—including speech, song, humor, legendry, ritual, custom, craft, and art—but it is tied together by its invocation of tradition and social purpose. Beneath the veil of play, student participants in campus traditions work through tough issues of their age and environment. They use their lore to suggest ramifications, if not resolution, of these issues for themselves and for their institutions.

Although the college experience of taking courses, getting through exams, and working with institutions is global, sharp cultural differences are evident in national systems. In this book, I focus on the United States because of the immense proportion of the population pursuing postsecondary degrees and the pivotal role of college life in shaping American culture. The American context is important to consider in the development of campus traditions because of the oft-reported lack of ritual passage into adulthood in American society and the varieties of collegiate experience that citizens in the United States expect to access in one way or another, whether as fans, neighbors, employees, or alumni. Another contextual national factor that affects American collegiate folklore is the foundational idea of higher education fostering democracy so basic to the American enterprise—and dream. The social tension in the American system that pervades lore is on the egalitarian, inclusive ideal of an educated, classless citizenry characteristic of democracy coming into conflict with the university's production, indeed encouragement, of an affluent, elite stratum to lead a competitive, hierarchical society.

I began documenting the folklore of American college students during the 1980s and published the results in two editions of *Piled Higher and Deeper*

(1990, 1995). Although the present book contains some of the material found in those editions, the revisions have been more sweeping and warranted retitling as a new work. In addition to reorganizing the sections, I have focused interpretation more on the relation of student life and lore to the campus environment. I also updated the status of student culture with more material on folkloric responses to new technologies, hazing controversies, and economic and political upheavals. I additionally revisited the historic material with more extensive treatments of sports, interclass contests, and the Greek system, and extended my previous social-psychological perspectives on these traditions with the idea of precarious, often paradoxical social "frames" students call upon to perform and empower cultural practices.

Let me take a moment to outline this frame theory at the heart of my interpretations (see Abrahams 1977; Bronner 2010; Goffman 1974; Mechling 1983). The concept is that students imagine boundaries between themselves and other campus interests, and consequently construct or engage with social frames for speech, actions, narratives, and rituals that might not be appropriate in another setting or in everyday practice. The intangible frames for traditional action understood by participants are useful strategies to deal with issues of aging and social connection that cause anxiety or ambivalence and are difficult to broach in everyday conversation. Strict Freudians, and a lot of parents, often assume that youths construct social frames only to channel trouble, but I also see great revelry and joy in student folklore. Sometimes the gaiety is a cover or compensation for inner turmoil (as in the folk saying "laughing to keep from crying"), but it can also be cultural work to express and harbor emotional abundance in socially designated situations. Sometimes the party atmosphere—in the stadium, the tavern, and the dorm—is just that, but it is often linked to a location and the student's stage of life marked by exuberance, emotion, and intensive social needs and desires.

Culturally sanctioned frames often work to contain paradoxes and ambiguities of college experience, and in the process effect symbolic communication (often in metaphoric oppositions, such as setting the free "natural" behavior of sex and defecation against the "artificial" corporate control of the institution) to validate what the framers are doing. Of interest to the analysis of cultural processes in the campus realm is the tendency for messages in the frame to become metacommunicative, that is, turned into commentary on the act of framing rather than the event being framed (Bateson 1955, 1956; Geertz 1972; Mechling 1983, 2008a, 2009). In other words, the lore expressed within the frame leads to commentary embedded in actions on the use of traditions in college. A famous example is Georgetown College's Grubfest, a food fight literally framed by the Quad and separated physically from its picturesque green surroundings by a slimy, muddy area covered with food products. Held early in the academic year shortly after students arrive on campus, the point of this unsightly mess is a defiance of "your mother's admonitions to stop playing with your food" (LeMaster 2005, 82; "Top Ten GC Traditions" 2011). A rite of collegiate separation, and sanctioned mayhem, the coming-of-age tradition points to the significance of another tradition associated with students' world of home and childhood. The compact nature of frames influences the production of symbolism that conveys referential knowledge in condensed form. For Georgetown, much is made of the inversion of the usual conventions of appearance in the crowning of a king and queen who are the dirtiest participants. Then the frame dissolves with a raucous and transformative "Race for the Showers." Students hold, and uphold, Grubfest in esteem as one of the college's "top ten traditions" alongside Songfest, a Christmas custom of Hanging of the Green, and ritual Midnight Brunch during finals (LeMaster 2005, 63; "Top Ten GC Traditions" 2011). The commentary in the form of text and action invites comparative analysis of how and why traditions arise and sometimes get adapted or dislocated. I pull out the messages and rhetorically analyze them as texts of practice within the context of campus life that both reflects and rejects the larger society.

Seeking out processes of inception, adaptation, and variation in myriad framed expressive practices on campus, I extract cognitive sources for the ways people act, or act up. Part of my methodology is to ask students about their motivations for engaging in traditions, but often influences and consequences exist outside of their awareness. Indeed, they may deny sexual, scatological, and other concerns of their life stage and campus context because they expose their vulnerabilities, or the very reason for engaging in some forms of framed play is to disguise, redirect, or morph ambiguities, emotions, and conflicts, especially in relation to life-course and social-relational maturation (Abrahams 2005, 96–110; Bronner 2011a, 196–247; Dundes 1976, 1994a; Freud 1966; Mechling 1980, 1986). In particular, I find that many college traditions as part of human development are not so bizarre, and indeed can be explained, when one recognizes the psychological processes of projecting, transferring, and symbolizing pent-up feelings onto the fictive or ritualistic framing of folklore.

Many of my psychological observations have addressed the symbolic meanings of campus traditions as responses to the peculiarities of students' betwixt and between state. Indeed, many student traditions appear to be condensed enactments of, or allusions to, this position to raise and resolve incongruities, emotions, and anxieties or at least contain them. Building on the observations of Gregory Bateson (1955, 1956, 2000), Sigmund Freud (1930, 1959, 1960, 2003), Arnold Van Gennep (1960), and especially Victor Turner (1967, 1969) for situations far away from campus, I find the "liminality" of this state crucial to the idea of tradition in the college experience. The physical campus often appears neither here nor there, representing a time out of time between childhood and adulthood, and between the past and future. In this state, scholars following Turner point out, symbols proliferate in special events framed as rituals or traditions to dissolve and then reorder reality. The symbols arise to confront the ambiguities inherent in the liminal situation (see Myerhoff 1982; Turner 1967, 93–111; 1969, 95–96). Transformation is therefore implied as one proceeds in and out of liminality by expressive markers such as folklore that participants recognize to externalize, and often play with, their inner concerns. Participants employ a degree of license in these liminal play frames to bend rules and defy norms of reality (see Dundes 1976, 1980, 1987a, 1987b; Mechling 1980, 2009). They also use these events and expressions to scrutinize, and often criticize, their culture, even as they form social attachments and identities based upon it. For my purposes of revealing meanings in the apparently bizarre stories and antics of college life, understanding campus traditions in the context of these frames is more effective for addressing critical issues of age and institutional cultures than, as popular media are often wont to do, dismissing student be-havior simply as boys and girls gone wild or the work of the devil.

Besides getting into the heads of students, I consider a social structural factor in the production of campus life regarding the odd political economies of universities. Consistently since the dawn of the new Republic, American higher education has fused feudal communal and industrial capitalist motives that have generated the subtexts beneath the expressive lore and affected the public perception of college campuses as distinctive, even anomalous or in-congruous cultural spaces. Campuses signal an idealized community inspired by a parcel of nature, but the components of this community struggle to stay in sync. Campuses paradoxically evoke images of pastoral, premodern landscapes along with futuristic buildings housing the latest gadgetry and human artifice. They are supposedly compassionate places where students build social bonds that last a lifetime and at the same time are rule-bound institutions that alleg-edly treat their residents like numbers rather than people. Campuses in the American imagination are environs for extremes of quiet reflection and rau-cous exuberance. These apparently contradictory profiles of the college space as a special location in an upward-aspiring individual's human development and the progressive country's built environment uneasily combine. Conse-quently, the fragile, shifting relationship of the two joined political economies, apparently at odds, command symbolic treatment in a host of ever-renewable jokes, legends, decorations, and customs. The uncertain ground of the campus inevitably produces border and ethical conflict—between the public square and the private worlds of the campus as well as among the camps of students, faculty, and administrators (Bailes 1977). A social landscape that is intrinsically unstable, the university has variously taken roles over time to act as a unifying, mediating organization—especially evident in campus traditions.

In addition to updating sources and adding perspectives with new scholarship taking up the challenge of explaining the outpouring of expressive traditions during the college years, I significantly changed the illustrations in the volume with new archival sources and fieldwork I have undertaken. All this effort has been made to broaden the representation of campus folklore in the twenty-first century as well as to locate more precedents for traditions in the too-quickly forgotten past. As part of identifying cultural processes on campus historically, I take up the question of traditions that have perished as well as those that have endured. Particularly in the chapter on "scraps" and "dinks" but also in sections on legendary locations and courtship rituals, I provide examples to analyze for discontinuity in addition to continuity from the past into the present and what that says about historical and cultural conditions in the legacy of American higher education.

The additional evidence has forced me to reexamine my previous characterizations of student culture and my explanations of the lore it embodies in the American context. My previous assertion that lore represents shifts in student experiences of the emerging, socially constructed period of adolescence and the cultural expectations of institutional life over time still holds, but I have had to adjust my thinking about customs from campus and dorm into cyberspace. Instead of presuming that new media allowing instantaneous global communication apparently free from concerns for place unsettles folklore and renders it obsolete, I find that the Internet and digital technology in collegiate sites and networks extend, and diversify, social identities—and traditions—of students. I locate continuities from American collegiate concerns in the analog days in the new communicative genres emerging on the Web and note that cultural response to anxieties of the age—in human and historical time—weighs heavily on students' minds.

That connecting the customs and lore of college students to a distinctive culture is still news bears out the popular resistance to thinking about academic life in terms other than classroom experience and its career payoff. People are more used to categorizing relatively remote, "othered" groups by language, geography, ethnic and occupational background, or lack of formal education such as Sea Islanders and sailors under folk culture. Like many folklorists, anthropologists, and sociologists concerned with the uncovering of grass-roots traditions, I had my eye as a budding professor away from campus. I had worked with blues singers deep in the heart of the Mississippi Delta, old-time musicians in the northern Appalachians, backwoods craftsmen in Indiana, gritty factory workers in Pennsylvania, Yiddish speakers raised in the Old Country, and Old Order believers in Amish settlements. Returning to the classroom to teach folklore studies, I drove home the point about customs emerging and maintained as a consequence of social interaction by pointing to the slang, stories, and rituals that students year after year repeated—and renewed.

The background of my expedition into the collegiate jungle is in a presentation Stanley Miller, an esteemed historian of education at Penn State, asked me to do comparing "natives" of traditional folk cultures to campus residents. He challenged me to test my assertion that folklore arose in temporary, learned organizations as much as in the cultural eddies of isolated locations that the public often fixates on as quaint, genuine "folk." Years later, "the book" on student traditions arose after my sifting through thousands of surveys, interviews, letters, photographs, artifacts, and publications. At the outset—organizing, referencing, and making sense of the astounding mounds of material—was Alan Mays, as skilled an archivist as one could ever hope for, and now a valued colleague in the library. The reference system he established has served me well over the years. Folkloric texts used in this book come from the surveys unless otherwise indicated.

On the organizational front, I am grateful to Sue Etter and, following her retirement, Jennie Adams, staff assistants in the School of Humanities at Penn State Harrisburg, for maintaining my files and keeping my head on straight. This book could not have been completed without the resources of Penn State's University Archives, and I am grateful to the special assistance of University Archivist Jackie Esposito, and before her, Leon Stout. Patrick Alexander, director of the Pennsylvania State University Press, kick-started the revision project, and Craig Gill at the University Press of Mississippi moved it into high gear. Students are the heart of this undertaking, and I am grateful to all the contributors who sent me their special versions of campus folklore. Deserving acknowledgment are dedicated excavators who dug deeply as Penn State Harrisburg doctoral students to find treasure troves of collegiate lore in person and online: Trevor Blank, Jennifer Dutch, Spencer Green, Amy Milligan, and David Puglia.

I owe many—too many to list here—community relations officers, student activity directors, archivists, historians, and student interns working in colleges across the United States for generously providing me with invaluable sources not available in publications. Professors at the institutions also came through wonderfully with student papers and commentaries. For providing provocative text and essential context about their institutional cultures, I want to especially thank Susan Asbury-Newsome of Berry College; the late Mac Barrick of Shippensburg University; the late Samuel Bayard, Bill Ellis, and Ken Thigpen at Penn State; Dan Ben-Amos of the University of Pennsylvania; Jan Harold Brunvand of the University of Utah; Robert Bethke of the University of

Delaware; Kurt Dewhurst and Marsha MacDowell of Michigan State University; the late Alan Dundes of the University of California at Berkeley; William Ferris of the University of North Carolina; Angus Gillespie of Rutgers University; David Horde of Purdue University; John McDowell and Linda Dégh of Indiana University; Jay Mechling and Patricia Turner of the University of California at Davis; Richard Meyer of Western Oregon University; Wolfgang Mieder of the University of Vermont; Danielle Roemer of Northern Kentucky University; Lonn Taylor of the Smithsonian Institution; Jacqueline Thursby and William "Bert" Wilson of Brigham Young University; Elizabeth Tucker of Binghamton University; and Tok Thompson and Alison Dundes Renteln of the University of Southern California.

Bill Nicolaisen, my first teacher of folklore, had the courage to talk analytically about the culture of college students, and the late Richard Dorson at Indiana University encouraged its serious study. Ronald L. Baker, for many years chair of the English Department at Indiana State University, also heeded Dorson's call and offered groundbreaking folklore collections of his own from Indiana and Illinois toward the understanding of the institutional, work, and play cultures of students. I learned from their work combining approaches of language, history, and society, and additionally from Cathy Baker, who brought a critical perspective from educational psychology to the subject. Many conversations among us, and later with the late Bill McNeil of the Ozark Folk Center, informed, indeed inspired, my writing.

I would also be remiss if I did not credit the other Professor Bronner, my wife, Sally Jo, who from her vantage of teaching undergraduates at Dickinson College and her experience as a student in the United States and Israel provided a comparative outlook that added to my knowledge gained from university teaching in Japan and the Netherlands. My children have contributed a good bit of drama. With this trait, they are well suited for college.

CAMPUS
TRADITIONS

1

GETTING IN

Orientation

"WELCOME TO CAMPUS, SCHOLARS," THE RESIDENT ASSISTANT barked with some sarcasm as I joined the other wide-eyed freshmen during campus orientation in my first dormitory meeting, far from home. Back a few months we celebrated "getting in," but now that we had arrived, uncertainty could be felt about the path ahead.

"You're no longer in high school, you're in college now," this senior student, apparently wise to the ways of higher learning, reminded us, as if we had safely crossed a huge abyss. He wanted to emphasize that being "on campus" was different from anything we had encountered previously.

He continued, "You've come to get your degree, and some of you may even go for the Ph.D." He paused, and his authoritarian air shifted to one more relaxed, as if he were an uncle giving us the lowdown on the rest of the family.

"You know what B.S. stands for, don't you?" Heads turned and glances were exchanged anticipating where he was going with this off-color reference. "M.S. is more of the same, and Ph.D.—well, that's the same thing, just piled higher and deeper."

As the first bit of lore given us on campus about student life, it was no doubt interpreted variously by the new recruits gathered in the lounge that balmy August day. The resident assistant meant it to give us the unofficial, insider's perspective on college and its demands, and to put us at ease with humor. Some folks in the room appreciated the refreshing reminder that the job of being a college student is nothing to be afraid of. For others, it bore the message that if they stumbled through their studies, it was not the end of the world. A few opined that college involved more than getting the degree: it was importantly a social experience. Yet undergirding all these views was the assumption drawn from the lore that degrees, represented by those magic letters, hold power.

I must have heard this bit about degree initials in one form or another hundreds of times in my college years, and I later discovered that others across the country had heard it, too—for generations. Still, if it had been the only bit of lore I recounted, I probably would have thought little about it. I found, though, a long string of college traditions revolving around campus life.

I heard, for example, that a sculpture of Pegasus over the entrance to the Fine Arts Building would fly off if a virgin walked into the building. (The sculpture is still there.) From students elsewhere I heard of columns collapsing, clocks on towers stopping, and statues altering their poses in the unlikely event that an innocent should graduate.

I listened intently as word spread about a popular seer predicting that a mass murder would take place at a college like mine. Curious how the story circulated around *several* campuses in the area just before Halloween, along with stories of lovers' lane murders and roommates done in because they recklessly defied warnings against going out into the scary night.

My ears perked up at stories of straight-A students committing suicide under the pressure of their studies, and of the ghosts of those students returning to warn the living. Questions arose in my mind about why most of these ghosts were women and why campus residences seemed to attract these ghosts more so than in town. If my roommate committed suicide, dorm mates assured me, I could count on a 4.0 grade point average (GPA) for the semester. My student cronies recognized the magic ring of "four" in the number of years to complete the degree and the gradations of teachers (instructors, assistant professor, associate professor, full professor).

In answer to the burning question of whether class would be held if the teacher does not make it to the room on time, I was given the student body rule that once in class, one waited fifteen minutes for a full professor, but only five for an assistant professor and hardly at all for an instructor. Later, as I set off on the trail to graduate school, I heard the business about the degrees and their meaning again, told this time to take a poke at the growth of graduate education everywhere—and to say maybe the paper chase is not so long and hard, if it all amounts to a familiar routine. With stacks of books and papers neatly rising around us, the shared lore led me, and others, to reflect on the distinction of the academic grind and its connection to our later work and life.

It was hard to escape the scatological metaphor of the diploma humor, and sexual or social symbolism in other examples of campus humor, belief, and legendry emanating from hormone-raging, coming-of-age teens adrift in a new place—physically and socially. There appeared to be constantly an opposition in these oft-repeated expressions between "natural" urges of defecation, intercourse, and socializing and the alienating, artificial institution. On the campus where adolescent strangers are brought together by institutions to engage in a competitive, intense experience of passage into a high-stakes adult world of individual independence, is the schoolwork unnaturally anally retentive, as

Freud might say? Is lore able to say some things that we felt uncomfortable blurting out to each other in conversation revealing our vulnerabilities and fears? Was this lore a cultural sign of the esoteric knowledge that identified us as students? In the fun and games of the material, are there serious messages about the negotiation, and transition, being made between our self and the temporary society we found ourselves in?

As background to answer these questions, consider the college years as a distinctly situated time of life. No longer stuck in place attending the local high school, adolescents desire to get into colleges on the basis of location, reputation, offerings, and often the campuses' academic culture. Students view the "college years" of the life course as a time to set one's goals for the future, to develop identity and one's "self," and to connect with a cohort intellectually and romantically. They want to be accepted, first by the university to which they applied, and then socially within campus life. They recognize, and resent, their lack of power in relation to professors and administrators, but they might be emboldened by their quest for knowledge inside hallowed halls and outside the classroom set off on some daring escapades with like-minded explorers.

College as the Time of Your Life

American society cuts campus-bound students some slack during the "college years" of the life course to regress a bit and engage in apparently childish behavior variously referred to in the popular press as mischief, antics, high jinks, and even cultish and dangerous activity. Another way of looking at the "acting-out" on campus is under the broad umbrella of tradition that contextualizes these escapades as part and parcel of social life at college. Socially connective and culturally rooted, tradition frames various activities as play, drama, and ritual that bring to the fore special concerns and roles college students have in their state of betweenness after being home with parents but before venturing out into the "real world."

The conventional mind-set about campus life is that never again in one's lifetime will a person be so free and open to new experience. Yet "being in school" can also bring forth a host of academic anxieties about making decisions such as declaring a major and making connections that will momentarily bring satisfaction and ensure future success. Much as students share concerns with, and loyalties to, their age cohort, they are also aware of competition for grades, pressure to excel, and status envy, particularly for prestigious campus roles and selective groups. Tensions also arise socially as well as academically concerning fitting in to various campus identities in the new unexplored terrain of the college campus and navigating emotional and sexual turfs with love—and hate—interests. Many of the long-standing traditions of college life respond to these anxieties by placing them in a play, dramatic, or narrative frame where they can be confronted—often in symbolic forms—so that others can comment comfortably in a way that would be difficult in everyday conversation or practice.

A large part of American culture involves college traditions, partly because college students abound in the United States and their setting is associated with high spirits exhibited in showy customs, rallies, humor, and speech. At the start of the twenty-first century, the United States boasted more than 4,300 colleges in all, educating over twenty million students. A century earlier, the U.S. Census estimated college enrollment at 238,000; that figure amounted to less than 1 percent of the total population. By the end of the twentieth century, the percentage increased tenfold. With the opening of the twenty-first century, half of all American eighteen- and nineteen-year-olds were in college, a 13 percent rise in thirty years. Despite predictions of college enrollment leveling off because of economic woes or reduced birth rates, the American college student population grew dramatically by 20 percent in the first decade of the twenty-first century. Sixty percent of high school graduates in the United States pursue some form of higher education, although only about half of them tough it out to graduation (Chronicle 2011, 31). This statistic has led some global educators to folklorize (and perhaps sexualize) differences between American institutions as "easy in, hard out" as opposed to the experience in other countries such as Japan and China of "hard in, easy out" (A & A International Education 2008).

Placing college student attendance in an international context, the United States ranks first in the number of students, lapping runner-up India three times. American students are more concentrated into fewer institutions, judging by the larger number of colleges in Mexico and India than in the United States, which ranks third in that category. The United States leads the world in the percentage of its population over twenty-five with postsecondary education overall (46.5 percent), more than double the rates for Sweden, Canada, Japan, and Germany (Kurian 2001, 376–77). The Americanness of colleges today in the United States relates to the perception that going to a university increases opportunities for success no matter one's background, and those chances should be democratically open to all qualified, often set against the notion that being a collegian, particularly at one of the super-selective "Ivies," breeds elitism.

Another international context in the pattern of coming-of-age in the United States contributes to the fascination with, and reliance on, college custom in American lore. Unlike other countries such as Japan, where reaching adulthood is marked by public, agreed-upon rituals, the United States is largely bereft of such conventions, and in fact vagueness exists culturally about when one gains maturity to merit being called an adult. Is it after puberty? Is it after high school? Is it when one gains financial independence from parents? Is it voting age or the legal age to consume alcohol and marry? The public has expectations that the "college years"—especially for undergraduates as they are generally defined between the ages of eighteen and twenty-four—will be a period of serious preparation for a career and lifelong values. Yet allowance is also given for immature playfulness in the presumably sheltered campus environment. The coming-of-age process certainly begins earlier in high school, but the association of college with being an unconventional place "away from home," a distinctive total institutional structure of residence and recreation as well as work, and a special location for intensive self-examination, adds to the notion that campuses should be ritual-filled or transformative sites. Children and parents alike often view being on campus not only as "away" but also "between." That is, the structure of college life into four class stages, from a "fresh" start or birth after high school to a "senior" finish or death and rebirth in the real world, is conspicuously transitional—between home and occupation, childhood and adulthood, parent and self. The sharply framed tradition of this sequenced path simulates a life journey in condensed form. Along the way, customs invoke the power of tradition to compel participation in initiatory activity that demarcates maturation and transformation.

Although the growing number of older students since the twentieth century threatens to upset the correlation of college with a coming-of-age experience, the majority of undergraduates are still between the ages of eighteen and twenty-four (Chronicle 2011, 31). Though more part-time students in the twenty-first century enroll in college than did in the twentieth century, most college students attend college full-time. Over 75 percent of the total college student population flocks to public institutions, which puts them smack in the middle of public discourse on the role of, and support for, American higher education (Chronicle 2011, 38).

Students are a socially mixed lot. Whereas colleges were primarily men's domains in the nineteenth century, more women than men attended America's colleges by the start of the twenty-first century (Chronicle 2010, 5). Another notable change over time has been the representation of minorities and international students, and the high valuation of ethnic and racial "diversity" on American campuses. By the early twenty-first century, a third of college students were classified as minority—Native American, Asian, black, and Hispanic—with the largest representation being African American (Chronicle 2010, 5). In at least three states—California, New Mexico, Hawaii—minorities constitute a majority of college enrollment, and the likelihood is that the number will increase in the future (Chronicle 2011, 42). Under 4 percent of students in American colleges come from abroad, and overall, most student bodies hail from nearby municipalities. Close to 90 percent of all postsecondary students attend a college in their home state, and it is no wonder, then, that most colleges, despite their worldly aspirations, display a regional cast.

The map of America's college students looks much like the population map of the United States with some notable exceptions. A large concentration of students resides in the megalopolis that runs from Washington, D.C., through Philadelphia, New York, and Boston. Another mass of students lives in a band of states from Ohio to Wisconsin, where large land-grant institutions became established during the mid-nineteenth century. A bunch of campuses boast more than 40,000 students each and constitute cities unto themselves. The mega-universities in size as well as organizational complexity include Ohio State University at Columbus, Penn State University at University Park, Miami Dade College, Arizona State University at Tempe, University of Florida, University of Central Florida, University of Minnesota–Twin Cities, University of Texas at Austin, Texas A&M University, University of Central Florida, University of Illinois at Urbana-Champaign, University of Michigan at Ann Arbor, University of Wisconsin at Madison, Purdue University at West Lafayette, Indiana University at Bloomington, University of California at Los Angeles (UCLA), University of South Florida, and New York University (Chronicle 2010, 29). Since the late twentieth century, the crowded American campus has been perceived as more of the norm with more than 100 universities claiming 25,000 students or more.

Universities in the twenty-first century are also increasingly arranged into mega-university "systems." The State University of New York (SUNY), founded in 1948, ballooned to sixty-six campuses by the start of the twenty-first century, and the City University of New York downstate had twenty-three units. On the West Coast, the California State University system, established in 1960, boasted twenty-three campuses, and vies with SUNY for the crown of having the largest enrollment in the nation. Other complex systems include the University System of Georgia with thirty-five campuses and the Florida College System with twenty-eight. Pennsylvania created an unusual arrangement in 1982 with a Commonwealth System of Higher Education with four state-related (in that they receive public funds but maintain independent control) rather than state-supported institutions (Penn State University, Temple University, University of Pittsburgh, Lincoln University, and Cheyney University) that spin off into thirty-three campuses (Penn State has the largest number with twenty-four). The state additionally has a State System of Higher Education with fourteen state-owned institutions divided into twenty campuses. Many of these systems have imperial rhetoric of flagship, main, branch, and satellite campuses.

A sign of the perceived worth in public perception of attending one of these systems as democratic entitlement is the growing number of applications for college admission. At large state university systems such as California

State University and SUNY, applications went over the 600,000 threshold in 2010 while single-campus applications went over the 50,000 mark at UCLA, St. John's University (New York), and the University of California at Berkeley (Chea 2010). Brigham Young University and Harvard University claim the title of being America's most popular university on the basis of the percentage of offers accepted, with over 75 percent (the service academies of U.S. Naval Academy and U.S. Military Academy have an even higher yield). Large public systems that rate in the top twenty in this category include the University of Nebraska, the University of Florida, the University of North Carolina, the University of Georgia, Texas A&M University, and the University of Texas (U.S News Staff 2011).

The small college tradition is still widely appealing, even if it is now viewed as an alternative, rather than the standard for high school graduates. The cultural expectation is frequently that campuses with less than 5,000 students provide a cozier, more relaxed, and nurturing environment. The South, often boasting a special regional identity with reverence to heritage, claims more colleges of this size than any other section of the country. Many of the smaller institutions, often taking on the identity of "traditional liberal arts colleges," flaunt a sense of community as well as tradition to prospective students. In fact, 80 percent of all institutions nationwide enroll fewer than 5,000 students each. Of the states, New York State has the most colleges with over 300, followed closely by California and Pennsylvania. The larger ones are often demeaned as party schools and impersonal seas of lost (or underqualified) souls, or extolled as exciting, intellectually stimulating dominions for studying everything under the sun and gaining a boundless array of experiences—practical and otherwise.

Judging from what college students study these days, the business of America is still business. This characteristic feeds into the American folk idea of college paving the way to commercial success, even though faculty frequently espouse the university experience as intellectually uplifting and broadening (English 2011). Business majors tap into the view of America as a commercial culture with the hope that with pluck and luck, and a sudden brainstorm gained along the way, anyone can be the next rags-to-riches corporate mogul. Another long-embraced major is engineering, which fits into the image of an inventive, technological society such as the United States (Pursell 2007, 100–106). On the rise between 1970 and 2010 have been arts and humanities (up two percentage points to 12.8, fueled by the growth of communications and media), social sciences (from 8.2 to 11.1 percent), and education (from 8.4 to 9.2 percent). Driven by modern health and environmental concerns, the sharpest rise of all was experienced by biological sciences, which nearly doubled to 8.6 percent. The National Postsecondary Student Aid Study substantiated these trends for all undergraduates by ranking business as the most popular declared major (23.3 percent) followed by health professions (16.3 percent), social sciences (15.5 percent), humanities (12 percent), and education (8 percent) (Cataldi et al. 2011). Students sometimes humorously set the different majors in rivalry with one another with a comment on the fragmentation of modern academic culture: "The business students tell the liberal arts students to find real jobs, and the B.A. students chide the business students for their lack of imagination. Both groups consider the engineers to be eggheads" (Yale Daily News 1990, 683).

Priding themselves on offering many choices, America's colleges also list programs that defy easy categorization such as humane studies, secular studies, applied living, and history of consciousness, along with a panoply of various transdisciplinary combinations and area studies. Curricular specialization is also apparent in majors such as auctioneering, bagpipes, and bakery science (Brown 2011). At many campuses, students can propose individualized majors of their own invention. And yes, one can earn degrees in folklore at a number of schools, including the University of California at Berkeley, Harvard University, George Mason University, Indiana University, the University of Louisiana at Lafayette, the University of Missouri, the University of North Carolina, the University of Oregon, Utah State University, Western Kentucky University, and the University of Wisconsin.

Besides making a choice about available majors, prospective students also weigh the social mix on campus. Colleges historically associated with African Americans and women have in particular been known for their special institutional traditions. Originally established in the nineteenth century to offer higher education to those groups historically blocked from the white male preserve of the elite "old-time college," black and women's colleges commonly instituted customs emphasizing a strong feeling of solidarity among students and faculty (Boas 1971; Horowitz 1984). The federal government counted 105 "Historically Black Colleges and Universities" (HBCUs) enrolling about 214,000 students at the start of the twenty-first century, or 16 percent of all African American higher education students in the nation. Historians of education have noted that after desegregation ushered in by the civil rights movement, enrollments at the HBCUs declined markedly, but the institutions have endured with expanded curricula and degree offerings as well as the admission of more white students. In the post-civil-rights era, a number of political leaders have called for merger of the HBCUs with state-supported schools, but advocates for continuation of HBCUs argue for the supportive social settings and cultural relevance they provide for African Americans.

Women's colleges, once prominent on the scholastic landscape, became transformed around the same time as HBCUs. In the wake of the sexual revolution and women's movement of the 1960s, the number of women's colleges dropped sharply from 233 (more than 10 percent of all higher education institutions in 1960) to 90 (2.7 percent of all colleges) two decades later. At the start of the twenty-first century about 60 remained (Peril 2006). Most all-male institutions went coed many years earlier, and the legal challenge to military academies at the end of the twentieth century ended former male bastions, but not their institutionalized hazing traditions. Some notable liberal arts holdouts for men's education are Hampden-Sydney, Wabash, and Morehouse. Hobart College is all male but has a partnership arrangement with a women's institution, William Smith College. Some universities organize constituent colleges by gender such as the University of Richmond, which has Richmond College for men and Westhampton College for women, or Yeshiva University with the all-male Yeshiva College and the Stern College for Women. More than fifty colleges in the United States retain a male profile as Christian seminaries or orthodox rabbinical institutions.

The Historical Context of Contradictory Political and Economic Systems

The history of American higher education is a story, at least in part, of widening access to, and increasing the size of, college education coinciding with debate over campus authority. What makes collegiate history unusual and relevant to cultural production arising out of social tension is its fusion of often contradictory political and economic systems. With the pastoral image of the campus invoking a preindustrial, precapitalist heritage, institutions of higher education still contain self-images as altruistic, intimate, feudal communities with professorial faculty lords and student vassals in a system of mutual dependency. Certainly there are many material reminders of medieval custom, including commencement gowns drawn from European universities and "Collegiate Gothic" architecture as a sign of learning and authenticity on many campuses (Mackey Mitchell Associates 2001). On campuses such as Princeton, where natural ivy creeps up the sides of buildings, facades intentionally convey the impression of the life of the mind. The castellated campus with Gothic Revival structures appears to promote a monastic spiritual quest for knowledge and communal connection set apart from materialism. Yet as mega-universities arose with complex management hierarchies and even small liberal arts institutions promoted their commercial brand, economies of scale were introduced suggesting more emphasis on the market-oriented outcomes rather than the emotional process of discovery. The "Cathedral of Learning" rising above the University of Pittsburgh campus (completed in 1934), for example, is an imposing tower reminiscent of the feudal age when cathedrals dwarfed pietistic towns and for a competitive, modern age, publicity blares its skyscraper rank for the university as the tallest educational building in the Western Hemisphere.

Concerned about displaying a progressive reputation, college presidents gush about their modern, multifunction buildings showcasing smooth surfaces, sharp angular lines, open spaces, and lots of windows and shiny metal. By design, the engineered elevations of "leading-edge" buildings on campus scream "corporate headquarters" and capitalized success. The University of Cincinnati's website touts McMicken Hall's old steeple for embodying "tradition and inspiration," and, at the same time, the slick metal and glass surfaces of the Campus Recreation Center bring to the campus, according to the website, a nature-defying "24-hour-a-day environment" (UC Photographers 2011; see also Bennett 2001; Dober 1996; Turner 1987). One might expect from histories of corporate American institutions an evolutionary model of displacement of feudal communities by capitalist bureaucratic systems, but the university, even more than the basic education that precedes it, retains features of both (see Bledstein 1976; Genovese 1989; Klein 1993, 81–107; Trachtenberg 1982). Cultural forms often comment on, and arise from, the tension between the dualistic aspects of the higher educational institution.

One prominent example is in parodies of college applications that purport to reveal the real motives of institutions as well as the character of the students. Often circulated to give the appearance of an official form, the application— after the usual lines for name and address—asks, "Are you a football player?" with a note "If 'Yes,' please skip to the last line of this application." The implication is that the athlete, lacking in intellectual skills, gets into the university because he pays off for the corporate organization. At some elite institutions, other parodies ask about the "number of hired servants in your household" and "type of BMW." A mock philosophical or social consciousness essay question from the University of Southern California (USC) poses this dilemma to the applicant, "You are trapped in a Beverly Hills mansion for one (1) hour with only ten thousand (10,000) dollars to spend. What will you buy? Why?" In a biting commentary on the significance of literary culture, the application parody frequently quizzes, "Have you read a book this year?" with the note "If 'Yes,' why?" Yet to get a laugh, it also asks, "Which gossip magazines do you read regularly?" It closes with a request for an official transcript (and translates the phrase to "your grades") along with the applicant's "tennis pro recommendation" (Dundes 1996, 157–58).

Colleges over time have fused both tradition and modernity into their representation of public culture, and in so doing have structured themselves as a separate location between the traditionalism of home and family prior to the student's arrival and the modernism of capitalist work and individual existence afterward. Social theorist Jay Mechling has suggested that American universities with their functions of bridging or negotiating between two worlds and a face toward each are prime examples of key "mediating structures" (or "megastructures" owing to their size and influence) representing "those institutions standing between the individual in his private life and the large institutions of public life" (Mechling 1989, 341; see also Berger and Neuhaus 1977). He asserts that the "study of folklore forms, content, and processes in mediating structures at the university may help us understand American culture as Americans actively create and modify it in their everyday lives" (Mechling 1989, 347). He points to the central campus quadrangle (designated as a "free speech" area) as a location where public and private realms collide and produce folklore to symbolize as well as culturally confront political as well as social relations on campus. He writes:

> The public university contributes universalistic values inherited from eighteenth-century French and English liberal political theory and deposited in our Constitution and in two hundred years' worth of interpretation of that text. The university's contribution to the public square, in other words, is the unique blend of Protestant Christianity and English liberal political theory that has come to be called, variously, America's "public religion," "public philosophy," or "civil religion." An important dimension of this American civil religion is that it is also a "religion of civility"; that is, the rules of discourse in the public square demand a certain civility in the free contest of private values in the public arena. (In fact, some folklore works to teach and sustain these rules, such as the proverbial phrases, "Everyone's entitled to an opinion" and "Your freedom of speech stops at my nose.") (Mechling 1989, 344)

At various points in educational history, often uncivil conflicts rose to the surface with competition among the groups on campus and of the megastructure with the larger institutions of public life. With each period of upheaval, public questioning heated up about the quality and purpose of American education (especially in relation to Europe), the character of students in light of publicized indiscretions, and access by ordinary folk to the university echelon. Eager reformers held up campus customs to expose, and symbolize, what was right or wrong with American youth and, by extension, with the nation's future prospects. Early in collegiate history, penalism by which underclassmen served their seniors and could be harshly punished for displeasing their masters was a matter of great debate. The age of penalism gave way in the mid-nineteenth century to the "rush and scrap era," referring to the widespread, controversial complex of rough activities pitting first- and second-year classes against each other. In the interwar period, sports arose as student outlets along with the corporate identities of many growing campuses. In the mid-twentieth century, the civil rights movement brought into question the inclusiveness of many college institutions and shook Americans' beliefs in the democratic foundation of higher education. Coming out into the open in the digital age of the twenty-first century were ways that cyber-technology changed learning as well as social patterns. Headlines from campuses and editorials for reform often concerned violence, sexuality, and drugs in the social lives, and folk activities, of college students.

A theme of political economy as well as cultural production that particularly informs the evolution of American campus traditions with the growth of a mass, technological society is the dramatic reformulation of colleges as homogeneous, often isolated collectives into gargantuan, complex organizations in which students are asked to assert their individuality. In 1636, the first American college, Harvard, opened its doors, followed by William and Mary in 1693, and a smattering of other schools through the eighteenth century. These early schools were small and struggling; they enrolled on average forty students apiece. By 1776, only 1 in 1,000 Americans had attended college. Those who went came generally from well-to-do white Protestant stock. The colleges educated mostly future clergymen, lawyers, and doctors in a controlled curriculum of Latin, Greek, Hebrew, logic, rhetoric, philosophy, and mathematics. Students aligned themselves with their entering class; all students in the class took the same courses. Tutors read from lessons, and students recited assignments from memory.

Civic leaders built Harvard, William and Mary, and Yale on the model of the English quadrangle, although they typically allowed for a more spacious feeling. Princeton distinguished its grounds, a centerpiece building fronted by a large lawn, from Harvard Yard, and with reverence for classical civilization called it a campus (taken from a Latin term for a field used for events in ancient Rome such as games, military exercises, and public meetings). The name and image of the campus have stuck to American colleges since (Turner 1987).

Another persistent label involved "classes" from freshmen to seniors in an arrangement of student bodies. An emphasis in learning at English universities that American educators recognized was debate between second- and third-year students. First-year students were referred to as "fresh-men" because they were novices. Supervisors of the debates called clever new arguments sophisms and their bearers, sophisters. The second-year students became known as junior sophs and the third-year students senior sophs. The designation of *sophumer* was inserted between the novice freshmen and the active juniors, and became in America the sophomore class. The freshmen were not simply supposed to stand by while the upper classes engaged in debate in English tradition. In keeping with an apprentice system associated with guilds, upper classes treated freshmen as servants and hazed them to offer initiation into the upper ranks. In the early history of higher education in America, the distinct rungs of freshman, sophomore, junior, and senior that students had to climb became even more rigorous than it did in England.

Further emulating the English, the colleges organized around residential plans. Under these cloistered conditions, schoolmasters controlled students by strict moral discipline. Acting in loco parentis ("in the place of a parent"), they reasoned that students were considered children in need of protection from worldly vice on their way to a professional calling. Masters confined students to campus except on certain days and sent them to bed without supper for infractions of the rules. College officials inspected their letters and packages, both incoming and outgoing (Schaeper, Merrill, and Hutchison 1987, 25). The college was a self-contained hamlet, with students housed alongside instructors, and they moved together through an exhausting uniform daily routine of prayers, meals, recitations, and studies (Rudolph 1962, 96–109).

Between the American Revolution and the Civil War, American colleges expanded into the rough interior of the new Republic and experienced religious diversification as well as reform of the master-servant relationship among students. European travelers remarked with puzzlement that most of the new colleges, and there seemed to be a lot of them, had their beginnings on the fringes of settlement. Consequently, they were skeptical of the institutions' exclusivity at the heart of a college education meant to cultivate a power elite, and of their quality as citadels of refinement (Fidler 1833, 38–48; Hamilton 1833, 1:356–64; see also Bevis and Lucas 2007, 36–40). As early as 1818, Saint Louis University was established west of the Mississippi, and in 1842 Willamette of Salem, Oregon, opened its doors on the West Coast. More than half the colleges founded before the Civil War were outside the original thirteen colonies. By the 1830s, thirty-seven colleges operated in Ohio alone, a state with three million inhabitants. England, with a population of twenty-three million, had only four universities.

For mushrooming towns in the United States, having a college anchored the community and represented a progressive aspiration. With a college campus in their midst, localities hoped to make their claim for higher civilization as well as for economic gain. Church leaders also saw in the colleges outposts from which to lead a missionary charge out to the edges of settlement. Many burgs with 500 or fewer residents, isolated from major centers, fought for the right to host a college. In this tradition, one sees emerging the common American image of the remote, bucolic college campus meant to reduce worldly distractions. The communal character of this kind of institution and its intensive round of intellectual work and social life combine to give it the appellation of the "old-time college" (Bledstein 1976).

State universities burst on the American scene in the antebellum period. The University of Georgia was the first to be chartered in 1785, and in 1795 the University of North Carolina opened as the first public institution of higher education. Thomas Jefferson founded the University of Virginia in 1819, and with eight separate colleges under its wing, the institution pioneered the multiple-unit system marking universities. Specialized institutions for the military and technical trades also opened during this period: Rensselaer Polytechnic Institute in 1824, and academies for the army and navy in 1802 and 1845, respectively. During the late 1850s, agriculture received its due at colleges such as Michigan State and Penn State. With the spread of their ilk, the sons of merchants and farmers claimed a place in college, and in professions serving an expanding America.

In the midst of this expansion—and during a time of national ambition and growth—students openly fought faculty for campus control. At Harvard, students planted bombs in classrooms, and at Yale they smashed windows in an out-of-control rage (Bledstein 1976, 228–34). Secret societies, forerunners of fraternities, emerged among the students as political as well as social instruments. They aired complaints about vindictive faculty, prisonlike conditions, and rotten food. Reports circulated widely in the 1830s of students fighting, burning, and looting; a common student ploy was to lock out faculty from their residences and classrooms (Rudolph 1962, 97–98). Incited by the expanding opportunities in this new nation, and with the memory of colonial rebellion against authoritarianism stamped into them, youth resisted being treated like servile children. Among their demands was control of extracurricular affairs and student councils formed to advise on policy in a shared college governance system.

Amid public calls for reform, the classical curriculum slowly opened up during the nineteenth century to include practical and modern subjects—science, English, economics, and geography. More lay scholars filled the ranks of the faculty, and, in a peculiarly American hierarchy, they divided by rank into assistant, associate, and full professors (Forrest 1940, 445). Schools eased requirements for attendance at morning and evening prayers, and relaxed rules for confinement of students to dorms. Oberlin in 1833 became the first college to admit women, Middlebury College in 1823 graduated the first African American student, and in 1854 another breakthrough was the graduation from Yale College of Yung Wing, the first Chinese student to receive a degree from an American university. With many colleges guided by Christian interests and prejudices, Jews combated exclusion (or hid their religious affiliation) in the nineteenth century and then assailed restrictive quotas in the twentieth century applied by prominent educational institutions. Historians recognize Amelia D. Alpiner at the University of Illinois in the class of 1896 (the university opened in 1868) as the first Jewish female collegian to be openly identified according to her religion (Turk 2004, 101–5). A Jewish-sponsored secular university would have to wait until the founding of Brandeis University in 1948. Following this breakthrough, Naropa University, a private nonsectarian institution, also dedicated to liberal arts, became in 1974 the first Buddhist or Buddhist-inspired campus to receive accreditation. In 2009, Zaytuna College opened in Berkeley, California, as the country's first Muslim liberal arts college.

Besides diversification of the academic landscape, another issue for administrators in the nineteenth century was programming for student life. The scholarly hard line was that the isolation of campuses fostered total devotion to the life of the mind rather than development, or enjoyment, of the body. In light of the college's primary mission to develop highbrow "aesthetics," the place of physical "athletics" desired by youth in college life was a matter of debate. Many school administrations in the nineteenth century expressed qualms about accepting "physical culture" with its boorish associations alongside intellectual pursuits but thought that it might be useful to redirect the aggressive energies of college men toward one another and away from their elders. Harvard and Yale began intercollegiate sports with a crew race in 1852, and other extracurricular activities gave students social outlets—or "a life," as some would observe.

Change in the college social as well as physical landscape accelerated between the Civil War and World War I. A boost came from the Morrill Act of 1862, which established land grant colleges. The act resulted in the creation of seventy-two new schools. They typically enrolled both men and women, were independent of church control, and offered a wide range of courses from the classics and humanities to agricultural and mechanical studies. The number of colleges in the United States hit 2,000 by World War I, a tenfold increase since the Civil War. By 1870, the young United States claimed more colleges than existed in all of Europe. After modest increases in graduates through the nineteenth century, college enrollment nearly doubled during the 1880s and 1890s.

The German model of education—the basis for the appellation of the "modern research university"—drew wider acceptance in the United States before World War I. This model, featuring a bureaucratic structure of self-contained departments, emphasized research to aid instruction and graduate study to advance knowledge in specific fields. Students took a field as a "major" and elected to take courses in other subjects or departments. The expansion of this model meant that the emphasis on class loyalty and general knowledge common in the old-time college was gradually replaced by connection to the major. Study became more individualized and research-oriented.

As strict administrative control of the student's routine subsided and more students entered colleges during the late nineteenth century, an extracurricular social life revolving around the collegiate experience emerged with greater strength. Phi Beta Kappa, established in 1776 at the College of William and Mary, is usually credited to be the first collegiate Greek-letter society, but Kappa Alpha, begun at Union College in 1825, had more of the social features of modern fraternities by being an exclusively student organization, emphasizing social activities, and instituting initiations into the group. As more women entered the college ranks, sorority chapters came into being following the establishment in 1867 of I.C. Sorosis (later known by its Greek motto Pi Beta Phi) at Monmouth College on the model of the men's fraternity. Pledging, hazing, and initiation subsequently became a regular part of college life, and administrative worries, at most campuses.

Intercollegiate sports expanded, and football rivalries gave focus to campus loyalties in the twentieth century. Mixing between men and women on campuses became more common, and students embraced courtship rituals as part of college tradition. Students also were a more noticeable force in the enclaves that surrounded the colleges. "Town and gown" divisions came into the American language, and students ventured off campus and into the community's streets with parades and festivities, as well as pranks. The town-gown distinction was not just about campus boundaries but largely about the cultural divide between the workaday world of the streets and supposedly indulgent student life. The press pointed to mid-century student stunts such as goldfish swallowing, panty raids, and phone-booth stuffing as signs of student frivolity. Often reporters editorialized about the dubious intellectualism and maturity of this crowd when students devoted time to these pursuits in the name of tradition (Bailey 1998, 187–89; Sloan and Fisher 2011, 19–20).

Psychologists explained collegians' high jinks by pointing to a modern stage of life between puberty and adulthood called "adolescence." Drawn from the Latin root for growing up, the period in Americans' eyes spelled trouble. Without clear ritual entrance and separation markers or rituals, the adolescent period was not easily defined either, although it was often connected to the onset of puberty and the imagined beginnings of adulthood after the school or teen years. Educators considered students to be freely acting out tensions caused by the difficult transition into the sobering responsibilities of adulthood, while social commentators worried about the effect on moral character of the extension of childhood into the college experience with the delay of occupational independence. In response to the spreading idea that collegiate antics were not a failure of character but a psychological condition caused by a combination of their human age and modernization, colleges began programming social as well as academic activities. Teens supposedly had extra "nervous energy" to release because of sexual and social frustrations, or perhaps a distinctive biological makeup, and many authorities pointed out that collegians' shenanigans provided natural outlets for their pent-up feelings or special conditions (see Kett 1977). Social activities, pragmatists argued, provided skills and experiences that carried over later into society. More organized festivities—some established by the college, others by the students—thus came into being to meet, or control, these needs.

During the twentieth century, Americans heightened their faith in, and politicization of, higher education as a stepping-stone to success for themselves and their children. The traditional elitist image of white Protestant–dominated colleges came into question as immigrants, blacks, industrial workers, and other groups called for the wider availability of colleges to the common person. Whereas the public expected colleges in the nineteenth century to be exclusive from their social surroundings, commentators fueled by Progressive Era reform increasingly called upon schools to represent the look of society and take action to improve it.

Enrollments sharply increased at several points in the twentieth century. After World War I, colleges enjoyed their rah-rah period, days of raccoon coats and flagpole sitting, as college enrollments and spirits grew. The class of 1929 nationally doubled the 1919 cohort. After World War II, some 90,000 veterans swelled the ranks of colleges and called for more applied studies in technological, business, and professional areas geared toward workforce development, ushering in a growing educational movement venerated and vilified as collegiate "vocationalism." Older and generally less tolerant of boisterous, supposedly immature fun than traditional students, the veterans influenced the decline of hazing and other initiation traditions at college campuses. In this period, the governmental trend was toward expanding existing colleges rather than adding new ones. By increasing the number of students within a single location, budgets and reputations—leaders thought—could be expanded. Many colleges merged or sought university status.

Enrollments leveled by 1953, but thereafter rose steadily toward the student explosion of the 1960s brought by the postwar baby boom. A doubling of enrollment occurred between 1960 and 1969, spurred at least in part by deferments from military conscription for college students as well as an expanding population in search of professional education. Large public universities grew, with campuses of more than 20,000 students becoming more common. Campuses added real estate and underwent a building boom in an effort to keep up with the population growth. Responding to public pressure to gain access to the collegiate ticket to success, federal and state programs made possible a rising level of loans and grants to needy students. Activists argued that attending college was a right, and increasingly a necessity, in a democratic society rather than a privilege of affluent citizens.

The baby boomers also asserted the student demographic as a political and cultural force. Student unrest over the Vietnam War and civil rights jumped onto national headlines, and students came off campus to march in the streets and rouse communities. Collegians actively challenged the role of the administration acting in loco parentis. Colleges dropped their supervision of visitation in dorms by the opposite sex and pulled back on dress and moral regulations (Bailey 1998). Administrators conceded to students a governance role. In surveys, students answered that seeking "meaning" for their lives was what they wanted out of the college experience (Pryor et al. 2007). In that search to change the world and express themselves, students signed up in large numbers for social sciences and humanities offerings.

Moving toward the end of the twentieth century, buoyed by the successes of social action, students assaulted the "ivory tower" image of the university. Collegians called for measures to ensure an egalitarian, compassionate example on campus for society. Students vocally protested the increasing alienation of being a lone cog in the large bureaucratic wheel of the university. Reflecting concerns about society at large, students lashed out at the educational giants for constricting, isolating, and depersonalizing them. They called for making the curriculum contemporary and relevant to social and cultural issues of the day; they advocated new majors representing an expanding set of identities, including Africana studies, queer studies, and women's studies. Student activists hurled barbs at the faceless "computerization" of students, with assignment of numbers to individual lives, and expansion of campuses signified by large lecture halls seating 500 and more course takers, or slackers. Administrators responded with the establishment of student assistance programs, small residential or alternative colleges within the large university structure, and vibrant ethnic and religious organizations to provide social support.

By the 1980s, campuses settled down, but new tensions threatened the self-assurance of the colleges. A barrage of reports criticized the education students were receiving. Two of the most notable were *College: The Undergraduate Experience in America*, by Ernest Boyer of the Carnegie Foundation for the Advancement of Teaching (1987), and *The Closing of the American Mind* (with the caustic subtitle, *How Higher Education Has Failed Democracy and Impoverished the Souls of Today's Students*), by Allan Bloom of the University of Chicago (1987). Citing the exodus from humanities and social sciences to narrow vocationalism—in a cafeteria-style curriculum run rampant—the collegiate critics shared the opinion that scholarly education had eroded, students were dispirited and ignorant, and colleges had become distended if not incoherent.

The National Commission on Excellence in Education, adding that general observation as well as the fact that standardized tests showed that American students were losing their edge in the world, warned in 1983 that the nation was "at risk" as a result of "a rising tide of mediocrity" (National Commission 1983, 5). The report came as a blow to an egotistic American belief in its education system as the pinnacle global example of progress and discovery.

Many colleges responded by restoring general education requirements and reexamining student life issues. In the meantime, with college presidents noting the escalating cost of maintaining their institutions, students faced more financial pressures with rising tuition outpacing the national inflation rate. Legislatures curtailed many federal and state aid programs along with cutting allocations to public universities. Feeling the pinch, students swelled the ranks of business, trade, and technical programs. They expected high grades to impress job recruiters and resented administrative attempts to elevate standards. Although an earlier generation of students had told pollsters that they primarily viewed the college years as a time for societal reform and seeking a meaningful philosophy of life, surveys of collegians moving into the twenty-first century ranked "being very well-off financially" highest (Hong 2004).

Enrollments stabilized again in the post-baby-boom years as the numbers of students drawn from high schools declined. Yet colleges often made up these losses with a relatively new clientele drawn from part-time and non-degree enrollees, foreign students, and employed adults. Commuting to large urban schools and attending college part-time became more frequent choices among cost-conscious students. Community colleges, trade institutes, branch campuses, and urban centers located where students lived arose as populist alternatives to the old isolated, campus nirvanas belittled as being "out in the middle of nowhere." Into the twenty-first century, expanding computer-delivered education into the privacy and comfort of the home, also known as "distance learning," "e-learning," or "cyber-education," further individualized (or alienated) the student and for some observers negated the need for campus centers that involved a crossing-over from the real world to a cordoned-off learning zone.

Meanwhile, the liberal arts college experience arose in the public mind as a path to success in response to the massification of mega-universities and the spread of distance learning. Traditionally located on an arcadian campus and offering roundedness to one's education rather than specialization, liberal arts colleges engaged in public relations campaigns to keep old-time college intimacy and general education relevant for postmodern times. Many of the older coeducational colleges attracted students with claims of a communal, idyllic atmosphere and personal staff attention lacking at the gargantuan universities. At these institutions, and increasingly at the larger campuses, student groups—fraternities and sororities especially—sought to restore traditions to forge a sense of community, and with it the school spirit, that had been lost during the 1960s and 1970s.

By the end of the twentieth century, administrators reclaimed some of their supervisory role over student behavior. Many colleges cracked down on drinking and drug use on campus, and banned smoking in college buildings and surroundings. While membership in Greek organizations came back strong during the late 1980s, colleges targeted for reform the abuses of fraternity and sorority life, often given to values of exclusion and rowdiness, and many colleges opted for banning the Greek system. Two national fraternities—Zeta Beta Tau and Tau Kappa Epsilon—tried to clean their own houses by eliminating pledging altogether.

Another sore spot, especially for the mega-universities, was big-time athletics. Intercollegiate sports had become big business in many schools, and the abuses to recruit and retain athletes came out into the open. Reports of payoffs, faked transcripts, sexual abuse, and academic dishonesty among athletes and coaching staffs made headlines, and public outcries forced college presidents to intervene. Several universities boasted stadiums holding more than 100,000 fans and huge arenas rivaling the facilities of professional teams. Banking on the returns from athletics, university administrators lived in fear of a National Collegiate Athletic Association (NCAA) "death penalty" for an entire program (notably the Southern Methodist University football program for the 1987 and 1988 seasons and the Morehouse College soccer program for the 2004 and 2005 seasons) or banishment from playoffs and bowl games. Once known for their quiet, serene environment, campuses became a hot entertainment venue. Universities built impressive athletic complexes to keep up with public demand and to be competitive in recruiting top athletes. Critics editorialized that in the race for championship trophies, academic standards as the core of the university became secondary or immaterial. Marquee sports programs, and especially their football teams, were touted as the "faces of the university," and prominent coaches enjoyed exalted, even deified status. Higher education officials worried that universities could maintain control over programs that accrued cultural capital from media attention and appeared insulated from institutional watch—and rules. These issues came to a head when scandals erupted in 2011 at Penn State and Syracuse Universities over allegations of sexual molestation by coaches of underage boys on university property (Wolverton 2011). At Penn State, the Board of Trustees removed the university president and fired legendary football head coach Joe Paterno. A national dialogue ensued on the academic priorities and moral responsibilities of higher education institutions, especially in the face of college athletic programs that pull in over $10 billion of revenue annually (McMillen 2011). National columnists such as Howard Bryant pinned much of the blame for failure to act on "so much bigness" of the university and the protection of the sports programs' power (Bryant 2011). In response, the university's message was that academics remain central in higher education and that the administration is committed to the protection of all youth on campus (Frantz 2012).

To get into business, Americans increasingly believed that a college education was an economic necessity. More than half of all new jobs created in the first decade of the twenty-first century required postsecondary education, and a third of the jobs would be filled by college graduates, according to the Bureau of Labor Statistics. Additionally, the bureau declared that half of the thirty fastest-growing occupations in the following decade would depend on college credentialing. The list included data communications analysts, financial analysts, theatrical and performance specialists, mental health counselors, family and marriage therapists, forensic science technicians, and physical therapists. Americans looked to colleges to do more than preparing students for these new jobs. They expected colleges to provide models for a better society, for basic education, for scientific and technological research, and for the way people lived and interacted on campus. These high expectations pressured colleges to guarantee results and be accountable to the public in a way they never had before, all with less support from legislatures.

Interpreting the Cultural Life of College Students

The intense public discourse during the 1980s about the role of colleges egged on scholars to explain new social and cultural meanings of higher education in America. A pivotal historical study was *Campus Life: Undergraduate Cultures from the End of the Eighteenth Century to the Present* (1987), by Helen Lefkowitz Horowitz. From the anthropologist's perspective came *Coming of Age in New Jersey* (1989), by Michael Moffatt. Horowitz described a progression of identities that dominated and shaped student life. In the old-time institutions it was the college men, followed by groups calling for their rightful place at the head, such as the rebels, the organized "frat rats," and the outsiders. The new self-centered outsiders in control in the modern period, she wrote, resist organization and seek achievement defined by money, goods, and status. They combine grade-consciousness and work habits drawn from the old outsiders with a nonintellectualism reminiscent of the old-time college men. She found historical roots of persistent modern student types early in the formation of American colleges when students used social capital to wrest power from the faculty and administration. Still needed to fill out the picture of campus life in the present were ethnographies and collections of student cultural practices.

Emulating an anthropological expedition to record primitive natives, Michael Moffatt narrowed his focus to a small group of students studied ethnographically at Rutgers. He found much more joy than Horowitz did in the modern student's life. Indeed, he suggested that much of the student's coming-of-age during a college stay is found in the intentional pursuit of social and bodily pleasures. "At least half of college was what went on outside the classroom, among the students, with no adults around," Moffatt observed, and he asserted that "college was about fun, about unique forms of peer-group fun—before, in student conceptions, the grayer actualities of adult life in the real world began to close in on you" (1989, 28–29). Humans need to laugh and have fun, but Moffatt observed that students, supposedly matured beyond childish tomfoolery, felt a compulsion for puerile play, probably as a defense mechanism. But Moffatt was hesitant to get deeper into the heads of the students or expand the collection of folkloric material for comparative purposes.

Following Moffatt's anthropological encounter with natives in the wilds of American college dorms, a middle-aged professor identified as Rebekah Nathan (a pseudonym) passed herself off as a student at an institution she identified as "Any U" and published her observations in *My Freshman Year* (2005). She gave attention to what students talk about informally, although she did not distinguish between everyday conversation and enactments of folklore as different social frames. Drawn to consideration of language and discourse, she expressed surprise that so little of student communication revolved around intellectual life. Related to folkloristic work is her consideration of the undergraduate "worldview," or general outlooks based on a set of shared beliefs and ideas held by natives in a group. She observed a divide between in-class and out-of-class messages. The official or formal university exists in class and is related to the realm of organized clubs and programs. Out-of-class discourse represents, in her observation, the "real" college culture "centered on the small, ego-based networks of friends that defined one's personal and social world" (Nathan 2005, 100).

The challenge of cultural, and especially ethnographic, explorations of college life is the paucity of materials, since historians, sociologists, folklorists, and anthropologists have not usually looked inside their classrooms for fields of study. It was for the purpose of raising memories among alumni that the first register of college lore was compiled in 1851 when Benjamin Homer Hall (1795–1884), a lawyer graduated from Middlebury College, amassed his 319-page *A Collection of College Words and Customs*. It was essentially a dictionary of distinctive college-student slang, showing the apartness of the experience from life before and after being on campus. Inspired by Hall's handy guide, Henry D. Sheldon (1874–1948), a young professor of education, added an important sociological chronicle of extracurricular life, largely focused on the rise of secret societies, in his *Student Life and Customs* (1901) to show the use of organizations by students to increase their position in a power struggle with administrations.

Folklorists in the twentieth century probably missed opportunities to collect from their students because they were preoccupied with preserving endangered oral traditions from remote or illiterate or what they called "primitive" populations (Baker 1983). In that context, an article puffed up with a scientific tone on college lore that appeared in the *Journal of American Folklore* in 1923 must have startled readers. Its author, Martha Warren Beckwith, announced that despite the notion that official learning displaces folklore, she collected abundant living "signs and superstitions" from quite literate, refined college women at Vassar. Unlike previous studies, hers analyzed a haul of material quantitatively and in the process raised psychological questions about the college experience, or its gendering. "Little interest," she wrote "exists in maxims regarding the weather, bodily ills, or nature; here modern science has eliminated folk-lore," but "eighty are signs referring to various forms of good and bad luck. Fifty-six refer to love and marriage. Twelve methods of wishing are elaborated" (Beckwith 1923, 1). Notions of luck, particularly at exam time and the occasion of the big game, are still evident on campuses, and merit explanation. It should also not come as a surprise that blossoming adolescents are anxious about love, and new questions arise about gender relations in the ever fragile rituals of courtship.

Expanding on Beckwith's pioneering balance sheet of students' beliefs gained and lost, Richard Dorson at Michigan State University collected material from over 1,000 students enrolled in his folklore classes. He shared his findings on "the folklore of colleges" in popular outlets such as the literary magazine *American Mercury* (1949) and the trade-press book *American Folklore* (1959). He also encouraged his own students later at Indiana University, of which I count myself one, to delve more deeply into what he viewed as the core of "modern folklore." His contribution was to show that folklore, particularly a trove of legends, was being created anew in various modern collegiate situations. He was the first to document "virgin test" beliefs as a response to the growing coeducational movement and "dumb star-athlete" and "lofty coach" legends as folk commentaries on the role of big-time sports in relation to the intellectual mission of higher education. He concluded that "the enterprising folklorist doesn't need to journey into the back hills to scoop up tradition. He can set up his recording machine in the smokeshop on the college grill" (Dorson 1949, 677). Intrepid folklorists have picked up his trail with twenty-first-century forays into supernatural stories in dormitory life (Barefoot 2004;

Bruce 2003; Tucker 2007), rituals in the stadium parking lot of big-time football games (Lindquist 2006), and paddling in fraternity houses (Mechling 2008b), to name a few notable studies.

Dorson's point was that modernity and tradition are not at odds with one another, but in fact rely on one another. Folklore expresses the identity, as well as anxieties, of all social formations, literate and illiterate. If anything, the college campus as a cultural scene breeds folklore. Stories of haunted halls persist whether or not students believe in ghosts because they have messages for students that bear repeating (Tucker 2007). More than adding to the inventory of horror legends well represented on the bookshelf, the awareness of the supernatural in adolescence invites psychological and cultural analysis, especially when sociological studies show that going to college increases students' belief in ghosts and ritual engagement and appears higher than at other stages of life (Farha and Steward 2006; Manning 2000; Tucker 2007). Folklorist Elizabeth Tucker has observed similarities between the greater independence, excitement, and stress of summer camp and going away to college shared by many high school graduates (2007, 19–23). Both camp and campus constitute a physical and social context in the congregation of youthful strangers within a liminal space for the generation of fantasy-filled lore, although the campus suggests more issues of entering adulthood. A physical distinction of the college campus that combines preindustrial pastoral landscapes to inspire individual contemplation and institutional buildings that suggest social regimentation presents tensions that are projected into narrative, ritual, and play.

Despite the image often portrayed in popular media, students do not become suddenly deranged once having set foot on campus. They use the imaginative, symbolic content, and sometimes escape and fantasy of folklore for strategic purposes of adaptation to the place, to their age, and to their social situation. Folklore provides passage from one stage to another through ritual, custom, narrative, and object. It defines and describes the subgroupings within the student's world: the "frat rats," the "grinds," the "jocks," the "profs," and all the rest. It is students' unofficial cultural orientation held through the college experience. The stuff offers parables to ponder, rituals to observe, values to honor. Folklore from the nation's colleges opens a legacy of creative expression reflecting student culture, concerns, and roles within an exclusive institutional setting. Most important for many students, the traditions embedded in folklore help guide them to identities within a new setting often large, mysterious, and imposing. Folklore is a place to begin, and a way to belong.

Left to figure out is the meaning of traditions that either appear to reflect or distort life, provide a stage on which to rehearse reality, or provide a frame for self-discovery and escape. Many traditional practices can look like good hardy fun, or else the play masks serious issues that students are not fully equipped to handle (Dundes 2007; Dundes and Dundes 2002; LaDousa 2011). From a historical viewpoint, I have shown a number of traditions to persist across generations of students, but I also see a difference between folklore on the collective, old-time campus and the mega-university associated with individualism as well as massive scale. Differing from the communal traditions found in small colleges in times past, much of the folklore of student life today, especially at mega-universities, appears to serve more individual needs. It is not as public, not as organized, having been fragmented into the personal realms of students. Replacing many of the old rituals and displays are narratives told by one student to another about the contours and dangers of college life. Customs still remain—albeit revised frequently for our complex times—from freshman initiation at Purdue to "senior prank" at Hood, from the "door slams" of the halls to the "lineups" of the fraternities, and from the "rat line" of Virginia Military Institute (VMI) to the "running of the rodents" at Spalding. In these conspicuous events, students draw attention to themselves as being apart from the novelty of mass society, or else they raise questions about the needs traditions serve or the identities they offer.

For some readers, the very idea that folklore is so common among what passes for America's educated elite is surprising. The formation of folklore, however, is basic to social interaction, and can be especially pronounced in situations where groups are in constant contact, respond to anxiety, or need cultural guidance. Folklore arises from the kind of learning we might call informal, typically outside the formal instruction of the classroom and published text. It relates to tradition by the process of expressive material being handed down or over among people, typically in a shared setting or community. Passed by word of mouth, practice, and imitation, folklore representative of the processes of tradition provides signs of a group's connection and legacy (Bronner 2011a, 1–92). By appropriating and transmitting special stories, words, and rituals associated with a campus, students open for scrutiny issues and concerns of a place and a time in their lives. This is true whether they attend an old-time college today adapted to modern times or a mega-university sprawling over the landscape, for both act as mediating structures between public and private social worlds in which values often conflict.

Students, especially if they are attending full-time a college away from home, seek out their social space within an institutional structure and material culture. Sharing a similar age for the most part, engrossed in the pursuit of a degree and grades, in frequent contact with one another through classes and residence, separated in status from faculty and administrators, and often isolated from the support of family and friends found at home, students seek the lore emerging from their common ground.

Other segments of the university have their lore too, but I have chosen to focus on traditions expressed by students, for they give life to college. More than faculty or staff, students are the most connected group on campus, and in their lore they reveal much about their society and the future society they will shape. Their traditions also tell of their social power to construct their own experience on campus, often in conflict with the official dictates of administrations. Folklore is indeed especially demonstrative, because often in the special domain of lore, with its generally long-standing character and allowance for going beyond the limits of formal rules, one finds deep-seated attitudes, fears, desires, and biases that cannot be comfortably expressed in everyday conversation.

"The traditions of a college," Fred Lewis Pattee (1863–1950), pioneering professor of American literature at Penn State, explained in 1928, "are those bits of history, mostly unwritten, those events, customs, ideals, men, about which every student and alumnus of the college is supposed to know, but which are next to impossible to find in any book or collection of books" (1928, 3). The irony of his words is that the university library bears his name, although he was a champion of human resources of knowledge who do not render their lore into print. Collegians nationally also owe to Pattee an early scholarly voice who pressed scowling administrators to accept traditions because they give each campus a unique character, and by virtue of their similarity in structure and style to those of other campuses, they express a shared culture. As Pattee told alumni, "Atmosphere has been created by the past of the college and this past comes to the student body largely by way of tradition; by a body of information and advice and counsel passed on by word of mouth from college generation to college generation" (1928, 3).

Pattee was not about to push administrations to artificially prop up and therefore entomb folklore. He advocated the free expression of students in campus culture, and suggested that faculty could learn a great deal from what students were wont to say and play. The structure of folklore is generally slow to change, folklorists after Pattee theorized, but when it does, it is often a sign of dramatic social and cultural shifts. One will find in this book particularly the move from customs reflecting the communal activities of the old-time college student looking for status and fellowship to the kind of privatized lore stressing the individualistic character of the modern student in search of identity and community. Some student concerns seem timeless—the quest for success, resentment of the "grinds," and the desire to turn the tables on professors—while others reflect the special regional, religious, and ethnic conditions of particular colleges.

The book moves from lore inside the classroom to outside on the recreation field. I begin with the tests and papers that have generated lore across the span of collegiate history. I then examine campus characters, starting with the professors—absentminded and all-knowing, according to legend—and looking at the other side of the desk to the pantheon of campus types. Subsequent chapters focus on campus speech and actions—including games, sports, songs, pranks, and rites—from analog to digital culture. I then give attention to the prominent organizations and settings of campus life, particularly the Greeks, and for independents the dormitories and hallowed halls of academe. Along the way, I cover major themes of coming-of-age on campus, through the acquisition of higher learning inside the classroom and outside, the experience of drugs and alcohol, sexuality, privilege, and prejudice. I close with graduation and ways that students transition out of campus identity with intriguing patterns of traditions into the "real world."

I invite you to appreciate the joy and travail of being a student. I ask you to think of colleges as organizations and communities on which cultural expression comments. Reflect, if you will, on campuses as settings for individual and collective development, social and psychological, which folklore signifies. There is much to learn while we are students, and much more to know about the experience as it relates to our individual lives and our society as a whole.

CHAPTER

THE STRESS OF GRADES
Tests and Papers

THE FIRST DAY OF CLASS, THE AVUNCULAR PROFESSOR CHEERILY welcomes the students to the course. He describes his interest in the subject and begins to tell something about himself. Suddenly, a hand shoots up. Taken aback by a questioner at such an early stage of the class, the prof calls upon the anxious student.

"Excuse me, will this be on the final?"

This often-told story reminds students that tests and papers produce the numbers that translate into all-important grades. Although professors and official campus literature relate the measure of accomplishment in a course as the learning that occurs, students look to high test scores. Or that is the message that folklore gives, and the stories students produce often are set against the college's administratively controlled image, broadcast widely in professionally presented publicity.

Where students gather to talk, folklore likely can be heard, contextualized as an answer to the college's official line. With the wide array of courses available to students today, for example, the choice of classes is a great topic of discussion among students. "What should I take?" they ask one another. The staff adviser's reply is courses that are good for your mind and career. Printed information at hand might be a rundown of requirements—how many tests, how many papers, how many books to read. At lunch with one another, students share what they have heard about the prof or the class. Students identify easy courses as guts, cakes, puds, puddings, cinches, snaps, skates, and breezes; hard courses are bitches, screamers, and ball-breakers (or busters). That may lead to narrative in great variation about how professors really grade or how they, as a lot, are weird and absentminded. Sometimes fanciful, often revealing, student slang, stories, and beliefs lay out a round of life fragmented into classes where the terrain always seems treacherous. The control students have over the situation is to know what to expect and consequently score the best numbers.

A look at Benjamin Hall's groundbreaking *A Collection of College Words and Customs* of 1851 shows some notable continuities from past to present in American student folk speech about the relation of studying to grades. He noted that "cram" was used in England to mean a tutor's preparation of a student for an examination, but in American colleges, it meant intensive study in a short time. "Cutting" class remains an emphatic statement of a student's intentional absence. Miss a class and you are bagging it, taking a mental health break, taking a powder, or blowing it off; finally get to studying and you are boning up, or pounding, hitting, cracking, buried in, or keeping a nose in the books. "Flunk" in Hall's day specifically applied to failing when called upon to make a recitation, but now more generally covers receiving an "F" in a course. If students missed a test in the 1840s, they would seek out a "makeup," much as they do today.

The student tradition of "cramming" involves taking in weeks' worth of material in a single night. A mid-twentieth-century collection from Southern Illinois University includes stories of students staying up all night and then, unable to stay up any longer, falling asleep and missing the exam. One persistent cautionary tale about drugs as an aid to performance is about a student using amphetamines to take exams (Meakes 2004, 110). As told by Alfred Rollins, the story goes: "At last, after several semesters of successful dope jags, he drops to sleep fatefully in mid-examination and has to be carted off to the infirmary" (Rollins 1961, 171). Students of the early twenty-first century talk similarly of inhaling caffeine and sugar-laden "energy drinks" to stay up and echo in their exam narratives similar results.

A variant of the "cramming drugs" story comes from C. W. Post: "There was this guy who took speed to get him through an exam. He stayed up all night studying and then came into the exam. Most people turned in one blue book, but he handed in four. The trouble was that he was so high that he didn't realize that his pen ran out of ink after the first few paragraphs, so he handed in four blank books and failed anyway" (Brunvand 1989, 199).

An earlier story related by folklorist Richard Dorson from the 1940s is about students seeking to relax jittery nerves before an exam. The cautionary tale from the University of Minnesota is about a student who calmed herself by downing some booze before walking into the final: "She thought the questions looked a little strange, but went at them with a will. Some weeks later she received a grade of B for a course in American political science, in which she was not enrolled, and a statement of incomplete for the course in American literature in which she belonged" (1949, 673).

Folklorist Elizabeth Tucker supplies another cramming story with an implied moral from Mount Holyoke College of the student preparing for exam week, presumably to relax her, by embroidering a fancy sampler with the words "I cram for the damn exam." It looked beautiful, but because she was working so hard on her sampler, she was distracted from studying. According to Tucker's narrative, "She flunked all her exams and had to leave school at the end of the semester" (2005, 111). Tucker reports a local context of the legacy at the college of women doing embroidery often of homiletic mottos, suggesting the "cram" motto is a parody of death portents such as "Prepare to meet your God" (Sebba 1979, 127).

Since students in these narratives are not about to study until they have to, the idea of a "pop" or surprise quiz gives them nightmares and inspires folklore. Especially at older college halls where doors have transoms, students tell the one about an athletic-looking professor who is asked by students whether he ever gives surprise quizzes. The professor laughs and tells the students that the day he gives a pop quiz is the day he climbs through the transom (or window)! A sigh of relief passes through the classroom. Then one day the transom began to creak open and, to the amazement of the students, in climbed their professor, grinning happily and clutching a three-page quiz in his hand (Major and Bray 2008, 245; Meakes 2004, 108).

Some reports attach the pop-quiz story to famed professors who might have had a stint as circus performers before their academic career. In 1979, Oliver Graves collected the story about Professor Menno Spann of the University of North Carolina, and Professor Guy Williams of the University of Oklahoma, who supposedly performed the stunt as early as 1925 (Graves 1979, 142–45; Brunvand 1986, 192–91; 1999, 436–37). To this list, I add history professor Guy B. Harrison, who was known widely around Baylor University from the 1930s to the 1970s. The story of the transom boast told by "Guy B." is part of the heritage of the Baylor campus, and has a basis in fact, according to an oral history interview with Professor Harrison (Keeth 1985, 46). Perhaps existing as a modern take-off on this legend, a story circulates about the journalism professor who promises never to give an unannounced quiz. He strolls in one day with test in hand. When the class protested that he violated his own rules by not announcing it, the professor pointed out that he had run an ad in the local newspaper saying "Unit Quiz Today in Mr. McDonald's journalism class at 2 p.m." (Brunvand 1989, 284).

Looking for Luck and an Angle

Even with cramming, students believe that success on exams involves some luck. Test-takers guess what will be asked, and they think it is not just a matter of knowing the material, but of giving professors "what they want." With that belief, students transfer responsibility from their own acquisition of knowledge, or lack thereof, to the professor's capriciousness or trickiness. With such uncertainty in the student's mind about what to expect (rather than what to provide), test-takers invoke magic for assurance. Surveying 600 students at the Universities of Oregon and Utah, Portland State, and Reed College, Barre Toelken (1986) found that more than 400 reported engaging in customs during finals typically intended to bring good luck on the exam. The most common acts had to do with clothing or grooming styles, such as growing beards (or not shaving, or, for coeds, not cutting hair), or wearing "grubby" clothes, especially if these clothes had been worn on "aced" exams. Students sought out "lucky" seats where they had done well on a test. They brought "lucky" pens, again made magical by association with a good exam. Accordingly, students reported as bad luck taking an exam with a new pen. They also clutch traditional lucky charms such as rabbits' feet, found copper pennies, and silver bracelets. Today's exams are often delivered on computers, but that has not diminished the use of accessories providing good luck. Rabbits' feet are still around, and copper and silver talismans are ever popular. Students are often unaware of the classical associations of these metals with mysterious powers of Venus and the Moon, respectively, but probably know associations of copper with lucky pennies and silver with warding off witches and hurting vampires.

Modern variations of lucky charms also appear, such as the request I received from a student at a candidacy exam in a computer lab to bring a felicitous mouse pad. The image was astrological, and I heard from others in the room about wearing attire they connected with a previous success (especially collegiate garb associated with sports victories), bringing clovers or small flowers, and wearing lucky colors (blue, also associated with Venus, is common, as are supposedly noble colors of purple, red, and yellow; green, representing ignorance, is almost universally avoided) and religious medals. A number of students reported being unnerved by taking the exam in the lab because they could not park in their favorite classroom seat, and several were horrified that the seats had a green cloth covering.

These beliefs of luck are among the most persistent of student folklore. Back in the early 1920s, Martha Beckwith collected the following luck-inducing behaviors from Vassar women: bringing rose petals to the examination, wearing or using at an examination something that belongs to someone else who is or has been considered a good student in the course, and sitting in the same seat in examination as you did when an examination went well (1923, 6). Modern reports of student belief comment on the growing list of lucky tokens often recalled from a student's childhood, suggesting increasing individualization (see Albas and Albas 1989). Patricia Clawges (1989), a student collector, gathered customs from her fellow test-takers as varied as the fellow from Case Western wearing a baseball cap to exams (a carryover from his hunting days when he turned his bill to the back in order to focus the scope of his rifle) and the student from Dickinson who believed that underlining exams with his lucky ruler ensured his high grade. For many students, the key is not just having the item but following a ritualized routine, such as taking a direct (rather than circuitous) route to the exam site and having the same meal that preceded a previous good score. These behaviors indicate the logic of sympathetic magic: like actions effect like results. In the case of the circuitous route, students imagine that it represents confusion; the meal has the added magical component of being digested (especially if it is sweet, thus, like a sweet birthday cake, ensuring fortune in the future), having a direct, or contagious, bodily effect, and maybe being compared to "digesting" information, in student slang.

Students are constantly on the lookout for omens. Seeing a dog on the way to an exam is bad luck, probably because "a dog" is considered in folk speech something bad, and the sound of it suggests the grade of D (Baker 1983, 109). Getting a three or a seven in a numbered seat or on a numbered exam is a good omen. Speaking of numbers, some students believe that using a no. 3 pencil ensures good luck. Some students may have their own lucky numbers, such as the date of their birth, but three traditionally represents completeness and is associated with magical repetition, while seven also conveys an idea of fruition (seven days in a week) and winning at games of chance (Dundes 1980, 134–59; see also Bronner 2007, 6–8). At meals before an exam, eating off a green tray is bad luck, green being singled out because it suggests the novice, ignorant status of the "greenie." Red trays, in reference to red as a symbol of vitality, bring good luck (Cannon 1984, 42).

Students rub various campus objects and statues for good luck before examinations, because ritualized touch has magical associations, especially with producing fertility and growth. At Brown, students rub the nose of the bust of statesman and author John Hay (class of 1858), presumably to transfer knowledge of the library named for him to the student (Tucker 2007, 29). Noses phallically stick out, and embody as well as extend the spirit of the person, usually male, or animal being rubbed (Dundes 1987b, 170–72; Fenichel 1953, 155–57, 221–40; Rabelais 1984, 316–17; Vasvári 1998, 126–28). At the University of Maryland, the campus archives calls the act of rubbing the nose of a terrapin statue "our most-enduring tradition" (University of Maryland Archives 2010). The statue was the gift of the Class of 1933, who lobbied for the university to adopt the animal as the official mascot. Shortly thereafter, students began rubbing the nose on the extended head of the reptile and drawing attention to the belief with the material evidence of the spot's sheen. The tradition evolved by the century's end into leaving objects at the statue at finals time as if the terrapin were a religious or memorial shrine. Among the recorded offerings are food, cigarettes, soda, beer, poems, computer disks, candy, flowers, and coins. Elsewhere, students say that rubbing the nose of Abraham Lincoln at the University of Illinois, Hamilton Holt at Rollins, and Warner Bentley at Dartmouth provides "touch magic" from the institution's ancestors to ensure success on exams (Korab 2011; Mills Memorial Center 2011; "Traditions: Here's the Rub" 2010).

The foot, another extremity replete with phallic symbolism, also gets a hand from students (Dundes 1980, 46–47; Róheim 1945, 87–91; Rossie 1993; Thomas 1995). At Texas A&M, Lawrence Sullivan "Sul" Ross, a nineteenth-century university president and governor, embodies "Aggie Spirit," and besides rubbing his statue's bronze boots students festoon him with pennies for good luck at exam time (Slattery 2006, 28). The feet of John Harvard's statue repeatedly receive a good luck pat from Harvard undergraduates before an exam (Wiseman 2007, 91). At Wofford College, a plaque devoted to the founder in the Main Building has a misspelling of the word "beneficent." According to legend, the eccentric president refused to have the plaque recast, leaving it instead to warn students about the dangers of sloppy work. Students now rub the misspelled word, seeking good luck and protection from the spelling gremlin lest some prof take points off (Stalker 2011).

At Roanoke College in Salem, Virginia, to bring good luck on exams students boot rather than rub the three-foot cement marker colloquially known as the "kicking post" between the Administration Building and faculty offices in Trout Hall (Kicking Post 2011). Standing in one of the busiest intersections when classes are in session, the swift kick symbolically knocks down a barrier to student mobility, right smack between their nemeses of the faculty and administrators. Usually, though, the more vigorous good-luck kicks are reserved for sporting events such as the long-standing custom of USC students giving a backward kick to flagpoles at the edge of campus to ensure the football team's success in the next game. Touching and rubbing transfer power from an object to the hand, which, like the body's tool, is perceived to effect labor and change (Bronner 2011a, 30–34; Wilson 1999, 48–49).

Students tell parents and friends not to bother them before an exam, and an argument portends misfortune on the test. Stepping over the school seal, as stepping on a sidewalk crack or manhole cover does in children's folklore, brings bad luck (Bronner 1989, 163; Dundes 1980, 41; Mullen 1997, 94). At Eastern Michigan University, for example, students on the way to an exam who step on the school letter "*E*" painted on the campus grounds will have difficulty passing. From Utah comes the omen that meeting a priest on the way to a test is a sure sign of failure on the exam (Cannon 1984, 43). The last belief may derive from sailor lore that seeing a priest on the way to a ship was an omen of a difficult voyage (Daniels and Stevans 1903, 2065). One may wonder why a priest would be bad luck, since students have long been known to pray for good results on exams. The connection might be similar to the naval lore in which priests arouse guilt among the youthful, imprudent lot, and therefore invite retribution. Following this thinking, the requital for sailor or student is sure to be stormy.

Distinctive folk religious traditions are associated with students taking exams. At Iona College in New Rochelle, New York, a Roman Catholic institution, students write J.M.J. (Jesus, Mary, and Joseph) and S.J.O.C., P.F.M. (St. Joseph of Cupertino, pray for me) on exams. St. Joseph (Joseph Desa, 1603–1663) is considered by Catholic students to be the patron saint of the stupid, and they can recite a prayer for exams in his name: "Saint Joseph of Cupertino, who while on earth did obtain from God the grace to be asked on your exams only the questions which you knew, obtain for me a like favor in the exam for which I am now preparing or am about to take" (Huguenin 1962, 145–48). Other saints used by students include St. Jude, St. Theresa, and St. Luke. Catholic students attend chapel before exams and sometimes bring rosaries to tests (Clawges 1989, 8; see also Carroll 1987).

A narrative with a moral that questions whether students put into action what they learn is the one about seminary students taking their final on Christianity and the life of Jesus. They meet at the appointed time and place for the test, and are directed by a note on the board to go to another building on the other side of campus. As they hurriedly trek over to the new location a shabbily dressed homeless person asks them for aid. They do not stop to help him because they are panicky about being late for the exam. As they approach the room, they spy their professor impatiently waiting for them. The instructor informs them that the beggar was an actor, put there to test their reaction. The prof tells them that they all flunked because they did not show that they acquired any compassion while studying the life of Jesus (Genge 2000, 253–54; Meakes 2004, 108; Nist-Olejnik and Holschuh 2007, 232).

Psychoanalysts suggest that fear of exams by youth derives from the association of tests with ritually passing into a new stage. Failing them means being held back, and thus leads to anxieties over infantilization or even thoughts of castration (as in the folk speech of "making the cut") (Blum 1926; Flugel 1939). The sexualization of exams is evident in a widely circulating story of the tough prof who gives students painful quizzes, which he irritatingly calls his "little quizzies." After the third or so ordeal with these quizzies, a coed tells her classmate, "If those are his quizzies, I'd hate to see his testes" (Meakes 2004, 111).

The chilling effect of the professor on sexuality is also apparent in the legend documented in many university folklore archives of the professor who bans knitting among his students with the explanation that it is a form of "socially acceptable masturbation." In the next class, one female student is knitting. The professor exclaims, "Young lady! Did you hear my last lecture?"

and the woman replies, "When I knits I knits and when I masturbates I masturbates" (Brunvand 1962, 62). With a commentary on male psychoanalytic narrow-mindedness, the story is sometimes attached to famous child psychiatrist Bruno Bettelheim (1903–90), who taught at the University of Chicago. The woman's retort in a version posted on the Internet is "You masturbate in your way, Dr. Bettelheim, and I'll masturbate in mine" (Zekas 2007).

Worth pondering is the relation of many good-luck talismans for exams that have fertility or phallic associations (for example, flowers, rabbits' feet, pens), suggesting that being placed in a submissive position, the test-taker asserts procreative power and can pass the test as kind of initiation into maturity. Tests are not supposed to be punitive, but many students see them as professors "out to get them." Some reform-minded educators try to get away from giving tests, believing that they are too stressful for students, but the alternatives of papers and projects often create different anxieties of a lack of a clear numerical representation of their status. Having passed an exam students feel initiated knowing that some have not made it over.

For others, examinations raise images of dehumanization in immense introductory courses where students are known by their identification numbers and, to add insult to injury, tests are machine scanned. If not bringing a lucky pencil, students produce lore of how they can foil the system. A commonly reported story is the ploy of applying lip products or petroleum jelly to the test sheets. As a result, the befuddled machine supposedly calculates a perfect score. The narrative often adds a specific location to smear the goo, including over the answer bubbles or along the black marks that resemble a bar code on the sheet's side. Variations include beliefs that connecting all the marks on the side with a pencil or pen will magically produce a perfect score, or shading answers lightly instead of creating the required dark spot will fool the scanner. Student tellers express a thrill in beating the authoritative machine with the infantile excitement of smearing. Barbara Mikkelson (2006) on the urban legend reference website Snopes.com reports that the schemes do not work. The optical-scan machines recognize a discrepancy and spit out an error message, signaling an instructor to hand grade the test, and that will bring the cheat to light. But maybe that is the point: a real person took notice of the student. The narrative additionally shows the storied significance of the quick and easy A, and, in the telling by students, the power of student ingenuity.

Mnemonic Devices and Crib Sheets

A memorable tradition around exam time is the use of mnemonic devices. Typically passed into students' oral tradition, these devices organize complex lists into sayings or names that help the student commit them to memory. In elementary school, students probably met the renowned "Roy G. Biv," whose letters help students remember the order of colors in the spectrum (red, orange, yellow, green, blue, indigo, and violet). Young musicians learn the phrase "every good boy does fine" to remember the lines of the treble clef. In college, the devices are often more elaborate, and many take a sexy—or sexist—turn. Electrical engineers learn the color code of resistors by remembering "bad boys rape our young girls but Violet gives willingly" (black, brown, red, orange, yellow, green, blue, violet, gray, white). Geology students learn the Mohs' scale of hardness as "The girls can flirt and fairly queer things can do" (talc, gypsum, calcite, fluorite, apatite, feldspar, quartz, topaz, corundum, and diamond). Anatomy students might learn the bones of the wrist as "never lower Tillie's pants, Mother might come home" (navicular, lunate, triangular, pisiform, greater multangular, lesser multangular, capitate, and hamate). The Harvard classification for spectral classes of stars—O, B, A, F, G, K, M, R, N, S—is rendered by the sentence "Oh, be a fine girl, kiss me right now, sweetheart." At the Naval Academy, students remember the list of elements to correct the compass as "Can dead men vote twice?" (compass, deviation, magnetic, variation, and true). When going from true to compass, one can recall "timid virgins make dull companions" (Dundes 1961, 139–47).

Students may decide not to trust committing the initialisms to memory and write them on one's hand or sleeve. For material not easily distilled into catchy phrases, "cheat sheets" or "crib sheets" (small pieces of paper with notes on them) may be prepared, tailor-made for gargantuan lecture classes with tests using multiple-choice and short-answer questions. If all else fails, the student might resort to glancing over at a strong student's answers. But aware of the old ploy, professors may deliver exams on the computer and scramble the questions and answers. Having given some of these computer-generated exams myself, I was interested naturally when students in a folklore-collecting project reported stories of heroic hackers overwriting the software to have all the answers to the multiple choice questions show up as "c" (see Brunvand 2000).

Computer software to discourage cheating only adds to the wide belief among students that teachers try to "trick" or "throw off" students on exams. Such a gaming metaphor suggests that students may contextualize cheating as combative sport between player and the system on the campus playing grounds, especially when headlines out in the real world blare revelations of pervasive cheating in the professional sporting ranks. To students, the exam is apart from "real life," and involves high stakes—the grade (see Mechling 1988, 359). The exam, after all, is a framed activity—like a game—with rules, time and space limits, and restrictions on the resources used within the frame.

In their folklore concerning cheating, students believe that professors have an unfair advantage in the game, and cheating is a way students can even things up. Indeed, some of the stories suggest that more effort is put into cheating than into the studying that the professor demands. Students might folklorically respond with the half-joking proverb, "If you are not cheating, you are not trying" (Doyle, Mieder, and Shapiro 2012, 37). Jay Mechling proposes that cheating may thus be a rewarding form of "deep play," meaning that it is intentionally framed to allow transgressive behavior with metaphorical connections to the power relations between student and professor. "Cheating," he writes, "may offer risks and thrills these adolescents and young adults find in few other places in their lives" (Mechling 1988, 360). Students typically keep the game to themselves, and may have some guilty feelings about cheating, for they think that other students disapprove on moral grounds. To be sure, more than thirty colleges—including Roanoke, Smith, and Hood—have a tradition in their revered student-enforced honor codes allowing for unproctored exams (Berger 1988, 9). Larger institutions tend not to, and this reinforces for many students the association of examinations with assumptions of student immaturity and mass society's imposition of rigid authority and facelessness.

Blue Books and Digital Scams

The iconic "blue book" used for many exams figures centrally in many student stories. The workbook takes its name from its blue cover. Inside it has eight to twenty-four blank white-paper pages with ruled lines. Blue books go back at least to the mid-nineteenth century, and in those days the whole book, not just the cover, was blue.

The most common blue book cheating story I collected is typically set in a large lecture class of 300 to 500 students. Alan Mays of Penn State recalled the story about a student in such a class who was obviously up to something: "The proctor was going to intercept him at the end of the test when he turned in his blue book. The student brought his blue book to the front of the room and shoved it into the middle of the stack of blue books already on the table before the proctor could stop him. He asked the proctor 'Do you know who I am?' Then he turned to face the remaining students still taking the exam to ask them, 'Do you know who I am?' No one responded and he ran out of the room. Since no one could identify him or his blue book, he presumably succeeded in cheating and in getting a good grade on the test." For the teller, the story raised the issue of the temptation to cheat created by a large, impersonal lecture class.

In many versions of the story with the "Do you know who I am?" tag, the student is not cheating, but has worked over his or her allotted time. The professor tells students to turn in their exams, but the student frantically keeps writing, wrapping up his answer. The student then scampers to the front of the room and turns in the exam. In many tellings, the narrative then relates the heated dialogue:

> PROFESSOR: "I won't take that. You continued beyond the allotted time limit."
> STUDENT: "Do you know who I am?"
> PROFESSOR: "I don't care who you are, I'm not taking this."
> STUDENT: "Do you know who I am?"
> PROFESSOR: "I told you, I'm not taking this."
> STUDENT: "Do you know who I am?"
> PROFESSOR: "Okay, smartass. I don't know who you are. Why?"
> At which point the student grabs the whole pile of finished exams on the professor's desk, throws his in with the pile, and flings the entire pile up in the air, where they naturally intermingle and fall all over the place (thus mixing his up with the other exams). (Emery 2010a; see also Chopra 2009; Tucker 2005, 113)

In this case, the professor is not just the unwitting dupe of the impersonal mega-university system with immense classes. The professor is portrayed as part of the problem because he or she rigidly follows the system's misguided rules, even though the student has abundant knowledge to impart. The professor is unfeeling and, in psychological terms, controlling or robotic, in contrast to the passionate student.

Many cheating stories are about "dumb jocks" who need a ruse to pass because they supposedly do not belong in college in the first place. From the University of California at Berkeley in 1982 comes this story of a stereotypical football player in a classroom of 500 students: "During the final exam the player got out his notes and began cheating. The teacher saw him and thought he would nail him when he turned the exam in. [The student] made sure he was one of the last students working. Instead of handing it to him [the professor] he took all the exams on the table, shoved his in between and knocked them on the floor. As he was leaving he said 'find it' and he got away with it." The collector's commentary recorded in the Berkeley Folklore Archives supports the idea of cheating as part of a collegiate game: "I see it as another example of students 'beating the system' in the game with the faculty."

In many versions of the story, the cheater in essence punishes the teacher for his or her lack of attention in such a large class. In other words, if the professor deprives the student of a reasonable class, then the student will deprive the instructor of a fairly taken test. In variants, the student keeps on working after the proctor orders the class to stop. The proctor, usually described as being haughty, stiff, and strict, threatens to punish the student, but the student pulls the trick of shoving the exam into a pile of exams and spreading the exams on the floor (see Brunvand 1986, 198–99; Meakes 2004, 109; Roeper 1999, 109–11). In another variant, the exam-taker is actually a paid substitute for an enrolled student. When the proctor tells the student that he does not recognize him, the exam-taker pulls the con.

Lew Girdler dates his earliest blue book legend to 1937, collected from a University of California at Berkeley graduate student:

> This student went into his final examination with an A-minus average. There were two essay questions. He knew nothing about the first one, but he was primed on the second. He filled his first blue book with just anything he thought of. Then he labeled his second blue book "II" and began it with what appeared to be the last sentence or two of the answer to the first essay question. Then on the second page of this second blue book he wrote "2" for the second essay question, and a beautiful answer to it. He turned in only the second blue book. A few days later he got a postcard from the instructor saying he got an A in the course and apologizing for having lost the first blue book. (1970, 111)

Another legend raising this issue concerns a two-page exam. The student did not recognize the material asked for on the first page, so he spent all his time on the second page. When the period ended, he slipped the first page into his notebook and turned in the second page. Once outside the classroom, he hurriedly looked up the answers and filled in the first page. Then he stepped on the page. He gave the page to a friend who had a class in the same room. The friend approached the teacher after class and said he found the page "in the back." The teacher took it, checked through the papers collected in the morning class, and sure enough, found the page was missing. He graded all the papers and gave the student an A (Girdler 1970, 111–12; see also Jeakle and Wyatt 1989, 83).

From San Jose State College, Girdler reports a moving blue book legend that brings in Mom into the plot:

> A friend of mine tells this about her brother Jack, a sometime student. Jack found himself sitting in the classroom during an important examination with two blue books, a pen, and a question he couldn't answer. Being naturally bright, if lazy, he thought of the following solution. In one of the blue books he wrote a letter to his mother, telling her that he had finished writing his exam early but was waiting for a friend in the same class and so was

taking the opportunity to write to her. He apologized for not writing sooner but said he'd been studying very hard for this instructor, who was a nice guy but had pretty high standards. When the time was up he handed in this blue book and left in a hurry with his unused one. He hurried to his text, wrote an answer, and then put the blue book in an envelope and mailed it to his mother in Boston. When the instructor found the letter he called Jack, who explained that he had written in two blue books and must have got them mixed up and if the instructor had the letter, the answer must be in the mail on the way to Boston. He offered to call his mother in Boston and have her send the envelope back as soon as she got it. He did, she did, and the blue book was sent back, with the inner envelope postmarked the day of the test and the outer envelope postmarked Boston. (1970, 112; see also Meakes 2004, 110; Roeper 1999, 111–13)

In some stories with a cautionary tone, the cheater is caught. One concerns a student at the University of Alabama who was not doing well in chemistry. Then he figured out a foolproof method of passing his written final. The room was on the ground floor, and his seat was next to the window. The ingenious student hatched a scheme for his roommate to wait outside the window, be slipped the exam by the student, and take it back to the dorm to answer the questions from the textbook. All went off as planned. The test went out the window, off to the dorm, back through the window, and turned in to the prof within the two-hour test period. The student walked out happy. But when his marks came back, he found that he had failed. It seems he answered the questions a little too well. The roommate had printed out his answers on a computer (or typewriter in earlier versions).

In a legend that shows professors may not be as dumb as they look, a University of North Carolina professor steps out of his office the day before the final exam, leaving the door open and the pile of the next day's tests on the desk. A student comes by to ask a question and, finding the room empty, steals one exam. The professor, though, had counted the exams, and did so again the next morning before going to the classroom. Discovering one missing, he cuts exactly one half-inch from the bottom of all the remaining exams. When the tests come in, the student with the long paper gets a failing grade (Brunvand 1989, 285–86; see also Meakes 2004, 112; Roeper 1999, 107–8). A student stratagem using the class window also is foiled in the following narrative from the California Institute of Technology about a brilliant student paid for answers with a drink or two. According to the story, a "student would slip his copy of the exam out an open window. Then, some of the most gifted students (legend has it that Robert Oppenheimer was one) who had already taken the course, answered all but one of the questions correctly. For the last question they wrote, 'I'm too damn drunk to write any more'" (Capri 2007, 103). Students come up victorious, however, in the tale of the professor who announces an open-book final exam for the lower-level undergraduate class. Asked by the undergrads what they could bring with them to the final, the professor responds, "Whatever you can carry with you." One cagey student arrived with a graduate student on his back and had him ace the test (Genge 2000, 251; Meakes 2004, 109; Roeper 1999, 109).

The blue book has survived into the twenty-first century, but it is quickly becoming a relic of the analog, or pre-personal-device age. Even in the digital age, stories surface with themes similar to those of the blue book legends, particularly the concern for inequity of power and individuality. Many of the twenty-first-century exam stories concern hackers breaking into exam files or substitute examinees being discovered. A persistent story at MIT, for example, is the narrative of the hackers who got around the restriction of user names and passwords for exams by obtaining a copy of the password file and posting it on an MIT bulletin board (Hansche, Berti, and Hare 2004, 69). Another narrative comments on software-generated quizzes for a class gathered in a computer lab to take a final. A weak student had paid someone who had previously aced the course to take the exam and gave him his password. He figured that the professor would be clueless about who took the exam if he or she had the password in the proctored lab. Trouble was that the student did not realize the webcam picked up who was logging in. There are holes in this "cheaters never win" story about the use of technology to catch students in the act, but the narrative incorporates an additional fear besides that of the pressure of a single test determining a final grade and the belief that professors are indeed out to get students—the watchful, secretive eye of technology. Occasionally, though, stories will surface about digital fallibility, such as the server going down in the middle of an Internet-delivered exam and losing all the student data. In that case, students draw on the "4.0 suicide rule" in relating the administrative decision to give everyone an A.

Technology also is a feature of the cheating narrative reported by a University of California at Berkeley student who heard a story as she was about to take a test of two young men who had come into a final exam, one with an arm cast and the other with a head cast. Thing is, they did not have casts on earlier that day. According to the teller, "it turned out that the casts were wired with hidden microphones that they were communicating with during the test, in order to cheat." Folklorist Elizabeth Tucker's commentary is that the story conveys a warning "don't plan to cheat because you may get caught," although at the same time admiration is expressed for the students' ingenuity. The proverbial professorial perspective is that "if they spent as much time studying as preparing casts with microphones, they would not need to cheat on the exam," while students held the view that it was a valiant attempt to "beat the system" (Tucker 2005, 112–13).

A student protest of examinations that do not really test smarts is of the woman taking a biology course with a unit on ornithology. She is a top student, and in preparation for the exam, she memorizes everything about birds, including the minutest details of their wings, beaks, and feathers. At the exam, the professor places five paper bags and requires students to identify the bird from the evidence under the bag. He lifts the first bag and shows the students a bird's feet and legs. The woman is dumbfounded, even though she is the smartest one in the room and has studied hard. By the time he reaches the third bag, she exclaims, "This is ridiculous, and you are an idiot." The angry professor retorts, "What is your name?" The woman raises her skirt up to her knees and yells, "You tell me!" (Brunvand 1989, 277; 1999, 442–43; Major and Bray 2008, 245; Meakes 2004, 110). The story indicates the popularity of clever alternatives to the blue book introduced by professors, but as educators Claire Howell Major and Nathaniel Bray comment, the legend expresses "concern of students that tests can be arbitrary and unfair, and to an extent there is only so much students can do to prepare for the wealth of routes professors can select in their evaluation decisions. Here, the student responds in a reactionary way that illustrates the frustration of being a part of a nameless mass of students as well as of being evaluated in such an arbitrary manner" (2008, 246).

Smart Answers

Another kind of story honors the noncomformist student who gives clever earthly retorts to lofty-sounding final-exam questions. Probably the most familiar is about the philosophy exam with the single question "Why?" While most of the students write lengthy essays, one student answers "Why not?" (or "Because") and gets an A (see Baker 1983, 109; Brunvand 1989, 286; Meakes 2004, 119; Toelken 1986, 511; Tucker 2005, 110–11). Variations include the exam instruction to "define courage (or bravery)," and the student writes "This is courage" before packing up her bags to leave (Brunvand 1999, 445).

Jan Harold Brunvand reports a version from Harvard concerning a course in freshman metaphysics: "When the students are settled for the final exam, the teacher places a chair on the desk in the front of the room. 'Prove that this chair exists,' he says. 'You have two hours.' As the students begin to chew their pencils and roll their eyes, one student leans back. . . . He writes, 'What chair?' submits his paper and leaves the room, just as the others begin to scribble furiously" (1989, 286). This student naturally receives an A.

A classic tale of clever student conciseness that flies in the face of the professor expecting a treatise is about the literature assignment for an essay discussing the themes of religion, royalty, sex, and mystery. "This will take time for you to write and integrate these themes," the professor cautioned. A minute later, a student raised his hand and announced he was done. The startled instructor said, "I don't see how that is possible." The smiling student replied, "Well, I have." Looking to embarrass the student he thought was slacking off, the prof told him to read it aloud to the entire class. Confidently, the student rose and blared, "'My God!' said the queen. 'I'm pregnant. I wonder whose it is?'" (Baker 1986, 194–95; Lebman 2004; 12; Legman 1975, 90; Meakes 2004, 111; Mikkelson and Mikkelson 2011a).

At the University of California at Davis, I was told of the story of the college entrance exam that asks for one word that describes yourself and an explanation. The student's response was "Terse." He was admitted. Even more minimalist is the philosophy exam that simply read "?" The high grade went to the response "!" This example prompted a discussion among my students of whether tests prepare students for "real life." Reflecting the interpretation of the popularity of these narratives representing student frustration over the importance placed on exams, one student offered that "people who are good in school have learned a bunch of strategies for dealing with all the stupid things governing tests." Giving insight to some student views of the "exam game," another student replied, "Test taking IS like real life in that you are no more likely to succeed in tests using an inflexible set of strategies than you are in real life. I never learned any such strategies, anyway—most teachers have their own bizarre variations to the rules, and you always had to be on the lookout."

One studious fellow who blanked out supposedly wrote on the final fall exam delivered to Professor William Lyon Phelps of Westbrook College in Maine, "God only knows the answer to this question. Merry Christmas." The good professor returned the exam with the note "God gets an A; you get an F. Happy New Year" (Healy 1972, 21). The story also appears as a more generalized college jest: "During a Christmas exam, one of the questions was 'What causes a depression?' One of the students wrote: 'God knows! I don't. Merry Christmas!' The exam paper came back with the prof's notation: 'God gets 100. You get zero. Happy New Year'" (Copeland and Copeland 1940, 375; see also Meakes 2004, 109; Mikkelson and Mikkelson 2011b).

Questioning the system of student knowledge measured by answering seemingly capricious questions is the widely circulating story of the big test with these disarming directions: "Write the best possible final exam for this course, then answer it." The question unnerved most students, who had memorized dates and names in anticipation of regurgitating facts, but one pupil calmly scribbled, "The best possible final exam question for this course is 'Write the best final exam question for this course, then answer it'" (Brunvand 1999, 446). The story often leads to student commentary on the key to success being the provision of "what professors want" rather than what students know.

Believing that exams often test ability to memorize a narrow range of material rather than awareness of general, pragmatic knowledge, science students may recount the following story. On a physics exam, a student was asked how to determine the height of a tall building using a barometer. His answer: take the barometer to the top of the building, tie a rope to it, lower it to the ground, pull it back up, and measure how much rope was let out. He flunked on the grounds that, though his answer would work, he had not demonstrated any knowledge of physics. When the student protested his grade, his professor agreed to reexamine him. This time the student gave five answers (still resisting the obvious rote response—differential barometric pressures at the top and bottom of the tower): drop the barometer off the roof, time its fall and calculate the height with a particular formula; take the barometer out on a sunny day, hold it upright, measure the length of its shadow, measure the length of the shadow of the tower, and determine the height of the building with a simple proportion; measure the length of the barometer, climb the tower marking off lengths of the barometer on the inside wall, and multiply; tie the barometer to a string, swing it as a pendulum at the street level and at the top of the tower, measure the value of "g" at both points, and calculate the height from the difference in the two values; and, the best and easiest way, take the barometer to the superintendent of the building and bargain with him thus: "Mr. Superintendent, here I have a fine barometer. If you tell me the height of this building, I will give you this barometer." The student received an A for the answers (Dundes and Pagter 1987, 158–59; Meakes 2004, 108; Moffatt 1989, 22).

A number of the legends about clever retorts touch on the student nightmare of "blanking out." Harvard alum Richard Dorson remembers the anecdote floating around campus about a trickster student's "feat in handling a pedantic question in American diplomatic history on rights to the Newfoundland fisheries. The student could not remember anything about the matter, so he wrote, 'This question has long been discussed from the American and British points of view, but has anyone ever considered the viewpoint of the fish?' He proceeded to give it, and was awarded, appropriately enough, a C" (1949, 673).

A story from Stanford with a commentary on the special treatment of athletes concerns an exam in comparative religion. According to the student collector:

Comparative religion was the snap course football players traditionally took to restore sagging point averages at Stanford. The professor who taught the course ... gave the same final exam year after year, and every fraternity had the exam in its files. One heroic quarterback taking the class during a hectic football season was thoroughly primed by his cohorts for the final, so that he could answer the prof's expected essay question.... The question was, "explain the significance of and list in chronological order five kings of Israel." Exam time arrived, and the confident gridder sat down to write his blue book. He was horrified when he saw the only exam question, one about which he knew absolutely nothing. The professor had finally wised up and changed his examination tactics by asking his students to "compare the significant aspects of Shintoism and Buddhism." Not to be so easily struck down, the football stalwart gave it the old college try, and handed in an exam paper which began as follows: "Far be it for me to intrude my humble intelligence upon so delicate a subject. Instead I will explain the significance of and list in chronological order five kings of Israel." (Ligotti 1987, 6; see also Meakes 2004, 110–11)

The story is similar to one reported by a male student at Harvard Divinity School in the 1950s. "A certain Old Testament professor," he says, "always included on his final exam the question 'List the kings of Israel and Judah in parallel columns.' One year, however, he substituted the question 'List the names of the major and minor prophets in parallel columns.' One student alone passed the course when he began his answer by writing, 'Far be it for me to discriminate among such worthy men, but the kings of Israel and Judah in parallel columns are ...'" (Brunvand 1989, 290). Apparently the teller from Stanford adapted the core of the story to express a parable for the special treatment of athletes within the university.

Alongside this corpus of devious professors and trickster students, one will occasionally encounter a story of a helpful professor. From mathematics comes the story associated with legendary Cornell professor Mark Kac (1914–84), who was of Polish descent. He administered a makeup oral exam to a struggling student. He asked what kind of singularity a certain function had and tried to give a clue by pointing vigorously to himself. The student stared back dumbly. Kac then supposedly asked, "All right then, what am I?" He still could not get a response from the student, so Kac supplied the answer: "A simple Pole" (Capri 2007, 27–28).

Finals, Primal Screams, and Naked Runs

Some legends suggest that the only way a student can turn in everything a professor demands on a final exam is to be out of this world. From Southern

Illinois University, for example, comes this testimony: "Everyone knows about the ghost exam. Prof. Adams of the History Dept. had it happen to him and it is one of the mysteries of campus. It seems that Prof. Adams gave one of his finals a few years back and this one girl turned in a nearly perfect paper. Now comes the truly weird part. It seems that Adams gave the exam on a Thursday but the girl had died in an accident, I think it was a car accident, the preceding Wednesday night. It is really strange but it is supposed to be true" (Procter 1966, 26). You hear these kinds of stories still around finals, especially during the dark days of winter.

The custom of the "primal scream" or "door slams" on campuses indicates the kind of tension that finals produce among students. A report from Franklin and Marshall College states, "a 'primal scream' at midnight from one senior—'I can't take it anymore'—soon was supported by every student within chanting distance" (Brubaker 1987, 46). At Southwestern University, faculty members cook a midnight breakfast the night before finals, and then during finals the students bellow out their annual scream. The tension from finals released by the scream is clear, but the connection of the scream to the quality of the meal is left somewhat ambiguous.

At Stephens College, students prefer to take out their frustrations by slamming doors en masse, which then signals the start of twenty-four quiet hours in preparation for finals. At the University of California at Berkeley, a cry around finals has taken on the name of "Pedro" usually drawn out to "Peeeeeeedroooooh," which reverberates over the campus on a late evening. Berkeley professor Alan Dundes explains the connection of Pedro with final examinations: "Typically, the president of the University (Wheeler, Sproul) or perhaps a dean or professor loses his pet dog. The sad owner announces that he will cancel finals if someone finds the dog. From that time on, students during the period of final examinations have called for Pedro in the hope of finding the lost dog and thus avoiding finals" (1968, 30; see also Farrell 2004; Hankey 1944, 29–35; Taylor 1947a, 1947b).

At Harvard, the primal scream kicks off the final-exam period with a lap in the buff around the north end of Old Yard (the western third of Harvard Yard around which cluster freshman dorms, including Massachusetts Hall, constructed in 1720, the oldest standing campus building). Students well aware of Harvard's long, studious legacy inherit the lore that the naked frivolity dates back to colonial days. The screaming part of the event derives from students congregating in the Yard for a loud stress-relieving yell for several minutes just before midnight. By the 1990s, according to campus chroniclers, the streaking at night became prominent, apparently countering the stuffy Ivy League college's image by day. According to a *Harvard Crimson*'s editorial writer, "It seems fitting that such a salient symbol of Harvard tradition should be comprised of several hundred nude Ivory Tower dwellers who, eager to escape their daily, uptight, and proper image, throw off the repression with their clothes and take to the Yard" (Barbieri 2007). A spin-off concocted by residents of the alternative-minded Dudley Co-op is the Lingerie Study Break. They claim distinction by stripping inside Lamont Library in view of hundreds of students cramming for exams the next day (Fox 2004, 157).

Stripping down in unison to Skivvies, and less, as a ritual of finals week has grown in popularity in the twenty-first century. At UCLA, students initiated the Undie Run in fall 2001 to replace the "Midnight Yell," which had been restricted by police ("Steps" 2008). On Wednesday evening of finals week, between 3,000 and 7,000 scantily clad students joined in a stress-relieving sprint through campus. Students added creative touches, including decorating their bodies with paint, carrying erotic props, and donning an assortment of accessories such as capes, helmets, or crowns. In the summer of 2009, the campus administration cited safety concerns in prohibiting future runs. The run lives on, however, at a number of other universities, including San Diego State, the University of Texas, Texas A&M, Arizona State, Syracuse, the University of California at Santa Barbara, Chapman, and the University of Houston. Not all of these are warm-weather climes where one might expect that skimpy attire may not be all that unusual. Some participants in the spirit of college rivalries post videos of the event on YouTube and declare their campus as host of the wildest and most creative run. Technology fostered mass participation by rallying students at the appointed time and place for a run through electronic tweets and instant messages circulating even faster than word of mouth.

A localized variation of an end-of-semester evening student romp is USC's Fountain Run beginning after dark and featuring seniors donning bathing suits and jumping rowdily, and sometimes drunkenly, into the campus's twenty-nine elegant fountains. Framing the transgressive event is the starting point of the sculpture that students affectionately call the "Finger Fountain" (officially, it is the Gavin Herbert Plaza) because it looks to them to take the shape of an extended middle finger giving an obscene gesture, supposedly aimed at UCLA (Steach 2011). The fountains distinguish the campus landscape and, with their planned design, have classical associations of a sober temple of learning, but in the framed parting ritual, students take over and transform the water into a playful fountain of youth before symbolically aging and leaving at graduation. The ritualistic function of the event is not lost on students. A twenty-two-year-old participant describing the event for the campus's folklore archives commented, "It is a liminal stage of transition to being an active, educated member of society. People employ such a tactic in order to also act against authority one 'last' time by participating in a festivity that would ordinarily have a certain degree of ramifications. It is altogether a way of ending an era, remembering it,

Fig. 2.1. The University of Southern California's Gavin Herbert Plaza fountain, known by USC students as the "Finger Fountain" (belief holds it is an obscene gesture aimed at UCLA), traditionally the starting point of the annual Fountain Run. (Photo by Simon Bronner)

and preparing for the life ahead" (Jordan 2011). Another student collector saw a social bonding occurring in the event: "There are no athletes, no sorority girls, no engineers, and no geeks. Everybody is celebrating the two things they have in common: being a Senior at USC, and being close to graduation." Also referring to the liminal status of participants, this participant-observer notes that "it's okay for people to get a little crazy" (Thomas 2011).

At Tufts, scores of students brave the December New England frost just before finals to dash around Rez Quad several times. According to some accounts, residents of West Hall originated the run in the 1970s and maintained it for several years without sanction by the university. Another storied explanation is that the event began as a protest against coed dormitories or the imposition of mandatory "quiet hours." During the 1990s, students revived the run as a local campus tradition, and it grew with attendant drinking and partying. In 2002, university president Lawrence Bacow sent out an open letter stating that "the combination of consumption of alcohol with a mad dash through an icy, hilly campus at night cannot continue" (Carol 2007). An ensuing effort with the cooperation of university organizations and police to tame the popular event resulted in the organization of a Nighttime Quad Reception to safely reframe the festivity. Additional problems arose, however, with the spread of compact visual technology such as mobile-phone cameras and miniature video cams causing many participants to worry about their privacy, especially when their visages appeared on social networking sites and blogs (Carol 2007). In the open modern campus, students faced a difficult time keeping their release from societal norms tightly within the frame of the event and out of the public spotlight. Nonetheless, many students want to keep the tradition going as a mark of Tufts' social distinction among national colleges. Besides, Tufts University police sergeant Robert McCarthy commented, "It's hard to stop it, and if it's going to happen anyhow, we try to do it as safely as possible" (Carol 2007).

Students associate studying for finals with staying up late and, to aid keeping the eyes open, downing a sweet doughnut for a sugary rush. Brown University students have institutionalized that connection with the Naked Donut Run. On the night before the first day of exams, naked students meander through campus libraries to hand out doughnuts to their comrades in study. It is less of a competitive run than a stroll for the participants; it may be a play on words that the "run" derives more from slang for students going out for late-night sustenance than for athletic endeavor. Students maintain the spontaneity of the tradition by recruiting students within twenty-four hours of the actual run and not announcing beforehand the exact time for their appearance in the library. The role of head organizer held by an upperclassman usually from one of the campus's coed fraternities or residential co-ops is secretly passed to a newbie every year or two.

Gaining an official stamp of approval has been Purdue's Nearly Naked Mile since 2008, apparently as a take-off with a service and outreach twist on other run-in-the-buff student traditions. Sponsored by the Purdue Alumni Student Experience (PASE, the student membership of the Purdue Alumni Association), the Nearly Naked Mile is intended to be a charitable event for donating clothing to the needy. Playing on the Purdue Boilermaker moniker, organizers come up with catchy mottos for T-shirts and banners such as "Boiler Up, Strip Down." Several hundred students arrive in outfits they want to part with, and, once exposed, make a dash to the end of the mile. University police are on hand to make sure that participants are not showing too much skin (thongs, a favorite at the mayhem of the Undie Run at UCLA, are a no-no at Purdue's Nearly Naked Mile). Students also have the option of wearing outlandish costumes for which they can receive prizes for being most creative, closest resemblance to a celebrity, and most spirited.

With so much hunkering down for study in the library that suggests an unnatural (at least to students) stillness, submission, and solitude at the behest of authoritarian professors, it should not come as a surprise that many students revel in stories of sex in the stacks that suggest getting "it up" or "doing the nasty" around finals time. Here is an interview, for example, conducted by student folklore researchers at Indiana University:

> Q: What, in your opinion, is the best or craziest story you've heard about this place?
> A: ... haha, come on. Do I actually need to say it?
> Q: I'm writing, so go for it.
> A: It's definitely the stuff about sex in the library.
> Q: Have you witnessed anything interesting first-hand?
> A: Oh no, I actually don't think I ever want to! That's *so* risky, oh man, I think I'd just die if I got caught. How embarrassing!
> Q: When you did you hear this legend, and why do you think it's been so popular for so long?
> A: Clearly it's still so intriguing because everyone wants to believe it really does happen a lot. It adds a certain culture and mysterious tradition to campus—like something more than just reading [at finals time] goes on inside these walls! (McDowell 2008)

The student in her narration of the belief structures the sex in symbolic opposition to the control (implied assignment of reading) and restriction ("walls") of study in the library. Another Indiana student, for example, thought of "sex in the stacks" rumors after noting, "Finals are coming up around the corner, and I need to buckle down to get all of my projects, papers, and finally, some studying done" (McDowell 2008). Students at other universities pipe in with their own stories of sexual encounters, usually placed in narrative in the library right around finals time. At Brown University, the thirteenth floor of the Sciences Library (with all the aura attached to the magical number thirteen) is reportedly a place for erotic trysts ("Brown University" 2005). At Cornell, a student responded to rumors of sex in the stacks with the observation, "It's the most classic college thing that you won't be able to do after you graduate" (Marcus 2010). "The senior-week schedule will screw you," a Harvard alum advised, and that vivid metaphor inspired the student answer to being placed in a passive position: "sex in the library is the undersexed scholar's study break" (Dean 2006).

Some folks may think that the apparent turn from ritualized scream to streak for relief from finals is another sign of an oversexed, exhibitionist society of the new millennium or confirmation of reckless adolescent abandon, but a symbolic logic can be discerned in the association between nudity and the organizational pressure of the initiatory "big" test. References in testimonies to the naked run as release not just from the rigors of studying but from a sense of "repression" suggest that baring all signals a stark contrast, and even resistance, of one's natural self to the authority and artifice of the hurdle that allows one to get out and move on.

Additional evidence is the importance of spontaneity and student control over the risqué festivity. That the exuberant performance of nudity, with its sexual overtones in public space, especially comes out at finals time implies the kind of desexualizing or neutering effect psychologically felt by students forced to prove themselves and compete with one another as organizational signs of passage. Students realize that streaking is counternormative, especially to an institution/society represented by elders administering exams that are all about control in mechanically assigning numbers, lining students up, and sublimating adolescent urges. With fear of inadequacy building among students, they display what they consider their best assets—their youthful bodies—and subvert the most serious, alienating, and individuating segmentation of reading or exam period of the academic year with the socialized play, magical, or ritual frame of a run on campus under the cover of midnight or darkness.

The clamorous and often sexualized public run counters the anal image of sitting quietly in place, separated from others, at a desk taking a test or hunched over in study. The run may appear more extreme than the scream or slam, but in its transgressive, unrestrained performance, the run shares with other forms of traditional release at finals time a social "up and at 'em" show of symbolically youthful and natural force, making students feel better about subsequently knuckling under. Of course only a portion of students participate in these adventurous escapades at finals time, and some campus cultures eschew the runs as unbecoming or debauched, but for many test-takers it is still important to know that a tradition representing, if not alleviating, their anxieties can be loudly heard and vividly seen.

Grading Papers and Other Mysteries

Next to finals, the assigned essays known as "term papers" worry students most. Because students expect high grades for their trouble, they are at a loss to explain the varying grading techniques of professors. Folklore offers allegories to which students can nod and smile knowingly. One story is that professors grade papers by throwing them down the stairs: those that land on the bottom get an A, those on the next step up get a B, and so on. Among the most widespread and persistent samples of folklore, the story carries an underlying belief that when it comes to papers, weight, not content, is what counts.

Variants of the story suggest that professors really do not treat students as individuals, or that they make up their minds beforehand about the student's success. William Tillson recounted that "at Purdue, with its scientific bent, the students knew that blue books were thrown *up*stairs in order that the grade distribution more nearly approximate the bell-shaped curve" (1962, 56). Richard Dorson told a story about his chemistry professor at Harvard who distributed his papers to his family: "he gave the Es himself, his son-in-law the Ds, and so on up to the baby, who, being the slowest, marked the As" (1949, 673). Then there is the tale of "the professor who customarily placed his papers in two heaps, representing the good and the bad students. When he came across an error by a good student he disregarded it, saying, 'He knows better than that.' When he saw a correct answer by a poor student he marked it wrong saying, 'He couldn't have meant that'" (Dorson 1949, 673). The imagery of dividing souls into good and bad (evoking "evil") suggests the power of a deity who apparently supports predestination.

Professors arbitrarily piling papers in anal-retentive style frequently appear in student stories. Here is one I heard about a Duquesne professor: "He shuffled the exams and blindly separated the one pile into several. The first pile he designated the As, the second pile the Bs and so on." The story was also reportedly told in the nineteenth century about famed Harvard professor Nathaniel Shaler (1841–1906), who packed blue books in a mountainous heap on his sofa. After they had aged a week, he plunged both hands deep into the mass and carried all he could to a chair on the opposite side of the room. A second week went by and he carried another armload to another chair, and he made a similar move after the third and fourth weeks. Those in the first chair he gave As, those in the second got Bs, and so on. All those that slipped onto the floor flunked (Cowley and Reed 1977, 35). Other belief legends question whether professors really even take the time to look at papers, especially those of large classes. If reading great quantities of written material is difficult for students, how could it be reasonably done by professors? Students thus tell about a paper handed in with a title page, a first page, and a bibliography. In the middle was a bunch of blank pages. The student received an A.

Students bemoan the hard grader in narrative, but provide warnings about the too-easy A. In one account,

> a professor was known for being an easy grader. The grades he gave for a survey course were based entirely on two exams, and the stuff on the exams was entirely covered in the textbook. So showing up for class wasn't a big deal. However, this started to get out of hand. As word of the course spread, each term more students showed up infrequently or not at all, except for exam days. Finally, it got so bad that about half of the students one term never showed before the midterm. The day of the midterm everyone came in, and a graduate assistant handed out exams. "Prof X is sick, so he asked me to give you your exams." There was only one question in the exam

booklets: "Which one of the pictures below is of Professor X?" "Obviously," the storyteller added, "the students who never showed up didn't know and had to guess. Many failed, while the students who had been showing up regularly got As." (Kandolf 1991)

Students have a great reputation for making excuses, and every semester it seems that grandmothers (apparently exacting more sympathy in cop-out lore than grandfathers) fall victim right around finals. Probably the best-known exam legend involving famed alibis is one that might be called "The Flat Tire Excuse," although online in student groups it is often labeled as "The Bastard Professor."

One weekend this past winter, four college students went away for a weekend while midterms were going on. However, it was not until late Sunday night that the students realized that they all had a Philosophy exam the next morning at 8 AM. This proved to be most unfortunate as none had even cracked a book for the course, and even if they had studied they would never be able to make it back to school in time for the exam. So, one of the students called their professor and told him that they had gotten a very bad flat tire, where the rim was bent. The mechanic said that he would not be able to repair it until Monday afternoon. Well, the professor was very understanding and told them to take their time getting back and to call him when they were on campus again. Well, the students thought this was great. They came leisurely back on campus Monday afternoon and called the professor. He said they could take the exam the next morning in the auditorium. Come the next morning, all four students arrived in the auditorium and were seated in each of the four corners of the room. The professor then proceeded to give the following instructions: "I know that you have all had a chance to talk with the other students in the class in order to find out what was on the exam. Well, fear not, because this is a very different exam. In fact, you will be very happy to know that there is only one very simple question on this exam. Are you ready to begin?" All of the students nod. "Okay, you will have ninety minutes. The question is: Which tire?" (see Meakes 2004, 109; Mikkelson and Mikkelson 2011d; Ochs 2006, 201–2; Roeper 1999, 113–14)

The majors in question often change in the telling. From Marshall University comes an account of two engineering students kept in separate rooms while they were given the simple question. Sometimes an explanation is given that the students were doing very well in the course and therefore decided to party before the final. At Duke, it was known as an anecdote about a renowned chemistry professor. Typical of many versions, that one has the question

"Which tire?" worth ninety-five points following a science problem that the students master for five points (Carroll 1994).

In the digital age, students imagine that professors probably use videogame software to assign grades. A post I spotted around the end of the semester is about hearing of a program that takes paper files and simulates hurling them toward the viewer. According to the student relating dorm humor, "Using the arrow keys (or a joystick) the 'grader' fires photon 'grades' at the attacking papers; each 'hit' is assigned a random grade according to preset curve data, thus assuring a double-random result (which self-evidently is as normatively 'fair' as any student could wish)" (Solove 2010). The post received a host of replies about the fabled program, but no one could track it down of course. A writer reflected that the age of the virtual paper has removed at least one professorial quirk—grading on the basis of the quality of the type rather than the content.

Recycling Paper

If a paper receives an A, however mysteriously, student stories ask, "why not give it another go?" Jan Brunvand reports the story from California about an instructor famous for his low grading scale: "After years of giving only D's and F's, one year he finally gave a paper a B-minus—his highest grade ever. Word got around campus about the grade. Then the paper became a hot commodity trading hand to hand. The lucky student sold the term paper to the highest bidder, who then turned in to the same professor. This time he gave it a B. The paper was recycled again the next year, and it received a B plus. Just as the students were beginning to lose respect for the professor, the roving term paper was turned in a fourth time. This time it got an A. The teacher's written comment was, 'I've read this paper four times now, and I like it better each time" (Brunvand 1989, 286–87; see also Meakes 2004, 114). The stories suggest that papers are goods to be traded and sold in a capitalistic society rather than monastic acts of discovery, as campus ideals proclaim.

From campuses where fraternities keep files of successful papers comes the story of the student who pulls a paper from the file to hand in to a professor. The professor writes on it, "A—When I wrote this theme when I was a freshman, it only received a C and I always thought it worth an A" (Baker 1983, 108; Brunvand 1989, 287; Cerf 1959, 114; Fitton 1942, 41; Meakes 2004, 114). In a variant replacing the fraternity conspiracy with an independent student's procrastination, the undergrad suffering from a writing block or simply from putting the assignment off finds an old paper in the library and retypes it to make it look fresh. The professor's comments in that case is "Twenty-five years ago when I wrote this paper, it got a B. I always thought it deserved an A," but the narrative adds a warning tag from the professor of "Try anything like this again and I'll have you thrown out of school" ("Old Man and the 'C'" 2007). The story has stuck around, often with the adaptation of the paper's source in one of the companies offering essays for sale on the Internet (Brunvand 1999, 441–42; 2001, 350). The narrative emphasizes the gulf between instructor and student, with the punch line referring to the disbelief by students that professors may have been once in their shoes.

Exemplifying the adage that "a picture is worth a thousand words" is a story about a particularly tough marine-biology course. A student scores a rare A on the paper with a slick illustration of a whale. A pal hands it in the next time the course is offered, but the third time around a student submits it without the illustration. The written comment from the professor was "I liked it better with the whale" (Brunvand 1989, 287; see also Meakes 2004, 114). To add to this cycle, Hope Coulter sent me her recollection of a large history course at Harvard called "The Great Age of Discovery, 1400–1520," nicknamed "Boats": "A guy who had artistic leanings took the course one year and for the paper turned in a not-very-impressive piece of prose, triple-spaced, with big margins, but with an intricate line drawing of a ship included. He made an A. The next year his roommate took the course and turned in the exact same paper, with the drawing. He made an A, too. The third year another roommate of theirs took the course and turned in the by now two-year-old paper, but he thought it was too risky to include the line-drawing again, so he tore it out. The paper came back to him marked 'C—where's the picture?'"

In a well-circulated narrative with another "gotcha" ending, the protagonist is a student at a loss for what to write on an important paper. Hearing that professors grade by looking at the beginning and end of the paper, the undergraduate composes a catchy opening and erudite conclusion. To fill the pages in the middle, he inserts the Gettysburg Address. The paper came back with an "F" and the inscription, "Ha, ha; I do read the middle part" (Brunvand 1999, 442). The story's credibility is based on the notion that much of student discourse in the form of shared beliefs is about professorial grading quirks. Added to this context is the idea that the paper is an odd form of communication that the student is unlikely to pursue outside of class. Comments following the stories of sham papers indicate that grading is "all a game," and professors must be as uninterested in reading papers as students are in writing them.

Unwritten Rules

Fitting in with student beliefs about the arbitrary nature of grading is the one about the "suicide rule." Students say that if your roommate commits suicide during the semester, especially late in the semester, you are entitled to an auto-matic "4.0" (an A in every course) for the semester. Although I have yet to find a college with such a rule, folklorists have found the belief at campuses from one coast to another. At the University of California at Berkeley in 2009, a first-year student described the action as an "unwritten rule" of the university. She heard the dictum from someone on her floor who heard it from a friend during summer orientation. To these self-confident, but impressionable, first-year students wondering about the grind lying ahead, the story confirmed the stresses of academic work and the importance placed on grades. A 4.0 for the semester, in other words, will make it all better, even the trauma of death close by. Reporting on Tufts University, for example, journalist Lisa Birnbach wrote, "People work for grades and the tension can get relentless," and then she quoted a student, "A lot of students think they'll die if they don't get an A in economics. You get a 4.0 for the semester if your roommate commits suicide" (1984, 177; see also Brunvand 1989, 295–98; Cowan 1989; Fox 1990; Meakes 2004, 117; Moffatt 1989, 88). Hollywood has fanned the belief's fire with film adaptations such as *The Curve* (1998) and *Dead Man on Campus* (1998). Although the former is a horror film and the latter a comedy, they both relate the moral to audiences that trying to take advantage of the rule is futile.

With costs of attending college spiraling upward, sometimes the compen-sation for students suffering legendary trauma is in tuition remission rather grades. At Indiana University, student collectors gathered numerous stories relating a policy of providing tuition to student victims of bus accidents (Mc-Dowell 2008), and I heard similar reports at Penn State's University Park cam-pus, also known for being a crowded "college town." The metafolklore of the policy, according to student narratives, is that "if you get hit by a bus then you would probably sue the school and that would be more than tuition" (McDow-ell 2008). With the more general context of lawsuits for corporate liability in the headlines and the more localized situation of lines of buses regularly cir-cling the campus, the story's credibility depends on the perception of modern America as a litigious society.

Other legendary speculations of campus policy concern close student rela-tionships other than roommates: "A law school student was sitting for his final exam. In law school, you don't have midterm exams or papers or anything, so your grade for the entire semester is based upon your performance on the one test. The guy apparently couldn't take it. He picked two sharp pencils, put one in each nostril, threw his head back, and then slammed it onto the desk in front of him. The pencils went straight into his brain. The guy died instantly. The other students in the exam were given credit for the exam, and an aver-age of their GPAs in the other courses was used to assign the grade for the final" (Major and Bray 2008, 246; see also Healey and Glanvill 1996, 233–34;

Mikkelson and Mikkelson 2011c; S. Williams 2007). Signifying the importance of the exam in a collegiate testocracy, students believe for other disciplines that if either a student or professor dies during a test, all the other students present pass.

On a related note, the bells of the campanile on the University of California at Berkeley campus play "They're Hanging Danny Deever in the Morning" (a mournful ballad tune to Rudyard Kipling's famous poem of 1890 about a soldier being executed for murder) the last day before finals (Dundes 1968, 30). Cal students annually since 1930 have had their own spin on Deever's story, often with reference to the memorable lines that Danny is "fightin' 'ard for life" before being done in by the noose of exams, and at the end of the poem, Deever's fellow young recruits "are shakin', *an' they'll want their beer to-day*, After hangin' Danny Deever in the morning.'" That the plaintive tune has a hint of the familiar bawdy folk and frat song "Barnacle Bill the Sailor" and the alliterative name sounds like an animated character add for some students to its appeal.

In folkloric allusions to death by examination, life is traded for the grade. In getting a 4.0 the student does not grieve, but rather takes the deceased student's place in line. The belief is so widespread that it has also entered into the grim humor heard around finals. A student from the University of California at Davis reported to me that if someone would say in anguish, "I can't take this anymore!" someone else would humorously tease, "Straight As for your roommate." She commented, "This kidding around usually eased the tension by assuring people that everyone else was feeling the same pressure."

Spreading Lore through Photocopiers and Computers

The personalization of technology to print and copy official-looking documents has been a boon to exam parodies. Appropriate to a technological form with an emphasis on appearance and a modern service role that emphasizes the bland formal front or performance, much of the humor is understated, mimicking therefore the style as well as the form of technological service products.

Students ridicule university entrance exams, especially for a rival university. One common example floating from photocopier to dorm room usually has twenty questions, probably in reference to the popular game "Twenty Questions." Q: Where do they bury people living west of the Mississippi? A: Please do not bury living people! Q. What is Smokey the Bear's middle name? A: The. Q: What can you fill a bucket full of to make it lighter? A: Holes (*Seventh* 1988, 10–11).

Other parodied entrance exams use the ancient rebus form, such as this one from Texas A&M (*Tenth* 1988, 14–15; see also Dundes and Pagter 1987, 139–41; Preston 1982, 104–21).

r/e/a/d/i/n/g	Reading between the lines.
Stand **I**	I understand.
o **M.D.** **Ph.D.**	Two degrees below zero.
ii ii **o o**	Circles under the eyes.
dice dice	Paradise.
he's/himself	He's beside himself.
ecnalg	Backward glance.
r **road** **a** **d**	Crossroad.
t **o** **u** **c** **h**	Touchdown.
death/life	Life after death.

Another popular piece of humor parodying the form of tests highlights what students believe is the unreasonableness of college exam questions, especially in the normal time given. Like other forms of occupational lore, this humor emphasizes the extraordinary demands on laborers to perform animatedly, to complete an unreasonable number of tasks and do them superlatively well (see Dundes and Pagter 1978, 1987; Bronner 1984). This particular example has been collected since the 1970s from California to England; consistent in the material is the time frame of four hours, and the closing of defining the universe, both symbolism for immensity (see Baker 2003; Dundes and Pagter 1987, 160–61; O'Bryon 2008, 350; Smith 1984, 84–85).

Instructions: Read each question carefully. Answer all questions. Time limit—4 hours. Begin immediately.

HISTORY: Describe the history of the papacy from its origin to the present day, concentrating especially but not exclusively on its social, political, economic, religious and philosophical impact on Europe, Asia, America, and Africa. Be brief, concise and specific.

MEDICINE: You have been provided with a razor blade, a piece of gauze and a bottle of Scotch. Remove your appendix. Do not suture until your work has been inspected. You have fifteen minutes.

PUBLIC SPEAKING: 2,500 riot-crazed aborigines are storming the classroom. Calm them. You may use any ancient language except Latin or Greek.

BIOLOGY: Create life. Estimate the differences in subsequent human culture if this form of life had developed 500 million years earlier, with special attention to its probable effect on the English parliamentary system. Prove your thesis.

MUSIC: Write a piano concerto. Orchestrate and perform it with flute and drum. You will find a piano under your seat.

PSYCHOLOGY: Based on your knowledge of their works, evaluate the emotional stability, degree of adjustment and repressed frustrations of each of the following: Alexander of Aphrodisias, Ramses II, Gregory of Nicea, Hammurabi. Support your evaluations with quotations from each man's work, making appropriate references. It is not necessary to translate.

SOCIOLOGY: Estimate the sociological problems which might accompany the end of the world. Construct an experiment to test your theory.

MANAGEMENT SCIENCE: Define management. Define science. How do they relate? Why? Create a generalized algorithm to optimize all managerial decisions. Assuming an 1130 CPU supporting 50 terminals, each terminal to activate your algorithm, design the communications interface and all necessary control programs.

ENGINEERING: The disassembled parts of a high-powered rifle have been placed in a box on your desk. You will also find an instruction manual printed in Swahili. In ten minutes a hungry Bengal tiger will be admitted to the room. Take whatever action you feel appropriate. Be prepared to justify your decision.

ECONOMICS: Develop a realistic plan for refinancing the national debt. Trace the possible effects of your plan in the following areas: Cubism, the Donatist controversy, the wave theory of light. Outline a method of preventing these effects. Criticize this method from all possible points of view. Point out the deficiencies in your point of view, as demonstrated in your answer to the last question.

POLITICAL SCIENCE: There is a red telephone on the desk beside you. Start World War III. Report at length on its socio-political effects, if any.

EPISTEMOLOGY: Take a position for or against truth. Prove the validity of your position.

PHYSICS: Explain the nature of matter. Include in your answer an evaluation of the impact of the development of mathematics on science.

PHILOSOPHY: Sketch the development of human thought; estimate its significance. Compare with the development of any other kind of thought.

GENERAL KNOWLEDGE: Describe in detail. Be objective and specific.

EXTRA CREDIT: Define the Universe. Give three examples.

For more extra credit you can answer the Shakespeare question, such as this one collected at the University of California at Berkeley (see Mitchell 1976, 223–24):

Identify each block in the table with one Shakespeare play.

miscarriage	
wet	
dry	
3"	
6"	
9"	

Moving left to right and down from the top, the answers are *Love's Labour Lost*, *A Midsummer's Night Dream*, *Twelfth Night*, *Much Ado About Nothing*, *As You Like It*, and *The Tempest*. In some versions the last block is *The Taming of the Shrew*.

For English 101, you might see a parody of the rules of grammar—otherwise known as the "rools of grammore" or "grammer as wrote." Here are some highlights from the list (*Ninth* 1982, 20; see also Dundes and Pagter 1978, 39–40; 1987, 121–22):

1. Don't use no double negatives.
2. Verbs has to agree with their subject.
3. Try not to over split infinitives.
4. Just between you and I, case is important to.
5. Proofread your theme to see is any words out.

Visual technology has circulated around campuses many parodies of songs once held sacred. "The Battle Hymn of the Republic" has long been a target for students since elementary school when they sang, "Mine eyes have seen the glory of the burning of the school, We have tortured every teacher and we've broken every rule" (Bronner 1989, 97–99). Here's a collegiate version, where the "final" battle between teacher and student occurs in thermodynamics (see also Monteiro 1976, 159; Pankake and Pankake 1988, 101). This repeatedly copied song sheet came from Wayne State by way of the University of Maryland, where it reportedly came from MIT, or was it Ohio State?

Free energy and entropy were whirling in his brain
With partial differentials and Greek letters in their train
With Delta, sigma, gamma, theta, epsilon and pi
Were driving him distracted as they danced before his eyes
Chorus:
Glory Glory dear old Thermo
Glory Glory dear old Thermo
Glory Glory dear old Thermo
We'll pass you by and by
Heat content and fugacity revolved within his brain
Like molecules and atoms that you never have to name
And logarithmic functions doing cakewalks in his dreams
And partial molal quantities devouring chocolate creams
They asked him on this final if a mole of any gas
In a vessel with a membrane through which hydrogen could pass
Were compressed to half its volume what the entropy would be
If two-thirds of delta sigma equalled half of delta pi
He said he guessed the entropy would have to equal four
Unless the second law would bring it up a couple more
But then, it might be seven if the Carnot law applied
Or it almost might be zero if the delta T should slide
The professor read his paper with a corrugated brow
For he knew he'd have to grade it, he didn't quite know how
Till an inspiration in his cerebellum suddenly smote
As he seized his trusty fountain pen, and this is what he wrote

Just as you guessed the entropy, I'll have to guess your grade
But the second law won't raise it to the mark you might have made
For it might have been a hundred, if your guesses were all good
But I think it must be zero 'til they're rightly understood
Final Chorus:
Glory Glory dear old Thermo
Glory Glory dear old Thermo
Glory Glory dear old Thermo
We'll try again next year.

Probably also drawn from children's folklore are parodies of carols and holiday verse. A favorite item circulated in emails and blogs is "'Twas the night before exams."

'Twas the night before exams and all through the dorm
Everyone was studying (and not looking at porn)
Their clothes for the next day draped over their chairs
Not necessarily clean (but who the fuck cares?)
Those ill-prepared were giving up the fight
Due to the fact that it was starting to get light
The 11th hour slowly drew near . . .
"Let's get it over with so we can all go get beer!!!"

You have probably guessed by now that being part of folklore, such texts invite variation, as in the following folk poetry featuring another dorm scene:

'Twas the night before finals and all through the dorm
Not a creature was partying, not even wild Norm
The students were studying so they wouldn't fail
And not make it through college and end up in jail
Boy that didn't work you see
They all flunked
And now are locked in a cell with no key
All this junk was for no good
The students felt dumb, stupid, and unnamed
For they studied the wrong subject
Boy they were ashamed! (cf. Dundes and Pagter 1987, 250–53)

Sure, parodied songs and rebuses have been around a long time, but one can note college folkloric genres generated by cyberculture such as repeated text messages left to signal that someone is away from his or her computer.

Examples playing with proverbial form and referring to college that I picked up are:

Gone to something my mother says I have nothing of . . . class
I have gone to get my learn on.
College is the snooze button on the clock radio of life.
College is great . . . too bad classes get in the way
A professor is someone who talks in other people's sleep.
School is practice for the future, and practice makes perfect. Nobody's perfect . . . so why practice?!?
Knot hear im at dat plaze cal skool getten mee a edgimicashon yoo shood tri it sumtim.
I'm not going to cheat on the test tomorrow, I'm simply going to study during it.
I wasn't cheating . . . I was just looking at the answers.
Ever notice how DYING is at the end of STUDYING? I don't think that was an accident!
Latin is a language, as dead as it can be, First it killed the Romans, now it's killing me.
I'm studying for finals—this defies the laws of physics by sucking and blowing at the same time :-/
I have this test tomorrow, I need to study you see, I probably will be on later, But don't wait up for me!
Grrr . . . studying hard for my finals. Talk to you later after my brain explodes :-)
No wonder why they call it "finals," it's your final day to live. (cf. Blumenfeld et al. 2006, 208–9)

Besides noting their stress in such messages, students also demonstrate the dread, as well as foolishness, of finals by giving mock definitions or humorous reflections:

Finals=academic suicide

Why do they call them finals? If you fail you have to come back :(

Why do they call them finals? It's not like it is really the final test we are going to take!!!

Finals mean the end to a lot of things. . . . End of classes, end of the semester, end of my diet, end of my sanity, end of my beautiful head—because it's ready to EXPLODE!

The folklore of ending the semester with finals emphasizes an extraordinary, excruciating, punishing experience because campus exams supposedly have nothing to do with the real world. In the student worldview, the tests are an unnatural way to gauge what students know or what they can do. Added to this disconnect in their minds between their academic and professional experience are the high stakes placed on finals. They strike terror because so much appears to be riding on them, and students are afraid that they will not be able to perform well on that particular day and time in that specific location.

Or students are sure that study time is not correlated with high grades. I recorded Penn State students jokingly telling me why they do not study. Senior Chris Detweiler made the proverbial pronouncement, "The more you study, the more you know, the more you forget. The less you study, the less you know, the less you forget. So why study!" The lines have been around at least since 1940 when they appeared in a collection by Lewis Copeland and Faye Copeland (1940, 375) and are still going strong on the Internet. Variations include "The more you learn, the less you know," and, for the computer age, "the smarter you are, the less you click." Or students following this proverbial structure may question the occupational status of being a student with "the harder you work, the less you get paid (earn)" (cf. "the harder you work, the more luck you have" in Doyle, Shapiro, and Shapiro 2012, 280–81). To this line, a student may humorously ask, "Are you working hard or hardly working?"

Parodying all the logical laws students must memorize as well as the ubiquity of rules on campus, students frequently circulate the "Laws of Applied Terror," which incorporate proverbial student attitudes toward studying. This one comes from Penn State Harrisburg. I first saw it hanging in a student club lounge, and it spread quickly from there.

1. When reviewing your notes before an exam, the most important ones will be illegible.
2. The more studying you did for the exam, the less sure you are as to which answer they want.
3. Eighty percent of the final exam will be based on the one lecture you missed about the one book you didn't read.
4. Every instructor assumes that you have nothing else to do except study for that instructor's course.
5. If you are given an open-book exam, you will forget the book. Corollary: If you are given a take-home exam, you will forget where you live.
6. At the end of the semester you will recall having enrolled in a course at the beginning of the semester—and never attending. (cf. Bloch 2003, 117)

These laws resemble "Murphy's Law," sometimes known as "Finagle's Law," circulating in many offices and labs around the country. So as not to expect success all the time, or so as not to be disappointed when things do not go the way they should, Murphy's Law boils down to "If anything can go wrong, it will" (see Dundes and Pagter 1978, 69–75; Doyle, Mieder, and Shapiro 2012, 101–2).

Besides laws, other revered texts such as prayers and scripture commonly receive parody in student life. Spoofs of this sort are known generally in American culture, but some have been designed specifically for the student's lament (see Monteiro 1964, 1976). A motto that many students post to remind us why so much student folklore about finals takes off from religious sources is "As long as there are finals there will be prayer in public schools." Here's a parody of the twenty-third psalm that circulated first in photocopies and then made its way to the Internet.

The professor is my quizmaster, I shall not flunk. He maketh me to enter the examination room; He leadeth me to an alternative seat; He restoreth my fears. Yea, though I know not the answers to those questions, the class average comforts me. I prepare my answers before me in the sight of my proctors. I anoint my exam papers with figures. My time runneth out. Surely grades and examinations will follow all the days of my life, and I will dwell in this class forever. (Gaither and Cavazos-Gaither 1999, 351; Cnytr 2005)

Another mock prayer takes off from children's bedtime prayers and again invokes the image of death from finals.

Now I lay me down to study
I pray the lord I won't go nutty
For if I fail to learn this junk
I pray the Lord I will not flunk
But if I do don't pity me at all
Just lay my bones in the dorm hall
Tell my professor I did my best,
Now I lay me down to rest
And pray I'll pass tomorrow's test
But if I die before I wake
That's one less test I'll have to TAKE! (cf. Davis 1956, 76)

One of the more common scriptural parodies floating around many campuses is about the last days of finals, just before the time of judgment (or destruction, calamity, or flood in other versions).

And it came to pass early in the morning of the last day of the semester, there arose a multitude smiting their books and waiting. And there was much weeping, and gnashing of teeth, for the day of judgment was at hand and they were so afraid. For they ought to have done, and there was no help for it.

And there were many abiding in the dorm who had kept watch over their books all night, but it naught availeth. But some there were who arose peacefully for they had prepared for themselves the way, and had made straight the path of knowledge. And these wise ones were known to some as the burners of the midnight oil, and by others they were called curve lousers.

And the multitudes arose and ate a hearty breakfast, and they came to the appointed place and their hearts were heavy within them. And they had come to pass, but some they were to pass out.

And some of them repented of their riotous living and bemoaned their fate, but they had not a prayer. And at the last hour there came among them one known as the instructor, he of the diabolical smile, and passed papers among them and went upon his way.

And many and varied were the answers which were given, for some of his teachings had fallen among fertile minds, others still had fallen flat. And some there were who wrote for one hour, others for two, but some turned away sorrowful. And many of these offered up a little bull in hopes of pacifying the instructor, for these were the ones who had no prayer. And when they had finished, they gathered up their belongings and went away quietly, each in his own direction, and each one vowing to himself in this manner—"I shall not pass this way again, but it is a long road that hath no turning."

The last line parodies sentimental sayings often spouted at memorial services by conflating the "I shall not pass this way again" often attributed to Quaker lore and the old English-American proverb, "It is a long lane [road] that has no turning" (Mieder, Kingsbury, and Harder 1992, 513; Whiting 1977, L29; Wilson 1970, 480).

Many of the parodies of letters, memos, and forms such as "And It Came to Pass" seen on college bulletin boards in the precomputer age have made their way in the twenty-first century to social networking sites on the Internet. Every new advancement in communication technology is an instrument for the circulation of student humor (see Smith 1991). The photocopier not only copied forms but also served students' social ends by spreading folk expressions put into a form with which they instantly associate—paper. A well-known piece of photocopied humor is a letter home from a young coed. Like the oral humor I have been surveying, the photocopied pieces repeat and vary, and are often anonymous in origin. One version that made the jump to the Internet catalogs students' views of parents' worst fears (see Dundes and Pagter 1978, 40–41).

Dear Mother and Dad,

It has been three months now since I left for college. I have been remiss in writing and I am very sorry for my thoughtlessness in not writing before. I will bring you up to date now, but before you read on, please sit down. You are not to read further unless you are sitting down, okay?

Well, then, I'm getting along pretty well now. The skull fracture and the concussion I got when I jumped out of the window of my dormitory when it caught fire shortly after my arrival here is pretty well healed. I only spent two weeks in the hospital and now I can see almost normally and only get those sick headaches once a day.

Fortunately, the fire in the dormitory and my jump were witnessed by an attendant at the gas station near the dorm, and he was the one who called the fire department and the ambulance. He also visited me in the hospital and since I have nowhere to live because of the burnt-out dormitory, he was kind enough to invite me to share his apartment. It's really a basement room, and it's kind of cute. He is a very fine boy and we have fallen deeply in love and are planning to get married. We haven't set the exact date yet, but it will be before my pregnancy begins to show.

I know how much you are looking forward to being grandparents and I know you will welcome the baby and give it the same love and devotion and tender care you gave me when I was a child. The reason for the delay in our marriage is that my boyfriend has a minor infection which prevents us from passing our premarital blood tests and I carelessly caught it from him. This will soon clear up with the penicillin injections I am taking daily.

I know that you will welcome him into our family with open arms. He is kind and although not well-educated, he is ambitious. Although he is of a different race and religion than ours, I know your oft-expressed tolerance will not permit you to be bothered by this fact.

Now that I have brought you up to date, I want to tell you that there was no dormitory fire, I did not have a concussion, or a skull fracture, I was not in the hospital, I am not pregnant, I am not engaged, I do not have a disease, and there is no miscegenation in my life. However, I am getting a "D" in history and an "F" in science, and I wanted you to see those marks in the proper perspective.

Your loving daughter. (see Brunvand 1999, 439–40; D'Pnymph 1988, 142–43; Dundes and Pagter 1978, 40–41; Meakes 2004, 121; Orr and Preston 1976, 65; Roeper 1999, 95–98; Smith 1984, 138)

Another favorite on photocopied sheets and computer printouts hanging in dorm rooms is the "Student Death Tag."

This tag is to be attached to a student only after death has been established using the following procedure.

If, after several hours, it is noticed that the student has not moved or changed position, the professor will investigate. Because of the highly sensitive nature of our students and the close resemblance between death and their natural classroom attitude, the investigation will be made as quickly as possible in case the student is asleep. If some doubt exists as to the true condition, extend a copy of an exam as a final test. If the student does not recoil, it may be assumed that death has occurred.*

*Note: In some cases the instinct is so strongly developed that a spasmodic shuddering and shirking reflex may occur after death. Don't let this fool you.

This bit of student folklore appears to be an adaptation of photocopied humor circulating around corporate offices since the 1960s (Dundes and Pagter 1978, 86; Smith 1986, 54). Sent from "Your Big Brother," the parodied memo is entitled "Instructions on Death of Employees." It notes that "a close resemblance exists between death and the normal working attitude of employees," and a paycheck is used as the final test. Whoever adapted this text to the college scene must have associated the conditions of mass corporate bureaucracy with his or her own in the mega-university.

No, life need not end with finals. But imagining them as potentially fatal emphasizes the accomplishment of completion when the student is reborn after the ordeal. The ritual practice of reciting folk story, saying, and belief about the stress of finals keeps many a student alert. A theme that keeps coming back into the folk material is the unnaturalness of grading as an arbitrary act by empowered professors who really do not know their charges. In student lore, grades corporately divide students into ranked categories of worth when, as a body, collegians want to express social solidarity. A constant theme in student narratives is that grades are the coinage of the realm. Campus lore conspicuously shows the culturally ingrained stress on grades at the same time that it tries to ease the anxiety they produce.

CHAPTER

PROFESSORS, COACHES, JOCKS, GEEKS, AND OTHER STRANGE CHARACTERS

IF CAMPUS IS AN UNUSUAL LIMINAL LOCALE WITH IMPOSING BUILDINGS and a landscape intended to inspire great ideas, then it follows that it is populated by characters who are probably out of place elsewhere. Humor and legend work hand in hand to reveal the idiosyncrasies of figures who draw suspicion because they appear strangely and singularly obsessed with their task. Lore may also especially express an ambivalence about professors as powerful elders who guide their student charges but at the same time from whom youths want to break away to assert themselves. Students also look around at their cohort and notice that quirkiness is hardly reserved for their instructors. They identify types in their lore and use narrative to question the norm of an abnormal place.

Students' slang identifies campus folktypes, especially those with privilege or specialty, who are knocked down a peg. Athletes are jocks, beef, meatheads, no-necks, and bulletheads. Those with aristocratic airs might be dubbed preppies, frat boys, or razor-necks (or pencil-necks). Popular students, or those that would like to be, are B.M.O.C. (big men on campus) or campus queens. It is worth noting that the slang for unpopular students—the drudges, nerds, and geeks—matches closely the argot for diligent students—the grinds. Religious students are Bible bangers, thumpers, and beaters; students of agriculture are aggies, grangers, and sodbusters; and geology students are rock hounds, mud smellers, and pebble pups. Those in the Greek system, or Greekdom, are frat rats and sorority bitches; at some campuses with large fraternity populations, those not in the frats are called 'siders or outsiders, hallmen, barbs, or barbarians (see Eble 1996; Hummon 1994; Lu and Graf 2004).

Professors get the bulk of attention in campus anecdotes because of the authority they hold. The narratives have a way of humanizing them, since they often appear to students to be in a pursuit that is somehow unnatural. After all, professors appear to never have left the infantilization of school and must have eschewed more lucrative lines of work to spend their time reading and writing. Raising ambivalent feelings in students, professors may seem parental because they tend to youth, but they are not the familiar faces of high school teachers. The narrated professor gives character to a particular campus and defines the student-mentor relationship. Humor and legend work to query as much as expose what the curious role, and world, of the professor is about.

Student folklore portrays professors as absentminded, arrogant, dull, impractical, or lacking common sense, immersed in their research to the detriment of their personal hygiene and awareness of the world around them. They are always in danger of going "over the edge" if they have not lost their mind already. These are people, students remark in various traditions, who lie outside the lines of normal society. It should not be surprising, then, that the most commonly reported anecdote about professors in my collection concerns those who walk around campus in a haze.

Absentminded and Disheveled Professors

Easily the most common story about professors emphasizes that they do not know whether, proverbially speaking, they are coming or going. Representative is an anecdote turned in by a student collector for the Berkeley Folklore Archives about a philosophy professor from Calvin College: "Professor Runner is a brilliant philosopher, but very absentminded. He walks around in a trance most of the time. In fact, a friend went up to Professor Runner one day on campus to ask him a question. When he was through answering the question, Runner asked if he had been coming out or going into the cafeteria. 'Out,' said the friend. 'Thank you,' the professor replied, 'then I must have already had lunch'" (see Toelken 1986, 507; Wilgus 1972, 25; Jackson 1972, 5). The backdrop of the meandering campus appears to reinforce the head-in-the-clouds professor's confusion because it is not organized like the town, and yet students are able to master it. Thus students contrast their own practical knowledge and navigation skills with the professor's impractical intellect.

In a later-reported variation, the student asks the professor the way to his office. The professor replies, "If it is that way, then I've had my lunch; if the other way, then I must be on my way to it" (Wyman 1979, 85). According to George Carey, the story as it is told at the University of Massachusetts has the vague professor answering a student's invitation to lunch with, "Which way was I headed when you stopped me?" "Toward Bartlett Hall," says the student. "Sorry, then," says the professor, "I can't join you. I've already eaten" (Carey 1988, 8).

Students also relate the same story about philosopher Irwin Edman of Columbia and mathematician Norbert Wiener of MIT (Cowley and Reed 1977, 37; Jackson 1972, 5; Wilgus 1972, 25). Indicating that this anecdote goes back well before those esteemed figures were around, a related narrative is told about Isaac Newton, the great English physicist who taught at Cambridge during the late seventeenth century. A friend paid the great scientist a visit one evening. The servant announced that his master was in his study and not to be disturbed. The visitor decided to wait since it was approaching Sir Isaac's dining hour. The table was set, and in a short time a boiled chicken under cover was brought in. Time passed. The fowl was growing cold, but Sir Isaac did not appear. Finally, being hungry, the visitor devoured the fowl and covered up the empty dish. At the same time he asked the servant to have another chicken boiled for Sir Isaac. But before the second bird was ready, the great man came down. He apologized to his visitor for his delay and added, "Give me leave to take my short dinner, and I shall be at your service; I am fatigued and faint." He then took the cover off the dish, and finding the plate empty, turned to the visitor with a wan smile. "You see what we studious people are; I forgot that I had dined" (Cowley and Reed 1977, 36).

The professor stories are mostly about men—dominant yet apparently clueless males. From Purdue and Illinois comes the story of the professor asked by his wife to change clothes for dinner. Finding himself in the bedroom undressed, he could think of only one reason to be there, and put on his pajamas and went to bed at 6:30 p.m. (Tillson 1962, 55–56; Dorson 1949, 672). At Gettysburg College, I heard about the professor who drove his car to Philadelphia to do research. Forgetting he had driven, he took the train back (see also Jackson 1972, 6; Taft 1984, 181–83). At Brigham Young University, similar absentminded professor stories are told about Hugh Winder Nibley (1910–2005), who specialized in ancient scripture. A common anecdote is about the time Nibley's wife sent him to the store: "Apparently he drove the car instead of walking like he usually does. Sometime later he came back carrying the groceries, and his wife said, 'I thought you'd taken the car. What did you do with the car?' And he could not remember where he'd put the car. It's simply his way of looking at things: his mind and spirit are preoccupied with other things than the mundane or trivial" (Brady 2005, 67). Richard Dorson offered an early version of the narrative type in 1949, with the additional detail that the professor "bawled out his wife for not meeting him at the station with the auto" (672). He also gave the related yarn of the Harvard professor who drops his wife at a mailbox (sometimes the location is a gas station restroom or convenience store) and then continues on his journey. Later he notices her absence and informs the police (cf. Taft 1984, 181–83).

Professors in folklore are often oblivious to personal appearance. One common anecdote is about the professor who wore an unidentical pair of shoes to class. A student respectfully asks the sage, "Sir, you know you're wearing two different shoes, right?" The professor scratches his head and replies, "Yeah, I don't know how it happened. I have one more pair like this at home." Students recall Brigham Young University (BYU) professor Nibley coming to the Mormon campus with suit pants that did not go with the coat, mismatched socks, and ties that clashed with his shirts. He reportedly wore the same attire repeatedly for weeks or donned scruffy clothes that obviously needed to be discarded. Verifying the connection of Nibley's appearance to his intellectual loftiness, one teller reflected, "None of this is because he can't afford to buy good clothing; he just doesn't think about it" (Brady 2005, 38). Another university resident noted that in death, "he's passed over into the mythic so that I'm sure the stories about him will continue and grow and get better and better—because of the emotional need it satisfies for the community of BYU—trying to make an uneasy marriage between the things of the spirit and the things of the world" (Brady 2005, 44). A professor of religion, Nibley invites commentary about the ideals of being intellectual and spiritual while giving attention to the practical details of everyday life.

Albert Einstein (1879–1955) epitomized the brainy professor uncomfortable with formal attire meant to impress others, and many stories are told about the famous physicist. One concerns his wife imploring him to dress more professionally when he went to the office. "Why should I?" he shot back, "Everyone knows me there." Supposedly when he was about to attend his first major conference, she begged him then also to dress up, and to that he responded, "Why should I? No one knows me there!" Einstein also represents the scientist who operates by his own logic. Students like to recall his observation that "when I was young I found out that the big toe always ends up making a hole in a sock, so I stopped wearing socks" (Calaprice and Lipscombe 2005, 111). Musicology professor Ron Pen, who began teaching at the University of Kentucky in 1991, not only quit wearing socks, he got rid of his shoes, too, in favor of flip-flops, even in winter. Not all is beachwear, however, for he sports colorful bow ties and dress shirts. His attire earned him a permanent place on a list of professorial "characters" about whom campus stories are told. The point of such stories that draw out the break of the campus characters with reality is not only recognizing professorial quirkiness but also their autonomy.

In addition to showing that professors are more mindful of their studies than of their loved ones, folklore suggests that professors view themselves as nobility who are used to having things done for them. Consider the story from Cornell of the professor who had announcements appear almost simultaneously of his new book and his wife's new baby. The professor, when congratulated by a friend about the "proud event in your family," naturally thought of that achievement that had cost him the greater effort. He modestly replied, "Well, I couldn't have done it without the help of two graduate students" (Keseling and Kinney 1956, 148).

Some of folklore's surest demonstrations of absentmindedness occur during the classroom lecture. For example: A biology professor comes into the class with a paper bag stuffed with something and announces that today the dissection of the frog will be demonstrated. He reaches into the bag to get the frog, but finds a ham sandwich instead. He scratches his head and says to the class, "Hmm. I wonder what I ate for lunch" (Jones 1977, 11–12).

In a variation commenting on female professors, the young English professor reaches behind her ear for her pencil. Instead she finds a tampon. Startled, she asks, "What did I do for my period this morning then?" A carryover from jokes in adolescent folklore, this story uses the tampon as a modern symbol of women's mobility and at the same time a reminder of the gendered hindrance of menses to show the vulnerability of women as they enter into professions (Bronner 1985, 39–49).

Several professor stories resemble old numskull tales like those in international circulation about the man who searches for an ax, which he carries on his shoulder, or who does not recognize his own horse (Thompson 1966, 169, motifs J2025.1, J2023). From the Berkeley Folklore Archives comes this story told by Carolina Clare, who learned it, she said, from another student at Arizona State University. "A professor came into class one day, took his wrist watch off, and placed it on the desk in front of him so he could watch it as he lectured. He began his lecture, stopped, looked at the watch, picked it up, and said, 'I find someone's wrist watch here on my desk. Did anyone lose it?' A student raised his hand and suggested that the professor take the watch to lost-and-found after class. The next day the professor came to class and announced that he had lost his wrist watch. He asked if anyone had found it" (cf. Taft 1984, 183–84).

Mac Barrick, a Dickinson College alum, told me of the history professor who wrote a list of things he had to do when he got home, walked to the post office, and mailed it to himself "special delivery." He hurried home so he would be there when it arrived. This reminds me of the numskull tale in international folklore about the fool who writes himself a letter. When someone asks what the letter says, he replies that he does not know because he will not get it until the next day (Baughman 1966, motif J2242.3).

From Cornell comes the story of the professor who eased back to his office after class. He found a long line of students waiting in front of the door, so he took his place at the end of the line (Cowley and Reed 1977, 36). This numskull story bears some resemblance to the one reported in 1940 about the professor who rings his house bell and is answered by a new housekeeper. "Um-ah—is Professor Thompson at home?" he asks, naming himself. "No, sir," she replies, "but he is expected any moment now." The professor turns away, and the housekeeper closes the door. Then he sits down on the steps to wait for himself (Copeland and Copeland 1940, 386). Or there is the absentminded professor who jabbers well into the night about theories with his guests. Finally, one guest says, "I hate to put you out, but I have to meet a nine o'clock class in the morning." It seems the professor thought he was at his own house (Cowley and Reed 1977, 37).

Sometimes forgetfulness is blamed on single-minded devotion to one's subject, often displacing connection to people. Richard Dorson gives the example of a University of Texas professor of ichthyology, famous for his studies of fish, walking across the campus with a colleague. A student greeted the professor, who answered impersonally. "Don't you know the name of that friendly student?" the colleague asks. "I have made it a point," replied the ichthyologist, "never to learn the names of my students. Whenever I remember a student, I forget a fish" (Dorson 1949, 672). The story also told about scientific specialists of birds, insects, and rocks dates from much earlier, for it appears in oral histories recounting the incidents of David Starr Jordan, who came to Stanford as president in 1891 after establishing an international reputation for his classifications of fish. In this story, however, the professor is less arrogant, for he "determined that he would also come to know each student by name." Several years later he was asked how he was progressing. Jordan sadly said he had given up. "I found that every time I learned the name of a student, I forgot the name of a fish" (Cowley and Reed 1977, 36).

Arrogant, Devious, or Deranged?

The arrogance of professors is nowhere better shown than in the migratory legend about renowned teacher-scholars who do not hold a Ph.D. When asked why he never pursued the degree, the professor haughtily snaps back "Who would examine me?" The story is frequently attached to famed professors George Lyman Kittredge and Bernard De Voto, who taught at Harvard from 1888 to 1936 and 1929 to 1936, respectively (see Reuss 1974, 306; Emrich 1972, 324). Yet the story is updated in our day to describe celebrity professors without the doctorate. For instance, the story is told about the noble-sounding Richebourg Gaillard McWilliams of Birmingham-Southern College, who presided over forty-two years of literature and composition classes (Raines 1986, 46); the previously mentioned Hugh Winder Nibley from BYU (Brady 2005, 115); and R. L. "Beowulf" Brown of Middlebury College (Carey 1988, 7).

Professors who irritatingly take the Ph.D. as a badge of their brilliance might have the migratory narrative told about them of a car ride shared with a younger associate. For five hours the great one reminisces about himself, his writings, and his friends in the field. Finally, at the end of this time, he looks at his junior companion and says, "Well, I've talked enough about me. Now you talk about me for a while!" (Reuss 1974, 313; cf. Graber 2011; "Roll Inverted" 2010).

Professors can do no wrong, or so they think, anyway. There is the college professor instructing a military economics class on technical terms. The professor explains the terms with the aid of diagrams on a chalkboard. When a student remarks that the professor had misspelled a word, he quickly answers, "Like I always said, I consider a person dumb if he can't think of more than one way to spell a word" (Mitchell 1976, 563).

The pronunciation of a word is key to turning the tables on a professor in a joke typically told about a professor of botany. "This twig, you will notice," he says, "is composed of bark, hardwood and pith. Of course you know what pith is." The class stared at him blankly. "Don't you know what pith is?" the professor repeated. "You, Ms. Brown, you know what pith is, do you not?" "Yeth, thir," she says (*New Anecdota Americana* 1944, 56). The narrative might be read as drawing attention to patriarchal relationships in the classroom to women, for the professorial figure is usually characterized as an authoritarian, stuffy man (with esoteric knowledge of pith, the soft, spongy tissue in the twig) in contrast to the insecure, lisping woman, who subverts this comprehension with her image of "piss." The humorous narrative, like other professorial anecdotes, also draws a symbolic opposition between academic pedantry, in this case of nature, and vernacular awareness of when nature calls.

In some stories, especially of grand pranks, students more aggressively fight back. One such story is frequently attached to the U.S. Military Academy at West Point, but can be heard about a number of demanding institutions. In one version, a young cadet was preparing a physics paper to prove that if all the toilets at West Point were flushed simultaneously, the water pressure would be sufficient to burst pipes throughout the plumbing system on campus. His professor returned his paper saying the idea was nice, but the figures and calculations used for the computations were in error, and it would not work. In a furtive attempt to prove his theory, the cadet arranged for the "West Point Flush." Plumbing burst all over campus, and supported his theory. He was still given a failing grade on the paper, but no one challenged it for credibility (cf. Lim 2007; Meakes 2004, 199; Mythbusters 2009). The story is also related as a ploy of mass student protest as students recall eras of campus unrest.

Students, aware of the "publish or perish" motto in academe, believe that professors selfishly treat them, and teaching, as secondary to their publications.

One story circulates about prolific literary critic Harold Bloom of Yale who, after not showing up at his office, was called at his home in New Haven by an advisee. Bloom's wife answered, "I'm sorry, he's writing a book." "That's all right," the student replied, "I'll wait" (Parini 1989, 1, 24). The story has been adapted for other extraordinarily productive faculty.

What contributes to these sometimes outlandish stories about professors? For starters, there is the fact that at many campuses, faculty members—involved in research, with offices far from student hangouts, or maintaining a professorial image—keep their personal distance from students. The distance allows for student speculation in story. At the same time, students think they need to "scope out" their professors, to know what they are like so as to know what to expect from them in class, on exams, and particularly at grading time. Students, in the best American antiauthoritarian tradition, recognize the power of professors over them and use folklore to bring the faculty down a notch or students up a few. Many of the stories humanize professors, reducing their superiority and showcasing their fallibility. As people priding themselves on intellect, professors are often shown to be lacking in sense, and especially deficient in mundane tasks. Yet there can also be detected in the stories a certain context worth appreciating of the campus as a location tolerant of eccentricities and deriving distinction for its freedom of expression.

If students delight in some professorial quirks around campus, they tend to judge their instructors' classroom performance more harshly. The most common sin is putting students to sleep, another way of saying he or she is boring (or that the student has no interest in the professor's esoteric knowledge). On more than one desk, one may find the following parody of the popular bedtime prayer:

> Now I lay me down to sleep
> The Professor is dry, the lecture's deep
> If he should quit before I wake,
> Someone kick me, for goodness sake. (Davis 1956; cf. Monteiro 1964, 46; 1976, 151)

The plaint is not just that a professor can be dull, but that he or she is in control, right or wrong, and sucking away vitality from students. From Wisconsin comes the story of the geography professor lecturing from faded notes, droning along about the Mississippi River dumping each year 9,989,000 tons. He turned the page and started another topic. A brave student asked, "The Mississippi River dumps each year 9,989,000 tons of what?" The professor turned the yellowed page back, and again intoned, "The Mississippi River each year dumps 9,989,000 tons," paused, turned the page, and said, "It don't say" (Wyman 1979, 85).

At Ohio State, the story gets around about the lecturer who began reading in a wheezy, cracked voice. At the bottom of page one, he turned the leaf and continued reading. What he read repeated the first page, and the third was the same. His staff assistant had delivered the notes to him in triplicate (Cowley and Reed 1977, 36; see also Carey 1988, 7). In a variation I received from Harvard, the story is about a famed philosophy professor who lectured on logic. Previous to the class, some graduate student sneaked into his office and disarranged his lecture notes. When the professor read through his notes, however, he did not notice the difference.

Circulating by email was the story of first-year students at the University of California at Davis vet school receiving their first anatomy class with a real dead cow. They all gathered around the surgery table with the body covered with a white sheet. The professor started the class by telling them, "In Veterinary Medicine it is necessary to have two important qualities as a doctor: The first is that you not be disgusted by anything involving the animal body." For an example, the professor pulled back the sheet, stuck his finger in the anus of the dead cow, withdrew it and stuck his finger in his mouth. "Go ahead and do the same thing," he told his students. With shocked look on their faces, the students hesitated for several minutes, but eventually took turns sticking a finger in the anal opening of the dead cow and sucking on it. When everyone finished, the professor looked at them and said, "The second most important quality is observation. I stuck in my middle finger and sucked on my index finger. Now learn to pay attention. Life's tough, it's even tougher if you're stupid." A medical school version has the instructor inserting one gloved finger up a patient's rectum and licking a different one (Margaret 2011; Mikkelson and Mikkelson 2010).

A contemporary variation playing on the fear of ingesting bodily fluids to teach a lesson involves a urology test. The instructor tells a class of medical (or biology) students that it is possible to detect the presence of too much sugar in the urine by tasting it. He demonstrates by sticking his finger into a urine sample and then inserting it in his mouth. He pronounces the sample too sweet and asks the students to try it for themselves. Each student repeats the test, some of them agreeing on the diagnosis. None of them notices, until their professor explains, that he had put his middle finger into the sample but stuck his forefinger into his mouth. To the students' chagrin, the demonstration tested their powers of perception, not their ability to taste sugar in urine (Brunvand 1999, 430; see also Meakes 2004, 120; Mikkelson and Mikkelson 2010; *New Anecdota Americana* 1944, 53).

The urine test story goes back to at least the nineteenth century when it was told about Dr. Joseph Bell, a model for Arthur Conan Doyle's characterization of Sherlock Holmes from his medical student days in Edinburgh. According to an account related by Dr. Harold Emery Jones in 1904:

> Bell was as full of dry humor and satire, and he was as jealous of his reputation, as the detective Sherlock Holmes ever thought of being.
>
> One day, in the lecture theatre, he gave the students a long talk on the necessity for the members of the medical profession cultivating their senses— sight, smell, taste, and hearing. Before him on a table stood a large tumbler filled with a dark, amber-colored liquid.
>
> "This gentlemen," announced the Professor, "contains a very potent drug. To the taste it is intensely bitter. It is most offensive to the sense of smell. Yet, as far as the sense of sight is concerned—that is, in color—it is no different from dozens of other liquids.
>
> "Now I want to see how many of you gentlemen have educated your powers of perception. Of course, we might easily analyze this chemically, and find out what it is. But I want you to test it by smell and taste; and, as I don't ask anything of my students which I wouldn't be willing to do myself, I will taste it before passing it round."
>
> Here he dipped his finger in the liquid, and placed it in his mouth. The tumbler was passed round. With wry and sour faces the students followed the Professor's lead. One after another tasted the vile decoction; varied and amusing were the grimaces made. The tumbler, having gone the round, was returned to the Professor.
>
> "Gentlemen," said he, with a laugh, "I am deeply grieved to find that not one of you has developed this power of perception, which I so often speak about; for if you had watched me closely, you would have found that, while I placed my forefinger in the medicine, it was the middle finger which found its way into my mouth." (Jones 1904, 15, 20)

Besides being offered as narrative evidence of professors' devious ways, the story may have persisted because of its strong symbolic suggestions of students punished for their adolescent eroticism. The professor is triumphant because of oral gratification gained from sucking his middle, or phallic bird, finger. Students' comprehension of phallic sweetness or, in the case of the cow, anal penetration, is debased, or as the cow story underscores, made "disgusting" by conflating anal and oral sensations.

If the symbolic sexual undertones of the urine test story are outside the awareness of most tellers, one can manifestly detect answers to the arrogant professor in narrative by students relating "preposterous professor" tales.

Science students like to tell about the faulty logic of their instructors, or even fellow students, with the story of the frog-jumping experiment. The scientist put the frog on the floor, told it to jump, and it jumped. He measured the distance and wrote down in his book, "Frog jumps 12 feet with both legs." Then he cut off one of the frog's legs, put the frog on the floor, and told it to jump again. It did, and the scientist measured the distance and wrote in his book, "Frog jumps 6 feet with one leg." Then he cut off the frog's other leg, put the frog on the floor, and told it to jump. The frog just sat there. After about five futile minutes of telling the frog to jump, the scientist wrote in his book, "Frog can't hear with both legs cut off" (Baker 1986, 101). Variations exist with fleas, flies, and grasshoppers (see Beezley 1981, 117; Mitchell 1976, 449–50). During the 1960s and 1970s, the story was frequently reported as a "Polack" joke, an ethnic version of the moron or numskull jest (Clements 1969b, type E6.8; Mitchell 1976, 334, 622–23).

A related story appears much earlier, in the 1840s, this one from Yale: "A young physician, commencing practice, determined to keep an account of each case he had to do with, stating the mode of treatment and the result. His first patient was a blacksmith, sick of a fever. After the crisis of the disease had passed, the man expressed a hankering for pork and cabbage. The doctor humored him in this, and it seemed to do him good; which was duly noted in the record. Next a tailor sent for him, whom he found suffering from some malady. To him he *prescribed* pork and cabbage; and the patient died. Whereupon he wrote it down as a general law in such cases that pork and cabbage will cure a blacksmith, but will kill a tailor" (Hall 1968, 433).

If a professor's thinking can be faulty, sometimes in lore it can appear downright deranged. The ultimate sign of going over the edge, especially in the worst dreams of students, is the failure to hand in grades. From Sul Ross State University in Alpine, Texas, comes the story of a man who hit the skids.

The man had gone to pieces. His wife had left him; and although he was reputed to be a good teacher, well liked by students, he had become troubled and embittered to the point of incompetence. On the last day of finals he started hitting the bottle with abandon. The three-day period for turning in grade reports elapsed. The dean, unable to locate the man at his home, finally reached him at a disreputable bar across the tracks. Since the drunk professor had no grades prepared, the dean attempted to read his class rolls to him and secure the grades in that manner. The effort proved useless, however, and the dean had to make some disposition of the grades himself, since the best response he could get to his calling off of the names was comments of the order, "That bitch? Give her a D!" or, "Hell, flunk ol' Gibson, the bastard!" (Bratcher 1972, 121)

Sometimes the story reflects on a professor who goes off the deep end because of a divorce. The professor cannot recall any names until Mr. Smith comes along. "I remember him now," he says, "Give him an A—poor devil, he's married" (Bratcher 1972, 122).

Again, one can locate a nineteenth-century precedent, this one from Cambridge in 1896. Describing elderly tutor Walter Pater, the author offers that

> his temperament, it is true, sometimes made it difficult to work with him. On one occasion, at the examination for scholarships, he undertook to look over the English essays; when the examiners met to compare marks, Pater had none. He explained, with languor, "They did not much impress me." As something had to be done, he was asked to endeavour to recall such impressions as he had formed; to stimulate his memory, the names were read out in alphabetical order. Pater shook his head mournfully as each was pronounced, murmuring dreamily, "I do not recall him," "He did not strike me," and so on. At last the reader came to the name of Sanctuary, on which Pater's face lit up, and he said, "Yes; I remember; I liked his name." (Bratcher 1972, 122–23)

Legendary Professors

As the last story shows, many collegiate narratives are attached to specific legendary characters. A strong cycle of anecdotes, for example, revolved around the renowned Harvard professor of literature and ballad George Lyman Kittredge (1860–1941), often referred to as "Kitty" by his many students of English. Characterized as a stately, imposing figure, possessed of a stern New England morality, Kittredge once encountered several undergraduates raucously singing "The Bastard King of England." He rapped his cane sharply on the brick sidewalk and ordered them to stop singing. He told them that it was ungentlemanly to abuse the night in such a way. "Behind those open windows," he said, "are ladies in bed who cannot help but hear the words you are singing." The students apologized profusely. As he left, he tapped his cane, turned, and told them, "By the way, the words you were singing to that last stanza were not quite correct. They should go like this . . ." (Emrich 1972, 323). When a brash character supposedly asked Kittredge how much time he spent preparing for his class, he cut in, with authority and dignity, "A lifetime!" (Rollins 1961, 168–69). The ending is reminiscent of an oft-repeated anecdote about literature professor Frank "Big O" O'Malley of Notre Dame (1909–74). At a reception honoring a pretentious visiting professor of psychology, the pedant condescendingly asks what

O'Malley's field of specialization might be. Eyeing the man coldly, O'Malley replies, "What field? Why, my dear man, the entire world" (Leary 1978, 134–35).

Stories also abound about the famous MIT mathematician Norbert Wiener (1894–1964). In the anecdotes, he appears absentminded, myopic, brilliant, savagely moral, egotistical and at the same time insecure. Although occasionally appearing scatterbrained, he is capable of prodigious feats of mind and memory. Wiener supposedly was able to tell students exactly where books, even the most obscure, were located in the library, but he could not find his own house. It seems that Wiener and his family bought a new residence. They had been living in the old place for years and years, and they needed a place with more room for the growing family, so they moved out of their home. Knowing of his absentmindedness, his wife gave him a slip of paper with the new address. She even put it in his coat pocket. Wiener took the train from their home to spend the day at MIT, and when he came home, just as his wife expected, he went straight for the old house. He remembers then that he moved and that his wife wrote out the new address for him. He begins to look through his pockets, but then remembers that the new address is in his raincoat, which he left at his office. A little girl passes by on a bicycle, and Wiener is sure she lives in the neighborhood, so he stops her and says, "Little girl, little girl, I'm professor Wiener. I used to live here, but we moved today and I don't know where the new house is. Do you know where my family moved?" She replies, "Mommy thought you'd forget, Daddy" (Jackson 1972, 4; Renteln and Dundes 2005, 32; Wilgus 1972, 25).

Mathematician Paul Renteln, collaborating with folklorist Alan Dundes, claimed that "the stereotype of the absentminded professor (mathematician) may contain a kernel of truth. The degree of concentration required to solve a mathematical problem is such that one is virtually obliged to put everything else aside for the moment to devote all of one's mental energies to working out a solution" (Renteln and Dundes 2005, 32–33). Still, some narratives give an extreme picture of what an absentminded professor, even a legendary one, forgets. Renteln and Dundes, for example, report the following anecdote about Wiener:

> One day, a student saw Wiener in the post office and wanted to introduce himself to the famous professor. After all, how many M.I.T. students could say that they had actually shaken the hand of Norbert Wiener? However, the student wasn't sure how to approach the man. The problem was aggravated by the fact that Wiener was pacing back and forth, deeply lost in thought. Were the student to interrupt Wiener, who knows what profound idea might be lost? Still, the student screwed up his courage and approached

the great man. "Good morning, Professor Wiener," he said. The professor looked up, struck his forehead, and said, "That's it: Wiener!" (2005, 32)

The characterization of the professor being "lost in thought" is important in many narratives showing a disconnection between what the professor is thinking and his or her ability to convey it to students. A joke that mathematics students like to tell is of the professor who writes an equation on the board and declares to the class, "Of course, this is immediately obvious." Upon seeing the blank stares of the students, he turns back to contemplate what he had written. He shuffles about the room, deep in thought. After about ten minutes, just as the silence was beginning to become uncomfortable, he brightens, faces the class, and says, "Yes, it *is* obvious" (Renteln and Dundes 2005, 32).

Wiener's work and the lore about it epitomize the bridging of science and the human condition. In one anecdote, a naval computer problem has all the experts stumped. He has designed the sophisticated, top-secret computer for a ship out in the middle of the ocean. When the navy bigwigs approach Wiener for help, he folds his arms behind his head and leans back in his chair. Then he thinks for a minute and tells the baffled officers to remove a panel in the computer, behind which they would find a mouse that has eaten through one of the wires (Jennings 1986, 16). Yet this is the same professor who, according to legend, walks into a first-year calculus class and starts writing difficult equations on the board. A freshman raises his hand, and after a while, Wiener notices him. "Yes?" "Ah excuse me, sir, but, I, um, think you're in the wrong classroom. This is freshman calculus." "Oh," Wiener said and walks out the door. Five minutes later, still waiting for their instructor to come in, the freshman notices that Wiener had come in the back door and begun writing differential equations on the black board in the rear of the classroom (Jackson 1972, 6).

Many Wiener stories are about his poor eyesight, a trait often attached in folklore to professors. The narratives imply that the great ones have worn out their eyes by overdoing their reading and writing. Supposedly, Wiener had moldings put in so he could find his way from his office to his classroom. According to a legend collected from MIT alumni, Wiener liked to read while walking around the room feeling for the moldings. But one day a class was in session inside an open door off the hall and Wiener walked right around the door jam and circumnavigated the classroom, before heading back out (see Jackson 1972, 12–13). He also went blindly around the room when he wrote on the board. He finished at the blackboard and kept on going, writing on the walls and the doors and everything that came into his way. He got into such a habit with this behavior that the school supposedly built a room for him with blackboards on four walls (Wilgus 1972, 24).

Legendary professors frequently are elevated above mortal colleagues by performing prodigious mental feats. Stories about literature professor Fred Lewis Pattee refer to his astounding memory when students annually ask about the reason for the campus library being named after him. One narrative concerns Pattee's handling the devotional part of the college's morning chapel services (or recitation of a long prose passage in lit class). He opened the big chapel Bible and proceeded to read, or so it seemed, a lengthy psalm. Admiring his delivery but suspecting some variation from the passage, a student took a look at the Bible and found a completely different text on the page. Pattee later explained to the student's amazement, "I forgot my glasses and had to read from memory" (Pattee 1953, 342–43). Similarly, the previously mentioned Frank O'Malley at Notre Dame gave an extended eloquent lecture on James Joyce. The lecture is by all accounts stunning in both its clarity and complexity. An admiring student offers congratulations as the professor fumbles to put away his notes, only to observe that these notes are blank sheets of paper (Leary 1978, 134–35; see also Woodward 1984). Indiana University's Felix Oinas (1911–2004) supposedly demonstrated his photographic memory by rattling off library call numbers for all the books listed in a bibliography. I knew him, and he indeed was an amazing bibliophile. The hyperbolic story owed probably to cards he constantly kept on hand with bibliographic information. His renown for recall grew, so that students believed that he had committed the library to memory. His Estonian background was evident in a distinctive accent, and students listening to him believed it was a sign of old-school European learnedness that was somehow more stupendous than that of his pedestrian American colleagues.

Students' nicknames for faculty are legion and imply a storied reputation. The names usually personalize the faculty, especially the ones who had been at the institutions for a long time, and by humanizing them often bring them down to the students' level. John A. McGeachy (1978) quantified nicknaming patterns given to the faculty and found that the largest percentage of names, almost 28 percent, were attached to personality traits, especially those displayed in class. The naming showed great variety, but some aliases reappear: "Fuddy-Duddy," for a fussy professor; "Bull," for an aggressive instructor; "Skinny," for a slim instructor; and "Leather Lungs" or "Boomer," for a loud faculty member (cf. legendary professors such as Wake Forest's Charles "Skinny" Pearson in Hendricks 1994, and University of Saskatchewan's Evan "Boomer" Hardy in Taft 1984, 170–71). Professors from Texas, especially if they have an accent, attract the moniker of "Tex" in different curricular generations. Other familiar names come out of the professors' research focus, such as "Birdman" and "Blood," especially if it forms an alliteration or rhyme, such as Maryland zoology professor Eugenie Clark, known as "Shark" Clark or the "The Shark Lady" (Reis 2005, 2).

The scientific rivals of Stanford's Paul Ehrlich, who professed doomsday predictions about the planet, and techno-optimist Julian Simon, from the University of Illinois, had nicknames of "Dr. Doom" and "Dr. Boom" conferred upon them, respectively (Haven and Clark 1999, 159; Wibeto 2010, 62–63). Faculty members tend not to collectively respond in kind with nicknames for their students (Dickey 1997, 264–65). Nicknames serve to educate students about a professor's persona ("Brass," "Happy"), appearance ("Skull," "Stretch," "Stringbean"), reputation as a strict instructor ("Max the Axe," "Terminator"), or favorite grade ("C," "Smiling C+") (McGeachy 1978, 282). Perhaps indicating the correlation of nicknaming with the stress of entering and leaving the institution, freshmen and seniors conferred the most nicknames on their professors.

McGeachy asked an additional question of whether the small, intimate college fostered more nicknaming than at a large university. He found that they appear at both in high frequency, but one difference is that at a small school, the knowledge of professors' nicknames is not limited to the student body, but is known to the individuals to whom they are applied (McGeachy 1978, 282). In the old-time college, the nicknames integrated faculty into the student community; in the larger institution, where faculty probably do not know the attribution, students believe that with the nicknames, they know the professors on a more human level or can anticipate their character. In this way, students' nicknames for faculty bear a comparable function to ones known among team and club nicknames on campus meant to show an intimate connection of members. Sometimes these names are based on wordplay or a clipping of a name, often to "Americanize" names, such as "Wiz" for Wizsniewski or "Pop" for Peter Popovic, or on a special attribute such as "speedy," "stretch," and "crazy legs" (Kennedy and Zamuner 2006). An added dimension in cyberculture are handles that students give themselves and then become familiar to others through social networking sites and blogs (Tufekci 2008). At least one Facebook site is devoted totally to professor nicknames—at Bethel Seminary. "This is not to rip on professors," the organizer assures members; the site invites suggestions "based on experiences in class."

Comeuppance and Condescension

In narrative as well as name, students tear into professors' pomposity, such as the vintage story of the bombastic Dr. Coffin who peppered his speech with obscure Greek and Latin terms to impress or confuse his students, and they responded with the pejorative nickname "Professor Sarcophagus" (Champney 1885). There is also the oft-told story about the pretentious instructor who comes into the class for the first time. Standing at the podium, he haughtily addresses the students. "If there are any dumbbells in the room, please stand up." A long pause ensues, and then a lone freshman stood up. "What, do you consider yourself a dumbbell?" asks the professor. "Well, not exactly sir, but I do hate to see you standing up by yourself," said the freshman (Keseling and Kinney 1956, 116; Copeland and Copeland 1940, 375; Wiseman 2007, 184).

Another narrative in which the professor is embarrassed concerns the professor lecturing on the Magna Carta. "You in the back," he calls out, "what was the date of the signing?" "I don't know that," comes the carefree reply. The professor exclaims, "You don't! I assigned this stuff last Friday. What were you doing last night?" The answer he gets is "I was out drinking beer with some friends." The professor angrily puffs, "You were! What audacity to stand there and tell me a thing like that! How do you ever expect to pass this course?" "Wal, I don't know. Ya see, I just come in to fix the radiator," is the man's cool response as the professor turns red (Copeland and Copeland 1940, 376).

As for professors' legendary pedantry, a story is told about the religious lecture at Hobart. The speaker uses the six letters forming the name of the institution for the headings of the subdivisions of his extended address. "H" stood for holiness, "O" for obedience, "B" for beneficence, "A" for adoration, "R" for righteousness, "T" for triumph. He gives fifteen or twenty minutes to every subject. As the students make their way for the exit, one student says to another, "Damned good thing we aren't attending the Massachusetts Institute of Technology!" (Copeland and Copeland 1940, 382). A related story concerns one Professor Brown explaining himself on the telephone. "No—not Bond— Brown. B as in Brontosaurus, R as in Rhizophoracae, O as in Ophisthotelae, W as in Willingbalya, and N in Nucifraga. Do you comprehend?" (Copeland and Copeland 1940, 383).

Reflecting the dramatic increase in the number of immigrants' children entering colleges during the twentieth century are a few dialect jokes in student repertoires that can be updated with the accents of the latest newcomers. I recall often hearing one such joke at story-swapping sessions while I attended Binghamton University. The school drew many children and grandchildren of Yiddish-speaking East European Jews from New York City. Students told of the parents who sent their boy upstate to the fancy-shmancy college (sometimes the school is Harvard or Yale), so that he could talk like a highfalutin educated American. They go with the boy to the school to ask the aristocratic English prof to give him special attention. "Oy, von't you tich ar' boy so he can spik vonderful?" "Harumph," the prof says in his best Brahmin English, "I shall see what I can do with this savage tongue to improve his diction." They return at the end of the year to find out how the boy is doing. They come into the prof's office and ask him his opinion. The illustrious scholar tells them, "Oy da boy spiks poifect" (Cottom 1989, 8; Leacock 1935, 181–82).

Still circulating is a variation of the dialect joke making the classic contrast between the professor as the epitome of campus sophistication and the student as the ignorant rube. Loyal Jones recounts the story of the southern country boy coming to campus for the first time. Feeling a little confused about the new place, he spots an English professor and asks, "Where's the library at?" The professor curtly answers, "Here we do not end sentences with prepositions." The country boy's retort is "Dang it, where's the library at, jackass?" (Jones 2008, 2–3; see also Baker 1986, xxxviii; Cottom 1989, 3; Sherzer 2002, 82; Wiseman 2007, 184).

Modern humor serving to put professors in their place often circulates on websites and photocopies. Labeled "the university hierarchy" or "the college food chain," the material serves to remind students of the power of the office staff in a bureaucratic organization.

The Dean
Leaps tall buildings in a single bound
Is more powerful than a locomotive
Is faster than a speeding bullet
Walks on water
Gives policy to God

The Department Head
Leaps short buildings in a single bound
Is more powerful than a switch engine
Is just as fast as a speeding bullet
Talks with God

The Professor
Leaps short buildings with a running start and favorable winds
Is almost as powerful as a switch engine
Is faster than a speeding BB
Walks on water in an indoor swimming pool
Talks with God if a special request is honored

The Associate Professor
Barely clears a quonset hut
Loses tug-of-war with a locomotive
Can fire a speeding bullet
Swims well
Is occasionally addressed by God

The Assistant Professor
Makes high marks on the walls when trying to leap tall buildings
Is run over by locomotives
Can sometimes handle a gun without inflicting self-injury
Treads water
Talks to animals

The Instructor
Climbs walls continually
Rides the rails
Plays Russian roulette
Walks on thin ice
Prays a lot

The Graduate Student
Runs into buildings
Recognizes locomotives two out of three times
Is not issued ammunition
Can stay afloat with a life jacket
Talks to walls

The Undergraduate Student
Falls over doorstep when trying to enter buildings
Says "Look at the choo-choo"
Wets himself with a water pistol
Plays in mud puddles
Mumbles to himself

The Department Secretary
Lifts buildings and walks under them
Kicks locomotives off the tracks
Catches speeding bullets in her teeth and eats them
Freezes water with a single glance
She IS God.

The humor is based on the iconic Superman, who was known in popular culture as "faster than a speeding bullet, more powerful than a locomotive, able to leap tall buildings in a single bound." Folklorists Alan Dundes and Carl Pagter found the parody originally as a guide to performance appraisal in corporate settings and thought it reflects an anxiety in a service and information economy over the ambiguity of one's effectiveness in a bureaucracy with uncertain criteria. They thought that the Superman model was particularly appealing because of the "American insistence upon exaggeration" and the "necessity for superlatives in personnel evaluations" (Dundes and Pagter 1978, 79; Smith 1984, 93; 1986, 62). It also reflects the critical role in the office of the secretary managing an organization filled with characters who seem unmanageable. With technology at the secretary's fingertips, it should come as no surprise that this figure considered low on the corporate chain of command has a hand in distributing the lore. The identification of the secretary as female in contrast to the male folktypes also indicates gender inequity in the organizational culture. In a university setting, the breakdown by title invites commentary on the differences between the formal and informal hierarchy in institutions that appear increasingly corporate. Students also will recognize in the lore a rubric format frequently given them for grading criteria. The parody additionally invokes religious metaphors of "talking to God" that sets up a connection of the modern bureaucratic organization in a service and information economy to a premodern transcendent spiritual community associated with social purpose.

One can note the sense of religious order and spiritual community in a freely varied set of "ten commandments of college" circulating among students, often introduced with the faux biblical verse of "Student was searching for divine inspiration. Student walked high on the mountain of knowledge and came across God. Student asked God how to live life as a college kid should. And God said unto him, follow these Ten Commandments and you shall be all a college kid is. And Student thanked God and it was good" (Seidell 2004; cf. Monteiro 1976, 152; Smith 1986, 109). First on most decalogues is "Thou Shalt Nap" (or the variant "Thou Shall Put Sleep Above All Else"). Why? One parody explains, "And God said, if you don't nap, you will not be able to stay up all night drinking" (Seidell 2004). Others that commonly make the posted lists are "Thou Shalt Gain Weight," "Thou Shall Not Begin a Paper Until the Last Minute," "Thou Shalt Wake Up Confused," "Thou Shall Not Covet Thy Neighbor's Music," and "Thou Shalt Hook Up" (cf. Smith 1986, 28–29). An implied reference in these commandments is guidance for being liberated from parental rule and yet bound by pressure to fit into what appears to be a liminal place and anxious time in one's life, with many distracting temptations. One student twist of the parable of Moses's delivery of the Ten Commandments, for example, emphasizes the need for "rules of living at college":

The graduate came down from the student center. Amidst the unwashed, sweatshirt-covered students before him, he presented a notebook containing these ten rules of living at college. These truths we hold dear. Follow them to the best of your ability, or face eternal damnation at the hands of your professors, memorizing the periodic table and writing expositions about dead composers. Behold these Ten Commandments of College Life. (Morain 2001)

With another biblical reference suggesting college as an inversion, or perversion, of normal life, many parodies conclude, "Follow the Ten Commandments of College or you will be smote!" (Seidell 2004).

Is there a moral message implied by the college commandments? The humorous commandments may appear to fuel the public perception of campuses as dens of iniquity, but they also raise questions about individual responsibility at a time when students are often on their own for the first time and away from the watchful eye of parents, ministers, and teachers. Reading between the lines, student writers seem to be asking whether one's choice of action really "was good." For instance, after "Thou Shalt Nap," one circulating decalogue included "Thou Shalt Get Sick All the Time": "Now God said to the Student, you must be sick all of the time. And student said why. And God said unto him, you shall share drinks, stay up too late, drink too much and make out with people you don't know. Therefore, God said, you shall be sick all year round. But God said, blessed are the sick for they have partied the hardest. And it was good" (Seidell 2004).

It is not surprising to find sexuality questioned as well, particularly with the folk construction of college as both intellectual and sexual awakening. Under "Thou Shalt Hook Up" (the colloquial phrase "hook up with" was reported by *American Speech* as referring originally to marrying, but in teen slang since the 1980s referred to finding a partner for romance or sex; see Glowka, Bonner, and Lester 1999, 84), a version labeled as "classic" related, "You shall go home with random people every weekend and forget about them the next day. You shall see them at class and be awkward amongst their company. You shall exchange saliva at bars and parties and it will be good. And Student became gleeful and God told Student to wrap it up because He knows where she has been, but Student does not" (Seidell 2004). As with many forms of folklore, this text frames and symbolizes behavior that may cause anxiety in the safe context of humor and fantasy, and serves to raise ethical questions in listeners' minds even as it appears to celebrate the liberating experience of college.

Soiling Scholarly Reputations

The character of a student body that carries over into the reputation of an institution is evident in lampoons of the all-important schedule of classes. In these parodies, students comment on odd professorial research or the rise of consumer-centered campuses. During the 1960s, a time of student unrest, a sheet went around about the course offerings at the University of California at Berkeley (sometimes Columbia or another school known for student rebellion was substituted). It listed freshmen courses as Riot 101, Insurrection 121, Russian 101, Lab (Riot Technique), Political Science 101, Dirty Books 101, Russian 102, Insurrection 122, Lab (Mob Rule), Arson Techniques 101, and Arson Lab. By the time the student gets to the senior year, the courses are Introduction to Free Love, Beard Growing 311, Sandal Mending 302, and Rules and Regulations for Understanding Welfare and Unemployment Collection (Dundes and Pagter 1978, 138–40).

The curricular parodies changed with growing materialism in subsequent collegiate generations. The most common humorous jabs at the growing vocationalism of the university course catalog listed Money Can Make You Rich and Talking Good: How You Can Improve Your Speech and Get a Better Job (see Dundes and Pagter 1987, 266–67). By the time the new millennium rolled around, humorous electronic posts circulated widely with a new list of ridiculous-sounding courses that poked fun at the bloating of the mega-university course schedule (and, it appears, the intellectualization of popular culture), including "The Simpsons and Philosophy," "The Science of Harry Potter," "Joy of Garbage," "Dirty Pictures," "Underwater Basket Weaving," "Tree Climbing," "Getting Dressed," and "American Degenerates." To show that folklore does not equal fiction, it should be noted that many of these courses in the top ten lists derive from actual titles in the course catalog.

The more standard courses of Geology and Psych 101, typically populated by students outside the major taking the classes for required general education or popular elective credits, breed their own lore. Many students across the country call an introductory geology course "Rocks for Jocks," a western history course "Cowboys and Indians," and a children's literature course "Kiddy Lit." Sociology courses on deviant behavior often become "Nuts and Sluts," modern art turns into "Spots and Dots," and introductory music into "Tunes for Goons" (see Sykes 1988).

In their courses, students have to load up on books, and they hurl some of their sharpest barbs at the titles of their overly academic tomes. Knocking their reading load, and showing considerable creativity, students of literature at the University of Delaware circulated a sheet with a technique to cut in half the number of pages to be read. They proposed combining at least two major works of literature into a single work. Some results were *Catch-22,000 Leagues Under the Sea* by Verne Heller, *As I Les Miserables* by Hugo Faulkner, *Dr. Faustus and Mr. Hyde* by Thomas Lewis Stevenmann, and *The Stranger in the Rye* by Camus D. Salinger. Other titles are bawdier and are reminiscent of spoofs found in children's folklore, although they often relate to problems in college, such as *The Worried Maiden* by Pastor Period, *The V.D. Symptom Book* by Urine Trouble, and *Wasted to the Max* by Iona Syringe (see Aman 1986–87; Clerval 1986–87; Doyle 1973; D'Pnymph 1988, 193–94; Dundes and Georges 1962, 224; Clerval 1986–87; Aman 1986–87). These titles add to the caricatures that might be offered when students look over their bookstore orders: *Big Fart!* by Hugh Jass, *The Spots on the Wall* by Hu Flung Dung, *Body Parts* by Anne Atomy, *Eating Disorders* by Anna Rexia, *Erotic Adventures* by Oliver Klozoff, and *Women Rule* by Iam Write (see Dundes and Georges 1962, 224).

Goldbrickers and Partiers

Legends and jokes arise on campus for students who defy the imperative to hit the books. Often this student type is called the "goldbricker" or "partier." The goldbricker term originally referred to a swindler who offered a fake gold bar for sale, and it was picked up in military slang for a loafer or someone who shirks his responsibility. In their distinctive landscapes, temporary residence, and hierarchical organization, campuses often invited comparisons to regimented military camps, and "goldbricker" is one of many army terms entering college slang (Bergera and Priddis 1985, 239; "Physical Education" 2010). Folklore collections include stories of apparent goof-offs who miss class and party, only to "ace" (student lingo for receiving an A) the tests. Alfred Rollins, for example, reported a collegiate story from New York of "the admired giant of the past who had a photographic memory. He could 'party' merrily for thirteen weeks, and then settle down to read the books and write the papers. Quoting verbatim whole pages of the textbook, he would take honors in his exams, despite his enraged professors" (1961, 171).

In most of the goldbricker stories, the truant is unrepentant and scores one over the professorial taskmaster. In what sounds like a good Munchausen tale, for example, Walker Wyman tells of the footloose student who, after answering to roll call on the first day, did not show up again until the final exam. He calmly took the test, and got a B. The professor called the fellow and asked him to explain this incredible feat. According to Wyman, "The student said that he thought he could do better than a 'B,' but the professor confused him a little when he attended class the first day" (1979, 82).

The wiseass often nonchalantly strolls late into the exam. In a frequently reported narrative, a student is tardy for a class and sees several math problems placed on the board. He is unaware that the professor had given them as insoluble problems, and he assumes that they are part of a test or homework. He ends up figuring out one or more of them. Folklorist Jan Brunvand has claimed to find the source of the story in the well-documented experience of famed Stanford University mathematician George B. Dantzig, but the appeal of student one-upmanship to generations of collegians has resulted in many localized, and dramatic, narratives of the solution of the unsolvable problem (Brunvand 1989, 278–83; Choron and Choron 2004; Meakes 2004, 114; Mikkelson and Mikkelson 2011c). The folkloric "truth" of the story now resides in the classroom expectations it reveals.

A variant of the "brainy goldbricker" narrative from Columbia relates the legend of famed theoretical physicist Julian Schwinger, who was a night owl and did not attend mathematics lectures scheduled for the morning. The professor noticed his absence and agreed that Schwinger could receive a grade only if he passed a rigorous comprehensive exam. He not only passed but, according to oral accounts, "of course, he knew everything" and got an A (Capri 2007, 27). For generations, students have commented on such unusual characters, perhaps to fantasize that absorbing all that material must come easily for some, but for the rest of us, it is hard to buckle down, especially with all the campus's distractions. In the twenty-first century, if the legendary photographic memorizer is not out partying, he (and the character usually is male, indicating some discomfort with taking a submissive student role deemed feminine) is wiling away his time on video games instead of studying.

Legends of remarkable drinking feats meanwhile highlight dubious achievements of the partier types. Frequently reported in my survey is the University of California at Berkeley's drinking legend of John P. Ergman, reputed to have caroused his way through school, always in the "recent past." "He was a notorious beer drinker, and he taught all the freshmen how to drink," one account begins. "J.P. was a true party man," another offers: "At one of the parties, the beer supply ran out, and J.P. was sent to get another twelve-gallon keg, and did not return. Some days later his dead body was found leaning against a tree, and the keg was empty!"

Jocks and Their Coaches

Often the legendary mass, indeed massive, consumers—of alcohol, food, cash, sex, and cars—are the men's football and basketball stars. With their reputations for privilege and excess, these athletes present a dilemma in student lore. While praised for the esteem they bring to the student body, they are scorned for taking advantage of the system and distancing themselves from the "regular" student. The nature of the taunting has changed from the late twentieth century to the early twenty-first century. The "privileged jock" has entered into student humor where the "dumb jock" left off (Beezley 1985; Moser 2002).

Wherever the jock is in these stories, the anxious, victory-minded coach is not too far behind.

Combining the stereotype of dumbness with excess is the joke about the new recruit who complained that the food at the training table was awful. "Every mouthful was terrible, just terrible," he went on, "and, to make it worse, the portions were too small." The recruit's appetite, and grasp of the situation, comes into play in the joke still getting around on the Internet:

> The huge college freshman figured he'd try out for the football team. "Can you tackle?" asked the coach. "Watch this," said the freshman, who proceeded to run smack into a telephone pole, shattering it to splinters. "Wow," said the coach. "I'm impressed. Can you run?" "Of course I can run," said the freshman. He was off like a shot, and in just over nine seconds, he had run a hundred yard dash. "Great!" enthused the coach. "But can you pass a football?" The freshman rolled his eyes, hesitated for a few seconds. "Well, sir," he said, "if I can swallow it, I can probably pass it." (Jokes4U 2008)

Recruits are brought to the university, lore professes, for their brawn rather than for their brain. To make the point, a legend of a coach traveling the backroads of farm country to find players is connected to several Hall of Fame coaches, including Notre Dame's Knute Rockne and Minnesota's Clarence "Doc" Spears. Tellers relate that the coach asks plowboys he sees for directions to the next town. If they point the way with their finger, he continues on his way. But once in a while, there is the exceptional specimen who picks up his plow to point the way (Baughman 1966, motif X941[b]; Baker 1983, 110; Beezley 1985, 218; Brunvand 1993, 156–57; Dorson 1949, 674; Randolph 1951, 170).

Lore has it that some recruits are given special oral entrance exams to bypass the normal academic route into college. Unfortunately, one star gave the wrong answer of "eight" when asked to compute the sum of three and three. "Aw, come on," the coach pleads with the examiners, "he only missed the right answer by one!" (Beezley 1985, 216; Baker 1983, 110; Wyman 1979, 86). Using a similar scenario, the story is told about the Kentucky basketball player who had to spell "dog" on his oral exam. "D . . . d . . . d . . . ," he stammered. Then the coach hit him on the back. "Oh, Gee!" he exclaimed. The player passed. From Wisconsin, meanwhile, comes the joke of the tough oral exam where the football recruits were asked not one, but two questions: "What color is blue vitriol?" and "When was the war of 1812?" (Wyman 1979). Another exam narrative concerns a lineman and quarterback taking an exam in English literature. The exam consisted of fill-in-the-blank statements. One of the questions had the lineman stumped: "Complete the nursery phrase, 'Ol' MacDonald had a . . .'" He whispers to his teammate, "What does Ol' MacDonald have?" "Dang, you're stupid," he replies, "that's a farm." He nods and begins to write the word in, but stops when he realizes that he cannot spell it. He whispers again to his teammate, "Hey, how do you spell it?" "Oh my God, you're dumb," the quarterback haughtily tells him out of earshot of the proctor. "Everyone knows 'farm' is spelled 'e-i-e-i-o,'" he says.

Some narratives suggest that the student body is not much sharper than the jocks, especially at places known as sports schools. Alan Dundes tells of the sterling presidential address extolling the great achievements of the university at USC's commencement. His concentration is broken by the growing chant "Let Bubba graduate" from the crowd. The flustered president turns to one of his deans and asks "Who's Bubba?" The dean reminds him, "Sir, you know, Bubba, the star of our football team. He's one unit short of the number required for graduation." The president ponders the situation for the moment and proclaims to the throng, "Who could forget Bubba who did so much for our university on the playing field. He's just one unit short of graduating. I'm going to ask him one question and if he answers the question correctly, he'll earn the unit and be able to graduate." "Bubba, how much is nine times nine?" Bubba thinks for a minute or two and finally answers, "Eighty-one." Immediately the crowd yells, "Give him another chance; give him another chance" (or "Let him try again") (Dundes 1996, 160; see also Davies 2011, 40). In other versions, the scene is not commencement but the locker room, where the star player's teammates shout "Give him another chance" (Falk 2005, 175; Saluja 2005, 34; Shubnell 2008, 40).

The privileged jock of folklore may be dumb, but he is not stupid, as the saying goes, for he is the one raking in bucks and having an easy time in college. And "How many jocks does it take to change a light bulb at Arizona State?" The answer? "Only one, but eleven get one course credit for it!" (Beezley 1985, 224). Many students at big-time colleges quip that they have the best teams money can buy or school (or science department) the football team can be proud of (Barra 2004, 34). Rumors fly about the numbers of cars and other amenities athletes receive (Beezley 1985, 219). In many versions, the appetite of the athletes for tremendous quantities of food, alcohol, and women is equal to the generosity of patrons (Beezley 1985, 22–23). Many swear that once graduated into the professional leagues, a star student-athlete was introduced as "the only college player in history who had to take a cut in pay to turn pro" (Beezley 1985, 220).

A disturbing racial reference often creeps into many quips, especially as it is sometimes expressed that stereotyped black athletes get into big-time, predominantly white colleges to play for pay. Even though the "dumb jock" is a fixture of lore questioning the place of athletics in academic pursuits of learning, the stereotyped male "black jock" appears way out of place and especially linked to basketball. After University of Maryland basketball star Len Bias died of cocaine intoxication in 1986, many "sick" jokes circulated, including "Why are so many blacks and other minorities enrolling at the University of Maryland?" Because they heard there is no bias there (Aman 1988–89, 271). Also during the late 1980s, a crude parody of a recruiting list made the rounds from photocopier to photocopier. In versions variously attached to the universities of Oklahoma, Wisconsin, Minnesota, and Miami, the list included the fictitious recruit Woodrow Lee Washington, 6 feet 8 inches tall, 198 pounds, from the Bronx, New York. "Third-generation welfare family. At 19 he is the oldest of 14 children. Mother thinks that possibly child No. 3 and No. 9 may have the same father. Expensive tastes; wants two floor-length mink coats and pink Mercedes to sign letter of intent" ("University of Wisconsin" 1986–87). The one from the University of Oklahoma was circulated in response to scandals involving football players arrested on criminal charges. It lists Cletis Quentis Jenkins, "running back. Set state scoring record out of Melrose High School, Charlotte, NC. Also led the state in burglaries. But has only six convictions. He's been clocked in the 40 at 4.2 seconds with a 25" TV under his arm."

In the twenty-first century, jokes circulate on Internet humor sites such as "What do you call a black guy who goes to college? A basketball player; "Why can blacks run so fast? Running from cops (alternative answer—the slow ones are in jail)." Black male athletes, even more than women, often report being celebrated on campus as collegiate heroes, and yet they also resent presumptions that they are not otherwise academically worthy or are genetically superior rather than working for their success (Hall 2001; Harrison and Lawrence 2004; Sailes 1993). Similarly, Jewish and Asian American athletes are aware of beliefs that they are not genetically or culturally suited for athletic competition. This prejudice comes through in humor suggesting that Jewish and Asian American male bodies are feminized or frail and their overbearing parents dissuade them from superfluous sports in favor of intellectual pursuits in contrast to the case of African Americans characterized by emotive physicality and hypermasculinity (Klein 2000; Konagaya 2005).

The persistence of deep-seated beliefs about the "black jock" among white college students convinced of their inclusive, egalitarian attitudes has raised speculation by scholars about the psychology that associates all black men with basketball. Sociologist Ronald Hall (2001) has insightfully pointed out that basketball more than other sports in which blacks are well represented suggests aggressive domination. The modern game, with its celebration of urban intensity, appears out of place on pastoral, elite campuses (George 1999; Greenfield 1999). A commonly expressed belief is that players are more likely to be pulled out of impoverishment, particularly in ghetto life, and therefore have pent-up anger that they release on the court. Their manly displays of chest-bumping, high-fives, and heart pounding draw notice as ethnically framed behavior and usually a blast of cheers. In their exposure of towering, skin-revealing tattooed bodies, quick pace, entertaining agility and trickery, and cheer-triggering "in your face" acts of "slam" dunking and jamming over opponents, black athletes have simultaneously generated raves and fears, according to Hall. He writes that "motivation for the 'dumb Black' stereotype is inherent in the ability of African American men to threaten America's masculine male power structure. By virtue of their dark skin, they are perceived as the most masculine members of the human species. Their athletic superiority and physicality are not irrelevant to that perception" (Hall 2001, 114).

African American basketball players draw attention to themselves more so than African American football players because of the visibility of their blackness on the court and economic success in the black-player-dominated pro ranks. They may thus be viewed as hired guns valued for what they can aggressively accomplish in a play frame, but feared for their representation of violence and physicality—and economic success—outside of the frame. One way to cognitively resolve that paradox is for European Americans to narrate black men into a safe frame of the playing court where, like gladiators, they dominate one another rather than threatening the campus (Robertson 2011). The stereotyped humor targeting African American men more than women demonstrates, according to Hall, that "by dark skin color, assumed virility, physical strength, and athletic prowess, black men as a subjugated minority are a societal contradiction to established ranks of wealth and power. This intensifies their ability to threaten the European-masculine status quo" (2001, 114).

In the wake of scandals since the late twentieth century concerning student-athletes arrested for violent crimes, bringing out issues of the control that coaches and administrators have over their players outside the field of play, humor has arisen about the "crooked jock" in addition to the "dumb one." The stereotype fits in with fear of the size—and presumed brutishness—of the players that goes against the image of the brainy student. After some arrests in 2008 at Penn State, the following jokes circulated that had previously been adapted to other troubled programs at Michigan, Oregon, Tennessee, Texas A&M, Washington State, Indiana, and Arkansas:

A lady in Boalsburg calls 911. Hysterically, she says, "Someone's just broken into my house and I think he's going to rob me! The police officer says, "We're really busy at the moment. Just get the guy's jersey number and we'll get back to you."

The Penn State team is expecting a 7-6 season this year. 7 arrests and 6 convictions.

What is Joe Paterno's biggest concern? Does the NCAA count bail money as a recruiting violation?

What do you call a drug ring in State College? A huddle.

There are four Penn State players in a car. Who's driving? The police.

The Penn State team has adopted a new honor system. "Yes, your honor. No, your honor."

Lore such as these "jock jokes" draws attention to the aggressive business of sport at big-time colleges. Related humor that circulates on the Internet, and previously in photocopied sheets, mocks the schedules of colleges who play soft opponents to inflate their winning record and earn profitable tournament invitations. Although the names of the schools change, the schedule of opponents is fairly consistent: Chicken Little Nursery School, Boy Scout Troop 99, Crippled Children's Hospital, School for the Blind, World War I Veterans Association, Brownie Scout Troop No. 13, High School Cheerleaders, St. Joseph's Boys' Choir, Korean War Amputees, and Veterans' Hospital Polio Patients. All the games are, of course, at home. The parody also lists important rule changes for the current year. Some of the notable ones are: The home team will be allowed to play with three footballs at the same time, and thirty-three players can be on the field instead of the usual eleven. The home team also has special rules tailored for the schedule. Implying that the home team would do anything to win, the rules stipulate that when playing patients with polio, the home team must not disconnect iron lungs; when playing the Brownies, the home team cannot steal their cookies; and when playing a team from the School for the Blind, home team players cannot hide the football under their jerseys. The joke also shows up in briefer oral replies to the question of who the home team plays in an upcoming weekend: Blessed (or alternatively, Little, Crippled) Sisters of the Poor. The old derisive jest caused public controversy when Ohio State University president Gordon Gee, in the heat of his institution's quest for a national football championship, told the Associated Press that high-ranked teams like Texas Christian University and Boise State University do not deserve to play in the Bowl Championship Series (BCS) title game because of their weak schedules. He underscored the point by saying, "We do not play the Little Sisters of the Poor" ("Ohio State President Atones" 2011; see also Little Sisters of the Poor 2011). With that comment is not only a questioning of the toughness of the schedule but also a reminder of the game as a test of manhood to show the superiority of the university. If the contest proves in folk lingo to be "not even a game," the ritualized win is not fully satisfying.

The coach epitomizes the pressure to instill toughness and win. In older collegiate lore in the context of a period in which athletics fought to be relevant to higher education, the coach often appeared confused or eccentric, but befitting the heightened role of collegiate sports, in contemporary lore the coach is mostly portrayed as aloof, commanding, and egotistical. Among the older texts are those attached to Ed Diddle, longtime coach of Western Kentucky's basketball team. Complaining that his players were eating too well and gaining too much weight, his trainer suggested that the boys could cut down on their milk consumption. Coach Diddle "stood up and beat on the table with his fists and said, 'Boys, I got an announcement to make.' He said, 'From now on you don't get a quart of milk each meal. You just get two pints.'"

Another time, one of Diddle's stars asked the coach, "Hey, do you hear that noise?" "What noise?" the coach replied. "Illinois" was the joking answer. The coach liked that so much that he later tried it on one of his assistants. "Do you hear that racket?" he smilingly blurted. "What racket?" "Pennsylvania," Diddle offered (Dawson 1971, 39).

Put in the context of twenty-first-century collegiate sports scandals about the lack of education athletes receive, the humorous motif of the confused coach surfaces in stories such as the one told sometimes about venerated football coach Tom Osborne of Nebraska. Osborne was getting on Penn State's Joe Paterno about his disappointing season, and Paterno quickly responded by pointing out the high percentage of his seniors graduating. Osborne defensively referred to his student athletes at Nebraska. "You see that big red 'N' over there by Cornhusker stadium?" he said. "That stands for 'knowledge.'"

Legendary coaches such as Bob Knight of Indiana, Dean Smith of North Carolina, and the late Bear Bryant of Alabama received more than big bucks for their effort; they got holy adoration. Witness a story and variations told with any of the three in the leading role. "There was a basketball player from Indy who died and went to heaven," one story begins.

> When he got to heaven he told St. Peter that it was all right that he died as long as they played basketball in heaven. St. Peter said they did, but instead of numbers on the jerseys they used letters. The man from Indy didn't understand, so St. Peter said he would just show him. When they got to the court he explained that the man with the "C" on his jersey was a center, the players with "G" were guards, and since the man from Indy was a forward he would have an "F" on his shirt. The player from Indy said he understood everything except who the man was with "BK" on his shirt. St. Peter just laughed and replied, "That's just God; he thinks he's Bobby Knight." (Baker 1986, 173–74; see also Beezley 1980, 198; Boswell 1976, 78)

Sometimes the story is not complimentary, as with this variation told by, not surprisingly, rival North Carolina State fans about North Carolina's Dean Smith (told also by Michigan fans of a later generation about Michigan State's Tom Izzo)

> Basketball coaches Norm Sloan of State, Bill Foster of Duke, and Carl Tacy of Wake Forest died and went to heaven. As they were being introduced around, St. Peter told them: "This is a nice place. Very few aggravations. About the only thing that might be considered unpleasant is the waiting. We have to wait in line for everything." Sure enough, at dinner that night, there was a long line of angels. Suddenly there was a commotion as a line-breaker charged to the front, pushing other angels out of the way. He grabbed the food and began eating; soon he demanded to be brought seconds, and the angels meekly complied. "Wow, who's that?" the coaches whispered to St. Peter. "Oh, that's God," said the saint. "Sometimes he thinks he's Dean Smith." (Beezley 1981, 115–16)

Pointing to, or deriding, the egos of coaches, tellers relate the story of the group of northern sportswriters who came to Arkansas to see Bear Bryant's birthplace. Bryant took them to a small barn. "Is this where you were born, Bear?" asked one sportswriter. "Yep," answered Bryant. Another sportswriter said, "I thought you were born in a log cabin." "That was Abraham Lincoln," Bear answered. "I was born in a manger." In another story about the coach's holy status, Bear takes a quiet, casual walk on the water, when he suddenly falls under. He gasps for breath and yells for help, until along in a speedboat comes the head football coach at Auburn, who assists Bryant into the boat. "Now you won't tell anyone that I fell in, will you?" asks Bear. "Not if you won't tell anyone that I rescued you," answers the Auburn coach (Boswell 1976, 77).

With the growing power base that coaches hold within the university and over their young charges, suspicions often arise about exploitation of their superordinate position. In conversation and narrative, speakers embed questions about whether coaches in big-time sports programs are above reproach by the university even when engaging in illicit behavior. Football players and their coaches especially invite commentary in legend and humor because of the sport's display of violence and hypersexual associations (Dundes 1978; Bronner 2011a, 350–97). Famous Ohio State coach Woody Hayes (1913–1987), who had a reputation for a volatile temper and roughneck manner, for example, was ultimately fired after the 1978 Gator Bowl for punching a football player from the opposing team when he intercepted the pass and ran toward the Ohio State sideline. Journalist Jack Torry (2010) reports variations of stories about Hayes and other coaches driving players hard at practice until they dropped from fatigue and frequently vomited with exhaustion. Hayes supposedly would tear his baseball cap to bits and dramatically throw away or stomp on clocks in a rage over imperfect execution on the field. His attention-grabbing tirades, whether rehearsed or not, signaled to players an all-night ordeal of pain-inducing drills. Hayes acknowledged some truth in the stories but swore that the fabled chuck of timepieces derived from his throwing away a malfunctioning watch (Torry 2010). Hayes is hardly the only coach to figure in narratives of verbal and physical abuse in the obsession with victory, although often tellers contextualize the stories as characterizing "old-school" types before a purportedly postmodern coddling of athletes and public intolerance for bullying.

Media attention to abuse by coaches in big-time college sports took a distressful turn toward child molestation in 2011 with headline-grabbing scandals of sexual assaults by assistant coaches at Penn State and Syracuse universities (Luciew 2011). Besides raising issues of institutional control over the programs, the allegations drew comment about homoerotic, homophobic, and predatory behavior in football. *New York Times* columnist Daniel Mendelsohn mused that if the victims had been ten-year-old girls instead of boys, the legal and cultural response would have been surely swifter and more open. He wrote that "in a culture that increasingly accepts gay life, organized athletics, from middle school to the professional leagues, is the last redoubt of unapologetic anti-gay sentiment" (Mendelsohn 2011). Folklorist Alan Dundes argued, however, that anxiety over masculinity in American adolescence is projected into football as a male initiatory ritual with abundant sexual metaphors of intimate male contact (1978, 84). Dundes pointed out that in the play frame of the sport, coming-of-age males display their masculine dominance by symbolically sodomizing, that is, feminizing, their opponent in celebratory displays of smearing, piling, and sacking (1978, 86–87). This explanation accounts for Mendelsohn's (2011) puzzlement over why "the familiar ferocious anti-gay swagger many athletes affect is likely meant to quash even the faintest suspicion that anything tender or erotic animates naked playfulness between men." The hypermasculine displays of throwing off tacklers and penetrating holes (and end zones) announce that the players are not feminine or else compensate for the fervid participation in activity that could be construed as homoerotic.

The sexual threat of football play and the characterization of aggressive coaches are evident in former player David Kopay's descriptions of the typical exhortatory folk speech of coaches.

> We were told to go out and "fuck those guys"; to take that ball and "stick it up their asses" or "down their throats." The coaches would yell, "knock their

dicks off," or more often than that, "knock their jocks off." They'd say, "Go out there and give it all you've got, a hundred and ten per cent, shoot your wad." You controlled their line and "knocked" them into submission. Over the years I've seen many a coach get emotionally aroused while he was diagramming a particular play into an imaginary hole on the blackboard. His face red, his voice rising, he would show the ball carrier how he wanted him to "stick it in the hole." (Kopay and Young 2001, 53–54)

The sexual interpretation of football is not the only one to explain the incredible appeal of the sport in America, especially at the college level, as I will discuss later, but it is certainly implied in a spate of jokes after news broke of the Penn State and Syracuse university sexual abuse scandals. A blogger at Syracuse University noted that "I went to the gym and all we heard was Bernie Fine [assistant basketball coach at Syracuse University accused of molesting team "ball boys"] jokes. . . . Titles for Bernie Fine's new book: Traveling Violations, Two Hand Ball Control, Teaching in the Shower" (Ducati 2011; cf. title-author jokes in Dundes 1962, 221; Doyle 1973). At Penn State, the character in the jokes is Jerry Sandusky, a retired assistant coach who started Second Mile (a charity for children) and who was accused of sexually abusing ten boys over a fifteen-year period. Invoking some of the football rhetoric mentioned by Dundes, one jest making the rounds of the Internet blared, "Penn State football: We start you at tight end, then make you a wide receiver." Photos posted on humor sites suggestively showed Sandusky as a coach standing behind a football player down in a three-point stance. Verbal jokes referred to predatory behavior such as the one about Jerry Sandusky, Tim Curley, and Gary Shultz (Penn State officials charged with perjury and failing to report suspected child abuse), who are on a plane with a bunch of Second Mile kids when suddenly the plane careens out of control and is on course to crash. Curley yells out, "Here, there are three parachutes!" "What about the kids?!?!" replies Shultz. Curley angrily replies, "Fuck the kids!!!" To this, Sandusky calmly asks: "Have we got enough time?" (Flynn2Doucet 2011). An example of metafolklore is the punning comment on one college football discussion board, "These Jerry Sandusky jokes are old . . . unlike those boys in the shower" (Flynn2Doucet 2011).

In fact, the plane-crash joke (also told with a sinking ship) and others were adaptations of humor circulating earlier in the wake of sex scandals for pop singer Michael Jackson, Catholic priests, and President Bill Clinton (amo1337 2009; Blank 2009; Chatikavanij 2012, no. 903; Frank 2011, 45–57, 173–76). All these cycles involved sexual impropriety with youth and brought out the fall from grace of prominent popular icons. Sandusky and Fine were not the household names of these previous characters, but they represented scholastic institutions and sporting traditions that the public expected to uphold rigorous ethical standards similar to churches and political leadership as the bedrock of society. Folklore about these figures conveyed the moral that they failed the trust placed in them by parents and communities. The humor addressed anxieties about the protection of youth in colleges and churches alike, suggesting the characterization of coaches as a priestly or noble class (Hruby 2011). The college sex scandal humor shares with joke cycles labeled by folklorists as "cruel," "gross," or "sick," and dating to the 1950s, the theme of the loss of childhood innocence and questions of abuse in a modernizing, self-indulgent culture in which communities do not exert the same moral control as they did earlier (Bronner 1985; Dundes 1987a; Sutton-Smith 1960). The prominent feature of the Sandusky and Fine jokes, whether infused with homophobia or concern for child abuse, is the violations of youthful male bodies in sexual assaults by revered, parental figures related to the mediating structures of liminal and supposedly insulated university campuses.

Grinds, Nerds, and Geeks

The brains on campus are as suspect as the brawn. Either the eggheads ruin the curve the professor was about to give or surely lack social skills and physical attractiveness from all that time spent in the lab or library. Before the nerds and geeks became the fools with smarts in campus lore, the overachieving grind was singled out for ridicule—and practical jokes. Benjamin Hall, in 1851, defined a grind as a long, difficult lesson, although the word with its image of someone single-mindedly bent over a grinding stone or wheel apparently evolved into a type of person who methodically and persistently studies (Dundes and Schonhorn 1963, 170; Gore 1895, 20; Green 2010, 2:554; Hall 1968, 153; Hummon 1994, 79).

In their slang, students created a contrast between the abnormality of a sedentary serious pupil alone at a desk and the sociable, athletic, playful sort of collegian who was depicted as normal and popular. An editorial in New York University's student magazine in 1898 proclaimed, "There is of course strong presumptive evidence of insanity where a man seems to prefer the classroom to the athletic field, and the applause of the faculty to the acclaim of his fellow students" (Barnes 1898, 126). The writer defined the grind as "the man who devotes his college life to classroom work and to classroom work alone" and implied in the delicate social equilibrium among students that his high achievement owed to his unnatural workaholism rather than intellectual superiority (Barnes 1898, 125). Apparently it was the lack of time for play, and casting one's lot with faculty, that marked the grind for derision. He or she could make the playful lot feel guilty about taking time away from the "grind" of college. Elbert Hubbard of Arts and Crafts Movement fame described the grind's physical type as "bulging forehead, round shoulders, myopic vision and shambling gait" (Hubbard 1904, 162). An anonymous writer for the *Harvard Advocate* in 1884 recognized the grind "with long hair and weak and spectacled eyes!" (Peletiah Gove 1885, 5).

During the nineteenth century, zealous students were called digs, fags, grubs, polers, or blues in addition to grinds. Grind remained in circulation into the twenty-first century, and additional terms arose for the workaholic or unpopular student such as grunts, gunners, gweeps, dweebs, drudges, and throats. Still implied in these appellations is a sexual displacement for those who study or, not so subtly, homosexuality (a fag in the nineteenth century was an underclass male who performed menial services for upperclass men [Hall 1968, 120]). Students of yore who gained teachers' approval were boot-licks, fishers, piscatorians, toadies, and coaxers. Now they are anally pegged as brownnoses and ass lickers and kissers (see Eble 1996, 131; Hummon 1994, 89).

The special derision in folk speech held for the laborious student comes from beliefs held by students regarding grading. Students are sure that professors grade according to a standard set by the leading pupil. That person is the "curve-buster," referring to an increase in points given to the class because the average score was low (Green 2010, 1:1465). To hear professors tell it, students follow a standard of work regardless of who is in the class. But "average" students think that they can do better if the grinds, marked as class traitors, would hold back their achievement and show solidarity with the middling sort. Another implication of the pejorative slang for hardworking students is that they are not doing better than others because of intellectual superiority but because they put in extra hours, thus making equally smart but socially conscious students look bad.

The "nerd" of college humor emerged in the late twentieth century as a folk-type usually characterized similarly to a grind for a lack of playfulness but is often distinguished in modern form by an obsessive devotion to science or mathematics. Dr. Seuss receives credit for first using the term in print for an animal in his children's book *If I Ran the Zoo* (1950), and a year later it showed up in popular parlance for someone not in step with current fashion (Lighter 1997, 647). Linguist Jonathan Green speculates that it has a folk origin, however, as a euphemism for turd or feces (Green 2010, 2:1796). By 1960, it became associated with students who appeared bookish, scientific, and socially inept (Green 2010, 2:1796–97; Lighter 1997, 647–48). The term became popularized with a slew of teen movies from *Revenge of the Nerds* in 1984 to *Nerds Fight Back* in 2010. "The Nerd Test" circulated as photocopied humor and email forwards to determine one's "nerdity." Examples of the questions are:

1. Do you wear glasses?
2. Are your glasses broken (e.g., taped)?
3. Have you ever answered a rhetorical question?
4. Do you sit in the front row?
5. Is your weight less than your IQ?
6. Do you have acne?
7. Do you have greasy hair?
8. Have you ever designed a multistep chemical synthesis?
9. Was it fun?
10. Are your pants too short?
11. Do your socks mismatch?
12. Do you own a pencil case?
13. Do you wear it?
14. Have you ever worn a calculator?
15. A pocket protector?
16. Did you ever work on a Friday night?
17. While there's a party next door?
18. Do you know more than three programming languages?
19. Do you know Maxwell's Equations?
20. Do you have them on a T-shirt?

Answering between 40 and 60 of the 100 questions with yes qualifies the test taker as a nerd. Students answering no to 80 or more of the questions get the message, "Totally cool, dude!" And what if the test taker answers with more than 80 yeses? Then he or she reads "Hail, O Great Nerd Master. I have sacrificed some virgin, untouched slide rules in your name."

The category of "nerd jokes" arose often concerning engineers, physicists, chemists, and mathematicians, and such jokes make the point that their narrow scientific way of thinking lacks common sense. An example is a joke about the math and engineering majors who take a psychological test. They sit on one side of a room when a naked woman comes in the room and stands on the far side. The attendant advises them that every time they hear a beep they could move half the remaining distance to the woman. After a beep sounds, the engineer jumps up and moves halfway across the room while the math major sits still, looking disgusted and bored. The attendant asks the math student why he chose not to move, and he responded, "because I know I will never reach the woman." The engineering major explains his activity to the attendant by saying, "because I know that very soon I will be close enough for all practical purposes!" (SpikedMath 2011).

The nerd, usually characterized as male, appears to have gone over the edge because he is uninterested in sex and fun. An example of humor with this theme is the story of a nerd bumping into another nerd riding on campus with a shiny new bicycle. The first nerd asks, "Hey, where did you get such a nice bike?" The rider nerd replies, "Yesterday I was walking home minding my own business when a beautiful woman rode up to me on this bike. She threw the bike to the ground, took of all her clothes, and said, 'Take what you want!'" The first nerd understandingly says, "Uh huh, good choice. The clothes probably wouldn't have fit" (SpikedMath 2011). Besides turning down sex for a contraption, the nerd is characterized as riding a bicycle rather than driving a cool car. In keeping with the nerd logic, the last line indicates an analytical way of thinking that appears out of step with others his age.

Aware of their nerdy image, engineering students at the University of California at Berkeley organized "E-Week" to show the rest of the campus they know how to have fun. "People tend to think of us as nerds and geeks," the president of the engineering honors society told a reporter, "but it's not true at all" (It's Newtonian 1989, 43). The society organized the event in springtime to encourage engineering students to take a break from their frequent all-nighters on the computer and long hours in labs. The *New York Times* observed, however, that these nerds seem to have a distinctly different idea of a good time (It's Newtonian 1989, 43). A featured event was the egg drop contest for which students built containers that would allow eggs to survive a fall of about eighty feet. Students also built elaborate bridges of cardboard, and, just to show they were not suck-ups to the faculty, they dunked professors in tanks of water.

Rhetorically, the term "nerd" implies that the obsession for work or gadget, as in the label of "computer nerd," "anime nerd," or "math nerd," displaces the brainy youth's sexual urges and renders him or her socially inept and likely undersized, bespectacled, and unkempt. Nerds may also be referred to as geeks, but this term evolved to particularly represent someone expert, but lost, in technology, especially computer work. Geek is hardly new slang. Shakespeare uses it in *Cymbeline* (1611) for someone peculiar or offensive, and nineteenth-century Americans were familiar with circus sideshow geeks performing sensational stunts (Dargan and Zeitlin 1983, 17; Green 2010, 2:366–67). Linguist Edith Folb during the 1970s collected it as uncomplimentary slang from Los Angeles black teenagers for a "studious person" (Folb 1980, 239). By the 1990s, however, "geek" in popular usage meant a technologically proficient person or computer programmer (Glowka and Lester 1997, 293). Probably showing the importance of technology in campus life, "geek" appeared to take on a more complimentary connotation for having the cultural capital of mastering cybertechnology. Still, students warned the techno-experts not to be a grind with a play on the proverb "work to live, don't live to work" with "geek to live, don't live to geek" (Glowka et al. 2006, 306).

In a variation of the Nerd Test, a Geek Test made the rounds of campus emails.

1. A friend opens a magazine full of scantily clad members of your pre-ferred sex. Do you:
   A. Openly Ogle
   B. Act Non-Chalant
   C. Comment "Gee, that's got to be at least 900 dpi, color!"
   D. Slip the hand down the pants for a bit of good, old-fashioned ex-ecutive relief.

2. You win a "Grocery-Grab" at a local supermarket. You've got one minute to pack a cart with as much stuff as you can. You start:
   A. In the Liquor Section
   B. In the Confectionary Lane
   C. At the Pencil Bar
   D. At the cash register

3. You've been hit by a car and your life flashes before your eyes. The thing you remember most vividly is:
   A. Your Mother's voice as a child
   B. Your first Love
   C. The ASCII table.
   D. The tire pressure was maybe a little too high

4. You told your best friend the first time you:
   A. Had Sex
   B. Had Oral Sex
   C. Got a Ram expansion
   D. Killed a cat.

5. No-one understands you like:
   A. Your Mother
   B. Your Father
   C. Your PC
   D. Your Parole Officer

The answer code assures the student choosing A consistently that he or she is "normal" (B warrants "mostly normal"), although it also sarcastically admon-ishes, "Boring Boring Boring. You're the sort of person who'll just fritter their way thru life enjoying themselves and having a good time. Shame on you!" The test implies that these answers, especially in reference to sexuality answering to adolescent urges, are natural socially and physically particularly in the play zone of campus (see Dundes and Pagter 1978, 119–24). Choosing C again and again, according to the answer code, is unnatural. It results in this warning: "Geek Alert! Break out the pocket protector!" As for the dreaded D, the test taker reads, "So you're a sociopath; But that doesn't mean you're a bad person. Just keep taking the Lithium and everything will be fine." The Geek Test has a precedent in parodies of psychological tests administered to corporate management candidates, often labeled the "situation adaptability evaluation" (Dundes and Pagter 1987, 153–56; Smith 1984, 82–83). The implied reference to the corporate exam, on the one hand, boosts the geek's importance as an agent of modern information economy and, on the other, questions the psychological health of the powerful figure.

Geeks answer back with their own inside humor using proverbial biblical parodies such as "the geek shall inherit the earth" (see Matthew 5:5, Blessed are the meek for they shall inherit the earth; Brunvand 2001, 64) and mock glossaries separating their superior technological knowledge from campus rubes:

Byte—Whut them dang flies do
Chip—Munchies for the TV
Download—Gettin the farwood off the truk
Hard drive—Gettin home in the winter time
Mega hertz—When yer not kerful getting the farwood
Modem—Whut cha did to the hay fields
Ram—That thar thing whut splits the farwood
Software—Them dang plastic forks and knifs
Windows—Whut to shut wen it's cold outside. (Glowka et al. 1999, 299)

The symbolic opposition of the superior intellectual in the college and the ignorant rube is an old one in college humor, but making this glossary significant for the information age is the additional contrast of computer technology as the center of the mass cultural enterprise to the earthy, premodern rustic (see Dundes and Pagter 1987, 22–27; Jones 2008, 2–3). With the emphasis on geeks' computer skills as the basis of their esoteric identity, "geek jokes" often refer to binary codes and programming languages. Indeed, the humor often identifies programmers as the geekiest of the geeks:

There are 10 types of people in the world—those who know binary and those who don't.
There are 10 types of people in the world—those who know binary and those who have friends.

Q: Did you hear about the Coder who got stuck in his shower for a week?
A: The instructions on his shampoo said "lather, rinse, repeat."
Q: How can you tell if a geek is extroverted?
A: He stares at your shoes.
    If u c4n r34d this u r34lly n33d to g37 l41d. (Miss Tech 2007)

Although these humorous lines, often posted on blogs and forwarded in emails, indicate self-aggrandizement because of the role of computer programming in the digital age, they also carry a self-deprecatory worry about mainstream perceptions of the group, as in the line about geeks not having friends or the last line in code indicating that the geek is sexually deprived (fifth example).

Playful codes, like children's secret language, communicate esoteric identities to geeks. Crowned the "king of the geeks" on the Internet, Robert Hayden is credited with inventing the Geek Code when he was a twenty-five-year-old graduate student at Mankato State University in 1993. According to Hayden, who has become a folk hero in cyberculture, "The geek code consists of several categories. Each category is labeled with a letter and some qualifiers. Go through each category and determine which set of qualifiers best describes you in that category. By stringing all of these 'codes' together, you are able to construct your overall geek code. It is this single line of code that will inform other geeks the world over of what a great geek you actually are" (Hayden 1996). The single letter stands for an attribute, such as C for computers, and plus and minus signs indicate the grade. Hayden's code, for example, is GED/J d- s:+ + a-: C+ + (+ + + +) ULU + + P + L + + E- - - W + (-) N + + + + K + + + w - - - O- M+ V - - - PS+ +$ PE + + $ Y + + PGP + + t- 5 + + + X + + R + + +$ tv+ b+ DI + + + G + + + + e + + h r- y + +. It reveals that he reads books, wears T-shirts with political messages, worships the television show *Babylon 5*, and is not considered hot dating material (Glowka et al. 1999, 320–21). Geeks may recognize the inspiration to the code of the Yerkes spectral classification system for describing stars. The code caught on in geekdom as a signature on emails, logos on T-shirts, and banners on blogs. According to *American Speech*, "the Geek Code has become part of Net Culture" (Glowka et al. 1999, 320–21).

When stories of purported computer geeks such as Harvard's Bill Gates (cofounder of Microsoft who, according to legend, as a teen modified his school programming code so that he was placed in classes with mostly female students), Berkeley's Steve Wozniak (nicknamed "The Woz" and "Wonderful Wizard of Woz" and cofounder of Apple Computer), and Reed College's Steve Jobs (featured in PBS documentaries *Triumph of the Nerds* [1996] and *Nerds 2.0.1* [1998], and cofounder of Apple Computer) rocketing to fame and fortune came to public attention, then the oddballs received admiration, and recognition that the cyberculture they appeared to command and code was rapidly becoming the core of society. Legends arose, for example, about the creation of the wildly popular and lucrative social network site Facebook by Mark Zuckerberg from his Harvard dormitory room in 2004 (fueled, no doubt, by the film *Social Network* [2010] and his selection as *Time*'s "Person of the Year" in 2010 at the young age of twenty-six) (Greenspan 2010; Grossman 2010). Legend has it that Facebook grew out of the geeky, pranking Zuckerberg's desire for social approval after not getting into any of the elite final clubs at Harvard, a story that Zuckerberg denies (Vargas 2010). Zuckerberg's version is that a *Harvard Crimson* editorial for a broader campus "face book" (a photo directory for a residential house) inspired his not-so-well-received nerdy revenge of "Facemash" to compare the looks of students to one another (Greenspan 2010).

Technogeeks feel empowered in humor that has them triumph over other formerly privileged high-achieving groups on campus. A joke using biblical references, for example, confirms the superiority of the computer geek over doctors and engineers:

> Students from medicine, civil engineering, and computer science are discussing whose profession is the oldest. "Surely medicine is the oldest profession," says the med student. "God took a rib from Adam and created Eve and if this isn't medicine I'll be damned." The civil engineer breaks in "But before that He created the heavens and the earth from chaos. Now that's civil engineering to me." The geek thinks a bit and then says: "And who do you think created chaos?" ("Computer Geek Jokes" 2010)

In earlier versions of this joke, the one creating the chaos is often the lawyer, politician, economist, or IRS agent, making a statement about institutional hierarchy in contemporary society. These occupations, like the computer geek, are often publicly stigmatized, although they carry weight in citizens' lives (Dolan and Irvin 2008, 13; Dougherty and Cohl 2009, 279; Flynt 2006, 15; Murthi 2004, 10). In its theme of competition for social or institutional authority, the joke bears a structural relationship to the popular narrative of body parts, also invoking a biblical parable (1 Corinthians 12) arguing over who deserves to be boss (see Uther 2004, Tale Type 293, 1:169). The brain asserts that since it does all the thinking and exerts control over the body, it should be boss. The eyes argue that they look out for the other body parts. The hands counter by saying, "Since we do all of the work and earn all of the money to keep the rest of you going, we should be boss." Finally, the asshole speaks up and demands that it be made boss. The other, more refined, body parts laugh at the idea. Angered by the response, the asshole refused to function, causing the brain to become feverish, the eyes to cross, and the hands to go limp. The body parts beg the brain to relent and let the asshole be the boss (Abrahams 1970, 214–15; Badhshah 2004, 82–83; D'Pnymph 1988, 317–18; Dundes and Pagter 1978, 100–101; Harris-Lopez 2003, 110; Shubnell 2008, 124; Smith 1986, 31). Both narratives suggest reluctant deference given to a socially stigmatized area of the body or institution. In most contexts in which I have heard the "chaos joke," tellers deliver the punch line pridefully and, as in the "boss joke," invert the societal expectation. They use humor to show their awareness of their often-troubled image and to assert their authority.

The geeks' view of themselves as the upstarts against the established law and medical students is evident from a frequently reported joke with geeks in the role of engineers or computer programmers:

On a college field trip, four engineering and four pre-law students were travelling on the same train. The law students each had a ticket, but the engineers had but one ticket among them. One of the engineers shouted "conductor's coming!" and the four engineers crowded into one of the bathrooms. The conductor comes by and knocks on the bathroom door saying "Tickets, please." The engineers slip their one and only ticket under the door. The conductor punches it and moves on to the next car. On the return trip, the four law students, impressed by the engineers' trick, purchase only one ticket. The engineers, however, have no tickets at all! Suddenly, one of the engineers shouts "conductor's coming." All four engineers head for the bathroom, and all four lawyers crowd into the other one. Then, one of the engineers slips out of his bathroom and knocks on the other bathroom saying "Tickets, please." The lawyers then slip their only ticket under the door, and the engineer picks up the ticket and joins his friends, waiting for the real conductor. (Galanter 2005, 54; "Geek Jokes" 2002; Platinum Press 2005, 206)

Judging by the frequency of hits in a Google search, this joke appears to be in high favor online. It received a "funny rating" of 4.46 out of 5.0 among "geek jokes" at JokesAround.com. Earlier reports of the joke refer usually to MBA, medical, or accounting students as the triumphant profession (Capps and Capps 2009, 22; Galanter 2005, 54, 295). The occupations in the joke have reputations for trickery and vie for duping the conductor overseeing the desirable societal train that, like the students, is presumably "going places."

While geeks have risen in status on campus, unpopular, eccentric, or unfashionable students still attract pejorative slang spinning off from the "grind" reported since the nineteenth century. Some of the labels drawing attention in campus-speak in the twenty-first century include "dork," "dweeb," "freak," "bloom," "twit," and "wally" (Lu and Graf 2004). The words do not always call out an egg- or tech-head but often imply someone who stands out in appearance or interests. For a long time, these appellations marked a contrast with the youthful effort to be "cool," "awesome," "sick," and "sweet"—all representing socially fashionable behavior among youth that separates them from the innocent cuteness of childhood, on the one hand, and the perceived mundaneness of adulthood, on the other (see Cross 2004).

A factor in the production of slang and narrative describing various odd types in college is that the campus encourages students to make individual, nonconformist choices at the same time that it often acts as the harbinger of popular culture trends. Folklore helps students organize the collegiate social landscape by locating various identities that are distinctive to campus and questioning their cultural capital on and off campus. It often invites commentary on the folktypes such as professors, coaches, jocks, and geeks—and questions their position in hierarchies on campus and in society.

CHAPTER

RUSHES, PRANKS, AND DINKS
The Rough-and-Tumble Campus

THE COLLEGE CAMPUS CAN BE A RUDE AWAKENING FOR STUDENTS who enjoyed their senior status in high school. They probably heard about their ascent into maturity with graduation, but once on the college campus they are probably made to feel like mere babes. Modern institutions of higher education have added an infrastructure to guide the new kids on the block, sometimes requiring a first-year seminar to go over the rigors of college. Counselors spring into action during orientation and provide programming and workshops throughout the year. That is not to say that students do not take responsibility for their own adjustment. Through most of collegiate history, managing the transition to campus, particularly its social structure, was a matter considered better left to the students. Ritual and pranks—legislated as campus traditions—did much of the work of keeping students in line, establishing social hierarchies, and orienting new arrivals to the institution's values.

The old-time college handled the transition—and transformation—by separating, and humiliating, the newbies as initiates needing to pass a series of ritual tests to gain passage to the higher status of upperclassman. As with rites of passage they had experienced probably religiously as children, an unusual attire clearly designated the neophyte. In the old-time college, frosh wore identifying coverings on their heads ("beanies," "pots," or "dinks"), or ribbons, often colored green to signify the novice state, on their clothes. In addition, they might have worn large name tags to identify themselves, but upperclassmen referred to them as a group by the pejorative labels of "rats," "greenies," "plebes," "fish," "scrubs," "slimers," "babes," and "booloos," as if the frosh needed reminders of their lowly biological status in the college environment.

At St. Olaf College, sophomores barked at first-year men to "Button Button Frosh." At the command, the newbie dropped his load, put both hands on top of the beanie's central button, and dutifully recited, "I am a little freshman as green as green can be, I wear my little beanie for everyone to see" (Sauve 2008; cf. the children's jump-rope and hand-clapping rhyme "I am a little Dutch Girl as funny [pretty] as can be, and all the boys are crazy about me" in Abrahams 1969, 69; Bronner 1989, 59–60; Opie and Opie 1985, 450–52). The resemblance of the chant to a girl's folk rhyme was not only a signal of the freshman's newbie status but also that the sophomores were symbolically much older than the one-year difference would indicate. The sophomores underscored this message with signs posted around campus warning the freshmen to "Tremble and Obey," "Beware," and "Expect No Mercy" (Dundes 1968, 21).

At Penn State in 1920, first-year students might have been taken aback by broadsides with the ominous heading "Frosh Death Notice: Twenty-Two Wants Blood." The theme of submission was strong, for the sophomore class admonished the frosh, "Class of Misery, Peruse and Obey These Fourteen Points of the MIGHTY SOPHOMORES Lest Thy Sins Be Washed Away in Muddy Searsville (2.75% Sulphuric Acid)." Among the points were prohibitions against wearing mustaches, removing dinks (except when "passing a superior"), and smoking. Calling freshmen cowards, imbeciles, and "dirty curs," another poster from the University of Wisconsin from the period commanded the newcomers to know the alma mater, to divest of all high school articles, to avoid stepping on grass, to wear green ties, and to attend all events. At different campuses, the signs carried headlines with similar blustery rhetoric, as these two attest:

> Suckling Frosh Beware! Ye mewling, pewking Babes, ye green and spineless Gonionemi, Taeniae Solia, Ascares Lumbricoides, Fasciolae Hepaticae of 1929, hearken to the edicts of the supremely ILLUSTRIOUS CLASS OF 1928. Grovel then, ye infants, before the thunderous reverberations of our ultimatum.
> (Franklin and Marshall College)

> Proletarians of ye measly, slimy, despicable, uncultured class of 1916 PROSTRATE yourselves to the most illustrious and omnipotent class of 1915. Now that you have absorbed sufficient knowledge into your sterile brains, to warrant your entrance into the sacred portals of RUTGERS COLLEGE the class of 1915 has condescended to become supervisor of your future conduct HARKEN ye boobs and obey these "15" commandments, bilaws [sic], and instructions which the honorable class of 1915 has deemed it proper to promulgate for your conscientious perusal and absolute assimilation.
> (Rutgers)

To learn the hierarchy of the campus, freshmen sometimes paid respect to seniors with a bow, performed stunts, and ran errands for upperclassmen. Here is a graphic description from the diary of one Penn Stater in the 1880s.

Fig. 4.1. A Boston University student models his freshman dink, 1950s. (Author's collection)

Soon after our arrival in town the visits from the sophomores began. They were usually dressed in black sateen shirts and corduroy trousers, and a slouch hat or a cap bearing the class numerals. Each carried a huge paddle which was sometimes used to induce cooperation on the part of the freshman. At those times the hazing took the nature of digging for water in the unpaved dusty road, praying for rain, barking at the moon or possibly delivering an impromptu speech. A favorite request was to deliver a three minute speech on Hereditary Barrenness. If the freshmen dared to resist the sophomore's tauntings they could very well find themselves in a molasses feed [see Figure 4.3]. The erring freshmen were required to take off their clothes and cover themselves with molasses. The sophomores provided them with a few coats of feathers until the humiliated freshmen looked something like a walking pile of leaves. (Bronson 1968b, 1, 4)

The persecution of the freshmen has origins in the master-servant relationship established between upperclassmen and first-year students, who were perceived as "novice apprentices" in early American colleges. An early-eighteenth-century broadside read by sophomores to the freshmen at chapel at Harvard College outlined the code of behavior, for example, with the title "The

Fig. 4.2. Poster targeting freshmen issued by the sophomore class at the University of Wisconsin, 1909. (Author's collection)

Customs of Harvard College, Which if the Freshmen Don't Observe and Obey, They Shall be Severely Punished if They Have Heard them Read" (Hall 1968, 317). According to Sidney Willard, who was at Harvard in the late eighteenth century, "they were read and listened to with decorum and gravity" (1855, 258). Among the forbidden acts were freshmen wearing hats in the college yard, leaning against walls in campus buildings, or being "saucy" to upperclassmen. The first-year student was expected to carry out errands hastily for "his Senior" and "give a direct answer if asked who he is going for" (Hall 1968, 318). Woe is the freshman who breaks "any of these customs," for "he shall be severely punished," the last item on the list declared. Willard, in his reminiscences, commented, "These customs had been handed down from remote times, with some modifications not essentially changing them" (1855, 258). The system of penalism, as it was known, meant that subservient freshmen were obliged "to go on any errand" and face severe consequences from upperclassmen for transgressions.

Fig. 4.3. Penn State freshmen feathered by sophomores for violating initiation rules, 1910. (University Archives, Pennsylvania State University)

Rushes and Scraps

The freshmen could be vindicated in the old-time college by beating the sophomores in a roughhouse competition generically referred to as scraps or rushes. Preparation for these contests built class unity and instilled male values of competition, toughness, and perseverance thought to be necessary for success in college and in the professions that awaited students after college. So prevalent were the scraps on college campuses that Fred Lewis Pattee characterized the period from the mid-nineteenth century into the beginning of the twentieth century as the "scrap era" of student life (1928, 5).

Many old-time colleges begrudgingly condoned these activities because they were thought to release the "animal spirits" of the students and redirect them at one another. The severe—if playful—indoctrination, schoolmasters thought, quickly made college men out of high school boys. It gave them no time to be homesick, quickly forged friendships among the classmates, and replaced old family or community loyalties with ones focused on the class and college. As with lifecycle rites of passage, freshmen initiation moved from a ritual separation of the new recruits to a transitional stage, where challenges and tasks are put before the initiates, to an incorporation stage, in which they are united into the community (see Van Gennep 1960; Young 1962; Vizedom 1976; Raphael 1988). Initiation served to ridicule the freshmen's pasts and set their minds on the future, specifically on achieving the privilege of upperclassmen. At the same time, upperclassmen learned to maintain their advantage and protect (somewhat imperially) their campus status over the lowly elements of society.

Another justification for initiating, or hazing, freshmen was that once past the manageable, playful traumas of initiation, students were more capable of withstanding the stresses (mild by comparison, they thought) of studies and examinations. Finally, as a preparation for the adult world of work and family, students were reminded of the hierarchical order of society. Especially when social evolutionary thought was in its heyday in the late nineteenth century, the idea of climbing from the lowly, despicable depths of freshman ignorance to the privileged pinnacle of senior enlightenment was akin to the struggle up the theorized social ladder from savagery to civilization. It led, some college officials thought, to a survival of the fittest in the academic evolution of students.

At its beginnings, "class rush" referred first to spontaneous engagements of one class against another in hand-to-hand combat rather than a game with rules. An example is detailed in Olive San Louie Anderson's *An American Girl and Her Four Years in a Boys' College* (1878), in which she underscores that freshmen and sophomores "meet wherever the spurt seizes them, and, with the best intentions, plunge at each other like mad in a hand-to-hand fight, and often an arm is broken or an eye knocked out, which is simply 'hard luck.' We were just coming out of Latin while the sophs were going up to trigonometry, and they met on the stairs and went at it" (1878, 51–52).

At the University of Michigan, according to university chronicler Edwin Emery Slosson, nineteenth-century "class scraps and 'horsing' have had no accepted restrictions or regulations." He described "hair-cutting, face-painting, house-raiding, and kidnapping" reaching "epidemic" proportions. He added, "Freshmen were treed and egged and put through such stunts as sophomoric ingenuity could devise" (Slosson 1910, 195–96). Slosson conceded that such antics were often "offensive to good taste and propriety," but thought that press reports exaggerated the "disorder" and overlooked their "redeeming factor, the good-natured boyishness of it all" (1910, 196). In his opinion, the display of roughness of young men toward one another was appropriate as friendly, gender-appropriate rivalry. Yet while often spontaneous, the rush was often framed as "boyish" play, which separated it from their current status as young,

Fig. 4.4. Illustration of the start of a cane rush at Harvard from *The Book of Athletics and Out-of-Door Sports* (Townsend 1895, 229). The writer referred to the class representatives holding the cane as "gladiators in the palestrae."

learned men. Attending Michigan was not the root cause of the roughness and uncouthness, Slosson declared, for "the Michigan boys do not, I think, behave any worse than those in other universities, but they make more noise about it" (1910, 196). Sheldon also observed public opprobrium against the rushes because of their association with hazing (1901, 106). He claimed that "the ordinary citizen" understood the contradiction between the brutality of hazing and the progressive expectation that higher education prepared "the *intellectual* leaders of the next generation" (1901, 106; emphasis added).

The reform of the rush usually involved the imposition of rules and the categorization of the rush into different types. Part of the thinking was that the rush gave freshmen more of a chance than indiscriminate hazing by the sophomores (Lutz 1911, 427; Sheldon 1901, 102). Educator Philip Lutz defended the rush against editorials calling for its abolishment by claiming that it was the best possible means "to enable the students to give expression of their class spirit. . . . It is the fairest means of applying strength to the force and is one of the few interesting events in college life that the student can look forward to with pleasure" (1911, 427). With reforms on campuses "where they [rushes] are systematized, officially recognized and carried on according to rigid rules," he offered to the public calling rushing a barbarous hazing practice, "hazing has become an obsolete practice" (Lutz 1911, 427). With issues of campus hazing still around in the twenty-first century, many colleagues of his time and historians of the present disagreed with him.

The rush as structured activity moved the action outdoors to an open field able to absorb the bumps and bruises of combat. It could be made public in a "fair test" rather than one side sneaking up on another and gaining advantage by strength of numbers. The "rush," as the name implies, typically began with a running start of the two sides against each other. Participants grappled, pushed, and pulled at one another; in most rushes a tangle of bodies was the result, with many being knocked to the ground. The contest was construed as a battle without weapons, although in some rushes participants hurled flour, salt, grease, and mud at one another, adding to the image of disorder and filth in the contest. Amid the pandemonium that often ensued, one might wonder how participants knew the event was over. Indeed, reporters sent to cover the rushes often mentioned confusion whether the outcome was the emergence of a winner or mayhem. A common objective was elimination of one side by pushing them off their designated area or a line. Another goal was possession of an object such as a flag, cane, cider, hat, or bowl. In the colleges of the late nineteenth and early twentieth centuries, students could expect several rushes of different types during the year. The school year in the fall might begin with a ball scrap or cider rush and culminate in the spring with the flag rush. Arguably, the rushes structured the student's ritual year as much as exams and holidays.

Among the earliest reports of organized rushes was the cane rush. Students from the first- and second-year classes tried to wrest control of the cane by placing as many hands on it as possible. The cane's significance as a status symbol for upperclassmen derives from German university custom (Dike 1994, 83). To reinforce this stately image, nineteenth-century collegians also used tall hats as a sign of maturity and refinement to replace the juvenile beanie (Dike 1994, 91). College women averted canes (but used ribbons, hairpieces, pins, sweaters, handkerchiefs, and neckties of coed status) suggesting, therefore, associations with male phallic symbolism and attainment of patriarchal power as a form of social dominance with control of the cane in the rushes (Peril 2006, 105–21). The cane rush was also an occasion not only for asserting coming-of-age by stepping into a dominant position with a claim to the hard rod but additionally for humiliating or infantilizing opponents by pulling off their trousers and exposing their underwear or buttocks. An account from Rensselear Polytechnic Institute (RPI) emphasized that "the sophomores began to focus more on pulling off the freshmen's pants than grabbing the cane" (Institute Archives 2009). Penn State's student newspaper, the *Free Lance*, in 1890 reported that, despite the presence of a referee, "Shouts, yells, curses and threats filled the air. The mass of men swayed, to and fro, and moved, back and forth, across the field. Fellows were tramped on, hacked, bitten and choked. For five minutes the fight went on in this way and then the cane and the men clinging to it went down" ("Locals" 1890, 64).

In answer to critics who called the rush brutish and unseemly for educated elite, defenders justified its place in colleges devoted to the classical curriculum by relating the rush to pursuits in ancient civilization of the body as well as the mind. A writer identified as "J.C." made reference to the enlightening "aesthetic" function of a college education in his editorial for a student publication at the University of Michigan in 1871: "Can his [a college graduate's] present refinement be due to the aesthetic influence of a college course which draws its refining qualities from ancient life, of which games were no insignificant part? If Virgil who paints then with the loving hand of a poet describes them truly, the ancient games did not differ so very widely from the modern rush; certainly were not more dignified, except in having nations to admire and great bards to sing them" (1871, 29). He found the rush to be "ennobling," and the "spectator must profoundly respect the supreme good-nature and hearty enjoyment both in giving and receiving the severest bruises" (J.C., 1871, 29). Arguing essentially that the play frame outside of the awareness of spectators prevents hostility leading to "rowdyism," J.C. opined that "our rushes have never been disgraced by an excessive ardor among the combatants, and we anticipate no danger from that quarter. If, however, an angry scene should arise, the rowdyism would lie in the loss of temper, not in the simple rushing. If the character of a play may be known by the character of the audience, surely our rushes lack no gentility" (1871, 29). J.C. dismissed the incrimination of barbarism against the rushes by pointing to the "Greeks and Romans to prove that there is nothing in rushing 'entirely unbecoming to university men or the character of gentlemen'" (1871, 29).

Other writers used the rhetorical argument of rushes having a role in college life because they reflect the pursuits of ancient civilizations. Contending that all healthy athletic sports necessarily have "a certain element of danger," Malcolm Townsend in *The Book of Athletics and Out-of-Door Sports* (1895) called the cane rush "one of the most exciting contests adopted by the restless college 'men.'" It was "planned upon a manly athletic basis, and controlled by the spirit of friendly rivalry" (226). Its benefit, he claimed, was enlisting a "Spartan element of honor." Without it, he claimed, "class union" could never be formed (Townsend 1895, 226). To show that it was appropriate for learned gentlemen, the Harvard grad argued that the cane rush could be traced to the "Greek boys of the Twenty-third Olympiad–twenty-five hundred years and more ago," where they "tugged and struggled for the mastery in the game of strength and muscle known to them as the pancratium" (Townsend 1895, 225).

To be sure, he was concerned that "the demands of courtesy and manliness are kept ever in view," especially when indignities of "the fray presents a gladiatorial effect; every man is stripped to the waist; the exposed parts have been rubbed thick with vaseline to produce a slippery surface that a grip will not hold" (Townsend 1895, 230). Illustrations drew attention to the rush's field of play as a "palaestrae," which college men steeped in the classics understood as the only places where nude athletics were permitted (Townsend 1895, 230). Captured in sketches as well as text, the cane rush drew attention as a "rough and tumble game" located on a "battle-ground" of young, half-naked men in embrace as well as in a "fight" (Townsend 1895, 227, 236–37).

Underscoring the manly endeavor of the cane rush, a *New York Times* article in 1884 noted that "year by year the colleges devoted to the education of girls are approaching more closely in all respects to the colleges designed for the other sex" ("Another 'Rush'" 1884, 4). One indication for the anonymous writer was the adoption of class rushes in women's colleges. But the author found it newsworthy that the women eschewed the cane rush, "everyone knows," for a "great back-hair rush." Instead of rushing for the right to carry canes, the frosh battled for the privilege of wearing back hair, or a hair bun, considered a sign of maturity. An unstated implication, too, is the feminine symbolism of long hair (for example, folktales of mermaids and sirens with long tresses; the biblical passage of "hair is a woman's glory" from Corinthians 11:15), and the representation of hair-pulling therefore as a particularly feminine display of hostility in distinction from the male show of domination by shoving, pinning, or knocking an opponent to the ground (Weitz 2004, 4–5).

An important message coming from the hair-rush article concerned the power of the students to dictate their own activities. The article informs readers that "for nearly half an hour the two classes struggled for the mastery. The campus was strewn with torn skirts and sowed thick with hairpins, and the Faculty, hanging on the outskirts of the combatants, and weeping and wringing their hands, were powerless to restore order." As with the cane, the back hair could be brandished as a fetish for the victors much as taking the tail of an animal does for hunters or a warrior brandishes a scalp. The astonished writer reported, "Gradually the Sophomores fought their way to the Freshwoman who wore the back hair, and finally they triumphantly tore it from her head. At the same moment the Freshwomen, inspired by a happy thought, simultaneously seized the back hair of their opponents and fled to their rooms, each bearing her trophy" ("Another 'Rush'" 1884, 4).

The cane rush involves a limited number of contestants trying to get their hands on the cane, but as colleges grew in size, other rushes that involved hundreds of participants vying for possession of an object grew in popularity ("Underclass" 1905, 3). The cider rush had a similar objective in having as many hands from a class as possible on a barrel of cider. In another version of the rush, the freshmen had five hours in the evening on a day before Thanksgiving vacation to bring a barrel full of cider on campus and deliver a libation of cider to any juniors. The objective of the sophomores was to foil the attempt. The class winning the rush kept the barrel as a trophy ("Underclass" 1905, 10). Similarly, the structure of the picture and banquet rush involved stopping attempts by the freshmen to hold a ceremonious event.

Variations of the "foil strategy" type of rushes at the University of California at Berkeley included the Bourdon rush in which sophomores attempted to prevent a burial ceremony on the model of a Roman funeral for a mathematics textbook. In this rush, described by one chronicler as a "grand rough-house and beer-bust," the "Bourdon" was placed in a coffin and consigned to flames, causing great rejoicing. Sophomores tried to storm the ceremony, kidnap speakers, or steal the coffin containing the Bourdon (Gregory 1905, n.p.; Pickerell and Dornin 1968, 27; Sibley 1928, 19). Begun by the class of 1878, the Burial of Bourdon lasted until 1897, when the university administration clamped down on the event after a student suffered a serious injury in the "wild, physical melee" (Park 1984, 57). Yet, according to one alumnus, the end of the tradition came when "advancing civilization attempted reforms and took all the kick out of it" (Morse 1930). The writer from the class of 1896 opined that "there were more thrills connected with them [Bourdon burials] than in your modern football game. For two or three days preceding the ceremony classes were practically suspended. Everybody cut. Sophomores gathered for the purpose of concocting schemes for busting up the affair and kidnapping the speakers." Convinced that "a university without traditions is poor indeed," the chronicler editorialized, "I would like to see the bourdon tradition brought back with all its aches and pains, its joys and thrills" (Morse 1930).

In the Charter Day rush, characterized as a "rough-house" in the University of California yearbook, sophomores attempted to prevent freshmen from placing class numerals on the hillside above the site where Charter Day, representing the university's public celebration of its own birthday, took place (Gregory 1905, n.p.). At Penn State, beginning in 1902, freshmen and sophomores vied at considerable risk of injury to paint class numerals on the "Old Main" building tower; according to one report, "the danger of the practice caused the scene of action to be shifted to the Armory after a few years, and there it continued for some time" ("Brawn over Brains" 1955). The ability to pose for a picture, emblematize the class year, or hold a banquet/ceremony represented victory and solidarity that the sophomores did not want to concede. The ceremonious events also showed control and independence because the group was reliant on themselves rather than being led to dinner or photographed by authorities.

Fig. 4.5. Flag rush at Amherst College, 1925. (Author's collection)

These kinds of rushes outraged the faculty because classes were often disrupt-ed by rumors of a planned photograph, resulting in classrooms emptying.

A culminating student-run event of the school year was the flag rush, usu-ally held before examinations in the spring term (N.W.B. 1900). Simulating a battle in which a flag represents a claim to territory, at Penn State the freshmen planted a pole in the ground and raised their flag before 6 a.m. The freshmen won the rush if they could stop the sophomores from tearing the flag from the pole before eight o'clock that morning. Climbing the pole was a formidable feat, and a sign of "natural" physical ability, evident in abstention from the use of mechanical aids. Student organizers formalized the ethic of primitive naturalness in the flag rush by instituting bans on the use of professional wires, hooks, straps, and pegs. Although the idea was to make the climb more chal-lenging, a consequence was that climbers frequently incurred injuries from falls. Another danger was the crush of competing crowds against the poles as groups tried to assist climbers to get up the pole by lifting them or allowing them to step over them. One frequently used strategy to reach the top was to hoist a small, light comrade over the heavier fellows at the bottom. The risks taken to climb the pole enhanced a wishful dramatic scenario in which an un-likely male hero without equipment or special status emerged from the crowd to grab the flag (N.W.B. 1900, 298; cf. Uther 2004, Tale Types 1073, 1611).

Despite the flag rush's popularity and regard among students as the ultimate "rush," it did not garner good off-campus press. The rush drew disdain, for example, from Dorothy Canfield in her novel *Rough-Hewn* (1922) as "a disorganized melee, rolling and tumbling, panting and struggling in a hundred separate encounters" (213). In her narrative, "the Flag Rush [was] unanimously deplored by the directing forces of the University; the Flag-Rush, that outburst of meaningless brutality so shocking to all the European members of the Faculty, secretly contemptuous of the prosperous, illiterate, childish country where they taught" (212). Turned into "young Berserk fighters, blind and furious with the delight of battle," "buoyed up by their mass, by being together," every one of the boys, according to Canfield, became "twice what he had been two minutes before" (212). She was not suggesting, however, a kind of behaviorism in which the positive reinforcement of "belief in their own increase" urges them on, for she contextualized their entrance by noting that tradition held sway over their conduct. She wrote that the freshmen participated because it was expected of them, and implied that they would not rush if not for the provocation of the sophomores.

At Penn State, the tradition ended, in the words of faculty member Fred Lewis Pattee, after "the number of students increased and classes began to approach the thousand mark . . . [and] the scraps assumed dangerous proportions" (1928, 5). At Tufts, administrators shut down the flag rush in 1900 after a freshman drew a pistol on a roommate (Miller 1966, 397). Princeton suspended its rush in 1915 after a student died of cardiac arrest on the field of play and the tragedy became national front-page news ("Princeton Student" 1915). The reputation of the rush as boisterous fun suffered when press attention focused on the mysterious disappearance of freshman Leighton Mount at Northwestern after a class rush in September 1921. His skeleton was uncovered two years later, and the investigation focused on whether he was hazed by being tied to a pier as part of the rush or suffered a random attack unrelated to the rush ("Students Examined" 1923). In a news report that became too familiar through the 1920s, Rutgers banned all rushes in 1929 after a student drowned upon either falling or being shoved into a canal. The student council voted to substitute "competitions of a safe character, such as tugs of war and field days" ("Rutgers Bans" 1929). Other schools embraced the pushball or cage ball on a field of play as substitutes for the flag and cane rushes, although inviting freshman and sophomore classes to battle it out by pushing an oversize ball into the opponents' territory did not eliminate injuries.

Pushball was a later development in the rush tradition promoted by physical education advocates who considered it a Progressive Era reform of boys' beastly play. It retained the traditional strenuous praxis of sides pushing each other, but introduced rules, organization, and scoring that reformers hoped

Fig. 4.6. Mud Rush, Los Angeles City College. (Courtesy Jay Mechling)

would bring order and involve more strategy in play with a large number of participants (Allison 1905; Cook 1898). Educators' concern for activities involving many players not accommodated in ball, chasing, and singing games responded to American expansion as a result of growing industrialism and immigration during the Gilded Age. They devised games involving a mass of people, particularly in growing urban playgrounds and schools in need of recreation. Moses G. Crane, for instance, in 1894 invented a field game played by two sides on a field and a ball six feet in diameter (Allison 1905, 47–48). Sides had designated positions, including forwards, left and right wings, and goalkeepers. In his system, pushing the ball under the bar counted five points, throwing it over the bar counted eight, and pushing a team back into its own end zone was worth two points. He claimed inspiration for use of the huge ball with a bladder inside from the bladder-ball used in a "dusty scrimmage" described in the classical epigrams of Marcus Valerius Martialis. Crane modernized the sport, in his estimation, by replacing the grappling of the rush with hands restricted to the ball (Hindman 1951, 369). In the pushball scrap, hands and feet often flailed at opponents as well as the ball.

Fig. 4.7. Pushball scrap at Penn State, 1920s. (University Archives, Pennsylvania State University)

Rules in the pushball scrap tended to be simpler than Crane's game, with all participants trying to push the ball over the opponents' end line. At Penn State, administrators envisioned pushball as a sporting substitute for the disruptive picture and banquet scraps. Pushball contests were held on the second Saturday afternoon following the opening of the college year. The contest consisted of three periods of ten minutes each, "the object of each class being to push the ball into the enemy's territory" ("Rules for Push Ball Scrap" 1912). A goal was worth two points, and "at the end of each period, the side that has the ball in the enemy's territory shall score one point." In a nod to the faculty who had raised concerns about the rushes in 1912, students asked a faculty member to referee, and another faculty member took a seat as a judge alongside the senior and junior class presidents. Although the pushball scrap seemed less injurious than the cider and cane rushes, students still could get trampled by the sheer number of participants in a growing freshmen class of 700 young men, about the size of the entire student body five years earlier. Women had been admitted since 1871, but a limitation on housing and isolation of the college, as in many other institutions in the country, kept the number of females below eighty in any one year (Dunaway 1946, 202–3; Sonenklar 2006, 9–32).

With the emphasis on lines and its play in the fall on a Saturday, pushball followed from football rushes that had been in vogue since the mid-nineteenth century. Like football, the pushball also had a "bladder" and involved the control of ground in scrimmage. At Penn State, the interclass football game was reserved for the festive season between Thanksgiving and Christmas

("Committee Report" 1904, 4). Students, whether they played or not, had class jerseys. Signs posted by the sophomores leading up to the event announced to the freshmen class of 1923, for example, that they "will tolerate your presence long enough to wallop you to a frazzle." Students recognized the importance of the game from a prominently displayed trophy engraved with scores of previous games. The freshmen had the added incentive of being entitled to carry canes if they won. Players did not wear much protection, typically just a nose guard, and injuries were common.

One adjustment to cut down on injuries in the 1920s was to introduce a number of rushes replacing hand-to-hand combat with that of tugging and tying, usually with rope. At Penn State, students organized a "tie-up scrap" involving binding opponents, a "pants scrap" with the objective of pulling down opponents' trousers, and a "shoe scrap" in which shoes were tied together. In the tie-up scrap, fifty men entered on each side for six five-minute periods. Contestants had a length of rope with which they tried to bind the hands and feet of opposing classmen. The class with the most claims of binding the enemy won. In variations, tie-ups meant kidnapping officers of the opposing class and holding them until the opposing class relented. These scraps introduced more humiliation and hilarity into the rushes than the beatings witnessed in the old rushes. Even in the tug-of-war held annually at Penn State through the 1920s, losers ended up having their faces muddied or falling into a pond or being doused with a liquid spray. At Emporia State in Kansas, until the 1950s freshmen normally removed their beanies at the homecoming football game, where they threw them up in the air at halftime, but they could remove them earlier by challenging the sophomores in a tug-of-war across a lake (Maxwell 1987, 11).

Localized versions of rushes that featured humiliation of losers by immersion in mud and water took forms such as mud rushes at Cornell and Los Angeles City College, the Tank Rush or Scrap at the University of California at Davis and Purdue University, the Flour Rush at Syracuse and Penn, and the Grease Rush at RPI. These varieties of the rush often had the most longevity, lasting well into the 1950s. Being able to take ridicule, apparently required to show collegiate friendliness and an air of fun on campus, replaced demonstrations of penalism. Comedies of engagement in the tugging and tying events supplanted the tests of strength and determination featured in the old "scrimmage" rushes. At RPI, the cane rush, for instance, was transformed into the grease rush, and in 1949 a comic element was introduced with the awarding of the "'tute screw" to the loser of the rush by three hooded fraternity brothers dubbed as "The Order of the Royal Screw." Against the backdrop of guffawing spectators at the halftime of a home football game, the screw carried the double meaning of a technological symbol appropriate to an engineering school and the phallocentric act of intercourse, clearly indicating the feminization of the losing team. In the play frame of the mock ceremony, freshmen were made to kneel down in a submissive pose before their upright, hooded elders (Institute Archives 2009).

Students devised a mystical narrative for the ceremony to endow the crafted, oversize screw with special, even if comical, significance. The narrative repeated over the public address system related the quest for a university symbol over seven continents to strengthen school spirit and identity.

> At last, in the remote regions of Tibet, three students stumbled on the site of the Macpus-Kwatapur Polytechnic Institute, founded far back in the dawn of time. When they left the Tibetan center of science, the wanderers were given the symbol of the Institute–a flat-head screw made of Himalayan cherry wood. The three pilgrims returned just in time to present this symbol to the Frosh. Each year a gold plate bearing the year of the losing Freshman class will be added to the shaft of the screw, which will be guarded in a glass case by the members of Sigma Phi Epsilon. Each year they will present it to the losers of the Grease Rush, always the Freshmen.

The detail of the trophy bearing a gold plate is an obvious reference to the heralded trophies of the old football rushes. To underscore the idea of taking ridicule as a sign of collegiate conviviality, the screw after the heyday of the grease rush was presented to the undergraduate recognized as the meanest student on campus.

Structurally, the rush emerged from its use as ritual initiation and release of aggression to be viewed as organized athletics by its competitive interaction and explicit rules. It was reported as sport by the late nineteenth century because of the level of physical exertion and institutional affiliation in addition to its intense competition. As physical education commentators noted in the early twentieth century, it contained a healthy element of strenuosity (critics called it violence and mayhem) that conveyed desirable qualities of manliness and hierarchy for the day. But the rush came to be seen as going against modern industrial principles of progress and cooperation and led to different forms of the event emphasizing playful ridicule in a dramatic show of social mirth. Despite the changes in the rush contextualized by perceptions of qualities necessary for success as a nation and individual, the structure of mass boisterous display remained in place so that the rush was still part of the expressive profile of college life through the 1950s. Students maintained control of the rush and the extracurriculum through the rush's history, but increasingly faculty and administrations exerted more oversight. By the 1960s, with universities on a massive scale becoming more of the standard and student rebellion against institutional dictates of tradition and affiliation, the rush fell into decline and quickly faded from institutional memory. Not coincidentally, this period also ushered in a sexual revolution that arguably led to less erotic displacement in contact sport and the breakdown of gender segregation in campus and dormitory life.

Why did sophomores pit themselves exclusively against the freshmen? A standard folkloristic answer in occupational studies is the need to indoctrinate the initiate denigrated as the novice into the responsibilities of the job. In this interpretation, the ability of the initiate to withstand pranks and abuse in a play frame will translate into success in reality and identification with the group (McCarl 1986, 71–72). Particularly in high-stress situations, the initiate is taught to lose his or her old identity and replace it with group solidarity (Tangherlini 1998). The theme for the Penn State sophomore class's hazing of the freshmen in 1920, for example, was to wash away the sins of the freshmen in a mock baptism marking induction into a new life. The broadside of "fourteen points" (parodying Woodrow Wilson's "Fourteen Points" of 1918) for freshmen to obey had the first letters of the points spell out "WASH THY SIN AWAY." By this thinking, their former lives constituted filth, and college life represented purity. "Water washes clean," they were reminded, and it was followed in the last letters of "AWAY" by:

> Away with that Prep school stuff. We know you are nothing without being labeled like an arsenal. You may wear gas masks to Frosh class meetings.

> You yellow streaked lumps of putty, listen. WE ARE THE ITS, YOU ARE THE NITS. You are buck privates in this man's army, permanently assigned to K.P.

Just in case the freshmen did not get the idea, a final comparison was to the "greenhorn" immigrants who needed to assimilate as citizens: "Those off the boat are in the water."

Despite the claims of students for the legitimacy of the rushes in the old-time college because of a classical origin, more likely precedents for the ritual victimization of new students rest in European medieval sources. In central Europe, illustrators and chroniclers documented a ritual "deposition" or "laying aside" in which upperclassmen removed horns and tusks worn by the new students to signal in an evolutionary fashion that even though they are grown, in the context of higher education they begin as animals or brutes and rise slowly to human level. New students were called *beani*, a Latinisation of the French derisive term *bec jaune*, for "yellow beak," and given mock baptisms, simulated planings (in which they are stretched on a board and metaphorically shaved or polished), and scatological ordeals. One indication of the persistence of this terminology in college lore is the imposition of beanies or small caps on new students. Another is the institutionalization of rat and beast lines as initiatory traditions in military colleges. Another related evolution in student passage besides an animal to human hierarchy is from dirt or earth to a clean, aboveground elevation.

Another possible historical source for the rushes is the tradition of wrestling matches at Harvard dating to the late eighteenth century (Hall 1968, 314–16). On the first Monday after arriving at Harvard to begin their studies, new students were expected to engage the sophomores in a series of wrestling matches purportedly inspired by classical events. The matches had a ritual feel as described by Sidney Willard in 1794:

> On some day of the second week in the term, after evening prayers, the two classes assembled on the play-ground and formed an extended circle, from which a stripling of the Sophomore Class advanced into the area, and, in terms justifying the vulgar use of the derivative word Sophomorical, defied his competitors, in the name of his associates, to enter the lists. He was matched by an equal in stature, from that part of the circle formed by the new-comers. Beginning with these puny athletes, as one and another was prostrated on either side, the contest advanced through the intermediate gradations of strength and skill, with increasing excitement of the parties and spectators, until it reached its summit by the struggle champion or coryphaeus in reserve on each of the opposite sides. (1855, 260)

The match was not exactly a fair test, because the odds were against the freshmen as a result, according to Willard, of the sophomores having "more and mightier men." Willard notes that at Harvard a form of a football rush superseded the wrestling matches. He believed that in its mayhem, the football rush was "groveling and inglorious" in comparison to the "art" of wrestling (Willard 1855, 261). At Yale at the end of the nineteenth century, sophomore-freshman wrestling matches were also linked to the "old-time rush" (Opening 1899, 1065). Wrestling matches were still being grouped together with rushes on the field of play at Penn State in the early twentieth century, with rules added to order what the student newspaper called "hitherto unwritten and often misunderstood customs of the past" ("Committee Report" 1904). The match was held outdoors on the second Wednesday after the opening of the fall term. Its linkage was not only the combat of the first two classes but also the action of grappling of the men with the objective of pinning the opponent to the ground that also characterized the mass rush. By driving opponents into the ground, winners showed their superiority by literally soiling the adversary, and in so doing, marked him as dirty or infantilized.

Even with awareness of these historical sources, the question still arises about the perception of natural enmity between the sophomore and freshmen classes, which Freud would have probably recognized as exhibiting a "narcissism of minor differences" (Freud 1930, 72; see also Bronner 2011b). This concept characterized a response to tension caused by similarities between adjoining groups by the exaggeration of their differences, often resulting in aggression. In the rushes, the sophomores have experiences of being excluded fresh in their memory, but build up a resentment of the new students because they threaten to perpetuate the sophomores' exclusion by an association with infancy and indeed virginity. It is apparently more important for the sophomores than the upperclassmen to use aggression to show their "fight" on the field of play, but sophomores must deal with the narcissistic conflict of embracing their enemies in intimate contact. More is at stake for differentiating themselves from the freshmen socially and sexually. In Sidney Willard's memoirs, for example, he notes that if the freshmen won their battle against the sophomores, one would have thought the next step was to challenge the junior class, but that did not happen. He reflected that the junior class was not involved because if the contest "had taken place, [it] could not fade from the memory of the victors; while failure, on the contrary, being an issue to be looked for, would soon be dismissed from the thoughts of the vanquished. Instances had occurred of the triumph of the Freshmen class, and one of them recent, when a challenge in due form was sent to the Juniors, who, thinking the contest too doubtful, wisely resolved to let the victors rejoice in their laurels already won; and, declining to meet them in the gymnasium, invited them to a sumptuous feast instead" (Willard 1855, 260–61).

The sophomores understood that they are "sophomoric" or still unaccomplished in the eyes of the upperclassmen, and show their worthiness by vanquishing the freshmen as a sign of elevated status rather than challenging the juniors and seniors with whom they want to ally. Indeed, Benjamin Hall's groundbreaking collection of college words noted that the Americanism of "sophomore" was "given them [students] in sport, for the supposed exhibition of inflated feeling in entering on their new honors" (Hall 1968, 288). The "mor" after "soph" was added to indicate "praise," one that appears self-imposed by the group and premature to older observers (Hall 1968, 288).

The sophomores in the rush forced the freshmen to show their sameness and lack of bodily extensions in hats, canes, flags, and spades. It was not enough to win a decisive victory but to maintain a system of repression whereby the freshmen fear reprisal that can be imposed through hazing. The system broke down, though, when the size of the lower class became too large to control, and the social structure of the campus divided not by classes but by majors and interest groups. One sign in the extracurriculum of a structural shift away from status hierarchy was the rise of intramural sports with teams deriving from organizations, rather than by classes. The hierarchical system also became vulnerable when the male pattern of social dominance was challenged by women, by scattered small-scale housing rather than communal living in a single "Old Main" or other central dormitory, and by a dissolution of curricular unity by class level resulting in more individualism. Arguably, the sophomores recognized that the freshmen shared with them an undervalued role as underclassmen, but as a result of their previous fear of reprisal from superiors, they aligned with the upperclassmen rather than with the group most like themselves.

If the system was designed to perpetuate itself through tradition or a fear of change, the question arises about how it could be subverted, especially if the rushes become the structuring events of the ritual academic year. In addition to the growing size of the student body and reports of fatalities, the shift away from the classical curriculum and assertion of administrative control of the extracurriculum had a large hand in doing the rush in. Out of place in an ethic of progress and heterogeneity associated with modern campus life, the rush became anachronistic instead of traditional. It became comical because of its incongruity with the new narcissism of individualism and incorporation.

Reviving and Adapting the Rush

Rushes in tamer forms are still evident at a number of modern campuses, often to invoke for students apprehensive about being isolated or alienated on campuses during the college years a sense of tradition with reference to an era perceived to possess a strong sense of community bonding. The modern rush custom with the most direct connection to the past is probably the Princeton Cane Spree. Despite the name given for the event, "cane wrestling," now held between women as well as men of the first two classes, is a small part of the event. Representatives of the classes also engage in badminton, basketball, cycling, field hockey, squash, table tennis, volleyball, soccer, basketball, and even "ultimate Frisbee." The "cane spree" title, though, evokes a sense of continuity with the past, and, in fact, posters plastered around campus implore students to participate and "Come Join the Tradition!" If that appeal does not do the trick, publicity reminds students that it is Princeton's "oldest intramural event since 1869."

Fig. 4.8. Sophomore women stop a first-year student in front of the opening to "The Cloister" at Juniata College's "Storming of the Arch," 2008. (Photo by Simon Bronner)

Another modern rush event is Juniata College's "Storming of the Arch." The "Arch" in the title is an entrance to a central campus residence called "The Cloister." It is not, as one would suspect, a revival of a nineteenth-century tradition, although the campus was established by the Church of the Brethren in 1876. The September ritual dates to the late 1940s when World War II veterans who were placed in the Cloister and were new to campus declared the dorm off-limits for dink-adorned freshmen. In the absence of documentation of the original event, the handed-down narrative is that freshmen rushed the passageway and fought their way through. From this spontaneous beginning, control of the Cloister became a matter between the freshmen and sophomore classes to settle. Subsequent first- and second-year classes agreed on a time and date coinciding with the opening of the new academic year to battle on the green outside the Arch. Fearing injuries, the administration shut down the event in 1995, but then found that the students held the rush surreptitiously, often in the dead of night, and that scenario raised graver risks. Negotiations between students and the administration resulted in adoption of rules about tackling and staying on the ground that would prevent harm. The rugby team took responsibility for the event as the representative of the sophomore class, and organized it as a fund-raiser, lest the impression be given that students were engaging in senseless violence. In a nod to egalitarianism, the storming included women after 1996. In the latest iteration of the storming, a crowd

Fig. 4.9. Freshmen and sophomores rush at each other in Juniata College's "Storming of the Arch," 2009. (Photo by Simon Bronner)

gathers to cheer and photograph the players, and many of the freshmen don outlandish costumes. To date, the freshmen never have broken through, but that does not seem to bother the first-year students much. In an act of social bonding after the event, students who "storm" for the first time are baptized by having water sprinkled on them, and they are given a nickname that sticks with them through their college days.

Even with all the rules set for the event, participants will suffer a fair share of bumps and bruises, and occasionally some spilling of blood. So why do it? Besides noting the "rush" the storming provided, most participants I talked to made some reference to tradition. They explained that either the storming fit with Juniata's appeal of having a campus intimacy because of continuing customs year after year, or else it gives the school a special distinction. Student Brenton Mitchell, also known by the nickname earned at the storming of "OT," told me, "As a player, up-holding a tradition that has taken place for years is a bit of a thrill. Also knowing that it's a bit of an 'unconventional' tradition is exciting." Another student, Meredith Eatough, touts its community-building function, especially for the first-year students: "I personally feel that this is an event that brings the entire campus together and also unites the freshmen together as a class from the start. In past years the freshmen class has held secret meetings to devise a plan to get through the arch which is just one step closer to the class getting to know each other and make bonds." She recognized that "some administrators are not fond of the event," but the dean of

Fig. 4.10. After Juniata College's "Storming of the Arch," a first-time participant is ritually baptized with sprinkling of water and given a nickname by sophomores, 2009. (Photo by Simon Bronner)

students extolled its benefits of providing "many students with leadership opportunities," and building "community amongst the students." Arguably, pointing to sense of community as an accolade is especially important because the relatively isolated student body of less than 1,500 students is well aware of the long shadow of gigantic Penn State to the north and an array of other historic liberal arts colleges such as Gettysburg, Susquehanna, Dickinson, and Wilson in the region. From this vantage, "Storming the Arch" is one of a "number of traditions that are unique to Juniata," according to the school's website, and give it a special badge of honor.

On some campuses where students have forged a new rush tradition, administrators have been less yielding than those at Juniata. A version of pushball called "bladderball" (a six-foot leather exercise ball) was an annual event held on Yale University's Old Campus from 1954 until 1982, when university president A. Bartlett Giammatti banned it because of a rising number of injuries, destruction to property, and dangerous pranks. One of the stunts that irked him occurred in 1976 when the Pierson College master outlandishly soared over Old Campus in a rented helicopter, littering the town with leaflets declaring, "Surrender, Pierson has won" (Muller 2001). The context is the rivalry between residential colleges enacted in the bladderball contests, whereas previously it was between campus organizations, and in an earlier day for freshmen and sophomore classes. The number of participants also swelled to dangerous proportions from the early days when it was a warm-up for the

Fig. 4.11. Students rush at one another in the "Epic Quad Battle," University of California at Davis, 2007. (Photo by Jay Mechling)

Yale-Dartmouth football game held on Halloween weekend. During the 1960s, sides in the battle rolled the ball through the New Haven streets to the Yale president's house, and police got involved at that point. The goal was to get the ball over the High Street gate on old campus, and the college that succeeded in seizing the ball then presented it to the university's president at his residence. Giammatti categorized it not as a game, however, but as "carnivalesque anarchy" (Muller 2001). In 2002, the Yale College Council (YCC) tried to bring back what the *Yale Daily News* called "this much loved tradition" but ran into a police roadblock. The end result was that students initiated another outlet for their pent-up energies: Spring Fling. The YCC president explained to a reporter, "When bladderball stopped, that's when Spring Fling started. It's more inclusive [than bladderball]. About every single Yale undergrad comes to Spring Fling, but you couldn't have 5,000 undergrads chasing a ball around" (Post 2004).

At the University of California at Davis in the twenty-first century, a battle between freshmen and sophomore classes out on the central grass-covered quad did not carry the meaning it might have when rushes were annual traditions in the early twentieth century. Instead, beginning in 2005 the "Epic Quad Battle" organized by students pitted residents of dormitories on the north side against those on the south side. Students armed with foam pool noodles and water balloons gathered as the academic year was wrapping up in June (Davis is on a quarter term system). Although the north-south confrontation echoes the rivalry of the American Civil War, and in California the fabled cultural clash of northern and southern sections of the state, the "battle" soon took on the look of classical and medieval wars. Students came adorned in duct-taped shields and helmets in a collective fantasy of heroic glory and honor earned on the field of battle. The connection to finals time supposedly was the demonstration of courage and self-discipline in the face of pain and adversity. Inventive students fabricated catapults and marched in columns reminiscent of the Spartan 300.

The action of the Epic Quad Battle resembled a flag rush because the sides fought to take down each other's flags. The gathered armies rushed toward one another swinging their noodles at one another like swords. If not to haze a subservient class, the rush nonetheless continued the function, at least in the view of the student organizers, of letting off steam at the end of the academic year before sweating out final exams. After three epic battles, the number of participants rose to over 1,000, and in 2007 a student was injured when hit by a noodle that had a pipe lodged inside it. In 2008, the vice chancellor for student affairs directed students who were organizing the fourth Epic Quad Battle to cancel the event because it "is not an authorized campus event and the University does not consent to or condone this event" (Nosek and Wood 2008). Under societal pressure to show intolerance of public displays of violence, the administration was particularly aghast at "the emphasis of past Epic Battle events on use of weapons and physical attack on individuals" (Nosek and Wood 2008). Yet the planned event promised to be the largest ever, and the university faced the prospect of several thousand participants, many from outside the campus. Recognizing the psychological and social outlets of the event, the administration offered to work with students to develop "an alternative means of marking the end of the academic year in a lighthearted, safe, and fun way." Although a round of banquets and musical events signify the end of the year at Davis, posters on the photo and video sharing sites still fondly recall the "rush" of the epic battles on the quad.

At Howard Payne University in Brownwood, Texas, a small Southern Baptist school founded in 1889, the focus of events is on the start of the year rather than its end. Planned events evoke memories of traditions past when freshmen were initiated. First-year students may wonder what is in store for them when told of the annual welcoming festival affectionately called the "Daze of Payne." The tradition has evolved from an earlier period when freshmen sat on the bottom floor of the auditorium, and the upperclassmen in the balcony threw toilet paper and other objects at the "fish," or freshmen, while shouting "poooor freshmen" or "fresh meat." The orientation still involves the pairing of an upperclassman, called a big brother or sister, and a series of competitive games, including a grand tug-of-war between the little brothers/sisters and the big brothers/sisters. Beanies in Yellow Jacket colors for the school mascot are decorated on Stinger Night. The campus features a "Fall Rush" in October, with competitions between campus organizations rather than between classes, including pedestal jousting and a potty race.

By hanging on to its all-male character, Indiana's Wabash College, established in 1832, recalls the old-time college today in many ways. One blogger summed up the lure of the college in one word—*tradition*—and respondents all seemed to agree (Amidon 2007). "That's the one word most often used to describe Wabash College by anyone who has attended the College, worked for the College, or in any way come into contact with the College," blogged Jim Amidon. Thus it should not be surprising that class competition and freshman initiation hailing from the "scrap era" still rear their head on campus. To be sure, freshmen beanies disappeared at Wabash much as they did at other colleges during the 1960s, but Wabash's freshman "pot" made a comeback in the twenty-first century with a reaffirmation of Wabash's commitment to retaining its legacy of an all-male liberal arts college (Gregerson 2006). The current pot is made of a green feltlike material, with a red bill and red button on top and worn by fraternity pledge classes. "I love the idea of the pots, and the idea of bringing back an old tradition," Kevin Long '10 said. John Dewart added, "I'm glad the brothers of Sigma Chi brought back the pots because it helps to restore traditions lost to time" (Gregerson 2006). Class competitions show up on the football team, where freshmen players square off against the upperclassmen in vigorous tugs-of-war (Harris 2006). The idea of the tradition is to bond the units and still maintain a whole. Coach Christ Creighton referred to this function behind many of the rushes after seeing fifty-four rookies piled on top of one another to celebrate their victory in 2006: "Now you've come together as a group in a short amount of time and have learned to work together. And you also learned that it's ok to compete hard against one another, but we celebrate together as a family when we're done" (Harris 2006).

The traditional connection of interclass contests with football suggests the rush's functions continuing in the modern intercollegiate game. Consider that the highlight on many college campuses is the start of the football season coinciding with the opening of the new academic year. The "kickoff" for the year, usually played in front of a massive crowd that exceeds the audience for any other sport, is two lines of men rushing at each other. The runner receiving the ball tries to gain ground while the other players push, grapple, and tackle one another. The "pile" in football is a sight familiar to participants in the class rush, as is talk of offensive and defensive rushes. The importance of the varsity game is to show the fight, and mettle, of the team representing the honor of the school; for participants of the rush, the loyalty shown in battle was to the class. Walter Camp (1859–1925), known as the father of American football, was particularly active on the college scene of the early twentieth century to advocate adopting football as an evolutionary advance over the class rush. In *The Book of Foot-ball* (1910), Camp cited the class rush of the mid-nineteenth century as a source for the intercollegiate sport he was developing, but he berated the rush as "little-disguised hostilities" and "degenerate" compared to the organization and skill of football (1910, 63–64). He kept hammering away at the superiority of coach-directed football over the mayhem of the rushes in a series of popular novels in which the young man "grows up" and finds glory on the football field whereas he mainly suffers bruises in the freshman rush (Camp 1909a, 1909b, 1911, 1914, 1915). Around the same time, physical education advocate James Naismith, renowned for inventing basketball and the football helmet, also used evolutionary rhetoric to deride the rush for its reliance on primitive brawn tied to a preindustrial era whereas the "skill, finesse, and concentration" of varsity college football was of "greater value to the business and professional man of to-day than weight of body or strength of muscle" (1909).

Notice of the evolution of the rush into intercollegiate football was made by historian John Allen Krout as early as 1929, when he reported the game as a distinction of American culture (1929, 235–39). As the interclass rush suffered banishment on many campuses at the time he wrote, intercollegiate football rose in popularity to the point that football was primarily known as a college game. Helping in this ascendancy were oversight committees that controlled the violence of the game with the imposition of rules about prohibiting unsportsmanlike conduct and dangerous tactics such as wedges and momentum plays. Students related to the game more because new rules also limited participants to bona fide undergraduates. In a previous era, colleges stacked their teams with nonstudents, who acted as hired guns, often offering their services to multiple institutions. Administrations channeled much of the campus fervor, and violence, for the interclass rush at the opening of the school year into intercollegiate contests, thus directing rivalry externally rather than internally. From having athletics run by students in a separate world from aesthetics— that is, the academic side of campus life—the new college scene was more organized or bureaucratized. Whereas in the scrap era, every able-bodied male student joined his fellows on the field of play, the rah-rah culture overtaking colleges promoted the specialist athlete. Professional coaches and trainers populated the campus, and the class rush looked increasingly like purposeless frivolity or perilous mayhem by comparison to their strict regimen toward the goal of victory. As part of this organizational effort, some of the first leagues and sport "conferences" were formed of schools with similar sizes and reputations in a region. But the shift of emphasis on campuses to varsity sports for the identity-formation of students also meant that the goal of having every class member participate in an athletic activity gave way to the student serving primarily as a spectator. Students became used to rooting for their team rather than rushing with their class.

Tugs-of-War

The tug-of-war, envisioned in the early twentieth century as a safe alternative to the rush, shows up today as a festive campus event, but is more often associated in the mega-university with fraternity and sorority competition than interclass contests. Like the rush, the tug-of-war had advocates claim connections to ceremonies of ancient civilizations and tout the importance of teamwork as well as strength. The contest may be familiar to many college participants from intramural competitions at summer camps and schools, and on college campuses it similarly is embedded into a festival rather than being viewed as sport. Its reference to "war" is one clue to this perception, because it implies an ultimate, decisive contest in which one side is metaphorically eliminated. The same term is often used to describe the college experience as one in which students feel caught in a tug-of-war. For instance, the article title "The College Tug-of-War" in the *Daily Princetonian*, echoed on many blogs, was not about some athletic contest but about the pressure felt by students, especially new students, between home and campus life, and even between different groups vying for students' commitment—and identity (Griffin 2007). This metaphorical tug-of-war may be behind the continued appeal of the physical tug-of-war as a campus custom, particularly for intramural contests, as a comment on college transition and the desire for certainty. Its action implies more than emotional "release" from the grind of study, because it suggests enduring pain as a trait of the successful student in addition to encouraging participation to uphold the honor of the group. The tug-of-war as a struggle of self is evident in the setup of the "tug" with evenly matched lines. Spectators view the teams as mirror images of each other. The typical motion is back and forth across a central divide suggesting, as one would say in folk speech, being tugged or pulled at in opposite directions.

At Hope College in Holland, Michigan, the tug-of-war is still an interclass battle. Beginning in 1898, the "Pull," as it is known there, has pitted freshmen against sophomores on a Saturday in September shortly after the beginning of the academic year. The teams consist of eighteen students each tugging a 600-foot, 1,200-pound hawser rope. Both have student coaches who work

Fig. 4.12. Freshman puller prepared for "war" in the Hope College Pull, 2007. (Courtesy Hope College)

their teams across opposite sides of the muddy Black River. The goal is to pull the other team into the river and face humiliation. One modern addition has been the "moralers," who cheer and comfort the contestants. Before 1995, all the pullers were men, and the moralers were women (known as "morale girls"). In a nod to gender equity, women began competing as pullers in 1995, and male moralers took up positions alongside the women. As the contest begins, the moralers provide drink and food, shout encouragement, tape wounds, and towel down the sweaty pullers. The pullers for their part dig pits in which they can lie down and brace their feet. Protective armaments are fashioned around the shoulders and chest with duct tape. Pullers apply war paint to their faces and inscribe inspirational messages on their arms. The modern rules call for pullers to remain flat on the ground throughout the Pull; in the contest's early years, pullers stood up, leading to some wicked falls. Bonding with classmates, showing endurance, and withstanding pain in the Pull are highly honored traits. According to one college official, "grueling though the experience is— indeed, in part because it is grueling—many participants compliment it as a highlight of their time at Hope" (Olgers 2009).

A huge banner with the year of the class and a motto like "cataclysm" (class of 2012), "inferno" (class of 2011), or "revolution" (class of 2010) hangs prominently over the line. Pullers, moralers, and rooters wear specially made shirts with the class year emblazoned on them. No longer a contest over the right to remove beanies, it is now a matter of pride and spirit at the liberal arts college.

The event also has a way of bringing men and women together in embrace. In 1977, the Pull lasted a record three hours and fifty-one minutes, in contrast to the two and one-half minutes of 1956. As a result of new rules allowing judges to call the contest to prevent injuries from a competition going too long, in 2005 the sophomores won not by dragging the freshmen into the river but by pulling them twenty feet, one inch. The modern world demands record keeping, after all. If you are keeping score, the sophomores have won most of the time, including a record ten years in a row beginning in 1997 until the freshmen won in 2007.

Students thematize the Pull as an expression of youthful campus spirit, continuity of tradition, and social bonding. One former participant reflected that the Pull provides a "sense of family and that sense of teamwork and also what you learn about yourself—that sense of your endurance" (Olgers 2009). Following up on the idea of the Pull as a metaphor for achievement after struggle, another former student observed, "There is no way that anybody can just get on a rope and pull for three hours. I'm convinced that it's physically impossible. The only way to do it is to go beyond what you ever think you can do" (Olgers 2009). "The Pull is a new discovery, and chance for self-discovery," Hope College editor Greg Olgers summarizes, and his emphasis on self in an intimate setting is significant for the function of the event that helps it persist at Hope, whereas it has faded as a campuswide interclass event at many other campuses.

Elsewhere, tugs-of-war are especially evident among fraternities and sororities, where they bring out the competitiveness among organizations touting their emphasis on tradition and social solidarity. The announcements of tug-of-war events as ultimate battles between Greek organizations have a familiar ring on many campuses. At the University of La Verne, Greek Week involves a series of physical challenge events culminating in the tug-of-war. "The winner has bragging rights; today is more for pride than points," a Phi Delta Theta member told a reporter for the college newspaper (Lampkin 2008). At Stephen F. Austin State University, instead of losers landing in a muddy river, sorority teams risked rolling into fifty-five gallons of green, squishy Jell-O. To give this gelastic scene redeeming value, the event is advertised as a charity fund-raiser (Morton 2002).

Organizers try to distinguish Tug Day at Western Kentucky University between fraternities and sororities as not being your typical tug-of-war. Held during Greek Week, as on other campuses, the students boast that they train and practice for several months for the one-day battle, known simply as "the Tug." Participants "get down and dirty with strategies and techniques when they are pulling on the rope," according to the campus website, a reference to the typically muddy terrain that tuggers plod through as they compete (WKU Greek Affairs 2009). Spectators are not immune from the muck. Chunks of dirt loosened from the tuggers' footholds shower spectators and cause screams mixing disgust and laughter. Besides cheering in the three-minute contest for a winner determined by which team's side the central bandana is on when the clock stops, a general delight is apparent from the muddy mess. Wouldn't you know it, a guy with the last name of "Pride" is director of student activities and organizations and told the campus newspaper that pride is a big motivator in the contest. He gushed that the Tug has been a part of Greek tradition at Western for more than thirty-five years and that it has been an outlet for Greeks to "display pride, prestige, and teamwork" (Thurman 2004). The campus newspaper followed the event with a poll asking a cross-section of students, "What was your favorite Greek Week event?" By far the largest number of respondents named "playing in the mud at Tug" (33 percent), but half of the students were not aware that Greek Week had even occurred (College Heights Herald Poll 2008).

A spectator favorite at many contemporary campuses is the sorority tug-of-war probably because it undermines, or reinforces, depending on your view of the risible scene, the perception of women as weak or spoiled sisters fixated on their precious beauty rather than flexing muscles and getting down and dirty. At the same time, participants use the tug-of-war to broadcast their social solidarity in a context where extreme individualism is more often the norm. If the solidarity is not with one's class, and is expressed not as part of campus culture, then it is channeled into one's organization at a subcultural level. Commonly held during spring festivals when role reversals and frivolities are culturally expected with the blooms of the new season, especially for youth, tugs-of-war are showcases for organizational exuberance on campus.

Of Rats and Men

Although "hazing" is the general term used for ordeals inflicted upon underclass subordinates or initiates, many derisive activities were framed as set forms. One often imposed on freshmen involved mock contests such as "peanut races" in which students had to push the nut with their noses. A variation indoors was a blowing contest in which freshmen got on their knees with hands behind their back. They had to blow at a Ping-Pong ball and try to move it out of the circle. These events emphasized the subservient positions of the first-year students, as they typically were forced to kneel or have their heads on the ground. With their buttocks in the air, and feigned enactments of fellatio, they were symbolically feminized, infantilized, or sodomized with erect elders standing above them. They also bent over to be mockingly beaten with paddles, sometimes while being forced to drink liquids upside down (resulting in spilling water or other substances over their face), or they were pulled out of the washroom, often in a state of undress.

Other male traditions tested new students' mettle with vomit-inducing trials. Caltech for many years had the "blowhard contest" for freshmen. Students stuffed oysters, juice and all, into a six-foot-long plastic tube. One frosh was put on each end of the tube, and at a signal each would blow as hard as possible into the tube. The loser would end up either swallowing or inhaling the oysters, usually leading to involuntary puking (Dodge et al. 1982, 45).

From Binghamton University come reports of "chunking," or vomiting, contests after the consumption of alcohol. The term "chunking," with its reference to pieces of regurgitated food, is meant to be disgusting and parallels another manly test of "chugging" down beers. After a violent vomit, a student had "loser" written on his arm during the night. A student who seemed more adept at "tossing his cookies," "driving the porcelain bus," "praying to the porcelain goddess," "hollering for Ralph O'Rourke," or letting out a "Technicolor yawn" was rewarded with a six-pack of beer. Students noted incidents and wrote commentaries on such performances on a "chunk list" posted in the underclass dorm (Raftery 1989). One also encounters descriptions of fraternity initiations where pledges vomit after chewing tobacco, another manly symbol (Raphael 1988, 87–88). At Caltech, students may even sing a song in a mock athletic cheer:

> I hurl Green and Gold
> The tequila was quite old
> The salt and the lime
> Came spewing up with mold.
>
> I hurl Green and Gold
> My world is in a whirl
> So for California Polytechnic
> Hurl! Hurl! Hurl! (Wilson 2010)

At Purdue, an initiation tradition in a men's dormitory in Cary Quadrangle dates back to 1929 (the dorm complex brags that it is one of the largest all-male housing units in the country). Serving to promote unity among these "hall-men" not aligned with the fraternities (Purdue has the third largest campus Greek community in the United States, with forty-six fraternities and twenty-nine sororities), the event reportedly began between five and six in the morning the day before classes start. Upperclassmen in the dorm woke the freshmen by banging on their doors with baseball bats and other noise-making implements. After being rousted from their beds, the freshmen were herded into the

Fig. 4.13. Freshmen hazed in a "peanut race" at the University of Wisconsin, 1910. (Author's collection)

basement, where they learned risqué folk chants and songs relating to life at Purdue. They were then led by a Cary "executive" to serenade various halls on campus. The vilest cheers were saved for fraternity houses on campus. "Drink beer! Drink beer!" they shouted. "Drink beer, goddammit, drink beer! I won't drink beer with any man, Who won't drink beer with a Cary Man!" (cf. use of the "drink beer" chant or toast in Frothingham 2002, 206, for Harvard; Johnny-zip84 2007 for Akron; Travelpunk 2003 for Ohio State). The walk home took on the look of a rabble, as the group shouted and gestured in a gang (Salmon 1983).

Football teams and marching bands, groups demanding cohesiveness, still carry on initiations. Two weeks before the football season, freshmen players at Michigan State University (MSU), to give an example, go through mandatory rites. "We had to stand up in the cafeteria during this thing called the Booger Show and sing 'I'm a booger snot,'" a new football player reported. "Some guys would tell us to go to the back of the cafeteria and do sit-ups and push-ups." MSU's marching band meanwhile takes its freshmen out on a midnight march or "hayride" and shows them what it takes to be a member of the band. "Freshmen are treated like any rookies would be on a sports team," a band member remarked, and added that nothing more strenuous occurs than what happens

Fig. 4.14. Freshmen in a "blowing contest" at Drake University, 1946. (Author's collection)

on the day of a game (Boettcher 1980, 1–2). Administrators at the University of Wisconsin–Madison suspended the entire marching band from a football game show in 2008, however, for hazing that went over the line of acceptable conduct. Marching band director Mike Leckrone referred to the embedment of hazing in the "band's culture," which he tried to change (Marching Band 2008). Among the infractions were female band members ordered to suck on sex toys, blindfolding of male members who then took off the underwear of fellow musicians, younger band members forced to run errands and refill beer cups for older band members, confinement of younger musicians in small bus bathrooms, and female band members commanded to kiss other women in the band to gain access to bus bathrooms (Wisconsin Band 2008).

Criminal investigations of hazing-related injuries in marquee marching bands at the historically black institutions of Florida A&M, Jackson State, and Southern Universities between 2008 and 2011 raised questions on national talk shows about whether HBCUs had a special hazing problem as well as marching band culture. At many of these institutions, the bands are under more than the usual pressure because they are nationally known acts in demand for high-profile parades and presidential inaugurations; they are more popular than the football teams for which they play. Becoming a member of these bands is accorded a high status worthy of initiation: "You get the fame, and you're kind of treated like celebrities," a band member explained to an investigating reporter. Students point to hazing functioning to produce a heightened

Fig. 4.15. Freshmen at Wayne State University drinking upside down while being hit with flexible tubes. (Author's collection)

sense of camaraderie; band members walk in packs and spend the majority of their time together (Sanders 2011). Investigative journalist Frank Deford (2011a) reported that new members, called "crabs," had to face choreographed assaults with wood planks, belts, baseball bats, and beer bottles. Other reported activities included running younger members through a gauntlet (often being paddled or slapped with female sex toys) and "dog piling" initiates (pinning the victim on the bottom of a tower of people) (Conan 2011). At Florida A&M, the award-winning "Marching 100" band came under a cloud in 2011 when police charged three band members who beat a woman with a metal ruler to initiate her into the "Red Dawg Order," a band clique for students who come from Georgia. The beatings resulted from her not being able to recite information about the "Order" properly (Three Students 2011). At Southern University, two first-year band members were hospitalized after being initiated into "Mellow Phi Fellow," a fraternity-like subgroup of the French horn section (Violent Hazing 2009). At Jackson State, the entire percussion section of the highly heralded "Sonic Boom" marching band was suspended for beatings inflicted after forcing freshmen to line up from the shortest to tallest and link up in a line interlocking one arm around the neck and waist of the person in front of them (Anderson 2009).

Explanations of the intense marching band culture at HBCUs frequently hinge on the historical models of the black male fraternities that often involve severe rituals and a heightened sense of solidarity (Copleand and Alcindor 2011). A belief underpinning the fraternity and marching band culture at HBCUs is that, as African Americans on display, they need to outperform white counterparts, particularly in response to anxieties about masculinity in a feminized collegiate environment and the stereotyped perception of African Americans as indolent (Jones 2004, 113–19). Affected by a history of exclusion, African Americans in marching bands at HBCUs view themselves as selective elite units that necessitate extreme requirements of membership. The initiation rituals following this belief do more than reform the initiates; they remake them (Jones 2004, 57). Rather than being viewed as one extracurricular activity among many in one's college experience, marching band membership is treated as a singular, total identity. With pressure placed on bands to perform precise formations in lockstep with one another, to impose strict discipline, and to accord honors for ranks within the band, the marching bands adopt military hierarchy and, in many cases, boot-camp dissemination of punishment for imperfection or insubordination. Although wanting to retain traditions that instill esprit de corps in marching bands and teams, administrators and students are increasingly on the spot to change collegiate subcultures that promote violence with more than tightened regulations and workshops.

Military schools have some of the most active initiation ceremonies. At VMI, initiation lasts a year. Called a "rat line," the tradition calls for upperclassmen to order freshmen to perform rigorous physical exercises. Classmates thus refer to one another as "Brother Rats," and work toward incorporation at "Breakout," the proud day when upperclassmen recognize the rats as a class worthy of the VMI name. On this day, the cadet is symbolically reborn, for students refer to the day as the class birthday. Many even engrave the date on their VMI class rings. According to one sophomore who got through, "It's a bonding experience. You learn quickly to respect the older cadets and the history of traditions of V.M.I." ("V.M.I's" 1989, 47). In 1997, VMI was the last military college in the United States to admit women. It argued in *United States v. Virginia* (1996) that keeping its exclusionist policy was necessary because of the grueling traditions of the Rat experience, but after the Supreme Court forced VMI to open its doors to women, the rat lines indeed continued with female participants. The women would not become "sister rats"; they were equally "brother rats" who endured the traditional fifteen-mile forced march together with the men, culminating according to tradition with a punishing crawl up a mud-covered hill (Strum 2002, 315).

At Texas A&M, the Corps of Cadets, some 2,000 cadets out of 36,000 students, vigorously maintain the "Aggie Spirit" in a tradition of initiation. The freshmen work from being lowly fish to their version of a "Breakout" at the "Final Review" nine months after entering the corps. They trade a cap with no braid for a cap with a black braid. Another act of transformation is to remove the black cotton belt with a small buckle and replace it with a black nylon belt with a large buckle. They then remove the flat brass, which they have found so hard to keep looking good, and replace it with curved brass, which they have customized. Before the Final Review, however, upperclassmen order each fish to "hit a brace" or "pop to"—stand at stiff attention and introduce himself as a fish. If the performance is not satisfactory to the upperclassmen, the freshmen cadet may have to perform push-ups or "sit on a pink stool," taking a position as if sitting on a stool, with his back against the wall and his legs bent at the knees at a ninety-degree angle with no support for his bottom (Graham 1985).

Making Status Visible

A strong feature of freshmen initiations is the recognition of material emblems of the campus and its hierarchy of privilege. The wearing of freshmen beanies early on established rank associated with dress. The frosh were anxious to remove the infantile head coverings often jocularly referred to as "dinks," also a slang term for a small or child's penis (Green 2010, 1:1614; Read 1935, 49–50). Sophomores often were labeled "hatmen" because of their fuller soft hats, while seniors got to wear stiff hats. At the University of Arkansas, seniors wore derbies; at Franklin and Marshall College, they wore high straw hats; and at the University of California at Berkeley, they wore sombreros. Decorated canes and pipes, associated with seniority and power, were other popular senior accessories forbidden to freshmen (see Brubaker 1987, 28; Miller 1966, 397; Boney 1984, 207). Corduroy pants were another sign of upperclass status. At Purdue, students decorated what they called the yellow "senior cords" with designs showing school spirit (Mohler 1977, 8). At Hood, sophomores wear blazers and juniors receive rings.

Letters, colors, names, and numerals all take on symbolic importance in the old-college class hierarchy. Freshmen were commonly prohibited from displaying their graduation year or school letter. At Georgia Tech, and many other schools, each class had its own color to honor and protect, and graduating seniors bequeathed their colors to incoming freshmen (Newchurch 1985, 14). This use of class colors evolved into the selection of school colors so common today; the most popular combination is blue and white, followed by blue or purple with gold (Snyder 1949, 257–59). Blue carries associations with male strength, power, and royalty (as in the popular label of "royal blue," and some college public relations officers give the interpretation of blue standing for opportunity and optimism afforded by higher education.

Some schools elaborate on the color scheme to form "Odd-Even" alliances among their classes. At Wells, women who will graduate in odd-numbered years join the "Odd Line" against women in the "Even Line," who will graduate in even-numbered years. The teams compete in singing, skits, and basketball games. The Odd's traditional colors are purple and yellow; the Even's colors are blue and green. Each class gives its color a special name and constructs a banner proclaiming itself; some examples are Imperial Purple, Blueberry Blue, and Blazing Yellow. In addition to having a color, classes at Keuka College in upstate New York take names of tribes in the Iroquois Confederacy.

Besides colors, the inscription of letters and names for all to see can take on significance in a college social world where one's class and the people in it leave after a short four-year stint. Especially at western colleges, it became customary for the freshmen to show their moxie by painting the school letter on a hillside while the sophomores tried to stop them (Dundes 1968, 24–25). The battle evolved into a joint pep effort before football Saturdays (Parsons 1988, 15–23). At the University of Puget Sound, an eight-foot-long, four-sided post became ceremonially important for incoming freshmen. On each side was a record of the graduating classes. Incoming freshmen would be marched in through the gate enclosing the post and pause at the monument in contemplation. Four years later, this same class upon graduation would march past the color post in the opposite direction (Earley 1987, 36).

An old inscribed sidewalk is at the University of Arkansas. Begun in 1905, the walk, according to legend, was a unifying response to freshmen-sophomore scraps at the turn of the century. Students inscribed their names and class year in the early years, but as class sizes grew the job was taken over by physical plant staff (see Wylie 1933, 168–72; Parler 1984, 26). At Western Oregon University, since 1962 the freshmen annually have left their mark in the cement on the sidewalk at the college's football stadium.

A sign of status on campuses is the right to roost. Campuses often had "senior fences" and "senior benches" kept off limits to freshmen. The University of Idaho had a cement seat traditionally reserved for seniors in front of the administration building. Underclassmen were told that they had no time to relax on this bench. Violators of the restriction were tossed into the nearby lily pond. At the University of California at Berkeley early in the twentieth century, use of the senior bench as well as some exclusive staircases was also kept from women as well as freshmen (Dundes 1968, 27). Sophomores at Pomona College claimed an arch in front of a college building and excluded freshmen from walking through it. At the University of Georgia, freshmen were forbidden to walk under an arch separating campus and downtown Athens. According to F. N. Boney, the tradition "persisted until the university grew so large that it was no longer possible to tell who the freshmen were" (1984, 165).

Despite this early semester friction, unity often came by the start of classes or later at homecoming. To stress this "incorporation" stage of rites of passage, many colleges have ceremonies before the start of classes that bring together the whole college community. Hood students attend a "pergola party." Upperclass women wake the first-year students at one or two in the morning and force them down to the pergola, an arborlike passageway with a roof on which climbing plants grow. First the first-year students run around the pergola. Then they and upperclass women all join hands around the structure. Dressed in ceremonial black robes and carrying candles, student leaders follow by walking down the center path to the pergola. In a spirit of unity, they sing the alma mater and lead everyone in song. After the ceremony, everyone goes to the dining hall to break bread together.

Called the "pumphandle" at Knox College and the "handshake" at Union College, an annual event involves students shaking hands with administration and faculty who then fall in line themselves, so that everyone has clasped hands in a touching ceremony. At Knox, the last person through the line ends up shaking hands with about 1,200 others.

The majority of today's freshmen undergo "orientation" rather than initiation. The orientation has more of a therapeutic style; it seems more psychological than cultural. Rather than displacing uncomfortable feelings of homesickness and transition through rites of passage, students are encouraged to discuss their feelings with one another. They share their emotions with one another in encounter groups. To discourage privileged cliques and competitions for dominance, students are encouraged to assert their individuality and from there to make their own connections based on common interests, regardless of class standing. Discarding an evolutionary model in favor of relativism, students learn that each position, each group, is relative in worth. One is not better than another, but rather different, and sensitivities are developed toward those varieties in a plural society. Students recognize the ideals expressed in this approach, but still yearn for an exclusive cultural identity to give them a place to belong, a tradition and loyalty to claim, in the transition that college life brings. Often bemoaning the effect of mass culture on a sense of belonging, many commentators have lamented the loss of cultural rites of passage—rites that undergirded transition in age, status, and responsibility—and criticized the self-indulgence of therapeutic approaches (Raphael 1988; Lears 1981).

Tormenting Faculty and Friends

One of the signs of passage could be successfully "pulling a prank" in public view because it was discerned as empowering for students. To warrant being the talk of campus, pranks aimed usually at the faculty and administration needed to show brazenness and at the same time creativity.

Farm animals figure prominently in pranks pulled on faculty, often with scatological implications or to indicate the disconnection of library-bound professors from the outdoors. Typically, farm animals with nonpet status are used to victimize instructors (see Steinberg 1992, 199–203). A report of a cow smuggled into the second-story classroom of an unpopular instructor occurs as early as 1876 (Dundes 1968, 22; see also Kilde 2010, 93; Manley 1969, 258; Mechling and Wilson 1988, 312; Mook 1961, 243; Rollins 1961, 165; Turrell 1961, 162). According to an account from Brown University, a cow was "led up the stairs of University Hall, to the roof, where her tail was tied to the bell, which she rang with determination. It seems to be a characteristic of cows that they will sometimes go up stairs, but they are reluctant to descend" (Worthington 1965, 53).

Animals also characteristically make a mess. At the University of Florida during the summer of 1986, veterinary students released a pig into a packed auditorium, and freed a sixty-pound porker into a faculty member's office. There they dramatically defied the boundaries between the formal, "unnatural" institution and informal nature. MIT pranksters placed a life-size fiberglass steer on the Great Dome at MIT, a symbolic center of the campus famous for its technological work because it houses the engineering library and overlooks the location of university commencement (Peterson 2003, 58–59). Although not the real thing, the animal nonetheless communicated the idea of the cow representing student triumph (MIT students had placed a live cow on the East Campus dorm in 1928) (Peterson 2003, 38–39).

Collegians derive great joy from the incongruity of animals in buildings or atop towers, and they defy authority under the protection of a playful frame. They also point out with this incongruity that the power relationship between faculty and students is "unnatural" and can be easily disrupted. This agitation comes most frequently in late spring when students anticipate graduation, or under cover of Halloween darkness. Cornell students around Halloween 1998, for example, wondered how a pumpkin was lodged on the top of the campus's 173-foot-tall McGraw Tower. Campus officials thought the pumpkin would rot quickly and descend on its own, but having been hollowed out before it was placed on the dome, it clung tightly to its perch. By March, campus officials hired a crane to remove the fruit. How it got up there, though, remains a mystery, leading students to offer up speculative narratives on the method to the prankster's madness.

Students also show their power by performing improbable feats. They regularly disassembled wagons and reconstructed them on top of towers or inside college rooms. Later, automobiles served just as well to astound the college community (Dodge et al. 1982, 10–11; Peterson 2003, 44–52; Taft 1984, 70–71; Utt 1968, 96; Worthington 1965, 53). The point of the stunt is to turn heads and to shake up the order of things. Reality is shaken by those without the power of dictating routine. Sometimes college icons, usually heavy and large, are moved. At Hamilton College, students lifted the half-ton statue of Alexander Hamilton off its base and transported it to a distant farm field. In 2009, MIT students relocated a large statue of the Greek goddess Athena, associated with her wisdom, from a more remote part of campus on the first day of final exams to a more conspicuous spot noticed by student passersby (IHTFP Gallery 2009).

Many outrageous pranks, sometimes called "hacks," come at the hands of engineering students who show off their ability to change the built landscape. Before Halloween in 1982, a telephone booth appeared atop a 148-foot dome overlooking MIT. Maintenance workers prepared to bring the booth down when the phone rang for them! A few years later, the dome sported a small house complete with mailbox and welcome mat (see Dodge et al. 1982, 35–38; Peterson 2003, 60; Steinberg 1992, 112; Theroux 1986, 60–65). Giving a speech at MIT on energy in 2009, President Barack Obama referred to this hacking tradition when he joked that his departure was likely to be delayed as a result of his motorcade ending up on the 148-foot-tall Great Dome. On the West Coast, Caltech students have their own pranking tradition. Two memorable stunts were the changing of the Hollywood sign to read "Caltech" and the rewiring of the scoreboard during the 1984 Rose Bowl game to show that Caltech was trouncing MIT (Steinberg 1992, 61–67).

MIT hackers differentiate their creative acts of relocation from "crackers," who break into computer systems. Still, the general collegiate parlance refers to hackers as technowizards circumventing security. Although campus technology officials worry about malicious and criminal electronic intrusions into their systems, a number of crackers foist memorable pranks on roommates, especially around April Fools' Day. In one widely reported trick that appears to have become a cybertradition, messing with one's autocorrect options to replace usage of "I" with "Mr. Poopy Pants" has been known to get a rise out of the user. Students also make an optical mouse go haywire by placing a tape over the unsuspecting victim's laser sensor (Holland 2008). Student programmers have also shared pranking software that inverts the Windows desktop screen and leaves the impression that indeed the world has been turned upside down. Another perennial gag puts a virtual earthquake on someone's monitor. The fix is embarrassingly simple—with a press on the keyboard, the shaking software will close (PCWorld.com 2001).

Before the age of computers, Penn State students took creative license at the end of the academic year to tease their professors by constructing a mock faculty graveyard. The idea was to turn the tables on faculty who had buried them in work. One headstone was a podium complete with book and notes on top. Mock memorials such as drinking jugs, coffins with students' nicknames for profs on them, and epitaphs proclaiming professors' fates dotted the grounds. One epitaph was in the form of a Western Union telegram to the students from the devil assuring them that one professor burned with lots of smoke and a pungent odor (Bronson 1968a, 1).

Into the 1950s, the idea of mock graveyards was picked up by freshmen who left verses in the ground for sophomores who hazed them. Some of them read "Here lies a Hatman who thought himself wise. He tried to make a 'frosh' wear two bow ties" and "Black Hatmen take heed! Here lies one who didn't. He rests in pieces." The mock cemetery still surfaces occasionally on fraternity front yards during homecoming, when they help to "bury" football rivals with gravestones that carry "R.I.P." messages. Halloween is also a favorite time to bring out mock memorials, wakes, and coffins with grisly messages about college community members. One of the more elaborate Halloween events is the Fright Fair at Pierce College's Halloween Harvest Festival, which includes lots of mock graves on the way to the "Factory of Nightmares" haunted house and "creatures of the corn" haunted trail.

At other times of the year, student groups stage mock funerals, sometimes for silly fun, sometimes in serious protest, but always to draw attention to the finality of the ritual at the end of life in the midst of youthful exuberance. Letting down their hair, fraternities at many campuses show their brotherly bonding in a mock funeral procession for the late "Ray Zor" and, in keeping with tradition, show their state of mourning by letting beards and mustaches grow. Often held at the end of the year, either to display the end of a long journey or represent maturity, mock ceremonies commonly involve references to the growth of facial hair, such as "Mustache May" informally organized by a group at Penn State Harrisburg, and in an earlier era seniors flaunted their high status by sporting mustaches at Purdue's Junior-Senior Parade (Bowlby and Gannon 1944, 34–35; On the Campus 2009, 78). Student organizations also use mock funerals and processions as a protest strategy, especially to show the death of higher education caused by slashes in public funding accompanied by rising costs for students. At the University of California at Irvine in 2010, attendees wore black and mourned the death of "public education" to protest rising student fees. At the same time, Cal State–Long Beach students brought a bagpipe player and a cardboard coffin with a dummy dressed in a cap and gown to the chancellor's office and erected fifty tombstones on the lawn. At Evergreen State College in the state of Washington, student pallbearers carried a coffin representing the corpse of public education from the campus to the state capitol.

Other traditional demonstrations may not appear to be political protests, but they serve as reminders of student appropriation of the campus. Reports through the year mention students tormenting faculty and administrators by stealing bells or clappers, placing privies (and now portable johns) in the middle of quadrangles, painting various college cannons and statues odd colors, and rolling cannonballs (now bowling balls) down steps to make a terrible racket. In another statement of incongruity, huge commercial statues of animated figures and animals from restaurants and convenience stores find their way to college courtyards (see Dodge et al. 1982, 31; Peterson 2003, 58–59). Revered statues are incongruously decorated with sunglasses, hats, and even lingerie. At Harvard, the statue of John Harvard is frequently dressed up in gaudy wear; stately sculptures of George Mason and Thomas Jefferson receive similar treatment at George Mason University and the University of Virginia, respectively.

One student prank in particular comments on the computer age and its impersonalization of the campus community. Students plant the name of a fictitious student and regale one another with stories of the success of this student slipping undetected through the electronic collegiate system. The stunt has precedents, however, in precomputer days. As the story usually goes, the fictitious student is enrolled in a course and receives a grade from the oblivious professor (see Dodge et al. 1982, 15; Stec 1985, 2). At Georgia Tech, a fictitious student named George P. Burdell emerged when Ed Smith, class of 1931, received two admissions applications by mistake. Working together with other students, Smith saw the mythical Burdell through to a bachelor of science degree, and legends circulated about the stunt yearly after that (Newchurch 1985, 12–13; Betterton 1988, 179; Shulman 1955, 93–104; Tucker 2005, 94–95). His memory lives on by having the name paged at football games, used to fool unsuspecting freshmen as one of Tech's greatest alumni, and set up with a Twitter account and website reporting his whereabouts. The legend also expanded with the report that Burdell married Agnes Scott College's own illusory student by the name of Ramona Cartwright (Li 2007). Princeton lore features Joseph Oznot, Bert Hormone, and Ephraim Di Kahble (Tucker 2005, 95). These named figures are hardly alone in collegiate folklore, as Mary Louise Fitton (1942) noticed when she announced, "Every campus has a tale about an imaginary student whose name turned up through some mistake on a class roll and whose existence was prolonged as long as possible by his gleeful colleagues" (40).

Here is how Walker Wyman ran into the variations of this legendary prank from Massachusetts to Minnesota:

> The story told when I was in college was that of the old horse that gradu-
> ated from Harvard. The students enrolled an old milkwagon horse named
> Bill, paid his fees each semester, and took his exams. Classes being so large,
> no professor ever had any occasion to know Bill. . . . The same story is told
> about the U.W.-Madison, and perhaps elsewhere in Wisconsin, about the
> enrollment of a student by name. But in the computer age, names are un-
> important, only numbers count. Students took this non-existent student's
> exams and finally graduated a *number* with an "A" average. Students at St.
> Olaf in Minnesota tell about graduating a dog." (1979, 89)

Pranks abound in the dorms for good reason. Like other restrictive institutions that throw strangers together, including summer camps and military
bases, college dorms often socialize residents through pranking (cf. Posen 1974,
299–309; Graham 1985, 105–21). As with freshman initiations, groups, especially male groups, bring a fresh recruit into the fold by what they perceive
as comical pranks. The pranks are usually not randomly chosen: they follow
a pattern of extending fears associated with living in an institutional setting.
Under the protective frame of play, pranks there focus on the fear of being
alone, of entrapment and confusion. Typical approaches are ritually polluting
another's clean space, bringing disorder to the order of things, and disrupting
routine. The fear is ridiculed, and one is expected to rely on or respect the
group rather than oneself for adjustment.

Common examples of pranks that bring confusion and disorder are moving furniture from a room to another spot, short-sheeting the bed, tilting cans
of water against a door so that they spill in when the door is opened, and
blowing talc into the room. During the nineteenth century, students "smoked"
(that is, ritually killed) freshmen by blowing smoke into their rooms, and in
the twentieth century "stinked" them (Hall 1968, 434; Simmons 1967, 230). A
favorite prank is "pennying in" doors of rooms in a suite. Pennies are jammed
between the door frame and door so that the person inside cannot get out to
the common room. A nineteenth-century precedent for this practice is "screwing up," or fastening the door shut with nails and screws during the night. During the 1960s, students also "Coked in" a door, by wedging a wooden soda case
over the doorknob so that the knob is tightly held inside the case (Simmons
1967, 228).

Especially in men's dorms and fraternities, many pranks expand on scatological and sexual themes that imply a test of manhood (or homophobia). In
the pranks, symbols of infantilizing the young targets might include exposing

rumps, snatching undergarments, and engaging play with toilets and feces. At Rutgers, Michael Moffatt observed male bonding in a group called the "Wedgie Patrol": "New male students and unpopular older ones were snatched from their beds, usually sleeping only in their underwear, and 'hoisted' by the tops of their 'wares' until the garments shredded, leaving them naked and confused, sometimes with cloth burns on intimate parts of their anatomy, at the center of a circle of laughing attackers. . . . The correct manly response to a wedgie attack, according to its perpetrators, was to take it in good humor" (Moffatt 1989, 86). As in other boys' play such as piling on an "it" trying to get away with a ball (sometimes going by the label of "Smear the Queer" or "Dogpile") and, some argue, football, the initiate shows his masculine mettle by metaphorically withstanding feminizing or homoerotic attack (Bronner 2011a, 355–59; Dundes 1987b, 178–96). In other words, the victim responds to being symbolically feminized and infantilized as a sign of a submissive role, but then gets to show dominance, and elevated status, as the prankster.

In a related custom frequently recorded in the Berkeley Folklore Archives, popular men were "pantsed" accompanied by the sexual double entendre of "rolling" the young, naive target. According to one student's observation, "First someone says, 'knock, knock' and others respond by saying, 'who is there.' Then the first person says, 'roll on' and the others say, 'roll on who' and the first person will give a name of a person. When this person's name is said, everyone runs to that person, gets him or her on the ground and takes off the socks and shoes and finally the pants and hides them. As the clothing is taken off this song is sung: Roll on you Golden Bear, For victory is in the air. For California's fame we'll be winning the game, And for Alma Mater fair" (cf. Yohe 1950).

Some of the scatological pranks—such as covering toilets with plastic wrap, filling toilets with gelatin, coating black toilet seats with shoe polish, covering other toilets with petroleum jelly or shaving cream, and feeding a cat a laxative and placing it in a car or room—take the form of orchestrated attacks and suggest a relation of feces play connected to an infantile anal stage of human development. The implication is that the prankster has matured past childhood to a normative sexual and social status in a bureaucratic organization, but the target has remained stuck in abnormal or revolting infantile play (see Dundes 1997, 105–7; Dundes and Pagter 1996, 16–17; Freud 1989; Jones 1961, 413–37; Kubie 1937; Mechling 2001, 199–205). The pranksters literalize the metaphor of smearing or "giving shit" by showing the victim's immersion in, and association with, feces.

In the student's folk categorization, a type of ritual pollution is reserved for rival hall or fraternity groups. In student lingo, these more malicious acts go by the name of "borassing," "ratfinking," "ratfucking," or simply "R.F." (Egan 1985, 179–80; Poston and Stillman 1965, 193; Simmons 1967, 227). To complete the raid, students may fling toilet paper across the front of the house or expose their buttocks to the rival students in an act of "mooning." The symbolic associations come together to belittle the rivals: the lowly rat, phallic dominance suggesting feminization, and anal infantilization.

Besides polluting rivals, students baptize their own with water. On their birthdays, and in pledging ceremonies, students are regularly thrown into showers, fountains, and ponds. Special dunkings occur on a student's twenty-first birthday or engagement. Unlike the whacks one received as a child, dunkings do not count age as much as recognize insider status within the group. The immersed birthday person is simultaneously set apart and brought into the group, humiliated and honored. He or she is now given new life by the water. The birthday person or pledge must rise from the dunking and come anew as if by evolution onto dry land. At the University of Washington, students are dumped into Drumheller Fountain, also known as Frosh Pond; at Indiana University, Showalter Fountain; at Texas, Littlefield Fountain. At the University of Alabama, the traditional tapping ceremony for the Jasons, a men's senior honorary society, includes a good dousing with muddy water (Wolfe 1983, 226).

Some traditional pranks involve student theatrics. An old prank that may be talked about more than enacted goes by the name of "Going to See the Widow." It was commonly played on a braggart who extolled his sexual abilities. The braggart was led by pranksters to believe that a widow (or O'Reilly sisters, trucker's wife, brakeman's wife, or prettiest girl in the county) who lives a few miles from town is interested in making his acquaintance. He was warned, however, that the widow has a suitor whose jealousy has been inflamed by rumors concerning her conduct. Once out at an isolated farmhouse, the group got out of the car and walked up to the house. A series of blasts from a shotgun rang out in the darkness, followed by shouts and threats. One of the group pretended to fall wounded. The braggart ran until informed of the joke played on him (Cohen 1951, 223; Grotegut 1955, 51–52; Hand 1958, 275–76; Sobel 1951, 420–21; Randolph 1957, 17–19; Starr 1954, 184).

One well-known stunt is the chemistry experiment with food. A student at the University of California at Berkeley reported it this way for the Berkeley Folklore Archives: "A chemistry major introduced Paul to the 'salt and butter reaction.' He put salt on a pat of butter and told Paul it was an exothermic reaction, giving off heat. Paul thought heat really would be coming from it, so he put his hand over it to test the temperature. The chemistry student smashed his hand down on Paul's, so that Paul's smashed on the butter." In 2009, I received the following from a Millersville University student: "I would gather various substances in [the] cafeteria, such as mayo, catsup, and mustard, and add ice. I would tell other people at the table that I had done this fascinating chemistry experiment. Then I wave my hand over the gooey mixture and say 'Yeah, it seems to be getting warmer." Keep doing this until curiosity overwhelms the unsuspecting onlooker. When someone waves his hand over the mixture, slam it down!" The prank is meant to reveal someone's gullibility, especially in a college setting where fellow students all seemed wise to the ways of the world. Be alert when in the company of people with B.S. behind their names!

Leaving One's Mark

Students also use artistic abilities to make their presence felt on campus. Every campus, it seems, has a rock, bridge, fence, wall, cannon, or water tower repeatedly given a fresh paint job. The painters traditionally come do their work in the middle of the night, so as to surprise the awaking campus community in the morning. Fraternities particularly like to leave their Greek letters or spirited messages on rocks, and classes often leave their special colors. Eastern Michigan's rock receives a paint job from fraternities and sororities every few days. The student newspaper estimates that the rock receives more than 5,500 coats of paint during the school year. When university officials removed a frequently painted rock from the courtyard at Northwestern, students answered with a papier-mâché model where it once stood ("Tradition Crumbles" 1989, 35).

At MIT, students regularly paint messages and "Smoot" marks—slashes of paint spaced five and a half feet apart—along the half-mile-long Harvard Bridge. The marks date back to 1958 when Lambda Chi Alpha pledge Oliver Smoot agreed to lie down and be the measuring unit for the bridge's 364.4 "Smoot" lengths plus an ear (Egan 1985, 127; Geeslin and Brown 1989, 93–95; cf. Dodge et al. 1982, 19; Peterson, 2003, 42–45). What is the point? Well, ever been in Boston during the bitterly cold winter? "Smoot marks make it possible for students to know how far they are from the other side without looking up," the frat president explained, "and you can stay huddled down in your jacket and still know how far you have to go." "Besides," Smoot himself added for good measure, they are "no more illogical than feet or yards" (Geeslin and Brown 1989, 94).

The paint never stays on long at a "senior bench" (officially known as the Thomson Memorial Seat, dedicated in 1905) at the all-male Wabash College in Crawfordsville, Indiana. In the bench's early years, freshmen painted the bench, usually green, to show their newbie status under the supervision of the seniors. Despite their work on the bench, they were not allowed to sit on it. A somber ceremony transferred ownership of the bench from graduating seniors to the rising seniors. By the 1980s, however, bench painting showed competition on campus among fraternities and clubs more than classes. In the twenty-first century, the bench featured designs promoting ethnic and sexual diversity on campus with images for Hispanic heritage and gay identity. School spirit is still evident in its coats of school colors before each home football game (Swift 2009).

College officials did not always look kindly on what they called "painting vandalism," however. When Vanderbilt engineering students painted the school colors on a much-venerated downtown cannon, officials dismissed three upperclassmen and suspended three freshmen for a year (Conkin 1985, 142–43; Steinberg 1992, 26). At St. Andrews Presbyterian College in Laurinburg, North Carolina, administrators encourage students to paint slogans and designs on the white surfaces of a wall on the east side of the campus lake as a "venue for free expression," but warn that "painting elsewhere on campus will be considered vandalism and misuse of College property" ("Student Activities" 2011). Recognizing that public overlays over official campus structures could be interpreted as a collegiate rite of spring, University of South Dakota police sent out a stern message to the student body with the arrest of students who painted red marks over the crotch and chest on the august statue of Professor William "Doc" Farber on campus. "Being 'college students' is no excuse for damaging property," an official commented (Kokesh 2011).

Campus pranks and scraps may appear at times to be a regression into childhood antics or an adult blossoming of creative effort that might have been put into studies. Between the dorm and stadium, between youth and maturity, students search for fun and find traditions that offer social connection on campus in the face of what appears to be an increasingly individualistic, acceleratingly changeful society. They seek cultural as well as academic passage through their absorbing, exhilarating, and frightening experience on campus. They pursue emotional release and self-discovery at a formative age when they feel they have to define human relations, morals, and limits for themselves. With campuses more subject to media attention and administrative regulation, their struggles and missteps in this process often make news and draw opprobrium, but the point is that looking for fun is hardly frivolous. From the tussle of class scraps to the intrigue of hacks, students have embraced social lessons that their courses have barely taken up.

CHAPTER

COLLEGE SPIRIT

Expressing Loyalty and Rivalry

EVEN THOUGH STUDENTS' TIME ON CAMPUS IS SHORT, THEY EXPECT to be infected while there with a strange sort of exuberance known as "college spirit." Brought back to campus, alumni typically complain that the current crop of enrollees lack the spirit their class exhibited. Or else they are convinced it disappeared with the growth of the school to immense scale. When asked to clarify what college spirit entails, many students and alumni state that more than cheering on their institution, it has something to do with their fondness for one another living in community. To exemplify college spirit, students point to a host of traditions, including homecoming celebrations, songfests, and sporting events. They may recall "school spirit" in their high schools, but usually perceive college spirit as being more public, more clamorous, and on a larger scale. They often reserve their most boisterous demonstration of college spirit for their designated institutional rivals. On its surface, spirit connotes devotion to the institution that is expressed through song, story, and custom. It is wrapped up with a sense of the institution's tradition or legacy and the concept of students taking part in an unbroken chain from the past to the future. But spirit is also evident in collegians' self-deprecation and certainly in organized stunts intended to quash the spirits of neighboring institutions.

Charles Franklin Thwing, president of Western Reserve University in the early twentieth century, gave the formula for the ingredients of college spirit as "love of teacher and student for the college, *plus* submission of the individual to the general academic good, *plus* appreciation by students of the highest ideals, *plus* songs and sports, as expressing college devotion" (1914, 126). Although he knew that students could get carried away with their rollicking pep displays, he saw college spirit as a function of the age of transition for youth in a last fling of social intensity before settling down into adulthood and going their separate ways in individual life pursuits. He proclaimed that "to make the fire of college spirit all the pieces of the kindling wood of the student life must lie close together. College spirits make 'college spirit'" (1914, 127). "College spirit" may sound old-fashioned and idealistic, but scholastic guides still refer to it as distinctions of various community-minded campuses. The annually updated *Insider's Guide to the Colleges,* which prides itself on featuring student obser-vations of their campuses, for example, advises, "When you come to UMD [University of Maryland], be prepared to cheer long and loud. If there's one uniting factor on this campus it's school spirit: 'Everyone has school spirit and, despite it being large, it feels very close-knit'" (Yale Daily News 2010, 349).

Spirit is not just about getting fired up at sporting events. The traditional liberal arts institution boasts college spirit as a feeling of engagement resulting from small classes, accessible professors, and overall its social and physical "we-ness" (Yale Daily News 2010, 190). At Harvard, students have a panoply of extracurricular organizations that embody college spirit, and there is a great deal of interaction with alumni, therefore emphasizing the lineage of the col-lege's spirited tradition. Harvard students tell me that they want to counter the perception that a reputation for excessive college spirit means a diminished intellectual orientation. Students materialize college spirit in displays of pen-nants, mugs, sweatshirts, blankets, plaques, and the like. At special occasions such as homecoming and pep rallies, student organizations go all out with grassroots constructions of floats, signs, and bonfires that convey their spirit for all to see.

At Colby College, when students think of college spirit, they refer to a re-gatta on the college pond where students make boats out of nonboat materials such as gardening pipes, balloons, and bicycles. The event represents for them the idea that students are "really involved in stuff on campus" (Yale Daily News 2010, 324). They also have their rivalry game, not so much on the football field but in the hockey arena against Bowdoin. Fairfield students, however, told the *Yale Daily News* staff that there is not much college spirit at their campus in Connecticut, whether as a result of disbanding its football team in 2003, ab-sence of an archrival, more concern for hitting the beach rather than attending organized school events, or the lack of fraternities and sororities. Fairfield folk express fondness for the institution, recognize a sense of community around its preppy image (its nickname is J Crew U), and have a high participation rate in intramural sports, but report that they do not have that rah-rah or combat-ive team worldview characteristic of nearby campuses such as Yale, Trinity, and the University of Connecticut (Yale Daily News 2011, 129–30).

Spirit evokes the past for inspiration and suggests the institutional affili-ation for the young man and woman coming-of-age is significant. Spirit is often code for a heightened sense of tradition on campus that is rooted in an altruistic bonding of students, faculty, and administrators. Yet befitting the historical fusion of feudal and industrial political economies on the campus, spirit can appear corporately orchestrated and is parodied in lore as fueling establishment norms, cultural homogeneity (and "mainstream" hegemony), and diminished social consciousness. The renowned social critic Thorstein Veblen (who gave us the concept of "conspicuous consumption"), for example, thought that the rise of athletics, clubs, fraternities, and organized student activities owed to the spread of a "business régime" (2007, 87). The "accessories of college life," according to Veblen "are held to be indispensable, or unavoidable; not for scholarly work, of course, but chiefly to encourage the attendance of that decorative contingent who take more kindly to sports, invidious intrigue and social amenities than to scholarly pursuits. Notoriously, this contingent, is, on the whole, a serious drawback to the cause of learning, but it adds appreciably, and adds a highly valued contribution, to the number enrolled; and it gives also a certain, highly appreciated, loud tone ('*college spirit*') to the student body; and so it is felt to benefit the corporation of learning by drawing public attention" (2007, 87; emphasis added). In short, his view was that college spirit is good for publicity and the incorporation of the college campus rather than for upholding the ideals of higher education.

Echoes of Veblen's view can be heard in contemporary reflections of university presidents. John A. Flower, president emeritus of Cleveland State University, described "the changed spirit and face of college life in America" in his memoir, *Downstairs, Upstairs* (2003), a play of words upon the Masterpiece Theater serial drama *Upstairs, Downstairs* (1971–75, 2011), in which a clear class distinction exists between servants downstairs and the elite family upstairs. The connection, in his view, is that changes of social class and political economy in college spirit occurred with the massification of universities in the twentieth century. He writes, "Groups from every level of humankind produce the students that now pour onto campuses—from the elite and exclusive 'upstairs' of economic and social privilege to the 'downstairs' occupied by vast millions" (Flower 2003, xii). He worried that it was not possible to create community or value education in ideas and concepts out of such a vast diversity. His critical view is that student spirit remains, and may even be louder, but it is often in response to market forces and entitlement to "customer satisfaction." He observes that "with the democratization of admissions and dramatically increased access to colleges in the public sector and in many nonselective liberal arts colleges, market forces for producing customer satisfaction have been added to the equation of delivering educational services and managing the affairs of campuses" (Flower 2003, 165).

Many students in mega-universities seek college spirit to have a sense of social belonging in a highly individualized mass society. The spectacles of competitive affiliation in sporting events, pep rallies, and campus convocations are appealing for providing rituals of solidarity and rootedness in a mobile, dispersed society. Often universities as mediating structures re-create qualities of traditional early socialization (such as family, religion, and neighborhood) in highly symbolic rituals and customs to foster identification with the institution. Sociologists Peter Berger and Richard John Neuhaus (1977) call this process "alternation" or secondary socialization and argue that it is never as successful as primary socialization. Folklorist Jay Mechling observes that folklore works to advance alternation and succeeds in sustaining a high-context culture whereby participants feel a bond and recognize one another possessing a distinctive tradition. Institutional folk processes "are designed" by university community members, he writes, to "establish a private, home-like world in a world away from home" (Mechling 1989, 343–44). In the examples that follow, tensions in the processes—between primary and secondary socialization, altruistic and commercial forces, little community and corporate mass society—generate symbolic meanings inherent in spirit as both an emotional state and expressive quality.

Homecoming

A prime frame for campus spirit is homecoming. Indeed, campus newspapers often proclaim a special "homecoming spirit" that channels the exuberance and devotion associated with college spirit into time-sensitive tasks of house decoration, parading, and rallying. Homecoming extends the family and community metaphor at many colleges into the streets and onto the playing field. Like Thanksgiving, which brings family members in this mobile society home to share in festivity, homecoming brings alumni back to campus to share their common bond with one another and with students. Spreading quickly during the mobile 1920s, the activities of homecoming were designed to heighten the rah-rah spirit of the college and remind one and all of the values of the college haven. For students, homecoming is an extension of rituals begun before classes started. For alumni, it is a renewal of old ties.

At the old-time college, homecoming often featured a bonfire into which freshmen flung their beanies and thus attained full-fledged student status. At Earlham, students liked to burn privies along with their beanies as a sign of leaving childhood behind. At the University of Florida's homecoming, called the Gator Growl, freshmen had to bring their weight in wood to the bonfire. (Local disfavor with the practice may have had to do with the frequent appearance in the pile of restaurant and city limits signs.)

At most homecomings today, students put on festivities—often around the central event of an intercollegiate football game—for the benefit of returning alumni and parents. Students decorate the halls and Greek houses on campus, sometimes adding the extra touch of toilet paper streamers in the treetops.

Fig. 5.1. Drake University homecoming float announces "Scorch Emporia [State University]". The sign in front of the float states "Drake's on the Warpath!" (Author's collection)

They prepare floats for an elaborate parade. Georgia Tech has its "Ramblin' Wreck" parade, and Auburn annually answers with its "Wreck Tech" parade. Onlookers at Auburn taunt sorority and fraternity pledges who must walk the parade route in their pajamas. At Tech, the parade features vintage automobiles creatively hacked, chopped, and sawed into mechanical sculptures. The battered cars serve as pregame symbols of anticipated victory on the playing field, appropriate to aggressive engineers showing mastery over their mechanical icons (Weales 1957; Rountree 1985).

The parade showcases student creativity and humor. First-year students, especially, parade in outlandish costumes, and provide self-mocking floats. At Western Oregon University, the homecoming parade becomes a "noise parade"; students make a riotous din with the help of car horns, fire engine sirens, whistles, and school bells. At the University of Arkansas, the big hit for many years in the parade was the "Freshman Story" float, a portrayal of the freshmen as untamed savages (Wylie 1933, 187). At the University of Alabama, in a well-established tradition, law students don formal attire for homecoming and, accompanied by dates, continue their celebration on flatbed trucks (Wolfe 1983, 214).

In the spirit of incorporation, the taunting in floats and house decoration is usually directed at the day's opponent, thus uniting the campus against a common enemy. Students construct environments such as the one directed against the Vanderbilt Commodores football team that showed gravestones and coffins. A huge sign in front blared the message "Commodores Will Be Coughin'" (Egan 1985, 112). At Lawrence, students built a large railroad engine and the sign "It's No Loco-Motive To Want To Run Over Carleton" (Lawrence 1988, 32). At western colleges, often sporting frontier-styled mascots of pioneers, trailblazers, and cowboys, it was common to have floats showing the scalping or scorching of the opposition. Fraternity and sorority houses join in the festivities by constructing lawn sculptures made out of crepe paper on chicken-wire frames.

Bringing aristocratic dignity to the homecoming procession, a Homecoming Queen accompanied by her court of maids rides majestically in the parade. Southwestern University, however, has a parody of this tradition. Not having a football team, Southwestern has homecoming nonetheless and parades a queen who is a man dressed as a woman. Chatham University, a women's college, puts on a tag football game and "cheap floats" led by a kazoo marching band made up of students from other schools. Cheerleaders shake pom-poms in the parades—never mind that they are not in the school colors. As for the floats, each "cheap float" committee gets 4,000 white paper napkins, three cans of spray paint, and a large wedge of plywood with which to work.

Many small colleges have another version of homecoming in parents and alumni weekends. Often a highlight of these events is a formal ring ceremony for the juniors, at which they ritually receive upperclass status. Usually the ceremonies are conducted in black robes, and, given romantic associations with receiving rings, often take on the character of a wedding—in this case a marriage to school and classmates. At Saint Mary of the Woods College, a Catholic women's college, the "Woods' Wedding March" is played. One junior expressed its meaning this way: "It links us to members of our class and every other class," and another added, "There's just a special bond, a certain kind of friendship there when you meet someone wearing a ring." At Mary Baldwin, another women's college, students receive their rings in November in a weekend devoted to the women's fathers, "Junior Dads' Weekend." Making the connection of football to masculine roles, many dads' days are held in the fall, and moms' days are reserved for the fertile, maternal spring (Bowlby and Gannon 1944, 26).

At VMI, cadets consider the "Ring Figure" the most important event next to graduation. In the ceremony, the rings are received twice—once from the superintendent of VMI and later at a ballroom ceremony from dates. Each year's

Fig. 5.2. Fraternity members construct an effigy for homecoming at Penn State University. Achieving a large-scale presence is an important aesthetic to the homemade constructions. (Author's collection)

class designs its own ring, and it becomes a source of pride because, cadets brag, at thirty-three pennyweight it is the biggest ring in the country. In a sign of bravado, wearers claim that if the ring were "any heavier . . . it would be considered a weapon" (Birnbach 1984, 414). In a variation, Wells women in Aurora, New York, receive "Junior Mugs" and celebrate their arrival with a rowdy party called the "Junior Blast." The first-year women celebrate by tampering with the juniors' rooms—moving their beds and leaving clues to their location—while the upperclass women are breaking in their mugs.

The University of Illinois is proud of bringing home to campus with festive dads and moms weekends, held in November and April, respectively. The idea of celebrating dads and moms separately has been a tradition since the early 1920s when, according to the campus history, "University spirit blossomed" (University of Illinois 2011). Presently, all parents are initiated into the Moms and Dads Associations and are supposed to help with the transition of students to campus and generate college spirit. Having a festive environment where activities are planned takes some of the sting out of independent-minded

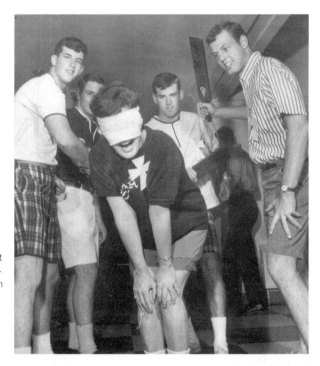

Fig. 5.3. A visiting parent is initiated into the Mother's Club of Sigma Chi on Moms Weekend at the University of Illinois. The woman's son is holding the paddle on the right. (Author's collection)

students having their parents around and reminding them of their childish past (eNotes.com 2011). Making a manly connection to the gridiron, the Dads Weekend revolves largely around a home football game, and a "King Dad" is crowned at a huge annual banquet. Moms Weekends feature crafts fairs, fashion shows, flower displays, and honors given to the "Mom of the Year." Some campus organizations have their own mother's clubs, such as the Sigma Chi fraternity, which has been known to hilariously initiate (and infantilize) frat members' mothers by giving them lighthearted whacks in the paddle line. They would not dare (or need to) do that to the fathers.

Fight Songs and Alma Mater Songs

At homecoming, students are likely to be called upon to sing the college fight song and alma mater. Fight songs performed to the accompaniment of the school band on the field of play pump up the crowd at football and basketball games. The oldest collegiate fight song in the United States is Boston College's "For Boston," composed by T. J. Hurley in 1885. Its lyrics set thematic precedents of often manly pride, glory, and victory that echo in the fight songs of more than 100 other schools afterward.

For Boston, for Boston,
We sing our proud refrain!
For Boston, for Boston,
'Tis Wisdom's earthly fame
For here, men are men,
And their hearts are true,
And the towers on the Heights reach to Heav'ns own blue.
For Boston, for Boston,
Til the echoes ring again!
Rah rah.

One of the country's most recognized fight songs is the "Notre Dame Victory March" written by Michael Shea and John Shea, who earned degrees from the university in 1906 and 1908, respectively. It contains a memorable chorus:

Cheer cheer for old Notre Dame,
Wake up the echoes cheering her name,
Send a volley cheer on high,
Shake down the thunder from the Sky!
What though the odds be great or small,
Old Notre Dame will win over all.
While her loyal sons are marching
Onward to victory!"

As with many revered refrains, Notre Dame's receives ample parody in collegiate folklore. In the two versions that follow, the cheer becomes a drinking song.

Beer, beer for old Notre Dame,
Bring on the cocktails, we want champagne.
Send the freshmen out for gin,
Don't let a sober sophomore in.
We never stagger, we never fall,
We sober up on wood alcohol,
All the loyal faculty lie drunk on the barroom floor!

Beer, beer for old Notre Dame,
Bring on the whiskey, bring on the dames!
We drink wine or beer or gin,
Don't let a sober person in!
We never stumble, we never fall,
We sober up on wood alcohol,

As our loyal sons go marching
Back to the bar for more! (Wilson 2010)

Boston's original fight song is not immune from scatological and sexual parody commonly found in college song, especially from rivals:

For Boston, For Boston,
The outhouse on the hill,
For Boston, For Boston
They suck and always will.
So here's to the outhouse on the hill,
BC sucks and always will! (Wilson 2010)

A number of lyrical parodies use a much-adapted tune of "The Battle Hymn of the Republic," which collegians undoubtedly adapted from childhood renditions of "My eyes have seen the glory of the burning of the school, We have tortured every teacher and we've broken every rule" (Bronner 1989, 97–99; Knapp and Knapp 1976, 172–74; Mechling 1986, 99; Monteiro 1976, 159; Sherman and Weisskopf 1995, 102–5). But instead of being directed at one's own school, the barbs are hurled at a rival at tailgate parties. Here is one sung by avid fans of the Georgia Tech Yellow Jackets aimed at their archrivals, the Georgia Bulldogs.

Mine eyes have seen the glory of the stomping of the dogs
We will teach those poor damn farmboys they should stick to slopping hogs
When the Jackets are triumphant we will raise a mighty cheer
"We'll do the same next year!" (Wilson 2010)

At Northwestern, the tune is used against the Iowa Hawkeyes:

Mine eyes have seen the glory of the shucking of the corn
They have outlawed education where the black and gold are worn
And when the game is over the Hawkeye fans will start to mourn
The Cats are marching on. (Wilson 2010)

Part of the reason the song tradition lives on is that it invites creative improvisation of the rhyme with the familiar tune. To the above chorus, for example, a fellow singer offered,

Although your homes are mobile your team is not on the go
We'll be out in Pasadena while you're sitting home in snow

You'll be nodding off at halftime while your band does park and blow
Yeah Bucky keeps marching on. (Wilson 2010)

A college fight song that has attracted a host of folk variations is "The Victors" from the University of Michigan. The notable feature of the song is the repetition of "hail" in the chorus:

Hail! To the victors valiant
Hail! To the conquering heroes
Hail! Hail! To Michigan
The leaders and best!
Hail! To the victors valiant
Hail! To Michigan
The champions of the West!

Louis Ebel composed the song in 1898 when he was a student following a late-game, championship-clinching football victory over the University of Chicago. The lyrics diverge from the usual lot of fight songs because they celebrate a win rather than exhort the team to victory. Thus the band plays the tune after the football team scores as well as when the team takes the field. The song is ritually performed at a number of university events, including freshman orientation and commencement. Students learn the customary accompanying gestures: standing and clapping in rhythm until the chorus, when they thrust their fists in the air at each repetition of the word "Hail!"

Rival fans play off the word "hail" in their creative parodies:

Fail! But remember our cheer
Fail! But just wait 'til next year!
Fail! Fail! We missed again!
Forever second best!

Help! Help! For Michigan!
Help! For the big game losers!
Help! For the choke excusers!
Help! Help! For Michigan,
Aid is needed here! (or the cesspool/armpit of the West). (Wilson 2010)

As the above parodies indicate, the school is a target not only because of its catchy fight song but also because of its supposedly haughty attitude gained from years of being at the top of the sports heap. The parodies roll the team and the fans in the lowly dirt and sardonically comment on the ubiquity of the song:

Hurl! Hurl! To Sing Again!
Hurl! To this wretched fight song!
Hurl! While the hounds bark along!
Hurl! Hurl! This fight song sucks!
Vomit and spew!

Hailing rather than hurling shows up in another college musical tradition of singing the alma mater, from the Latin for "nourishing mother." The revered song typically performed at university convocations serves as the institutional anthem. Colby College's alma mater, in fact, uses the tune of the Canadian national anthem and opens with "Hail, Colby, Hail! Thy people far and near stand at thy call, Our Alma Mater dear."

"Glory" also is featured in many alma mater songs. Penn State's anthem, for example, is kicked off with "For the glory of old State, For her founders strong and great, for the future that we wait, Raise the song, raise the song." The lyrics were composed in 1901 to the hymn "Lead Me On" by Penn State professor Fred Lewis Pattee, who as a writer on folklore wanted to establish a song tradition to instill college unity and loyalty. His concern for the college experience turning boys to men was expressed in lines finding students standing at "boy-hood's" gate waiting to be "molded into men." That changed in 1975 during the International Women's Year to "When we stood at childhood's gate, Shapeless in the hands of fate, Thou didst mold us, dear old State." Remaining was the reference to the maternal college in "Rest, O Mother dear, with thee, All with thee, all with thee."

Pattee had graduated from Dartmouth and became familiar with its school song, "Men of Dartmouth," written by Richard Hovey of the class of 1885. These Dartmouth men, Hovey, wrote in the song,

Set a watch lest the old traditions fail!
Stand as brother stands by brother!
Dare a deed for the old Mother!
Greet the world, from the hills, with a hail!

In 1988, Dartmouth revised the title to "Alma Mater" and changed the lyrics to recognize women at the college (the school had become coeducational in 1972). The second line, for example, was changed to "Stand as sister stands by brother!" Men's sports teams and some fraternities continued to sing the old version, raising protests from an anonymous student group called "The Daughters of Dartmouth" (Buntz 2007).

One of the best-known alma mater songs is Cornell's "Far Above Cayuga's Waters," composed around 1870 by student roommates Archibald Croswell

Weeks and Wilmot Moses Smith. They set the lyrics to an earlier ballad tune, "Annie Lisle," which became a common accompaniment to other school songs. In a folk process of imitation and variation, Weeks and Smith's opening line, "Far above Cayuga's waters with its waves of blue, Stands our noble Alma Mater glorious to view," was later adapted by many other colleges, including the University of Kansas ("Far above the golden valley glorious to view, Stands our noble Alma Mater towering toward the blue"), Wofford College ("On the city's northern border reared against the sky, Proudly stands our Alma Mater as the years go by"), Lehigh University ("On the breast of old South Mountain reared against the sky, Stands our noble Alma Mater, Stands our dear Lehigh"), Lewis & Clark College ("Standing by Willamette's water, Towering o'er its blue, Rises our dear Alma Mater, Proudly to the view"), and LSU ("Where stately oaks and broad magnolias shade inspiring halls, There stands our dear old Alma Mater, who to us recalls, Fond memories that waken in our hearts a tender glow").

With the kind of circulation in staid ceremonies enjoyed by "Far Above Cayuga's Waters" far and wide, one should not be surprised by the steady stream of folk parodies. The most widely collected verse is "High above Cayuga's waters, There's an awful smell. Some say it's Cayuga's waters, We say [know] it's Cornell" (cf. Sherman and Weisskopf 1995, 122). At Kansas, students sing "Across the stagnant water, Beneath the sky so blue, Lies an abandoned outhouse, That they call KU." The scatological smear continues at LSU, where one may hear orally recited or see emblazoned on a T-shirt, "Where rotten oaks and bent magnolias shade gators and raccoons, There stinks our dear old alma mater 'neath a Cajun moon, Foul memories that waken in our gut like a bad crawfish pie." The parodies take a good-natured poke at the school in the spirit of many childhood mockeries of ceremonious songs associated with assembly such as "Joy to the World" and "Here Comes the Bride" (see Bronner 1989, 104, 108; Knapp and Knapp 1976, 167; Sherman and Weisskopf 1995, 112–13).

The theme of innocence in alma mater songs is frequently dashed. After proclaiming that "we pay thee devotion, In the fervor of youth that is strong," Mount Holyoke College's heartrending lyrics of loyalty are "So from east and from west now we gather, And united in firm love to thee, All years are as one and their loyal pledge, Mount Holyoke forever shall be." The pervasive parody that alumni remember is:

O Mount Holyoke, we pay thee tuition,
In the fervor of youth that's gone wrong;
Each year it gets higher and higher,
My God, Alma Mater, how long?

So from barroom to bedroom we stagger,
And united in free love for all,
Our drinks are too strong and our morals gone,
Mount Holyoke, what's happening to me? (Sherman and Weisskopf 1995, 121)

Another aspect of folk parodies of alma mater songs worth pondering is their reflection of repressed sentiment. Many of the songs have a lineage to the Victorian era, which emphasized sentimentality especially related to a religious devotion to the harmonious, domestic maternal role before children emerged to encounter the harsh world of business and industry. Full of worshipful and tearful loyalty to the campus as a nurturing mother, the odes tout sheltered familial unity of students as they depart for rougher terrain. The original songs urge students to remember the good old days and keep mother in their hearts. Sentimentality came under modernist attack in the early twentieth century with what Elliott Oring calls a "profound sense of alienation and its [modernism's] utter repudiation of certainty and virtue" (2003, 77). A conflict arose for students in the campus environment as universities increasingly embraced individualistic modernism and reduced their parental oversight. According to Oring,

> To the extent that modernity succeeded in creating an extreme self-consciousness of and uneasiness about sentimentality, modern humans have been left in something of a quandary. They continue to experience feelings of tenderness, affection, admiration, and sympathy. They continue to be moved by the display of these qualities in others. But as modern people, they have also learned to discount these sentiments as "mawkish," "maudlin," "corny," "corn-ball," "hokey," "schmaltzy," "sloppy," or just plain "sentimental." Those who would claim for themselves any measure of urbanity, education, and sophistication have had to suppress the least trace of their sentimentality. (2003, 78)

In their advocacy of higher learning, universities led the charge for passing such sophistication to students, and yet as the institutions grew and became seemingly impersonal, they strived to maintain social ties based on emotional attachments to a fondly remembered maternal campus "home sweet home."

Faux alma mater singers in their enactment of the humor of parody deflate the tender images of an intimate family while demonstrating their affiliations with the institution. Externalizing this suppression to the institution appears to aggressively and scatologically devalue sentimentality, although drawing attention to the school anthem recognizes the possibility of affectionate longing for the college mater. Much as sentimental verses of "Roses are red, Violets

Fig. 5.4. Lorado Taft's Alma Mater sculpture, at the University of Illinois, unveiled on Alumni Day, June 11, 1929, was inspired by the university's hymn with the themes of learning and labor. Behind the lead maternal figure in scholastic robes "generously greeting her children" are the twin characters of Labor and Learning joining hands. The inscription at the base is "To thy happy children of the future, those of the past send greetings." (Author's collection)

are blue, Sugar is sweet, and so are you" expressing affection for one's mates upon moving to another stage became ritually parodied in schoolchildren's autograph books in the twentieth century with "Roses are red, Violets are blue, You look like a monkey, And you smell like one too," mockery of the alma mater in the college years creates an emotional detachment in preparation for separation (Bronner 1989, 83–94). A difference with the alma mater is the extra symbolism of the child breaking away from the "dear mother," thus showing the maturity and passage effected by the college experience. Modernist revisions to make the lyrics egalitarian have apparently accentuated the aggression of the parodies.

Rivals, Their Women, and Aggies

One way to show loyalty, or college spirit, to one's alma mater is to deride the school's chief rival. At many universities, riddle-jokes abound to demean regional rivals, and students occasionally turn them on their own schools. The sources of derision are typically the rival's lack of sophistication, brains, or career.

What's the difference between yogurt and Davis? Yogurt has culture.

What's an Indiana University martini? A beer with an olive.

How many Purdue students does it take to screw in a lightbulb? One, but he gets three credits for it!

How do you get a Pitt graduate off your porch? Pay him for the pizza.

What is the only sign of intelligent life in Bloomington [Indiana]? West Lafayette [Purdue]—187 miles.

The joke on the diminished likelihood of success for a rival can also be set up with some straight answers:

What does a Penn State engineering graduate say? How does it work?

What does a Penn State accounting graduate say? How much does it cost?

What does a Penn State marketing graduate say? Who can we sell it to?

What does a Temple graduate say? Do you want fries with that? ("School Rivalry" 2006)

Jokes in narrative form frequently turn on the "rube revealed" motif. For example, students at Temple University, a state-related institution in Philadelphia, like to tell the story about one of their own on a flight with a grad from Penn, an Ivy League school in the same city, who had the seat next to him. Halfway through the flight, the Temple guy says, "Hey, you must be a graduate of Penn." The Penn alum replies, "Why, yes I am. How could you tell? Was it my wit, my sophistication, my savoir faire?" The Temple fellow says, "Nope. I saw your class ring while you were picking your nose" ("School Rivalry" 2006; cf. Beezley 1981, 112; Best 1976, 4; Mitchell 1976, 480–81).

Aware of the glut of rivalry jokes, the following numskull story refers to the joking tradition in a self-referential form that could be called metafolklore because it is a traditional narrative about the meaning of joking:

A group of Indiana University backpackers were sitting around a campfire one dark evening when a stranger asked to join them. Glad to have the company, they agreed. Soon the conversation turned to jokes, and one of the camping group started to tell jokes with Kentucky being the butt of jokes. The stranger who apparently graduated from Kentucky got angrier and angrier at each joke. So he finally had enough and pulled out his razor and began to threaten the group with it. Fortunately for the jokester, the stranger couldn't find an outlet to plug it into. ("School Rivalry" 2006)

Tellers sometimes change the setting to a bar or hunting camp, other social frames where camaraderie is expected. The act of joking should bond the gathered group, but instead the stranger takes offense. In the punch line, he shows his true numskull colors, and the implication is that the fiction of the jokes about the stereotypical stupidity of Kentucky grads is not absurd. I should note, though, that the story can easily be reversed so that the Indiana (or other neighboring rival) stranger is the butt of the joke.

A raft of jokes embodying the rival school's problem is exemplified by the character and appearance of its women. Perhaps most common among the riddle-joke variety is the question, "Why doesn't State put Astroturf in the stadium?" The answer, drawing a comparison to an unattractive cow, is "Because they wouldn't have a place for the homecoming queen to graze." University of North Carolina students ask about the difference between a North Carolina State coed and a trash can. The answer? Trash gets taken out once a week (Costner 1975, 111). North Carolina State students meanwhile inquire, "What do you call a good-looking girl at Carolina?" A visitor (Beezley 1981, 114). Coeds at rival schools presumably compensate for their ugliness with sexual aggressiveness. University of Washington students pose this question: "What's the first thing Washington State girls do in the morning?" Pack up their things and go home. They also ask, "Why do Washington State coeds wear bibs?" So they don't get tobacco juice on their overalls when they spit. But State students might reply, "Why couldn't they hold a Christmas pageant at the University of Washington?" They couldn't find three wise men or a virgin (cf. Boswell 1976, 78; Beezley 1981, 115; Costner 1975, 111).

Similar barbs are hurled by students from women's colleges. Wellesley women smear their rivals as sluts with the joking question, "What's the difference between a Smithie and a Ferrari?" Most men haven't been in a Ferrari (Birnbach 1984, 182). At Hood, one might hear "Goucher to bed, Hood to wed," while Goucher women say the reverse (cf. Carey 1988, 8). Or suggesting a suspicion about the economic-class background of women, the story is told about the carload of a rival's fans who were late for the game because they saw a sign advertising "clean restrooms" and stayed to do the job.

If one of the rivals is an agricultural college, its supposedly hardy men may be accused of bestiality, and its field-toughened women may be taunted for having masculine traits. The university men known for their intellectual snobbery, rather than manual labor, may be accused of being effeminate or gay. University of North Carolina (UNC) students, for example, are fond of taunting North Carolina State as a place where the men are men and the sheep are all nervous. UNC is meanwhile described as a place where the women are women and so are the men (cf. Mechling and Wilson 1988, 310–11; Birnbach 1984, 82; Wyman 1979, 82; Egan 1985, 128). And "how do they separate the men from the boys at North Carolina?" With a crowbar (Beezley 1981, 114). "Why did the guy from State marry the cow?" a UNC student may ask, and supply the answer, "Because he had to" (Costner 1975, 108). The reply to this insult from the North Carolina State student might be "better ag than fag" (Beezley 1981, 114).

A whole sheaf of jokes, often built on numskull motifs, concerns Texas Aggies. As a book from Texas A&M professed, "The Texas institution that is talked about and bragged about—in addition to being joked about—perhaps more than any other is the Texas Aggie. Because Texas Aggies are not like the rest of the world (thank goodness), the 'Aggie joke' has become a part of the folklore of Texas A&M. People talk about Aggies because they are different, and Aggies are proud of it. Aggies tend to be 'a little bit square'" (Adams 2000, 4). The story is told, for example, about two Aggies who climbed a tree at the border of a nudist colony so they could see in. "Why you can't even tell the men from the women," one exclaimed. The other replied, "That's because they don't have any clothes on" (Mitchell 1976, 518). In a similar formula with moronic logic, the news is shared of the drowning of four Aggies riding in a pickup truck: "How's that? They couldn't get the tail-gate down" ("School Rivalry" 2006; cf. "little moron" jokes in Bronner 1989, 119–20; Davidson 1943; Leventhal and Cray 1963, 162; Sims 1944; Wolfenstein 1978, 131–38).

Usually told by students at the University of Texas, many Aggie jokes parallel the style of ethnic slurs, such as "What do you call 144 Aggies in a room?" Gross stupidity (Mitchell 1976, 711; cf. Clements 1969b, type E1.3; Dundes 1987a, 134–35; Baker 1986, 109–24). Around many offices, emails circulate that contain a string of joking questions that start out, "Did you hear about the Aggie who . . . ?" Among the listed lines that complete the question are: "studied five days to take a urine test," "took a roll of toilet paper to the crap game," and "thought 'no kidding' meant birth control" (cf. Boswell 1976, 81–82; Bronner 1989, 119–20; Davidson 1943, 101–4; Sims 1944, 155–61).

Aggies may offer this rejoinder: "What do you call an Aggie five years after he has taken his first job?" Boss! (Adams 1979, 3). Or they may tell about the Aggie who got into a boasting match with some natives on a visit to Alaska. "We may not be the biggest state in the Union anymore, but we're still the toughest," declared the Aggie. The Alaskan laughed and said, "We Alaskans can't be beat. Every man here can drink a fifth of whiskey in one gulp, wrestle a grizzly bear bare, and make love to an Eskimo woman all in one night." "Shucks, any Aggie can do that," huffed the Aggie. So he downed a fifth of whiskey, and went looking for a bear. A few hours later, the Aggie staggered back with his clothes in tatters and bruises all over his body. "Okay men," bellowed the Aggie, "now where's that woman you want me to wrestle?" (Best 1976, 11; see also Badhshah 2004, 97–98; Rovin 1987, 115).

Several jokes making the rounds refer to prejudice against the Aggies presumably because the name is associated with images of rubes and dirt as a result of their agricultural label (cf. the description of the UC-Davis Aggies in Mechling and Wilson 1988, 303–17). In one, a University of Texas student approached St. Peter at the gate to heaven. St. Peter greeted him warmly, and said, "Welcome to heaven. We have a simple entrance exam here. Spell God." He spelled it with no problem. A student from Southern Methodist approached, and he took the same exam, which he passed. Then the Aggie came. "We have a simple entrance exam here in heaven," said St. Peter. "Spell Nacogdoches" (*Best* 1976, 151; for references to persecuted ethnic groups such as Mexicans and African Americans filling the slot of the Aggie, see Knott 1982, 47–48; Potter 1979, 48–49; Xavier 2004, 118). Aggies take the message to be that they have to be united and even more spirited about their special (or persecuted) minority identity.

In a variation of the theme, an Aggie, a T-Sipper (a derisive term for snobs from the University of Texas), and an Oklahoma Sooner were survivors on a wrecked ship in the middle of the ocean. When a helicopter came to rescue them, the pilot said, "There's only room for two. The two who answer my questions correctly can come aboard." The Sooner received the first question, "What was the famous ship that went down when it hit an iceberg?" The Sooner replied, "The *Titanic*." Next the pilot asked the T-Sipper, "How many people died on it?" The T-Sipper smugly answered, "1,517." The third question was for the Aggie: "Name them!" (*Best* 1976, 164; see also Burns 1976, 52; Galanter 2005, 105; Singh 2004, 28).

Texas A&M is not the only state university to show a bit of inferiority complex when compared with other colleges. One example is a parody of a "Dear Abby" letter. "I have two brothers," the text begins, and then there are many variations, but it might follow like this one from my archives. "One attends Penn State University and the other was sent to the electric chair. Mother died in an insane asylum. Since I was three years old, my father has had a narcotics problem. One of my sisters is a successful and highly paid prostitute, the other is the common law wife of a local executive of the Mafia. Recently I met a wonderful girl (shortly after she was released from prison for smothering her illegitimate child). We are very much in love and expect to be married just as soon as her venereal disease clears up. My problem is, should I tell her about my brother who attends Penn State?" (cf. Clements 1969b, type L5.10; Beezley 1981, 113; *Best* 1976, 144; Boswell 1976, 79; Dundes and Pagter 1978, 15–16; Walton and Wilkinson 1981).

Many jokes compare the various responses of students from different colleges in a region. In northern California, students told me that in response to a professor's greeting of "Good morning," a University of California at Davis class writes the greeting down. At Stanford, the reply is "Good morning professor." At the University of California at Berkeley the class retorts, "Hey, don't lay your trips on me!" A variation is told in New England where Smith students typically write down the greeting, Mount Holyoke students stand up and salute, students at Amherst bark back "Prove it," and those at the University of Massachusetts inquire, "Will that be on the final exam?" Finally, the students at Hampshire look at one another and say, "Hey man, far out!" (Carey 1988, 6–7).

In a similar vein, raconteurs talk about a test of Ivy League chivalry in reaction to a pretty woman entering a room. A "Yale man" asks if someone else should bring a chair for her. The "Princeton man" dramatically brings one, and the "Harvard man" sits in it (Copeland and Copeland 1940, 407). The Indiana University Folklore Archives contains similar comparisons in the vein of an Indiana student shuffling his feet, the one from Purdue asking her for a date, and the fellow from Notre Dame phoning the coach for instructions.

Some rivalry jokes are metafolklore by virtue of being *about* rivalry jokes. For example, there is the story of an ardent Auburn fan who overhead two Alabama graduates telling Auburn jokes. Just as the 'Bama grad was starting another joke, the Auburn grad interrupted and said, "Just a minute, buster. It so happens I'm a graduate of Auburn University." "In that case," the 'Bama grad said, "I'll tell it slowly" (Walton and Wilkinson 1981). The story serves to say that joking drives as well as reflects the rivalry. So familiar is the repartee that a popularly prearranged routine opens with "Have you heard the latest Auburn joke?" often in the company of people in a car. "Shhh," warns one of the passengers. "There's one riding in this car" (Walton and Wilkinson 1981).

Many jokes concerning traditional southern rivals such as Auburn and Alabama or Mississippi and Mississippi State refer to the schools' agrarian surroundings. One plays upon scatological references to play up the rivalry in earthy terms:

A man was driving along a country highway when his interest was sparked by the sight of an antenna on an outhouse. He stopped his car in front of a rickety farmhouse. On the porch was a farmer rocking back and forth and spitting tobacco. "I'm kind of curious," said the traveler. "Could you tell me what an antenna is doing on top of an outhouse?"

"Well, I tell ye," said the farmer, "I've been rentin' that room to two of the Auburn students."

On his return trip, the traveler was once again overcome with curiosity. Now there were two antennas on the outhouse. He stopped the car and asked the farmer the reason for the second antenna.

"Them Auburn boys got mighty smart," said the farmer. "Why, they went and rented out the lower floor to two Bama students." (Walton and Wilkinson 1981)

The narrative suggests a source of the rivalry jokes in the similarity of the collegiate identities, and indeed, the story can be easily adapted to make the other school the butt of the joke. The narrative constructs difference out of two similarly spirited institutions.

Although apparently localized, many tale types known more widely for ethnic putdowns are adapted into collegiate rivalry jokes. With students often relating themselves to animals who are tamed (and cleaned up) by the civilizing process of education, one migratory narrative that has persisted in college lore degrades the rival for being dirty or smelly: "A contest was being held to see who could stay in a pig pen the longest by students from Alabama, Georgia, and Auburn. On the first day the Bama student left, the Georgia student left on the second day, and on the third day, the pig left" (Baughman 1966, motif X691.5.1*; Clements 1969b, Polack Joke Type G4.4; Baker 1986, 120; Bronner 1989, 141–42; Buehler 1964, 154–55; Walton and Wilkinson 1981). Many stories with the motif of the pig leaving because it cannot stand the odor of the student feature ridiculed ethnic or national characters. The implication of the insult is that the derided figure is subhuman. In the collegiate context, the story's substitution of institutional affiliations suggests the university identity is a mark for life.

A "field test" of ability in many college rivalry jokes is in hunting and fishing, particularly because of the popular image of setting out on one's own against the forces of nature. The allusion is to the lone student able to make his or her way around the strange grounds of the campus. The narrative setting of the woods or lake also raises questions of whether the "nature" attributed to students on the institutional grounds carries over to the ageless environment. Mississippi State students, for example, might relate the story of two Ole Miss students finding some tracks while hunting. They followed them for some time until a train ran over them (Clements 1969b, Polack Joke Type E5.7.1; Walton and Wilkinson 1980).

A Mississippi student might come back with the story of the Ole Miss and State guys out hunting. Suddenly a gorgeous young woman emerges from the bushes. The pair of ogling hunters are stunned and stare silently at each other in disbelief. Finally, the State guy asks, "Are you game?" "Why yes," she sexily replies. So the State guy shoots her (Clements 1969b, Polack Joke Type E5.7.2; Walton and Wilkinson 1980). Or if the image of an Ole Miss and State student hunting together is unbelievable to listeners, a teller might relate the joke of two State hunters who come upon a pile that looks suspiciously like excrement. One says, "I know, I'll taste it to make sure of what it is." "Yep, that's crap all right, and we sure are lucky we didn't step in it!" (Clements 1969b, Polack Joke Type E6.9).

Presuming the familiarity of rival coaches of rival institutions, students like to emphasize the diminished intelligence of the "other" school in another country "field test" of fishing. The way Mississippi State tellers relate the story, the State and Ole Miss coaches find a place on a lake where the fish are plentiful. All day long the fish are biting, and they pull up fish after fish. They decide that they had better find a way to mark the spot for a later time. "I know," says the State coach, "we'll just put an 'X' right here on the side of the boat." "Now, that's stupid," replies the Ole Miss coach. "We might not even get this same boat next time!" (Baughman 1966, motif J1922.1; Clements 1969b, Polack Joke Type E5.6.2; Uther 2004, Tale Type 1278, 2:97–98; Baker 1986, 115; Walton and Wilkinson 1980).

Fishing stories thematize a simple task into the life lesson of an elementary food-chain relationship: humans above the water reel in fish below them. In college lore, fondness for fishing implies being admirably down to earth, "naturally" secure in one's environment, and confident in one's role within it. The inability in various fishing stories to recognize the harmony of humans to their surroundings signals a problem. An example of a joke pointing this out is about the Arizona State University (ASU) diehards driving through the desert outside Phoenix complaining about how everyone makes fun of Sun Devil fans. They come across a guy in a rowboat wearing Sun Devil gear trying to row across the sand. The driver stops, gets out of his car, and yells out, "What the hell you doing?" The guy in the boat shakes his head and answers, "What does it look like I'm doing you dumbshit, I'm fishing." Astounded, the ASU guy on the road exclaims, "It's ignorant guys like you who give ASU a bad name." The fellow in the rowboat shoots back, "Oh yeah, what are you going to do about it?" The driver screams, "If I could swim, I'd come over there and kick your ass!" (Zanes 2010; cf. Kentucky and blonde jokes in Boyd 2011; Nunn 2007).

Rivals on the Court and Field

Sports, as the most visible part of the university to the public, figure prominently in stories showing the superiority of a school in collegiate rivalries. For many rivalries, the sports field becomes a way to settle the dispute between effete "snobs" at the state university and the dumb "hicks" at the land-grant or agricultural college. The nation has many of these fierce rivalries, including those between North Carolina and North Carolina State, Michigan and Michigan State, and Washington and Washington State. The story is told, too, about the Texas A&M coach who resorted to prayer to reverse his team's fortune on the playing field. His Aggies beat Baylor and SMU by big margins on successive weekends. Appealing to God once again before the big game against the Texas Longhorns, the Aggies' bitter rival, the coach came out on the field full of confidence. But the Aggies lost 99 to 0. After the game, the coach beseeched his Maker, "Why, oh Lord, did you let us down this time?" Black storm clouds gathered in the sky, a streak of lightning flashed, and a deep, solemn voice boomed, "Hook 'Em Horns" (*Best* 1976, 12–13; cf. Baker 1982, 173).

Although football reigns as the mass spectacles for rivals to settle their score with one another, college basketball arenas have steadily grown as a festive venue, particularly around tournament time when "March Madness" sweeps America. With many arenas holding upward of 20,000 fans in close quarters, the indoor setting can give rise to major carrying-on. At Notre Dame, the first basket by the Fighting Irish is rewarded by a storm of confetti from the student section. Spirited types at a number of venues might wear a basketball shell, sometimes complete with a small hoop, over the head. Students paint their faces and chests in school colors and vigorously wave cloths. Fans in the student section also try to distract opposing players, waving Styrofoam noodles and shouting when a foul shot is taken, taunting a player who missed the rim on a jump shot by repeatedly chanting in unison "air ball, air ball." Fans also mimic the "high-five" hand slaps and fist bumps used by the players on the court.

Traditions involving boisterous fan celebration are not restricted to big arenas. Taylor University in Upland, Indiana, with fewer than 2,000 students, plays up its "Silent Night" game every year on the Friday before fall semester finals week begins. Pajama- and Skivvies-clad fans pack the campus's Odle Arena and remain deathly silent until Taylor scores its tenth point. Then the crowd erupts. Students scream and jump, throw confetti, and jovially carry on for several minutes. They then lock arms around each other's waists and sway back and forth while singing "Silent Night." After the game, students attend a campuswide Christmas party, listen to the school president read a Christmas story, and compete in gingerbread house and cookie-decorating competitions. Not all rival coaches appreciate the tradition, but the school's sports information director defends it as "one of the premier events on our campus. . . . It's become one of the things you can't miss as a student" (Norlander 2010).

In the televised era of mass spectator sports, many rivalry jokes concern the behavior of fans. Michigan Staters tell about the easygoing Spartan student who went to the lavatory at Michigan's stadium. He passed by some snooty Michigan fans on his way to the urinal. When he was done, he turned to leave the facility. The Michigan fans stopped him, and one scolded, "I don't know the way they do things at State, but here we wash our hands after we urinate." The Michigan Stater quickly replied, "Well, where I come from they teach us not to piss in our hands!" (cf. Beezley 1981, 112; *Best* 1976, 150; Jacoby 2008, 679; Levine

1992, 47–48). The story can also be told with three regional characters, in this case from the vantage of a Georgia Tech partisan:

> Three graduates are peeing in a bathroom. The University of Georgia graduate finishes, goes over and washes his hands very well using lots of soap and water, and says "at UGA, they teach us to be clean." The Clemson graduate finishes peeing, and washes his hands with a very small amount of soap and water and says "at Clemson they teach us how to conserve resources." The Georgia Tech graduate finishes and walks right toward the door. On his way out he says "At Tech they teach us not to piss on our hands." (Wilkinson 2004; see also Thripshaw 2010, 556; and Baum 2010, 162 for reference to being "environmentally conscious")

Although the joke is frequently told about various closely matched rivals, the implication is often that one has a reputation for being snooty, and the school accused of being unsanitary, that is, beneath the other school's standards, soils the rival.

At Indiana University, students say that Purdue fans wanted to tell everyone they were number one, but they could not figure out how many fingers to hold up (Walton and Wilkinson 1977). Purdue students meanwhile hung photocopied sheets and then blog posts blaring "Not All Indiana Fans Are Assholes," under which is a drawing of a fan with a face strangely resembling a man's genitals. In the cyber age, Facebook pages such as "I Bet This Outhouse Can Get More Fans Than Purdue" and "Can This Outhouse Get More Fans than the Texas Longhorns" create long threads of traditional dirt for students to ritually fling. The outhouse humor is thick with directions to the rival's stadium: go west until you smell it and south 'til you step in it (Browning 2003, 95; Emmanual 2004, 170; Flippo 1975, 48; Oates 1999, 247).

Emails with humor are also forwarded that look like news reports (see Frank 2011, 180–95). Ripping a headline from the newspaper about law enforcement authorities checking out suspicious powdery substances left in public places, the text reports that the FBI has been called out to a football stadium or that a practice has been delayed pending an investigation of a report of a strange white material on the field. According to the report, team members who called in the report had never seen anything like it before. The authorities find that it is the goal line (Green 2006, 4:230–31; "School Rivalry" 2006).

Jokes about athletes, coaches, and fans address the importance of sports in big-time colleges. In many jokes, sports figures evade or triumph over the academic mission of the university. For many tellers, the stories thus carry a mixed message. The stories illustrate the public notoriety of sports for the campus as a source of pride and spirit for students, yet also demonstrate the abuses that reflect badly on the college's attention to the needs of students. At bottom, the stories about sports, usually told at large universities, are about the incorporation of the big-time colleges. Apparently driven by the profit motive, administrations have, according to the nonvarsity students, exploited sports as much as athletes have exploited the colleges.

A common way to demoralize one's college rival in sports is to kidnap the mascot and then fervidly spread stories about it. A North Carolina State alum recalled the following pranks pulled on rival North Carolina: "I think it was 1941 or 1942 when the football games with UNC featured a freshman team game one week and the varsity game the next. A group of State students kidnapped the UNC ram. The UNC administration threatened to cancel the varsity game if the Ram was not returned. He was sheared and dyed with good textile dye—red on the head end and blue on the other" (Beezley 1981, 114). When security for mascots tightened, students bought paint to get their message across. In a legendary incident after the Franklin and Marshall–Lehigh game in 1948, students whitewashed "F&M" over walkways and awakened the Lehigh student body in the middle of the night (Brubaker 1987, 131). Collegians might also go after an opposing school's statuary. At USC, the statue of the USC Trojan is wrapped in plastic before the UCLA-USC game to protect it from crosstown raiders.

Threats of kidnapping are part of the intrigue of rivalries between the military academies. An event that has lingered in legend is the kidnapping of Navy's Bill the Goat by West Point cadets a week before the Army-Navy football game in 1953. According to the humorously elaborated story, the cadets grabbed the goat from behind the stadium and stuffed it in the backseat of a convertible. The plot was foiled when they stopped at a gas station and the goat's horns shredded the convertible top. Army cadets raided the Naval Academy dairy farm before the 2007 game to nab several Bills and in a digital-age twist posted their escapade on YouTube. Showing their military spirit, the cadets dubbed the successful maneuver "Operation Good Shepherd" (Robacabras 2007). The video sparked a host of memorable comments, including the legendary account in answer to the question of why Army's mascot mule is not as vulnerable. The answer? "The last time Navy tried to capture the Mule it kicked the side out of the trailer and escaped" according to TomBrooklyn. Studinthemaking snidely wrote, "Glad to know that 4 years of school and 150,000 $ of money we spent training you all paid off!" to which the poster replied, "It paid off well, it was a well executed operation that resulted in the capture of all three goats. If you want to be bitter it's actually closer to $500,000." Mo15094 summed up, "The Army/Navy rivalry is good spirited fun."

Some digital-age heists have an electronic twist. At Yale, Davenport and Pierson residential colleges have long been fierce rivals. "D'porters," as they are known in folk speech, have a beloved gnome mascot the residents thought was immune from theft because of its hefty weight of 300 pounds. Originally brought by a student to decorate his room in 1997, the statue was donated to the college and given reverence by students as the college mascot in 1999. On an April morning in 2010, Pierson students awoke to an email announcing the successful removal of the gnome from Davenport and subsequent placement on the Pierson roof adorned in a bright yellow freshman "move-in day" Pierson T-shirt. Once news spread about the burglary, a war of emails erupted. A group of Davenport residents urged their fellows to spam the more than 400 Piersonians to return the gnome. Pierson administrators brought the mascot back to its prominent location of the dining hall server, where residents can keep an eye out for it. Residents cared for, and maybe fetishized, the mascot all the more as a result of its absence. "It's like having your little brother stolen," a student commented, indicating the role of the mascot in emblematizing a social as well as institutional connection (Gasso 2010).

Spirit Clubs

Whereas spirit in the old-time college was considered a quality that arose spontaneously on campus, many universities institutionalized it with the organization of student "spirit clubs." Much of their activity revolves around sporting events, but they will also take responsibility for maintaining campus traditions. Hillsdale College's Spirit Club, for example, states that the group's mission is "encouraging game attendance, reviving traditions and hosting events that bring the campus together through Charger spirit and pride" (Spirit Club 2007–9). Some spirit clubs (also organized as squads or teams) costume themselves in cheerleading and dance outfits and entertain, or "spiritlead," at home football and basketball games. Additionally, they compete in state and national competitions with elaborate choreographed routines involving cheers, gymnastic and dance movements, and formations.

Student-activities officers often tell club leaders that they all embody college spirit by virtue of their organizing student participation on campus. At Daytona State College, the student government sponsors Spirit Wars to epitomize this view. Often these intracampus competitions feature games that can involve everyone. The highlight of Daytona State's was a relay contest to move water only with the help of a sponge from a garbage can in the center of the campus square to a small bucket. Hilarity ensues as participants inevitably get soaked in the commotion.

Off campus, spirit clubs mean something different from the cheerleading and dance crews on campus. They often comprise alumni who gather for television "Watch Parties" with appropriate accessories for members. One such club for Nebraska Cornhuskers in Pennsylvania gathered for a football game with oversized foam hats in the shape of corn, red beer to root on "Big Red," and a full set of plates emblazoned with Nebraska logos.

Many spirit squads include a mascot who also runs through traditional routines. Perhaps the most dramatic since its inception in 1978 is Florida State's Chief Osceola riding atop a horse named Renegade. The chief is supposed to embody the renegade spirit of the Seminole people that is transferred over to the university's football team. The chief and horse gallop into Florida State's Doak Campbell Stadium, and the chief hurls a burning spear at midfield to begin every home game. To show the special rivalry with the University of Florida, when the football team plays Florida, Chief Osceola jumps off the horse before hurling the spear. At USC, a classically dressed Trojan warrior rides Traveller, a white horse that serves as the mascot. Introduced in 1961, Traveller gallops around the track after every USC score in a football game and pumps up the crowd. At the University of Oklahoma, the Sooner Schooner, a covered wagon pulled by matching white ponies named Boomer and Sooner, takes a victory lap. It first appeared in 1964 and became the school's official mascot in 1980.

LSU's Mike the Tiger appears as the real thing in a cage on wheels and as a costumed character. At home football games, the cheerleaders, Mike the Tiger, and the Golden Band from Tigerland march down a hill between Tiger Stadium and the Assembly Center prior to the kickoff. In a grand show of spirit, thousands of fans line up on both sides of the road to cheer for the LSU Tigers. The cheerleaders park Mike's cage on wheels by the opponent's locker room at the southeast end of the Tiger Stadium. According to tradition, LSU will score a touchdown for every one of his roars on game day. The buildup to a game with a march or ritual walk is hardly unique. The University of Southern Mississippi is proud of its "Eagle Walk" tradition. Eagle Walk Drive is converted into a street of gold every fall with a fresh coat of gold paint. Two-and-a-half hours before every home kickoff, a cannon is fired, and the marching band strikes up "Southern Miss to the Top!" as the Golden Eagles march into the stadium. To welcome the team at the beginning of the second half, children form a human tunnel called the "spirit line."

Spirit clubs take a leading role in promoting student frenzy at pep rallies on Friday nights before home football games. Among the best known is Notre Dame's, known for the marching band's trumpet section playing inside the Golden Dome and a drumline formed at midnight to lead students in cheers. The college mascot of the Leprechaun, along with the cheerleaders decked out in green uniforms, incites the crowd in what many observers view as a "throwback to yesteryear" because of its total campus involvement (Lost Lettermen 2010).

At Texas A&M, the night before the game is devoted to yell practice. In a loud demonstration of spirit, elected yell leaders use various hand signals that coincide with different yells to guide the fans. Helping to make yelling popular is the tradition of "mugging down," meaning kissing one's date at the Midnight Yell before the game and every time the Aggies score points during the game.

The organization and intervention of spirit clubs raise questions about the perception of tradition as a factor in forming campus unity. The work of the spirit clubs suggests organizational needs to appropriate the label of tradition for types of activities that reinforce the institution rather than allow spontaneous student customs that threaten to subvert it. Social theorist Eric Hobsbawm offered "invented tradition" to describe a process within modern societies of rule-governed practices that "seek to inculcate certain values and norms of behavior by repetition, which automatically implies continuity with the past" (1983, 1). The infusion of invented traditions does not mean that old ways or grassroots movements are no longer available or viable, but that organizations desire to formalize or idealize their relationships to constituents and legitimize themselves (Hobsbawm 1983, 8). The appeal of invented traditions is the promised consequence of socially engaging community, and emotion or "spirit," which will temper the alienating effects of enlarging bureaucratic structures. Hobsbawm emphasized the artificiality, and often ideology formation, of invented traditions and the tendency of these practices to wrongly displace, diminish, or politicize "authentic" customs (see also Becker 1998; Cantwell 1991; Handler and Linnekin 1984).

Another view that is especially evident in the self-conscious defense of spirit clubs and their appeal to, and sometimes manipulation of, tradition is that they facilitate social connection among disparate participants and cultural expression of identity. Spirit club members prefer the message that a feeling for tradition as a way to belong and act on campus would suffer if they were not involved. Yet they embody "symbols in tension" because their very existence is an admission that spirit deriving from tradition, or their version of it, has been weakened by modernization (see Mechling and Wilson 1988). In their opinion, spirit leaders generate action that might otherwise lay fallow in an individualistic, mass society. They resist the idea that they control or politicize spirit; they rather see it as boosting and framing it in social scenes that instill pride in one's subcultural affiliation. Taking this perspective, spirit clubs extend the praxis of organizing and symbol-making inherent in the performance of folklore (see Jones 1991; Jones, Moore, and Snyder 1988). They act on behalf of the institution, and work to validate its norms and values, although to be accepted they constantly need to counter the perception that they are authoritarian or anachronistic (see Beyer and Trice 1988). In exercising agency by forging a large-scale corporate identity even as they evoke a sense of "old-fashioned" subcultural spirit, community, and tradition, they reveal symbols in tension. The social frames the clubs establish for visceral, exuberant behavior—at rallies and events—work to contain these ambiguities by encouraging emotional expression and drawing attention away from the "club" to the desirable action.

Generating spirit has become a ritual specialty on campuses, often related to drumming up support for football and basketball teams. The spirit leaders exaggerate the role of spirit with dramatic performances involving being thrown with elaborate gymnastic flips, forming dangerous human pyramids, and riveting crowds with rousing dance numbers. The spirit leaders serve to uphold and even invent traditions that build an active devotion to campus as a totalizing identity. As campuses have become less bounded physically, and grown and democratized, spirit leaders vie with other loyalty or interest builders in an open market. The rhetoric of spirit extends to adolescent passions not just for the university brand but also for multiple pursuits of social belonging. In representing both the old-time college communalism and mega-university incorporation, traditions of college spirit exhibit the contradictions of campus as both natural and artificial, cultural and institutional space.

CHAPTER

CAMPUS EVENTS

Holidays, Games, and Sports

BENEATH THE JESTS ABOUT GOING TO COLLEGE BEING A WILDLY "GOOD time" and delaying "real work" (and responsibility) is anxiety about getting away from the safe haven of home or embarking on a daunting new endeavor. With reference to their dormitories and distractions, institutions of higher education present themselves as places for immersive study and personal growth apart from the child or adult worlds. The environmental description of "campuses" gives another kind of separation: the college from surrounding towns. Away from home, away from family and friends, in the competitive pursuit of learning, students on campus are set out on their own—and naturally seek other young, kindred spirits. And they have more of those same-age fellow travelers in and out of class than they ever had in high school or will later in life. A host of games, rituals, and festivals promote social bonding, cultural growth, and self-development in the process. In the old-time college, students often took charge of their festive needs as members of a select society, but in the modern mega-university, administrations keep a watchful eye over student activities or else students fend for themselves, often under the illusion that as modern iconoclasts they need no bonding or bridging. Their folklore often proves otherwise.

Halloween

More than other holidays, Halloween on many campuses brings out student high jinks. In collegiate history, it was traditionally a time of costume parades, parties, and pranks, tolerated because the holiday marked not only the time when nights get longer and colder but also when the harsh realities of exams and studies set in (Curley 2005, 142; Walden 1987). At Stetson University, memorable stunts at Halloween included toilet-papering the campus and moving vehicles up onto the tower of Elizabeth Hall (Lycan 1983, 151). At

James Madison University, students organized a mass wedding ceremony on Halloween of about 100 people to bananas (Applebaum, McNally, and Pittman 2006, 93). For most campuses, as folklorist Jack Santino observed, "Halloween meant a masquerade party," frequently featuring cross-dressing, supernatural, and sexual themes (1994, xxv).

One cannot forget the pumpkins on campus at Halloween, not so much as a decoration as one might find on front porches but as ritually messy performances of disorder. A continuing tradition at Butler University is a long procession of men in white bedsheets entering the dormitory courtyard behind a leader carrying a pumpkin. The hooded figures form a circle around the leader, who murmurs eerie incantations. The crowd is hushed. The leader ceremoniously pulls a baseball bat from beneath his sheet and smashes the pumpkin to a pulp to the delight of a large gathered crowd. At Muir College, students cheer the dropping of a mammoth pumpkin from the eleventh story of Tioga Hall. When the conspicuous orange globe splatters, a load of candies discharges for the students to pick up ("25 Craziest College Traditions" 2011).

At Transylvania, appropriately, students ghoulishly celebrate Rafinesque Day around Halloween. The day is named for Constantine Samuel Rafinesque (1783–1840), a professor of natural history and botany known for eccentricities and unceremoniously storming out of town for good in 1826 after a tiff with the college president. Supposedly this foreigner left a curse on the college, and students to this day tell the story that shortly thereafter, the president died and the college burned. Transylvania students came up with a "tomb" for Rafinesque (actually he was cremated, and the remains there are someone else's) in Old Morrison hall, a place for tellings of spooky stories about the irascible prof. On Rafinesque Day, students build a bonfire, and dressed as undertakers, solemnly carry a black coffin around the fire, against a background chorus of blood-curdling screams from classmates (Boewe 1987).

Christmas

The old-college calendar typically started later than today's popular early semester system, so students were still in school up to, and sometimes after, Christmas. Denominational schools, especially, came up with communal festivities for the event. Typically these festivities involved special meals and lighting ceremonies for trees and Yule logs. At Oglethorpe University, trumpets still sound in each quadrangle as a summons to Christmas dinner. Students carry a roasted boar's head on a silver tray accompanied by a procession and singers into the college hall. The provost presents the chief singer with the orange from the boar's mouth, and then distributes among the company the bay leaves, rosemary, and holly springs from the tray. The school explains this tradition with a reference to a medieval legend about an English student attacked by a wild boar. The student was reading Aristotle and rammed his book down the throat of the animal, thus using wisdom to conquer "even the treacherous beast." Victorious over the boar, the student brought the animal, Aristotle and all, to the college cook for Christmas dinner. Belief spread that diners grew wiser with every bite. Today, the dinner at the small school of about 1,000 students reaffirms that the college is a close-knit community.

At the University of Findlay and at Juniata College, what made the Christmas banquet special for many years was that faculty members served students. At Hollins University, faculty members come unannounced to student residences and sing Christmas songs. Several Christmas festivities, including a dinner for students, are annually held at Mary Baldwin College in Staunton, Virginia. Prior to the dinner, seniors dedicate the Christmas tree to a Mary Baldwin family in need of the college's support. Reaching out to the community, students also sponsor "Christmas Cheer," consisting of carol singing and a reception on the candlelit campus. A similar event occurs at Stetson University every year. Called by the chimes in Hulley Tower, nearly 500 students sing carols by candlelight and let a Yule log burn away the troubles of the past year. Out West, such things are done big, and Western Oregon University holds a ceremony claiming to light the nation's largest Christmas tree, a 122 ½-foot giant sequoia—until a storm in 1972 took away the top 9 feet.

Back at the dorms before Christmas, one is likely to run across "Secret Santa" customs. Students in a hall draw names of residents for whom they will serve as Secret Santa. As Santas, the students do good deeds for, or bestow small gifts on, the person they selected, but the identity of the do-gooder is kept secret until a party just before Christmas. In his ethnographic foray into a Rutgers dorm, Michael Moffatt thought at first that the Secret Santa custom was too innocent for the enthusiasm it generated among students who view themselves as iconoclastic and wild. His observation was that the custom in coeducational settings had a sexual undertone framed by the jollity of performance sessions applying the license of carnivalesque Halloween and Mardi Gras masquerades. In his report, "To get each gift . . . you had to meet a challenge; you had to perform an embarrassing stunt, sometimes in public outside the dorm, more often in informal performance sessions held in front of your floor friends in one of the lounges two or three evenings during the Secret Santa week. . . . Transvestite males. Nearly nude females and males. Other outlandish costumes and carryings-on. Mardi Gras! Carnival!" (Moffatt 1989, 104). In the work cycle of the semester under the cover of fun, "it was widely considered to enhance floor sociability at a time when the beginning-of-year friendliness had petered out" (Moffatt 1986, 171). A shy young man was challenged to take a shower in the women's room while singing "I'm a Virgin" (after Madonna's hit single of 1984); a first-year woman jock was required to give a weight-lifting demonstration in a skimpy bikini (Moffatt 1989, 106–11). What is the connection, then, if, as Moffatt observed, many of the stunts seemed demeaning? The answer, he muses, is using an American concept of friendship in a convivial frame to mask end-of-semester tensions. In his words, there is "the American cultural rule, You should be willing to make an idiot of yourself in front of your friends. If, under the ritual circumstances of Secret Santa, you make an idiot of yourself in front of your coresidents on a dorm floor, you are then reenacting all of them *as* friends. You are making them all back into friends—or at least into friendly acquaintances, whatever tensions and conflicts you may have had with one another over the previous three months" (Moffatt 1989, 134–35).

Women's colleges have a particularly strong tradition of Secret Santa, and they tend to play up the feminine theme of nurturing benevolence. Students leave cheery notes and small gifts, and arrange for kind favors for the "Santee." When not called Secret Santa, the custom might be called Spider and Fly, as it is sometimes at Wellesley College; Elfing, as it is at Mount Holyoke College; and Peanut Pals, as it is at Cedar Crest College. In Peanut Pals, the do-gooder is the "shell," protecting her "peanut." The practice is also adapted to other holidays. At Occidental College, students engage in Secret Sweeties for Valentine's Day, and at Millersville University, they have Bashful Bunnies for Easter and Secret Pumpkins (or Haunted Honeys) for Halloween.

Who Started All This?

Founder's Day or Charter Day is often the occasion for building continuity with the past revolving around icons of campus heritage. Founder's Day at Hollins College occurs in mid-February and honors Charles Lewis Cocke (1820–1901). At noon, members of the senior class and one female member of the community chosen by that class walk to the Cocke family cemetery and place a wreath on his grave. Founder's Day at Sweet Briar College involves the big sister–little sister tradition. Seniors pass their academic robes down to the juniors, and the juniors' little sisters "sew pockets filled with goodies into their big sisters' robes" (Birnbach 1984, 408). Pomona College has a "Ceremony of the Flame" at its Founder's Day on October 14; accompanied by singing, students light one another's candles in a darkened hall.

Berry College in Rome, Georgia, has a long-standing tradition of Mountain Day, which celebrates the vision of Martha Berry (1865–1942) for whom the institution is named. Generations of students learn that she never married and devoted her life from the 1890s until her death to developing on land inherited from her father the schools for children of poor landowners and tenant farmers that became Berry College. There is a message in narratives about her that the students became nurtured as if they were her children. Following the college's founding in 1902, she called students to join her for a birthday picnic on October 7. In the years since, students together with alumni, faculty, and staff have feted her founding vision with an annual pilgrimage on the first weekend in October to the foot of Lavender Mountain. The trek begins with a "grand march" down the slope of the mountain. Students wear ceremonial uniform colors of the original students (blue for underclassmen and white for senior men; pastel pink for first- and second-year women and light blue for the seniors). They ritually drop pennies as gifts to the school's founder in the amount of their age in a basket. The event, often cited by alumni as the college's premier tradition, has expanded into a weekend festival, with "Mountain Day Olympics" pitting residence halls against each other in pyramid building, hula hoop spinning, and tug-of-war. There are plenty of southern-styled picnics on the campus in tribute to the original birthday outing. Another throwback to the past during the event is the operation of Berry's Old Mill, which produces old-fashioned ground corn for thousands of attendees.

At the University of Nebraska at Lincoln, Charter Day, February 15, became Ivy Day to plant eastern collegiate foliage out on the dry plains. Seniors marched to the steps of the library, planted ivy, and affirmed their loyalty to the university. The university has grown tremendously and has many colleges, each looking for its sense of self, under its wing. Architecture college students satirically came up with Hinsdale Day, a special event commemorating two urinals in the ground floor bathroom of Architecture Hall. Traditionally observed November 1, the celebration includes a twenty-one-flush salute to the urinals, once a fixture on campus, made by university faculty member Winfield E. Hinsdale in 1910. Explaining the event, a student responded to my survey by stating that "since Hinsdale Day is a tradition unique to the Architecture College, it helps give the college an identity."

At other campuses, party weekends carry jovial themes related to localized circumstances. At the University of the South, three party weekends—fall, winter, and spring—have a formal charm. Various social organizations host parties evoking memories of the institution's historic roots in Anglican ecclesiastical and academic traditions. There are the Wellingtons, for example, who wear British-looking gowns and collars, and the Highlanders, who wear Scottish kilts and capes. The tone is more grassroots at the University of Texas at Austin, where students party much less formally in the name of Eeyore, the gloomy gray donkey in A. A. Milne's books, supposedly because the character believes his friends have forgotten his birthday, but they have planned a surprise party for him. The depressed figure living in rundown surroundings is obviously in need of cheering up. After a long academic year, the founding students longed for a shot of merriment in the spring and named the event for Eeyore to draw attention to their dejected state and ramshackle surroundings. Held since 1963, the annual spring event invites guests to dress in costume, and features a Maypole, honey sandwiches, lemonade, and birthday cake. The spring event has expanded since the 1960s into a major annual festival featuring loud live bands and drum circles along with novelty athletic contests such as sack races, costume contests, and egg tosses.

Students at SUNY Fredonia welcomed spring with Fredonia Marxonia, a frolicking homage to the Marx Brothers, in 2009 after a twenty-year hiatus. The Marx Brothers connection goes back to the 1933 film *Duck Soup*, a comedy set in a mythical kingdom called "Freedonia." Regaling each other with stories of supposed Marx Brothers visits to the northern town, students get in a partying mood by donning Groucho glasses en masse. Although tucked away in an upstate New York village, the campus demonstrates with the celebration that it is on the national popular culture map and, like the Marx Brothers' fictional country (historically an alternative name for the United States emphasizing "freedom"), do not want to be relegated to obscurity.

Rites of Spring

Spring seems to bring out the most hilarity in students. Spring festivals, known as "riots," "rites," "flings," "fevers," and "storms," serve notice that the school year is almost over, the days are longer and warmer, and the sun is shining once again. Typically, students also refer to release of tension shortly before finals in the jovial festivities.

A pattern to this release is recognizable in folklore. One source is ancient: the connection of spring with birth and renewal. People come out of their womblike homes and emerge outside to flourish. Spring is also a time when the ground becomes fertile, and many college festivities respond with tree- and flower-planting ceremonies. Spring to the ancients was also a time of transformation and merriment accompanied by more than a hint of sexual arousal. Practices related to the blossoming of the season signal human as well as natural fertility and stimulation. The awaking light replaces the sleepy dark, the lush green replaces the decaying brown, the rousing warmth replaces the frigid cold. In keeping with this idea, many spring festivities feature comical reversals. Men dress as women, students take faculty roles, and adults act like children.

As temperatures rise in the spring, soon time and life will be theirs, students think, but not before the last repressive hurdle of finals. In the student's spring

Fig. 6.1. This cigar-chomping, diapered threesome entered a single hat in the "Mad Hatter's Parade" competition during Penn State's "Spring Week," 1957. (University Archives, Pennsylvania State University)

events, parody and antithesis are particularly evident. Parody serves to take control of collegiate icons, those lessons and institutions drummed into the heads of students as part of sober everyday existence. Antithesis turns things on their heads to defy adult or administrative norms of control and maturity. Especially appealing to students is turning the intellectually rational into the socially absurd.

Student riots of fun have precedents in the old-time college. From 1853 to 1859 at Harvard, after a long winter in Cambridge, Massachusetts, students bellowed "Heads out!" from their windows during the spring. The cry called students out into a raucous crowd that swept through the grounds and into town. After 1900, the cry became "Oh Rinehart!" The real Rinehart, John Bryce Gordon Rinehart, apparently was a teetotaling, studious Harvard Law School student whose classmates continually called for him to go out on a spree (Baum 1958, 292).

Since the nineteenth century, the rallying cry to mischief at the University of Pennsylvania during the vernal equinox has been "Oh, Rowbottom!" The facts are less sure here, but according to legend, "Rowbottom or Rowbotham had a roommate who kept late hours. The stay-out was often locked out and could be heard in the wee hours calling for Rowbottom to let him in. Somehow, Rowbottom's name became connected with campus carousing" (Baum 1958, 293).

In the 1920s at the University of Illinois, students held the "Spring Riot." As one alum remembers, "It occurred on no particular date, but broke out spontaneously on one of the first warm evenings in spring. It was heralded by students throwing open their windows and yelling 'Yahoo'" (Hankey 1944, 34). These "riots" often involved storming theaters, throwing rocks and water balloons, breaking furniture, and raiding dorms for undergarments.

Partly to channel these outbursts into manageable festivities, colleges allowed organized spring rites on the campuses. In the Spring Fever at Saint Louis University, students sponsor a triathlon consisting of an egg toss, White Castle hamburger-eating contests (replacing goldfish eating), and Jell-O wrestling. Viterbo College holds the Courtyard Carni in the campus courtyard. There are kegs of beer, mattress races, egg tosses, and water-bucket brigades. The college president submits to the dunk tank; students who hit a target drop the proud president into the water. Students collect cash to sign arrest warrants on faculty members who are confined in a mock jail.

The University of Nevada at Reno has Mackay Days, named for a benefactor of the mining school. Held since 1914, the annual spring festival now includes contests in beard growing (celebrating fertile growth) and pie eating (celebrating excess), drilling and mucking contests out of the mining tradition, and dances that invite students to move freely once again.

Fraternities and sororities took the lead in promoting Spring Week at Penn State in isolated State College, Pennsylvania, beginning in 1949, and went all out to garner nationwide attention for a grand collegiate festival. Publicity blared that the event was intended as a "celebration of forgetting the winter past and the final exams to come"; it would serve as a carnivalesque "time out of time" (Penn State Alumni Association 2006). Held during the last weeks of April, Spring Week included an amusement park with sideshow; a parade with costumed musical bands and humorous floats often bordering on the offensive; hilarious sporting contests including donkey basketball, tricycle races, and strongman events; an outrageous Mad Hatter's contest; colorful fireworks; lots of cross-dressing; Greek sing finals; and coronation of Miss Penn State. The week's events were connected by a theme that often linked the isolated campus to the entertainment world—Disneyland (1957), television (1958), world's fair (1965), and "frakshured" fairy tales (1973). A changeover to a semester system dampened enthusiasm for revelry late in the academic year, and campus organizations organized an array of spaces around spring break (occurring actually well before spring arrives on the March equinox).

Notre Dame has an annual three-day spring extravaganza called "An Toastal" (Gaelic for "festival"). A good bit of drinking occurs, and a competition is held for the tallest stack of beer cans. One can also witness dubious achievements in Jell-O tossing contests and kissing marathons. In a display of parody,

Fig. 6.2. A regular carnival feature at Penn State's "Spring Week" was a target throw at sorority sisters' backsides. (University Archives, Pennsylvania State University)

students hold events designed to humiliate and defile contestants—events such as egg tossings, mud volleyball games, and "flour-blowing contests" in which contestants blow at flour in pie pans until a coin at the bottom is revealed. The festival also has three other features commonly found at other campuses: a bizarre animal race, a parody of a beauty pageant, and parodied theatricals or follies (Leary 1978, 140–41).

At Notre Dame's bizarre animal race, students brought their pet beasts—turtles, cockroaches, flies, snakes, and ducks—to the main quad for exhibitions of speed, such as they are (Leary 1978, 141). At Oregon State, sororities entered turtles into races at Gill Coliseum; each turtle came with a rooting section. Earlham College, located in the state that gives us the Indianapolis 500, had a racing tradition of its own in the Bundy 500. Bundy was an old dorm on campus, which by reputation had a problem with cockroaches. Bundyites held a contest to see who could catch and raise the biggest and fastest cockroach.

In the state famous for the Kentucky Derby, we have Spalding University's annual Running of the Rodents, which, according to publicity, is "the most exciting two seconds in sport." Held the week before finals, the event is run on the faculty parking lot, transformed for the day into Spalding Downs. The starting gun goes off at high noon, and entrants run for the winner's bowl and a custom-made garland of Fruit Loops. Along with the event, the festivities include a Rat Ball featuring the election of a Rat King and Queen, a Rattus Parade full of frivolity, and even a Human Race. In the twenty-first century, such events are often challenged by animal-rights activists, who have succeeded in virtually eliminating greased-pig contests, once a staple of campus spring festivals.

Other starting guns on college campuses during these crazy spring days mark bed, tricycle, raft, and more human races. After the bedpan and wheelchair races and pie-eating contests are done at Hahnemann University's annual spring event, the highlight is the hospital bed race. Six-person teams push decorated beds, which vie for prizes honoring creativity and humor as well as speed. In 1987, the Fleet Enema Team's chocolate-pudding-covered bed lost out to the balloon-bedecked Happy Birthday Team's bed for funniest entry. Best Overall was Oral's Angels, a bed satirizing television evangelist Oral Roberts. Four "angels" and dollar bills surrounded a nursing student.

Going back farther in tradition are various raft races and mock regattas honoring the thawing of the rivers at springtime around campuses. At the annual Harvard Raft Race, students construct makeshift rafts and race them a short distance down the Charles River. Most of the rafts, such as a cardboard replica of a pink Cadillac with a poster of Elvis at the front, sink, and it does not help that spectators pelt the contestants with eggs and other food projectiles. The challenge at the College of New Jersey's Annual Lake Crossing is to build a craft costing $10 or less. At Swarthmore College's Crum Creek Regatta, students construct makeshift boats out of inner tubes.

Students of Indiana University at Bloomington are quite serious about their spring tradition of the Little 500 (known around campus as the "Little Five"), a bicycle race held at a distinguished outdoor stadium where fraternities seek bragging rights by entering the winning team. Originating in 1951, the event was made famous by the movie *Breaking Away* (1979) and has grown as the centerpiece of what student organizations call "the world's greatest college weekend" with a week of activities, including a major concert and alumni races (Schwab 1999). As many as 30,000 onlookers turn out for Penn State's annual Phi Psi 500, held since 1968. This human race winds through the streets of State College and stops at six bars for refreshment. Along with this race is the "Anything Goes" competition, which parades contestants in thematic costumes down the street. Faux Hare Krishnas pray to a keg, three dancers dressed as a popular snack entertain as Big Fig and the Newtones, and seven runners bedecked in bulbous black costumes with fuses atop their heads spell out "BOMBED."

Events such as the Phi Psi 500, where drinking is conspicuous and crowds are unwieldy, are changing or ending. This turn reflects less tolerant societal attitudes toward the excesses of alcohol consumption, even if framed as a spring rite of release. At the Phi Psi 500, for example, bars now serve runners nonalcoholic beer, and costumes are more closely monitored to prevent offensive messages. The raucous Beaux Arts Costume Ball, formerly featuring themes such as "The Court of Charlemagne" and "An Evening on Mars," held at Carnegie-Mellon University in Pittsburgh since 1915, was canceled in 1989 after administrators barred it from campus. Especially since Pennsylvania enacted legislation making universities liable for drinking incidents on campuses, college officials were naturally wary of the spring blowout sometimes attracting more than 1,200 students and causing thousands of dollars in alcohol-related damages. In 1987, staff at Cal State–Chico canceled Pioneer Days after 2,000 mostly drunken students smashed windows, pelted police, and damaged cars when parties in preparation for the festival spilled out into the street. At Colorado State University, police resorted to tear gas canisters to disperse 3,500 students, many throwing rocks and bottles, gathered for the school's annual College Days. Administrators threatened cancellation of the event, a festive tradition going back to the turn of the twentieth century.

St. Patrick's Day is a major holiday in many college towns because of its association with drinking. At Penn State's University Park campus containing more than 40,000 students, fans of St. Patrick's Day, upset that its date fell during spring break, began "State Patty's Day" in 2007 as a pre–spring break version of the holiday with bars opening earlier and stores stocking green and shamrock-covered clothing. After problems with public drunkenness and bar brawls in 2009, police units began coming out in full force in a spring equivalent of handling massive fall football game celebrations. In 2010, 160 arrests were made, and nine taverns were given citations for selling to intoxicated or underage patrons. The big schools are not the only locations for problems arising with spring festivity and fall victory celebrations. At Colby College in Waterville, Maine, with less than 2,000 enrollees, students celebrated graduation with "Senior Champagne on the Steps" at the campus's Miller Library. Police estimated that 200 bizarrely dressed students became intoxicated and unruly. One student obviously surprised by the police response told the local newspaper, "We're just having fun" (Harlow 2006).

Despite the warnings about student fests getting out of control, many students view the events as enhancing the reputation of the institution as a "party school," a convivial place to be, much to the chagrin of faculty and administrators emphasizing the university's academic credentials in its recruiting. Popular publishers such as the Princeton Review and magazines such as *Playboy* have issued rankings of the top party schools since the 1980s, but previously the accolade of top party school has been believed by students at different campuses to be all their own based on the number of campus bashes and lots of sports and festivities distracting students from studying. Showing the inexact science of rating campus partying, Princeton Review did place Penn State at the top of its list of party schools in 2009, but the university was not even on *Playboy*'s list of the top twenty-five in 2002; the dubious distinction of being on top of the list went to Arizona State University. Despite rampant student declarations to the contrary, *Playboy* has not compiled annual rankings of America's top party schools (it has done so only three times) (Mikkelson 2008).

Having heard assertions from students talking about campus culture, often before the school year began, that "this campus was rated as America's top party school," or told more as a boast, "*Playboy* rated us the top party school ten years in a row," and in what sounds like a folkloric elaboration, "they dropped us from the competition because we won it so much," I went back to my notes and found that many of the institutions where this belief was pervasive compared themselves to supposedly more elite institutions—Dartmouth to Harvard in the Ivy League, Michigan State to Michigan, Penn State to Penn and Carnegie-Mellon, Ithaca to Cornell—or sought to gain attention because they were not as well known nationally (for big-time sports or academics)—Chico State, Oneonta State, Montana State, the University of California at Santa Barbara, Plymouth State, and Providence. Other student bodies waving the party school banner appeared envious of cosmopolitan institutions because of their remote locations: East Carolina University, Ohio University, Heidelberg University, Southern Illinois University ("PubClub.com's Top 10" 2010). One can detect compensatory thinking in the expression of the belief. Folklorist Jan Harold Brunvand adds in a survey of urban legends that mentioning the rumor on the web of the officially named top party school in a supposed competition akin to a national sports championship resulted in a "flood of responses" (1993, 193). The beliefs were couched in a joking narrative "A survey—supposedly published in *Playboy*—of the best colleges for partying had not listed the University of Wisconsin because 'we don't rank professionals'" (Brunvand 1993, 193). Brunvand cited variations of the story reported from the Universities of Florida, Maryland, Kentucky, and Virginia, as well as Boston College, Ohio University, Villanova, and West Virginia University. By announcing the distinction of being officially *declared* by national consensus a top party school, students subvert the usual collegiate claims to fame of being academically outstanding or excessively large and conspicuous with the rating that matters most to students, or so they imply, of having socially intensive fun.

Follies, Flings, and Frolics

At northern colleges, where the coming of sunshine and warmth follow endless months of gray and cold, students also hold sober rituals, even if done tongue-in-cheek. At Binghamton University in often frigid upstate New York, students observe the "Stepping on the Coat Ceremony" to mark the end of winter and the start of the all-too-brief warm season. A proclamation is read: "We are here today to celebrate an occasion of great importance to you all. It is a time of rebirth, a time of new awakening, when flowers emerge from the dead soil and bodies emerge from beneath the heavy layers of winter clothing. A miracle has occurred and we are in the midst of it. Look around you, you can see that it is true—once again after the winter of our discontent there is, once more, grass on the campus." Attendants remove a coat from a well-bundled student and help him to ritually stomp the symbol of cold discontent in this ceremony held for more than twenty years near the center of campus.

At the University at Albany, thousands of students celebrate a related spring ritual known as Fountain Day. As the university president throws out the first Frisbee, streams of sobering cool water rise in an enormous fountain on campus, and students wade in. The ritual is a symbolic reawakening of life. As one junior professed, "So many people are dormant the rest of the year, that an event like this, people resurface and show their faces." Another commented, "It's a big university, but today makes everyone feel a lot closer" ("Everybody" 1989, 54).

In the spirit of reversal, many campuses during the spring host theatrical "follies" and "frolics," satirical musical skits by students poking fun at student leaders, faculty, and administrators. Often first-year women, such as those at Mary Baldwin, take up the follies to tease their upperclass "big sisters" who have perhaps been too motherly. Students commonly take as their models satirical skits put on earlier in their lives at summer camps and high schools. Besides liberal arts colleges, professional schools of business such as the University of Pennsylvania's Wharton School have their follies. The plot of one memorable production targeted Wharton's dean as the "Silver CPA" (he has white hair and formerly headed a big accounting firm) who "buys" faculty from other schools ("It's" 1989, 1). In a skit about business ethics, the cast sang the following to the tune of Michael Jackson's "Beat It":

I cheated, cheated
And I probably sound conceited
You're probably angry
I'm overjoyed
I work on Wall Street
You're unemployed.

Law students nearing the end of their academic trials participate in the University of Virginia's "Libel Show" and Duke's "Flaw Day." Professors may be portrayed as lecturers inducing snoring or fiendish monsters enjoying the suffering of captive students (Clawges 1989, 11). In the stressful atmosphere of the medical school, follies are intended—often through dark humor—to break tensions associated with a bloody profession. As Anne Burson observed of one teaching hospital in Philadelphia, "An anesthesiologist may be portrayed as a Samurai who obtains blood samples by making a screaming lunge with a sword at his patient (many anesthesiologists in large city hospitals are Oriental). A pharmacist may sing a Gilbert and Sullivanesque patter song listing the drugs supposedly unavailable in the hospital. A skit about those doctors who treat the genitourinary tract may be entitled 'Pomp and Circumcision' and contain a song such as 'To Pee the Impossible Stream'" (1982, 29; see also Burson 1980).

This humor comprises "inside jokes" meant for a specific audience to laugh at itself. They contain not-so-veiled complaints about the student's education within the playful context (see Hufford 1989, 136–37). But such skits can verge on the cruel, and often they deal in offensive stereotypes. For this reason, the curtain closed on follies at Penn State's Hershey Medical Center, Cedar Crest College, the University of Arkansas, and the University of Northern Colorado. Franklin and Marshall's answer was for administrators and faculty to join students in its "Fum Follies." The president of the expensive private liberal arts college came out as smiling, lying, television pitchman Joe Isuzu and told the throng that his college tuition is only $5.95, and he showed a photograph of the new residence hall—the Taj Mahal.

Other dramatic reversals common at college campuses involve men playing women's roles. Oregon State University claims the "Junior Follies," an all-male musical show, and a men's theatrical group holds a similar event every spring at Penn. The Oregon State extravaganza includes a singing chorus and dance line in drag. At Shorter College in Georgia, college men held a womanless wedding (Gardner 1972, 329), a mock marriage ceremony theatrically performed by an all-male cast, connected to a community tradition in the southeastern United States of womanless weddings as fund-raisers sponsored by churches, fire departments, and civic clubs (Woodside 2009). At Juniata, men uproariously served women breakfast on May Day. In the 1930s, students at Western Oregon State held a male May Day pageant, a ritual usually reserved for women. Since 1976, men from Butler Hall at the college have been holding the Butler Beauty Pageant. In a parody of the Miss America pageant, male contestants taking fake names such as "Ima Fox" dress in women's evening gowns and swimsuits, at times appear to be pregnant, perform stunts in a talent competition, and answer questions with empty-headed remarks. Looking at the event critically, however, more than a reversal of gender roles in the name of spring is apparent. Such ritual displays reinforce male dominance, especially

Fig. 6.3. "First Hat Girl" carried to class, Hat Hunt, at Milwaukee-Downer College, 1950s. (Author's collection)

in tense situations or ones where threatening signs of change are about, by directing attention to the absurdity of men taking women's roles (cf. Spradley and Mann 1975, 134–35). Moreover, lacking the ability to get pregnant, the men appropriate the procreative, feminine associations of the season.

Comical displays in collegiate ritual reversals by women are infrequent. Influenced by changes in social dating patterns, reversal events for women such as Sadie Hawkins Day at Houghton College and Dutch Treat Week at North Texas largely met their demise by the end of the twentieth century. At these events, women approached men for dates and paid the bills. Lee University in Cleveland, Tennessee, still advertises its "Sadie Hawkins" festivities (begun in 1962), including a "chase day" in which women run after men, as the institution's oldest social event. At Abilene Christian, the pursuing woman tradition is going strong and affectionately known as "Sadies," lasting an entire week in November. Helped by free activities sponsored by the Campus Activities Board, women are encouraged to ask men to join them on dates each night of the week. It kicked off with complimentary smoothies on Monday and culminated in a movie on the weekend (Gutierrez 2008).

For more than seventy years women at Milwaukee-Downer College (now part of Lawrence University in Appleton, Wisconsin) fought over a man's top hat in the "Hat Hunt," held in the spring. According to legend, the hunt dates to 1894 when one Parson Ames wearing a tall silk hat visited Downer College to address a chapel audience or visit a faculty member. Some oral histories claimed that mischievous first-year women took off with the headgear, while others insisted that seniors swiped it for their theatrical production. The interclass rivalry became the heart of the event years later. Upperclass women hid the hat, and first-year students looked for it, often having to wade through streams, chisel through rocks, and dig in the earth. One year it was found inside a stuffed seal in the college museum, and another year it was suspended from a register in the chapel. The hunt began by tradition on April 29, and the first-year women were given until May 29 to come up with the prized possession. If they did not find it, they had to entertain the sophomores; if they did, the upperclass women gave the frosh a banquet. The first-year woman who found the hat was carried by her classmates on a huge wooden tray used in the dining hall. For the next twenty-four hours, students carried her to classes. The finder also received the honored title of First Hat Girl, and she, the president of the first-year class, and another student selected by these two hid the hat for the hunt the following year. The significance of the find is indicated by the remark made to a reporter in 1944, "I would rather find the hat than be class valedictorian." But the disruption the Hat Hunt brought to campus for a month disturbed some college officials, who for years threatened to put an end to it. The president of the college during the 1920s protected the event, saying, "You must understand that it is with young women as with young men, in the spring their blood gets a little warm and Hat Hunt helps to take out a little of the ginger" (Peterson 1964, 31–36).

At Penn State, the clamor created by freshmen parading in hobo outfits disrupted classes during the 1920s and 1930s, and briefly during the 1950s, when the university administration clamped down on the prespring custom known as Poverty Day (Sophs 1953). Students ran through campus and marched into classes wearing barrels, burlap bags, sarongs, and tin-can armor in creative combinations. Poverty after the Great Depression set in was no laughing matter, and the "hilarity and abandoning of regulations" in Poverty Day was replaced by "Freshman Frolic," although it still involved dressing down as hobos and "starving students" in an abandonment of traditional ties and button-down shirts worn by students at the time. The theme resounded on other campuses across the country such as the University of Kansas's Hobo Day. Variations of the transgressive-dress frolic also carried on in "pajama parades" and campus Halloween costume competitions in which students defy societal norms, at least in the frame allowed by the event.

A continuing tradition at Brenau Women's College is the "Spade Hunt." Two shovels, one small and one large, adorned in ribbons of the class color, are

Fig. 6.4. Costumed students pose for Hobo Day at the University of Kansas, 1931. (Author's collection)

hidden somewhere on campus by the seniors, and juniors have three days to find the prized item. Women go out in search of the shovels in military or hunting camouflage outfits (Andrews 1988).

For scale of an event involving a search, few festivities today match the extent of the University of Chicago "Scavenger Hunt" (or "Scav Hunt"). The annual four-day team-based scavenger hunt held in May began in 1987 and involves acquiring as many as 300 items, such as an elephant (worth 500 points), sousaphone (300 points), and umbilical cord (96 points). Participants may also be asked to embark on a road trip, craft objects, compete in "Scavenger Olympics," and rally in one of the university's main quadrangles while students are in class. Team names are as colorful as some of the items they are supposed to retrieve. In 2010, the top finishers were "The Hitchhocker's Guide to the Snellaxy," "Dr. Scodel's League of Atrocious Wonders," "Hooked on Phoenix," "The People's Liberation Front of Scavistan," and "Enrico Fermi's Scarlet Sex Machine." A registered student organization at the University of Chicago, Scav Hunt boasts that it is the largest scavenger hunt in the world.

Students often represent their major rather than their class in modern spring events. A rite of spring held around St. Patrick's Day at Cornell, in often chilly Ithaca, New York, calls for freshmen in the College of Architecture to design and build a paper dragon thirty to forty feet high and then parade their creation around the Ivy League campus. Architecture students in costume follow their creation. Onlookers have been known to throw eggs and oranges at the "dragon of winter." The festivities end when the students, showing their rivalry with the future engineers, set the dragon afire on the engineering quad. As the construction burns, the "dragon of winter" has been slain.

Engineers at many campuses take special interest in spring events around St. Patrick's Day because St. Patrick was, by legend, an engineer. At the University of Missouri at Columbia, engineers added to traditional St. Patrick's Day events with a parade, snake killing, a mass "kowtow" to St. Patrick, the collecting of shillelaghs from the woods, bringing St. Patrick into town on a manure spreader, and performing drill-team figures with lawn mowers.

At the University of California at Davis, Aggies have their spring event called Picnic Day. The festivities kick off with a cow-milking contest, usually won by the campus chancellor, and usually eliciting sexual wordplay. Headlines proclaim "Chancellor Puts Squeeze on Big Teats." Related to this theme, T-shirts and bumper stickers read "UC Davis . . . The Best Dairy-Air for 75 Years." The highlight of Picnic Day, however, is a parade with floats. Several mock drill teams, such as Alpha Falfa Oink, the animal science department's precision shovel drill team, add levity, but much of the parade admiringly showcases horses. (The campus's mascot is the mustang.) Other attractions include a rodeo, sheepdog trials, dachshund races, a dog Frisbee contest, and a polo match—events showing the athletic abilities of dogs and horses often working in conjunction with humans. Cows, pigs, and goats—less a human extension than dogs and horses—tend to be ridiculed during the events, and as the T-shirt slogan suggests, the animals are associated with the scientific aspects of Aggie work. Aggies proudly bring out their humanistic work with nature by giving reverence to horses and dogs, but the other animals, given to nonpet status and much potentially disturbing animal experimentation at the university, attract derisive humor. According to Davis faculty members Jay Mechling and David Scofield Wilson, this festival thus serves to deal with cultural ambivalence caused by the nature of work on campus. The event orders categories for participants in this college culture who both admire and exploit animals (Mechling and Wilson 1988, 303–17).

Tree Fetes and Surprise Vacations

Nature also enters heavily into college culture in ritual tree plantings. They get special attention during spring events for many symbolic reasons. Plantings fit the theme of growth presented by both spring and the college experience. Further, the pastoral campus with large shady trees and flowerbeds has historically been the ideal image of campuses because it embodies the peace and contemplation evoked by nature. In addition, trees planted by a class preserve the presence of that class long after its members have left.

At Vassar, each class chooses a tree on campus or plants a new one to become its class tree. Tree planting as part of an elaborate spring ceremony— complete with a Tree Day Mistress—was a regular part of Tree Day held during the spring at Wellesley for almost ninety years. It fell victim to the lack of patience during the 1960s for formal programs and the redirection of student attention away from campus (McCarthy 1975, 236–40).

At Simpson College, a special campus day devoted to cleaning the grounds developed out of Tree Day. It may not sound like fun, but in an assuring spirit of community on a surprise day, usually in April, the chapel bell rings in the morning to announce that all classes are canceled. Students, faculty, and administrators work side by side to clean the campus. At noon, the campus community joins together in a picnic and games (see also "College" 1856, 378–80; Kern 1984, 144). The yearbook of the University of Puget Sound claimed that "more college spirit and enthusiasm prevails on this day than on most any other occasion" (Earley 1987, 37).

The idea of a surprise vacation day, sans cleanup chores, exists at many campuses. At Keuka College, it is called the "Senior Scourge" and held during the spring. Seniors plan a picnic and party for the juniors and then surprise them with the location. At Mary Baldwin, the name given for the fall event is Apple Day, secretively organized by the sophomore class. Each spring at Coe College in Cedar Rapids, Iowa, the retiring student body president is honored with the task of calling the day when no classes will be held. The chosen day supposedly remains a secret, but students expect it to fall ten days before finals. The victory bell sounds at six in the morning, and the student body president and crew run through the dorm halls yelling "It's Flunk Day!" and delivering the Flunk Day newspaper lampooning members of the college community. The whole community heads to a nearby park for an all-day picnic.

Knox College in Galesburg, Illinois, also has its Flunk Day at which students are roused early in the morning by Old Main's bell. They are then treated to a carnival atmosphere on the grounds with pie-throwing free-for-alls, tugs-of-war with the Fire Department, and fireworks. A mysterious group called the "friars," composed of seniors, plan the event and receive kudos for making it into the inner circle. According to tradition, the day is "when no one cares how many 'flunks' you receive" (Polk 2010).

This kind of surprise vacation day most popularly goes by the name of Mountain Day (Juniata College, Elmira College, Smith College, Mount Holyoke College), but it is also known as Stop Day (Stephens College), Spree Day (Clark University), Tinker Day (Hollins University), GIG Day ("Get into

Goucher," at Goucher College), Fox Day (Rollins College), and Toe-Dipping Day (Chatham University). Juniata College touts its Mountain Day held in the fall as the college's oldest tradition, dating to the late nineteenth century. Students try to guess the date for the day when classes will be canceled because it is not announced in advance. A special feature of the campus emptying to go to a state park in the region is a spirited coed flag football game between the faculty and the seniors.

Special privilege is given seniors on a special day at several campuses. At Houghton and Mary Baldwin Colleges, seniors are excused from class for a day usually associated with revelry. At the University of Nebraska at Lincoln in 1898, the senior class staged the first Seniors' Day or Sneak Day. Seniors entered the chapel and sounded horns, tin whistles, and squeaking dolls (Manley 1969, 264–65). At St. John's College in Annapolis, Maryland, seniors without warning still hold "Senior Prank": they signal the closing down of campus by decorating campus and performing a comical skit. Memorable pranks lingering in college lore include bricking in the dean's office, piling twenty-five radial tires on the college flagpole, and rolling a 300-pound Trojan horse made of papier-mâché onto campus. Seniors interrupted Monday night philosophy seminars wearing Greek dress and presented a parody of Homer's epic *Odyssey*. The next day, the class threw a feast that drew 450 students, faculty, and staff—a nice turnout considering that the school's entire enrollment is under 500.

Since the 1930s, senior pranks have also highlighted Caltech's Ditch Day. Seniors devise elaborate mechanical defenses on their doors, and leave campus for nine hours. Underclassmen, through ingenuity rather than strength, try to get past the defenses and get to the booze and sweets left as rewards for their efforts. Underclassmen, for example, successfully talked their way past a computer with a voice synthesizer. Prompted by a keyboard outside the door, the computer sentry dispensed a series of clues and plaints as the underclassmen got closer to the password that would open the door (Ellis 1987, 102–4).

May Day

Senior women frequently get special treatment during May Day celebrations. At Bryn Mawr, sophomores wake up early on May 1 to pick flowers and put them in baskets for the seniors. Baskets in hand, the sophomores proceed in a group through the dormitory at dawn. They approach a senior's room, knock on the door, and wait for signs of life. Then they sing a traditional song such as "The Hunt Is Up," which carries the lines "Awake! all men, I say again, Be merry while ye may! For Harry, our king, is gone a-hunting, To bring his deer to bay" (Briscoe 1981a, 221). The sophomores hand the risen senior her basket, and she usually jokes appreciatively with the crowd before going back into her room and preparing for the day's activities.

The day lets underclass women say good-bye to the seniors. The seniors are given adoration before being symbolically excluded from the student community. The seniors, for their part, perform dances and dramas that stress their refinement and maturity, their achievement and vitality. Some of these traits emerge especially clearly in ceremonies with more than a hint of sexual awakening—from the presentation of flowers to the dance around the Maypole. With the fertility of the merry month of May comes feminine rebirth into a new stage of life.

It is still early morning at Bryn Mawr when the seniors come down to be the sophomores' guests of honor in a champagne and doughnut toast. Then the seniors take a turn waking the college president, and the college bell rings in May. In a connection to the medieval tradition at Oxford, seniors sing the Magdalen "Hymn to the Sun" from a tower on campus (see Judge 1986, 15–40). Breakfast includes the special treat of strawberries and cream. After awards and a procession of heralds, dancers, and the May Queen, students dance around Maypoles. The May Queen is crowned, morris dancers complete their figures on the green, and the audience then gathers for the annual springtime drama in which the feminist-heroine slays the decidedly masculine dragon of winter. Picnic lunch follows, with wandering minstrels, jugglers, and fencers. Theatricals and art exhibitions, often on an Elizabethan or medieval theme, fill the afternoon. In a farewell gesture of fertility, the seniors plant a tree and bring ribbons, coins, and trinkets to hang on it.

After a medieval banquet and renaissance choir concert, the last step-sing of the year occurs under cover of darkness (Cohen and Coffin 1987, 165–66). It concludes with the "Good Night" song, during which the seniors file away from the steps. Their chorus is distant indeed by the time the song ends. In a "moving up" ritual, the juniors occupy the positions held by the seniors on the steps, and the other classes move up in turn. After a moment of contemplative silence, the students give two cheers, one for the seniors and one for the college, and then complete the evening with an English country dance (Briscoe 1981a, 240–41).

Features of the Bryn Mawr May Day, held since 1900, occurred at many campuses, particularly from the early 1900s to the 1960s. The inspiration for the event is the English folk celebration, connected often to Elizabethan tradition. Students gather flowers and greenery at dawn for the event. Making the link between femininity and the fertility of the spring season, a royal court of maids and children crown the youthful May Queen with flowers. Further in keeping with this fertile awakening theme, young women costumed gaily in virginal white, ribbons in hand, dance around the Maypole (Long 1977, 66–75).

Fig. 6.5. Maypole dance during May Day at Bryn Mawr College, 1935. (Author's collection)

The athletic, artistic, and feminine components of the festival appealed to many women's colleges when they took it up during the late nineteenth century, a time when medieval rituals of many sorts swept through society (see Lears 1981, 141–82). To the Elizabethan motif of May Day, schools frequently added Greek dances, hymns, hoop races, and exhibitions invoking classical symbols of higher civilization. At colleges such as Oregon Normal (now Western Oregon University), May Day was considered "the biggest and most colorful event of the year" ("Tradition" 1935, 1), and at Hampton it was "the prettiest and most attractive of our social gatherings" (Kenwill 1886, 70).

Various changes did May Day in by the 1960s. The semester calendar became dominant over the term system, and with that change, May Day came perilously close to finals. Students were unwilling to devote time to the preparation required for the event. Students were less inclined to focus their social energies on campus, since they were doing more things as individuals away from the college. The pomp of the event meant less to iconoclastic students of the 1960s, and they sensed that the ceremony conveyed stereotypes of women as dainty and dramatic. Women wanted to be less associated with the stillness of nature and more with the activity of modern production, especially in the corporate workplace. Women no longer displayed their athletic and artistic prowess through May Day activities as they once did. They sought outlets more integrated into the mainstream political economy. Colleges during the 1960s commonly replaced May Day with madrigal dinners, parents' weekends, singing competitions, earth days, and spring homecomings, or eliminated it altogether.

Some colleges have revived or revised the event in recognition of the need for reestablishing traditions. At Wells College, May Day was celebrated from 1922 until the early 1960s, and then it began anew in 1979. According to the senior student coordinating the event, "The idea appeals to present students because it welcomes spring in a symbolic and nostalgic way" ("Of Queens" 2004). First-year women kick off the festivities with a "Freshwomen Dance Around the Maypole," accompanied by English medieval music. Two May Queens, members of the junior and senior classes, are crowned, but in better accord with modern sentiment, the crowned students are picked by drawing lots. Formerly the queen's spot was reserved for a senior who represented "the highest tribute which could be paid to beauty." Against the background of a Grecian temple, a pageant of women and children made an invocation to a tree, and after the coronation wound ribbons around the Maypole.

May Day at Earlham College, celebrated since 1875, has probably been the college's longest continuous social tradition, and now is bigger than ever in its revised form. The Olde English theme is played up more than the feminine display, and works to build an intimate sense of community for the college. "Through the day a spirit of rural festivity will pervade the campus-village and bring pleasure to thousands," according to publicity for the event. Queen Elizabeth leads a procession to the green, children frolic, and students raise a Maypole and then sing and dance around it. Stage performances of episodes with classic legendary and romantic themes such as *St. George and the Dragon*, *Pyramus and Thisbe*, and *The Mad-Cap Marriage of Beatrice and Benedick* enliven the festivities.

As the subjects of the plays suggest, love and marriage is normally a strong motif in May Day activities. Coming before the traditional wedding month of June, May Day celebrations at some schools looked more like wedding ceremonies than college assemblies. The women proceeded in formal white dress with trainbearers, attendant maids, and flower girls—in front of parents and friends. At Mount Mary College, May Day called for the crowning of the Virgin Mary's statue before the Queen of May, "dressed as a bride while her attendants . . . wear long pastel shaded tones" ("May Day" 1939, 1). At Wellesley, officials presented the winner with a wedding bouquet and flower wreaths.

Hoop exhibitions and races, with all their vaginal symbolism, were regularly part of May Day celebrations, and the races regularly rewarded winners with portents of marriage. The winner was, by tradition, the first from the class to be married, and Bryn Mawr students add that the *runner-up* will be the first to get the Ph.D. (McCarthy 1975, 247; Briscoe 1981a, 235; Betterton 1988, 170).

Hoop races are often part of other occasions besides May Day. At Barnard, they are part of Greek Games; at Cedar Crest, they are part of Soph-Frosh Day. In this new day, Wellesley women give the hoop race, now held in April, a new interpretation. They say that the winner will become, in a sign of the dominance of commercial culture, a corporate chief executive officer.

At Brenau, juniors still use the occasion of May Day to honor departing seniors. Juniors wrap the Maypole, make ivy chains and crowns, and offer the seniors an entertaining skit (Andrews 1988). Wells juniors and seniors make up the court of the majestic May Queen, complete with jesters, while frosh dance around the Maypole.

A particularly elaborate celebration occurs at Keuka College. It begins with "Freshman Stunt," in which students spoof the college and honor their Big Sisters, Big Buds, and Senior Pals. On Saturday, classes gather in chapel for "Moving-Up Ceremony," in which classes officially advance in rank. Interclass crew races follow. The May Day Court at Keuka recognizes women chosen from each class who have been active in the college for the past year. Finally, a festive dinner dance caps the May Day weekend celebration.

Football: The College Game

May Day may have celebrated femininity, but at most campuses the main spectacle of manly competition, and by extension, of college spirit, is on the football field. Since 1869, when Rutgers met Princeton in something of a grudge match, football has caught on as the event bringing out the most people from the college community (McCallum and Pearson 1971; Moffatt 1985a, 5; Rader 1983; Rudolph 1962, 373–92; Watterson 2000). Often compared in its early form to rugby and class scraps, American football evolved into America's favorite collegiate sport. Once looking like a series of bodily piles, American football added distinctive features by the early twentieth century of the scrimmage line, forward pass, and specialty positions (tailback and receivers), which opened up the game and also drew new comparisons to the organization and precision of industrial society (Riesman and Denney 1951; Robertson 1980, 253–57).

In contrast to women's associations with the blossoming spring, men looked to the cool brown fall as the setting for football battles in the dirt. A common exhibition of men at football pep rallies at many colleges was the noisy pajama or nightshirt parade, either before the big game or after a victory. At the University of Kansas well into the 1950s, male students "participated in the Nightshirt Parade, an event held the night before the first home football game. The men assembled on campus dressed in nightshirts or pajamas, marched to Massachusetts Street downtown, and snake-danced to a bonfire and a rally at the bridge, followed by free movies" (Nichols 1983, 8). A pajama parade dating back to Stanford-California football games around the turn of the twentieth

century at Berkeley evolved into a "Pajamarino," featuring costumes emphasizing the elaborate and fantastic (Dundes 1968, 30).

Bonfires literally fire up fans and players at pep rallies held on Friday night
before a Saturday home game. In Texas, the "Aggie Bonfire," after its initial
burning in 1907, became a long-standing tradition to pump up the football
team and its fans for its big game against the University of Texas around
Thanksgiving time. Fresh-cut logs, neatly stacked into a wedding-cake structure, went up in flames. Over time, the size of the tower grew to dangerous
proportions. The rally made headlines when, in 1999, a collapse during the
tower's construction killed eleven students and injured twenty-seven others.
Mourners placed flowers, stuffed animals, T-shirts, drawings, and posters at
vernacular assemblages at the location (Grider 2000). University officials
halted the bonfire event after the tragedy, but in 2002 a student-sponsored
coalition created an unsanctioned, off-campus bonfire to continue the tradition. Back at the original site, a permanent memorial was dedicated in 2004 in
an area named "Traditions Plaza" ("Thousands Attend" 2004).

A remaining bonfire tradition is the Big Game Bonfire Rally held at the
University of California at Berkeley campus. The "big game" is between Cal
and Stanford. A Rally Committee sets up the bonfire and refuels it during the
rally. Egged on by chants of "Freshmen More Wood," first-year band members bring out pallets of wood for the fire. Students cheer a rendition of a
traditional Maori war dance traditionally performed by a yell leader from the
alumni. The culminating ritual of the rally is igniting the bonfire, with students
watching in awe at the flames shooting up four stories high. But that is not all.
The rally closes with a ritual recitation of "The Spirit of California" (known as
the Andy Smith Eulogy) in honor of the legendary Cal football coach who led
the team to five straight undefeated seasons beginning in 1920, before dying
unexpectedly in 1925. During the speech, students hold lit candles and sing the
campus alma mater, "Hail to California."

Stanford is rallying, too, but since the 1990s has staged a laser light show
known as the "nonfire" in lieu of a pyre. Implying a put-down of the boorish-
ness of Cal students, the Stanford side also hosts the "Big Game Gaieties," a
musical extravaganza dating back to 1911. The show, with titles such as "Daze
and Calfused," is written by students and performed to a packed house in
Memorial Auditorium (holding 1,700 seats) in anticipation of Stanford winning the game against Cal. As the name suggests, the Gaieties is an exuberant production with singing, dancing, Cal-bashing—and often nudity (Laing
2008). On the field of play, the schools battle for the Stanford Axe, an ax head
mounted on a large wooden plaque. The story oft-told about the ax relates to
its original use in 1899 during a Stanford rally (Steinberg 1992, 43–47). Yell

leaders used a lumberman's ax to decapitate a straw man dressed in Cal colors while chanting the Axe yell:

Give 'em the axe, the axe, the axe!
Give 'em the axe, the axe, the axe!
Give 'em the axe, give 'em the axe,
Give 'em the axe, where?

Right in the neck, the neck, the neck!
Right in the neck, the neck, the neck!
Right in the neck, right in the neck,
Right in the neck! There!

After suffering losses at the hands of Stanford and fearing that the ax (and its castrating gesture) jinxed the team, Cal men stole the ax and hung on to it for thirty-one years, despite Stanford's best efforts to retrieve it. In an elaborate ruse after a Cal rally, Stanford students grabbed the ax and sped away. Realizing the symbolic significance of the ax, the two universities agreed in 1933 to make the ax the trophy awarded to the winner of the big game. Scores for the game were dutifully inscribed on the plaque.

The bonfire at Cal and other campuses might bring back memories for students of the close circle around the campfire from their youth and therefore signal a social unity and dedication that help prepare the college team for battle. Yet it differs markedly in its scale and its connection with college life. Lighting up the evening invokes magic because it defies nature with a human constructiveness. If the darkness and cold can be altered with the rite of the bonfire, apparently rendered sacred, other obstacles, such as the rush of another team, seem insignificant. The connection to the "big game" as a manly battle is apparent in the militaristic outdoor fire (rather than the fire of the domestic hearth) linked to the enlarging, destructive power of the living element. The bonfire dwarfs humans and instills veneration and wonder in attendees as the flames shoot upward in a sign of triumph. Men are charged with, and emboldened by, the symbolic power of the pyre and are incited to burn the opposition. Students enlarge themselves by noisily "firing" the structure, turning natural, tame wood into skyward-shooting flames (simulating in some accounts the actions of harnessing lightning). They may even then give the traditional boisterous chant led by the cheerleaders: "Fire it up (clap, clap), Fire it up (clap, clap), Fire it up, and up, and up, and up, and up!"

Folklorist Jay Mechling discerns a sexual component of the campfire that can be applied to the bonfire (1980, 50–55). To explain why such events are

Fig. 6.6. Football pep rally and bonfire at the University of Chicago, 1957. (Author's collection)

construed as appropriate to teenage men, Mechling cites Freud's idea that fire in its phallic form, the heat of passion, is a symbol of the libido (Freud 1964). To be sure, women, too, participate in the event and support its function of boosting the team, and, by extension, the reputation of the institution of which they are a part. But the bonfire is about pumping up the men on the team. Through the ritualization, even magical transformation, of the fire into shooting flames representing the phallic ejaculative power of the team, the sacralized event compensates for the expected competition among the men by unifying the collective into an aggressive and communal unit. Applying Mechling's psychoanalytic perspective, the bonfire centers a play frame in which hypermasculinity is displayed and thereby allows for references for feminizing and infantilizing the opposition (Mechling 1980, 53–55).

Some of the factors given for the decline of the manly "scrap" tradition have contributed also to putting out the bonfire tradition. As campuses grew in size, the bonfires expanded, and the number of participants increased to a massive, unmanageable scale. Administrations worried about injuries, spreading fires, and damages. Organizing such events became complex, expensive endeavors involving police and fire departments. With fans outside the student body taking intense interest in the outcome of big-time sports, the event blurred the lines between campus and community. Some protests could also be heard about the militant values inherent in the rhetoric of the bonfire, often expressed in hyperbolized, hypermasculine messages in carnivalesque orations and theatrical gaieties carrying over into cheering and celebrating at the big game that appear to outdo indoor basketball or outdoor baseball by comparison (Deford 2011b).

Fig. 6.7. The University of Alabama football team makes its way down the Walk of Champions before the Iron Bowl (Auburn vs. Alabama) in 2010. (Photo by Matthew Tosh, Wikimedia)

Spectators at college football games have a variety of traditions to guide them. Even before the game begins, fans revel in elaborate tailgating customs that express both a religious "sacred" fan devotion and outdoor "profane" party. "Tailgating" is slang for dining and jollity in open areas around stadiums before, and often after, football games. Many tailgaters have adapted, and enlarged, American picnic and camping traditions to the signature fall outdoor events of "gameday" with grilling all-American fare of hamburgers, sausages, and hot dogs (and, for the showy crowd, higher-status foods of steaks and lobsters accompanied by candelabras and fine tablecloths) and playing lawn or drinking games, including "beer pong," cornhole, ladder toss, quoits, and sholf (see Henderson 2006; Lindquist 2006). Some notable tailgate locations include "The Grove" at Ole Miss for colorful tented gatherings before home games in a central area of campus shaded by oak, elm, and magnolia trees. The prime spot in The Grove is the area around the "Walk of Champions" because the Ole Miss Rebels football team before kickoff ritually proceeds like a victorious army under a brick and metal arch into a cheering throng of "grovers" (Bragg 2011). Ritual marches of football teams through large tailgating crowds are also cherished traditions at Auburn (Tiger Walk), Alabama (Walk of Champions), Southern Mississippi (Eagle Walk), University of Tennessee (Vol Walk), and other schools. Auburn's is often credited with being the model for others in which the team members, led by the coaches, encourage supporters to pat

Fig. 6.8. Students parade "Big Bertha" (named after a super-heavy German howitzer), touted as the world's largest drum, before a University of Texas home football game. The drum is wheeled onto the field for the halftime show and is played after touchdowns. (Author's collection)

them on the back and shake their hands as they parade like gallant warriors through fan tailgating venues into the home stadium.

Inside the stadium, Texas A&M fans are known for their Twelfth Man tradition. According to legend, after underdog Aggie football players were put out of commission by numerous injuries in a 1922 game against Centre College, then the nation's top-ranked team, the coach called a student-athlete out of the stands to suit up (the Aggies won the game 22–14). In subsequent seasons, the Aggie student body stood up to indicate their readiness to serve as the twelfth man for the team (Adams 1979, 118). The symbolic gesture evolved into the custom of the student body standing throughout the game to show its exuberant support of the team. Since the 1980s, fans have also waved white Twelfth Man towels to add to the effect. The spirit of bonding with the team is evident in the handed-down student adage, "when the team scores, everybody scores," which translates into the action of dates flauntingly kissing each other in celebration after A&M gets a touchdown.

Aggies may also give the "Gig 'em" sign by clenching their right hand as if calling someone out in baseball. Since the 1980s, fans of the Florida State Seminoles have conspicuously performed their chopping motion of a tomahawk

Fig. 6.9. Chief Osceola, riding the horse Renegade, begins every Florida State home football game by hurling a burning spear at midfield. (Wikimedia)

swinging down accompanied by a war chant reminiscent of western movies. Florida has its version of a collective gesture known as the "Gator Chomp." Fans extend their arms in front of their body with the palms of the hands facing each other and imitate the action of an alligator's mouth opening and closing. It not only is used to cheer but also to jeer opposing players. Accompanying the chomp is the frightening "Gator Jaws" melodic chant (dunt-dunt-dunt) from the movie *Jaws* (1975). Probably the best-known gesture in college football is the "Hook 'Em Horns" sign introduced to University of Texas Longhorn fans in 1955 (Berry 1983, 18). Made by extending the index and little fingers and tucking the middle and ring fingers beneath the thumb, the signal is sometimes jokingly turned upside down by Oklahoma fans at Oklahoma-Texas games, creating the sign of the horns hitting someone in the rear end.

Kansas Jayhawk fans out in America's breadbasket "wave the wheat" by stretching their hands over their heads and moving them back and forth. They have also been well known for their haunting "Rock Chalk, Jayhawk, KU!" chant since the late nineteenth century (the Jayhawk rhyme referred to the chalk rock on Mt. Oread, the university's campus). At Penn State, the massive football stadium traditionally reverberates with the sound of one side yelling "WE ARE!" and the answer "PENN STATE" coming from the other. (According to legend [Sedor 2009], the cheer derives from Penn State's refusal to play in the 1948 Cotton Bowl, whose segregation-era officials insisted on black

Fig. 6.10. University of Michigan student fans play "beer pong" at a tailgating party. (Photo by Trevor Blank)

players being left behind; a player supposedly exclaimed at a team meeting, "We are Penn State. We don't do that.") This is the same crowd that has a tradition of irreverently singing "We don't know the goddamn words" over and over when the school song is called for, and during the game throwing marshmallows dyed in the school colors at one another. Theirs is not the only chant from different sides of the stadium. At Florida, those in the east and south stands yell "orange," followed by "blue" from those in the west and north stands.

Cheerleaders spur on the fans. The familiar "Rah, Rah, Rah" of college cheers comes from the "Hip, Hip, Hurrah" of British yells. Many American cheers spring from the old cheers of the Ivy League (Spectorsky 1958, 220–22). Here are two from Yale and Princeton:

Brekekekex, ko-ax, ko-ax,
Brekekekex, ko-ax, ko-ax,
O-op, O-op, parabalou,
Yale, Yale, Yale,
Rah, rah, rah, rah, rah, rah, rah, rah, rah,
Yale! Yale! Yale!

H'ray, h'ray, h'ray,
Tiger, tiger, tiger,
Siss, siss, siss,
Boom, boom, boom,
Ah, ah, ah,
Princeton, Princeton, Princeton!

And here's a 1930s variation from Roanoke College:

Brackety-ackety-ack
Brackety-ackety-ack!
Hullabaloo! Hullabaloo!
How-do-you-do?
How-do-you-do?
Roanoke!

Cheers today are often leaner and meaner, urging the warriors on the field in short bursts. Roanoke cheers today, for example, include "We're tough, we're mean, That's why we call it the Maroon Machine!" Ole Miss fans feel downright proprietary about "Are you ready? Hell yea! Damn right! Hotty Toddy, gosh almighty, Who the hell are we? Hey! Flim Flam, Bim Bam, Ole Miss by Damn!" Alabama's "Rammer Jammer Cheer" also raises hell and in fact is adapted from Ole Miss's cheer (Berry 2003). It has caused some university officials embarrassment because of the charge of its unsportsmanly ridicule of the other team's fans. The crowd cheers "Hey [nickname of the other team such as Vols for Volunteers]! Hey Vols! Hey Vols! We just beat the hell out of you! Rammer Jammer, Yellowhammer, give 'em hell, Alabama!" The references at the end are to a student newspaper at Alabama from the 1920s called the *Rammer-Jammer* and the state bird, the yellowhammer. At Florida, one hears "Go, Gators, go, Fire up tonight! Fight, Gators, fight!" while at Arkansas, home of the Razorbacks, the stands resound with "Woo—Pig—Soie." Florida is renowned, too, for "Two bits, Four bits, Six bits, A Dollar, All Florida Gators stand up and holler!" Gator fans also claim as a tradition linking their arms and swaying while singing "We are the boys from old Florida" at the end of the third quarter. And many cheerleading teams have versions combining gestures and chants of "Knock 'em down, Roll 'em around, Come on defense, work, work" and "Sack (clap, clap) that quarterback, Crash through that line (slap down)! (Traditions Cluster 1981, 43–45).

College football victories result in towers lighting, cannons firing, and bells ringing. At Texas, a thirty-story light tower emblazons the night sky with the school color of orange when the team wins, while at the University of North

Texas the sky turns green. Also at Texas, cannons boomed for years when the Longhorns scored a touchdown, until the Southwest Conference, fearing an accident, outlawed cannons for conference games (Berry 1983, 62).

A contested tradition is the use of Native American mascots and names. The Tribal Council of the Seminole Tribe of Florida confirmed support for use of Osceola and Renegade at Florida State football games because, in the words of the council's chair, "We don't look at it as a mascot, we look at as a representation of the Seminole Tribe. They work with us in representing our heritage" (Fitton 2010). Chief Illiniwek of the University of Illinois did not fare as well. The chief performed a dance at halftime of Illinois football games starting in 1926. Protests of the figure as inauthentic and demeaning to Native Americans began in 1989. In 2007, the Oglala Tribal Council formally issued a resolution that the university cease using the Chief Illiniwek mascot, and the board of trustees complied with the request. The university kept the "Fighting Illini" name, but at other universities administrators also changed the team monikers: the Arkansas State Indians became the Red Wolves, the Eastern Michigan Hurons transformed into the Eagles, Knox College's Old Siwash turned into Prairie Fire, and the St. John's University (New York) Redmen adopted the weather reference of Red Storm.

If performing a Native American war dance became a politically incorrect tradition at football games, bell ringing at many campuses was an old alternative. At women's colleges, it used to signify a student's marriage and now often indicates acceptance into graduate school or first job offer, as at Agnes Scott College. At Franklin and Marshall, bell ringing for a football victory was a regular tradition from 1890 until 1958, when the college president put a stop to the racket. When the team beat regional rival Gettysburg College, students regularly went to the president's house to call for the celebratory cancellation of Monday's classes (Brubaker 1987, 69). At Brown, the bell on University Hall still calls students to classes and signals football victories. Celebrations of victory often spill out into the street and occasionally turn into riots (O'Toole 2002). The most common mass response to a big game win at home is to storm the field and tear down the goalposts.

Besides ringing in the news of victory, some campuses hurl objects. At one of Auburn's oldest intersections, Magnolia Avenue and College Street, students gather after football victories with rolls of toilet paper in hand and decorate, or "roll" in folk speech, what they call "Toomer's Corner." The corner carries symbolic significance as the border between the campus and the city marked by the historic Main Gate and the anchor spot of Auburn's original 1856 campus. Toomer's Drugs has been operating at the corner for over 100 years and achieved iconic status among Auburn students. Auburn alumni are also fond of two massive oak trees at the corner that hold the streams of toilet paper thrown by gathered celebrants. According to legend, rolling the corner began when Toomer's Drugs had the only telegraph in the city. To visibly signal a victory when the team was away, store employees rolled the oak trees.

Auburn's trees leapt onto national headlines when, in 2011, an older fervid Alabama fan was arrested for poisoning the beloved hardwoods, supposedly in retaliation for pictures of an Auburn T-shirt taped to Bear Bryant's statue outside the stadium that bears his name on Alabama's Tuscaloosa campus (the same obsessed fan had named one of his children "Bear" and the other one "Crimson" in honor of his team). *USA Today*'s interpretation hit the mark when it reported that the sacrilegious act went over the line of playful collegiate rivalry. It reported the crime as symptomatic of the elevation of personal investment in sports to provide identity and well-being as sports moved from being a campus interest to mass-mediated culture. Mike Lopresti editorialized that "one problem is how so much emotion is hyper-injected into the more rabid followers of this sport, encouraged by round-the-clock media and Internet and whatnot. If you're from Alabama and you live with beating Auburn 365 days a year, what happens when your team doesn't win? A game is inflated into a matter of civic pride, and there is nothing wrong with that, so long as everyone understands how to act after the clock runs down" (2011). The sacredness of the tree tradition to Auburn fans is apparent in the administrative decision to allow rolling Toomer's Corner to continue, although in the continuing effort to save the hardwoods, the university replaced use of high pressure hoses to hand clean the foliage.

Colleges traditionally leave their fiercest regional rivals for the last game of the season, and, just to heighten the stakes, play for a named trophy. This game also brings out the most revelry from students, complete with pranks, songs, jokes, parties, and public displays. Purdue and Indiana battle for the "Old Oaken Bucket," Michigan and Minnesota vie for the "Little Brown Jug," and Oklahoma and Oklahoma State play for the "Bedlam Bell." Some others you might not know about are the "Bronze Turkey" fought over by Monmouth and Knox Colleges, the "Goat" signifying victory for Carleton or St. Olaf College, and the "Coal Miners Pail Trophy" for the winner of the California University of Pennsylvania and Indiana University of Pennsylvania. Publicists also promote the rivalry with colorful names that draw on tradition, such as the "Backyard Brawl" between Pittsburgh and West Virginia (played since 1895), "Holy War" joining Boston College and Texas Christian (since 1899), and the "Duel in the Desert" pitting Arizona against Arizona State (since 1899). At least two big games are known as the "Border War": Colorado State and Wyoming (since 1899) and Kansas and Missouri (since 1891); fans and media hype the game between Oregon and Oregon State as the "Civil War."

Why is so much placed on the line in these "big games" of college football? Why indeed are colleges associated with the football field? And why do universities outside of the United States not view the campus's "bragging rights" from the sport in the same way? One symbolist answer is pointing out the material significance of lines on the field as points of reference for ritual passage and the conceptual emphasis on linearity (moving forward expressed in the masculinist values of triumph in charging "straight ahead," "up the gut," and "up the middle"). As James Oliver Robertson points out, the football "gridiron" is distinguished from basketball and baseball in the holy trinity of American sports by its profuse use of lines that players repeatedly cross and in so doing reach their "goal" of achievement (1980, 256). The lines structure the game as well as the field as many ritual tests and transformations because plays begin with the "lining up" of offensive and defensive "lines." Gaining property is important because an offense stays on the field by acquiring a "first down" measured in official ten-yard increments. The team's objective is numerically presented in the number of yards remaining to get a first down, such as "second [down] and eight." Excitement builds when a third-down play has a short distance to go and teams close up their lines in anticipation of grappling bodies. The expectation in such recurring situations is that the running back will be "shot through the line," suggesting a double meaning of gun and phallus. The pent-up, potent energy resulting in either a cheered release for the offense or a stop for the defense, thereby showing the offense's impotence, implies an adolescent male sexual praxis tying acquisition of property to sexual gratification. In the ritual action of crossing lines, men are arguably conquering nature as well as exhibiting sexual potency (Ortner 1974; Bronner 2011a, 350–97).

Although other sports have a ritualized sexual component, arguably football gains prominence as the college game because of the importance of its location as an autumn spectacle on a field of battle. Unlike most American team sports, the action in football is measured with players advancing across a line. The point of emphasis is the scrimmage line, also known as "the trenches," which are movable. The defense wants to pin back the offense and smack or pound (a sexual double entendre) the players to the turf, preferably placing them in a feminine position by placing them "on their butt." The defense wants to hold its ground or pin the offense back "deep in its own territory." No team wants to "give ground," feel pushed around, knocked down, or thrown for a loss. Coaches scream at players to hold their spot and get up, so as to show their mettle, their pride, their manhood.

Particularly in American football, associated with young male participants, teams want to move unchecked up and down the field. Players are lauded for their toughness but also for their youthful energy, mobility, and organization in "gaining ground." Broadcasters like to talk about a team taking "real estate" or having "property" behind them as a sign of success that separates the men from the boys. Listeners to sports talk shows know that callers are concerned when their team "sucks," in an obvious reference to taking a passive homoerotic position, but they are happy if their team triumphantly kicks butt (Dundes 1978). They complain if in a loss the team looked like boys to the other team's men, because they were crushed, or worse, nailed or sacked (with the explanation that the defensive line got "penetration in the *back*field"). In victory, though, college spectators charge the field, occupying it with great jubilation, and may tear down the goalposts in a sign of taking control of the land.

The property metaphor is critical to the drive toward victory and reference to America's mythology of conquering the frontier. Many colleges built upon this metaphor in their team names of Cowboys, Broncos, Mavericks, Pioneers, Mountaineers, and Chargers, and the early development of football (such as the nationally publicized games in the early twentieth century between Carlisle's Indians and college teams from Army, Nebraska, Minnesota, and Wisconsin) (Adams 2001; see also Bronner 2011a, 366–72; Oriard 1998). Each of the two teams is said to have "territory," and as a team advances, it acquires ground, even though the designation of territory is nowhere written on the field. A milestone is crossing into the other team's territory past the fifty-yard line, thereby acquiring it by pushing the opponent off its turf. One gains control in the game by "eating up big chunks of yardage." The goal is a precious piece of land. Scoring a goal implies that the other team has been eliminated; it has been demoralized by being driven unrelentingly off the field. For the defense, the goal line is protected, and the ultimate test is the goal line stand, treating the end zone as precious ground that is distinguished from the field by stripes or decoration.

Football gains importance as a matter of school pride because it represents a televised war of narcissistic rivals on the field of battle aspiring to move from adolescence to adulthood (Bronner 2011a, 372–82). This becomes especially significant when the institutions are deemed similar because of their proximity or reputation (for example, Auburn-Alabama, Mississippi–Mississippi State, Oklahoma–Oklahoma State, Michigan–Ohio State, Army-Navy, Harvard-Yale). References to rivalry are coupled with demonstration of social domination by emasculating the opponent in ritual performances of spiking the ball, engaging in war dances, and raising helmets or index fingers. Players are egged on to get the opponent on his back, showing that the team has "kicked ass." Invoking images of hunting, players on the run are chased down, and players are caught in the "open field." In a merger of hunter and soldier, quarterbacks are said to have a rifle arm and be on target. With the naturalistic image of a brown leather football, the thrower wants to hit his man "in the chest" while the defensive player, in sports talk, "brings down his prey." With some phallic implication, speech about players in trouble refers to them being creamed, shot down, and hit hard.

When they are "slammed down to the ground," players are symbolically stuck in the mud or symbolically joined to feces. Carriers have to keep the ball "clean," that is, it cannot touch the ground or else it becomes symbolically contaminated. The player by being dragged down to the ground is not just being overtly feminized as he is tainted by being stuck in infantile feces. The contrast is going into the end zone "untouched" or avoiding being put down into the ground. Manhood is represented in such a case by overcoming the infantile desire to play with dirt or feces. Toughness is shown by "grinding out" or controlling "yards" (= dirt/land). The end zone is also known as "the house," and the runner who takes off down the field is said to be "bringing it to the house." As a frontier metaphor, this rhetoric suggests the transversal of hostile ground to create a settlement. Skill with the ball means that the prize possession is kept off the ground. Thus time of possession, represented by control of the ball allowing an offense to stay on the field, is an important statistic. The context that makes sense to Americans is the property grab, so that owning land by eliminating its previous occupants is the sign of dominance (Bronner 2011a, 366–72; Smith 1950).

The connection of football with autumn was apparent in the game's formative years even before colleges took it up as a ritual opening of the academic year, often following campus rushes that set the whole freshmen and sophomore classes in full against each other. As in football, the rushes or "scraps" involved often brutal contact as players tried to push a ball over a line, and therefore declare the campus grounds as theirs (Bronner 2011b; Krout 1929, 235). If baseball came to be the springtime ritual of going to the well-kept "park," bask in the sun, and witness the blossoming greenery as a sign of renewal, football was meant to be dirty, befitting its gritty image by being played on grounds. It marked a time of natural decay when provision would be gained by hunting rather than cultivating. Following the drama of the hunter myth, in the absence of greenery, humans looked beyond their domain and sought to expand. The narrative that it suggests for autumn endeavors is that adventurers showed their courage under conditions of scarcity and decline, and provided for family and nation/community by venturing out and battling fauna vying for survival (Paolantonio 2008, 15–32).

As is common to hear in football narrative, the goal of the rugged warrior was to be the "last man standing," "laying on a big hit/score," "butting heads," and "dishing dirt" in a particularly "punishing sport." The prominent symbol was not the blooming garden but the dirt below their feet and its association with the untamed field of battle where men engage in events greater than themselves. Arguably, the culmination of this process is the high-stakes championship or "big game" as the new year approaches. The "big game" has a finality to it, with a subsequent anticipation of "next year." It regenerates life with emphasis on masculine control of land and labor to show transition from adolescence to adulthood. Football shot up in appeal since the 1960s because it hybridized the regeneration of an American frontier exploit with postindustrial characteristics of layered organization and urbane individuality in the midst of a social and political environment in which the sport provided a bounded cultural scene for an aggressive victory culture. Football frames a release through vicarious spectator experience from the pressures of routinized everyday life, and even a location for socially sanctioned immaturity.

Ritualizing Drinking in Games and Customs

Whether tailgating at the football game or celebrating in the bars and dorm rooms, students engage in festivities involving consumption of alcoholic beverages, despite the forceful steps of universities to curb drinking on campus. The long list of terms for drunkenness offers an admixture of invitation and warning. Students smilingly refer to being "trashed," "wasted," "blottoed," "wiped out," "blinded," "pickled," "fried," "damaged," "smashed," and "shitfaced." They also freely give advice on ways to allow you to "drink others under the table": drink milk, milkshakes, and water before drinking; eat steak, ice cream, chalk, baked potato, and bread coated with olive oil. For that inevitable discomfort after "pounding" beer, "When you go to bed, put one foot on the floor and your arm on the bed. Swallow a raw egg and drink salt water to make you vomit." And there is the proverbial hair of the dog that bit you, or taking a stiff drink the next day (Cowie, Mackin, and McCaig 1983, 2:248; Mieder, Kingsbury, and Harder 1992, 273).

As if to dubiously welcome a youth into adulthood, his or her twenty-first birthday may well involve "taking shots," that is, quickly downing small glasses of hard liquor, sometimes combining it with mugs of beer, in front of friends to induce a ritual display of drunkenness. Recognition of becoming "legal" at twenty-one with the ability to buy alcoholic beverages is not limited to students, but studies have shown that the chances that someone engages in this "bingeing" increases if he or she is a student (Jayson 2008). For students, the age of twenty-one also represents approaching graduation and separation from one's social cohort. It implies being on one's own with adult responsibilities. The dangerous ritual behavior of taking shots marks a passage by enacting a symbolic drowning death among friends and then rebirth away from one's group.

If taking shots appears to leave behind the student's cohort, drinking games serve to integrate them among relative strangers and raise questions about

peer pressure to be congenial by losing control or being willing to be humiliated. During the 1940s and 1950s, students, particularly men, popularized the
"chug-a-lug," in which each drinker in a group downed a glass of beer in one
fell gulp. Whoever failed to do so had to buy the next round (Dorson 1959,
265). It was a show of manly achievement and, at the same time, of bonding
with buddies (Spradley and Mann 1975, 138–39). "Chugging" now generically
refers to finishing off the glass and is the main penalty in many folk games
played by students, both male and female.

Among the games that can be played in large groups is "Thumper." Students
clap and thump on a table rhythmically while one person asks, "What's the
name of the game?" to which the group responds, "Thumper!" The questioner
says, "How do you play?" and the group responds "Fast and Dirty!" "Why do we
play?" the person asks, and the crowd answers, "To get fucked [messed] up!" At
this point the person provides a signal, such as pulling on an ear or snapping
fingers. The next person repeats what this person has done and adds a signal,
and so on down the line. If someone forgets a signal or botches the order, then
that person must chug his or her beer.

A related memory game with gestures and table beating is "Indian." A difference is that players sit around a large bowl called the Buffalo Head filled with
liquor. Players devise an identifying gesture such as the "Hook 'Em Horns"
sign. The group then beats on the table. While that is going on, one person
flashes his or her sign; the next person needs to perform that one and add his
or her own. On down the line it goes. The person who forgets the sequence
drinks a portion of booze from the Buffalo Head (McDowell 2008; Reuss 1965,
173).

The game, reminiscent of children's folklore, can also be played by the demand to name something rather than give a signal (Duda 1987; Griscom et al.
1984, 39; Egan 1985, 167–68). Examples are cigarettes and cars. In a variation
called "Bizz-Buzz" that uses numbers, players count off numbers in sequence
from one. For all multiples of five, a person must say "bizz," and for multiples
of seven, a person must say "buzz." If a player misses, then he or she has to chug
(Duda 1987; Griscom et al. 1984, 79–80; Egan 1985, 168). These games play on
the effect of drinking on concentration as well as memory.

The drinking game of Turtles, which has antecedents in English pub contests, challenges players to avoid drunkenly slurring their speech. In the game,
usually played in smaller groups, the object is to repeat what the first person
says. If this cannot be done, everyone must drink, and the person who made
the mistake must try again. Players can step up the difficulty by playing in the
round, so that the caller starts off with the first line and waits for all to repeat
it. Then the participants drink to the completion of a round (Douglas 1987, 55;
cf. Egan 1985, 170). The lines are:

One fat hen

A couple of ducks

Three brown bears

Four running hares

Five fat fickle females sitting sipping scotch

Six simple Simons sitting on a stone

Seven Sinbad sailors sailing the seven seas

Eight egotistical egotists echoing egotistical ecstasies while eating an eggroll

Nine nude nublings nibbling nuts, nats, and nicotine

Ten I never was a fig-plucker or a fig-plucker's son but I'll pluck figs till a
   fig-plucker comes.

Adding stimulation to the game are slips of the tongue while reciting the last line, which causes the repeated utterance of a taboo word (see Clements 1997, 793; Mook 1959, 294; Nilsen 1981, 81).

Other games test physical dexterity and its impairment after consuming alcohol. The most common of these is Quarters, a game with many variants. The object of the game is to bounce a quarter into a cup. If the player makes it, he or she can order another student to chug. Super Quarters uses two full cups and one empty one, and players square off against each other—if a player inadvertently lands a quarter in a full cup, he or she must drink its contents. In Chandeliers, each player has a full cup, and one sits in the center of the table. Players try to bounce quarters into opponents' cups. If one makes it, the opponent must chug. If a quarter lands in the center cup, everyone must drink together (Duda 1987; cf. Griscom et al. 1984, 73–74; Griscom et al. 1986, 53–55).

Students in my survey often referred to beer pong as the ultimate sport of drinkers. It has components of carnival games and bowling as well as table tennis in its play. A table is set up with two arrangements of ten cups at opposite ends of a table. Players arrange the cups in a pyramid shape, with the longest row on the edge of the table. The game begins with players on either end looking each other in the eye and counting to three. On three, they simultaneously throw or bounce the ball at the opposite end, with the goal of landing the ball in a cup. If one player is successful, then the opposite team drinks the cup. Adding excitement in many versions, the opposing team can grab or swat the ball before it lands in the cup. If both players score, then a "send back" occurs. In a field report submitted by a female student at Indiana University, she observed a sexual undertone to the game: "As players get more intoxicated, they become more rowdy. Frequent cheering took place as well as cursing. When all males were playing, the game seemed to be much more competitive, and when females were playing with males, the game seemed to be much more of a flirtatious interaction" (McDowell 2008).

Several drinking games depend on signs and numbers, whether from cards, dice, or television. In "Up and Down the River," a dealer hands players five cards face down, and then the dealer turns a card from the deck face up. If the card in a player's hand matches, then he or she must drink that number of times. Sometimes, reversals are allowed; the player with a match can make someone else drink (Duda 1987; Griscom et al. 1986, 94–99). In "Kings," participants distinguish between actions for red and black cards. If someone receives a red card from two to eight, he or she takes the number of drinks indicated on the card. If it is a black card, the player distributes that number of drinks to others. Nine is a special card that is greeted with the chant "nine, nine, bust a rhyme." The person receiving it utters a sentence, and the others in the circle must give another sentence that rhymes. If a person in the group cannot rhyme, he or she must take a drink. If a player pulls a ten card, then everyone drinks together. Similarly, an ace demands, in folk lingo, a "waterfall": the cardholder starts drinking and cannot put the cup down until the person next to him or her does. Pulling a jack calls for the person to initiate a version of Thumper in which someone gives a name within a category, such as types of beer, and each subsequent participant must remember that and add one. If someone falters, then he or she must take a drink. Pull a queen and you get to make your own game rule. For a king, the player gets to pour an amount of beer into a cup placed in the middle of the table. The fourth person to pull a king must drink the entire cup, and then the game is over (McDowell 2008).

In "Mexicali," "Mexican," or "Liar's Dice," two dice are placed in a cup. One player rolls the dice inside the cup and slams the cup to the table. The player peeks under the cup and tells the next player the result of the roll, perhaps truthfully, perhaps not. The nonroller has the option of believing the roller, rolling to beat the call, or calling "bullshit." If bullshit is called, the cup must be lifted to reveal the dice. If the roller is caught bluffing, he or she must drink, and it is the next player's turn. If the roller was not lying, the player calling bullshit has to drink, and the roller goes again. If a 3–2 shows up, then everyone must drink, and 21, or "Mexicali," is the highest roll possible (Duda 1987; Dundes and Pagter 1975, 5–7; Egan 1985, 171; Griscom et al. 1984, 71–72; McDowell 2008).

Paul Douglas documented a whopping sixty-five drinking games from Towson State students, and comparable extensive collections exist in folklore archives at the University of California at Berkeley, Indiana, Penn State, and Wayne State. Douglas found that previous generations of students knew of drinking games but did not engage in the frequency and variety of games as do contemporary students in the mega-university age (1987, 57). Drinking games are played normally by underage drinkers from high school to college, but usually trail off as one nears graduation. Drinking in these games is made social and playful to initiate young drinkers. Alcohol, after all, is an acquired taste. Many of the new drinkers, Douglas found, were women who felt uncomfortable about drinking beer associated with manly behavior. For them, games eased their anxiety about engaging in publicly assertive behaviors. Fifteen percent of the students, Douglas found, played these games at least twice a month.

For some participants in drinking games, the play frames are not about drinking but about socializing in the sense of "making friends," or flirting. In a college setting where one meets strangers, they allow for relating to others. They break the ice, as students are fond of saying. The attitude reveals a pattern referred to often in modern American culture of people seeking mood-altering substances to mediate their social relations with strangers, but apparently intensified in the campus environment attracting residents unknown to one another previously. "Fun," used so often to describe what students are after in college outside of, or to compensate for, the grind of coursework, first means engagement of others through conviviality, and second, the release from everyday reality, which suggests the loosening of inhibition. One also senses a performance of friendliness in which collegiate camaraderie includes being willing to be humiliated and please one's mates by showing self-deprecation (the opposite of stigmatized, individualistic "snobbishness" and grim, antisocial "bitchiness") (Moffatt 1989, 40–45).

The emphasis on showing vulnerability in collegiate culture may stem from a realization that students are in competition with one another, separated by grades, position, and sports into higher and lower status. In addition to this competitiveness that drinking games mimic and at the same time subvert, students realize the temporariness of the college experience. Collegians, when they unwind from studies, set up a sanctioned frame for the kind of activity they will not engage in again and indeed, social ties that probably will not be maintained. Rituals of drinking serve to equalize relationships tailored to college life and usually bring the controlled, sober, narcissistic student down. Students expect to form "gangs" of friends while at college according to different interests (students in my experience distinguish between their sports, residence, and study friends) and shared stresses, such as being in a difficult class together or living in a dorm. Anthropologist Michael Moffatt observed at Rutgers, for example, that "though many incoming students had hometown friends at Rutgers, almost all of them believed that they would not benefit from higher education unless they also made new friends in college. And most of them did so very quickly" (1989, 42).

In drinking games one finds mixed messages toward America's favorite intoxicating substance. Although the outcomes of physical and mental impairment in the games *should* convey the warning that drinking adversely affects memory, concentration, movement, decorum, and speech, they also are perceived as actions of play, a type of equalizing friendly, if risky, fun. Unlike other games in children's folklore, drinking play is not designed to select a winner as much as to isolate a loser. Typical of many pranks, players will in fact "gang up" in these games on someone they feel cannot handle drinking. The sickness that one may suffer is the ultimate embarrassment, and at the same time a sign of belonging to a group that strangely gives incentive to participate. By being willing to be foolish, players may be thinking that they are being friendly—and bonding into a clique considered essential for navigating campus life. Another special characteristic of drinking games is that they focus on *how* the game is played rather than on the achievement of the winner. Is the message then to avoid drinking, or to drink heavily if one is to fit in? For many, the answer is ambiguous.

Killing and Being Killed

Students categorize other games in college, sobering in their content, as "serious fun." This category of campus games is often referred to as a "live-action game" because it involves students moving about in their daily lives instead of a playing field or stationary game station. Live-action games such as "Killer" and all its variations swept college campuses beginning in the 1980s. Variously called "The Hunt," "Assassin," "KAOS" (Killer as an Organized Sport), "Gotcha," "Kisser," "Juggernaut," "Battle Royale," "Elimination," "Circle of Death," Paranoia," "Eradicator," and "Seventh Victim," the game appears to be an outgrowth of the classic movie *The Tenth Victim* (1965), although most players of the game are unaware of the source (Johnson 1980, 81–101; cf. Fine 1983). The movie was set in the twenty-first century when huge wars have been replaced by millions of small ones. Computers pair players who play alternately as assassins and victims in ten games. Some reports give a student at the University of Michigan credit for introducing the game there after the movie came out (Editors 1982, 84). A later movie, *The Murder Game* (2006)—about a group of teenagers devising a game in which one will be secretly designated "the killer" and must creep around to eliminate other players before he or she is identified—took a cue from the campus tradition and may have reignited interest for the twenty-first century. The fact remains that regardless of origin and promotion in popular culture, the game is played with rules often passed by word of mouth by students from one coast to the other, in colleges big and small.

Here are some versions taken from responses to my surveys:

> *Assassin:* Each person in a dorm has a water gun and picks a person out of a hat that they are supposed to kill with the gun. When you kill your

person they have to give you their person. Then you go after that person. That goes on until there is one person left, who is the winner (Hood College).

Catch Me If You Can: Students sign up for this campus-wide watergun competition. Each "agent" receives the name of another agent they must hunt down and shoot. "Dead" agents forfeit their list of victims. The agent who lasts the longest and has the most catches wins (Biola University).

Gotcha: Everyone gets an index card. You wrote your name on it, and then they are collected and mixed up. They're distributed so that everyone would have someone else's name. Everyone is given a dart gun with suction cup darts, and they're supposed to "kill" the person on the card with the dart gun. You had three tries to get someone. When you "killed" someone, you got their card and had to "kill" the person listed on their card, too. There were prizes for the winner (York College).

KAOS: You fill out a form describing your class schedule and habits. You have to stake out your victim, take him by surprise, and shoot him before he catches you. You have to make a kill in seven days or else you're terminated, taken off the roster. There's an obituary list where scores are registered, and the obits are pretty funny with sexual references and creative prose. Awards are given for the best shots as well as the survivor (UCLA).

Students did not describe the game setting futuristically, but rather as a spy or nihilistic fantasy. Many students considered the game a way to meet other students, especially of the opposite sex. The student at Hood who described "Assassin" added that it brought a dorm together at the beginning of the school year, and was complemented later in the fall semester by another secret-identity custom: Secret Santa. Sociologists commenting on the assassin games cite the growing tolerance for violence in America that allows such play to thrive (Johnson 1980, 92–93). University administrations have discouraged the practice, especially in light of concerns for school shootings (for example, the headline-grabbing Virginia Tech "massacre" in 2007 and the murder-suicide at Northern Illinois University the following year). In 2008, the University of Nebraska banned playing of "Assassin" after police were called out to a classroom by a report of a masked gunman. Officers responded within two minutes and found a student in a ski mask, armed with a toy gun that shoots foam darts. The resident of Neihardt Residence Center explained that he was playing a version of "Assassin" called "Live Free or Neihardt" at the dorm. Investigation revealed that other residences had their own variants, such as Smith Hall's "Cupid's Rampage." The actions were similar: players attempted to assassinate their targets by hitting them below the head with foam darts or paperclip bullets. At Bowdoin College in Brunswick, Maine, assassins used socks, and elsewhere water pistols were the weapons of choice. Although students meeting with administrators insisted that "they were just doing it for fun," Nebraska's vice-chancellor for student affairs declared that the game "is at least disruptive, and could be dangerous if anyone misinterpreted a toy gun to be real" (Lampe 2008).

Folklorist John William Johnson, however, is more supportive of the game, and points out that it provides an outlet for "surrogate sin," feeding on new freedoms young students are finding in college, "but in a very safe way." He interprets the game in its college context, suggesting a "cathartic function." He explains: "Such a game lends itself readily to the highly tense atmosphere of university life, which involves many forms of academic pressures: deadlines, exams, identity crises, term papers, and the questioning of traditional mores and values. The establishment of life-and-death scenarios totally within the realm of fantasy can help relieve the tension of college life through the medium of Killer, especially at the moment of killing or being killed" (Johnson 1980, 92–93).

I also suggest that the text of the assassin games provides a model of success in what students anticipate to be a radically individualistic postmodern world featuring constant contact with strangers. "Killer" is playful, high-risk preparation in a cyber age in which the line between private and public space is blurred because one can always watch others and be seen, and information can be gathered about him or her. It emphasizes more than other games the role of an individual alienated from any group. Faced with the prospect of diminishing expectations of success, each participant looks out for himself or herself, simultaneously acting as attacker and victim (Jackson 1992). It is a role protecting privacy, yet remaining always vulnerable. It is simultaneously and tensely competitive and cooperative. To a large degree, the modern college with its intensity and divisiveness accentuates this individualistic character of narcissistic self-indulgence coupled with fear of losing social connection, resulting, many would argue, in a cultural paranoia (see Sennett 1977; Bellah et al. 1985).

Variations of live-action games that also appear to comment on the vulnerability of students about to enter the big, fearsome world include "Humans vs. Zombies," again probably influenced by popular culture—a spate of mass-market American zombie movies such as the Halloween favorite *Night of the Living Dead* (1968), continuing with *Night of the Living Dead 3D* (2006) and *Zombieland* (2009). In the game, players start out as Humans and try to survive with Zombies beginning to rise from the dead. Humans are given socks or dart guns to stun unarmed players identified as Zombies. The goal for Zombies is to tag the Humans to gain a kill and avoid "starvation," which would force them out of the game. The game ends when all Humans are turned into Zombies, or the Humans endure in a set amount of time, usually over the course of a weekend. Goucher College credits two of its students, Brad Sappington and Chris Weed, with creating a Zombie event with seventy participants in 2005 to be a gentler, contained version of "Killer." After receiving enthusiastic response on campus to the game, the students created a website with information for other universities to adapt their own versions of "Humans vs. Zombies." The game grew in popularity, with player counts rising to as many as 1,000 at Cornell, Penn State, Bowling Green State, and the University of Maryland, among others (Nuckols 2008; Wexler 2008). A student editorial at Bowling Green State (BGS) explained the appeal this way: "Sometimes people just need to have some violent, but not too violent, fun to get some of that stress out of their systems. What fits that description better than humans and zombies fighting to the death? This is exactly the kind of release that students could use" (Warrick 2010a).

But many observers could not distinguish between play and the real thing. At Alfred University in 2008, a faculty member reported a student seeing a student with a gun, and campus officials quickly locked down for hours, in keeping with its emergency plan. Police cornered a student with a plastic Nerf toy who reported playing "Humans vs. Zombies" with sixty other players. Prompted by real-life school shootings, Alfred officials consequently issued a moratorium on the game on campus ("'Nuff Nerf" 2008). The University of Colorado allowed the game to be played by replacing Nerf shooters with balled-up socks (Fantz 2009). At BGS, where the game was called "Undead," students had to agree to keep the game outside of school buildings; make sure that the brightly colored Nerf shooters or marshmallow blowguns were not painted to look more like guns; refer to the weapons in communications as "blasters," not guns; and identify players with conspicuous bandannas (no masks). Some students worried that the regulations dampened the folk spontaneity of the game and would force more intense play underground. In blog and newspaper exchanges, students viewed the simulated violence as thrilling, socially unifying, "a much-needed break from class," and even sexually rousing. This was "real fun," BGS student Bryan Warrick (2010a) wrote. By that, he meant an opportunity to regress into an age perceived to be freer than the college years. "Humans vs. Zombies" allowed his fellow players a chance, he opined, "be a kid again" in "the ultimate game of tag." Yet they also looked ahead beyond their time on campus by carefully considering the experience in line with the personal "energy" and reliance on new technology to "fight" and "survive" in a new age (Warrick 2010b).

The Women's Way

If women now share with men the masculine displays of killer games and tugs-of-war in campus festivals, they also maintain their share of customs all their own. Artistry and creativity, rather than brawn, typically are the order of the day in the women's rituals. At Hope College, first- and second-year women compete in performing arts for the coveted Nykerk Cup, established in 1936. Professor John Nykerk, founder of the campus's music department, established the contest to give women their own event because most competitive activities were reserved for men. The rhetoric of the early contests in fact referred to challenges of upperclass women by the first-year women to a "match of muscles." Nykerk presented a silver cup to be handed down each year to the victor of the contest involving one oratorical number, one musical selection, and the enactment of a one-act play. Ritual builds anticipation for the big event. A candlelight service occurs the week prior to the competition, with a candlelight walk through campus that makes a stop at the president's house. The competition for the cup occurs at the Holland Civic Center as a highlight of Parents' Weekend. "Song women" sit properly unbent with gloved hands on their laps; "morale guys" offer support with booming cheers and thoughtful gifts. Several hundred women present a play and an oration, and participate in the chorus. Although judges determine a winner, the women—in the spirit of feminine cooperation—have a ritual "meeting in the middle," a chaotic conglomeration of all the happy participants in which losers cannot be separated from winners.

Vassar upperclass women welcome the frosh the first week of school by serenading them in their dorms with class songs and carrying banners. Amid beer and Vassar Devils (ice cream with chocolate cake and sauce), the first-year students kneel to the seniors and respond with a song composed for the occasion. The event climaxes when each house sings for administrators, and the senior class officers and the president of the college select a winner. The Vassar tradition is related to a widespread older campus custom of "step singing" among women. The steps symbolically represent a transitional location between the house and the wider world, and the singing encourages the occupants of the steps to move to bigger and better things. At Sweet Briar College in Virginia, for instance, seniors sit on "Senior Steps" in special robes. Juniors sing a combination of serious and teasing songs, culminating in the traditional "Holla, Holla":

Here's to the [seniors, first-years, and so forth] Holla, Holla, Holla
Nothing that you cannot do!

Here's to the [seniors, first-years, and so forth], Holla, Holla, Holla
Nothing that you cannot do!
Work for the good and work for the right
Always doing something and doing it right, so
Here's to the [seniors, first-years, and so forth], Holla, Holla, Holla,
Nothing that you cannot do!

Step singing has been recorded at Wellesley College since 1899, where students assemble decked out in a class color (purple, red, green, or yellow) on the chapel steps several times a year, including the tension-filled first and last days of the semester. Each class has a song mistress charged with making sure that her fellow students learn and perform the songs. Distinguishing the step singing from a choral recital are cheers poking fun at the other classes in between songs.

At Chatham University (originally Chatham College for Women) in Pittsburgh, Song Contest began in 1921, but unceremoniously died during the turbulent 1970s. In 1985, alumni encouraged the revival of the tradition. In the new version, the victorious class wins a cup for singing the traditional Chatham song and a song of their own making. The original song offers the students a chance to lampoon themselves. The winning entry for a recent winning song was "Our Favorite Things" set to the tune of the same name:

U of Pitt doctors and CMU hackers
Tartans and Panthers and Steeler linebackers
Duquesne musicians they all come to call
We've mixers and parties and dates with them all.
Fall Fling and Egg Nog and Thanksgiving Dinner,
Cookies and turkey won't help us get thinner,
Candlelight Service the joy that it brings,
These are a few of our favorite things.

Song Contest is the culmination of the annual "Battle of the Classes," which includes planned activities such as tug-of-war, scavenger hunts, window painting, and karaoke.

Sometimes called "songfests," or "stepsings" when they are traditionally held on the steps of a college hall, the contests often coincide with parents and alumni weekends early in the fall semester. At Hood College, each class prepares two songs—one on a theme for the competition and another for the big sisters of the class. Each class enters the chapel in a different way. The frosh, for example, run in with one hand on their dink-adorned heads and the other at their sides, and at the signal of the "song leader," the line stops and sits down. The sophomores, in class skirts and blouses, jog in with their hands behind their backs; the juniors, decked out in class blazers, saunter in snapping their fingers; and the seniors, befitting their lofty status, walk in slowly wearing black robes. Since 1923, a similar tradition has thrived at Cedar Crest College, a small women's college in Allentown, Pennsylvania, where, according to school publicity, "Song Contest is to Cedar Crest what football is to Ohio State—the tie that binds."

Many women's colleges also have "lantern nights" early in the first semester. At Bryn Mawr near Philadelphia, a lantern-giving tradition begun in 1896 celebrates Athena, the goddess of wisdom. Representatives of the three upper classes present wrought-iron lanterns to new students at a solemn ceremony in October. Dressed in black academic gowns, participants assemble at dusk in a cloistered garden at the heart of the campus. Upperclass women sing a Greek hymn as they present the lanterns, and the new students respond with one of their own after they receive the gifts (Briscoe 1981a, 119–50). Since 1921, alumnae at the University of Pittsburgh's "Lantern Night" have offered the gift to incoming women to light their way in the search for truth over the following four years. In a variation at Cedar Crest, students use candles to symbolize carrying on the spirit and tradition of the college. During the first vespers service in September, each "big sister" lights a candle from the flame at the altar and then turns to brighten the unlighted candle of her frosh "little sister."

The big sister/little sister tradition is a long-standing institution, especially at women's colleges. Big sisters help underclass women get set up at the college. They throw parties for them, show them the ropes, and generally look after them. At schools such as Agnes Scott and Hood, the student body is organized by sister classes. Juniors are sisters to first-year students, and seniors are sisters to sophomores. The sisters are often bound in a mock wedding ceremony.

At Cedar Crest, little sisters present big sisters, dressed in black, with long-stemmed yellow roses at a candlelight dinner. After the meal the little sisters form an arch through which the juniors walk to a ring ceremony. At Wells College in Aurora, New York, a school of approximately 500 women, every first-year student is assigned a "sister" from each of the three upper classes. Introductions are made in surprise summer letters with unknown addresses. This nurturing relationship develops a family tie on campus. At Wilson College, first-year students receive an "Aunt Sarah," a graduate of the college who corresponds with the student once each month.

At Keuka College, about the same size as Wells, each sophomore chooses a "Little Bud," who is not aware of the Big Bud's identity until a ceremonial breakfast. If a Big Bud has two or more Little Buds, they are commonly known to each other as Budsters. A Big Bud's Big Bud is known as Grandbud, and her Big Bud is a Great-Grandbud. Juniors select frosh to be their "Little Sister," and seniors select first-year students to whom they will be a "Senior Pal." In a special ritual called the "Pow Wow," juniors leave campus and leave clues to their whereabouts. Their Little Buds have to find the juniors before breakfast at 6 a.m.

If congenial big sister traditions and feminine displays of refinement smack of blue-blooded gentility, many modern campus women appropriate manly football games to assert their equal, active stake in campus, and public, life with a popular show of grit. At campuses big and small like Quincy University, Lindenwood University, Southern Methodist University (SMU), Mansfield University, Rice University, Texas State University, and Fairfield University, women take the field for an annual "Powder Puff" game, usually at homecoming, or they engage in league play for an entire season. Rules and number of participants vary, but usually the games follow the model of flag football, with players wearing bright-colored cloths on each side of the hip. Defensive players pull (rather than tackle) the ball carrier down and relieve her of the flag to get her knee to touch the ground and stop the action. Passing is allowed, and, adding excitement in most versions of the game, all players are eligible to receive passes. In a sign of reversal, many Powder Puff games feature male cheerleaders who perform a mock half-time show. The Powder Puff label implies softness, but as the Texas State newspaper reported, "Powder Puff football is anything but dainty. . . . [It] begins innocently, but usually ends as fierce as any game of tackle football with sprained ankles, broken wrists and pulled muscles" (Gaddis 2009). At East Texas Baptist University, the game means class war as first- and second-year students square off against junior and seniors. Still, some events play on voyeuristic interest in women cavorting in the mud with self-deprecating themes in the name of fun (and fund-raising), such as the "Blondes vs. Brunettes" and "Bikini Bowl" games and racy team names like Hot Chicks, Down N' Dirty, and Bad Girlz (Thompson 2007).

The fun and games of a college, from a student's viewpoint, distinguish the college as much as its intellectual reputation. The "events on campus" may appear to be a round of entertainment, but digging deeper reveals those cultural markers that structure the year and identify the campus's denizens. The events may be gendered to remind students at women's colleges of their legacy or massified in the big football game to broadcast institutional power from the actions on the field. A process of negotiation between students and administrators is apparent in the organization, or alternation, of socializing events in the production of campus culture. The institution touts its special holidays and commemorations as its distinctive corporate traditions of ingathering, often with solemn overtones, while students seek smaller social frames with their own spirited ideas of fitting in and letting go.

GREEK LIFE

FRATERNITIES AND SORORITIES OFTEN VIEW THEMSELVES AS UPHOLD-ers of tradition and collegiate spirit leaders. Many fraternity and sorority members declare Greek letter societies as a traditional place in the college where "me" becomes "us." Fraternal organizations sing the praises of fellowship, ritually honor "brothers" and "sisters," and parade the value of civic engagement, particularly in an individualistic, self-absorbed mass society. But as organizations that enclose themselves in separate houses and carry the stigma of secret societies, fraternities and sororities are subject to suspicion, restriction, reform, disparagement, suspension, and, at many campuses, banishment. Greeks recognize in a kind of double consciousness that many college characters see them as despoilers of campus integrity or social progress. The conflict of perceptions is especially acute in the public square because of the fear that the Greeks form an insidious cartel that, even if small, wields power over the collegiate superstructure. Questions naturally arise about the power and abuse the fraternities and sororities exert, what they are up to, who got in, and who did not.

The Greek system is intended to foster lifelong benevolent values of fellowship and service, its defenders declare. Yet there is a public, and often administrative, apprehension of the exclusivity of the fraternities and sororities. The organizations are often assumed to be elitist and therefore arrogant, if not troublesome, and even defiant subcultures at the same time that they carry a line-toeing establishment aura. Another paradoxical combination of images is evident in traditional practices associated with fraternities and sororities of crude hazing, rowdy singing and pranking, pledging, initiation, and partying set off against their publicized activities as big-hearted service organizations, campus boosters, and well-mannered socialites. The debate heightens as universities have grown and the purposes of fraternities and sororities as debauched private worlds in a mass democratic society become matters of national concern.

Greek-letter fraternities have come a long way from their eighteenth-century roots in the founding of Phi Beta Kappa at the College of William and

Mary. Latin-letter fraternities had already existed, and John Heath (1758–1810, destined to become a U.S. congressman), after failing to get into two of the organizations, created a precedent with the use of Greek-letter initials for the creation of an honorary society. Membership in the organization was more about academic status than brotherhood, and members included faculty as well as upperclassmen. Kappa Alpha at Union College in Schenectady, New York, organized in 1825, is credited with establishing the model of a modern fraternity with an exclusively student organization and elaborate initiation. Sigma Phi, formed in 1827 also at Union, became the first national fraternity when it opened a second chapter at Hamilton College in 1831. That led to the creation of other fraternities on the same campus to form a Greek system: Alpha Delta Phi in 1832 and Psi Upsilon in 1833 at Hamilton, Beta Theta Pi at Miami of Ohio in 1839, and Alpha Sigma Phi at Yale in 1845. Evolving from literary and debating societies, the early fraternities provided fellowship outside the control of college faculty and administrators.

Students saw an advantage in forming fraternities, often ten or fewer in a chapter, where the support came from one another in an intimate setting. In answer to the regimentation of students in formal study, the fraternities provided a location for the social, fun side of college life. Sometimes fraternities attracted members looking for escape from the dismal dormitory life in the nineteenth century. Greek houses appeared much more attractive and independent, and also allowed for cooperative arrangements among students to work on exams and papers that were generally frowned upon in the Old Mains of many campuses (Syrett 2009, 13–50). More broadly, sociologists have observed, fraternities offered a counter-society within the faculty-derived parental authority of the campus that could extend into the society at large. This counter-society rested power not in the father-figure and male-provider role, but in a hierarchical group of brothers that could be called fratriarchal (Brod 1995, 245–47). Pointing to the American fratriarchal context, social theorist Jay Mechling's explanation is that "there is a strong individualistic, antiauthoritarian element in American culture, filled with distrust of patriarchal authority. Male power in American society lies with the fraternity, the male group (generally white, upper-middle class, heterosexual, and Protestant). American men's anxieties about male power, hierarchy, and acceptance, then focus less on the father and more on the brothers" (2008, 67).

Fraternities also promised something for the long term: the professional contacts one needed after college. The fellowship of the Greek society would last a lifetime, members vowed, and serve to garner favors. The undergirding principles were about the privileges of a fraternity of like-minded, like-acting, and often like-looking social climbers. Invoking Greek civilization in their name, fraternities held up lofty ideals of enlightened and often entitled youth, and claimed to build manly traits of strength and competition to succeed as the "fittest" in a Darwinian vision of an evolving society. By the mid-nineteenth century, women broke through male bastions of college campuses, but faced rebuff from the men's fraternal strongholds (Turk 2004, 14–42). To participate in fraternal life, women would have to organize their own groups. The first college organizations for women such as the Adelphean and Philomathean societies resembled the Latin literary clubs more than fraternities. Early women's organizations built on the model of a men's fraternity were I.C. Sorosis (later Pi Beta Phi) in 1867 at Monmouth College in Monmouth, Illinois (it added a second chapter a year later at Iowa Wesleyan College), Kappa Alpha Theta in 1870 at DePauw University, Alpha Phi in 1872 at Syracuse University (where the term "sorority" was coined to replace the masculine-sounding "women's fraternity"), and Sigma Kappa in 1874 at Colby College (Turk 2004, 165).

Characterized as white Christian institutions that promoted ties of brotherhood, the model of fraternities in the old-time college was adopted by Jews and African Americans aspiring to social equality but excluded from the Greek-letter societies. The groundbreaking Jewish organizations were Pi Lambda Phi, founded in 1895 at Yale, and Zeta Beta Tau, established in 1898 by students attending the Jewish Theological Seminary and New York colleges. The separation of Jews in these organizations followed the parallel development of Jewish and non-Jewish law firms, summer camps, sports leagues, and hospitals. The rate of fraternal membership by Jewish college students was high up to World War II: as many as one-fourth to one-third of all young Jews from 1920 to 1940 attending universities outside New York City joined Jewish fraternities (Sanua 2003, 25).

The emergence of African American college fraternities responded to a common ghettoized situation on many northern campuses. Black students were typically isolated from the general student population and had an abysmal retention rate. At Cornell, the six African American students admitted in the fall of 1904 did not reenroll for the 1905–6 academic year. A student committee sought to retain the remaining black students and took note that Cornell fraternities and sororities could help by providing students with housing, study groups, and social networking. On December 4, 1906, seven black brethren decided to create Alpha Phi Alpha, and a second chapter was established at the historical black institution of Howard University a year later (Ross 2000, 5–7). Other fraternities followed in quick succession: Kappa Alpha Psi in 1911 at Indiana University, Bloomington; Omega Psi Phi in 1911 at Howard University; and Phi Beta Sigma in 1914, also at Howard University. The first African American sorority was founded in 1908 at Howard, and a second chapter was chartered in 1914 at the University of Chicago. Delta Sigma Theta also emerged from Howard University, in 1913, with a second chapter established at

Wilberforce University a year later. It grew to be the largest historically black Greek-letter sorority.

In their organizational rivalries, Greek-letter societies perpetuated the competitiveness of the old-time college. But they often acted together in college politics, taking charge of many student governments across America, and they stood up for student concerns against many college administrations. "Rushing" to attract fraternity and sorority members became a major campus event to rival the old scraps. Pledging and gaining a pin were signs of status indeed. Once initiated, the "pledge" transformed into an "active," with the expectation that he or she would be a lifelong member and participate fully in campus fraternal events. To serve their social ends, the Greek-letter organizations instituted initiations, rituals, and customs to select appropriate members. The Greek customs saw to it that close friends were made quickly, more quickly than students thought they ever could back in the dorms. Social labels of "hallmen" or "independents" used by fraternity and sorority members for the non-Greeks implied lesser participation in campus life and even narrower popularity and vivacity. In addition to their pins, canes, and paddles, Greeks adorned themselves with shirts, pants, bags, jewelry, and key chains, sometimes transferred from seniors to juniors in pass-down ceremonies. Some fraternities and sororities have nicknames such as Sig Pigs for Sigma Pi, Yak-Yaks for Acacia, Sammies for Sigma Alpha Mu, and Gumbies for Sigma Tau to go along with the kinder names of Tri Delts for Delta Delta Delta, Phi Psi for Phi Kappa Psi, and Delts for Delta Tau Delta.

The dramatic social widening of colleges in the post–civil rights period to include more traditionally excluded groups changed the role of the college fraternities and sororities. They were still about fellowship and position, but with the number of "independent" students growing, they could not exert the control they once did, and on most campuses they no longer spoke for the student body (Horowitz 1987, 82–150). To maintain their prestigious social niche, fraternities, sometimes as large as 200 members to a chapter, threw the big parties and gained status in athletic competitions, often at a considerable cost to intellectualism (Egan 1985, 223).

Student affairs officials cited civil rights legislation to end discriminatory racial and ethnic practices in the fraternities. In the wake of the women's movement, some coed Greek houses have been organized, thus ending the sharp gendered split between fraternities and sororities. Some minorities such as Latinos, Native Americans, Asian Americans, homosexuals, and Muslims created fraternal organizations to declare their identities more out in the open (see Guardia and Evans 2008; Yeung and Stombler 2000). Other fraternities and sororities such as Epsilon Sigma Rho established in 1986 at Cal–State Sacramento were self-consciously formed to encourage multicultural participation.

Administrators concerned about their institutions' liability exerted more supervision over the Greeks in response to complaints about the initiatory and celebratory practices of fraternities (Syrett 2009, 229–84). This regulatory pattern became especially critical as frat parties, sometimes packing in hundreds of students—often caused problems with violence, alcohol, and sexual abuse (Fischer 1982, 208–9). Greeks often pointed to the parties as proof of their popularity and vitality, although campus observers speculated that sociologically they compensated for the declining prestige of fraternities and sororities (Syrett 2009, 309). A sexual factor cannot be ignored either in the changing fortunes of the Greek system. Since the 1960s, coed dorms diminished some of the appeal of the frat as a place to mix with, and impress, the opposite sex.

Though some pundits expected that frats would face extinction in the wake of 1960s iconoclasm, a resurgence of the frat occurred during the American economic bubble years toward the end of the twentieth century (see Horowitz 1987, 273–79; Syrett 2009, 229–84). Undergraduate fraternity membership doubled in a decade to 400,000 in 1990, and more than 1,000 new chapters formed. Sorority memberships increased similarly to a total of 240,000 (Betterton 1988, 179). Still, more than 90 percent of college students bypassed Greek involvement. A number of campuses held on to the identity of being Greek-dominated. Fraternities and sororities claim more than 40 percent of the student body at some forty-five colleges. DePauw is the most Greek at around 80 percent, and other campuses with strong frat representation are Washington and Lee and the College of William and Mary.

Although many of the colleges with strong Greek systems tend to be of moderate size, at larger universities the frats and sororities are making inroads. The intimacy of the Greek house sometimes seems more attractive to students facing mass campuses of more than 30,000 students and dorms holding hundreds of students. One of those mega-campuses at Arizona State University in Tempe claims the crown for the largest Greek system in the world with over 100 fraternities and sororities. Another factor influencing the resurgence of frats is that when drinking ages rapidly moved up from eighteen to twenty-one and colleges cracked down on alcohol in dorms, many Greek houses became underage drinking clubs. Fraternity and sorority membership opened up to more campus types, although joining still came in cost-wise at a premium compared to staying independent.

Addressing their exclusiveness and shady reputations as sadistic hazers, many fraternities during the early twenty-first century reduced the length of their pledging periods, and softened or eliminated their initiation practices. Some sororities meanwhile benefited from women forsaking the coed dorm and its atmosphere of sexual competition. Students also reported to me the need to have a small group to rely on and support, a surrogate family in a homelike setting that would nurture them through what they perceive to be difficult years socially as well as academically. The status associated with an organization one had to be initiated into held appeal in a society that had few rituals for the transition from adolescence to adulthood. Initiation also suggested a kind of status associated with being part of a firm or organization as a sign of success in the corporate or political world many aspired to join. An American belief still holds, conspiratorial or not in nature, that fraternal organizations, enhanced by their secrecy and ritual, are paths to, and bulwarks of, power (Robbins 2002). The hierarchical model of fratriarchy fostered by the Greek system gave members a sense that, as a group, they could make a difference: they advanced with experience and the support of a network. The related perception that future financial security is a primary goal of college had an influence on other students. The feeling that jobs are more competitive, especially in business, also restored the role of fraternities and sororities as a place to make future professional contacts.

But if the independence of the Greek organizations was going to be maintained under renewed administrative, faculty, and even community scrutiny, the image, and some of the roles, of the fraternities would have to be changed. Yes, maintain tradition, give students a peer support group, encourage community service and college spirit, administrators admonished, but do not harass, exclude, or abuse other students. At Bucknell, Gettysburg, Colgate, Colby, Amherst, Franklin and Marshall, and Middlebury, faculty voted to eliminate the Greeks altogether after reports of sexual and racial harassment, injuries caused by hazing, and drug and alcohol abuse. Two national fraternities—Zeta Beta Tau and Tau Kappa Epsilon—moved to improve the Greek image by eliminating pledging. Zeta Beta Tau also closed two chapters. While maintaining pledgeship, four other national fraternities—Alpha Gamma Rho, Kappa Delta Rho, Phi Sigma Kappa, and Alpha Epsilon Pi—announced programs to eliminate hazing (Quinto 1989, 27–28).

In 2004, journalist Alexandra Robbins scored a national best seller with a critique of the American college sorority system in the twenty-first century. She laid the blame for its ills squarely on tradition as a hammer of authority swinging with brutal force on young people. Robbins made news with her charge that sororities' "revulsion to change, euphemized as a devotion to tradition, is what keeps the sororities ignorant and intolerant" (2004, 322). She indicted sorority chapters for perpetuating drug use, violence, psychological and verbal abuse, prostitution, racism, forced binge drinking, nudity, cheating, and eating disorders all, in her words, "in the name of tradition" (Robbins 2004, 11). As evidence for the oppression of tradition in fraternities and sororities,

Robbins quotes a sister who seemed horrified at the author's suggestion that practices such as running girls through a gauntlet (known as "Pigs' Run," "Running of the Bulls," or "Squeal Day") could be challenged: "You don't even question the tradition. You just do it" (2004, 2). In response to the added charge that sororities do not embrace diversity and multiculturalism, a campus official tells Robbins, "This is a system steeped in tradition, and I think that's part of the problem. Chapters are afraid to go first. I think there's an unarticulated pressure toward sameness, which fosters racism and a homogeneity they'll never see the rest of their lives" (Robbins 2004, 237). In the above rhetoric, tradition is both a mode of thought involving fidelity to precedent and a kind of practice that draws attention to itself because of its ritualistic, symbolic content. Either way, it sounds bad, even loony.

Many sorority pledges indeed accept, if not venerate, the attachment of sorority institutions to the power of tradition, not because of ignorance or intolerance, but because of what they viewed as an admirable process of gaining sisterhood in the midst of a larger, often alienating campus culture. Complaining that modernity has also brought an overwhelming mass culture that makes people feel lost as small faceless specks in a giant corporate superstructure, organizations like sororities and fraternities market their sense of community, their social solidarity and mutual aid. Sisters mention tradition in relation to sororities as old institutions featuring social bonding and identity building that routinely occur in a lineage through many generations. This aura of tradition is conveyed through rituals, songs, secret passwords, and initiations that senior sisters pass down to younger pledges in an annual, much anticipated round of activities known as "rush." Rather than remaining static, the rush tradition had been subject to reform since the late twentieth century, including the increased regulation, and in many cases elimination, of pledging and hazing.

In his own journalistic investigation, Alan D. DeSantis found dismay from sorority sisters that tradition had eroded instead of, as Robbins tells the tale, there being much of it. DeSantis reported a reaction from sisters that would have horrified Robbins–a call for a "return to tradition" (2007, 187–88). "We need to start pledging again," a representative senior Omega told him, with the explanation, "I think we would be much tighter" (DeSantis 2007, 187). He quotes another sister who does not mince words to form her opinion of the elimination of pledging traditions: "These girls are great, beautiful, blah, blah, blah, but they suck. Nobody pledges anymore, so sororities are nothing more than girls' clubs. They do nothing that makes them respect their chapter; *there's nothing they have to do*" (DeSantis 2007, 188; emphasis added). Tradition, for her, is not only sorority rhetoric or an unwritten guide to action; it gains its significance from practice, or purposeful activity that contributes to fratriarchy.

She is not convinced by all the blurbs about tradition being important in the official chapter literature. For her, tradition translates to ritualistic action, and it is a vital force for an organization that purports to provide social attachment for its members, the kind of intimacy associated with a tribe or family.

Pledging

So as not to distract new students, many colleges prohibit initiatory rushes until at least the second semester of a student's freshmen year. Others insist on waiting until the sophomore year. Students choose from a number of fraternities and sororities, many with reputations for a certain ethnic or racial membership, social atmosphere, and outside interests such as athletics or business. The Greek organization offers the prospective student a "bid" to pledge with the fraternity or sorority, which the student can accept or refuse.

Alpha Chi Omega for many years held a formal dessert in which a piece of "dream cake" was given to rushees. A story and song accompanied the cutting of the cake; they concern a lonely princess who dreamed of having many friendships. Actives tell the rushees to take a piece of cake and wish upon it before they go to sleep. If they receive their bids, their wish will come true, and they will have many friendships (Christner 1967, 11–12; Glavan 1968, 195).

Pledges also learn special blessings referring to the deep social bonds of the organization. Here is a toast collected at Indiana University from the Tri Delts:

Now we ask, O God of might
Keep our crescent over bright;
Help us our noble aim to keep
And bless our friendship bond so deep. (McDowell 2008)

Gamma Phi Beta has a grace blessing with a similar sentiment:

O let thy blessing, Father dear,
Rest on each sister gathered here,
Our order bless, help us we pray
True lives to live from day to day.

Many songs are specific to an organization. Delta Gamma's symbol is an anchor, and its colors are bronze, pink, and blue (often emblazoned on the sorority house). Not surprisingly, the sorority has adapted "Anchors Away" in a song sung during rush to potential pledges:

Anchors away DG we're setting sail
Fresh breeze and running tide
Our ship will never fail to anchor
Colors on high DG bronze, pink, and blue
All hands on deck
Because we're sailing on
Because we're sailing on
With you! (McDowell 2008)

Sisters sing to the pledges at other sororities to reassure them, often using classic tunes such as "Consider Yourself" from the Broadway hit *Oliver!* The fratriarchal reference underscores the image of the lost soul separated from parents and able to connect with peers.

Consider yourself at home, consider yourself in the family,
We've taken to you so strong, it's clear we're going to get along
Consider yourself well in, consider yourself part of the furniture
There isn't a lot of space, who cares what ever we got, we share.
Nobody tries to be la-de-da and uppity, there's a cup of tea for all,
We've a sisterhood devoted to each other, we're quick to answer any call.
Consider yourself our mate, we don't want to have no fuss.
For after some consideration, we can state, "Consider yourself one of us."
(McDowell 2008)

Many sororities throw a pledge dinner honoring the students accepting bids (Washburn 1976, 2; Glavan 1968, 192–98). Some frat members have a custom called a "shakeup" or a "jolly up," celebrating the acceptance of a bid by lifting the student over their heads and tossing him around (Egan 1985, 28). Others may have a big brother or Dad's night. As explained by Jacob Phillips to collectors at Indiana University, "This is when all the upperclassmen in the house pick one of the pledges as their son. That night, the pledges get their father which gives them a mentor to look up to for the rest of pledgeship. That night is one of the times the pledges get to hang out with the house during pledgeship. It is a really good night for the pledges because they just get to drink and have a good time" (McDowell 2008). Frat members learn drinking songs for the occasion, such as this one from Alpha Tau Omega reportedly taught "on the first day of pledgeship":

Ru Ra Rega
Alpha Tau Omega

Hip Hura, Hip Hura
Three cheers for Alpha Tau (*followed by loud screaming*). (McDowell 2008)

Unofficial songs are learned on Dad's night and used in inter-Greek competitions to root on the team. Sigma Pi, for example, is known for crying out with male bravado the following spoof of the Ole Miss fight song, "Hotty Toddy":

Hidy tidy, Gosh almighty
Who the hell are we
Hey flim flam, bim bam
Sigma Pi by damn
Hidy tidy, gosh almighty
Who the hell are we
Hey flim flam, bim bam
Sigma Pi damn it
And don't you forget it! (McDowell 2008)

Sororities usually more kindly call the pledging period Inspiration Week, Initiation Week, or the euphemistic Help Week, but it is still colloquially known as Hell Week—the climax of activities designed to initiate the "pledge" into the fraternity or sorority. For weeks before Hell Week, the pledge has learned songs, followed rules of address and etiquette, and fashioned special clothing or emblems. Pledges are assigned big brothers or sisters, and as a "class" they take part in sports, drink-offs, barbecues, walkouts, and singathons (Egan 1985, 45–46). To hear a national frat executive explain it, "Pledging is the period of time when prospective members of fraternities participate in planned, non-esoteric activities to familiarize themselves with the organization and its members before they make the decision to be inducted as a full member for life. In the great majority of cases these activities are developmental and supportive of the pledge/associate member. Hazing is an aberration of this process" (Martin 1990, B3). Nonetheless, actives during Hell Week often resort to hazing to test the mettle of pledges, to instill values of the organization, and to build unity before crossing over to the status of "active" brother or sister. Many critics question how much hazing involves mental or physical abuse. Most chapters, however, view initiations not as hazing but as invoking traditional tasks and ceremonies to bring out the special status of Greeks in close fellowship with one another.

Here is a list, for example, of prohibited hazing activities issued by Kappa Kappa Psi fraternity and Tau Beta Sigma sorority at Purdue University. The chapter defined unacceptable hazing as "any actions taken or situation created, intentionally or unintentionally, to produce mental or physical discomfort on or off campus involving members and/or prospective members, which may cause embarrassment, harassment, and/or ridicule" ("Fraternity Policies" 2009).

1. Expecting participation in any activity in which initiated members themselves will not participate.
2. Drinking alcohol or any other substance.
3. Using any drug, narcotic, or controlled substance.
4. Eating spoiled foods, raw onions, goldfish, or anything a reasonable person would not eat.
5. Dropping food or other substances (eggs, grapes, liver, etc.) into another person's mouth.
6. Tying a person to a chair, pole, anchor, tree, or any other object or to another person.
7. Causing fatigue through physical or psychological shock.
8. Branding.
9. Paddling of any nature.
10. Performing physical exercise (sit-ups, push-ups, runs, rolling up or down hills, crab walk, etc.) except in the case of organized sports and Marching Band activities.
11. Pushing, shoving, tackling, or any other physical abuse not associated with organized sports.
12. Throwing anything (whipped cream, garbage, water, paint, etc.) at a person or a group of people.
13. Exposing oneself indecently or appearing nude or in a way that is considered by a reasonable person to be offensive.
14. Verbally addressing prospective members in a demeaning manner.
15. Misleading prospective members in an effort to convince them that they will not be initiated or that they will be hurt during initiation.
16. Carrying any items (shields, paddles, bricks, etc.) that serve no constructive purpose or that are designed to punish or embarrass the carrier.
17. Waking prospective members at odd intervals or permitting fewer than six continuous hours of sleep each night.
18. Conducting membership education activities between the hours of 1 a.m. and 6 a.m.
19. Participating in or conducting lineups (actives or prospective members, separate from members, in order to answer actives' questions).
20. Conducting activities that do not allow adequate time for study and/or classes.

21. Wearing apparel or accessories that are conspicuous and in bad taste or wearing items that cause discomfort.
22. Wearing more or less clothing than the temperature or weather indicates.
23. Defacing property (trees, grounds, buildings, cars, etc.).
24. Stealing any property (composites, trophies, etc.).
25. Compelling a person or group to remain at a certain place or transporting a person or group anywhere without their consent (road trips, kidnaps).
26. Assigning or endorsing pranks (stealing, panty raids, harassing another organization, etc.).
27. Acting like animals or objects.
28. Engaging in public/private stunts or buffoonery that causes mental or emotional trauma and/or injury to any individual.
29. Yelling a prescribed phrase of chant, as an expectation of the membership education program, when entering, passing through, or leaving any building.
30. Intentionally "trashing" any area for the purpose of annoying others or for having others clean the "trashed" area.
31. Disallowing prospective members to speak, as an expectation of the membership education program, with the exception of exams and rituals.
32. Performing marching maneuvers individually or as a part of the membership education program.
33. Blindfolding and parading individuals in public areas or privately conducting blindfolding activities that serve no constructive purpose with the exception of when entering the ritual room immediately prior to the beginning of the ritual or joint ceremony.
34. Having prospective members perform personal chores or errands under the threat of negative repercussions.
35. Placing or receiving phone calls or answering doors with a prescribed chant, riddle, song, or rhyme.
36. Having only prospective member perform wakes and phone duty.
37. Allowing perspective members to use only a particular door when entering or leaving any building or to use only a certain stairway within a building.
38. Conducting quests, treasure hunts, scavenger hunts, paddle hunts, big or little sibling hunts, or walk-outs in a manner unrelated to membership education.
39. Entering or leaving any building in a dictated manner (hand over hand, backwards, crawling, sideways, etc.). ("Fraternity Policies" 2009)

The presentation of the list implies that these activities were familiar to fraternity and sorority members. Fraternities and sororities delineate these prohibitions in response to a host of antihazing laws passed since the 1990s (forty-four states as of 2010) and bad publicity from media coverage of hazing-related deaths (no official statistics are issued for hazing deaths, but unofficial antihazing sites monitor them; see hazing.hanknuwer.com) (Nuwer 1999, 2004).

What is left to do if so many activities are banned? One response has been to eliminate initiations altogether and maintain organizations as open-enrollment clubs. The bulk of fraternity chapters seek to maintain their exclusivity with sanctioned rituals, because in folklorist Jay Mechling's estimation, controlled forms of hazing (separating real or abusive hazing from playful "stylized humiliation") serve "important functions in creating and maintaining the male friendship group" (2009, 58). Chapters usually require pledges to clean and repair the Greek houses. Chapters may also require pledges to wear special clothing to identify them with the fraternity or sorority. Pledges might carry a pledge brick and wear ties and jackets, for example, or, for sororities, pledge ribbons with the house colors and symbols. Pledges also sleep—or spend sleepless nights together—in the house during the week, and may be mobilized for a "borassing" raid (pulling a prank such as toilet papering a lawn) on a rival house (Green 2010, 639). Despite official prohibitions, there have been reports that anytime day or night pledges are herded to a "lineup" or, as sororities know it, a "call-out" (Egan 1985, 42–45; Acri 1989, 5; Glavan 1968, 197). At the lineup, the actives remind pledges of their lowly status, calling them scums, worms, slime, lowlifes, maggots, pledgettes, and rats. The actives bark esoteric questions to pledges arranged neatly in line. Some examples are "What is my middle name? Where do I come from? What am I majoring in?" (Dalkoff 1974, 5). If the pledge does not know the answer, the active punishes the pledge by some kind of physical task, such as push-ups or work detail. In addition, the pledge may have to withstand teasing about some personal characteristic, such as being short, skinny, or stout, and submit to accusations of sexual inadequacy (Raphael 1988, 83).

Other physical demands on the pledges may include forced cold showers taken while singing a fraternity song (Raphael 1988, 82). Some frats will require members to make runs through town or campus, sometimes dressed down to undergarments (Britton 1987, 6–7; Egan 1985, 230). Or there is the controversial use of the symbol-laden fraternity and sorority paddle. Although typically outlawed today, hitting pledges on the rear with a paddle in initiations surfaces in reports (T. 1976, 6–7; see also Egan 1985, 57; Mechling 2008). One old fraternity prank that plays on this fear involves taking a pledge into a closed room while the other pledges wait outside. The person in the room is told to yell and scream each time the paddle is hit on a table and chair, thus creating anxiety among the waiting pledges. One pledge after another is taken in to the room, until all are in on the joke (cf. Raphael 1988, 88).

One former pledge describes a variation from Beta Theta Pi, whose symbol is a winged dragon:

> A guy would say to me, "I am the Brother of the East who brings you the blessings of light and knowledge." And, "I am the Brother of the North who brings you strength and fortitude. Now prepare yourself to meet the dragon!" So they took me over to what they called the dragon's balls, some kind of round, smooth spheres. They told me to take my pants down and lean over to grab hold of the dragon's balls. Then they took my blindfold off and showed me this huge guy with a polished hack-paddle, wood, about two feet long. They told me that my final test would be to take one hack with that paddle. They said that people had been injured in the past, so I'd have to pull my balls up and cup them with my hands. So I pulled my own balls up and leaned over.

The paddler gives his most threatening advance, and the actives give their best screams to scare the pledges waiting outside, but the pledge ends up getting a light tap on the butt. Then the actives announce, "You made it! Congratulations!" (Raphael 1988, 88).

A similar relief comes from an initial lineup reported by Robert Egan:

> The pledges are requested to bring a carrot to the line-up—an innocent vegetable in itself, but an instrument of loathing to wide-eyed pledges who have heard those stories about frozen hot dogs during Hell Week. The pledges' worst fears seem to be justified when, as soon as the line-up begins, they are asked to take their pants down. Not to worry. The actives just want to see, in the words of one brother, "if the pledges are wearing 'grown-up' boxer shorts or if Mommy still has them in Fruit of the Looms." Nothing happens to the guys in boxers—but the guys in "Fruits" get wedgies until they say they will change their evil ways. Then the pledges eat the carrots. (1985, 43–44)

There may be more going on in fraternity practices than first meets the eye, such as shots on the rear with a paddle. Because the bonds among the men are supposed to be intimate, a fear arises that this may suggest homosexuality. Thus many of the demands placed on pledges to appear sexually aggressive to women, or the taunts hurled at them for acting like "fags," compensate for the risk of physical intimacy among the men. There is a psychoanalytic interpretation that the strike on the rear with the paddle symbolizes anal penetration, which the pledge withstands to show submission to the group (Mechling 2008b). The decorated paddle particularly associated with Greek organizations becomes an icon for members because of this association. In a visualization of the brotherhood in the organization, the fraternity member may have fellow members inscribe their names on the paddle and hang it in a conspicuous location in his residence.

Alan and Lauren Dundes theorized that paddling infantilized pledges by replicating spanking, and, as the obstetrician spanks the newborn as he or she enters the world, paddling serves as a type of rebirth into an identity as a fraternity brother (2002, 102–3). More in keeping with the idea of the Greek system representing a societal fratriarchy, Jay Mechling counters that pledges understand the role of the older members as brothers, not parents. He observes that pledges occupy the feminine role and derive masochistic or homoerotic pleasure in taking that position for the liminal play frame of the paddling. In his words, "paddling literalizes the fantasy, 'I am being beaten by my brothers, who really love me'" (Mechling 2008, 67). In this thinking, the presentation of the buttocks is less likely to suggest fraternal incest than unsettling overtly erotic play with genitals. There appears to be a relationship of this anal reference to the friendly "pat on the butt" among athletes. Showing the buttocks, often portrayed as effeminacy and submission in popular culture, in the American fraternal context becomes, ironically, the visual marker for male strength and sexuality. A problem arises in the play frame of the paddling breaking down, however, when the masochistic position is exploited and sadistic behaviors go dangerously awry.

The demand on pledges to undress probably suggests different social lessons. To be sure, pledges learn not to treat the state of undress as a sexual threat to one another. Lineups, for instance, are frequently held in showers (Egan 1985, 43–44). Further, it lends a feeling of youthfulness, even primitiveness, to the pledge, in contrast to the clothed, civilized "active." As a prospective fraternity member, the pledge is reminded that he or she is different from nonmembers. Successfully running through quadrangles in undergarments turns what could be an embarrassment into a socially shared triumph. The pledge has proudly defied the expectations of others. As with tasks asking for physical strength, the "undie runs" ask for mental strength. With the support of brothers and sisters, pledges triumph over their inhibitions, or so the thinking goes.

One young man who experienced rigorous frat hazing—and might have been expected to resent it—described it this way:

Hell Week brings the pledges together. It forever gives them a point of departure, a common center with which to identify. By the mere fact that a pledge class goes through Hell Week together, each pledge cannot help but feel a certain kinship with his fellow pledges. And the importance of this cannot be overestimated. In a fraternity that survives because its members consider themselves brothers, unity is vital. . . . The activities associated with Hell Week thus serve to divert the tension surrounding the pledge's introduction into the house. When the week has ended, pledges and actives are fully familiarized with one another. (Klein 1975, 19)

Mechling also points out the rich visual culture of frat hazing kept in photographs meant to capture and literally frame the play, and, he argues, the enjoyment of the "stylized humiliation" intended to bond men together (2008, 45).

Ray Raphael records similar responses in his study of men's initiations. As one informant told him, "I have good, strong memories of the comradeship that the fraternity developed. We had a real acceptance of each other. You did not have to prove yourself anymore—after you had proven yourself during Hell Week" (Raphael 1988, 89). A former pledge related this comment to me about Hell Week, "I thought it was going to be stupid, and at first I probably did feel silly sometimes, but, you know, as I accomplished more things and went through it with my brothers, it gave me strength. I did something special, and I had an identity others didn't have. I never felt lost again like I did when I was a freshman. I belonged to something, and others belonged to me."

Although fraternities have generally toned down hazing, the dividing line between traditional initiatory practices and criminal abuse continues to be tested in the courts. Several cases show the risks when initiations go overboard. At the University of Lowell, six fraternity members were charged under the state's antihazing law over a stunt that sent a pledge to the hospital with a body temperature of 109 (members had bundled him in a sleeping bag and turned on heaters nearby) (Nuwer 1990, 26). In 2011, a mother of a sophomore initiate sued Sigma Alpha Epsilon at Cornell University after her son died from alcohol poisoning. The suit alleged that pledges kidnapped the student from his room and brought him to the fraternity house. They tied him up and made him answer trivia questions about the fraternity. When he answered incorrectly, he was forced to do exercises and consume various food and drinks that contained sugar, flavored syrup, and vodka. The victim passed out, but rather than taking him to the hospital, the pledges left him bound on a couch in the house's library. His blood alcohol level was measured eventually at five times the legal limit (Webley 2011). A pledge at the University of Delaware claimed in a lawsuit that he was seriously burned when an active dumped caustic oven cleaner over his head during a fraternity "Hell Night" (Kaplin and Lee 2006, 208–9). Often the questions judges ask in their decisions on the

criminality of hazing are about whether injuries were foreseeable (or acciden-
tal) and whether the fraternal organizations had malicious intent (Kaplin and
Lee 2006, 209).

Besides denouncing hazing for its potential mental and physical abuse to
pledges, feminists at the University of Pennsylvania decried fraternity initiations for perpetuating a "phallo-centric sexual culture" that sanctions violence
against women. One anthropologist cited an incident in which pledges were
blindfolded with a sanitary napkin, stripped naked, and forced to put a heat
ointment on their genitals while other fraternity brothers urged them not to
act like "fags" or "wimps" (Collins 1988, 3B). To Lionel Tiger, the reason for this
aggressive testing of pledges is the special need men have to clarify their ambiguity about sociosexual roles in adolescence—especially in American society,
which does not provide society-wide rites of passage for a boy to become a
man (1969, 190–92).

Reforms have been proposed to stress the positive aspects of initiation
(Quinto 1989, 27–28). Eliminating pledging altogether and substituting open
admission is one, but some observers argue that hazing will continue regardless (Mechling 2009). Calls have also gone out to bring back the kind of strong
in-house supervision by faculty or professional housemothers that was common during the 1950s (Krattenmaker 1989, 9, 12). Worried that these measures
ineffectively police rather than culturally guide fraternities and sororities, Jay
Mechling (2005) has suggested use of cultural workers and folklorists as ritual
specialists to guide the initiation process. Still other reforms have been floated,
including institutionalizing coed and multicultural fraternities, eliminating
separate residences for Greeks, and providing stronger social alternatives in
the dorms.

In the name of building brotherhood, fraternities are nonetheless hanging
on to their ritual "dousings" and "reversals." Some houses use dunking of initiates in a nearby pond or in the showers to mark the passing from a pledge to
an active; others use it during Hell Week. At Duke, one student recalled, "the
threat of being hauled away encouraged you to move in packs," thus forcing
pledges to rely on one another. Tempers did flare occasionally, however, and
punches were landed (DeParle 1988, 45).

One way for pledges to release their frustration of submitting to their elders
is reversal weekends. During this time, the pledges act like actives. They are
relieved of work details and pledge tests, and they get the run of the house (T.
1976, 6–7). In other versions, the pledges borass the house or lock out the actives by constructing elaborate barricades. Another ploy is to kidnap an active
and take him along on a walkout to another campus or site. They leave behind
a message in the form of, say, taking all the silverware and dishes from the
kitchen (Free 1982, 3). In a variation, the pledges take the kidnapped active to a

hiding place and give the other actives clues to his whereabouts. If the actives discover the victim before receiving the last clue or before time runs out, the pledges have to throw a party for the actives; if they do not make the discovery, the actives serve the pledges dinner (Egan 1985, 50–52).

The discovery of a missing item, namely the active, by figuring out clues is a reversal of the long-standing fraternity tradition of scavenger hunts for pledges during Hell Week. Often held dusk to dawn, the scavenger hunt requires pledges to bring back, by a deadline, items on a list prepared by the actives. The hunt challenges pledges physically and mentally, and forces them to work together intensely. Sometimes the items on the list are open to interpretation. An example is the request to bring back a "bird," which was answered by pledges extending their middle finger in an insulting gesture at the actives. As the example suggests, many of the items are sexual in their nature. Frat pledges haul in large bras, contraceptive devices, and autographs on bodily parts (Egan 1985, 53). Another common requirement is to bring back photographs of deeds accomplished ranging from "mooning" a hotel to hugging a policeman.

Then there are "walks," "ditches," or "dumps." In this custom, actives haul pledges miles away from the house to a remote spot, often take away some of their clothing or give them some outlandish clothing to wear, and tell them to make it back by their wits and small change. In a variation, the actives "walk" the pledges, requiring them to do tasks along the way, or to check out places associated with ghostly legends. At DePauw, pledges had to throw their shoes and socks into a pile, and the footgear was mixed together. The pledges were given only a few seconds to retrieve their goods before setting out. The mad dash meant that the pledge often ended up wearing another person's shoe. Reversal is possible here, too. Tradition sometimes calls for pledges to dump, ditch, or walk the rush chairman (Egan 1985, 62).

Collegiate observers note that a shift is apparent in the twenty-first century as a result of legislation and public criticism of physical hazing toward psychological challenges or pranks. At Florida Southern, according to Assistant Dean Alexander Bruce (2003), actives in one sorority place the pledges in the chapter room. Every fifteen minutes a sister will come in and forcefully grill the pledges about sorority customs and the chapter's history. If they are asleep or cannot answer, they are removed. He reports another custom he categorizes as psychological rather than physically demanding: the pledge is placed in a coffin often causing trepidation, but then she is ritually raised back to life and told she is "reborn" as a member of the sorority (Bruce 2003, 86). Bruce acknowledges that even if pledges are no longer dragged off campus or ditched somewhere, fraternities and sororities rely on deception to initiate pledges. He gives the example of a narrative by the new type of pledge humiliated by the actives' trickery who saw nothing wrong with playing it on others when he became a brother:

I was told by a certain fraternity that the school Jell-O bounces off the cafeteria floor. What they would do is that they would get an innocent freshman and tell them that the Jell-O bounces and the freshman, who would
say, "No, it doesn't." The upperclassman would then proceed to grab a piece
of Jell-O and pretend to bounce it off the floor (actually, he would pretend
to bounce with his hand under the table, then flick his wrist upward and
throw the Jell-O up). This would be done several times perhaps by several
people and then they would ask the freshman if he/she wants to try. They
would say "yes," then grab a piece of Jell-O and throw it to the floor. Obviously the Jell-O would splat on the floor and that person would try to make
light of it. (Bruce 2003, 84)

Such "tricks" are reminiscent of initiatory customs known in children's folklore
such as the "snipe hunt" in which the young person who aspires to join a group
of older boys or girls is given a bag to catch a mysterious bird. The youngster
draws laughs at being left literally "holding the bag" and, as a result of being
made aware of his or her gullibility, joins the group (Bronner 1989, 169–71;
Chinery 1987; Smith 1957; cf. Baughman 1966, motif J2349.6 Snipe hunt, a variation of Thompson motif J2349 Fool's Errand). The snipe routine will probably
be well known to the fraternity initiate, but likely not the gelatin or other splat-
tering substance (until now, that is!). The initiatory effect is to infantilize the
pledge by symbolically reverting him to an anal stage of development in which
he is literally smeared in his mess. By cleaning him up and making him aware
of the ridiculousness of his "childish" belief, he is in the "know" and allowed to
move "up" into the mature (and apparently more phallic) fratiarchy.

Distinguishing pledging in historically black fraternities is the use of
"lines," "step shows," "signals," and occasionally "branding." Although pledges
now rarely are shackled or tied together "on line" by their fraternity brothers,
as they once were, they may still be seen walking across campus in formation with military-style synchronized steps. Pledges line up in size order, wear
uniforms—often of their own making—and speak in unison. Many chapters
require black pledges to refrain during the pledge period from drinking alcohol, eating sweets, and having sex (Egan 1985, 44–45; Jones 2004, 47–66).
The regimen of black pledging provided the backdrop of Spike Lee's movie
School Daze (1987), in which he critically dramatized the severe regimen of
being "on line." Twenty years later, another African American director, Sylvain
White, more sympathetically showcased in the movie *Stomp the Yard* (2007)
stepping competitions at the fictitious Truth University. The "Yard" in the title
derives from black slang for a campus (Mould 2005, 81–82). For many black
pledges, being "on line" is designed to develop even more unity than found in
many historically white fraternities. Black pledges as minorities among the

Fig. 7.1. African American fraternity pledges "step on line" at Indiana University. (Photo by Simon Bronner)

frats as well as in society show in their performances that they have to be tougher, more creative, and more united than members of other organizations (see Mould 2005; Scott 2011). Also at stake is a lifelong commitment, for while many white fraternities and sororities serve their main purposes in the college setting, black Greeks maintain their activities well after college in community chapters (Gadson 1989, 34–36, 136–37).

Elizabeth Fine traces stepping as a pledging ritual among historically black fraternities and sororities to the 1920s, when "probates," as the pledges were called, demonstrated their newfound brotherhood or sisterhood by walking together across campus, all wearing their group's colors and symbols (2003, 16). The uniformity was meant to promote lofty fraternal ideals of "unity, trust, and devotion" (Fine 2003, 16). Early reports did not mention more than foot stomping. By the 1950s, Fine reports, "marching on line often involved singing or chanting and syncopated and synchronized movements," apparently combining the marching with Greek singing events (2003, 18). Props and specially prepared apparel began appearing in the ritualization of the lines. For instance, Fine observes in the Howard University yearbook for 1943, "Twelve young men in suits and ties, with dog collars and long chains around their necks, [posing] behind the university's sundial ('the Dial'), a traditional gathering spot for Omega Psi Phi (the 'Q-Dogs'). . . . In another photograph of a public skit,

Fig. 7.2. African American soror-
ity pledges "step" at Indiana
University, 1978. (Photo by
Simon Bronner)

young men gather around a man who is on his knees and wearing a long,
Egyptian-looking headdress, a common ritual costume of Alpha Phi Alpha"
(2003, 17–18).

Based on African American musical forms, the stepping by six to nine
pledges is a study in coordination and unity. Pledges in their lines break into
a series of precisely synchronized steps, which create a syncopated beat. The
pledges accompany the steps with chanting and singing proclaiming loyalty
to the fraternity or sorority. As a Hampton graduate elaborated, "Stepping is
a form of precision and motion. It's competition, it's publicity, it's emotion. It
relates back to Africa, to African tribes and the movements they do. It's a tight
bond we have of being brothers" (Gammage 1989, 2B). Many steppers have
experience in predominantly black high school drill teams, and the influence
of military marching, a source of manliness for many black men, can also be
discerned in many stepping routines. Stepping originally emphasized percus-
siveness of the feet accompanied by chants, often with no musical accompaniment, but in later step shows musical background, particularly drawn from
hip-hop and other urban styles, became more pronounced.

When I first encountered a step show at Indiana University during the
1970s, it was a private affair performed by men for other black fraternities
and sororities. The show started about 1 a.m., and for a few hours distinctively
costumed lines from different fraternities presented songs, dancing, and recitations to the sharply syncopated beat of their marching. Besides proclaiming

their loyalty to a particular fraternity, the lines also hurled barbs at other frats, and the audience noisily encouraged them. Despite the distractions, negative or positive, of the vocal crowd, the pledges were expected to maintain their serious, concentrated looks and continue their routines. During the 1980s, competitive step shows went public, being presented to the whole campus community in prime time at Virginia, Michigan State, Northwestern, Penn State, and North Texas, among other well-publicized locations (Anderson 1987; Gammage 1989; Nomani 1989, 1, 4; "Fraternity" 1989; Moore 1989). Often they were staged as judged competitions with points given for intricate precision stepping to complex rhythms, costumes, production, and creativity. Originally viewed as a masculine performance by fraternities, sororities got into the act with elaborate moves all their own to popular acclaim. Moving from gyms to grand auditoriums, step shows emerged as the major annual event for the historically black fraternities and sororities. Enjoying the attention, a member of Alpha Phi Alpha observed, "Step shows are the soul and spirit of black fraternity social life" (Nomani 1989, 1).

But voices of concern could be heard about this preoccupation with the shows playing to outsiders in packed houses. Changes have occurred in routines, and some members say also to the function of stepping in this new performance venue. The "cracking," or stylized ritual insulting, that occurred formerly "on line" is often muted or eliminated for the largely racially heterogeneous audiences who attend the shows (Mould 2005, 95–99). Although in private such stylized insulting served the purpose of promoting fraternal identity and verbal artistry, in public, a fear exists, according to Elizabeth Fine, "that audience response might become too heated or that the public will misunderstand the intent of the performers" (2003, 148). Organizers worry that audiences will perceive divisiveness among the black Greek groups ("the Divine Nine," as they are called, for the nine historically black Greek-letter organizations that make up the National Pan-Hellenic Council: Alpha Phi Alpha Fraternity, Alpha Kappa Alpha Sorority, Kappa Alpha Psi Fraternity, Omega Psi Phi Fraternity, Delta Sigma Theta Sorority, Phi Beta Sigma Fraternity, Zeta Phi Beta Sorority, Sigma Gamma Rho Sorority, and Iota Phi Theta Fraternity) and often compensate by encouraging themes of African American as well as Greek unity. Some critics have also been concerned with the perception of young African Americans as entertainers rather than learned, community-minded students and the commodification of the shows. They also note that the fraternity performances descend into stereotypes of black machismo as they play up to audiences' expectations of sexual display. A further complaint is the increasing amount of time and expense taken by fraternities and sororities to prepare for the shows, taking away from the service and fellowship roles of the organizations (Fine 2003, 147–48).

Folklorist Tom Mould has described the difference between men and women stepping in the shows this way: "Men's stepping should be bigger, higher, and more athletic than women's stepping. Men's stepping should include more hopping and stomping and less hand clapping than women's. Men can be wild, nasty, aggressive, and sexually suggestive, where many women feel they need to convey a persona of femininity, to be ladylike" (2005, 92). With pressure on stage to downplay divisiveness resulting from "cracking" (also known as "mauling" and "dissing"), themes sometimes emerge of sexual competition, especially for men who consider the campus a feminized space compared to the military and urban environment. Women on stage and in the yard seem in control, and men vie to assert their presence. Zeta Phi Beta women, for example, chant "Zeta, oh sweet Zeta; Always held in the highest esteem; Sisterly love, cultural advancement, working for all; That's what Zeta means." And on stage, they remind one another of relations between the sororities and the fraternities:

> He's not your brother, he's not your frat
> You're not related, so stop all that
> If you weren't founded, one by the other
> He's not your bro, he's not your frat, he's not your brother
> If you wear red (OOOOO-OOOOPs), and he wears gold (Q-Bark)
> He's not your brother, haven't you been told?
> If you do this (Sigma Rho sign), and he does that (Kappa sign)
> He's not your brother, he's not your bro, he's not your frat
> If you're a pearl (skeee-wee), and he's a jewel
> He's not your brother, you silly fool
> We're here to tell you, one simple fact
> That we're the sorors, that have true frat
> Zeeeeee-Phiiiiii! (McDowell 2008)

The step shows present a set of symbols that often act in conflict because of the ambiguity of who the performance is for. Reaching the black audience means emphasizing the superiority of the organization, its claim to "run the yard," in exaggerating its attributes of racialized manliness (or femininity) and deriding the other groups for their lack of appeal. The skits and routines seek vocal approval from the audience as a recruiting, and according to Mould, a courtship ritual. Aware of the distorted image this hyperbolic performance may convey, historically black fraternities and sororities in white-dominated settings also negotiate in their public presence on stage social acceptance on the campus as bona fide students who are inexorably linked to, and supportive of, one another (see Hughey 2008; Mould 2005, 103–8).

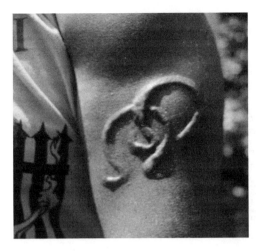

Fig. 7.3. African American fraternity member shows Omega symbols
branded on his arm. (Photo by Sandra
Mizumoto Posey)

Different black fraternities and sororities have distinctive hand signals and calls they sound at step shows, parties, and picnics. Omega Psi Phi members bark "Woofa, Woofa!" and form an inverted Omega with their hands over their heads. Deltas make a triangle with their fingers and holler "Oo-ooo-oop!" (Egan 1985, 120–21). The different signals, signs, and calls are likely to be apparent at massive reunions that black fraternities and sororities run in many cities. In addition to social activities, the fraternities and sororities mobilize politically during these reunions. For instance, black Greek organizations worked together to spearhead the letter-writing campaign to declare Martin Luther King Jr.'s birthday a legal holiday (Gadson 1989, 36).

A controversial practice among some African American fraternity members is branding as part of initiation rituals. Members voluntarily take homemade heated irons and shape Omega or Sigma symbols on their arms or backs. It may be administered by a brander called a "hit man" or at branding parties (Battle 2007). The practice is not endorsed by any of the Divine Nine, but scars in the form of the fraternity symbols on African American men can regularly be spotted on campuses. The brands are often conspicuous because of the apparent tendency to form a keloid scar, a raised overgrowth of scar tissue, on black skin (Battle 2007). Some students I have talked to refer to the solidarity conveyed in the brand with enslaved African ancestors who were branded. Others see it as a manly display of sacrifice and devotion to one's fraternal identity, because of the pain that is endured and the distinction it accords (Posey 2004). At Michigan State, the local press condemned Omega Psi Phi for the practice, and a branded member responded, "It's just an individual's way of showing how much he loves his fraternity," and "It represents a common bond of brotherhood" (Boettcher 1980; Egan 1985, 67). An Alpha Phi Alpha member from the University of Wisconsin–Milwaukee showed his brand to a reporter in defiance of the chapter president and commented, "I love that it has been done because it makes me a different individual in my society right now" (Battle 2007).

If the theme of brotherhood and toughness representing a fratriarchy links both black and white fraternities, sororities often build up ideals of family, femininity, and expressiveness (Robbins 2004; Young 1962, 379–96). "When I became a sister," one student explained, "it was like entering into a big family. Every pledge got a Big Sister and the pledge class had a Pledge Mom. Pledging usually lasts about six weeks and begins with an induction ceremony. This ceremony begins with the sisters in an open circle, which means that they are united but welcome new members. They all recite the creed of the organization and they have candles. One person lights a candle and the flame is passed on. Then the pledges receive their pledge pins and ribbons to wear throughout the pledge period" (Acri 1989).

Sororities place great demands on pledges to show care-giving qualities and creative abilities to one another. Fraternities, often in manly military style, reward values of grit and toughness. Sororities reward creativity and coopera-tion. Alexandra Robbins, in her exposé of sorority pledging, complained that an added dimension is an obsession with the right appearance that translated into humiliation for pledges who gained weight, wore unfashionable cloth-ing, or had unkempt hair. She thought that too much emphasis was placed on impressing the opposite sex rather than supporting one another, but sorority sisters often have a self-perception of a bond among them that is stronger than the bond among men. For the sororities, the risk of intimacy is not perceived to be as great, since women are socialized to express themselves more physi-cally and emotionally toward one another (they regularly kiss and hug each other in greetings and farewells), and they tend to avoid imitating the implic-itly homophobic practices of many fraternity initiations.

In some sorority chapters, pledges must earn "pearls," twenty-two in all, which symbolize the pearls placed in their sorority pin once they are initiated. Pledges earn pearls for passing pledge exams, attending campus events, and doing service work. A progressive search for clues is used to lead the pledge to her "new mother." As a sister explained, "The clues lead the girls through the house and finally to the informal living room, where the sorority moms are seated under sheets to which their social security numbers are pinned" (Wash-burn 1976, 7). Sororities, though, have their share of pranks and escapades, especially walkouts and pranking. At Shippensburg, actives took pledges to a remote cemetery and related a ghostly legend about the founding of the soror-ity. They blindfolded the initiates and ushered them to the grave of a woman who supposedly founded the sorority. Actives tell the pledges that this woman wants to meet them. With her heart beating fast, a pledge steps forward, and a skeleton hand with clay and a sponge around it is put in her hand, causing her to scream.

Another sorority tradition is the humorous skit produced by the pledges for the actives. The material pokes fun at the senior members, especially at their vanity and their relations with men. If the skit goes off well, the pledges are given pledge points or smaller work loads (Egan 1985, 49). Song is another important artistic expression. Although fraternities also require singing, sororities tend to use it more extensively. Pledge classes serenade the actives at dinner, in front of the house's fireplace (occasions called "firesides"), on the lawn at night, and at other houses (Egan 1985, 49; Christner 1967; Taboada 1967; Maurer 1976). Some critics complain, however, that pledges are sometimes made to serenade in undergarments or bikinis. In so doing, they emphasize their sexuality rather than other attributes as strengths.

Songs of the Greeks

Beyond this occasional hazing, songs are used as forms of address as well as entertainment. Sororities have songs for welcomes, congratulations, and farewells. Songs explain the significance of pins and activities, and voice the values of the sorority. Spaced out through the week, serenading can take on a different character depending on what night it is. Monday night songs are typically formal and inspirational. One example refers to the "lyre," the sorority pin (Christner 1967, 7; see also Glavan 1968, 194–95):

> Our love is faithful to the lyre
> The symbol of our lives.
> Together let us seek the heights
> Together let us strive.
> Alpha Chi, Alpha Chi,
> To you we'll always be
> A steadfast loyal guardian of
> Our precious symphony.
> And so our pledge is made.
> Our harps are found.
> The harpstrings of our lyre
> Ring forth again to tell the world of our fulfilled desire.
> We dedicate this song to you,
> Our dear fraternity.
> To Alpha Chi, to Alpha Chi,
> Everlasting loyalty.

Congratulations and other informal salutations are offered in song during the week. Here, for example, is a congratulatory song from Alpha Chi at UCLA:

Here's to (name)
We'll never let her down!
Here's to (name)
We'll never let her down!
And when she hits that line,
There'll be no light at all!
There'll be a hot time in the old town tonight!
Here's to (name)! Yeah!

Variations, however, extol drinking and are frequently sung to losers of drinking games, such as "Bizz-Buzz" and "Indian," when the supposed penalty of chugging is imposed. Examples are:

Here's to (name)
She's true blue.
She's rounder through and through.
So drink chug-a-lug, chug-a-lug,
So drink chug-a-lug, chug-a-lug.

Here's to (name)
She's OK
Think she's going to heaven
But she's going the other way.
So drink chug-a-lug, chug-a-lug
So drink chug-a-lug, chug-a-lug. (Reuss 1965, 173–77)

Many of the songs express the distinctions between the many sororities, such as this song from Kappa Kappa Gamma:

Oh honey, would you love me any
Better if I lied like a Gamma Phi
If I partied like a Delta Delta Delta
Or cheated like a Pi Beta Phi, Beta Phi
If I danced like a Chi Omega, ugh
Or strutted like the Thetas do,
Or shot a hot line like the damn
Delta Gammas 'stead of kissin' like the Kappas do?

Incidentally I'm a Kappa, too
Let's go out and pitch a little woo! (Taboada 1967, 36)

Friday night is reserved for "rasty" songs often about sex and drinking:

Who says Alpha Chis never stay out late?
Who's that swinging on the fire escape?
Just another Alpha Chi with her lovin' date
She came home early for a class at eight. Oh-h
Alpha Chi girl . . . Gotta have her lovin'
Alpha Chi girl . . . Just another smooch.
Alpha Chi girl. . . Gotta have her lovin'
She came home early 'cause she ran out of hooch,
Ran out of hooch boys! (Christner 1967, 20)

One of the more persistent fraternity folk song complexes has been around the line "No there are no . . . "

No there are no AZDs down in hell—Hell no!
O there are no AZDs down in hell—Hell no!
'cause they all are up above drinking beer and making love
No there are no AZDs down in hell—Hell no!
But there are AZDs at Penn State—Hell yes!
But there are AZDs at Penn State—Hell yes!
And the Kappa Delta Phis all sleep with Delta Chis
And the AZDs sleep at TKE!

No there are no Alpha Xis down in hell—Down in Hell!
No there are no Alpha Xis down in hell—Down in Hell!
'cause they all are up above drinking beer and making love
No there are no Alpha Xis down in hell—Down in Hell!
Oh there are no Alpha Xis on the bed—On the bed!
Oh there are no Alpha Xis on the bed—On the bed!
'cause they're all on the floor rolling round and screaming more
Oh there are no Alpha Xis on the bed—On the bed!
So here's to the men that we love—that we love!
And here's to the men that love us—that love us!
If the men we love aren't the men that love us
So oh, what the hell [screw them] here's to us! (cf. McDowell 2008; Reuss 1965, 31–35; "Songs/Chants???" 2000)

The last four lines can also be extracted for a drinking toast or fight song (see Adams 2004, 233; "Famous Toasts and Sentiments" 1888, 302; Ford 2003; Wright 2002, 89).

To this kind of selection must be added a host of risqué fraternity songs full of braggadocio on drinking and sex (Craig 1974; Reuss 1965, 31–35; T. 1976). A perennial favorite is a parody of Cornell's "Far Above Cayuga's Waters":

> High above a Pi Phi's garter well above her knee
> Stands the symbol of her honor, her virginity
> Roll her over, oh, so gently
> Down in the grass
> This is what men fight and die for
> A piece of Pi Phi ass. (T. 1976, 18; see also Egan 1985, 195; McDowell 2008;
>   Reuss 1965, 76–80)

The same song can be used against a rival fraternity:

> Far below Acacia's standards,
> There's a motley crew
> One hundred and twenty sons of bitches
> Known as Sigma Nus
> Half the world is white and pure
> The other half is Sigma Nure. (Reuss 1965, 154)

Other lyrics that have been around a long time with many variations is a convivial parody of "Put On Your Old Gray Bonnet":

> Bring out that old silver goblet with the ZBT on it,
> And we'll open up another keg of beer,
> For it ain't for knowledge that we came to college,
> But to raise hell while we're here.

In one common variation, the last line is sung as "prevent virginity" (Reuss 1965, 160–64).

Or a bunch of fraternity boasts parody college cheers:

> We are Pi Kapp raiders
> Raiders of the night
> Dirty son of a bitches
> We'd rather fuck than fight
> Singing highty, tighty, Christ almighty

Who in the hell are we
Rat shit, bat shit, dirty ole twat
Sixty-nine assholes tied in a knot
Yea, rah lizard shit
a-a-a-a-a-ah, fuck! (McDowell 2008)

Songs are preserved on photocopied sheets and included in privately circulated "pledge manuals." Six are listed, for example, in a Theta Epsilon pledge
manual I received, concluding with the "Pork 'Em Song."

O Theta Epsilon our name and we always do our best
To keep the girlies satisfied we never take a rest
And on their knees they beg us please for sexuality
For we're the fucking studs of the GOD fraternity

CHORUS:
O we'll pork em in the morning
And we'll pork em in the night
And we'll pork em if they're broken
And we'll pork em if they're tight
And on their knees they'll beg us please in actuality
For we're the fucking studs of the GOD fraternity

O our services are rendered entirely for free
And with each package comes a life time guarantee
That they'll be coming back next week in hot expectancy
Cause we're the fucking studs of the GOD fraternity. (*Theta Epsilon* n.d., 12)

If that content sounds misogynist, consider some lyrics circulating among
sororities and fraternities alike. Theta Epsilon's song titled "Seal Song" is

Just put her in a corner
And hold her tight like this
Just put your arms around her waist
And on her lips a kiss.
And if she starts to murmur,
Or if she starts to frown,
Just tell her it's the sacred seal
Of Theta Epsilon. (*Theta Epsilon* n.d., 10; see also Reuss 1965, 42–45; Beta
    Theta Pi n.d., 37)

In a variant collected at Indiana University from Sigma Delta Tau sorority, the second verse is altered to force a rhyme with the name of the sorority:

And when he starts to murmur,
And looks at you with awe,
Just tell him that's the sacred seal
Of Sigma Delta Tau. (Reuss 1965, 42)

A different rhyme concludes the song at Theta Nu: "If he starts to holler, if he starts to coo, Tell him it's the sacred seal (or grip) of dear old Theta Nu" (Reuss 1965, 43). Beta Theta Pi's "Sweetheart Song" adds:

Her eyes are blue as Beta skies,
Here cheeks are like a rose,
She's different from all other girls,
How I love her no one knows;
And in my fondest memories,
Never shall we part,
For she is my dear one, and I am her dear one,
She's my sweetheart in Phi Kai Phi. (Beta Theta Pi n.d., 37)

Such sweet sentiments invite parody, such as this bawdy verse reported by folklorist Richard Reuss from fraternities at several campuses:

Grab her by the ankle, throw her into bed,
Wrinkle up her nightie, kiss her pretty head,
When she starts to whimper, when she starts to sigh,
Just slip her that which is the pride of old Pi Lambda Phi. (1965, 44; see also
    Letcher 2010)

The implication is that the fraternity man is not interested in a romantic attachment that could tie him down and emasculate him, or at least this is the message that he playfully shares with his brothers. On the fictive plane of the song, he maintains his manly independence and dominance with sexual aggression.

Survey responses tell me that the group singing tradition among the brothers and sisters has declined to a few occasions, and to be sure, more than a few hall men and women know their share of bawdy songs as well, but Greeks especially use singing to showcase their many voices singing as one. Their shared knowledge of the songs points to their shared cultural bond; it is a form of ritual communication and release—and often a representation of gendered values.

Parties in Greekdom

Besides singing, Greeks are often known for partying. They have the houses for it, and, as a mark of distinction, each frat commonly devotes its organizational skills to giving the parties creative themes. Given their association with scant dress, vacation, and released inhibitions, tropical themes are favorites for campus parties. As might be expected, Phi Gamma Delta, called "Fijis," take special pride in throwing parties encouraging students to go native. Great effort goes into making the house over into a tropical isle complete with huts and war shields. Other tropical parties brag "Give Me Samoa," "Let's Get Lei-ed," and "Taiwan On" (Egan 1985, 143–44).

The movie *Animal House* (1978) saw to it that toga parties have become old hat by now, but other ancients—Vikings, Neanderthal Man, Egyptian kings, medieval knights—are celebrated and fantasized in fraternity parties (Egan 1985, 145–47). American popular culture gets its due in Wild West, Barn Dance, Las Vegas, and Hollywood parties. Costuming at Halloween and Mardi Gras are favorites for midsemester festivities.

Sigma Alpha Epsilon is known for its annual Paddy Murphy parties, which uses a Prohibition-era theme. Murphy, according to legend and song, is an Irish drunkard hero given to womanizing and rowdiness (Baker 1983, 111; Dorson 1949, 676–77; Egan 1985, 150–51; Reuss 1965, 302–6; South Carolina Delta 2011; Virginia Delta 2010). Murphy is given a mock funeral procession and Irish wake, surrounded by guests dressed in Prohibition-era outfits. The party that follows often includes the singing of Paddy Murphy songs, mock sermons, and theatricals on Murphy's life or ghost.

To the chagrin of Greekdom's detractors, animated parties like Murphy's often build on ethnic stereotypes. At the University of California at Davis, a "Sombreros and Cervezas" party outraged the Chicano community, who protested the party's stereotypes about alcoholism and laziness in Mexican society, and a "Godfather Night" stirred outcries from Italian Americans (Mechling 1989, 295). At Juniata College, a "Bridal Party" raised eyebrows when the mock wedding caricatured Poles. The party had beer, Kielbasa, and polka music, and participants took on faked Polish names.

Parties advertised as "Halloween in the Hood" and "Compton Cookout" at Johns Hopkins University and the University of California at San Diego, respectively, raised the ire of campus administrations and civil rights groups for their racist tones. The advertisement for the "Halloween in the Hood" party invited attendees to come in costume "from our [Baltimore] locale" such as "fur coats, copious amounts of so-called 'bling bling ice ice,' 'grills, hoochie hoops, white Tee's and Air Force Onez.'" After sending the university' community liaison officer to investigate, Hopkins suspended activities of the Sigma Chi fraternity after the event (University Statement 2006). At San Diego four years later, the "Compton Cookout" was not an official Pi Kappa Alpha fraternity event, but because members of the fraternity were identified as organizers, Greek organizations in general took the heat for promoting bigotry. Promising a taste of "life in the ghetto," the Facebook invitation for the "Compton Cookout" urged women to dress as "ghetto chicks" who "usually have gold teeth, start fights and drama, and wear cheap clothes." Menu items, according to the invitation, included chicken and watermelon. In response, the fraternity condemned the event, and the university arranged a teach-in on "mutual respect and civility" (Gordon 2010).

"Greek Slave Auctions," a long-standing fund-raiser for fraternities, similarly drew fire when a black member was auctioned at the University of California at Davis (Mechling 1989, 292–93). The intent was to build on the Greek theme to offer the services of a member for a day to a high bidder, but to the public, the event was taken as an insensitive reference to the enslavement of Africans. A Davis faculty member's description of the controversy is revealing for its commentary on the different worlds of the fraternity and the campus community:

> The fraternity members, including the black member, were puzzled by the outcry. The fraternity was integrated and, indeed, united in conducting the event. To have excluded the black member from participating in the auction would have been discriminatory in the eyes of the fraternity members. Where the fraternity had miscalculated was in its assumption that it could move a ritual from the relatively high-context, private world of the folk group into the public realm of strangers who did not share the group's intimacy or their frame for interpreting the ritual. . . . What the fraternity took to be an expression of solidarity was interpreted as racist and divisive. (Mechling 1989, 293)

Greeks engage in many community service and charitable fund-raising events, and point to them as the civic benefits of fraternity and sororities. Fraternities and sororities raise millions of dollars each year for charitable causes (Egan 1985, 134). Greeks sponsor health fairs and blood drives, serve in Big Brother and Big Sister programs, and volunteer for community projects and hospital duty. Fraternities and sororities are also typically among the most active organizations helping the campus. They often serve as university ambassadors, guiding visitors and ushering events.

Holiday telegrams are a favorite fraternity and sorority fund-raiser. For a price, Greeks will personally deliver a note to another student on campus. Around Valentine's Day, it's a Cupidgram; for Christmas, it's a Santagram; at Halloween, it's a Pumpkingram. You can also buy "wake-ups" or "tuck-ins" for friends: the sorority sister will wake the person and present him or her with a card and a cup of coffee, or tuck him or her in with a stuffed bear and read a bedtime story (Egan 1985, 134). Greeks sponsor marathons, Special Olympics, and contests of dubious achievement (for example, ugly bartender, kissing). On some campuses, fund-raising and fun combine in versions of Greek Week or Derby Days. During Greek Week, you are likely to encounter chariot, bathtub, and bed races; eating contests; and keg tosses—all for a good cause (Egan 1985, 115–18). Derby Days, Phi Mu and Sigma Chi's fund-raiser, includes wacky field events and the Derby Chase, where sisters get points for plastic derbies grabbed off a Sig head (Egan 1985, 140).

Fraternities and sororities do not have a monopoly on fun and games on America's campuses, and they vie with a growing number of organizations such as clubs and teams with claims of providing a sense of community spirit on campus. In this competition for being "the one," that is, the main identity-forming group in a student's life, tradition is often invoked as a lure, and Greeks play on their historic legacy and venerated rituals. Arguably, students also turn to the Internet, as pre-cyber-age generations could not, for play and networking in the midst of a learning environment that demands, on the one hand, seclusion and, on the other, compensatory release.

The constant quest by students more than other campus constituents for fun is more than a function of youthful exuberance. Often students construct or use play frames to deal with conflicts and tensions in their variety of transitions—from home to campus, from campus out to the real world or back home again, from high school to college, from minor to adult. The rhetoric of fun in Greek talk and action—escape, release, break—signifies the intense experience associated with college life coupled with an apparently contradictory emphasis on social responsibility and image maintenance (represented distinctively in service obligations and rounds of "formal" social events). Students' conceptualization of fun is inherently social, brash, and eventful. They contrast its wildness with the tameness of study, and as a result might be attracted to the Greek life because of its social construction as wild (or at least spirited) and at the same time normative. The apparent paradox of roles in many ways exaggerates the contradictions of the university fusing private feudal and public capitalist political economies. Another conflict can occur psychologically: the Greek houses can appear old-fashioned with their reverence to tradition in a modern university setting, and yet as a rule-bound organizational structure also seem corporately contemporary. Realizing that students often go by some elder's rules in their studies, the Greek system beckons members with come-ons of social connection within a private world that promises a measure of control over its affairs.

LEGENDARY LOCATIONS, LAUGHS, AND HORRORS

PASSING THROUGH THE ELABORATE GATES POSITIONED AT THE college's border with its neighbors typically creates the impression of entering a mythical kingdom. Past the bustle of streets and stores one finds on almost every campus a winding path through nature and around proud edifices often showing medieval faces. In this commercial-free zone, there seems to be a unity of purpose, a march of thought. The pantheon of distinctive images meant to inspire passersby stretches from the dormitories around the library and past the halls of academe. Giving focus to the domain are campus markers—clock and bell towers, columns, obelisks, statues, friezes, and quadrangles.

Students coming to a campus feel a need to adjust to this environment by connecting themselves to those who have come before. The continuity provided by the "real story" of folklore allows them to understand the personality of a place, to learn the lessons of the ancients, and to know the portents ahead. When campus residents relate folk names and legends to newcomers, they humanize imposing buildings and make them socially accessible. Among the most frequently encountered collegiate nicknames are those told in jest for schools and buildings. Some of these nicknames reach well back in collegiate history. A source from 1851 lists "Brick Mill" being used for the University of Vermont (Hall 1968, 38); today, "mill" is more often attached to large public universities dubbed "diploma mills." Other common ones heard today are Zoo Mass for the University of Massachusetts, Suitcase U. for Kent State, Silo Tech for Iowa State, and Moo-U for Michigan State. These often change over time. Franklin and Marshall College has attracted multiple monikers, including Fast and Mushy, Frank and Marsha, and Fumble and Mumble. Music students at the University of North Texas refer to the Music Recital Hall as the Purple Palace; at Millersville, when you go to study at the Helen A. Ganser Library, you're going to visit the Hag.

With universities commonly going by initials such as UK for the University of Kentucky (not to be confused with KU for the University of Kansas), inevitably college folk fill in the meanings of the letters. The expensive private Los Angeles institution USC (University of Southern California) is widely known as "University of Spoiled Children." USC followers might chime in with variations such as "University of Second Choice" or "University of South Central," and jab the rival public UCLA with "University of Caucasians Lost Among Asians" and "University of California for Low Achievers." Other rivalries are frequently expressed in college initials, such as references in South Carolina to CU (Clemson University) as "Cow University" because of its large college of agriculture, while Clemson's supporters in the Piedmont retort that the initials of the University of South Carolina, whose mascot is the game-cock, stand for "University of Sick Chickens" (Eisiminger 1978, 583–84). The University of Texas goes by the initials of UT, but Texas A&M students refer to their nemesis as "t.u." (intentionally lowercased) to stand for just another Texas university.

If some of these folk names are localized, others cross campus lines. Many science buildings are known as bughouses, chemistry buildings are chem halls, and student centers are unions or stud buildings. In colleges with examination rooms, the name "sweatboxes" is commonly applied. More than one instructional technology office is located in a basement area to keep equipment cool, and such offices are dubbed dungeons. References abound to quads for the rectangular grassy areas where students meet. Recreational centers are clipped in slang to "the rec" with an obvious play on the word "wreck."

Fears and joys of campus life come out in narratives that can edge toward laughter or tears. Whether ghostly legends or bawdy jokes, they raise emotions, entertain and teach, and offer release in the grind of life around the sobering college landscape. They allow the expression of feelings, values, and hopes. In the special imaginative frame that folklore provides, fears and joys are translated into symbols and telling events, and given plenty of room to operate. The stories may be told as true, but more often as half-truth with the elaboration of a twice-told tale. That does not detract from their value. Indeed, it adds to it, for the "truth" of the narratives lies in the belief and sentiment expressed—the cultural perception, if you will—in this "unofficial" version given from one student to another in folklore.

Students often favor legends and jokes because they invite participation or response. In legend, tellers build enough moral ambiguity into them to invite listeners to comment about the lessons in them. In jokes, laughter or outcry may provide judgment, especially since many are told to a group, and more often than not compel one's audience to come back with one of their own.

Lore of the Land

A number of campus legends begin with the Native American presence that gave way to the college. Raconteurs often spin such narratives toward the romantic side. When students take in the landscape around them, they often get a dose of American Indian lore to explain the human relation to old trees, streams, and hills, presumably precious to the early inhabitants of the land. In their retellings, the stories evoke thoughts of love and romance, so dear to the hearts of students. At the University of Texas, the "Battle Oaks" still standing on the northwest corner of campus are said to have learned the American Indian tongue: "Later the tree brought happiness to an Indian brave by whispering to him of the maiden who loved him, for beneath the branches of the tree she had cried out her love for the warrior. . . . The University grew and the oaks became a favorite spot of the students" (Berry 1983, 58–59).

At Tennessee Wesleyan College, students hear an "Indian tale" revolving around hackberry and oak trees on the north end of campus, well known as a meeting point for young lovers. According to this legend, a hunting party of Cherokees found a young English officer wounded not far from where the college stands. The Cherokees brought the officer back to their settlement, and there the officer was nursed back to health by No-ca-too-la, the beautiful daughter of the chief. The two fell in love, and the officer was given the name Con-ne-sto-ga, meaning "The Oak." The officer met a tragic end when a jealous warrior ambushed and killed him, and the Indian maiden killed herself rather than live without the officer. The grief-stricken old chief placed a seed in each of their hands—an acorn in one and a hackberry in the other. From these seeds grew the two trees, symbolizing undying love and devotion.

Stories of Indian spirits carry special meaning for colleges serving Native Americans, such as Haskell Indian Nations University in Lawrence, Kansas. At the school's 120th anniversary celebration in 2004, Scotty Harjo told people gathered at the university's powwow grounds that "for as long as anyone can remember, Haskell students have shared stories of encountering Indian spirits on campus." But they are not roaming on the open plains, but playing near the school's football field and in the swimming pool (Ranney 2004). The spirits translate their legacy of revering nature (land and water) to the campus that has served Native Americans since 1884. Some stories, though, have a tinge of protest because tellers connect narratives of spirits to the experience of the "Haskell Babies," who died because of harsh living conditions at the boarding school and were buried on the school grounds. According to folklorist Elizabeth Tucker, the child ghosts have become protectors of students on the college campus (2007, 163).

Fig. 8.1. Library tower at Binghamton University. (Photo by
Simon Bronner)

At Binghamton University, Tucker reports that the encircling landscape, a
ring of hills near the confluence of two rivers, may have fostered the connection between narratives featuring Native American forebears and the campus
(2007, 171). Hall names play up the connection. The residential "College in the
Woods" has dorms labeled Mohawk, Onondaga, Oneida, Cayuga, and Seneca.
Students pass rumors of Indian spectral sightings in the woods and bodies
of water; as in a number of campuses built up on formerly undisturbed land,
stories circulate about development over Indian burial grounds (Tucker 2007,
172–73). Tucker finds connections of these stories to children's folklore students remember of Indian ghosts from summer camp. The campus can appear camplike with its natural surroundings, common social spaces, and youth
population housed in close quarters. As with camp legends that treat nonna-
tive children as intruders (fostered by counselors wanting to keep their charge
out of the woods), campus Indians can sometimes appear hostile, and they are
used to explain accidents such as boating mishaps at the hands of spirits of the
lake and structural problems caused by resentful woods wanderers.

Most campus revenants appear ancestral and do not inflict harm. They
may be narrated to imply a tie to the present student inhabitants of the land.

Students relate their wildness and struggle, or society's othering of their liminal identity, in the "natural element" of the campus green away from home to the authentic existence of Native Americans. Students appear to appropriate through the legends an ethnic legacy; they stand in for the Indians who no longer populate the region (Tucker 2007, 153). They may also serve as reminders of student temporariness. They are passing through spaces that belong to someone else, even if signs of settlement rise menacingly from the ground.

Miracles and Follies

Historical legends about buildings on campus often provide reminders of the college's mission. Houghton College in upstate New York is an evangelical Christian institution, and some of the stories of its expansion suggest divine intervention. When the main auditorium went up, students hear, bad weather over a weekend prevented completion of the roof, and snow threatened the interior. The building superintendent called for prayer and workers. When workmen braved a snowstorm to come to the rescue of the building, they strangely found no snow on campus and were able to seal the roof. The legend is also told of the college's need for native river stones for its buildings. The stones were in a field owned by a farmer demanding a sum much higher than the college could afford. "For that price we'll just let the water wash over 'em," he told them. Through the winter the water did wash over them, and moved them onto another farmer's land. The new farmer gave the college its much-needed stones.

Convinced that colleges construct their buildings on a shoestring and have, despite their reputation for intelligence, a knack for fouling things up, students on almost every campus have architectural folly stories. I went to school hearing that the old library tower at Binghamton University was leaning or would topple over sometime soon because campus planners foolishly placed it in the path of the fiercest winds in the region. Maybe mistrust of the building arose because it was the tallest building on campus, and students suffered as they braved winds to enter its grim, uninviting doors.

The University of Massachusetts library is the tallest building in the central part of the state, and it attracts similar stories. Students assure each other that the structure is sinking into the ground. After all, they offer, the architects failed to compute the weight of the books into their designs. That must be why many shelves are left unfilled to this day (Carey 1988, 9). Northwestern University students for generations have also explained their sinking library building on the neglect of calculations of the weight of books. They add that the building was constructed on a section of campus colloquially known as

Fig. 8.2. Hammond
Building at Penn State–
University Park. (Photo
by Simon Bronner)

the "lakefill," suggesting the arrogance of engineers who messed with Mother
Nature by pushing back the waters of Lake Michigan (Brunvand 1999, 435).

At Indiana University (IU), storytellers use the story not only to comment
on architects' grip on reality (that is, what a library is for) but also on the boom
in campus enrollments. Tracing the building's construction to the 1960s, as if
its origin in that decade meant craziness, students at the end of the century
told IU folklore collectors that architects did not foresee "all of the students
and teachers who come in everyday" in addition to the weight of the books
(McDowell 2008). In a variation found at several campuses, students claim
that the building went up on unstable soil, and the only way to erect the edifice
was to limit the amount of books or equipment in the basement labs (Brunvand 1999, 435–36).

An RPI engineering student, perhaps defending the honor of his chosen
profession, related to me that designers planned the library with the concrete
floors bowed upward so that when the books were added the weight would
level the floor. But the construction crews thought it was a mistake and built

the floors level. Now the floors all bow downward. The library is a central symbol of learning on campus, and the neglect of the building, the stories imply, says something about tarnish on the ideal of knowledge on campus and administrative bungling of educational management. Sometimes there is a commentary on the source of the problem—budget cuts—that is timely because of the cant of belt tightening that students and faculty hear from administration.

Building stories often involve the modern rivalry between architects and engineers for professional authority over society's built environment. At Penn State, on College Avenue by the entrance of the University Park campus, is the Hammond Building. Built in 1958 as an engineering hall with severe straight lines and unfriendly glass and steel, it stretches along the street for what seems like an eternity (it is 609 feet long). To explain this monstrosity, regarded by students as the ugliest building on campus, those apparently in the know tell the tale that architects designed the structure to be nine stories tall. Realizing that engineers had misrepresented the ability of the ground to hold the structure, the architects had to divide the building into three side-by-side sections. In a variation that adds a student superiority theme, it is said that after the first three floors were built, graduate students went over the calculations and found the mistake. The original design is, in fact, the blueprint for the building that went up, but that does not stop students from pointing out its legendary folly.

Some building stories suggest that when engineering instructors have to engineer, they do not fare well. "While at Montana State University," an alumnus told me, "I remember hearing rumors that many of the buildings on campus were designed by the architectural/civil engineering programs. Several of them had major flaws. One of the dorms was constantly raining large chunks of itself onto the sidewalk below." There is a kind of student justice when the flaws emerge in the engineering building. "Here at Pitt," a reply came online, "the sinking building is Benedum, the engineering building. Supposedly, it was built above an underground river, and is now slowly sinking." Here's one from the same thread that combines the beliefs about the roles of engineering and library on campus: "At SMU [Southern Methodist University], when the CS (computer science) floor was being added to the Engineering Library they forgot to take into account the thickness of the walls. That is why you have to go through one office to get to another."

Some building legends arise as explanations for designs that seem to students to be odd or unnecessary. Other narratives knock the privileged status of engineering programs on campus, similar to the way that humor about campus athletes questions the rise of sports as big business over the mission of liberal arts education. Some stories also serve to illuminate the relative position of other groups on campus, or the priorities of the school, such as this one I collected from a Yale alumna: "Yale University has a miserable graduate dorm called Helen Hadley Hall that was built in the 1950s. It is poorly ventilated and very hot in the summer. Reliable sources say it was designed to be air-conditioned and then at the last minute the air conditioning was deleted as a cost-saving measure. The important thing about Hadley is that it was built for graduate women at a time when the undergraduate school [Yale College] was still all-male. And it is widely recognized as an indicator of the low status of women at Yale at the time."

If such stories suggest that students doubt the wisdom of seasoned professionals, especially those hired by universities, other fresh postings imply that present-day students, accused often of being politically apathetic, wonder whether the rebellious students of another generation influenced the institutional look of their buildings. An Ohio State student asked online, "Ever notice that the buildings on West Campus have almost no windows? Like prisons? This is because they were built when riots were common in the early 1970s. A related story says that the South Campus area used to have lots of brick walkways, which are now covered with asphalt. They were paved over because the rioters were digging up the bricks and throwing them at buildings." A reply came from Edward (Alex) Sobie at the University of Oregon, who reported that Bean complex has only two exits from the quads. The explanation? "This feature, rumor goes, was to allow police to block off the building in case of student riots." Sobie, who works for the Housing Department, and therefore heard the rumor often, decided to investigate. According to the architectural firm, the design owed to budget and technical constraints rather than a prison model or fear of riots, although the firm built a women's prison after completing the dorm project. The narrative resonates many years after the period of student unrest because of the frequent comparison that confined collegians make, tongue-in-cheek, of higher education institutions to jails.

Students from Georgetown University, Brandeis University, Binghamton University, the University at Buffalo, the University of Washington, the University of Illinois at Chicago, Columbia University, City College of New York, Wesleyan University, the University of California at Santa Cruz, the University of California at San Diego, the University of Michigan, Swarthmore College, Boston College, San Francisco State University, and Sonoma State University all appeared surprised that their school was not the only one with the prison rumor. Students frequently reported the additional belief in the presence of secret underground tunnels from the administration building so that administrators could escape if a riot occurred. Some students added variations that comment on what they consider a bizarre architectural environment: the University of California at Santa Cruz campus was built to move troublesome Berkeley students, a graduate center at Brown was designed by an architect for the Nazis, a Penn State hall was a secret atomic test site, dormitories at Pitt and Flagler were failed hotels, and a residence hall at Rhodes was designed to confuse intruders. Sometimes strange-shaped buildings attract trouble, such as the round of rumors of psychic predictions around Halloween time that a mass murder would occur on a college campus in a U-shaped (also reported as T- and L-shaped) building (sometimes with the added characteristic of a cemetery or river near the building or the large scale of the building) (see Ellis 1991; Brunvand 1993, 116–19; Linker 1980).

Students often believe that the unusual appearance of a building is the whim of an eccentric donor, or the administration bending backward to please a rich benefactor. The student center at Brandeis, for example, by one posted account, "looks almost like a moonbase, with pods/wings connected by under-ground and above-ground passageways." According to students at the school, two rumors circulate to explain the design. One was that it minimized the chance of a student takeover, and the other was that it facilitated the admin-istration to solicitation of six large donations for each of the wings. A student from Washington University in my survey reported that he often heard that the reason for so many dogs running freely on campus was that "some alum left a substantial sum to the school on the condition that the dogs would be allowed."

Students elsewhere explain the presence of an anachronistic swim test by a condition of a deceased donor. Responding to a rumor at Harvard that the swim test was a memorial to a victim of the icy depths around the *Titanic*, students from Cornell and Bryn Mawr recalled a story about endowments that carried the condition of the swim test established by alums who drowned. Similar to the "donor's revenge" narrative is the posting about the University of North Carolina library dome: "Seems that the guy who gave the money for the bell tower on campus originally wanted to endow the library but was turned down. So, he just gave the money for the tower, on the condition that he get to design the tower and select its location." According to the legend, the dome design appeared to be a "dunce cap" if viewed from the chancellor's office. Such narratives with remarks about administrative "selling-out" for donations with Faustian implications and penny-wise and pound-foolish "budget cuts" iterate the perception that money rather than mission drives the modern university.

At the University of Arkansas, upperclassmen tell freshmen that the North Tower of Old Main is taller than the South Tower because the architect was a Northern sympathizer in the Civil War. The fact is that Old Main is a replica of University Hall at the University of Illinois, unbalanced towers and all (Parler 1984, 26). At Florida Southern College, students relate the apparent pattern of walkways forming a pentagram owing to the architect's "satanic bent" (Bruce 2003, 29). They throw in an administrative twist by asserting that an arena, pool, or amphitheater that was supposed to go up on the site was dropped as a result (Bruce 2003, 29). Undergraduates also comment on the modernist design of a choir screen in Annie Pfeiffer Chapel. Students swear that the arrows point down although they should have been angled upward. Other conspiratorial themes are in campus building stories of a cover-up:

> [The mistake] was not discovered until after the massive center section was completed and was too late to modify it. It had been designed by Mr. [Frank Lloyd] Wright as "circles to frame the choir members," but upside down showed only their legs. Even the tallest choir member could not be seen through the inverted circles. An elaborate cover-up was designed to protect the on-site supervisor although it is easily observed that the entire balcony wall is upside down. (Bruce 2003, 26)

Some versions place the blame, or playful subversion, on student workers. Others claim that an additional tier was put up that allowed the faces of choral members to be seen, but "a hurricane came through and ripped off the top and in order to prevent it from happening again, when they rebuilt it, they put one less tier on it" (Bruce 2003, 27–28). The teller suggests that the architect was not particularly aware of the specific campus environment or the supervisors (ah, the ever-present and powerful "they") were negligent.

The adaptability of campus buildings, particularly student residences, to regional climes frequently enter into college building legends. The narratives often question the campus's relation to its location or the administration's attention to student comfort. At Penn State Harrisburg, the one-level residences for upper-division students in an area called Meade Heights had large, drafty sliding doors. In blustery northeastern winters, students complained of the chill. They asserted that there is a second Meade Heights in Georgia (or Florida or South Carolina). As the story goes, when the two housing areas were being constructed, the plans for the houses must have been mixed up, for the ones down there look like northern fortresses against the cold. Compare that narrative with a classic legend of another administrative misstep in the British Empire. According to Scotsman Gordon McCulloch, army barracks in frosty Glasgow, Scotland, had drafty swinging doors and breezy internal courtyards. McCulloch reports that the "buildings are reputed to have had the plans mixed up with plans for a barracks to be built in India 'with draughtproof doors and large open fireplaces.' The legendary mix-up was held to be typical of War Office maladministration" (1987, 113). Perhaps stories of this type migrated from army camps to campuses that are imagined to be institutionalized and bureaucratized as military complexes are. In fact, Penn State's Meade Heights had once housed air force officers, and part of the campus had been a military installation.

Variants of the switched building narrative often imply the problem of bureaucrats not invested in the special needs or conditions of a single campus. They often appear to students to be outside the educational sphere, and hence stories are told of the University of Virginia's chapel plan switched with one intended for Notre Dame or Cornell and the Oberlin library built from a design meant for the University of Florida (Brunvand 2001, 434). Tellers will also comment in stories that the error may have stemmed from a misguided attempt to save a buck. In the cool climes of Cal State–Hayward, students explain the lack of air conditioning in a campus building, for example, by the adoption of a design meant for a school in the steamy San Fernando Valley. According to a student raconteur, "When the building was put into use [at Hayward], since the windows faced the sunny side of campus and couldn't be opened, the inside became hot as an oven. I heard that there were several cases of student heat exhaustion in that building every year" (Brunvand 1993, 303–4).

Many building legends are perpetuated through campus tours given to prospective students and their parents. Student guides give the legends to spice up the morsels of information on the jaunt and frequently convey the message that the campus is student centered, as evidenced by the student giving the lowdown on an imposing institutional building. Folklorist Kimberly Lau found this pattern, for example, at her alma mater, the University of California at Berkeley, where student guides made a point of giving an architect legend about Dwinelle Hall. Officially, the building houses humanities departments, and most undergraduates have classes there at least once during their time at Berkeley. The building is the second largest on the campus and was completed in 1953 and expanded in 1998. Unofficially, Lau reports, Dwinelle Hall is "better known for its dead-end corridors, uneven floors, bizarre numbering, narrow and hidden staircases, and seemingly infinite 'ground floor' entrances and exits" (1998, 5). Campus tour guides tell that the mess arose from an irreconcilable argument between the building's two architects (sometimes identified as brothers). Unable to agree, they each designed their own plans at the university's behest, and the two halves of the building were eventually joined in the center. Variations referring to fiscally driven decisions detrimental to student use refer to the project originally being two or even three buildings, but a university administrator, or sometimes governor (former governor Ronald Reagan is often mentioned by name, although he was not in office at the time of construction), decided to go the cheapest route and fuse the different plans into one structure. Actually, the building's design owes to a team of architects who conceived of the north wing aligned with Berkeley's older buildings

Fig. 8.3. Sather Gate at the University of California at Berkeley, 2008. (Photo by Simon Bronner)

and the southern wing with the new section of campus including Sproul Hall, formerly housing the campus administration.

Lau recognizes that stories told on the tour anticipate reactions from recruits to the malformed structure and prepare them for frustrations as newcomers trying to navigate through the building's labyrinth. At the particular moment the tour stops at the building, a memorable narrative assures potential students that the commanding institutional icon apparently out of whack with human expectations, or, for that matter, their high school experiences, is an anomaly. That might suffice to account for the narrative's impact on the tour, but Lau also comments that the legend is retained well after the campus tour because of its metaphoric, antiadministration message. The disconcerting design and in-house feud come to epitomize, according to Lau, "the seemingly endless, nonsensical administrative rules and regulations that hinder students from accomplishing what they intend, expect, and hope to do. In addition, the legend highlights the administration's incompetence by emphasizing the fact that even after arbitrating the situation, the administration allowed this building to be built according to two architectural plans" (1998, 7–8). Students can figure out from the story that the university's bureaucracy is immense and complicated, and the administration has a lasting, if often invisible, impact on students.

Often to drive the point home in narrative, students may follow up the Dwinelle story with one about Sather Gate, originally marking the university's south entrance near Sproul Hall. Underwritten by university benefactor Jane K. Sather in 1910, the gate's prominent features are eight metal panels of bas-relief classical figures of nude men and women representing various disciplines of learning. According to legend, the administration caved in to the prudish Sather's demand that the panels be removed (in contemporary legends, the disgruntled donors are her descendants) until a professor or faculty team finds the panels years later (the 1960s, again, in narratives is a favorite era for student and faculty empowerment), and they are restored (Lau 1998, 8–10). The panels were, in fact, designed rather than found by a professor—sculptor Earl Cummins—and they were removed for restoration in 2008 before being reinstalled the following year. Regardless, the story often paired by student informants with the Dwinelle legend, according to Lau (who became a University of California administrator), conveys the idea that "the administration 'sells out' the university and the very ideas for which it stands" (1998, 10). On the student side, at least in this narrative, are professors who find the panels and restore their "rightful position on campus" in defiance of the administration. In a location known for hotly contested issues of academic freedom, the faculty uphold ideals rather than buckle under to the whim of wealthy patrons (Lau 1998, 10).

Although Dwinelle's architects, as in most building legends, are unnamed, one architectural celebrity who is the stuff of campus legend is Frank Lloyd Wright. At Florida Southern College, Wright designed nine buildings on campus into an "integrated architectural complex," beginning in 1938, with the last one going up in 1958. Perhaps fueling campus legend, construction workers came from the ranks of students. Succeeding generations of the buildings' dwellers attributed the complex's follies to Wright's quirks. Students explain the low clearance of the Esplanades (just over six feet) with the observation that Wright was short (his autobiography claims he was five feet eight inches, tall) and did not think they posed a hazard (Bruce 2003, 30; see also Adams 1984). They also tell that the lovely lights behind the stained glass insets in the concrete block walls provided beauty to the buildings, but "when the bulbs burnt out, there was no way to change them since they were sealed up in the wall" (Bruce 2003, 30). The theme of Wright as overbearing task-master is evoked by the green coloration after time of the copper fascia on the Esplanades. In one collection, a student more than sixty years after Wright began his project offers the legend she heard: "We were told that when Frank Lloyd Wright build the Esplanades, his workers were not allowed to take bathroom breaks. So they urinated right there on the Esplanades. Apparently, the 'lining' of the Esplanades is copper, and when urine mixes with copper, it produces a greenish color. And if you look today, you'll see the same greenish color I'm

referring to. So, if you ever wondered how it got to be green . . . now you know!"
(Bruce 2003, 31–32). A variation that circulates attributes the green color not
to Wright's prohibition on bathroom breaks, but on his bizarre demand that
workers urinate on the copper to increase the oxidation process (Bruce 2003,
30–31).

At the University of Pennsylvania, students swear that the Irvine Auditorium, referred to as "that bizarre pile," was designed not by a famed architect
but by a student who flunked out of the school of architecture. According to
many versions of the legend, the student's father gave it to the school as revenge (Hine 1980, 1). The story does not check out, but it highlights folk narrative's power to point out deviations from the norm, especially in imposing
structures such as public malls and museums as well as lofty college buildings
(see Brunvand 1989, 253–58; McCulloch 1987, 109–16).

Legend asserts that campus structures—and by extension, engineering
"progress" past human scale and control—have it backward. At Stony Brook
University, students look to the "bridge to nowhere" to make their case. Built
in 1970, the bridge leads from the second floor of the union building to the
north wall of the library where it stops in a dead end. According to legend, the
bridge was supposed to go into the library, but the library was built backward.
"There are skylights in there that point the wrong way," students say (Birnbach
1984, 262). Folklorist Jan Brunvand meanwhile reports the case of an apartment building built for students on the Bloomington campus of Indiana University that students maintain is "backwards." It "was supposed to have been
curved the other way to be more in harmony with the shape of the hill." It must
have been the fault of the engineers, students observe, because "the architect
was very disappointed when he came to Bloomington and saw what they had
done" (Brunvand 1989, 257).

Sometimes in collegiate legendry rifts between university trustees and a
builder cause problems. Narratives about Howard Payne University concern a
bid for rock work on Old Main given to someone whom the board suspected
of tipping the bottle. Supervisors decided to fine him $100 every time he was
caught drinking on the job. According to legend, he owed the college money by
the time the work was finished. Legend has it that straitlaced trustees at Indiana University objected to the extra endowment given the breasts of a sculpted
female figure in the central fountain. The sculptor supposedly responded spite-
fully by making things worse: he placed fish between the figure's legs (Waymire
1978, 2–3). Students might add that when a virgin graduates from Indiana University, "the fish will swim out between the legs of the lady in the fountain" or
"the fish will swim around the pond" (McDowell 2008). It is true that at Hamline University, trustees, worried about undignified art, ordered the removal
from a residence hall of a gargoyle that portrayed a freshman, beanie and all.

The eventual fate of the whimsical statue is a matter of folkloric speculation. At Case Western Reserve University, freshmen swear that the gargoyle facing west from the Gothic chapel sticks out its tongue at Case's trustees (Cramer 1976, 355).

Suicidal, Loving, and Sick Ghosts

By far, most legends about buildings on campus get students where they live, including the dormitories and fraternity and sorority houses. As if to both personalize the place and underscore its strangeness, new students are introduced to a resident ghost. A warning is often embedded in the stories—the spirit may belong to a student who met a tragic end by studying too hard or not enough, or by loving too much. The majority of revenants are women, and many of them are restless because they took their own life. The ghosts are rarely malicious, but they do act up enough to let their presence be known. Students also refer to their activity to explain lost articles, disturbed sleep, and mysterious creaking sounds.

At the University of North Alabama, students tell of Priscilla, who committed suicide in a women's dormitory. Some say she was distraught over failing exam grades; others whisper she was involved in an unhappy love affair with a professor. Some say she jumped down the stairwell; others are sure she hanged herself in the second floor elevator shaft. Her ghost haunts the halls of the old dorm, especially around exam time. Today, the Guillot University Center stands on the original location of the dorm, but reports circulate of strange sounds emanating from the second floor (Y. Williams 2007).

At Oberlin College, students answered my survey with a related story about the spirit of a student who committed suicide during the 1950s. "She was having trouble dealing with the high pressure situation in Oberlin. It was near the end of the semester and the work was piling up. The weekend before finals her roommate was gone and she had a huge fight with her boyfriend. Feeling lonely, frustrated, and depressed, she took an overdose of sleeping pills. Her boyfriend found her the next afternoon when he had come back to apologize. Students say she returns to the room periodically looking for the young man. Her sobs drift through the room and her shadow can be seen in the window, beckoning for someone to help her."

Folklorist Elizabeth Tucker identifies a series of college legends about suicidal women associated with the sound of marbles falling. From Oneonta State in upstate New York comes a story, for example, told about two separate dormitories in which a young woman hangs herself, "and when she did her foot knocked over a jar of marbles off her desk" (Tucker 2007, 57–58). The origin narrative explains the sound of marbles dropping one at a time overhead. At the University of Northern Colorado, students name a resident ghost Edith. A victim of a prank involving the rolling of marbles above her room to "freak her out," Edith hanged herself, and, according to legend, she "rolls marbles in the attic to scare the [resident] girls" (Tucker 2007, 56). Tucker finds symbolism in addition to the characterization of the vulnerable, emotional woman in the narrative. The dropping of marbles represents insanity, as in "losing one's marbles," and death, as in "kicking the bucket," or in this narrative "the jar." "In college," Tucker observes from her experience as a faculty master in a residential complex, "students feel pressure to be rational, controlled, and successful in getting good grades." Symbols such as marbles falling "represent just the opposite of a desired future: irrationality, lack of control, and failure" (Tucker 2007, 58). The marbles, connected with childhood, provide a clue to the transition in age as well as location. They draw attention to the unexplainable noises in institutional settings, and suggest the importance of mental stability amid social tensions with resident strangers as well as the strains of work and being away from home.

Besides odd noises, mystifying smells in old campus buildings invite legendary speculation. At Penn State Harrisburg, I had heard stories of a "death smell" in a building used for admissions that had once housed students. I had to agree that despite renovation, some rooms held an odor that reminded me of sterilization liquids. Upon investigation, I learned that the building had actually been an infirmary, and the walls had absorbed the aroma of chemicals. As walls were replaced, the scent subsided, but students persisted in telling tales of youth cutting their own lives short as a result of going over the edge. Variations of campus legendry with the conspicuous feature of the ineradicable smell due to a student hanging are evident at the University of Georgia, where student tellers add a cover-up motif of the administration "bricking up or closing off that wing or section" in Joseph E. Brown Hall (Kelley 1992, 143). At Smith College, disputes about the presence of a "death smell" in a residence hall signaled the need for confirmation of a spectral presence by smell if not noise (Tucker 2007, 68; cf. "the Death Car" belief legend about a luxury car sold at a bargain price because the smell of death cannot be removed: Baker 1982, 196–98; Brunvand 1981, 20–22; 1990, 18–21; 2001, 107–8; Dégh 2001, 71; Dorson 1959, 250–52). In the collegiate "death smell" narratives, the college campus exudes youthful energy—epitomizing life, indeed a new life—but students in a construction of a cognitive binary of life and death associate failure and isolation with death—symbolized by hanging. The presence of a ghost often is immaterial. The crucial detail—or warning—is about the distress that students face, and with which they feel they have to cope alone. The administrative cover-up motif is a signal in the elaborative commentary of the story of the external image of the campus that appears to differ, at least through student eyes, from the internalized angst of college experience.

Suicides in legends far outnumber those in real life. In narrative, the harsh contravention of suicide serves to warn students about letting the pressure do them in, especially in this modern day when students seem more self-absorbed and competitive. An abundance of cautions can be heard in a legend given me by a student from Bethany College in West Virginia:

> It was said that some years ago, a Bethany College student had leaped to his death from the tower that overlooks the campus. It was rumored that the student had recently broken up with his girl, was on academic probation, and was under pressure from his family to excel in school. It was spring and finals were only a week or so away and he wasn't prepared for them. He left a note in his dorm room apologizing for not being able to live up to everybody's expectations. Ever since that night, people have said they have seen his ghost near the bell tower during final exam times. Some people even say that the ghost has made the clock strike the wrong time or not ring at all, causing many a student to miss his final exam.

With courtship such a prevalent distraction for students, it is not surprising that lovers' ghosts frequently haunt campuses. At Stephens College in Columbia, Missouri, students still recount the story of a young woman who found a wounded Confederate soldier in the tower of Senior Hall. The student nursed the soldier back to health, and the two fell in love. The couple decided to elope, but when they crossed the Missouri River the woman fell in, and the soldier died trying to save her. Tellers relate that the ghosts return to Senior Hall where they found their happiness. In a more cautionary variation, a student offered that the soldier left the student, vowing, however, to return to marry. "I've heard one thing," the raconteur emphasized, "that she had his baby and he never came back and she went crazy. It was just her ghost that comes back each year" (Shutan 1972, 5).

A similar story is told about Norland Hall at Wilson College—like Stephens, a women's college. The college's location in Chambersburg, Pennsylvania, site of a Civil War battle, is the backdrop for several stories of Colonel Alexander McClure, builder of the elaborate Victorian-style Norland Hall, and his beautiful daughter (who, by the way, never existed). A Union soldier with whom the daughter was in love came back to warn the family to flee because the Confederates were coming to destroy the town. The daughter hid the injured soldier in the attic and fled. When she returned, she found him dead. He is said to be buried in the garden, and red flowers tended by the daughter mark the spot. Students say one can hear his ghost knocking in the tower attic room. In a variation, the colonel hid the daughter from a Confederate soldier and chased the soldier into a tunnel. When the tunnel collapsed, both were killed. The daughter committed suicide in the tower room after hearing that her father and lover were killed. The ghost of the daughter haunts the tower, while the ghosts of Colonel McClure and the soldier roam the tunnel, which is now Prentis Hall (Ohlidal 1981; Varounis 2009, 29–33).

Students sometimes take measures to contact the ghosts, especially if the revenants have names attached to them. More than one blustery fall night in the dorms has been devoted to Ouija board play. Often use of the board involves looking for a "sign"—a knock, a ring, a blowing wind. The board's appeal to adolescents acting in groups has been psychologically interpreted as a way for youths to ritually control perceived dangers in the real world outside the protection of parents and in loco parentis institutions (Ellis 2004, 174–96; Quarentelli and Wenger 1973).

A popular form of occult "play" that swept campuses in the early twenty-first century to summon not just one ghost but a whole gang and bring the natural world even closer to the supernatural is "100 Candles." The activity stems from a ancient Japanese pastime called *Hyaku-monogatari Kaidankai* (A Gathering of Hundred Supernatural Tales) and might have been introduced into the United States by the modern global popularity in youth culture of Japanese *anime* (animated cartoons) and *manga* (comics), in which the ritual is frequently featured (Brenner 2007, x–xii). Of relevance to the collegiate scene is the reference made to the ancient practice not just as a storytelling frame but also as a warrior test of bravery (see Foster 2009, 52–55). A new-age interest in Asian spirituality and mysticism also might have had an influence on American adolescent adaptation of the custom (Pike 2004, 83–84).

In the American collegiate version of "100 candles" a group of students seated in a circle gathers around midnight and lights 100 candles. Each person tells a paranormal experience, and after the telling a candle flame is blown out until all 100 are extinguished. Players believe that, as a result, 100 spirits arise in the area and trigger supernatural activity. Participants often relate cautions to one another that to be effectual, the stories told have to be true and the players need to believe in the supernatural (cf. "Bloody Mary in the Mirror" pre-adolescent rituals in which spirits are summoned by chanting such as "Bloody Mary, I Believe in You" in a darkened room, often accompanied by lit candles; see Bronner 1989, 168–69; Dundes 1998; Knapp and Knapp 1976, 242; Langlois 1978; Tucker 1977, 408–9). Although considered a play frame, initiating "100 Candles" also comes with the dire warning that stirring up spirits can spell trouble.

At Penn State, the "game," as it was called, was supposedly responsible for bizarre sightings and events in East Hall. A frightened student there claimed that her room had become permanently haunted as a result of playing "100 Candles." She saw a girl in the bed next to her, although her roommate was not in the building. Other students witnessed dark forms or sensed a presence (Buell and Petrucha 2010, 97–109; Swayne 2011, 30–31). Reports in the media of dorm activity involving Ouija boards and "100 Candles" are often taken as sensational evidence of the influence of satanic cults on youth, but usually the activity is spontaneous play that frames curiosity with one's comrades about the relation between the living (in the "normal" world) and the dead (in the "paranormal" or mythic realm). Situated in a strange place cut off from home, asking what happened in the past to those in similar positions to them is a way for students to inquire about their navigation of the present with other worried souls and about the prospects for the future on one's own (see Purnhagen 2011).

Student storytelling does not always use a ghost to bring the point home about the emotional challenges facing students. An example is the suicide legend recorded about Schulze Hall at Penn State. According to a student teller, a coed "had been dating a guy quite seriously. It was expected that at any time an engagement would be announced. One night these two lovers had a real bad argument. Everybody thought it was just a lovers' spat. Evidently it was more than that, at least to the girl involved. Nobody heard or saw the girl that night or the next day. Finally a maid opened the door and had quite a surprise waiting for her. The girl had hung herself." Although there is no ghost, students sometimes add a little magical twist by stating that grass did not grow on the poor girl's grave (cf. Baker 1982, 52; Carey 1988, 9; "Grave" 2002; Taylor 2000).

To be sure, strange noises and occurrences on campus are typically blamed on ghosts. A discernible pattern to the finger-pointing stories is that the revenants were vulnerable young women meeting a tragic end, often by their own hands. At Kutztown University, unusual sounds emanating from the top of Old Main are explained by the story of a coed who took her dog to the top floor. She hanged herself, and the dog was found dead later. The sounds must be the young woman's dog who is howling for her. That is why you cannot go up to the top story today, students say to support their case.

At Indiana State University, a whole cycle of stories is told about Burford Hall. Students report hearing moans, laughs, cries, and even vomiting sounds made by a resident female ghost (Baker 1982, 219–21; Thomas 1991). Folklorist Jeannie Thomas reported the following experience narrative with the supernatural (folkloristically labeled a "memorate") taken from a resident assistant at the dorm:

> I had an encounter with the Burford Ghost one night about 2:30–300 A.M.
> It was on a Friday night. I was in my room doing some homework and went
> to the restroom. I heard someone—sounded like throwing up in the rest-
> room—as I was walking to the restroom. When I opened the door, I did not
> hear anything at all. I went ahead and went to the bathroom and was getting
> ready to head out the door. As I was opening the door, I heard the throwing
> up again. So I shut the door and went to get a drink. I went back in to see if
> anyone needed help or if everything was cool. As I went into the bathroom,
> I looked underneath the stalls and did not see any feet there. It seemed real
> weird, so I proceeded back to my room. As I got outside, I heard the barfing
> again. I never saw anyone in the restroom. (Thomas 1991, 27–28)

The ghost is supposedly responsible for alarm clocks turning off and toilets
flushing themselves. The story behind the story of the Burford Ghost (also
affectionately known as Barfing Barb) relates usually to a timely social justice
struggle of a woman who hanged herself. During the 1960s, students explained
that the ghost contained the spirit of a Black Power advocate driven to madness. As the 1990s rolled around, Thomas collected versions claiming the ghost
was part of the gay and lesbian rights movement (1991, 28). The teller typically
indicates the irony of the ghost dying for a cause that has been generally accepted on campus. In early-twenty-first-century versions, the ghost is a coed
gone wild, with the implication that she may have been too hungry for social
approval. She puked herself to death after one too many frat parties in this
variant (Parker 2003). Even in this fun-loving ghost, one discerns a reference
to the special need for social adjustment by a woman because the revenant
is always female. The question raised by the narrative is whether she drank
to have fun or out of social discomfort. As a suicide ghost, Barb draws attention to frustration—socially as well as politically—related to students' liminal
status up against powerful, imposing forces. A message may also be embedded
within the legends that patience and perseverance pay off in the end or that
moderation, particularly in the conservative Indiana political culture, is the
best road to take.

You may ask, "Why does this political ghost reveal herself by barfing in the
bathroom?" As a common area in which people are alike by heeding nature's
call, the bathroom carries a symbolism about social equality. It also has an
air of mystery because it is both private because of the stalls and public with
access. Students feel vulnerable in that space because of their potential humiliation by being undressed or in a compromised position relieving themselves.
Hearing unexplained noises invites speculation, and ghosts, associated anyway
with watery areas, have a credibility in campus lore. Students have been known
to vomit in the bathroom after a binge, and that is why in the narratives the

sound at first is not extraordinary. But the teller becomes alarmed when no afflicted person is found. The ghost cannot seem to stomach the current political situation and like many students cannot tolerate the social situation. With a folk gesture, students may indicate a dislike for another student by sticking a finger in their mouth and imitating a barfing motion, or even say "oh, barf!" The ghost narratives about Burford Hall trigger commentary about the frustrations of holding unconventional views and identities.

At Wayne State University, the ghost of yet another suicide case is blamed for unusual happenings: "She was supposed to have the other side of the room and keeps coming back, pulling things from the cupboard and making a pest of herself. I guess her spirit never rested, she was so unhappy" (Kreston 1973, 4–5). At Olivet College, students refer to "Ellen" or "Eileen" of 307 Dole. Stories range from security guards hearing orchestra music to someone whispering names when no one else is in the room (Sigler 1988, 1). In addition to being lovelorn, these ghosts as perfectionist or nose-to-the-grindstone students often could not face failure, which they defined as receiving less than straight As. Unable or unwilling to relax and partake in the campus's entertainments, the students' bad experience live on in ghost stories to remind listeners to preserve their mental health by keeping grades in perspective and letting go once in a while. The theme relates to migratory legends about outstanding artistic individuals who commit suicide if the products of their genius turn out to be less than perfect (Dégh and Vázsonyi 1978; McCulloch 1987). The applicability to student lore is the cultural notion that the life of the mind is often obsessive, and those who follow this life, including students, risk insanity. Tellers give more than a hint of abnormality to learned pursuits and worry that on a campus populated by all these intellectual types, trouble is likely to brew. The story conveys the message that students need to be more balanced—or more like ordinary folk.

Students at Georgia College maintain that a woman who hanged herself in Sanford Hall produces spooky lights on the vacant third floor, sounds of footsteps, and warm spots in the east wing. At Coe College, a first-year student stricken by pneumonia—"Helen," as she is called—is the guilty ghost. She hangs around a grandfather clock donated to the college in her memory and kept in the drawing room of her dormitory. According to legend, Helen would appear once a year at midnight in the old clock. After the clock was moved in 1980, it began to break down at exactly seven minutes to three—the time of Helen's death, or so it is rumored. Meanwhile, students living in her former room reported mysterious rearrangement of their things. Today, Helen inhabits the old dumbwaiter in the dorm. The women report hearing strange noises coming from behind a sealed door located on the first floor.

At Bethany College, students tell of a lone grave up on a hill overlooking campus. According to legend, a coed pined so much over a broken love affair that she died and was buried at the spot where she went to cry. A trip to the grave is a favorite social excursion for new students who come to check out the legend. The deceased about whom the legend is told, especially if interred in an isolated spot, is sometimes not a student, but a child, emphasizing youthfulness on campus and the tragedy of a life cut short. As other stories attest, many of these characters are on a first-name basis with new generations of students taking up residence on campus. At Lees-McRae College in North Carolina, a cemetery on campus invites narration and particularly one grave marker with the evocative inscription, "She is not dead but sleeping." The victim is known as Emily, who supposedly died of tuberculosis. Tate Hall occupies the stone building that housed a hospital where Emily died. Students on the fourth floor of Tate report windows opening and closing by themselves and noises sounding like footsteps (Barefoot 2004, 110–14). Truman State University's appropriately named Grim Hall has the ghost of Charlotte, who, depending on whom you listen to, went into a diabetic coma when she could not get insulin over winter break or succumbed to hypothermia because of the cold. Students in the dorm report feeling cold sensations and hearing doors rattling. As with many female ghosts, she is often spotted in a white dress, representing her innocence. Students view her function as assuaging loneliness by getting people together and sometimes think of stories about her as warnings not to sacrifice their health for the grind of college work. The dorm, after all, students note, was a residence for nursing students (Wolcott 2003).

Elizabeth Tucker reports a contemporary variant about a lonely diabetic student from the University of Scranton. The teller emphasizes that to assuage her depression, she inhaled sweets "even though she knew that they were bad for her" (Tucker 2007, 92). She ended up dead, found slumped over her desk (representing seclusion and the grind of work) by maintenance workers. Turning into a ghost, she reminds new dwellers to be welcoming to others. Sometimes a nursing student confirms for the workers that she is dead, because apparently the staff do not recognize students passed out over their desks as unusual. According to the student informant, "My friend says that the RA [resident assistant] from the first dorm that she lived in sees the dead girl all the time there. The ghost walks around at night around the doors of the people who gave her the most trouble when she was there. Things are always missing from their rooms as well" (Tucker 2007, 92).

One may wonder about students being on a first-name basis with their ghosts. Women often treat the ghost as a resident guest, albeit a sometimes difficult one. She is often a lost, plaintive soul struck with heartbreak, and thus her antics are understandable, students say. Women at Brenau College, for example, have "Agnes"; at Smith, there is "Lucy" at Sessions House. These figures, like those from Wilson and Olivet, have similar legends told about them. In the

Smith variant, there is the extra mysterious feature of a secret staircase to add intrigue to the tale. As folklorist George Carey collected the legend,

> In revolutionary times British General Bourgogne stayed in Sessions House and while there fell in love with the owner's daughter, Lucy. To keep their affair hidden, they met as frequently as possible on the stairway. Another account has Lucy falling in love with a soldier in Bourgogne's army, again using the secret stairway for their trysting place. In this version, her lover eventually leaves with the unfulfilled promise to return, and Lucy pines away. To this day her ghost returns to startle students near the stairway and in the house. Residents returning to Sessions at night have seen a light in their room and a figure standing there looking out. They reach the room only to find it dark, and their roommate gone from the building. (1988, 8)

Sometimes the ghost reminds students of the need to reach out to one another. At Huntingdon College in Alabama, undergraduates talk about "Martha," also known as the "Red Lady," who wanders around Pratt Hall. Forced by her father to leave her New York home for the school in the Deep South, Martha, whose trademark was wearing red garments, had trouble adjusting to her new environs. One roommate after another left her, calling her behavior "strange" and "aloof." Even the dorm president made a gallant try, and when she prepared to leave, Martha cried, "I was beginning to think you really wanted me to be your friend—but you hate me just like the rest." After the president's departure, Martha slashed her wrists and bled to death. Students today report seeing flashes of red shooting out into the corridor (Barefoot 2004, 11–16; Windham and Figh 1969, 97–103). Collegians make various interpretations of this story, from a daughter's sad lot when she cannot express her wishes to her father, to the need all residents have, no matter how different, for a friendly presence in the dorm, and finally to the regional differences that sadly divide students.

Men are not immune to the ghostly bug. At Michigan State's Holmes Hall, students reported seeing a ghostly male figure standing by the door at the end of the hallway, and they called out, "Hey, you." They followed the figure out the door and down the stairs, but he was nowhere to be found. They then figured that the spirit was none other than that of fabled computer whiz James Egbert, a seventeen-year-old student who committed suicide in 1980. Also at Michigan State, the story circulates about the ghost of a male student who died on the fifth floor of Wilson Hall. "Now the elevator always stops there," a student in my survey explained. "Whenever you press the button it has to come down from the fifth floor first. They hired elevator workers to come in and find the problem, but the workers could find no mechanical reason for the elevator continually stopping on the fifth floor."

A migratory legend that appears to deliver warnings to college students is about the pressure of overwork and the dangers of resorting to drugs. Elizabeth Tucker reports hearing the following at Binghamton University:

> See years ago there was this kid who went to Bing [Binghamton University] and his parents put all this pressure on him to do well and become a successful doctor but no matter how hard he tried he just wasn't able to do well. So he'd spend all his time studying and his roommate and everyone would call him a geek. So around finals time he was in the library studying. He had been there for a couple of days and wasn't able to stay awake. Well, this kid passed by trying to sell Adderall to people in the library and he figured there was another way he'd pass his orgo [organic chemistry] final, so he took some Adderall. Only he didn't know that it was really speed, and he started going crazy. He thought he was invincible. So he snuck up to the top of the library tower and jumped. Now his ghost haunts the library tower. He is still there trying to study for his orgo final. (2007, 85)

The narrative refers to parental pressure, competitiveness of college, and the stress of landing a status career—familiar sources of distress—but the essential message is that students need to do what is right for them rather than follow others' expectations. Tucker's summary is "a well-balanced life matters more than a push toward perfection. Excessive studying can ruin a student's life, dooming him to study in a library's tower forever as a shade of his former self" (2007, 86). Variations include the spectral sighting of an engineering student who took too much OxyContin, a narcotic pain reliever teens call "kicker" and "hillbilly heroin," referring to its high. "He . . . passed out in the third floor library," a student reports from Northeastern University, "and never woke up. Some kids say they see him still sleeping at the same table" (Tucker 2007, 86). Amid frequent talk of pulling all-nighters and taking drugs to enhance performance, stories of students never waking up bring home a powerful point in dorm talk about whether the advantages gained are worth the risk.

Greek Ghosts

Fraternity and sorority house ghosts tend not to be suicide victims. Selfishly taking one's life would go against the spirit of brotherhood and sisterhood prevailing in Greekdom. But like so many "real-world" ghosts, fraternity spirits are restless because of an unnatural death, often in a car accident, and they come home to the Greek house where they seek comfort. The elaborate designs of many frat and sorority houses, with dark paneling and multiple hallways, also invite legendary speculation with comparison to Hawthorne-like mysterious dwellings of the seven gables. Lurking in the fraternity or sorority house, in the best tradition of Greek high jinks, the ghost commonly causes disorder. He or she opens windows after they have been closed, turns on lights in the middle of the night, and mischievously knocks over books or dishes.

According to a student from Bucknell University in my survey, "One of the first things you learn at Bucknell is the story of the ghost on the Beta Gamma suite in Hunt, situated on the third floor." The ghost was a sorority sister who was called back home. Her house had burned, and when she arrived she discovered that her parents were dead. She decided to return to school, but the way was treacherous. Heavy rains soaked the road on her nocturnal trip. She lost control of the car and was killed in the accident. "Now, on stormy nights," the student told me, "people sometimes see a young woman wearing a drenched raincoat standing in the stairwell of the Beta Gamma suite."

Many accounts of ghost legends are told as personal experiences. Tellers worry that contemporary audiences will be skeptical of reports of how a ghost came to be; they often feel compelled to describe an encounter with the ghost to affirm its reality, even if it happened to a friend of a friend. That student from Bucknell, for example, made sure to add:

A fellow Beta Gamma was in her room studying one stormy night, with only her desk light on. It was late and she was just about to fall asleep when she heard a knock on her door. Wondering who it could be at such a late hour, she opened the door and saw someone standing there in a raincoat, dripping wet. I don't recall if the stranger talked or not, but Cathy somehow understood that she wanted to use the phone. Leaving the door open, she turned around to get the receiver (she was going to dial for her), but when she looked at where the girl had been standing, she wasn't there. She knew she wasn't crazy because there was a wet spot on the floor from the rain off her coat. Cathy stepped out into the hall to see if she could see her, but no one was there.

Shades of the Vanishing Hitchhiker legend! You have probably heard of this internationally known story of the young woman hitchhiking along the side of the road, often in the rain. When a car pulls over, she asks the male driver to take her home, but when the man stops where she is supposed to go, he discovers that she is gone. Confirming her presence, however, is a wet spot or sometimes even the raincoat. The hitchhiker, it turns out, had died on that very night, often as a result of a car accident (see Baughman 1966, motif E332.3.3.1; Bennett 1998; Bennett and Smith 2007, 287–301; Bronner 1989, 146, 307–8; Brunvand 1981, 24–40; 2001, 463–65; Goss 1984). As the hitchhiker legend often points to the security of home during teenage years when the rebellious youth seeks to drift away, so the vanishing sorority sister avows the significance of her Greek home.

Student raconteurs often confirm the fraternity spirit by identifying the pitiful student out of a yearbook or fraternity composite photograph. At Penn State, students at Alpha Sigma Phi talk about Lou (or John) Amici (or Ameche). "He was a good athlete and involved in all house activities," a student shared with me. He continued:

> All of the brothers were very fond of him. After graduation, Lou moved from State College and settled down somewhere else, where he was killed in a car accident. One night when a brother was asleep in his bedroom, he was awakened for no apparent reason. He opened his eyes to see Lou's ghost kneeling at the side of his bed. He lashed out with his arm but felt nothing. A cold wind began to blow through the room. A week later he was looking through Alpha Sig's yearbook. All of a sudden he noticed a picture that looked very familiar. It was the same person who was kneeling down beside his bed.

From another fraternity brother comes this variation: "One time, a brother was asleep in his room with the door locked, as he locked it every night when he slept. When he awoke the next morning, all of the furniture in his room had been rearranged. He happened later to look through some pictures of old brothers and found a picture that matched the image he had seen. It turned out that the ghost had lived in that room." Again there is a connection to the Vanishing Hitchhiker legend. In many versions the driver accompanying the ghostly passenger recognizes the ghost after seeing her picture inside the home to which she had asked to be driven (see Brunvand 1981, 28–29).

At Indiana University, members of Sigma Phi Epsilon relate similar encounters with the ghost of Michael Frang (also rendered as Pfang in folklore collections). He is the fraternity house's version of the headless horseman (Baughman 1966, motif E422.1.1). As the story goes, Michael died during a homecoming parade. He was atop the Sig Ep float when the cannon aboard misfired and decapitated him. After that tragic end, Michael came as a revenant to the fraternity house, lurking mostly in the dark basement (called "the swamp" in reference to its murky depth) where he once lived. As one might imagine, strange occurrences are blamed on Michael's restless—and headless—spirit. Students told investigating folklorists, "When anything weird happens in the house we know that it was him. Some of the guys claim they have seen him walking around or knocking things over in the house" (McDowell 2008). Several accounts mention books flying off a shelf of a bookcase in the "swamp"; others swear that drinking glasses mysteriously fell off another shelf. One frat member called attention to a venetian blind that fell. "The window wasn't open so it couldn't have been caused by the wind," he explained. Several students talked about lights going on after they had been turned off and doors mysteriously unlocking after being locked. And then there is the time the trophies from the locked case mysteriously were strewn about the room (Battreall 1987).

The University of the South at Sewanee also has a headless ghost, who belonged to a fraternal organization called the Order of the Gownsmen, although students treat this figure from the more distant past less reverently than the Sig Ep brothers do Michael. The gownsman lost his head when fisticuffs with fellow students ensued after some late-night studying (overstudying, and the pressures that go with it, students speculate). Notwithstanding that the college public relations office assured me the headless gownsman had not made an appearance lately, it was reported to the end of the twentieth century when this account was taken: "Each year someone claims to have some sort of scuffle with the ghost or sees the ghost in his room. It is said to come down the stairs and then count the stairs as it comes down, always the right number of bumps per the number of steps it comes down. Normally, it only shows up during the exam period" (McNeil 1985, 74).

The spirits of sad characters who are not fraternity brothers or sorority sisters are known to roam Greek houses. Once again the scene of the crime is the basement. At the Sigma Chi house at Penn State, various stories are told about an unsolved murder that occurred there. According to legend, the house cook and her daughter were viciously murdered by an unknown assailant when it was a sorority house. In some tellings, the cook belongs to the fraternity and the daughter to the sorority. Supposedly the restless ghosts appear around four in the morning when a brother is alone in the house. In a variation, the ghosts are carryovers from the days before the house belonged to the fraternity. A devil-worship cult inhabited the place, and one night a member was found on the back steps with his throat cut. The murder was never solved, but the cult was cleared out of the house. "Through the years," students report, "various brothers have heard strange sounds and happenings. The house is haunted by the murder victim. Brothers are afraid to stay in the house alone or over vacations because of the ghost." As one may surmise, being in a fraternity, or a fraternity house, is not about being alone. At another level, the frequent reference to past Satanism in collegiate legends distances and at the same time externalizes the idea that one explanation for the present strange behavior of students is that they must by possessed by demons (see Ellis 2000, 199–219; Flanagan 2012).

Fraternity houses that mysteriously lock and unlock, windows that open and shut without someone there to do the task, and lights that peculiarly come on and off by themselves are also found at Indiana University (IU). Old IU buildings have their share of strange noises, but one, the sound of babies crying at a house occupied at different times by several fraternities, receives special attention in legend from students. Again, the story refers back to the days before the house was inhabited by a fraternity. "The story I have most often heard concerning the ghost," a student reported, "is the one involving the baby. From what I have heard, a doctor and his wife were some of the first inhabitants of the house. The good doctor supplemented his income by performing abortions. Because abortions were illegal, the operations were performed in the basement, at night, with instruments which were crude by design" (Rosemeyer 1976, 11). There are many variations. Sometimes the doctor is thought to be linked to the builder of the house. After all, "signs" exist in the basement, such as a newly bricked-in area in the shape of a roughly made cross, or thick steel doors. Occasionally, as the story goes, the doctor performed the abortions on sorority members. He was variously arrested after slipping up, or he went insane, or he killed himself. Crying sounds are attributed to fetuses he threw in a coal bin or buried behind a wall (Lecocq 1980, 265–78; McDowell 2008; Rosemeyer 1976; cf. Baker 1982, 84–85, Murdered wife buried in wall of the Preston House; Baughman 1966, motif E334.2.1g, Ghost of sailor haunts house where his skeleton was buried in wall).

Once more, one hears the personal experience stories to chronicle the hauntings: "I was in my room studying late at night for an exam and I believe everyone had gone to bed. I was becoming drowsy. Suddenly I heard someone begin walking from south to north along the long second floor hallway. The walk was not normal. One step was muffled as if one foot or leg was crippled. It ended its march down the second floor hallway and stopped by the stairway door. Everything was silent. I waited to hear the door slowly being opened onto the stairway. I waited perhaps to hear a brother step out of heavy shoes and scamper barefoot back to his room, laughing to himself hysterically. I heard nothing" (Rosemeyer 1976, 13–14). Beyond the personal experience, an appeal is made to the encounters of others: "From what I've heard, while the house was empty for one and a half years before we moved in, many persons claim that, as they walked down the sidewalk next to the house at night, they would hear crying coming from the house" (Rosemeyer 1976, 12). The coincidence of the legend with debates over legalized abortion in the United States is noteworthy, for, in the telling, the legend frequently sought comment: Was the detail that the doctor performed abortions the horror, or was it that he was forced to do it illegally? (cf. Dundes 1987a, 3–14). Beyond the historical and political comments that can ensue, the narrative implies a cautionary message for the present about pregnancy resulting from premarital sex.

Residents of Phi Mu Alpha house at Illinois Wesleyan University have for many years told the story of a doctor in the Victorian home with deep wood wall coverings and lots of twists and turns. A botched abortion of the physician's daughter in the house resulted in the woman's death, and the distraught father dismembered the body and buried her remains in the floor of the basement. Students swear that the bricks placed above her grave sink into the ground no matter how many times they are replaced. Phi Mu Alpha brothers have reported different sightings of the revenant since the 1960s. One has her wearing a white veil as though she was anxious to get to a wedding. Some late-night sightings report her lounging on a couch. Having withstood the ravages of time and weather over the years, the house has been protected by her, residents say. They point out a symbol of a cross on a door near the grave. They say that as long as the cross is maintained, the fraternity house will be safe. Historical research shows that a physician did live in the house, and he indeed did have a daughter, but she did not meet a tragic end; she married in 1903 and lived to raise several children to maturity. Today's fraternity brothers still refer to the basement's mysterious sinkhole as her grave and point to a simple panel of plywood resting atop the legendary resting place as proof that one cannot pave over the burial spot (Deters 2003).

In another legend with a modern ring to it, some resourceful fraternity spirits call in their orders. Here is the way a Phi Kappa Psi member at Penn State told me a story with the theme:

Each morning at precisely 6:40 a.m., the house phones at the Phi Kappa Psi fraternity on Locust Lane begin to ring. And each morning they ring just three times. If answered at any time before the three rings are up, there is heard from the other end of the line nothing more than a common dial tone. It's been happening for about two years now . . . ever since the death of the house's founder John Henry Frizzell. John Henry, as the boys all used to call him, had practically devoted his entire life to his fraternity. Next to his family, Phi Psi was his true love. It is said that John Henry himself is responsible for ringing the phones each morning, each ring representing the mystic Greek words that are represented by the letters Phi, Kappa, and Psi.

At Illinois Wesleyan, a resident staying alone in Adams Hall, home of the Acacia fraternity, reported a series of phone calls that he assumed were pranks. He removed all the phones from their sockets and took a nap, only to be awakened by the sound of more ringing. The inexplicable rings were attributed to calls from the spirit of a woman named Frances who perished in the house. The ghost lives on in the belief that Frances is most active when residents are not taking care of the house, and the fraternity members are reminded then to get the place in order to stop her intrusions (Deters 2003).

The phone call from the deceased is apparently a migratory motif. Ronald Baker collected several stories from Indiana State University students about a phone installed in a nearby mausoleum. In one version, the deceased, before he died, had promised his wife that he would call her. Several years later his wife suddenly died of a heart attack, and when the police found her, she was still holding the phone in her hands. When they checked the mausoleum, they found the receiver off the hook (Baker 1978, 72). At San Jose State University, the mysterious phone ringing is a sign of desperation from a woman of yore who was gang raped. Often associated with Moulder Hall, tellers swear that one can hear a phone ring and the sound of a girl screaming. Tellers explain that "she ended up in the phone booth," and the booth is no longer there. Sometimes students may reflect that its removal was linked to the event: "They couldn't get all of the blood out of the phone, so they removed it; late at night, occasionally you'll hear a phone ringing down where it used to be located." Faculty investigators have not found evidence of a death in this building or over in Hoover Hall, where similar cautionary legends abound (Spivey 2004; Tucker 2005, 76).

Communication technology, especially gadgetry that astoundingly sends disembodied voices and pictures, invites speculation about the ability to hear from the dead. A connection may also be made to religious beliefs about bells summoning the supernatural. In the Greek house context filled with references to tradition and the house's or chapter's long-standing historical legacy, legends connect contemporary residents to those who came before and remind them of their upholding of a special status—often tinged with belief, mystery, and secrecy. As Anna Deters (2003) reported from Illinois Wesleyan's fraternity houses, "the antique ambience of an old house can materialize into ghostly apparitions" that engage fraternity and sorority tellers more than their independent, rationalizing fellow students. The implication drawn from stories told by brothers and sisters is that the Greek domain is something of another realm, and it is not for the faint of heart.

Tragedy and Murder Most Foul

Students out on their own, away from the protection of home and family, listen particularly attentively to eerie legends, sometimes ghostly, of unsolved murders on campus. Franklin College in Indiana has a murder legend that has persisted among students for more than fifty years. Many variations exist, but the plot usually centers on a student, sometimes a sorority pledge, who is found dismembered in a dresser drawer, trunk, or wall. When the story uses the character of the sorority pledge, it typically follows in the telling that after an argument, a crazed active fatally knifed, chopped, and then hid a pledge. Otherwise, the identity of the assailant and details of the motive remain a mystery, students say.

But there must be reports in newspapers or college records of this bizarre case, you say? Well, students add that there was a cover-up of the grisly crime. "You can find the yearbooks over in Hamilton and the picture will be gone. You can go down to the administration office and check back records and nothing's in there either. Everything's just been removed. It's really strange . . . you know that room is still here, except it's been changed. It's no longer lived in" (Till 1976, 189). In students' minds, either the college administration or the daughter's rich father worried about his reputation is responsible for keeping it all hush-hush. Some students ask, "Could it be because the daughter was pregnant?" The location of the crime, Bryan Hall (a women's dormitory), is thus susceptible to strange noises produced, naturally, by the ghost of this victim (Till 1976, 187–95). The story has the earmarks of a migratory legend, for a dismembered victim with similar circumstances supposedly resided at the University of Kentucky and Indiana University.

For example, in a variation stressing the need for harmony among room-mates, an Indiana University student told this legend:

> There was a strange noise coming from one end of the hall. I never thought much about it 'till the next night when I heard it again. I asked some guys on my floor about it the next day, and there was this one guy, an upperclass-man, that told me that one night a long time ago when there were some girls living in Bryan, there were two girls who were roommates. Well, they got into a fight and it ended up one girl killing the other, stabbing her with a knife. After she did this she put her behind some panels, or something behind the wall, and no one even noticed. Well, a couple days later some girls started complaining of a smell. They thought it was rats or something, so they had an exterminator come, and when he came he found the girl, and I guess the other girl was convicted or something. But the funny thing about the whole thing is that you can't find anything about her even being here at I.U. It's a real mystery. (Waymire 1978, 4)

Far back in collegiate history, students resided with the spirits. Statesman and scholar Edward Everett recalled his freshman year at Harvard in 1807 with strange goings-on in a place students forebodingly called "the Den":

Just at the corner of Church Street (which was not then opened), stood what was dignified in the annual College Catalogue—which was printed on one side of a sheet of paper, and was a novelty—as "the College House." The cellar is still visible. By the students, this edifice was disrespectfully called "Wiswal's Den," or, for brevity, "the Den." I lived in it my Freshman year. Whence the name of "Wiswal's Den" I hardly dare say: there was something worse than "old fogy" about it. There was a dismal tradition that, at some former period, it had been the scene of a murder. A brutal husband had dragged his wife by the hair up and down the stairs, and then killed her. On the anniversary of the murder—and what day that was no one knew—there were sights and sounds—flitting garments daggled in blood, plaintive screams—*stridor ferri tractaeque catenae*—enough to appall the stoutest Sophomore. (Everett 1852, 66)

The mysterious "Den" is also the setting for a nineteenth-century Harvard legend about Mr. Wiswal's second wife, who raised suspicions because she happened to be the nurse for the recently deceased first wife. Students speculated that the first wife got her revenge in the "Den." As the story goes, when the second wife opened a dresser drawer filled with the first wife's clothing, a ghost or even the devil himself appeared and drove the second wife to insanity and eventually death (Hall 1968, 156–57).

Students confirm many of the murdered victims that return to haunt college students by pointing out ineradicable bloodstains (Thompson 1966, motif E422.1.11.5.1, Ineradicable bloodstain after bloody tragedy). At Florida Southern, for example, freshmen in Joseph Reynolds Hall, a dorm constructed in 1922, learn folklore about the "bloody balcony." Drawing legendary treatment is a splatter mark on the white paint that supposedly cannot be covered over. "There was a lady who supposedly got murdered out on our balcony," one student related, and explained that "it has like, blood all over the outside of the balcony on the left hand side of the building facing the Buddha pond on the second floor." Often tellers realize that this sounds preposterous, so add a confirming narrative: "Supposedly it looks like bloodstains, but then someone said that it was egg. But someone told me that it was blood and that they did tests on it, and that they painted over it and it still shows through" (Bruce 2003, 107). Embellishments to the story of the murdered victim indicate the use of the story to caution others, particularly women, about the potential intentions of strangers. Students speculate, for example, that the young woman was raped and "got her throat slit on her balcony" or had "her head [face] . . . bashed in on the balcony" (Bruce 2003, 108–9).

The ineradicable bloodstain is apparently a warning from the dead about what students regard as the ultimate violation—penetrating (rape), obliterative (the distortion of the face or head as destruction of individuality), and castratory intrusions (throats slit) (cf. the ineradicable bloodstains from hanged Mollie Maguires reported in Kline and Newell 1964 and from a husband's cut throat in Sanderson 1969, 250). Not only are these murder details particularly unseemly bodily violations, but they also refer to the presumption of trust among campus members and safety in the ideal surroundings of campus. An indication of this symbolism is the contrast of the bloodstain to a pure or holy place shown by the white coloring of a wall or church floor in other comparable narratives (see Baker 1982, 51–52; Taylor 1945, 32).

If bloodstains do not remain after a grisly death in legends that students tell, what looks like a face might appear. The image often appears on top of a lake or in a window—surfaces that provide reflections reportedly appearing "ghostlike." Sometimes the death comes as a result of fraternity initiations gone wrong and drownings (often associated in narrative with drugs or alcohol abuse—or too much celebration). The legends frequently invite commentary on culpability in the tragic event. With the narrative, tellers ask, "Was it an accident or planned?" At Binghamton University, Elizabeth Tucker collected "face in the water" narratives such as the following: "A guy pledging a fraternity drowned in the lake on campus. No one knows exactly how it happened, except that a few guys were swimming in the lake and one drowned. Many of the students on campus say that late at night you can see a reflection off the top of the lake that resembles a man's face. I have yet to see it because I'm afraid to walk around the lake late at night since this tragic event" (2007, 77). Tucker rightly points out that this is no mere echo of a fixed text of bygone days (cf. Wilgus 1970; Price 1999, 57–48). It reflects what she calls a cognitive process of "spectralization" appropriate in a campus context: a student who has died in a terrible accident turns into a ghost—a face reflected from the top of the lake (Baughman 1966, motif E334.2.2c Ghost of drowned person haunts spot of drowning; Tucker 2007, 78). "Through spectralization," Tucker writes, "the lost student remains with his or her friends and teachers, delivering a warning that may prevent them from risking their own lives" (2007, 78).

Farther upstate at the University of Rochester, a variation of the process is evident in stories of tragedy on another body of water that appears to disrupt the presumption of a campus being a grounded landscape of greenery and buildings, or else represents the temptation to literally "dive in" to danger. Tellers explain that the pond by Tiernan Hall freezes during most of the school year because of dipping temperatures. "So one night," a teller offers,

> these two kids go off into the woods with all of their other friends. Anyway, it gets really late and the two of them start to walk back to the dorm. Except that it's so cold and there was a blizzard the day before so they couldn't

really see where they were going very well. They were also really stoned and without realizing it, they walked right onto the frozen lake. The ice cracked under them and they went under. It was so cold that the ice froze back over where they fell in right away. The next day when everyone realized they were missing, they sent out a search party. When they walked out near the lake, they stared down and saw the faces of the two missing students frozen in the ice looking back up at them. If you walk out near the lake at night on the coldest night of winter, their faces will appear frozen and trapped under the ice. (Tucker 2007, 83)

Often heard during first-year orientation, such narratives deliver warnings about the temptations of drugs and alcohol in the years ahead of freedom from parental authority. The tragic circumstances are often rendered as if they were headlines from a newspaper but set vaguely in the recent past to an unnamed victim. The events supposedly happened "a while ago" or "a few years back." The aberrant 1960s sometimes creep into drug stories of strange goings-on, such as college students high on LSD who stared directly into the sun until they lost their eyesight ("Blinded" 2007; Brunvand 1993, 109). As if to say that drug takers are blind to reality, students might repeat (reportedly propagated by antidrug organizations) a variant using the destroyed eyes motif for youth under the influence of PCP (known by the folk name of "angel dust") who pluck out their eyes (Brunvand 1993, 109). To be sure, these legends are often associated with the druggy past when tellers relate that users were less savvy, but apparently in every collegiate generation, students swear either as warning or boast that today's marijuana or other controlled substances are more potent than before. Youths may resort to the Internet to find confirmation of the unfounded claim and there also find social networks abuzz with rumor (and fake photographs) that tobacco companies are preparing commercial brands of cannabis such as "Marlboro Greens," a signal to comment on the relation between the escapism of their youthful underground society and that of adult commercial culture ("Marlboro Greens" 2008).

The Cadaver Arm

Well before cautionary stories circulated on campus of the drug trip gone bad, a different type of warning went up in stories labeled by folklorists as "The Cadaver Arm." Folklorists even assign the common motif of an innocent victim ending up insane or dead, often as a result of a practical joke, with a number (Thompson 1975, motif N384.0.1.1) and trace narratives about the trickster's replacement of a human arm with a cadaver's into antiquity (Hansen 2002, 362). Here is a modern version from Indiana University: "One year in McNutt Quad, some girls played a joke on another girl [who] lived on the same floor. They put a severed hand in her room one night, and when the girl came back to her room they didn't hear her scream or anything, so they went to her door to see what happened. When they got there they found her chewing on the hand" (Waymire 1978, 3). Often the detail is added that the victim's hair turns white, he or she makes gurgling noises, and sometimes even that the victim dies of fright (Thompson 1975, motif N384.0.1 Madness from fright; see Baker 1982, 216; Barnes 1966, 305–6; Baughman 1945a, 30–32; Carey 1971, 80–81; Dorson 1949, 674–75; Parochetti 1965, 53). The story tells partly about the risks of pulling pranks, and it also offers a lesson about the vulnerability of students, especially new female ones, who seem to live closer to the edge in the strange college environment than most realize.

The most common variation of "The Cadaver Arm" concerns students preparing for medical careers. The story often involves a novice medical student or student nurse who is falling behind in studies. In most versions the student is also given antisocial characteristics; he or she is an arrogant snob, a loner, a grind, a braggart, or a snoop. The ending is also extra poignant in a medical context because the nurse or doctor turns into a patient. The ending of insanity, in fact, suggests not only the fragility of students pursuing this competitive and high-stress line of work but also conveys a message about the worst-case scenario of mental illness because the medical professionals are powerless to "fix" it. Probably the first collected version from oral tradition came from a Penn medical student in 1942:

> For some reason Jane was unable to get along with the other nurses in the hospital, and was constantly quarreling with people. They purposely did things to annoy her because they felt she deserved it. One night after Jane had been particularly trying, they decided to do something particularly unpleasant. One of the nurses on surgery duty agreed to bring an arm which had been amputated that day to Jane's room and slip it in her bed after she was asleep. They knew this would frighten her, but they thought perhaps it might force her to be more agreeable in the future. The arm was carefully and quietly put in the bed and Jane did not wake up. The next morning she did not appear, and no sound came from her room. The nurses, thinking she might be sick, went to investigate. They opened the door slowly and saw Jane sitting on the bed. Her hair, which had been black, was now completely white, and she was gnawing on the arm, making low gurgling noises all the while. (Baughman 1945a, 31; cf. Baker 1982, 216; Cerf 1945, 16)

The prank of placing a fake arm of rubber or plastic sticking out of a couch or under an automobile tire is an old one in the annals of practical jokes, but elaborated in the narrative are the special motif of the arm coming from a cadaver, indicating a heightened fear of dismemberment, and the medical school—or dorm—setting, indicating the unusual high-stress environment in which rhetorically (as failure) or literally (as corpses) death's presence must be confronted. The detail of the victim's antisocial character is important because the question raised in the legend is whether she needed a hand reached out to her or was being punished for her lack of connection to others. It might also refer to a real phenomenon of ganging behavior in competitive, hierarchical situations by stronger group members on their weaker colleagues that results in institutionalized "horizontal violence"; among nursing students, this has been proverbially called a pattern of "animals *eating* their young," referring to the expectation of harsh treatment dished out to shaky students (Dunn 2003; Longo 2007; McKenna et al. 2003; Thobaden 2007).

According to the theory of horizontal violence, harassment among members of the group redirects pressure that students feel from the institution or their superiors to one another, because they feel disempowered to change the attitude of their elders. They may internalize their frustration with the belief that the failure of another student "holds them back" or that the seclusion of a colleague points out their own failing to isolate themselves for study. Students who feel that they are vulnerable to "going crazy" with stress find that the cause is external: peers have created the condition. The problem therefore is not with them, but with others. If that sounds as if it can create paranoia, keep in mind that students describe the story as a caution about what they imagine to be a distinctive social system and something of a plea to be more supportive of one another.

From the Berkeley Folklore Archives comes this account integrating several details of the student's antisocial character, status as a novice, and failure to make the grade: "This is a new med student. He went out on a date and got back late and his roommate and a bunch of the fellas decided to play a trick on him. This guy was really struggling and he was a new student, and feeling the pressure of all of it. And they didn't like him very well—he was kind of a study type—he worked late in the lab and he was really trying and he was kind of a teacher's pet kind of creature, not a very strong character. And they put the hand of one of the cadavers that they had worked on that day in his bed. And they're all waiting for some huge noise or something and nothing really happens. So they go in, and they find him and he's sitting in the closet chewing on the hand and his hair's all white." In the story, the stress of the situation mentioned as "feeling the pressure of all of it" is coupled with the accusation that he is actually favored by the superordinate power ("teacher's pet"). In a projective inversion, the novitiate suffers from his peers what they do not get from their superior. As an opening emotional defense, the feeling of "we hate her" becomes "she hates us" in the narrative. In the end, the victim bites the wrong hand, not the one that feeds him but those of his fellows who are in the same position.

In many versions, the pranksters tie the arm to the light switch in the lab, shut off the lights, and wait in the next room. As a former premedical student from Butler University elaborated to me, "The unsuspecting student enters the lab as expected, reaches for the light switch, and inadvertently grabs the arm. The pranksters next door hear a blood-curdling scream and rush into the lab, laughing hysterically, but their fellow student is nowhere to be found. Neither is the arm. They search all over to no avail. Finally, someone hears a faint gnawing sound. They open a cabinet door to find their 'victim,' his hair turned white, crouched down in the cabinet, stark raving mad, chewing on the cadaver's arm" (cf. Baker 1982, 216; Brunvand 1986, 99).

The backfiring prank also comes up in a variation in which students work a cadaver's arm into a sleeve and attach money to its palm as if offering change. Then they drive to a tollbooth (or subway token stand) and extend the arm to the toll taker. When they zoom off, the toll taker is left with the arm and, according to legend, dies of a heart attack (see Brunvand 1989, 299–301; 1990, 301; 2001, 447; Dundes 1971, 31–33; 1990, 103–4; German 2010, 76–77; Longley 2008, 7; Meakes 2004, 119). In a version that adds elements from stern professor anecdotes, police officers come in after the event and trace the arm to a school lab: "The anatomy professor and the police matched the hand to the body, then confronted the students with the incriminating evidence. The pranksters supposedly were not expelled—but the professor flunked them in anatomy, since they had put a right hand into a left coat sleeve" (Brunvand 1989, 300). In some narratives, though, the medical students are expelled, suggesting some moral retribution (German 2010, 76–77). The insertion of punishment in the stories raises consideration of folklorist Alan Dundes's interpretation that the detail of giving money suggests an ethical dilemma that is projected onto the narrative: doctors make money on the sick, dying, or dead and cannot afford to get too attached, but are also expected to be compassionate to their patients (1971, 32). "By offering the cadaverous arm with the coin attached to the toll-booth attendant," he writes, the medical students, in anticipation of their future, "are reversing the normal roles" (Dundes 1971, 32). There is literally a detachment from the person from whom the cadaver comes, and, as Dundes points out, more often than punishment, the students objectify the cadaver and leave the arm behind, as if their actions in the lab or operating table need to be left behind (1971, 32; see also German 2010, 76–77; Pekkanen 1988, 11). The story often elicits comments on the limits of medical professionals' detachment as well as scruples. Surgeon John German's critical take on the legend is that the medical students' morals were better suited for lawyering (2010, 77).

Students of medicine and anatomy, so used to dealing with the dead, typically appear, well, cold as a cadaver in their legends. Some stories imply a student response to superiors' insensitivity by mistreating a working-class member of the institutional community the group considers below them. Consider the narrative of the students who plugged electrodes into a cadaver and left the switch near the entrance of the room. That evening while the janitor was cleaning, he touched the switch, and the cadaver sat up. The janitor, so the teller says, "nearly had a heart attack" (Baker 1982, 50). Further, when the victim is not a fellow student or professor, it is often a blue-collar worker such as a janitor, vendor, or toll taker. The stories reinforce the superiority of the medical professional over the common worker. Although the nonacademic is often depicted as physically tough, the medical professional's mental and emotional toughness gets, if I can say it, the upper hand. An occasional narrative will feature student revenge against a superior, such as the one about medical students who replaced the cadaver with one of their very alive colleagues under a sheet. When the professor stepped to the body, the student sat up, frightening the professor to death (cf. Hafferty 1988, 347).

In other stories, the dividing line between life and death becomes blurred. An example with this theme is the narrative about a recently deceased cadaver sitting up and occasionally even uttering a word (cf. wake and funeral stories such as Baker 1982, 50; Bennett and Smith 2007, 266–69; Christiansen 1946, 32; Dorson 1967, 328–31; Harlow 2003, 85–97; Montell 1975, 203–4; Narváez 1994, 270; Súilleabháin 1967, 67). Some medical students at Penn State's Hershey Medical Center with whom I have discussed this story interpret the narrative's message as one reminding them to be sure about the condition of the patient and not be too quick to judge him or her dead. A few mentioned the repressed fear the story represents of a person who could have been saved, and the words have the effect of the patient "talking back" as a way of "getting back" at, or haunting, the doctors.

Medical students also tell of bringing a cadaver to a homecoming football game where it shocks a vendor or someone in the stands (Hafferty 1988, 347). In a related story, the future doctors arrange two cadavers in a sexual embrace and cover the two with a sheet. When an unsuspecting victim removes the sheet to begin work, a scream reverberates through the hall; sometimes it is a male member that is inserted into a female cadaver. Carrying this sexual theme further, a story circulates about a condom on a cadaver's penis that provokes shock in a wet-behind-the-ears student (Hafferty 1988, 347). Another variant questions student insensitivity when confronted by a familiar face. Usually identified as a new medical student, the protagonist is about to work on a cadaver when he or she realizes, in horror, that the body is none other than a relative, usually an aunt (see Bennett and Smith 2007, 247–48; Brunvand 1984, 99–102; Quigley 1996, 199).

As with most legends, the built-in moral ambiguity of the narrative allows for several interpretations, depending on how the story is told and to whom, in addition to the often unstated symbolic connection to horizontal violence. The cadaver stories may remind medical students that death and dismemberment, while second nature to the world of medicine, are horrifying to most people. Indeed, the medical student who works with dead bodies to take care of the living, according to the gruesome ending of the legend, appears to be a short step from cannibalism. The stories may suggest a cold attitude necessary for success in medical school or anatomy class, while maybe mildly reminding students to be sensitive to the other world marked by an emotional response to anatomical sights. To medical students, the cadaver is depersonalized; it is neither capable of having a personal identity nor of having sex. When located in a lab, the stories draw attention to the inappropriate behavior of screams or emotional expression. Regardless, the lasting power of this story—it apparently has legs—in college lore merits explanation.

Commenting on the stories in a scholarly journal for health professionals, Frederic Hafferty emphasizes that "cadaver stories stress that within the culture of medicine, the cadaver should exist as a learning tool and an object for manipulation rather than as a formerly living human being. In these stories, students who fail to behave accordingly, and thus threaten the emotional equilibrium of lab, are held up to ridicule and to the possibility of further torment at the hands of their peers" (1988, 350). Hafferty points out that the stories additionally deal with the significance of gender to health professionals. Most stories show males as the "emotionally transcendent and detached perpetrators," and cast women as the "emotionally vulnerable victim," a further reflection, he claims, of traditional attitudes in the culture of medicine (Hafferty 1988, 352).

Fatal Initiations

As fraternity and sorority lore, "The Cadaver Arm" is often embedded in a cycle of stories about fatal initiations (circumscribed in Baughman 1945b; 1966, motif Z510; see also Bennett and Smith 2007, 251–53; Brunvand 2001, 145; Tucker 2005, 3–4). The Indiana State University Folklore Archives contains narratives about a cadaver arm attached to a light switch; the victim is a fraternity pledge who ends up scared to death after grabbing hold of the limb (Baker 1982, 35). In popular culture, movies such as *Terror Train* (1980) and *Cinco* (2010) appropriate the story for horrific visual effect, and probably inspire retellings of the legend (Koven 2008, 130).

In most fatal initiation narratives, the supposed "harmless" lie of the fraternity actives in setting up the pledges for a scary experience turns out to be real and fatal. The most common scene of the crime in stories given to me is in a haunted house. Here is an extended narrative I received from a Penn State student:

> There were three fraternity pledges who had to spend the night in a haunted house as part of pledging. So a few of the fraternity brothers took them over. They unlocked the door, and the three guys went in. They told them all they had to do was spend the night, and the brothers would come and get them in the morning. So the brothers locked the front door so the pledges couldn't get out, and started to leave. They were walking down the front steps, which were really rotting, and the steps collapsed underneath them. The guy that was holding the key dropped it through a crack in the stairs, and they couldn't get it back. Well, while they were trying to get it, they heard these screams coming from the house—they really sounded like desperate screams, not just scared screams. So they ran back to the car to get a crowbar, and they jimmied open the door. All they heard was a weird, steady creaking noise and a constant banging coming from somewhere. They ran through the ground level, and there wasn't anybody there. Then they ran down to the basement, and there wasn't anybody there. They ran upstairs and started checking the bedrooms. When they got to the second one, the creaking noise got real loud, so they went in. One of the pledges was hanging by his neck in the center of the room, above a pool of blood; his arms and legs were cut off. The creaking came from the rope swinging back and forth from the ceiling. They still heard the banging noise, so they ran into another bedroom that had a big closet. They opened up the closet, and it was empty, but there was no ceiling to it; it was just open to the sky. So they pushed one guy up, and he got up on the roof. He found the second pledge up there on his back—his hair was stark white, and he didn't have any eyes left; they were gouged out. He had a hammer in one of his hands, and he was just banging it on the roof. They never found the other guy. (cf. Grider 1973, 13–14)

In its formulaic structure, this fatal initiation story is reminiscent of playful horror tales often told at summer camps (Bronner 1989, 154–59; Clements 1980, 280–81). In these tales, a ghost comes closer and closer to the final victim until the teller startles the listener by grabbing him or her or feigning death.

Adapted to the college scene, what might be called the "initiation curse" story is sometimes told as a personal experience by actives to pledges:

> Pledges and I had to go into this haunted house. Each one had to enter the house by himself, armed with only [a] flashlight. The first guy went in and we watched him shine his flashlight through the entire first floor. We watched his light on the second floor, but when it should have appeared at the middle window, we didn't see anything. We waited some time, thinking it was a joke, but he still didn't shine his light. Finally we decided that, pledge project or not, we were going to go in together. We followed his footsteps through the downstairs to the second floor. It was very dusty in the place, so we had little difficulty. His steps led to a door. Frightened, we opened the door, only to find an empty closet. No one's ever seen this guy since. That was ten years ago. Since then, something has happened to everyone else. Two years after this guy disappeared another was killed in an automobile accident. Five years after that, the third was killed in a boating crash. Now I'm the only one left and AAAARRRRRRGGGGHHH! (teller screams and feigns death). (see Baughman 1945b, 50, 1966, motif N384.0.1a Fraternity initiation requirement is that pledge must enter old house at night, usually with matches which he is to light in the window of each floor to show his presence; Carey 1971, 78; Tucker 2005, 85–86)

In most of the fatal initiation stories, the pledge's imagination produces the final frightening blow. In a story known internationally to folklorists as Uther Type 1676B (labeled "Frightened to Death"; see also Aarne 1964, Type 1676B "Clothing Caught in Graveyard"), a pledge goes to a graveyard to stick a knife into a grave. As a Colgate student tells it, "Some of his fraternity brothers drove a pledge to the cemetery, watched him lean down to plunge the knife in, and then drove off. It was a cold, foggy night with snow on the ground. The initiate was wearing a muffler and heavy overcoat. He leaned down, stuck the knife in, and started to walk away. He took one step, felt someone grab at his coattail, and fell dead of fright. Alarmed at his absence, his fraternity brothers checked for him at the graveyard the next morning. They found him dead, with the knife stuck through the tail of his coat (see Baughman 1966, motif N384.2 Death in the graveyard, person's clothing is caught, the person thinks something awful is holding him, he dies of fright; Baker 1982, 76–77; Bronner 1989, 146, 307).

A series of fatal initiation stories concern the fate of blindfolded pledges. One of these with a long lineage is sometimes called the "pseudo-decapitation" (Baughman 1966, motif N384.4c), which could be related to fear of castration, especially since the victim is usually male and involved in a coming-of-age ritual. According to the legend, actives decide to give a pledge, often characterized as particularly disobedient, a scare. They tie him to a chair and show him an ax. They blindfold him and strike him on the neck with a wet towel. When the actives lift him up they discover that he died from the shock (see Baughman 1945b, 52–53; Bennett and Smith 2007, 253; Bronner 1989, 169; Hartikka 1946, 80). The legend has been traced back to British university tradition in the eighteenth century (Hobbs 1973, 183–91).

In a variation, "the brothers told this guy they were going to slash his arm and let him bleed. What they did was to run something cold and sharp across his arm but they did not cut him. They had water dripping off of his arm into a bucket so that he would think they had really cut him. Everyone then left the room for a few hours, and when they came back they found him dead" (see Baughman 1966, motif N384.4a Initiate dies from loss of blood; 1945b, 51–52; Bennett and Smith 2007, 253). A similar narrative has the pledge threatened with branding. After the pledge is blindfolded and tied to a chair, a hot poker is pressed against raw meat at the same time that a piece of ice is held on the pledge's skin. The pledge smells the burning meat, and thinking it is his own, crumples up dead (Baughman 1966, motif N384.4b Initiate dies from supposed loss of blood; Bennett and Smith 2007, 252–53; Dorson 1949, 674; Hartikka 1946, 79).

The fear of being trapped, especially by the legendary motif of being tied up in a scary situation, is the subject of several fatal initiation stories, typically told by nonfraternity members to draw out abuses of hazing in the Greek system. An example is the frequently collected legend about the pledge who is tied to a railroad track. The actives drive away, certain that the train would not be coming or would come on the opposite set of tracks, and they return to find the pledge dead from fright after hearing the train. At Kenyon College, the narrative of the fatal fraternity initiation is attached to a specific trestle bridge on the Kokosing River and has an additional ghost story about the victim (affectionately called "Stewie") looking out at the train tracks from a fourth-floor window of the Delta Kappa Epsilon house (MacLeod 2007).

Some versions of the "tied-up pledge" story have a grisly ending. Here is how a Penn State student related an example: "A young pledge was given his initiation one night. He was tied to a chair in an old abandoned house and left there. To become a member, he must free himself within one hour. This was impossible because of the ropes and the knots used by the frat brothers. Determined, however, the young pledge decided he would cut them off on the broken glass in the window. As he started to try to cut the ropes off, he slipped and fell on the window and beheaded himself" (Baughman 1966, motif Z511; 1945b, 52–53).

Some of the horror stories use the familiar creepy feature of the cadaver arm to get revenge on the actives. From Indiana University, for example, comes the story of a pledge tied up in a chair at an isolated cabin in the woods. The actives produce blood-curdling noises from the outside of the cabin throughout the night. When they check on him in the morning, they discover that he is no longer in his chair. His ropes are broken, and his chair is overturned. The actives then hear a creeping noise coming from the attic, so an active goes up to check it out, but he does not come back for a good while. Another active then hears something dripping from the attic and goes up to investigate. He finds the active lying dead, his arm removed, and blood dripping down to the floor. The now-crazed pledge is beating the active with the arm (cf. Baughman 1945b, 51–52; Bronner 1989, 148).

Told in college, the horror variety of initiation stories is frequently related to explain why a campus does not have fraternities or sororities. Reporting "scary stories" from Purdue, for example, JoAnn Parochetti recounted the belief legend that fraternities were forbidden after a boy was killed when a tombstone to which he had been tied toppled over, crushing him (1965, 52–53; cf. Baughman 1945b, 50–51; 1966, motif Z512; see also Baker 1982, 221–22). As place legends, however, such stories, with variations usually stressing the ghastly details of death in an isolated, treacherous, or dreary location, are often heard well before students enter college. They often relate to specific mysterious places in a teen's life, which include devil's elbows, haunted hollows, cemetery ridges, spook light hills, not to mention lovers' lanes. Heard at slumber parties, camps, and summer outings, the stories may inspire heartbeat-raising trips, complete with retellings, to the scene of the crime (see Bird 1994; Dégh 1969a, 54–89; Ellis 1983, 61–73; Hall 1973; Meley 1990; Thigpen 1971, 204–5; Tucker 2007, 182–85).

Legend Quests

A favorite rite linking legend to practice is to take green first-year students or pledges in tow along with a generous supply of beer on a gloomy night to a purported spooky spot. I vividly remember my legend-quest experience at Indiana University. It was a foggy summer night with a full moon just barely visible above. Inspired by a round of talk about haunts in the area, a group of students jammed into a car to search for an out-of-the-way graveyard where, according to legend, the outline of chains appeared on a tombstone after a man killed his wife with the links, although some riders in the car insisted it was an overseer who killed a slave (see Baker 1982, 72–74; Clements 1969a; de Caro and Lunt 1968). We discovered that indeed it was out of the way, but it was hardly a lonely site, since it attracted several other carloads of teens who arrived at the cemetery from different points about the time we did. The essential difference between a trip off campus to spot some eerie sight such as spooky lights or colors in the sky and a legendary quest is the experience of enactment and discovery in the latter. In the quest, houses with creaky floors might be entered, and students may walk a graveyard wall waiting for a signal (Meley 1991; Tucker 2006; 2007, 182–210).

Students from Ventura, Oxnard, and Moorpark Colleges in Ventura County, Southern California, believe that their location is among the most haunted and explorable in the United States. The frequent fogs, history of shipwrecks along the coast, and rugged and unspoiled wilderness, coupled with signs of old Spanish and Native settlement (Mount Pinos is sacred to Chumash Indians), invite narrative about spirits. A favorite destination is the Olivas Adobe, the hacienda of Rancho San Miguel, built in 1847. The historical park around the site plays up the importance of the building representing the rancho period of California history, but students late at night check out the edifice for a ghost lady in a black dress walking on the balcony and a ghost girl in a white night-dress in the second-floor window (Swanger 2009). Another dare for students is to go to Memorial Park, established in 1965 in Ventura, the site of a cemetery abandoned in 1944. They verify rumors of spirits roaming the grounds. According to legend, satanic rituals conducted there forced the revenants to wander the lot forever; further extending the satanic association with youth, students may hunt for signs of diabolical rites and crypts holding vampires (Swanger 2009; cf. Ellis 2000, 202–39; 2004, 112–41). They also may be on the lookout for the sight of a swinging body in a tree from a suicidal teenager and confirmation of cold spots and an eerie presence undoubtedly caused by the buried souls beneath the pastoral landscape.

Back east, folklorist George Carey tells about a favorite student rendezvous outside Baltimore called by the haunting name of Druid Ridge (1971, 83–96). There students seek out the resting place of "Black Aggie," a spot once inhabited by a grieving statue with the word "Agnus" embossed on the bottom. A variety of stories, many with gruesome details of a horrifying murder, circulate to explain the notoriety of the grave smack in the center of the cemetery. Here is one:

> A long time ago the caretaker of that cemetery lived right there on the grounds with his wife. Her name was Agnus. Before she died she asked her husband to bury her in the middle of the cemetery. Well, he buried her where she wanted to be and he had this big statue put over her grave. That statue is cursed because Agnus had a sister who moved in with her husband after she was dead. She was his housekeeper at first, but later on she became his mistress. Since she was buried in the center of the cemetery where she

could see everything, she noticed this affair was taking place and wished to take revenge on her sister. So one night at midnight, Aggie's body rose out of the grave and killed her sister. I've heard that the two of them are buried head to head under that statue of Black Aggie. (Carey 1971, 83)

The story has a striking resemblance to early-nineteenth-century stories of Wiswal's Den at Harvard, which I discussed earlier (see Everett 1852; Hall 1968, 156–57). The theme of infidelity, along with the message of crimes discovered and exposed, especially when teens are increasingly asked to make independent moral decisions and face issues of commitment, apparently holds attention through the years.

Carey also reports that when the statue was up, fraternities and sororities called for pledges to pass the night in the statue's lap or to look into the statue's eyes at midnight. "The rigors of the exercise increase," Carey points out,

as the helpless victim hears accounts of what has happened to others who faced the same catharsis. He is told, perhaps, of the two Towson boys who went and sat in the statue's lap. When nothing untoward occurred, they jeered loudly, jumped back in their car and left the cemetery. As they pulled back out onto Reisterstown Road, a truck plowed into their car and they were both killed instantly. Other accounts held that if you sit in Aggie's lap at midnight, her arms will unfold and squeeze you to death. Steve Bledsoe of Baltimore tried it on a fraternity hell night. Just at midnight his friends, who were waiting nearby, heard his screams: "It's moving, it's moving," but fortunately he slipped Aggie's grasp before she had a good grip. Another pledge was not quite so lucky. His fraternity brothers left him in Aggie's lap all night and when they returned in the morning, his corpse lay at her feet, the hair snow white. (Carey 1971, 85)

Some sites are specifically identified as abandoned campuses, raising the specter of untimely ends for college students. Trips to such a site, according to Elizabeth Tucker, take the quality of a "quest" in which they experience in a dramatic frame the sensation of being "scared to death" (2006, 35). The visits may demonstrate maturity in the mind of youths by defying societal expectations of moral norms by trespassing on sacred ground, but the line between frivolity and fear is thin indeed, as laughter often turns to screams when weird noises and unearthly movements cause a startle. Or as they absorb rationalist thinking in their higher learning, students want to experience firsthand phenomena that appear inexplicable. Whether mindful of the success of *The Blair Witch Project* (1999) and a successive host of ghost-hunter shows on television, or out to verify what they see, students may take camera in hand to record their experience. A good example of these various qualities of the legend quest is at Tudor-designed, sprawling Briarcliff Lodge (built in 1902) perched on a hilltop in Briarcliff Manor, New York, formerly the site of King's College (1955–94). Students may hear of stories such as "Many, many people have seen and heard parties going on in the ballroom. Sometimes the faint smell of alcohol would traipse up the stairs of the Men's dormitories. As you know, King's was a dry college. The piano would play at night, and lights would go on in the attics and other rooms where no one was living, especially in the summer" (Yasinsac 2000). They heighten the action by reporting that it "became a very popular place for suicides, murders, and vanishings. Death loomed over the lodge, and it was soon closed and abandoned for having this bad reputation" (Tucker 2006, 37). Students from a number of colleges in upstate New York converge on the location with video cameras and turn their on-site experiences into retold narratives, often involving strange quirks in the technology:

> My friends and I decided it would be a fun time to go to the abandoned college and make a video of the trip. Three friends and I drove to the college at night and entered the old, crumpled main building. The building was in fact decaying, as it consisted of rubble, rocks, and debris. Upon entering the building we heard strange noises that faded, grew louder, and then faded again. . . . We didn't realize this at the time, but by inspecting the video, we realized that in one of the windows where noises were coming from you can distinctly see a face lean into the window and then lean out again. It is a clear image of a human face. However, we didn't see this image at the time, so we continued to explore the building. Upon entering the stairwell to go up, the footsteps came back, as well as faint sounds of people whispering and murmurs. The video camera had full battery and was in perfectly good condition, yet it mysteriously turned off during this time. The camera gave no indication that it stopped recording, and my friends and I thought that it was in fact still recording. Only when reviewing the tape did we realize that it had shut off by itself for no reason. We wandered the house for fifteen more minutes that the camera did not record. Everything on the camera said it was still recording, yet the film was blank. The noises kept coming closer and then going far away again, but we were never able to discover what was making the noise. We left the college confused and scared. (Tucker 2006, 37)

The students were on a quest for the truth, so to speak, and downplay the fright factor by emphasizing the experience that would, it appears, be a walk in the park. The narrative indicates that at least in the beginning, a healthy dose of skepticism and frivolity accompanies their journey, but as they continue deeper inside the bowels of the complex, they get more than they bargain for. That the building was once a college adds to their excitement because they relate their present status and age to the unseen inhabitants. If they do not fully own up to the presence of spirits around them, they project ghosts into the machine. They leave the site scared, and questions remain not only about the supernatural but also of their passage in life. Tucker, the collector, observes: "They learn about supernatural presences that seem real and past injustices that seem almost unbearably painful, as well as deaths that are inextricably related to everyday life. As they talk about what happened to them, students remember the intensity of their emotions during confrontations with the supernatural" (2006, 37).

The legend quest, with its simultaneous thrill and loathing of supernatural encounter and its frequent recounting of morality plays in story, brings students face to face with the challenges of reaching out beyond their safe campus havens to terrifying situations out in the real world. On these playfully framed trips, students talk to one another about frightening scenarios under the cloak of legend, and they experience for themselves the reality of the spooky sites, even as they confront their own cloudy fears and doubts.

Murderous Rumors

Another kind of rearguard penetration that strikes fear in students is getting axed. Narratives often describe the fatal blow to the rear of the head and the culprit as a male outsider viciously bringing a coed to her knees and cutting a young man down to size. Tellers add a creepiness factor by emphasizing that the attacker snuck up on the victims from behind. Ax and knife murderers probably figure most prominently in a story about a psychic who predicts a mass murder around Halloween at a college campus. According to the story, the psychic gives clues that lead students to believe their campus is the one that will be victimized. This murderer is characteristically not a school shooter brandishing a rifle but a knife- or ax-wielding maniac who frequently goes after women in a dorm, supposedly often a residence in vaginal shape of a U (or a nonphallic X), or at a university with a supposedly feminine first letter such as the circular O or vaginal K and a flat or watery landscape ("Campus Halloween Murders" 2007; Emery 2010b; O'Brien 2007; Roeper 1999, 91–94).

A panic erupted on campuses, for example, at Kent State University in 2007 and earlier at Kansas State University in 1998, when rumors circulated that a psychic (often identified as Sylvia Browne) appearing on Oprah Winfrey's or Montel Williams's television show predicted a mass murder would take place on Halloween. Despite denials from the shows' staff and psychics that no such prediction was made, the Kent State administration posted an email assuring students that "during the Halloween weekend there are increases in police staffing" (O'Brien 2007).

Such rumors have been reported since 1968, when the psychic in question was Jeane Dixon supposedly on a radio program and the murder weapon would surely be a hatchet or fire ax (Brunvand 1993, 116–19; Dégh 1969b, 70–74; 2001, 454; Grider 1973, 14). Students needed to beware because the male attacker likely cut down his unsuspecting victims from behind. Inviting comparison with hook man and roommate's death legends, the would-be killer was undoubtedly a deranged maniac who probably came from the mental institution near the school but did not draw attention to himself in appearance until it was too late for the victims. The dark and decay of the Halloween season in the northern clime influenced the spreading belief in a foreboding menace once students hunker down in studious isolation. Adding to the mystery was the identity of the target; its name began with a D or a B, was located near a body of water, or had oddly shaped dormitories (Brunvand 1993, 119). Even without the motif of the psychic prediction bringing a supernatural element into the narrative, the story involves fear of intrusion into the campus as a secure home. Elizabeth Tucker, for instance, related this narrative from her memory of residence at Mount Holyoke College: "The hatchet man is coming. He already killed a bunch of students at some other colleges, and he's heading in this direction. Nobody knows where he's going, but he might be coming to a New England women's college with the initials 'M' and 'H.' You'd better be careful riding back [on bicycle] to your dorm alone" (2005, 90; cf. "The Hatchet Man" legend in Grider 1980).

Folklorist Linda Dégh connected the rumor to media attention to the brutal rape and murder of eight student nurses in their Chicago rooming house in 1966. The features of the psychic's prediction and a hatchet murder are consistent with the latest scare. "Didn't Jeane Dixon predict Kennedy's death before she told of this massacre?" students asked. The Indiana University student newspaper ran a story on the rumor less than three weeks before Halloween 1968: "A rumor reportedly rampant on campus that seer Jeane Dixon has predicted the axe murder of 10 coeds on a midwestern university campus has been quashed by her New York publishing syndicate office. Robert Gillespie, who handles Miss Dixon's material for the *Newsday* syndicate, said she has never made a prediction of that nature [see also Linker 1980 for denials by Dixon]. Gillespie said the rumor started about six months ago in Oklahoma and had spread throughout the Midwest. In various forms, the rumor depicts an axe slaying on either a Midwestern or Big Ten campus" (Dégh 1969b, 71; see also Baker 1982, 219; Swayne 2011, 48–50). The rumor made it out to New York State, where reports said the prediction held that the attack would be on, variously, a women's dorm starting with an A (or B, C, or D), at a state school, at a private school, or near a mental institution, and between the "witching" hours of 9 p.m. and midnight (Dégh 1969b, 70–74).

As the 1968 rumor seemed to be about fear of real-life horrors repeating themselves in the vulnerable world of institutional dorm life, so other rumor cycles made indirect references to the news. In 1983, a rumor circulated around campuses from California to Massachusetts about a hatchet murder predicted by a psychic, but with the strange twist that the attacker was going to dress up as a feminine nursery rhyme character such as Little Bo-Peep (Brunvand 1993, 116–19; Ernstberger 1983; Tucker 2005, 40). At the University of Massachusetts, the rumor additionally called for the attack occurring at a party at a sorority house. The rumor was taken seriously enough there to cause several parties to be canceled (Berberoglu and Hilliard 1986). It is true that in June 1983, news magazines gave splashy coverage to the hatchet murder by escaped prisoner and former mental hospital patient Kevin Cooper. He attacked an innocent family at a California horse ranch, leaving only an eight-year-old, his neck slashed, barely clinging to life. According to *Newsweek*, "Local police called it the most gruesome murder scene in memory" (Alter 1983). Previously, he had attacked and raped a seventeen-year-old in Pennsylvania, although the crime did not occur at a college. A drag queen fear manifest in the "Bo-Peep" rumor may be evident in tabloid headlines in 1983 of a sensational transvestite murder case in New York City, although the cross-dresser was the victim rather than assailant (Wadler 1983; cf. the movie *Psycho* [1960]). Beyond these narrative adaptations ripped from headlines may also be anxiety beyond the women's movement implied in previous fearsome rumors to gay rights awareness of transsexual and transvestite identities.

Another major outbreak of the rumor was in 1986 when, according to an account I collected from Shippensburg, "the psychic predicted that there would be a mass-murder in a Pennsylvania state school. It would take place on Halloween night in a single-sex dorm which is near railroad tracks." If the listener appeared skeptical, the teller might point out that the famous psychic predicted other disasters. Similar rumors were heard at the same time at East Stroudsburg University, Lehigh University, Dickinson College, Slippery Rock University, Bloomsburg University, Penn State University, Susquehanna University, Mansfield University, and Kutztown University, all in central Pennsylvania (Donovan 1989). According to some students, the residence to be attacked was a freshman dormitory, or the largest residence hall on a campus, or a women's dorm where the attacker was predicted to rape as well as kill. The psychic was said to have appeared on television shows hosted by Phil Donahue, David Letterman, Johnny Carson, Oprah Winfrey, or Joan Rivers. Narrators characterized the killer variously as a crazed student, professor, maintenance worker, escaped convict, or maniac from an "insane asylum." The psychic appeared on none of these television shows, and the weekend passed with no incidents. Nonetheless, some students took no chances and rushed home for the weekend. Others laughed it off and went to Halloween costume parties dressed as murderous hatchet men. After the weekend was over, one enterprising student sold shirts showing a bloodied undergrad with a hatchet through his skull and the message "I Survived the Kutztown Massacre."

As students were arriving at school in 1986, they probably heard the news report of a massacre by a gunman in Oklahoma. A letter carrier unexpectedly opened fire on fourteen fellow workers in the Edmond post office (Pedersen 1986). There was no college connection in the news of the massacre, although it also brought up accounts in the media of a shooting rampage twenty years earlier by a student at the University of Texas at Austin firing at campus pedestrians from the university's tower. One still detects in the resurfacing rumors how students sublimate horrifying incidents into the celebration of Halloween: they make the murderer one of the campus's own. The coincidence of the rumors with the darkening fall season, the mistrust of the security of institutional life—especially for students away from the haven of home—and the setting of many campuses in isolated arcadias undoubtedly feed the rumors.

One also has to wonder about the influence of popular "slasher" movies, typically appealing to adolescents, and the incorporation of traditional legendary motifs into their plots (Danielson 1979; Schechter 1988, 25–48). *Halloween* (1978), *Friday the 13th* (1980), *Candyman* (1992), *Scream* (1996), *Urban Legend* (1998), *Hatchet* (2006), and *Blood Night* (2009) and their many sequels are perennial teen favorites that inspire legend telling (Koven 2008, 113–34). They regularly feature a knife-wielding attacker escaped from a "loony bin," who, with Halloween mask in place, slashes a young woman. Many slasher films, such as *Black Christmas* (1974), *Final Exam* (1981), and *Sorority Row* (2009), use college settings as backdrops (see Egan 1985, 122–24; Danielson 1979, 212). The Draculas and Frankensteins of popular horror films past have been traded in for ordinary-sounding Freddies, Michaels, Marys, and Jasons. Today's monsters in legend and life roam around reality (Russo 1990, 10).

Probably not coincidentally, the heyday of the rumors paralleled the era of eased restrictions on dormitory visitation. With colleges giving up their in loco parentis role, the campus seemed a more open but less protected place. It was potentially open to dangerous strangers. When the massacre rumors were related by students, they become folk tests of fear, invitations for commentary (both serious and humorous), and reminders to keep alert generally, particularly in an individualistic culture where students feel out on their own (see Rosnow and Fine 1976, 54–62). In the later iteration of the rumor-panic at Halloween in 2007, the background included earlier campus shooting tragedies such as the Virginia Tech massacre that occurred on April 16 of that year and the gunning down of five students by a pair of nonstudents following a dance at Duquesne University in September 2006.

One can detect some change in the pattern of the rumors over the years. Whereas the victims in the early rumors were typically women, suggesting the questioning of the adaptability and risk of women in college during a period when numbers of women were increasing, later rumors added victims of either sex in "large dorms" and "state universities." This additional detail raised the insecurity students felt as smaller and smaller units of growing mega-universities. And the ubiquitous psychic in all this? The characterizations of female psychics project the concerns of women's vulnerability onto the prediction in the context of growing feminine power and prestige. They add a touch of the supernatural appropriate to the season, to be sure, but also speak to the future, at a time when students are looking ahead with uncertainty and seeking predictability in their fates.

Murder in the Stacks

Rumors of a murder about to happen or having just happened are often attached to campus libraries. At many campuses, the library is the largest structure and comes to represent the mad mix of students coming and going. Women are often victims, and the stories include the frightening detail of screams not heard because the building was so large or students so indifferent or preoccupied by their studies. From the Indiana University Folklore Archives, for example, comes the account that "the library is so big that this guy came up to her and grabbed her and threw her on the floor. She screamed once but then he pulled a knife and she stopped screaming. No one who was studying around her came to see what the scream was about and so the guy just raped her."

In 1969, the fatal stabbing of a female graduate student actually occurred in Penn State's library, and it provided the basis for cautionary legends going by the name of "the murder in the stacks" ever since, especially because the culprit was never found. Further adding fuel to narrative speculation, police did not uncover a likely motive. "Stay away from level two," first-year students are warned each fall; "maybe the murderer will come back some day." Often the date of the murder is moved up to "just last year or so," and it is sometimes predicted that it might have been the first in a string of killings (Anthony 1989, 1, 4; Swayne 2011, 18–23).

The known facts of the case are that Betsy Aardsma, twenty-two years old from Holland, Michigan, was last seen on level two in what is known as the core area between 4:30 and 4:45 p.m. on November 28, 1969, and was found at 6 p.m. on the floor surrounded by books with little visible blood from a knife (a one-edged blade 3½ to 4 inches long, according to the autopsy report) wound to the chest (Dekok 2008a). In narrative versions, the dead woman (sometimes a senior, a graduate student, a narcotics agent, or policewoman) is usually not discovered for days. The victim reportedly was "minding her own business," "doing research," or "doing undercover work." In a variation, a student said: "This girl got locked in the library and she went to sleep or something and she woke up and heard noises and there was this guy in there. She saw him and she ran away into the stacks. And he finally caught her and he had a huge knife and he dismembered her body" (T. 1979, 5). A memorable detail that often enters into contemporary accounts of the death is a red dress, which, as it turns out, she really was wearing at the time of her death. The red dress raises images for many tellers of a possible sexual connection since, in addition to the suggestive color, it appears odd in students' eyes that she would be formally dressed in a location calling for casual wear. Also figuring in the narrative is either the idea that she screamed and no one heard her in the library labyrinth or else she did not yell, indicating the killer was someone she knew (her boyfriend, usually the first suspect, was cleared by state police).

Decades after the case students relate theories about her cold case that suggest various campus anxieties. The idea that it was a random act apparently is unsatisfying. Looking for a reason, students speculate still that she witnessed a drug deal in progress and was killed to keep her quiet. With this account is the narrative that she was an undercover agent or her parents were involved in law enforcement (they were not). Another encounter she should not have seen, some stories offer, is a homosexual tryst, and narratives may add that a bunch of pornographic paperbacks were found stuffed among the shelves where Aardsma was stabbed (Dekok 2008b, A7). Another popular explanation is that she was slain by a serial murderer, and sometimes the notorious Ted Bundy is mentioned, although his murderous rampage was in Washington State, and he strangled rather than stabbed his victims. It is true that because of Aardsma's Michigan roots, police investigated possible connections of the murder with the so-called coed killer John Norman Collins at Eastern Michigan University. Perhaps because of concern for scandalous relationships arising from professor-student romances, some students speculate that she was killed by a professor who knew her. Police investigated a teaching assistant in English at Michigan, but ruled him out as the culprit (Dekok 2008b, A7).

University Park residents sometimes explain the failure to land an arrest in the case with an administrative cover-up—probably, they surmise, because drugs were involved, and maybe the university was even hiring students to spy on others. (This last motif surfaces elsewhere: at Brigham Young University, a

Mormon-affiliated school with prohibitions on alcohol and tobacco, rumors fly about paid informers in the dorms on the lookout for the contraband; see Bart 1983).

Generations of students later, cool drafts blowing through the stacks, crying sounds, and sensations of an eerie presence on the upper levels of the library are attributed to the victim's spirit roaming about the narrow aisles. Some sightings include reports of a woman in out-of-date clothes with her feet elevated off the floor (Swayne 2011, 21).

Despite the deviation from the known facts, the legends reveal the truth of student attitudes toward the dangers of large public places, especially for women, and, by extension, the danger of the university's growth in general. Echoing motifs of the dormitory hatchet-man stories, in "murder in the stacks" legends, students have, as a result of the university's growth, become indifferent to one another's welfare and even distrustful of their comrades.

Phantoms in the Theater

Besides resounding through dorms and libraries, word of strange incidents often comes from the campus theater. The drama, mystery, and pathos enacted there lend to speculation about phantoms lurking in the darkness. Besides, theaters, usually intimidatingly cavernous, often have trap doors, shadowy basements, and multiple dank passageways. At the University of Delaware, students point to Mitchell Hall, which houses the theater, as such a place. Students in the theater department tell of "Elmo," a revenant who hangs around the theater. According to legend, Elmo was a stage technician who met a tragic death after he slipped and fell from the crow's nest into the concrete subbasement that now bears the label "Elmo land."

Elmo's spirit now watches over the place, often looking out for accidents and their victims, usually thespians. In an often-told story, an actress is running through her steps ("running some blocking," in theater lingo) on stage. She hears a mysterious voice from stage left. She ignores it, but the call continues. She heads over, just as an immense light crashes into the stage where she had been standing. Had Elmo saved her from a nasty end? Could be, but he is also blamed for mischief such as resetting control panels behind closed doors. Stories of Elmo bring out the dangers and responsibilities of technical theater work and bind technicians through lore. Technicians often feel upstaged by thespians, and get a chance to show the reliance of actors upon technicians in narrative (Roskin 1988).

At Birmingham-Southern College, students learn of the ghost of a previous drama director named Charlie who inhabits the theater. In 2003, numerous versions of narratives about him were collected from oral tradition for a folk-lore class. One student explained his introduction to the many stories about Charlie: "When we got here as freshmen, we were told Charlie stories jokingly. There were Charlie believers and Charlie skeptics, but in either case everyone talked about him. Most Charlie references are, 'Hope Charlie doesn't get you,' or 'Watch out for Charlie'" (Clements, Sheaffer, and Smith 2003). Whether the humor comes out of nervousness about being on stage with all the stress of performance or a legendary intent to initiate new students into the thespian order, Charlie is a frequent subject of conversation, especially noting possible personal encounters. Students explain that he was a longtime presence in the department and died suddenly only months after his retirement. Stories of his presence remark that he apparently is still at work, indicating his commitment to the stage that all students require. One personal experience narrative comments on his presence after hours:

> I have been playing my guitar in a very obscure stairwell in the theatre. This stairwell echoes like crazy and offers amazing acoustics, so I go and sit down on the stairs and play my guitar. The first time, I was in the theatre by myself—I had checked everywhere to make sure that [I] wouldn't be disturbing anyone. After I had played for a little while, I paused for a moment. In that moment, I heard a voice. The voice was coming from inside the stairwell . . . it was unmistakable. Although I couldn't make out exactly what it was said, but it sounded like "thank you" and "good job." As much as I appreciated the compliment, it literally sent chills down my spine. I ran to the mainstage to see if anyone was there . . . no one. I also checked Theatre One . . . no one. So I decided to leave . . . again very quickly. The last time I had two other friends with me because I had told them about my Charlie experiences and they wanted to check it out. We went back to the stairwell. After I had played for maybe 20 minutes, we heard what sounded like a door close. But that was the only sound. There were no footsteps that followed it. Again, we checked to see if anyone had come in, but no one was there but us. And yet again, I left very quickly. I hope this is of interest to you. To be completely honest, I am NOT a superstitious person, but I firmly believe that there is something odd in that theatre. However, he seems to like music . . . so maybe I'm on his good side. (Clements, Sheaffer, and Smith 2003)

Other accounts relate voices coming from the stage as actors were arguing about a scene and copiers running full-throttle. The implication is that people are working furiously in preparation for a production. Students often comment in response to such narratives that the theater brings performance anxiety, and the stories may be reminders of the drive, and need for approval, in drama circles.

Schwab Auditorium is sometimes called the most haunted building on Penn State's University Park campus, a belief probably driven by the curious location of former university president George Atherton's grave by the structure. Some students claim he haunts the auditorium, while others identify the spirit as steel magnate Charles M. Schwab, for whom the building is named, as inhabiting the auditorium built in the first years of the twentieth century. Students implicate the spirits for taking away personal effects, moving curtains, lowering seats, and issuing a cool breeze in the stuffy interior (Swayne 2011, 33–35).

Actors are perhaps the most common theater revenants. Usually they are so devoted to the theater that they stay in costume around the stage late at night. Hamline University has its "Pink Lady," for example, fabled to be an actress from the old theater, which was later replaced. She wore a flowing pink gown that has become her ghostly trademark. Upper Iowa University's best-known ghost belongs to Zinita B. Graf, who died in 1950. A devoted alumna of the school, she went on to become a professional actress. During her lifetime, she returned to the school during the summers to reside. Her spirit mischievously likes to move things around in Colgrove-Walker Auditorium, especially before opening night, but she is generally benevolent. Her costumes still reside in the theater closet, and play programs thank her spirit for aiding the production.

Theaters also seem to attract suicide legends. At West Virginia Wesleyan, students talk about the odd sounds coming from Atkinson Auditorium. There a young student supposedly hanged himself during the tumultuous 1960s, and now his disturbed soul haunts the balcony and sometimes moves to the long dock under the stage. Often students feel his spirit during rehearsals. Maybe the talk of his presence displaces their anxieties about the performance they need to perfect. Consider the report of the student who said: "We were on stage for 'A Man for All Seasons.' While Mr. Presar was giving us directions, we both saw something walk into the light booth, yet we knew there was no one else in the auditorium. Somehow our eyes were both drawn to the same point in the balcony above" (Barlow 1989).

Those involved in drama are often known on campus as flamboyant, nervous types intensely devoted to the stage. Some of their nervousness is apparent in a host of beliefs about ensuring a good performance attributed to the actor set, including the strange-sounding good luck wish of "go break a leg" and "knock 'em dead." Folklorist Alan Dundes (1994b) argues that the phrases refer to taking a bow involving bending the head downward, construed metaphorically as breaking a neck, and bending the knee appearing to be breaking a leg. The bow met by applause is the sign of an acclaimed performance when the final curtain falls (bringing the curtain down as if the actors are knocked dead and the actors are brought out for a "curtain call"). The injurious content may owe to the common belief that one should never say "good luck" to a person before a performance, for it will bring bad luck (Gross 1961, 258).

Beliefs in theater ghosts learned by campus dramatists complement a host of beliefs that, in the words of veteran actor Dan Gross, "emphasize the tension of the stage, and the courting of favorable auspices." Examples are "Study your part just before you go to bed and you will wake up with a good recollection of it; never quote Shakespeare during another rehearsal or play or the play will be a flop; if an actor is not nervous before a show, he or she will give a bad performance; mockingly kick or 'boot' a fellow actor for good luck on opening night" (Gross 1961, 258).

Restrooms and Stalled Expressions

Sitting in restrooms across the country, students also offer humorous commentaries on school and the world in the form of graffiti. The special themes of the wall scrawling related to the contrast of the natural excretion in bathrooms to the artificial institutional production outside the stall has led to designating restroom graffiti "latrinalia" (Dundes 2007). In the confines of the stall, comparable in students' minds to their classroom seats, students connect, at bottom, feces to a transgressive smearing impulse in front of their eyes. But in this seat, nature calls, and its work stands in stark contrast to the artifice of the institution outside of the privacy of the porcelain throne (or "temple" as the campus outhouse was known at Bowdoin College). The environment is often an irresistible location to express students' baser desires and concerns about sex, drugs, violence, and society. To be sure, campus maintenance regularly paints stalls and substitutes materials to challenge the bathroom writer. Yet traditional latrine rhymes and phrases appear anew, as noted by the triumphant poet who inscribes, "They paint these walls to stop my pen but the shithouse poet has struck again" (Mays 1980, 3).

Befitting the anal retention of academic work, the tension of student life in the institution may bottle up the writer. It should not be surprising then that good places to look for graffiti are in the library and classroom buildings connected with sitting for long periods taking in knowledge, and a frequent subject of running commentary in a seated contemplative position is on constipation and flatulence. One reads, for example, "Here I sit, broken hearted; came to shit but only farted" and "Here I sit, smelling the vapor, Because some bastard stole the paper; How much longer must I linger, Before I am forced to use my finger?" (Mays 1980, 3; Dundes 1966, 99; Read 1935, 50). In a variation

I recorded at the University of Texas at Austin, a writer complains, "Here I sit I'm at a loss, Trying to shit out taco sauce, I'm know I'm gonna drop a load, I only hope I don't explode."

Students link the practice of writing and defecating in the classic rhyme: "Here I write on shithouse walls, Roll my shit in little balls" (Dundes 1966, 101). Even for those not taking pen in hand, appreciation is expressed for bathroom wisdom:

> Some come here to sit and think
> Some come here to shit and stink
> But I come here to itch my balls
> And read the writing on the walls. (Dundes 1966, 100; Read 1935, 74)

Proverbial wisdom, representing adult admonitions, becomes unsettled in parodies such as "He who sitteth on an upturned tack shall surely rise," "Man who stand on toilet is high on pot," and "Man who drop watch in toilet have shitty time" ("Confucius Say Jokes" 2011; see also Mechling 2004; Mieder and Litovkina 2002).

The restroom seat is given reverence in a frequent inscription as "the porcelain god," especially when bowing or praying after bringing a night's worth of partying back up through the mouth rather than the anus. In another oral-anal line, students connect the "hot air" of professors' talk with the act of breaking wind in their smears (see Blank 2010, 69). Or else they comment on farting as an indication of their frustration with "getting stuff (shit) out" and liminal status as a student—digesting a lot of material but either not being able to get it out to their utter satisfaction or not expressing it well so that they are accused of being "full of shit." In fact, seated in a contemplative position that requires some effort to accomplish a productive task, they may read, "Frustrated, nothing seems to come out right? Tough shit!"

Soiling the glorious image of the college degree, many writers craft signage above the roll of bathroom tissue, "Diplomas [or arts degree], Take One" (Mays 1980, 5–6; Birnbach 1984, 265). Or the scribe may advise, "If you can't go to college, go to State" (Egan 1985, 128). Men use bathroom walls to elaborate on life in the university: "State is like a dick, When it's soft you can't beat it, and when it's hard you get screwed" and "State is like a whore. Pay money and get screwed" (Mays 1980, 7–8; Nilsen 1981, 81). They may also wax poetically, "I wish I was a ring, Upon my true love's hand, Then every time she'd wipe her ass, I'd see the Promised Land" (Mays 1980, 4; Read 1935, 83). If that is not enough of a smear, writers offer this meaning to the routine end of a thoughtful bathroom session: "Flush hard; it's a long way to the dining halls" (Mays 1980, 11; cf. Dundess 1966, 95; Read 1935, 20).

Women have feminist expressions to inscribe on bathroom walls. Often pointing to male dominance, women writers leave, "Balls said the queen; If I had them I'd be King." But they receive pleasure from lines such as "Here I sit, I have to pee, Just pissed out a member of R.O.T.C." and "Adam was only the rough draft" (Jachimiak 1978, 1). Writers often receive answers from those who take their place in the stall (see Gordon 2003). At Indiana University, a woman's stall carried the message, "All females get rid of boys and war, hate, poverty, greed, and rape will die out. Matriarchal revolution is here. Women Unite!" "Unfortunately so will the human race," was the commentary inscribed underneath (Jachimiak 1978, 1). Another favorite political statement is "Eunuchs of the World Unite! You have nothing to lose." Women can match the men in expressing sexual play, "Long and thin goes further in, but short and thick does the trick," but they may also counsel, "Look homeward pregnant angel" (Golden 1974, 5; Nilsen 1981, 84). A frequently reported difference between men's and women's scrawlings is that males tend to be more aggressive and frequently homophobic, while females support one another and write messages in long threads, often in answer to confessional notes (Vosgerchian 2009).

Some latrines express the distinctive wordplay of subgroups within the college. In a math department restroom at Penn State, I found "The angle of the dangle is directly related to the heat of the meat," to which a reply was penned, "Don't forget the mass of the ass." In music, one might read, "I think I'm in love with my French horn," to which the replies might be, "It's the only thing worth being in love with" and "Horns are as fickle as any woman or man" (Gates 1976, 37; cf. Dundes 1966, 99). Or frustration might be expressed in rhyme: "Here I am to sit and ponder, While over these keys I do wonder, But right notes I just can't hit, I think this piano is full of shit" (Jachimiak 1978, 4). From a women's bathroom comes, "Voice students should practice topless, lets the chest breathe deep," while from the men's one finds "A concert violist named Leo, Was seducing a flautist named Cleo; As she took off her panties, She exclaimed—No andantes, I want this allegro con brio!" (Jachimiak 1978, 4; Mays 1980, 5).

The bathroom walls are places for students to voice cynicism of politics. Wondering about the society they will soon inherit, students may write, "The future of America is in your hands" (Dundes 1966, 97; Mays 1980, 7). During the 1950s and 1960s, writers offered, "In case of nuclear attack, hide under this urinal. Nobody ever hits it" (Dundes 1966, 97). During the 1990s and 2000s, however, students more aggressively used "nuke" to deal a decisive blow to various targets: "Nuke Iran," "Nuke Iraq," "Nuke the Whale Hunters," "Nuke the Whales," and "Nuke Steeler Fans." Drugs receive comment in the commonly seen line, "Reality is for people who can't handle drugs" or as a comment on a school's performance in the big game, "What do marijuana and State have in common? They both get smoked in bowls" (Mays 1980, 10; Lockwood 1978, 11). Showing skepticism of divine intervention, or a repression of sentiment in the unholy bathroom confessional, students may write, "God is dead, but don't worry, Mary is pregnant again" (La Barre 1979, 275; Wyman 1979, 90; Gach 1973, 287). A reply to this last observation often is attached, "God isn't dead. He just doesn't want to get involved" (Gach 1973, 287; La Barre 1979, 275).

Apparently emerging out of the latrinalia tradition is the practice in university environs reported since the early twenty-first century of inscribing often edgy or subversive punning phrases in the tiny spaces of grout between tiles. Students label the form as "groutfiti" and devote websites to sharing memorable examples. With lines such as "Grout Expectations," "Grout Gatsby," "With Grout Power Comes Great Responsibility," and "Three Strikes and You're Grout," anonymous writers want to show their intelligence and at the same time engage viewers with what it means to write in the grout rather than on the tiles (Caprio 2011). One observer commented on the *Urban Dictionary* website that "it makes sense that it [groutfiti] exists primarily around Universities where people are intelligent, yet very young and therefore still trying to amuse themselves and others by doing things like writing on walls" (Raiks 2005). From a material culture viewpoint, it has become easier to write in the grout instead of new glossy tile surfaces on which graffiti is wiped clean. Nonetheless, students who admitted to me engaging in the practice reflected that their writing represented a postmodern feeling of diminishment within mass culture compared to the graffiti of old splattered on the stalls. The new latrines had become even more somberly institutional with little room for human vitality. At Boston University, a student even gave a pun to say that groutfiti shows that collegians and their expressions fall "between the cracks" (cf. Caprio 2011).

Graffiti writers also ply their trade on desktops. "Oh, Oh! Somebody wrote on this desk," one might find, or referring back to the latrine gallery, "These desk top poets, so full of wit, should have their names engraved in shit" (Lockwood 1978, 8; Gach 1973, 285; cf. Read 1935, 73-74). Some of the most common inscriptions express boredom or frustration: "40, 35, 30, 25, 20, 15, 10 minutes to go of this class," "I can't take it anymore," and "Let me out of here!" (Lockwood 1978, 4–5; cf. Brunvand 1998, 157; Nilsen 1981). Influenced by the different generations of *Star Trek*, a favorite of students writing on desktops is "Beam me up Scotty!" (Lockwood 1978, 5).

Perhaps discouraged by the synthetics replacing old wooden desks and the increased protection of bathroom stalls from the mighty pen, some creative folk poets, identities still typically veiled, place more personally directed messages in campus newspapers and social networking sites. Student writers especially mark important rites of passage in the student culture such as the twenty-first birthday and graduation. "Arteries are red, Veins are blue, A year from today, You'll be 22!" one reads (Fagan 1981, 338). Writers also honor holidays significant to students such as Halloween, Christmas, Valentine's Day, St. Patrick's Day, and April Fools' Day. Many of the messages, as one might expect, carry sexual references. From the University of Oregon, for instance, comes this sample: "The next time you want me to share your salami, take off the wrapper," "You are the tootsie roll in my candy bag of life," and "If you haven't had a ball until now you've got one comin'" (Fagan 1981, 340). Students might read the columns simply for their witty, off-color content, check the columns regularly to see if they received a message, and then figure out whom it is from, or read messages to see if they recognize other recipients.

Homegrown Mormon students who attend Brigham Young University, the University of Utah, or Utah State University have been familiar since their high school days with the tradition in Utah of sending creative dating invitations and often elaborate in their college years (Eliason 2006; Wenger 2005; Young 2005). That is why the following ideas for memorable dating ideas published in the Brigham Young University student newspaper do not seem so unusual when understood in the context of the creative courtship custom.

> Give your date a "TOP SECRET" envelope with code names and a tape of instructions. Make sure the tape includes "Mission Impossible" music and have your date meet you at a certain location and time where they can accept their mission. Remember to tell your date that the tape self-destructs. Dress in spy costumes and call each other only by code name. Buy photos in a booth and paste them on spy ID cards. Set out on the scavenger hunt of your choice. Prepare in advance hidden notes or food in unusual places. Make sure it's challenging. (Hodson 2000)

At the University of Utah, senior student journalists had a creative not-so-secret code for years printed in the last issue of the student newspaper. Beginning as a senior leave-taking stunt in the 1980s to see whether readers would notice that the enlarged first letters of columns formed words like "drunk" and "tipsy," two decades later the words became increasingly vulgar, and in 2010 the administration did not look kindly on the spelling out of words for female and male genitalia (Leonard 2010). In the cyber age, the students' clever or crude parting message, depending on your point of view, went viral on social networking sites and blogs.

Computer Stations Everyone

The computer lab was once a specialized part of campus where strange pencil-necked geeks dwelled and mammoth machines flashed and whirred well beyond human scale. The high-tech location generated a raft of stories about inventive, apparently magical wizardry in the often windowless mysterious space, frequently containing the themes of the dire consequences of artificial intelligence given to computers (think of the renegade computer "Hal" in the classic movie *2001: A Space Odyssey* [1968]) and the unlikely young student hero striking it rich with a astounding software creation. The narratives usually invited comment on what is really going on with curious characters working long hours in an isolated room with blinking lights and reverberating machines. One persistent legend is of the eccentric student who gives away his software code rather than making a mint on it. Engineer and raconteur Robert Glass gave the student the pseudonym of Beardly Sandalfoot to draw attention to the prodigy's rebelliousness against the corporate "suits," but suggested that the oddball student was "crazy like a fox" because he charged for servicing the software (1991, 51–52). Glass's comment is that "Beardly Sandalfoot's capitalistic tendencies may well be at least as healthy as those of the rest of us! They're just hidden behind a subtle disguise" (1991, 52).

The story emerging out of countless computer departments of the incredible giveaway underscores the idea that students who dwell in the tech labs are a different breed who challenge the ways things are conventionally done. Characterized as more freewheeling and bohemian than the bottom-line managers in the real world, the tech-heads associated with futuristic progress and social ideals nonetheless have commercial interests at heart, or so tellers viewing college as the path to economic success reassure themselves. Glass, who taught at Seattle University, dubs them "Theodore Theory" fresh from the lecture halls of "Ivy-clad University" in contrast to "Preston Practice" from the corporate world with the idea that all that time in the lab has put their head in the clouds and they do not grasp practical consequences (1991, 10–12). The narratives wrap perceived conflicts in the university's role as a utopian haven for discovery and an incubator for commercialism (and greed) into a location that represents a global technological future.

With the digital age after the 1990s, the computer lab featuring personal devices is for everyone to take advantage of. Entering this public space, or working their private units at home, students could very well hear numskull tales of naive computer users (calling the university help-desk and being told the fix is to simply plug the electrical cord into the wall socket), uncanny legends of ghosts in the machine (or those with a "minds of their own"), and provocative rumors about a modem tax and exploding components (Brunvand 2001,

86–88; Green 2006, 4:262–64). Tellers often break the tension of the room with humorous references to the gender of computers perhaps because of the historic reputation of computer labs as men's hangouts. Women might quip that the machines are masculine because as soon as they commit to one they realize that had they waited a little longer, they could have had a better model. Men might respond by noting that as soon as they make a commitment to "her," they spend half their paycheck on accessories for it (Ochs 2006, 202–3; Rubinstein 2000, 25; cf. "Why Cucumbers Are Better than Men" and "Why Beer Is Better than Women" in D'Pnymph 1988, 372–75; Dundes 1987a, 82–95; Dundes and Pagter 1991, 406–9).

The glisten of the monumental culture-changing computer is often contrasted in lore to old-fashioned utensils for defecation. Photocopies and printouts (and an occasional screensaver) of drawings might hang at computer stations showing a toilet with the captions "Understanding the Computer Technology" (with arrows pointing to the input and output areas and a backup system consisting of a chamber pot) or "The Job Is Never Finished Until the Paperwork Is Done!" (if not a toilet, an outhouse is pictured) (Bronner 2011a, 440; Dundes and Pagter 1975, 160–62; 1991, 161–62; 1996, 120–21; Smith 1984, 69). Engineering students have been observed pinning up a parody of a flow chart beginning with the question "Does the Damn Thing Work?" The arrow for "No" leads to a command box plainly advising "Shitcanit" (Bronner 2011a, 404). An ultimate expression of frustration is the widely circulated cartoon of an animated duck wielding a sledgehammer; the caption borrows from the all-too-familiar computer directive to "Hit Any Key to Continue" (Dundes and Pagter 1991, 167). Broadsides might also show a picture of a roll of bathroom tissue turned with pedals at the base of a commode. The contraption connected to the top of the tank is "Paper Recycler" (Dundes and Pagter 1987, 174; Smith 1984, 109).

Not intended to be funny are cautionary tales about disastrous "crashes," slang for computer malfunctions. Stories abound about tragedies befalling hasty students who neglected to save "back-ups" of papers, just as a previous generation was regaled with sad tales of students who failed to copy theses and their professors who lost them (Brunvand 1993, 322–24). One academic veteran recalled in my survey, "Certainly we passed around a lot of cautionary tales about people who had to wait another semester to get their degrees because their computer crashed, was hit by lightning, and their only draft of their thesis was lost." A frequent motif in student talk is about the student who runs back into a burning building, not to rescue animals or heirlooms, but to recover his or her thesis files.

The scariest legends for computer users may be those about computer viruses that bear a resemblance to the narrated fear of AIDS (Ellis 1995; Green

2006, 221–22; Jennings 1990, 143–58; Lundgren 1994). The computer virus is a program that can replicate itself and cause damage in the host computer. Users live in fear that they become "fatal," that is, wipe out a computer drive. Beliefs circulate that dangerous viruses are rapidly spreading and are difficult to detect. Suggesting a thickening plot, many narrators of computer lore blame the spread of the deadly viruses on young student "insane geniuses" or "oddball misfits" seeking attention or pointing to the dark side of technology.

A favorite thread is the revenge factor that motivates the clever or deranged collegiate "hacker," the term used for computer aficionados who live for the machine and vie with professionals for inventiveness. Karla Jennings, chronicler of the personal computer revolution, reports that although statistics show that hackers are just as likely to be women as men, narratives tend to emphasize the man seeking retribution for a woman denying him a date (1990, 151). Bill Ellis, however, documented accounts of a shady female figure named Cathy who reportedly sends a message with the subject line "Good Times." The message contains a virus that, if downloaded, will destroy the user's hard disk (Ellis 1995). "Good times" is a euphemism for casual sex, and with the virus Cathy hands down punishment to the user for falling for the temptation of the subject by wiping out the sexually suggestive "hard drive." After investigating the incidence of the virus, Ellis found that "more people were affected by the alert than by any 'Good Times' file." The "Good Times" virus scare (which followed an overblown panic widely reported in the press about a deadly "Michelangelo" virus) then inspired in-group humor (the group of computer users, that is) in the form of a number of parodies such as online chain letters and alerts threatening exploding components (Ellis 1995). Some real computer viruses, such as the "Myparty worm" from the early twenty-first century play on typical student discourse of posting photographs from a party. The worm spread in messages with the message "My party . . . It was absolutely amazing!"

Although these virus scares spread beyond campus, they especially get noticed around universities because students are intense computer users for work—and play. The polling organization of the Pew Internet and American Life Project has consistently shown that the highest percentage of American Internet users are of college age, and more than other groups, students tend to use mobile devices and text message one another (Chronicle 2011, 51; Pew Research Center 2011). The forms that have emerged in the process of college-age students creating traditions online bear watching. Student users appear more likely to construct diagrams that identify themselves at the bottom of their messages often accompanied by sayings that play on tradition. Multiple formats including instant text messaging, social networking sites, and blogs provide opportunities to converse, and folklorize, online, often with computer-specific language such as the exclamatory favorites LOL (Laugh Out Loud), OMG (Oh My God), and WTF (What the Fuck). With the world getting more wired all the time, many sites specifically target students as a community of users, often with lots of rumors, humor, and legends in narrative and visual form, such as campusgossip.com, CollegeACB.com (Anonymous Confession Board), CollegeOnly, and CollegeWallofShame. The question raised in many narratives and posts by the extent of the reach of mobile communication is whether there is any place left to be gadgetless or "natural."

Cybercommunication takes distinctive forms that typically emphasize simulation of conversation, peppered with sayings that draw attention to themselves by suggesting folkloric references. Leaving messages much like writing graffiti on a wall, a student from Rensselaer offered a proverbial twist on Twitter (which limits message "tweets" to 140 characters), "It is better to lurk and be thought a moron than to post and remove all doubt." The line appears to be an update of the traditional "Confucius Say" humorous twist on philosophical proverbs associated with adult or authoritarian wisdom: Confucius say it is better to remain silent and be thought a fool than to open mouth and remove all doubt ("Confucius Say Jokes" 2011; Doyle, Mieder, and Shapiro 2012, 83; Keyes 2006, 145–46; for structural analysis of the form, see Dundes and Georges 1962, 223).

Other humorous one-liners and sight gags often relating to adolescent lore are evident on Facebook at wildly popular pages such as CollegeHumor, which indicate the appeal to the university crowd of cultural expression through social networking. Favorite forms on the site are mock lists, glossaries, rules, and typologies, parodying all the guides students endure. They also comment on the need to scope the social types one encounters in the institutionalized world of strangers on campus. Some of the most frequently "shared" (that is, reposted or emailed) lists are "The 6 Types of Studiers" ("The BMOC," or big man on campus, is the legendary "guy who hasn't been to class since the very first day"), "7 People You See in Your Dorm Bathroom" (relating to older photocopied lore, the list includes "The Overly Modest One" and "The One Who Isn't Modest Enough"), "The 100 Worst Nicknames to Pick Up during Orientation Work" (particularly bad are "Dumpy" and "Chunderbucket") (cf. Dundes and Pagter 1975, 61–68; Smith 1986, 86).

Streaking across the bottom of a screen in dashes and slashes, a Valparaiso student's diagram that caught my eye is accompanied by the rhyming proclamation, "Only the tough can run a Code in the Buff," an apparent play upon the proverbial comment on competition, "Only the strong [or tough] survive" (Honeck 1997, 30). The potential folkloric reach of an international network inspires an occasional cry of "This seems ripe for some sort of rumor . . . anyone heard any? Wanna make one up?" Of folkloristic significance to students is that Internet practice is widely viewed as yeast for spreading stories calling for an evaluation of their truthfulness (Bronner 2009, 58; see also Blank 2011; Oring 2008). That process invites vernacular commentary on what really happens in one's college environment—from the public square or lab to the private room or even bathroom stall—and how that relates to others.

What is the connection of the cyber wall to the bathroom stall? Arguably, the computer station establishes a play frame that allows release from the restraint of workaday society, and the "wall" symbolically becomes a discussion board and canvas on which creative messages and drawings are sequenced (Longenecker 1977). Many Listserv postings, too, are framed as informal rather than business and relay rumors with the invitation to give feedback. Accusations of students "playing on the Internet" often imply that the users are engaging in "chatting" or rumor-mongering with others. The privatized context of defecation in a public institutional setting invites consideration of a psychoanalytic interpretation of graffiti and threading as using an infantile smearing impulse to signal human freedom, especially in the symbolic equation of playful writing and anality that bears application to the pose of extended sitting in front of a screen (Bronner 2011a, 437–46; Dundes 2007). Indeed, Facebook's primary form of communication is privatized "writing on the wall," suggesting graffiti scribbling. More directly, following legends of an "iLoo" computer attached to a toilet in the early twenty-first century, a popular iPhone app called iPoo adopted by students offered a "virtual stall" where one can view and post drawings and messages ("iLoo" 2007). Collectively, those expressions are called a "poo stream." On users' desktops, odious messages labeled junk, "spam" (from stigmatized canned luncheon meat), or colloquially as "crap" (a popular software program for cleaning up a PC-drive is called "Decrapifier") suggest a repulsion to being defouled or smeared (expressed in the satire of the modern proverb "To err is human, to really foul things up takes a computer"). Excretory references to digital work are also apparent in the common computer-lab adage of "Garbage In, Garbage Out" (Doyle, Mieder, and Shapiro 2012, 94). To be sure, other themes are apparent in lore revolving around computer stations, but notable in this prevalent student discourse is the cognitive need to gain control over the machine by linking technological and naturalistic metaphors in folklore.

Across the campus landscape students have plenty of cultural codes to decipher and lots of social distractions to dodge. Some diversions have to do with the distinctive, often mysterious college environment, while others connect to the growing pains of the student's age. Legend, humor, and custom remind students of issues and decisions they need to face by themselves. As liminal home, the campus presents students with more options, but fewer protections, than in years past. Students learn to be alert for hazards in the treacherous landscape they must cross from dorm to library, and the mindscape they must cross from adolescence to adulthood. Independent of parents and community, indeed often feeling unguided even prior to coming to campus, students adapt, create, and share folklore with their peers to reflect on matters of sex, courtship, fidelity, drugs, and security. These matters are typically discussed outside of the curriculum, and they fill up much of the time students spend on talk—and on symbolic, dramatic narrative.

SEX AND THE SINGLE STUDENT

PUT YOUNG MEN AND WOMEN INTO CLOSE QUARTERS OF THE COLLEGE campus and inevitably the question of sexual behavior comes up. Although sexual issues have increasingly come out into the open since the twentieth century, the topic still presents anxieties that are apparent in numerous stories, songs, and practices. Sex has a special relation to college life because the kinds of life decisions that are being made by youth in their studies are also played out in their social, and amorous, connections. Much of the lore about sex in college questions power relationships as well as erotic practices among professors and students, men and women, and same-sex partners. Sex as a weapon, sex as recreation, sex as indulgence (along with drugs and alcohol), sex as a sign of self-worth (often tied into body image and notions of "sexiness" as social attraction), sex as sign of romance, and sex in relation to marriage (and adult commitments) all come up in often awkward scenarios of jokes and legends. The storytelling traditions may offer cautionary tales or parade sexual bravado; in either case they often call for commentary by listeners. They provide a social frame and fictive space to deal with thorny issues that are difficult to broach in everyday conversation.

One obvious concern is peer pressure to be sexually active and even experimental as a sign of modern liberation. Contemporary students are typically convinced that "everybody's doing it." Yet a number of surveys of sexual practices suggest that while students in the twenty-first century are more active than their twentieth-century counterparts, they perceive their cohort to be more promiscuous than they actually are (American College Health Association 2009, 482–83; Kadison and DiGeronimo 2004, 118–20). Collegians report stress to be the major health impediment to their academic performance and concerns related to sex often top their list: romantic involvement and commitment, pregnancy, inadequacy, disease, harassment, abuse, and violence (American College Health Association 2009, 480). To be sure, sex is also viewed as a pleasure, perhaps even an expectation, of campus life without in loco parentis or religious prohibitions, but students recognize risks that accompany being sexually active. In so doing, they often weigh the passion of the moment, symbolically declaring one's independence from constraint, against a future life commitment or societal conscience that constitutes much of college social life.

Historically, college campus courtship traditions have changed from the old-time college's ritualized mixers that involved culturally enforced protocols for dating to postmodern hook-ups at parties, "meat markets," and "booty runs." Although appearing emblematic of more open attitudes toward sexual dalliance, the practices ushered in by the sexual revolution of the 1960s also brought uncertainty, and often trepidation, into students' social encounters. Decisions about, and practices leading to, sexual activity became tempered into the twenty-first century by fear of AIDS and STDs, unwanted pregnancy, proper gender power roles, and awareness of diverse sexual orientations. University administrations stepped up sexual abuse education, which also left many questions in students' minds about their vulnerability and ethical stance. Campus institutions promoting romantic commitment and dignified public formals and mixers received renewed attention. Back in the dorm, narratives expressing the dilemmas of the age served to work through the dizzying choices and consternation many students faced. Indicating the paradox of sex as potentially providing both individual triumph and social ruin, the lore can be couched as horror or humor. As this folkloric response demonstrates, the experience of the college years preparing for the future became entangled in attitudes toward sex.

Sex in the Classroom

A great deal of student humor about the classroom involves sexual themes. In these stories, the young student who has sex on the brain is contrasted to the crusty professor who conveys the innocence, or self-denial, in intellectual pursuit. One frequently reported joke is about the professor discussing the question of human and divine origins. The graybeard prof asks the young coed, "Who made you, little girl?" She answers, "Originally or recently?" (Legman 1968, 75).

Pretty coeds are often suspected in folklore of getting ahead on the basis of their sex appeal. In a frequently collected jest, a young attractive woman visits her male professor's office and seductively says that she will do anything for a good grade in the class. "Anything?" the professor asks with a smile. "Yes, anything," she coos. The professor leans closer and startles her by saying, "Try studying then!" (see Carey 1988, 7; Mr. "J" 1981, 92; Rogers 1987, 203; Rojstaczer 1999, 22; Toelken 1986, 505; 1995, 3; Williams 1999). The story questions the social capital of sexuality and youth in opposition to intelligence and age represented by the professor. According to psychologist Timothy Rogers, tellers imply territoriality with their renditions of the story. He explains: "The professor has (owns) something (presumably knowledge and standards) and these are his to protect and dole out when earned" (Rogers 1987, 203). The fact that the story inevitably involves a female, though, suggests gendering of the unequal power relationship between the young woman who is distinctively ascribed sexual assets that she tries to cash in and the male professor who is imagined to be not above exploitive urges.

Probably the most common off-color story concerns the professor who instructs the class to write an essay including four subjects: religion, royalty, sex, and mystery. The prof coldly announces, "It'll take quite some time to write an essay of this nature and smoothly incorporate all subjects, so please begin." About fifteen minutes later, a young man raises his hand and announces that he is finished. The startled prof says, "I don't see how you can be finished with an essay of that nature in that short a time." "Well, I have," said the smiling student. "If you think so, read it aloud." The student reads, "'My God,' said the queen, 'I'm pregnant. I wonder whose it is?'" (Baker 1986, 194–95; see also Legman 1975, 90). In a collection from the University of Arkansas at Fayetteville Folklore Archives, the responding student is an Aggie transfer student who turns in two sentences: "'Good God,' said the homecoming queen, 'I'm pregnant. Who did it?'" In a variation from USC, the instructor demands brevity, religion, royalty, and modesty. The student finishes quickly and reads the result, "'My God,' said the countess, 'take your hand off my knee'" (Carlinsky 1971, 117). Judging by Gershon Legman's recordings of a version as early as 1935 from the University of Michigan (1975, 90), the story has had a long persistent appeal on campuses, not just because of the tables turned on the imperious, windy professor but also because of reference to a self-indulgent woman choosing multiple partners (even if society expects her to be chaste) and the risk of pregnancy. Probably even older are related lingering Wellerisms that base their humor on the licentiousness (or penis envy) of the royal woman: "Fuck me!" said the duchess, more in hope than anger, and "Balls!' cried the king: the queen laughed because she wanted to (two) (Partridge 1986, 39, 141).

A widely circulating joke that relates to the phallic double entendre is about the waggish (or smug) male professor of anatomy who asks, "What organ of the body enlarges to six times its natural size?" No one answers. The professorial sage on the stage redirects the question to a young female student. Taking affront, she blurts out, "Well, I, um, I don't see why I should be called on to answer such a question!" The male mentor then commandingly announces, "Everybody gets zero for not studying today's lesson. The only organ of the body that can enlarge to six times its natural size is the pupil of the eye." In some versions the instructor looks at the embarrassed young woman and says,

"And as for you, you're due for a terrible disappointment" (Legman 1968, 140). In a variation, the question is "What portion of the body becomes harder than steel?" and the answer is "the fingernails. And as for you, you're nothing but an idle dreamer." Sometimes the coed flees from the embarrassment, and the professor innocently asks the class, "What's so bad about the pupil of the eye?" (Toelken 1986, 507).

The scenario that drives the double entendre narrative is the sexual tension between the masculine scholar who plays on the adolescents' erotic preoccupation and young women supposedly intimidated or seduced by the power of the male authority figure. The professor maintains his superiority in the narrative by showing his intellectualism in contrast to the students' base sexual interests. The narrative employs the ambiguity of exposure: although the male professor appears to be going over the line of decency by referring to, that is revealing, himself, he ends up *exposing* the students and even questioning whether they belong in the classroom.

The narrative relates to a folkloric form with which collegians will be familiar from adolescence: the pretended obscene riddle (Brown 1973; Dundes and Georges 1962, 225). An example is "What goes in hard, but comes out soft?"— chewing gum. As with the double entendre narrative, the riddle usually questions the concealment, as well as threat, of the penis, as representative of gender power conflicts after puberty between the attractive, shapely female and the developing male aspiring to be physically enlarged and socially superior (Bronner 1985). In the joking frame, the teller as trickster exposes the listener's preoccupation with sexual intercourse in which the male is dominant. Examples of this trope that I heard among men into the young adult years were "What's better than honor?—in 'er," and "What's indecent?—when it's in long, hard, and deep, then it's in decent" (see Brown 1973, 95). The riddles can mimic intellectual tests and therefore show the binary between the natural "real" world and the artificial, and therefore asexual, classroom. An example is the joking question of a four-letter word beginning with *f* and ending with *k*, with the additional information that if it does not work one could use fingers—the answer is a fork (Dundes and Georges 1962, 225). In double entendre narratives about the college setting employing the characterization of the embarrassed female recipient of the question, the phallic reference extends the gender conflict in coming-of-age to the relationship between the male professor and the coed.

Anthropology professors soberly delivering their graphic descriptions of exotic rituals figure in a similar context with a widely circulating joke, sometimes told as a legend. The professor describes a tribe in Asia, South America, or Africa whose men are endowed with penises fifteen inches and longer when in the state of excitation. At this point two or three coeds get up and start to leave the room, either because they are offended or need to go to another class. He shouts at them, "It's no use being in a hurry to get there, girls. The boat probably won't leave for another week" (Brunvand 1960, 250–51; Tillson 1962, 55; cf. Brunvand 1962, 62). In a twist that bears a resemblance to the plots of some international tale types, the professor, this time of anatomy or biology, purposely describes the male tribe members' parts to shock coeds right out of his class. All but three leave when he cites the measurement, and the rest walk out when he delivers the punch line (Brunvand 1960, 251; see Tale Type 1828* [Aarne 1964, 499; Uther 2004, 2:433] about the parson who preaches so that half the congregation weeps and the other half laughs. It turns out he preached without breeches.).

The story about the wisecracking professor has been collected in America since the 1940s at Columbia, Michigan, Purdue, Detroit, and Indiana, and it is still getting around. A possible precedent is in a story attached to English anthropologist A. C. Haddon (1855–1940), who taught at Cambridge. "He was discussing Sociology," according to an account, "and, as happened so often when he was talking about his Torres Straits Islanders, had exceeded his hour. He was describing how in some islands the women, not the men, make the proposals of marriage, when the women students from Girton College, knowing that their cab would be waiting impatiently outside, unostentatiously slipped out at the back. The temptation was too great. He called out, 'No hurry, there won't be a boat for some weeks'" (Brunvand 1960, 250).

A Milton scholar supposedly walked into his classroom on the first day and asked all the young women in the front row to cross their legs. "Now that the gates of Hell are safely closed," he says, "we may begin our discussion of *Paradise Lost*" (Toelken 1986, 505). A memorable quip in American folklore is most often attributed to Albert Einstein after a comely young woman proposes marriage to the wild-haired professor, who was not known for his handsome features. She explains to the famous teacher that with her looks and his brains they could have wonderful children. The professor responds, "But my dear, what if they had *my* looks and *your* brains." The legendary union is not just about Einstein's mind alone; it has been traced to exempla in European medieval manuscripts (Johnson 1960, 248–49).

When students are not claiming merely to be having a laugh at the expense of the unusual college situation, they may use the jokes as weapons in the battle of the sexes played out on the campus battlefield. In some mixed settings, students use jokes for sexual teasing, especially at their age of sexual awakening, although college men's risqué humor tends to be more obscene and hostile (Mitchell 1985, 163–86). Some campus humor distinctively aimed at women warns about unwanted pregnancy in the sexually open environment of the campus. A classic one is about the rustic grandmother who calls "Diploma" to a child toddling along behind her. A fellow on the street hearing this asked why she called the child "Diploma." She explained, "Well, you see my daughter, she done went off to college last year. And she told me that she was going to bring back a diploma." Pointing to the child, she said, "That's what she brung back" (Davis 1956, 9; Levitt 2002, 75).

Evidence of humor responding to women as student researchers is in this joke making the rounds of the campuses for years:

> This man was sitting in a bar one night and an attractive young woman came in alone and sat down beside the man at the bar. After a few minutes the man attempted to start a conversation by asking her for a match, but to his surprise she said in a loud voice, "What kind of girl do you take me for?" Now the man was very embarrassed because everyone in the bar glared at him so he turned away and went back to his drink. After a few minutes the woman was still sitting beside him and he began to think that possibly he had been a little forward and might have offended her somehow. So he said, "I'm sorry if I appeared forward when I asked for a match. I was only trying to be pleasant." The woman answered in a loud voice, "How dare you make such insinuations? If you don't leave me alone I'll have the police called!" The guy still could not figure out what he was doing wrong, but he realized that he had better just leave and avoid any real trouble. He finished his drink and quickly headed for the door, but before he could leave the young woman had caught up with him and said, "I think I owe you an explanation. I'm a graduate student in sociology and I'm studying people's reactions to an embarrassing situation. You were a good subject and I'm sorry if I upset you." To which the man replied, "Fifty Dollars?!" (Mitchell 1976, 512–13)

Men known for their sexual bravado are not immune from embarrassment in the classroom. A joke rating high marks on Internet humor sites, for example, is the one about a professor wrapping up class who starts talking about the final exam the next day. He admonishes that there would be no excuses for not showing up tomorrow, barring a dire medical condition or an immediate family member's death. One smart-alecky stud shoots his hand up and asks, "What about extreme sexual exhaustion?" and the whole classroom burst into laughter. After the chuckles subside, the prof glares at the student, and declares, "That's not an excuse, you can use your other hand to write" (Lebman 2004, 172).

The White Witch

The automobile, a prominent symbol of adult mobility, plays an important role in many legends in getting students beyond the campus borders and off beaten paths into zones of erotic mystery. The recently acquired vehicle full of bodies brushing up against one another adds to the excitement of independence and discovery. It also enters into legendary sightings by romantic couples. Stories often referred to as "lovers' lane" legends have the earmarks of the horror tale recounted early in adolescence and later elaborated in legend quests or group setting back home. Typically the backdrop for the legend is a couple out parking, that is, necking in a car in a secluded spot. As the lovebirds pursue the pleasures of embrace, all sorts of dangers lurk outside. The perils outside, of course, point to the venture inside the car of going too far sexually. The car has metaphorically gone too far by being parked by the fertile woods, high on a mountain, or out beyond town by a cemetery.

One frequently mentioned danger is the "white witch." At Berkeley, she appears in Tilden Park; at the University of Arizona, a lonely road from Patagonia; at Indiana, a limestone quarry off a country road. The "white witch" or "white lady"—sometimes a ghostly jilted lover or rape victim, sometimes a real-life maniac—has her ways of driving couples from the parking spots. At Berkeley, "she would try to scare them away by tapping on the roof or windows with her long diamond fingernails. It seemed that her daughter had been raped while parked up there and the White Witch's goal in life was to prevent the same thing from happening to other girls" (Samuelson 1979, 18). At Indiana, "if you are out on a date with a girl and you park your car alongside this quarry and at midnight on a moonlit night, this girl who was abducted and raped will come running over this hill and she'll be throwing rocks at your car. She'll go to the girl's side of the car and start beating on the window." Near Altoona, Pennsylvania, the ghostly white lady is so called because she appears in a wedding dress. She is part of a couple who eloped, but traveling down the Buckhorn Mountain, the car went out of control and crashed. The woman's body was never found, and she haunts the mountain on dark and rainy nights scaring away young lovers (Bronner 1989, 147; Shoemaker 1950).

In these various stories, the woman bears the responsibility for keeping limits on the romantic enterprise. It is her window that is scratched, and it is the young female victim (and sometimes the victim's mother) who returns to clear the spot of lovers. In many versions, the woman is more violent and seeks revenge on the men. At the University of Arizona, students tell of men picking up what appears to be a beautiful woman by the side of the road. But she turns into a devilish figure and kills the men (Leddy 1948, 272–77; Chambers 1983, 31–39).

The wrath of the white witch is often aroused because of the brutality of rape. With the concern of college women out at night alone, they commonly tell cautionary tales, sometimes ghostly, of the dangers of rape on campus. Many of the tales concern places on or near campus where ghostly screams can be heard at scenes of the crime. At Indiana, women tell of strange ghostly cries at midnight coming from a small stream that runs through campus (Waymire 1978, 3). In New Orleans, students say that a cloud or mist that comes down in City Park late at night and makes crying noises is the spirit of a rape victim (Chambers 1983, 34–35).

At Colorado State University, the motif of the crying sound as a warning is built into a white witch legend concerning an outdoor theater. In one version, the victim's mother swore that she would get revenge for her daughter's fate. As a student told the tale in a dorm one night, "Supposedly she waits on the stage of the ampitheatre [sic] at night with a hatchet to kill anyone who comes there. Her bloodcurdling screams can be heard as a warning to stay away. It's been said that people have died up there—not from falling off the rocks" (Samuelson 1979, 36).

The Hook Man

The most iconic male figure to haunt lovers' lanes in student legendry is probably the "hook man." In these legends the locales change, but the plots usually involve a romantic couple parking in a secluded spot outside of town or campus. Many tellers set up the scene by noting that the guy puts on the radio to set a seductive mood. The couple is getting deeper in embrace when a newsflash comes over the radio. It warns that a maniac or killer has escaped from a nearby institution (sometimes an insane asylum, sometimes a prison). The dangerous character can be identified by a hook replacing one hand. The woman typically becomes scared, but her date assures her that she has nothing to worry about. She persists, so he agrees to take her home. He zooms off, perhaps showing his disappointment. After he pulls up to the house, he comes around the car to open her door, and to his horror, sees that a bloodied hook— presumably from the escaped maniac—is in the door handle (see Baker 1982, 78–79; Barnes 1966, 310–11; Bronner 1989, 148–49, 310–12; Brunvand 1981, 48–52; Carey 1971, 78–80; Dégh 1968a, 92–100; Thigpen 1971, 183–86; Tucker 2005, 87–88). Folklorist Bill Ellis speculates that the rise of the legendary villain might owe to publicity surrounding the arrest in 1948 of Caryl Chessman in Los Angeles for attacking parking couples and forcing the woman to perform oral sex (1994, 63). Chessman had both his hands, but had the nickname "Hooknose" because of facial deformities.

Legend tellers documented during the 1950s and 1960s did not make the connection to the Chessman case but focused their accounts frequently on the "hook" as a weapon and the idea of a maniac on the loose who preys on young couples parked in cars. Linda Dégh mentions that the legend is frequently told by men to scare girlfriends as they escort them to lonesome spots, while other tellers elaborate on the guilty feelings of fearing people with disabilities (1968, 98). Alan Dundes makes a case that from the point of view of the women, the story is a warning about the aggressive sexual advances of men: "The 'hook' could be a hand as in the expression 'getting one's hooks into somebody,' but a hook could also be a phallic symbol. The typical fear of the girl might then be that a boy's hand, signifying relatively elementary necking, might suddenly become a hook (an erect, aggressive phallus)" (1971, 30). Dundes supports his claim by pointing out that "if the hook were a phallic substitute, then it would make perfect sense for the hook to be severed as a result of the girl's instigating the sudden move to return home. The attempt to enter the 'body' of the car is seemingly a symbolic expression of the boy's attempt to enter the body of the girl" (1971, 30–31). The "news" or "police" announcement on the radio of a killer on the loose represents the voice of parental authority. A joke I collected multiple times from college men bears out the symbolic equivalence of the police in this role: "A couple was out parking and making out in a secluded spot. A cop car pulled up and they stopped to see what the problem was. The guy rolled down his window and the cop said, 'You'll have to leave.' The guy replied, frustrated, 'But officer, we weren't doing anything wrong. We were only necking.' The cop told him, 'Well put your neck back in your pants and go home [get out of here].'"

Skeptical of the sexual interpretation of the hook man legend, Dégh notes that if the story demonizes the aggressive male, why would the telling of the "scary" story by the man, as she observed, result in the woman drawing closer to the man, "seeking protection from the 'fearless male'"? (1971, 65–66). One answer might be that the story has in it a social map of teenage transition between childhood and adulthood. The car, a sign of teenage mobility and maturity, is parked on the fringes of the community, far from authority or constraining forces. Indeed, the car is often located near an "insane asylum" or "mental institution," indicating that rationality is absent in this outlying zone. The radio bulletin, emanating from town, warns the couple to head back to the fold; the female, usually stereotyped as more cautious and homebound, typically insists that the couple return. When the couple returns home, the boy acts more like a gentleman. They have traveled the road of transition from the home to the edge of the community, from childhood to the freedom of adulthood. In some versions, the narrator comments that the girl "was laugh-ing at herself for being so silly" as to have childish fears, but discovers in her driveway that the dangers are real and she need not feel embarrassed about wanting to go home (Bronner 1989, 311–12).

With the popularization, and often parody, of the hook man legend in film and television, the character has arguably become less scary, and more of a nostalgic reference to sexual anxieties of a more innocent generation. A short list of films featuring the hook man, for example, includes *Meatballs* (1980), *Campfire Tales* (1991), *I Know What You Did Last Summer* (1997), *Lovers Lane* (1999), and *The Hook-Armed Man* (2000). The theme continues into episodes of the television show *Supernatural* (2005) and video game *Campfire Legends—The Hookman* (2009). In the video game, the hook man ruins the romantic getaway of a female protagonist by the name of Christine. Apparently confirming the predation of the hook man on women, the game involves her escaping and finding life-saving objects to save herself. Although the hook man character is prominent in popular culture, he has been less evident in folklore. Folklorists report a decline among oral collections after 1980, although the bloody hook with apparent reference to the legend rather than to a pirate theme is observable in Halloween costuming (Ellis 1994, 65–66). In college, students recall hearing about the hook man early in their adolescence and report to me a hidden hook pulled out as a prank played on unsuspecting or sleepy roommates. They may be arrogantly making fun of the need of previous generations to park to get the privacy to engage in sex, but still retain anguish over the risks of evening trysts away from campus. Even as a "playlike legend," as folklorist Bill Ellis calls the hook man narrative circulating after 1980, it nonetheless still attracts comment, perhaps with a tinge of humor, if not fright. Ellis suggests that playfulness about the hook still constitutes "a rich vocabulary of convenient language that allows teenagers to discuss a range of feelings and emotions about the fears, ambiguities and thrills of adolescent courtship" (1994, 71).

Another function of the hook man moving into the category of camp and children's folklore from his previous campus haunt is that he becomes a point of reference for supposedly more realistic characters encountered in contemporary campus scares. As the narratives in this chapter attest, most of these characters are not disfigured or beastly, although they may be guilty of monstrous deeds. They are often the unassuming kid next door who keeps to himself or the trusted brother inflicting a fatal initiation. Whether related deadly seriously or in fun, the narratives typically get a reaction that is likely to reflect on one's adolescent vulnerability in love and life, as well as the truth out there.

Troubled Roommates and Boyfriends

Many lovers' lane stories feature a "fearless male" character whose bravado is misplaced. He is especially at his self-assured best in the iconic story of the "boyfriend's death" that often complements stories of the hook man and the white witch. In the most frequently collected version of the legend, a young fellow drives a car with his date out to a country road surrounded typically by woods. The steamy romantic scene is interrupted by the discovery that the car has run out of gas or is somehow otherwise incapacitated. The man volunteers to go in search of gas, but the woman is scared for him as well as frightened of being left alone. He asserts that he will be fine out in the dark, and to calm her fears, devises a knocking signal that he will use for her to let him back in. He instructs her to lie down out of sight in the backseat to avoid sexual predators. The fellow does not return for some time, and in many versions the detail is added of her falling asleep. She hears a scratching or dripping sound coming from the roof, and she shrinks in her seat in fear. At daybreak, the police rescue her (sometimes it is still dark, and she is aroused by the headlights of the police car). They lead her out of the car but warn her not to turn around. She of course then looks back and sees her boyfriend hanging dead from a tree above the car. The noise coming from the roof is explained by toenails (fingernails if he is hanging upside down) or blood dripping (see Amick 1980, 1–17; Baker 1982, 201–3; Barnes 1966, 309–10; Bronner 1989, 148, 310; Carey 1971, 79; Dégh 1968b, 101–6; 2001, 105–7; Glazer 1987, 93–108; Roemer 1971, 12–13; Thigpen 1971, 174–77; Wilson 1998).

Most commentators have cited the story as a cautionary tale about the dangers of adolescents away from parental authority moving too quickly in sexual encounters represented by the isolation of parking, especially during a period of increased sexual freedom during the 1960s and 1970s. After all, the boy "gets it in the neck" for being the sexual aggressor. Although the story may appear to be about the dangers lurking for the independent, sexually active couple from crazed predators, this may also be a projection of the angry parents' reaction who throttle the transgressive male. But another theme is the disregard of the boyfriend's attempt to reenter the car. So the story has the message to the boy of being less foolishly macho and to the girl of being more aware of what is happening outside the car.

This last theme is especially evident in a spin-off of the boyfriend's death story to one about dormitory life. In the "roommate's death," a woman's roommate leaves late at night to study. Fearful of a maniac attacking the roommate, but really fearful of mistaking the returning roommate for the maniac and opening the door, the woman requests a knocking signal. Late at night, the woman hears a scratching at the door, which she does not answer. But when she opens the door in the morning she discovers her roommate dead on the floor (frequently with an ax lodged in her head), and her fingers on the door as if she had been desperately trying to get in the room (see Barnes 1966, 307–8; Brunvand 1981, 57–62; Carey 1971, 75–77; Dégh 1969b, 55–74; 2001, 105–10; Tucker 2005, 88–90).

In a variation, two women stay in different rooms in a dorm over Christmas or Easter break, while everyone else has gone home. Because of their fears of being alone, the women decide to call each other on the phone if help is needed. Sometimes a report comes over the radio that a hatchet murderer, a man who kills young women, is on the loose. The phone goes dead, and one woman locks herself in her room, sometimes going so far as to move furniture in front of the door. She hears a body being dragged upstairs or a scratching at the door. When all is quiet in the morning, she opens the door (sometimes there is a male, blue-collar rescuer) to discover the other woman dead with an ax in her head and her fingers bloodied from trying to scratch at the door for help (see Baker 1982, 217–18; Grider 1980, 147–78; Parochetti 1965, 53–54; Tucker 2005, 88; Waymire 1978, 3–5).

The lingering question for the listener, then, might be whether responsibility for the tragedy belongs with the victim who took the risk of going out late at night or with the person in the room who did not answer the door because of her fear of the murderer. The issue of responsibility commonly underlies the climax of both the boyfriend's and roommate's death stories, and in each type, extreme fear and courage could be shown to create problems in a period of newly acquired adolescent independence.

The roommate's death story's attachment to women suggests other nuances. The story creates a feeling of horror because of the presumption of women's vulnerability and the expectation of violence against them when they are out alone or late at night. Many of the victims in these stories get it in the pretty "head," dying with large masculine tools like axes embedded in their brains or backs. The implication of the ax-wielding male attacker lurking in a dormitory threatening to penetrate the female victim is often of sexual violence. In many stories, the woman is threatened because she has chosen to stay in the dormitory over vacation while everyone else has joined their families. When she is attacked, she is typically out studying late (or smugly going out partying after the semester is over), therefore defying obstacles to her use of intellect. Stumbling back to her room, she loses her feminine, sexualized fingernails scratching for help. For Beverly Crane, "The points of value implicit in this narrative are then twofold. If women wish to depend on traditional attitudes and responses they had best stay in a place where these attitudes and responses are best able to protect them. If, however, women do choose to venture into the realm of equality with men, they must become less dependent, more self-sufficient, more confident in their own abilities, and above all, more willing to assume responsibility for themselves and others" (1977, 147).

Yet another variation of the "roommate's death," especially prevalent in my collection from the 1980s and again in the 2000s, tests the various interpretations of the legend. From Shippensburg University comes a representative narrative: "These two girls did everything together. They studied together, ate together, and partied together. They were always together, up until one night. The one girl decided to stay in and catch up on schoolwork. The other went out. When she returned to the room, she was very careful not to wake her roommate. In the morning, she found her roommate dead and on the mirror, written in blood was 'Aren't you glad you didn't turn on the light last night?'" (cf. Tucker 2005, 91–93).

Sometimes a blind date is blamed for the murder, as in this version recorded in the Berkeley Folklore Archives:

A girl who was a student at the University of Chicago had gone out on a date one night and gotten home fairly late. As she was standing in front of her dorm room looking for her keys she debated whether or not to turn on the lights to her room, but she decided not to because she didn't want to disturb her roommate. So she got ready for bed in the dark and then went to sleep. The next morning she woke up and looked over to her roommate's bed, and saw her roommate hacked apart into bloody pieces. There was a note pinned to the sheets of the bed which read, "If you had turned on the lights last night you would have looked like this too." It turned out that her roommate had gone out on a blind date that night and had invited him back to her room, and the guy had turned out to be a psycho, and had still been in the room when the girl had gotten back that night. (cf. Baker 1982, 218–19; Britton 1987, 2)

Women reported hearing the story in conversation about the hazards of dating in a world of strangers, and fears emanating from the sensational news of serial killers such as Ted Bundy (1946–89), who broke into Florida State University's Chi Omega sorority house in 1978 and strangled two women to death. Before then, he had raped and strangled college women in Washington, Oregon, and Utah. His story, and the lessons from women being taken in by his charm and good looks before being victimized, live on for subsequent generations of college students in a bunch of movies emphasizing his role as a seductive stranger, beginning with *The Deliberate Stranger* (1986) and continuing with *The Stranger Beside Me* (2003) and *Bundy: A Legacy of Evil* (2008).

The "mirror" story also frequently comes up in conversations about dorm security. In fact, a detail is sometimes added to the legend that the two women agreed, foolishly, to leave the door unlocked because one did not have the key. In these instances, the story strongly conveys warnings to undergraduates. But in other ways, the story bears out the "points of value" given by Beverly Crane (1977). The woman who is killed by the male attacker is often studying, but to say that we have an anti-"grind" motif here is probably off the mark. The woman is variously dating and studying, and either way she is hacked up like "meat"—an offensive slur often hurled at women. So, is the woman who does not turn on the light feeling guilty for her decision to "stay in the dark," or is she relieved? The answer is left for the listener to provide. When I turned the question back on tellers of the story at Penn State, I heard that the roommate who had been out should feel responsible for the one who stayed in. Indeed, the detail of one roommate being spared, and the fear that it inspires in the telling, seems like a punishment for going out, usually on a date, with an uneasy dependence on male provision or seduction.

The story also invites reflection, so to speak, because of the key detail of the mirror into which the survivor looks. As if invoking the fairy tale formula of "mirror, mirror on the wall," she is given a message about her body, still in one piece, and her morality as she looks at the image of her face (a symbol of her personality or self) with the words scrawled over it. The dualism of the reflection is indicated by the twin possibilities of the red lettering as lipstick (for the buoyant, vital face looking out) and of blood (from the dying, consumed body taken in). The bathroom in which she stands is where she starts her day and reminds her of her natural self. The words are her wake-up call, it appears. She is forced to see herself (and an obsession with male attention and feminine beauty) in a new light. As she looks at herself, she must ask why she survived. The answer leads to the question of what she, and other women, should do now.

The story's references to mirror, blood, bathroom, and death suggest a developmental connection to a childhood ritual known as "Bloody Mary" familiar especially to young women (see Bronner 1988, 168–69; Dégh 2001, 243–46; Dundes 1998; Langlois 1978; Tucker 2005, 94–107). In that custom, often enacted in institutional settings of a school or camp, girls typically gather in front of a mirror in a darkened bathroom repeatedly chanting a name such as "Bloody Mary" (reported alternatives are "Mary Worth," "Mary Wolf," and "Mary Whales"), frequently with the additional line of "I believe in you." The expected, if feared, result is the appearance of a face in the mirror representing an innocent young female victim who may be bloodied from a past tragedy. A story frequently accompanies the dare to summon Mary; she may have died in a car accident or was molested. The avowed importance of believing in the chant stems from avoiding Mary's punishment of scratching disingenuous or doubting children in the room. Many accounts, Elizabeth Tucker points out, feature the mirror to "tell the truth about aspects of the maturing self that are difficult to acknowledge" (2005, 96). In providing a reflection related to a daily ritual, the bathroom mirror raises incidents or images from the past and also warns of danger ahead. In the campus legend ending with "Aren't you glad you didn't turn on the light," the survivor looks at herself rather than waiting for someone else to appear with whom she can relate. She imagines herself, though, in her roommate's position in the light in a way she did not in the dark.

AIDS, Contamination, and Conspiracy

A significant development in the circulation of roommate legends focusing on the presence of violence and the vulnerability of women is the fear of contracting AIDS. At the core of the story is a woman inflicted with AIDS who intentionally passes it to men. "AIDS Mary," as she is sometimes called, invokes the image of the famed Irish servant woman Mary Mallon, nicknamed "Typhoid Mary" by the popular press. From 1906 to 1915, she was accused of spreading typhoid to families for whom she cooked, even after tests showed that she carried the disease. She denied the presence of the disease, however, and angrily blamed ethnic antagonisms for her troubles (Kraut 1994, 101). As most contemporary students know Mary, she is a striking woman who picks up men. In the morning, her partner sees a note written in red lipstick left on the bathroom mirror: "Welcome to the world of AIDS." In discussions of the story online and in dorms, one learns of different interpretations by men and women.

When I was a visiting professor at the University of California at Davis in 1990, I surveyed the large class of close to 100 students and found that more than 70 percent had heard the story and other references testified to the prevalence of the narrative cycle (Bennett and Smith 2007, 45–47; Fine 1987; Smith 1990; Goldstein 1992; 2004, 100–115; Whatley and Henken 2000, 67–80). Probably reflecting the fact that an AIDS cure had not been found and the disease was considered an ominous threat, twenty years later at Penn State the story was still among the best-known legends, although more students reported the Internet rather than another student as a source for their information. Discussing the story with the classes, I found that women often believe a revenge factor is present. AIDS Mary is getting back at men for infecting her, or the sexual injustice or power imbalance she feels. Some of the beliefs given in response to the legend follow from this interpretation. One frequently reported message from women was that a fraternity held a blood drive, and most of the frat donors tested HIV positive (see Ellis and Mays 1992). Another was the view that fraternities had the highest rape rates on campus. Men tend to view the legend as a warning about anonymous sex, or perhaps the lure of attractive women over which they have no control. Some report that women have the upper hand in relationships. In a variation told by women, the man rapes the woman, sometimes on the first date, only to discover the scary message (Brunvand 1989, 195–202; Fine 1987). The discussion of AIDS Mary draws attention to the theme of a deathly scare found in many cautionary legends, but in addition, it sets sexual practices against the background of gender power and the assumption of a free atmosphere for sex on campus.

Subsequently, a male counterpart of the AIDS Mary story made the rounds (dubbed AIDS John or AIDS Harry by some folklorists) (Brunvand 1999, 133–34). The setting is often a spring break vacation where a college woman meets a man described as kind and good-looking. They get to know each other and engage in sex. As the moment nears for her to return to school, he gives her a gift and instructs her not to open it until she gets back. She is emotionally touched by this classy move, but later becomes impatient or suspicious. On the plane she opens the package and discovers a tiny coffin, sometimes a dead rose, with a note saying "Welcome to the world of AIDS." Appearances are deceiving, the legend suggests, especially in a sexually active society. Another story concerns a woman attracted to a handsome fellow in a dark bar. She takes him home, and to her horror in the morning light she discovers AIDS-related sores on his face. The story has the signs of a cautionary tale for women, especially in light of acceptance of the sexual aggressiveness of women related in the narrative.

The newly found power of women appears in a cycle of stories concerning feminine revenge against rape. Frances Cattermole-Tally has recorded several legends about women who attack a man with a dildo, so that he feels the pain of rape. In one variant, several women surround the macho man, and he is at first delighted by the prospect of sex until they hold him down and attack him. Tellers explain the inattention to the attack in the media by reporting that he was too ashamed to report the event to the police. In a campus version, sorority sisters attack a frat rat accused of getting women drunk and taking advantage of them. The man at first laughs at them, but soon cries for mercy as the attack begins. The sisters throw the dildo weapon into the fraternity house as a warning. In some versions, a female hero strolls through dangerous areas and invites trouble. She cuts down would-be rapists with martial arts and violates them with the dildo. In Chicago, the story is told that the female heroine "Amazalia, aged nineteen," during periods of the full moon "would go to Hyde Park at midnight and stroll around." She is "still at large," tellers report, because "her male victims are too embarrassed to press charges" (Cattermole-Tally 1990, 45).

AIDS shows up in a contamination legend that I first heard in 1993 at Penn State. The story brings up a legendary student obsession—pizza. Supposedly, a pizza delivery man infected with AIDS ejaculated on a pizza delivered to students. In many accounts, students describe a revenge motive, or a suggestion that they are being punished for their sexual appetite. The target of the pizza has significance, not only because of student fondness for the saucy food but also because it is communally shared, gleefully grabbed with the hands, and generally associated with the intimate informality of eating at home. It suggests epidemic proportions and sexual overtones. In the story, students worry because the food tastes bad or someone gets sick. Sometimes a tag to the story is given as "the pizza was analyzed at a local hospital or that the delivery man was arrested." There is a hint, too, that the "kind of people who work at the place" become suspect, suggesting some assumptions of class difference or corporate negligence. One student newspaper trying to disclaim the story went to great lengths to assure students that the pizza deliverers were often students themselves, and the establishment was locally owned (King 1993; Tucker 2005, 103–4).

The pizza contamination rumor, to this day unsubstantiated, circulated so widely that many student newspapers reported drop-offs in pizza delivery business for a while (King 1993). It followed a cycle of rumors about tainted mayonnaise on hamburgers bought at a fast-food franchise (Brunvand 1999, 199–200; 2001, 252; Goldstein 2004, 41–43). The burger contamination rumor might have drawn on newspaper coverage during the 1980s of a case of typhoid fever in suburban Maryland traced to an immigrant worker at McDonald's, dubbed Typhoid McMary by the press, who had removed plastic gloves when mixing vegetables (Kraut 1994, 97). According to rumors, a fast-food worker with AIDS sought revenge by ejaculating in a jar of mayonnaise; the tainted mayo then gets passed to customers on hamburgers (Langlois 1991). The narrative is one of many examples of contamination legends told by consumers about fast-food chains, such as the batter-fried rat or worms in the fast-food burger, maybe because of the unnaturalness connected to a mass cultural phenomenon of corporate preparation and mass consumption of fast food (Brunvand 2001, 90–91; Fine 1992). A related campus narrative ties the product to feces, indicating that digesting it is foul: "In the cafeteria at my school [James Madison University], someone ate a burger that had so much Ex-Lax in it that they were in their room, on the toilet for two days. When he finally came out of his room, his roommate and suitemates had gone to sleep in their other friends' rooms and everyone on the floor had hung air fresheners outside the door" (Tucker 2005, 104–5). In this version, the student is the unwary victim, whereas in occupational lore, the insertion of laxative by fast-food workers is retribution against difficult customers. In one "conversation" I recorded, a report of a delivered pizza contaminated with semen was followed by the following exchange among the students: "I used to know a guy from Burger King who would spit on burgers of people that pissed him off in the drive thru. . . . I knew some people at Domino's that would do that . . .

HAHA . . . HEH!" Folklorist Jan Brunvand additionally mentioned in 1984 an "urban legend" about an employee of a doughnut chain who masturbated into the batter (1984, 121). The doughnuts fit into the pattern of foods narrated for representations of stimulating, high-fat foods favored by stressed students.

Added twists in the AIDS contamination legends are the revenge and invisibility of the virus, although a rumor documented since the 1980s about invisible traces of LSD placed in paper tattoos popular among children invites comparison of these themes (Brunvand 1989, 55–64; Emery 2010c; Renard 1991). There might be a connection to rumors reported in England where semen is detected by customers in curry or yogurt sauce served in Indian or Chinese restaurants. In versions from Europe reported online, the semen (often provided by STD-infected men) is revenge by the establishment on customers complaining about service or food quality ("Secret Sauce" 2007). Folklorists typically interpret the beliefs as reflecting distrust of ethnic minorities associated with supposedly exotic cuisines (Brunvand 2001, 70–71). Do American contamination legends, then, speak to a fear of items made too fast and on a massive scale, or consumed too voraciously? To be sure, a number of American contamination legends, even some recent rumors about Vietnamese restaurants, refer to ethnic prejudice, but the AIDS cycle may very well be a variant that is especially concerned with the vulnerability of the healthy population (particularly sexually active youth) to the deadly virus, especially in a society aware of deadly drug tampering and terrorism.

The Gay Roommate

Many of the AIDS legends circulating on campus refer to the fear of contracting the disease through heterosexual activity because the angst expressed is that practices that had been considered par for the (inter)course had suddenly become dangerous. Activism for AIDS awareness and public discourse about equal rights for gays during the period increased discussion of homosexuality, and homophobia, on campus. Judging from campus legends, anxiety was at work particularly among men. One such legend that began drawing notice in the 1990s and that has gained new life on the Internet in the twenty-first century has been labeled the "Gay Roommate" or the "Chloroformed Roommate" (Brunvand 1999, 431–32; Green 2006, 204–5; Whatley and Henken 2000, 95–99). In most versions, a male student goes to a doctor or student health center to complain of headaches, nausea, or soreness in the rectal area, or a combination of these. The narrator of the story might relate that the student figures that his trouble is a case of hemorrhoids. The student is surprised as well as outraged when the doctor insists that his problem is caused by anal sex.

Returning to the room, the student searches his roommate's possessions and finds a bottle of ether or chloroform. Sometimes the student takes the doctor back to the room, and the doctor discovers the knockout drug. The implication is that the sleeping student had been an unwilling sexual partner for his roommate.

Folklorist Jan Harold Brunvand collected variations such as traces of ether or chloroform discovered in the student's blood, often with the insinuation that the student had been infected with AIDS. Brunvand pointed out that the campus legend had connections to stories reported as far away as Australia and as long ago as 1886 about men who return with a sore rear end from a party where liquor was flowing freely (Brunvand 1993, 310). This reference may explain one online remark that students sometimes faked evidence of homosexual activity as a prank on a passed-out, drunk roommate. Some commentators piped in with examples dating back some years about drugged seduction among soldiers and dentists (Ellis 1990). The story may also have been influenced by a campus cautionary tale about a woman who wakes up in a fraternity house after a party and discovers that she had been gang raped after having had a drug slipped into her drink (Greenberg 1973). The stories suggest a fear of rape (as signs of violence in a sexually open society and individual vulnerability among hostile strangers), and in the case of the masculine version, discomfort with the intimacy (or sexual tension) of a male roommate in close quarters.

The setting of the university is significant because of the uncertainty about the background of roommates. Little is known about roommates in the modern setting, and this adds to the mystery in the narrative. Gershon Legman recounts a cognate in what he called the "well-known joke" set in another institutional setting putting strangers together—a hotel. In his story recorded in the 1930s, a homosexual guest violates an oblivious bellboy plied with champagne (Legman 1975, 156). As in the postmodern college game of "Assassin" reported earlier in this book, the individual in the "gay roommate" story must be on the lookout for hidden dangers from anyone, even those supposedly close to him. In folklore, the university appears less socially predictable than the old-time college.

The ambiguity of roommate selection is apparent in a popular email text reported by folklorist Thomas Green in 2006:

Recently I had a conversation with my resident advisor who told me about a guy a friend of his knew here at aTm [Texas A&M]. Apparently this guy had gotten a potluck roommate who was nice but more or less kept to himself. The guy would awake morning after morning to find his rectum sore and red. This problem persisted so he saw a doctor about it. Well the doctor said he had a torn sphincter, which is typical of anal intercourse. The man remarked that he was not gay, and therefore this could not be the cause. He returned home and went to bed puzzled, thinking about what the doctor told him the entire time. As the hours rolled by he was still awake, though laying as asleep, when he noticed his roommate get up and fool with something on his desk drawer. His roommate then casually approached him and attempted to cover his nose and mouth with something. Apparently his roommate had been putting chloroform on a handkerchief and incapacitating him, and then having anal intercourse with him. This story was told to me not as a joke, but as true . . . really. (2006, 4:204–5)

The reference to the "potluck roommate" sets up the scenario whereby the heterosexual protagonist is unaware of the sexual orientation of the roommate—or much else about him. A tip-off of trouble that runs through several campus legend types is the incriminating trait of not being sociable. The story emphasizes, though, that the protagonist did not suspect a problem with the roommate. He was like "anyone else," but the story eventually shows him homophobically to be an "other" with a dirty secret. In some versions, the ether and Vaseline are above board, on top of a dresser, but they do not arouse suspicion because the student is an "entomology" major (Whatley and Henken 2000, 95–96). Nonetheless, the message is that homosexuality, like the products under the bed, is hidden, and as a result of the apparent sexual frustration, the gay roommate resorts to aggressive subterfuge to be sexually satisfied. Folklorists have mainly referred to the story's homophobia by pointing out that the narrative plays upon heterosexual male fear of being anally penetrated as a submissive receiver (Whatley and Henken 2000, 98).

A historical aspect is the challenged heteronormative manliness in the emergence of the fashionable, cosmopolitan sexually ambiguous "metrosexual" as background for the urgency of the story (Bronner 2005, 37–38; Miller 2005). The object of the gay roommate's advances has to swear, often repeatedly, that he is not homosexual, because others assume that he, as the representative college man in the feminized college space of the campus, has engaged in homosexual activity or at least harbors the possibility of being gay. In some versions, the attending doctor, concluding that the patient is homosexual or bisexual, matter-of-factly suggests to the protagonist, "This is easy to cure. The rash is from the condoms you're using; just change condoms." But the young man insists "No, it can't be; I'm not gay." Often a repeat of the visit is included in the narrative: "So he goes away, and the rash gets worse and he goes back to the doctor, who says, 'I told you, just change your brand of condom.' And the guy still says, 'I'm not gay.' Then he's back in his room, and looking in his roommate's drawers for something, and this box of condoms rolls out" (Whatley and

Fig. 9.1. The 32.7-foot-tall obelisk (also known as the polylith) was erected on the front campus of Penn State–University Park in 1896. More students know the virgin-test legend about it than its original purpose as a geologic column showing the diversity of Pennsylvania stones. (Photo by Simon Bronner)

Henken 2000, 97–98). As the narrative ends there, it may invite comment on the ruse by which the protagonist has become a sexual object and "feminized," and further, how he has become attractive to another male, bringing his heterosexual domination and manly identity from the real world to the campus into question. The story suggests that homosexuality is closer by, and probably more internalized, than previously imagined.

Virgin Tests

Outside the theater and dorm, students are likely to rehearse explanations attached to the many towers, statues, and columns that typically dot campuses. They are not likely to reiterate the stately official meanings of these proud structures, however. They have their lighthearted accounting for these intrusions on the landscape. The structures stand so rigidly because they are monuments to the sexy student body. In the unlikely event that a virgin graduates, or walks by the structure, students hyperbolize, bizarre events ensue. At the Universities of Missouri, Michigan, and Cincinnati, stone lions roar. The statue

Fig. 9.2. On the Rutgers–New Brunswick campus, the statue of William I, Prince of Orange, known widely as William the Silent, starts talking, according to legend, if a virgin graduates. (Wikimedia)

of the seated Pioneer Mother at the University of Oregon and of the seated Lincoln at the University of Illinois stand, while at Michigan State the figure of the standing Spartan and the alma mater statue at the University of Illinois–Urbana sit. At Upper Iowa, the sculpture of the Green Goddess bows; at Duke, the venerated monument of James Duke tips his hat. At Cornell, the icons of Andrew D. White and Ezra Cornell leave their pedestals and shake hands; the quizzical sight of footprints between the statues annually painted in the university's colors of red and white fuels retellings of the belief (Tucker 2007, 28). At the University of North Carolina–Chapel Hill, a statue of a soldier known as "Silent Sam" fires his musket (he is "silent" according to legend because a virgin has never graduated). At Rutgers, Willie the Silent (also called "Still Bill" for the Prince of Orange, national hero of the Netherlands) starts talking if a virgin passes. Statues of Italian patriot Giuseppe Garibaldi at New York University and Civil War soldier George Morgan Jones at Randolph-Macon College draw their swords. At Tarleton State University and Southern Illinois University at Carbondale, an honored cannon fires. At the University of Nebraska, classical columns crumble, and at Penn State, a proud obelisk falls. At Binghamton University, the sculpture of Pegasus, a campus symbol, flies off its perch atop the entrance to the Fine Arts Building. At the University of Arkansas, Old Main collapses. At Indiana University and Bucknell University, tower bells ring for all to hear (Mikkelson 2007b).

Students put one another to the test. They jokingly dare friends to walk by the all-knowing structure to see if it stays still—and, of course, it does, confirming the teen's badge of honor: awakened sexuality. The very symbols used on college campuses to mark their proud intellectual heritage are converted in student lore into sexual monuments. In a kind of parody play, students thus imply that the school really belongs to them, or that beneath the stiff intellectual exterior sex is the primary preoccupation.

Yet despite this general interpretation, the fact remains that the virgin test is most often directed at women. Most of the venerated statuary are phallic—cannons, obelisks, towers, and columns. Instead of staying rock hard and secure, the objects collapse and move when a virgin, associated with feminine virtue, graduates. Especially during the turbulent 1960s, the accounting of the statuary was accompanied by legends of the "one remaining virgin," usually a woman. At Knox College, for example, when the last virgin walked by the statue of a wounded soldier, it "would rise up and chase her out to the outlying cornfield to personally alleviate this condition," according to an interview in the Berkeley Folklore Archives. Another report notes that at Southern Illinois University, "it is said on campus that each time the cannon has been mysteriously painted during the night another unwise girl has succumbed to masculine persuasion and has lost her virginity." The outline of green hands above a former women's dorm at the University of California at Berkeley is sometimes explained with the tall tale that the campanile (the "campus phallic symbol," according to student accounts) wandered over to the dorm looking for sex.

Folklorist Barre Toelken points out that these accounts are "a revealing expression of male concerns over the rapidly developing status of women at universities for the 1940s onward. The movement of women into domains previously thought of as male and rapid changes in women's habits (smoking, drinking, voting) have often brought out charges that sexual promiscuity was also somehow involved" (Toelken 1986, 522). Relating tongue-in-cheek stories of collapsing columns and shooting cannons also establishes campus as a zone of social freedom rather than constraint. The campus operates by its own rules and laws of nature, virgin test narratives imply, and if one is skeptical, campus inhabitants can be shown to be "put to the test."

Charmed Spots for Romance

To emphasize the importance of courtship on campus, students also point to spots inspiring romance. Indiana University (IU) and Franklin College have well houses that have long been used for the purpose. "I heard that if you're sitting in the Well House," one IU student said, "and you're not doing anything romantic, the fountain will gurgle." Most often reported, however, is that "a girl isn't a coed until she's been kissed by an upperclassman in the Well House for the full twelve strokes of midnight" (Waymire 1978, 1–2). The twelve strokes of midnight also come up in stories of kissing the person one wants to marry in the chapel for his or her "dream to come true" (McDowell 2008).

At Michigan State back in the 1940s, Richard Dorson reported that "a girl becomes a coed when kissed in the shadow of Beaumont Tower at the stroke of midnight" (1949, 674). At the University of Michigan as late as the 1960s, coeds became "official" when they had been kissed under the arch in the engineering building (Cannon 1984, 42). At Eastern Michigan, the ritual kiss occurred under the lamp posts on the college mall. Cedar Crest women had "Wishing Steps" behind what was once the president's home. Some students claimed that wishes came true if the man and woman each counted the steps silently and arrived at the same number before sealing the wish with a kiss.

The University of Arkansas has a "Spoofer's Stone" where couples met. This piece of limestone was left next to Old Main after its construction in 1872. When campus rules early in the century prohibited "all intercourse between boys and girls," the stone proved useful for the leaving of love notes on the sly. Later it evolved into a favorite resting spot reserved for upperclass couples (Wylie 1933, 192–96). Oregon State also has a rock, of marble, a gift from the class of 1901 placed under what was known as the "Trysting Tree." Grove City College has several "sweetheart trees" on campus where couples left their mark by initialing the tree with a pocketknife (Gray 1969–70). Bethany College has "Centenna Stones" in the center of campus marking the spot where the first college building stood. According to tradition, relationships are ready to commence when the couple has kissed while standing atop the stones.

Other spots invite communing with nature. Western Oregon University has its "Cupid's Knoll" and Northern Colorado its "Inspiration Point." Loving students at Juniata College go to the "Cliffs," a high rocky area overlooking the Juniata River. At the College of William and Mary couples kiss on the bridge over Crim Dell Lake. (Some say this is a sign of future marriage—unless the woman throws the man into the lake.) Rutgers, in New Brunswick, New Jersey, still has a pond romantically minded students fondly call the "Passion Puddle." Located on the border between Cook Campus and Douglass College (Rutgers's residential women's institution), the lush, fertile area around the puddle represents a geographic meeting point for men and women. The romantic associations of the area come out in a legend that if a man from Cook and a woman from Douglass hold hands and walk around the pond a magical three times, they will soon be engaged. These spots inspire the kind of sentimentality typical before the days of coed dorms.

With segregation of sexes and visitation rules in dorms largely dropped during the 1960s, the romantic rendezvous was more likely to occur indoors. The coed dorm has relaxed sexual prohibitions, but arguably has also improved attitudes between the sexes. As Michael Moffatt concluded after being a participant observer of a Rutgers dorm, men in coeducational situations tend to treat women less as sexual objects, and to build intellectual and social friendships (1989, 45–49, 181–86). Indeed, Moffatt reports that "the sexual ambience of the coed dorm floors—the conventions of the mixed-sex groups in the lounges—was in curious ways more like older American erotic sensibilities than one had any reason to expect" (1989, 182).

Using traditional signals, students show that sex is still a private affair. One might still encounter a white towel used by women or a tie used by men on the doorknob to urge a roommate to stay out. For the less formal, a sock around the doorknob gets the message across. On a Saturday night especially, it is customary to knock three times before walking in on your roommate, or alert the most blurry-eyed roommates to pay attention to the hotel "do not disturb" sign left on the dorm door.

Courtship Codes

Engagement customs that fell out of favor after the sexual revolution of the 1960s made comebacks in the twenty-first century as rituals to mark a special state, especially if one's college buddies cannot attend the wedding (Potter 2008). Most common are women's "candle-lighting" or "ringing" ceremonies. From Bryn Mawr comes this account: "The women sit in a circle and pass a lighted candle from hand to hand. The candle is usually decorated with flowers and ribbons, with the engagement ring attached in some way. After a number of complete circles around the group, the engaged woman blows the candle out and then receives congratulations from the other women" (Briscoe 1981a, 11).

At many colleges, candle-lighting belongs to the tradition of sorority life. Typically the identity of the engaged woman is a secret until she blows out the candle. Usually only the best friend, housemother, or chapter president of the engaged sister knows, and she summons the others to the candlelight. In many sorority ceremonies, each pass of the candle, often to the accompaniment of a sweetheart song, represented the progression of a relationship; one time was for laveliering, twice for pinning, and three times for engagement (see Cochran 1981; Egan 1985, 131; Glavan 1968, 193–94; Hale 1968, 274; McDowell 2008; Preston 1973, 271–74; Toelken 1986, 515–16). Some houses add a pass of the candle for friendship and have their own songs, such as these collected at Birmingham-Southern.

Alpha Omicron Pi
There's a longing in the heart of each AOII for the man that lives in her dreams
Someone to share all her sorrows and cares, just a regular fellow it seems
For the red and white colors are the ones he loves so
They'll bring him to me, someday I know
For I love him so and for him I would die
He's the sweetheart of an AOII!

Zeta Tau Alpha
Deep in the heart of each Zeta there's a man who fills her dreams
One who is true to the grey and blue
He's the one for her, it seems
To him, the girl with the crown and shield is the best he'll always say
He loves her more than all the rest
Oh, how I wish he were with me tonight, for he's my Zeta sweetheart. (Wenke 2010)

As described by Christie Wenke at the college, candle lighting involves the women forming a circle in the campus amphitheater, taking each other's hands, and singing as they pass a single candle around the circle. As the candle makes it around the circle for a fourth time, representing a quantity considered as the years it takes to graduate an abundant amount, the newly engaged sister blows out the candle. Elsewhere on campus, the folklore collector reported, fraternity members tie the engaged brother to a tree and in a scatological rite of smearing douse him with chocolate or molasses. This marks a change, she notes, from the old days of baptizing him into his new engaged status by throwing him into the campus fountain (Wenke 2010). The contrast in ritual represents the view that women embrace the union while men consider matrimony as an end to individual freedom (Scott 1965). Nonetheless, the more elaborate preparations for the woman also suggest that she takes more of a risk and needs sisterly support, including a later bridal shower. As in ritual celebrations outside of campus, men will hold a stag bachelor party, but brides-to-be since the 1980s have increasingly enjoyed a rip-roaring time of their own known as the bachelorette bash (Williams 1994).

On some campuses, bells announce an engagement. Wheaton College in Illinois has an elaborate bell-ringing custom. Atop Old Main sits a tower bell once used to summon students to chapel. Today, when a couple get engaged, they gather their friends around, and the group climbs five floors of rickety stairs, through the attic, into a small area with a ladder up to the bell. Tradition calls for the couple to ring the bell three rounds of seven times for good luck. While the couple rings the bell, their friends paint their names wherever they can find a spot on the ancient wood. Some couples hang their pictures or other mementos from the rafters.

Both engaged men and women frequently have a forced shower or ponding to look forward to. Often the shower occurs for women after the candle-lighting ceremony, if one is held. In a sign of community, women might also dump an engaged sister in a bathtub full of perfume donated by everyone in the house (Hunter 1977, 25–26). Men, when they are dumped, are likely to emerge with a less flowery odor. Typically a lake is chosen for the ritual event. At Union College, an engaged man's cronies kidnap him during the night and dump him in Holmes Lake near campus. They forcibly remove his pants, and if the engaged man goes in the lake alone, he will get them back before returning to campus. If he manages to pull in someone with him, that person has to walk back to the college with the engaged man.

At campuses with a strong Greek life, the exchange of fraternity pins was an event just a notch below engagement. It was celebrated as engagements are with a good dumping or a "swirlie." In the swirlie, the poor fellow's head was held down into a flushed toilet. Afterward, according to one witness, "you run like hell, because he's going to come and get you" (T. 1976, 5). Pinned brothers could also face a "poling": "Six or eight guys will grab him at dinner, usually the pledges, and haul him outside, tie his feet together, hang him up in the tree upside down and throw garbage on him and leave him hang there for about an hour" (T. 1976, 18). At West Virginia Wesleyan, the pinned brother or sister might be tied to a statue of John Wesley and have food and mud hurled at him or her. In a variation, a fraternity brother pinned to a Delta Gamma was stripped and tied to the sorority's large anchor on the front yard. His brothers pelted him with food or dumped water on him, until the pinned sister came out and kissed him. In the meantime, some of the sisters also got into the act by photographing him and rating his attractiveness (Birnbach 1984, 112; Egan 1985, 133).

Indications are that these kinds of courtship customs have declined or gone underground with campus crackdowns on hazing. Some surveys also regard candle-lighting as old-fashioned and overly sentimental, more in keeping with the communal old-time college (Wenke 2010). Nonetheless, celebration of the student's change of status from single brother or sister to a new family, particularly in the already liminal status of the college campus, frequently demands ritualization.

Many colleges emphasize romance in the campus air by facilitating weddings and commitment ceremonies in campus buildings. Beck Chapel in the heart of the Indiana University campus, where couples also believe that their matrimony is foretold with a kiss during courtship, hosts many student weddings. Texas Woman's University is proud of its "Little Chapel-in-the-Woods" as a wedding venue. The story is told that 300 students and faculty members helped build the chapel in 1939, and the building was dedicated by Eleanor Roosevelt after its first wedding was held there. A prized possession of the university related to the chapel was the "Bride's Book," which recorded every marriage from 1939 to 1979, when it filled up. A new Bride's Book was unveiled during Homecoming on April 10, 2003. The university enshrined the old one in its Balgg-Huey Library (Haynes 2009). The Cadet Chapel at West Point is famous for providing military honors, in the form of a ceremonial saber arch, rendered at the conclusion of the service. The University of Nevada at Las Vegas, in case you are wondering, does not have an Elvis-styled wedding chapel, but it does host weddings at the Stan Fulton Building on campus. Fairfield University students since 1996 have enacted a mock wedding every spring involving bachelor and bachelorette parties, a love boat cruise, hilarious exchanges of vows by brides and grooms, and a full-blown reception with a wedding cake. The intoxicating event has become a separation ritual for seniors who come dressed as either brides or grooms (Caso 2009).

Digestive Rumors

Wondering about the college's efforts to control students' courtship activities, rumors circulate every once in a while that the administration slyly had the dining hall food saltpetered, particularly on Fridays. Students speculate that the reason the practice has not been uncovered is that deans intercepted a sample sent to a lab by enterprising undergraduates (Hunter 1977, 131). The rumors may have sources in military lore, which veterans spread about doctored food in repressive training camps (Mikkelson 2007a; Rich and Jacobs 1973; Wyman 1979, 88; cf. Hand et al. 1981, 552).

As soldiers had their jocular names for institutional food, students also refer to the strange, odorous wonders of dining-hall cooking as "griddle pucks" (hamburgers), "garbage barges" (tuna boat sandwiches), "mystery meat"

(UFO—unidentifiable food object), and "shit on a shingle" (in soldier slang referring to chipped beef on toast and in student argot generalized to a number of dishes, including sloppy joes and various stews). Referring to scatological and sexual rhetoric, students complain that cafeteria food "stinks" and "sucks." Many food names carry castration references: "Pigmy dicks" (miniature carrots), "monkey dicks" (link sausages), and "horse cock" (ring bologna) (Egan 1985, 129; Aman 1984–85, 284). Further adding to the image of victimized students' plight, rumors regularly fly about fingers, worms, and insects in the food, and mice and cigarette butts in soda cans (Brunvand 2001, 90–91; Domowitz 1979; Fine 1979; Wyman 1979, 88). Convinced that college dining halls reduce the chance of food poisoning by limiting the time that the meal is in the body (or alternatively to avoid bloating and weight gain, especially during the period of the fabled "freshman 15 [or 20]" pounds gained after arrival on campus), students spread the belief that dining hall staff mix laxatives into the food they serve (Mikkelson 2009). Barbara Mikkelson's investigation concluded that the rumors were false, but she rationalized the belief's association with campus life because "the balanced and regularly spaced meals enjoyed at home give way to a constant eating binge wherein junk foods are especially favored. Since junk foods are generally high in fat content, and fat does have somewhat of a laxative effect, it's no wonder those indulging in unfettered gluttony find themselves blasting the seat off the toilet" (2009). In this psychology, a process of externalization is evident, drawing blame away from oneself and redirecting it to the institution. Another cognitive effect may be at work by which expectations that the food "tastes like shit," especially with the institution hardly measuring up to the comfort of home and the parental provider, become projected into narratives containing a symbolic equivalence of food and feces.

If students complain that the dished-out food acts as a sexual depressant, they may counteract the effect with items believed to act as aphrodisiacs. One still hears about oysters, radishes, hard-boiled eggs, bananas, yeast, chocolates, and peppers stimulating sexual passion (Cannon 1984, 157; Hand et al. 1981, 551). A whole series of aphrodisiacs known for some time are green because of a symbolic association with fertility: olives, celery, asparagus, and avocado (Hand et al. 1981, 550). That might explain the modern rage for the media-promoted aphrodisiac of green M&Ms (Brunvand 1986, 111–13; 2001, 178–79). True, you do not get too many green ones in a pack filled with brown, yellow, and orange bits, and the few green gems (usually ten or fewer out of fifty-seven), and sometimes the red ones, are treasured by college students to induce sexual desire (Clarke 1987). Mars, the manufacturers of the candies, played up the belief by running an advertising campaign in the early twenty-first century portraying M&M "spokescandies," including a seductive female green character sitting on a lip-shaped couch.

One detects a modern imaging of pills for mood alteration in this association of M&Ms as aphrodisiacs. Most college women are aware of medical birth control pills and devices, but have reportedly added to their contraception or anaphrodisiac measures by eating grated nutmeg and parsley, and douching after intercourse with cola, lemon juice and water, and vinegar (Fish 1972). My students doubted that these practices continue into the twenty-first century with sex education widely available, but they offered observations that tight jeans cause impotence in men (it is true that sperm count can decrease) and that pregnancy is unlikely to occur in a hot tub (immersion is not going to decrease sperm count but repeated exposures over time might) (Whatley and Henken 2000, 36–37). Women also share folk "remedies" for debilitating cramps such as drinking cranberry juice, ginger tea, and dill pickle juice, and avoiding chocolate and carbonated beverages (see Whatley and Henken 2000, 45–46).

Although conception is to be avoided, appearing "sexy" is usually an admired trait. Convinced that looking pencil-thin makes one sexually attractive, women tell one another about "wonder" diets, using magical formulas of three or seven in structuring diets or relying on the fabled "calorie-burning" effects of grapefruit (Brunvand 1986, 186–90; 2001, 121; Dundes and Pagter 1991, 54–56; Smith 1986, 88; Tucker 1978, 142–43). Perhaps making a feminist comment on the sexual implications of this dieting craze, the riddle-joke "What would women be without men?" is answered by "fat and happy." The obsession with magical diets is also ridiculed in humor about the "30-day reducing diet" (one part Metracal, one part Ex-Lax, one part Spanish fly, one part bourbon/scotch). The result, according to the sheet, is that "you will be the skinniest, sexiest, shittiest alcoholic in the world" (D'Pnymph 1988, 301; Dundes and Pagter 1987, 236; Legman 1995, 361).

Sexual passion is not always desirable in college lore. College women may hear a cautionary tale about a drugging that results in unwanted seduction. In these stories, an underclass woman, usually a first-year student, goes on a blind date with a fraternity brother to a party at his house. During the course of the evening, the boy slips a drug into the woman's drink, which causes her to lose consciousness. In some versions, she wakes up just as he is molesting her.

In other warning narratives, the victimized woman wakes up the next morning and finds her clothes are gone. The teller speculates that she was raped or frighteningly did not know what happened to her. Folklorist Andrea Greenberg observed that the legend is a response to the tension of the coed arriving on campus on her own. She has a newfound freedom to experiment sexually, but she often feels, even more strongly than men do, parental disapproval. "The opposition," she points out, "is resolved by a forced sexual experience which places all responsibility for the sexual act on the male, who then becomes a surrogate for past parental responsibility. In this way, the girl achieves both goals: sexual experience plus irresponsibility" (Greenberg 1973, 134). The story is a warning for women to maintain control, particularly as women are believed to be more susceptible to the effects of alcohol than men. In addition, the legend reminds women that although they may be flattered by many social invitations in college, they may indeed be treated as sexual objects (or "hit on," in student lingo), especially, narratives suggest, in male domains such as fraternities.

As with other campus cautionary tales, anxiety is expressed about the actions of strangers with malign intent, especially in the twenty-first century with the popular designation of crimes related to the use of the drug Rohypnol (the commercial name for flunitrazepam) known by the folk term "roofie rape" (Burgess, Donovan, and Moore 2009, 849; Greenberg 2010, 3:582). Criminological surveys find that "there is no evidence of widespread use of flunitrazepam in sexual assault. Alcohol remains the substance most frequently associated with this type of crime" (Hindmarch and Brinkmann 1999, 225; see also Burgess, Donovan, and Moore 2009, 849). Despite the conclusion, American students denied in interviews the influence of alcohol on date-rape crimes (Burgess, Donovan, and Moore 2009, 855). Convinced that drinks are widely spiked with date-rape drugs, women clearly changed their behavior, affected by what a national police official called an "urban legend" (Burgess, Donovan, and Moore 2009, 849). A survey of women in their late teens and early twenties found that 77 percent held their drinks even when they went to the bathroom. Only 8 percent admitted that they "leave their drink on the table and hope that no-one touches it" (Burgess, Donovan, and Moore 2009, 849). Although fellow students were sources of advice such as "not letting anyone buy you a drink," respondents reported receiving their most frequent warnings, often embedded in narratives, from mothers and grandmothers. Students shared with one another personally experienced "bad-night-out episodes," including loss of memory, blackouts, sickness, and dizziness, which they narrated as owing to tampering of drinks rather than the quantity of alcohol consumed (Burgess, Donovan, and Moore 2009, 858–60).

Another narrative cycle making the rounds of social networking sites about date-drug rape concerns a supposedly new drug called Progesterex. Tapping into the widespread belief in drink spiking, students forward email messages to one another warning that the drug created for animals would surely be the next big thing on campuses. Here is a sample email text:

> There is a new drug that has been out for less than a year, Progesterex, that is essentially a small sterilization pill. The drug is now being used by rapists at parties to rape AND sterilize their victims. My best friend's mom works

at a pharmacy and she said the drug is available exclusively to veterinarians to sterilize large animals. But I have heard from several of my friends that are still in grad school up north that at frat parties at their schools (Columbia and Penn State) the drug is being used with Rohypnol (roofies), the date rape drug. With Rohypnol, all they have to do is drop it into their drink. The girl can't remember a thing the next morning of what happened the night before. Well now Rohypnol is not being used alone. Progesterex, which dissolves in drinks (alcohol or soda) just as easily, is being used with it so that the woman doesn't conceive from the rape and the rapist doesn't have to worry about having a paternity test identifying him months later. But the drug's effects AREN'T TEMPORARY. Progesterex was designed to sterilize horses. Any woman that takes it WILL NOT HAVE CHILDREN EVER IN HER LIFE. All guys have to do to get their drug is just know someone, like a friend, who is in the Vet school of any university. It's that easy, and Progesterex is about to break out big on campuses everywhere. . . . Please! Forward this to everyone you know, especially girls who might be headed to college or live in college towns. ("Progesterex and Cons" 2007)

The information in the email also figures in later narratives reported about a woman gang-raped (usually the figure is five men) at a nightclub or bar and dumped in a secluded spot (usually a bay). The epilogue involves a blood test on the victim showing use of Progesterex intended to sterilize her. If the story is passed along online, there might be a tagline, "Boyfriends and girlfriends, take heed. Good guys out there, please forward this message to your lady friends" ("Progesterex and Cons" 2007). According to the legend investigation site Snopes.com, the information is pure hoax: "No drug called Progesterex exists, no pill for permanently sterilizing horses or other large animals is used by veterinarians or sold on the market, no campuses have reported any students becoming the victims of sterilization-by-drug" ("Progesterex and Cons" 2007). The assumption in the narrative that rapists will remain anonymous because no child is delivered is also false, because authorities use bodily fluids and scrapings to identify the perpetrator.

Progesterex as a drug name certainly sounds authentic, all the more so because it carries the ring of medical "progress" and the use of "rex," representing the power of a king. The narrative presumes the attraction of college students to drug experimentation and the susceptibility of women on campus to sexual predation. Comparing the story to other historically documented sterilization rumors that carry a conspiratorial tone, one might conclude that coeds as an othered class of people are rhetorically punished in the narrative for their promiscuity and individual freedom. Folklorist Patricia Turner has collected, for example, legends in the 1990s of urban black men unsuspectingly sterilized by eating the very foods that mark their ghettoized state (they were often sold in black neighborhoods)—Church's Fried Chicken and Tropical Fantasy soft drinks (1993, 137–44). The rumors also arose at a time of growing mobility and political power by African Americans. Turner finds that the popularity of these rumors indicate that the African American community perceives itself as vulnerable to the hostile desires of the dominant population, "which, it seems, will stop at nothing to inhibit the growth of the minority population—including the use of polluted food to weaken individual sexual capacity" (1993, 144). If the use of sterilization and violence toward an othered group can constitute a linked symbolic narrative trope not only in African American rumor but also in other victimized groups who are breaking out of a repressive past, then a possible reading of the Progesterex legend is that the key feature of sterilization plays upon the culturally entrenched perception of colleges providing women unprecedented independence (Peril 2006). The culprits to watch out for in the narratives are not women's fellow learners, but representatives of the tradition-centered town or the old patriarchal order (that is, fraternities). For their sexual power in the stories, women are physically dominated and denied maternity.

Other campus legends bear out the use of the ambiguity of truth to comment on women's sexual assertiveness. From Minnesota college men, Gary Alan Fine and Bruce Noel Johnson collected many versions of the "promiscuous cheerleader." The legend tells of a young female cheerleader who has sexual relations (often fellatio) with members of an athletic team (as in the Progesterex legend, five is usually the number of men, probably deriving from the "starting five" players in basketball). She becomes ill, sometimes while cheering at a game, and must be rushed to the hospital. There doctors pump her stomach, removing a miraculous amount of semen (Fine and Johnson 1980, 120–29; see also Beezley 1985, 223). During the 1970s, a period of female assertiveness, Fine and Johnson argue, the legend was both a "warning to sexually aggressive women and the implication that it was perfectly acceptable for members of the team to take advantage of the cheerleader's sexual proposition" (1980, 128). George Hornbein and Kenneth Thigpen recorded a fraternity brother telling a variation of the "promiscuous cheerleader" legend in their documentary film *Salamanders* (1982). Commenting on his fraternity's ritual of swallowing salamanders at an annual party, a ritual replete with sexual symbolism, the brother told of a former member who had an extraordinary capacity for consumption of the amphibian. The heralded member complained of an upset stomach one day, so he went to the hospital. There an x-ray revealed slews of the creatures crawling around in his stomach (cf. legends of rockstars having their stomachs pumped and doctors finding an astounding amount of semen: Fonarow 2006, 732–33; Young 2002, 134–35).

As the "drugged and seduced" legend speaks to the fears women have of their sexuality being abused, the "promiscuous cheerleader" story tells of the fears men have of their sexuality being rejected. In the men's fantasy, the promiscuous cheerleader effectively saves the man from embarrassment about sexual maneuvering by offering herself to him. The cheerleader usually has a clean and wholesome image, and here she seems to yearn for giving pleasure to men, particularly those who adhere to the manly model of strength and dominance. The story thus reinforces the male bonding of the athletic team, which often comes to represent the school itself. Some ambiguity exists, however, in the appropriateness of the activity to the locale. Sometimes the story is offered as a derisive tale about the debauchery of a rival school.

The "promiscuous cheerleader" and "stomach pumped" legends, like other sexually tinged collegiate stories, tell of excess and risk. The main characters in the legend are suspect, because they represent an oversupply of brawn or spirit. With these fulsome attributes, when compared to norms of the run-of-the-mill student, athletes and cheerleaders receive a tense mixture of disapproval and envy through the legend that begs for commentary. Students have doubts about overachievement in social pursuits, much as they do about it in academic performance. Narratives of sex in legend and humor recognize erotic urges characteristic of the college years and also provide caution, and even opprobrium that often redirects attention from the student to the indulgent environment. Campus life is supposed to be intense and excessive, students firmly believe, but they also voice worries about the limits of its hedonistic tendencies and their loss of individual control.

10

GETTING OUT
Graduation

GRADUATION, AFTER FOUR LONG YEARS, IS THE MOMENT STUDENTS have been working, waiting, and suffering for. To freshmen, graduation seems impossibly far away. Adding to this feeling is the timing of completion after four years, rather than three. The length of time in college is not based on an assessment of how long it takes to be learned. Instead, it is ritually based on a cultural association of four with ampleness.

Whereas "three" in American society is a symbol of completion, "four" translates into a specific quantity representing abundance (Brandes 1985; Bronner 2007, 6–8; Dundes 1980, 134–59). Three distinct sizes represent a range—small, medium, and large—but the fourth category that comes to mind is *extra* large, or more than enough. To travel "the four corners of the earth" is to see it all; to "cover all your bases" (four in baseball) is to go all the way from home and back; to win a series in four straight is to make a clean sweep.

"Three" suggests magical power, as in the phrase "third time's a charm," while "four" stresses rational human control, as in the basic building block of a four-sided square or the adage that wisdom comes with figuring out that "two and two make four." Maybe that is why there are normally four passing grades: A, B, C, D, and a 4.0 GPA signals thorough mastery. Four is the number of seasons, after which another cycle begins. Related to the idea of completion of college as a coming-of-age transitional period structured into four stages is Arnold Van Gennep's concept of "rites of passage." He pointed out that such rites in response to life changes typically have three phases of separation, transition, and incorporation, but with the critical transition stage often divided into two parts, one can usually observe four components to cultural passage. Especially during initiation rites between puberty and adulthood, the transition stage comprises two sections of postseparation and preincorporation, both stressing the initiate's state of being at a threshold (Van Gennep 1960, 65–115). The initiate-child symbolically dies during this transition stage and is reborn with a new status as an empowered member of a special community (Eliade 1958; Turner 1967, 93–111). Death and rebirth is symbolized at "commencement" in word and action. The ceremony literally represents a beginning into a new life after symbolically leaving behind the "senior" status of the student's collegiate maturation. That senior status culminates an intellectual and social journey from the first to the fourth year of studies, although many students tell the tale that the tough part is in the first three stages. Reflecting the belief that by the fourth year, students have had "enough," collegians might refer to their culminating senior year as a "waste" or time to "cruise" and prepare for departure.

Moving Up

Ceremonies of transition do not wait for the end of the fourth year. Befitting the symbolism of three as a natural cycle of completion, the recognition of graduating senior status begins at the end of the junior year. A special occasion on many campuses, particularly smaller communal ones, is Moving-Up Day. At Chatham University, Moving-Up Day coincides with closing convocation, in which classes receive the color of the class to which they are moving up. The dramatic climax is when the senior class bestows its color in the form of flowers to the juniors, who then become seniors. At Wells's Moving-Up Day, each of the three underclasses compose songs to sing to the departing class. In a sign of farewell, the seniors sing about their dorms and faculty. At Bryn Mawr, the four classes gather on the administration building steps. Seniors claim the central seats with the other classes in a hollow square around them. After a hearty round of songs about college life, the seniors sing the college's traditional "good-night" song, and then they leave. The juniors move into the revered places held by the seniors (Briscoe 1981a, 239–41). At larger campuses, where moving up is less an honored tradition, students may joke about being on individualized "plans" ranging from five to seven years.

At Huntingdon College, a school with around 1,000 students in Montgomery, Alabama, an elaborate "Oracle Hunt" marks the traditional passing of the senior class title. Near the end of the school year, the seniors direct the juniors in a quest for the oracle. The seniors offer questions, and progressively, as the juniors figure out the answers, they come closer to the treasured item. When found, the oracle can only be touched by the newly elected senior class president. The officer presents the oracle to the outgoing president, who reads the scroll contained in the oracle and confers the senior class title. Intermittently since 1914, Shorter College seniors similarly hid a decorated wooden crook from the juniors, but they did not encourage the juniors to find the stick. They pronounced their superiority by their ability to foil the juniors before they officially handed it over for them to guard as seniors (Gardner 1972, 196–98, 255–57, 322–24, 451–52).

At Vassar's spring convocation, juniors officially become seniors, and the new officers of the student government take office. The day is filled with much festivity as tradition requires juniors to ring the bell on the roof of the Main Building or they will die virgins. The "moving up" of officers is a feature of older Moving-Up Days that has persisted through the change to larger and less unified classes in the old-time college. Sometimes called Class Day, Insignia Day, or Senior Class Day, the event no longer marks peace among the scrapping classes at the behest of the departing seniors (Miller 1966, 396–97; Hall 1968, 68–76; Wyman 1979, 87).

On Class Day at Williams College, seniors plant ivy to leave a permanent mark on campus and test their future fortune in a watch-dropping ritual. The ritual has students looking up as the watch is dropped from the chapel tower onto the concrete below. According to tradition, if the watch breaks, the class will be ensured good luck in the future. On Class Day at most old-time colleges in the past, classes united to honor the departing seniors, but now they might gather in an awards convocation often recognizing achievements in various departments and organizations.

Class Day at Meredith College occurs on the Saturday of a commencement weekend. A distinctive tradition at the private women's college is unveiling the results of the "crook hunt." Each spring the seniors hide a wooden crook representing maturity from the juniors. The juniors, armed with puzzling clues, spend a week searching the campus for the stick, usually unsuccessfully. If the prized item is found, students bring it into Class Day festivities with a black ribbon for mourning. If left undiscovered, the crook is festooned with a ribbon of the senior class colors. The crook hunt dates to 1906 when an instructor presented the stick with a curved handle to the seniors, and the event has been staged annually since 1929 (Meredith College 2010). The tradition emphasizes class identity, and particularly the close relationship of juniors to seniors, because the sophomores have a different status as "little sisters" to the seniors.

A formal convocation frequently occurs during the fall to mark preparations for the graduation year. At convocations such as Sweet Briar's and Cedar Crest's, seniors wear their caps and gowns for the first time, and join faculty and administration in the academic procession. Seniors at Vassar also join the faculty and administrators by wearing their academic robes at fall convocation. Additionally carrying ribboned sticks, the seniors thus announce their separated status to the rest of the college community. The president of the college, the head of the Vassar Student Association, and a special speaker usually chosen from the faculty deliver addresses during the convocation. At Lawrence University, the fall convocation is called Matriculation Day, and the spring one

Fig. 10.1. Commencement procession through the old campus at Yale University, 1934. Class Day is observed the day before. (Author's collection)

is designated as Honors Day. At Hood, the fall convocation is followed by a "balloon launch" to signify the students' upward aspiration.

The official countdown to graduation often begins 100 days before commencement (multiplying two officious numerations of ten). At Wells, seniors celebrate the first of "One Hundred Days" by wearing caps and gowns and sharing a champagne breakfast together in the dining hall. The first-year women create a special calendar for the seniors counting down each day until graduation. Each day the calendar requires the seniors to do or wear something unusual, such as wearing their clothing inside out or wearing brightly colored lipstick. At Keuka, juniors ring the tower bell 100 times in honor of the seniors. At Notre Dame of Maryland University, "100 Nights" is the occasion for a special dinner followed by awards given by students to one another and a slide show meant to evoke laughter and some tears.

Yale University holds its Class Day the day before commencement. In a tradition traced back to the 1860s, seniors pull out clay pipes. The custom is for students to fill the pipes with tobacco, take a few puffs, and then trample on their pipes as sign that the pleasures of college life are over. Afterward, they sing the alma mater, "Bright College Years," often wrapping their arms around one another and swaying to the music until the last line of the song, "For God, for Country and for Yale," when they raise their arms high in the air to wave good-bye to Yale with white handkerchiefs. Since the late twentieth century, students have added to the tradition by wearing bizarre hats during these customs. To represent the mark left by the students during their stay on campus, Class Day chairpersons usually plant an ivy symbolizing permanence in honor of their class, continuing a tradition begun in 1852, when the first ivy vine was placed near the wall of what is now Dwight Memorial Chapel. An ode is composed for the occasion, which invokes sympathetic magic to connect the growth of the ivy vine with the flourishing of the graduating class (Gonzales 2002).

Ritual use of building steps is honored as a commencement tradition at several notable institutions. Commencement at the University of Notre Dame is the first time a student walks down the front steps of the campus's Main Building. The campus lore is that the tradition of the steps being off limits until commencement originates in nineteenth-century porch etiquette and smoking rituals. Only after successful completion of a degree program was a student deemed worthy to ascend the steps and to smoke on the porch with professors (Schlereth 1991). After commencement, students proudly have their picture taken on the steps.

A similar prohibition exists for students walking through the campanile at the University of Kansas. Students learn early in their campus experience not to walk through the tower before commencement or they will not graduate. The tower was constructed in 1950 to honor students and faculty who died in World War II. Students ceremoniously walk through it at the beginning of the commencement procession "down the hill" from the campanile into Memorial Stadium.

The end of classes or finals occasionally marks the beginning of some graduating senior activities. On the morning of the last day of classes at Wells, seniors don their robes and dance around the old sycamore tree in front of the main building. The sophomore sisters present the seniors with roses, and then for luck they kiss the feet of Minerva in the front entrance to the main building. At Chatham, seniors burn early drafts of their senior theses in a bonfire in front of the chapel. Seniors at Wooster march in an annual Independent Study procession, which celebrates the completion of theses required of every graduate. Having submitted their papers to the registrar, students receive a Tootsie Roll and a gold button proclaiming, "I did it." About 400 students and faculty members join the parade, complete with trumpeters, drummers, and a mock throne held up by brooms ("Agony" 1989, 31). A similar ceremony celebrating the submission of the senior thesis at Reed College uses a costume theme, a fire-breathing thesis dragon, and a makeshift band (Betterton 1988, 172).

During the nineteenth century, funeral processions as well as ritual pyres and burials for books and courses were much more common than they are today. At the University of California at Berkeley, robed students carrying Chinese lanterns paraded caskets filled with Bourdon's *Elements of Algebra* and Minto's *Manual of English Prose*. The books were set aflame and buried, and a huge party followed (Stadtman 1970, 164; Dundes 1968, 21–22). At Yale, the book so mourned was Euclid's *Elements*. Benjamin Hall described the ritual skewering of the classical text in the mid-nineteenth century: "The huge poker is heated in the old stove, and driven through the smoking volume, and the division, marshalled in line, for *once* at least see *through* the whole affair. They then march over it in solemn procession, and are enabled, as they step firmly on its covers, to assert with truth that they have gone over it—poor jokes indeed, but sufficient to afford abundant laughter. And then follow speeches, comical and pathetic, and shouting and merriment" (Hall 1968, 41).

At Syracuse, Purdue, and Bucknell, particular courses were ritually cremated and the ashes buried; at Syracuse, it was calculus; at Purdue, mechanics and hydraulics; and at Bucknell, geometry (Huguenin 1961; Oliphant 1965, 186). Purdue students' burning of their books was preceded by an over-the-top funeral for fictional scholar I. P. C. McCannix, complete with satirical eulogies (Bowlby and Gannon 1944, 39–40; Goldsmith 1929, 602). Excessive "vulgar slurs and sacrilegious tendencies" aimed at professors drew administrative ire, and the event was shut down in 1913 (Goldsmith 1929, 602). Well into the twentieth century, students at the University of Texas joined together in a huge book-bonfire at Class Day, when each senior tossed in a book (Berry 1983, 73). Book burning by seniors ceased at Agnes Scott College during the 1960s. Commenting on the tradition's demise, the archivist told me that students had more control of their time then and became less inclined to remain on campus after spring exams. At Franklin and Marshall College, the practice of cremating zoology and analytical geometry textbooks in elaborate ceremonies faded as the curriculum expanded and the whole class no longer shared a required course (Brubaker 1987, 36–37). Undoubtedly also influencing the decline of the incendiary tradition is the reaction against Nazi book burnings during the 1930s.

Wills and Ceremonies

In the spirit of "moving to the great beyond," a persistent collegiate tradition is leaving wills and gifts to the college. One early parody from Harvard in 1794 opens with the declaration, "I, Charley Chatter, sound of mind, To making fun am much inclined, So having cause to apprehend, My college life is near its end, All future quarrels to prevent, I seal this will and testament." To "friends of science and of men" the writer left "naught but thanks bestow[ed]." The next lines explain: "For, like my cash, my credit's low; So I can give nor clothes nor wines, But bid them welcome to my fines" (Hall 1968, 476–79). The leaving of wills mocking professors and students is still a part of "Senior Prank" at Hood. At Cedar Crest, the tone became so caustic by the 1960s that administrators halted the tradition.

Senior classes may still leave gifts to the college, often in the form of a class bench, tree, or statue. Of late, class gifts often appear less symbolic and more pragmatic in the form of equipment or a contribution to the scholarship fund. In times of yore, gifts in the form of "transmittenda" were handed down from some lucky class member to the next. Mid-nineteenth-century chronicler of college customs Benjamin Hall reported that a jackknife was given to the ugliest member of the senior class at Harvard, who passed it on to a member of the next class. Apparently inspired by a tradition at Cambridge, Yale seniors offered the chair of the prom committee a wooden spoon usually implying that the recipient was the weakest student in the class; at Lawrence, the wooden spoon belonged to the homeliest man (Hall 1968, 492–97).

Through the twentieth century, seniors puffed and ceremoniously handed down "pipes of peace" at places like Colby College with intense interclass rivalries (Wyman 1979, 87; Miller 1966, 396–97; Pattee 1928, 5; Briscoe 1981b, 11). Another symbolic gesture was to "bury the hatchet" by handing over a hatchet from the seniors to the juniors (Earley 1987, 27, 37, 52; Gardner 1972, 115). After competitions at Randolph College between odd and even classes in singing and defense of their respective class tree, and an occasional water balloon fight, before graduation a senior presents a hatchet to the most spirited junior to symbolize coming together in friendship. When the tradition started in 1915, the ceremony had more of a Native American motif with class presidents serving as chiefs, but this aspect fell away (Minter 2008).

While many of the war symbols ceased to be handed down with the fading of class scraps, other items representing school memories remain. Trinity College seniors bequeath a wooden lemon squeezer that has traded hands since 1857. The squeezer had been used in the making of a renowned Trinity "punch," and inscribed with class mottoes and ribbons attached, the school pressed the relic into service as a symbol of class pride (Morris 1969). At Houghton College, the "Senior Chapel" concludes with the "passing of the mantle," a long strip of cloth to which each graduating class attaches its own embroidered insignia and graduation year done in the class colors. The graduating class also has a class banner that hangs in the auditorium at commencement, and is then given to the rising seniors, who use it as a homecoming decoration.

At Upper Iowa University's "Passing of the Gown" ceremony, the president of the senior class wears a special gown embroidered with the numerals of

Fig. 10.2 Fourth-class midshipmen lock arms and use ropes made from uniform items as they brace themselves against the Herndon Monument at the U.S. Naval Academy in an attempt to scale the obelisk. The monument was smeared with 200 pounds of lard, and the Midshipmen were hosed down during the annual event, which teaches them much about their own abilities and limitations, as well as the advantages of working as a team. (Photo by Photographer's Mate Second Class Damon J. Moritz)

that year's class. The senior president delivers a brief speech about the state of the college and challenges the junior class. The gown is then passed to the junior class president, who makes a response. At that time the senior class gift is presented to the university president.

A common pregraduation ceremony of transferal is a lantern procession. Every year on the Saturday night before commencement at Tusculum College, seniors turn over robes and lanterns to the juniors to mark the passing of responsibilities for the college. While this is going on, the seniors offer the lantern song: "From thee, our Alma Mater, we depart, These our lanterns symbolize the glow that's in our hearts." At Mount Mary College, seniors give juniors lanterns symbolizing the passing of the light of learning. Gathering around a reflecting pool in front of Notre Dame Hall, the seniors proceed around Madonna's circle with their lanterns. An induction of seniors into the alumnae association takes place, followed by the seniors moving to the front steps. There they sing farewell parodies to parents, faculty, and underclassmen.

Graduation week may also bring first-year students into the fold. At the Naval Academy, the new students, taunted as "plebes" and "the lowest of the low," rise to the top through a recognition ceremony to the delight of cheering seniors. Each spring, upperclassmen grease a twenty-one-foot-tall obelisk called Herndon Monument and place a plebe's white cap on top. Then hundreds of the fresh midshipmen try to climb the slippery stone and replace the white cap with an upperclassman's gold-trimmed hat. Resorting to teamwork, some plebes form a human webbing around the monument with legs resting on shoulders of midshipmen below (Robertson 1989a). The plebe who is successful is a big man on campus indeed. The midshipmen are likely to carry their hero to the steps of the Naval Academy chapel, where the superintendent might present him with an admiral's shoulder boards mounted on a plaque. Tradition holds that the plebe to reach the top will be the first admiral of the class. "There are two main points in a midshipman's career—Herndon and graduation," explains one plebe, now declared a "fourth classman" (Robertson 1989b, 1).

Originally reserved for men, the ceremony is replete with male phallic symbolism. The sexual implications of the climb are not lost on participants, as those who are not bare-chested don T-shirts with messages such as "I like it on top" and "Go all the way." With a nod to gender equality in the military, beginning in 1977 midshipwomen joined the climbing ritual (Cohen and Coffin 1987, 191). Some female participants complained, however, that men prevented them from reaching the top or even pulled them off the obelisk (Gelfand 2006, 184, 189; Barrett 2002, 162–63; Johnson and Harper 2005, 53–54). In addition to supervisors' worries about the public representation of the military in the event, officials have threatened to shut the event down because of the risk of injury from falling climbers and collapsing holders. The scene also bothers some visitors to graduation who find the ungentlemanly ruckus disturbing.

Senior Chains and Garlands

The "Daisy Chain" is the best-known women's pregraduation tradition. An emblem of fidelity, the daisy has many associations with women's divinations. Women pluck its petals for fortune-telling charms to predict the identity of a future husband and the number of children the union will bring (Bronner 1989, 165, 329). At Meredith College, a women's college in Raleigh, North Carolina, daisy chains in commencement programs materialize the campus family ties of little (sophomore) and big (senior) sisters. Little sisters construct the chains as long as 100 feet for ceremonies in the college's outdoor amphitheater. White-clad sophomores hold the daisy chains and sing as their sister class marches through the chains. Alumnae sister classes from odd-year classes wear black gloves on their left hands and give their little sisters wishbone charms for luck. The even classes give their little sisters bags of sticks and stones "to protect them from the Odd Spirit's bones" (Meredith College 2010). At the conclusion of the event, the chains form the class numerals of the graduating class. The seniors then form a circle and celebrate with their classmates.

Many women's colleges abandoned the daisy chain because its old-fashioned ties to courtship and floral representation of womanhood appeared out of step with feminist values. Until the 1960s, for example, the daisy chain was a regular part of sophomore duties at Agnes Scott College. By tradition, the sophomores began collecting late Friday or early Saturday morning and completed the 150-foot chain by 4 p.m. in time for a special ceremony at the May Day Dell. The seniors offered a class poem, and the sophomores give the chain to the seniors, who then formed it into an *S* on the dell. Seniors make their mark now by climbing into Agnes Scott Hall's tower and ringing the bell to announce acceptance to graduate school or a job offer.

At Vassar, as far back as 1889, sophomores picked daisies to decorate the old chapel for Class Day, the day before commencement. A chain of daisies first roped off a section of the chapel reserved for the seniors to sit in while attending the Class Day exercises. Credit is given to the senior class marshal of 1894 for picking a few especially comely girls to carry the chain. With succeeding years, the chain became longer and heavier, until the length became fixed at 150 feet. With the school going coed in 1969, male ushers took their place in carrying the chain. With the influence of feminism, seniors claim that selections of students for the honor of carrying the chain are made on the basis of academic merit and not beauty (Vassar Historian 2004).

At Hollins University for many years, sophomores prepared the daisy chain to pass on to the seniors at the close of Class Day ceremonies. Then the seniors draped the garland over the lawn in the outline of the class numerals. At Howard Payne, seniors chose a junior as a "chime-out partner," and in a ceremony the night before commencement under the college's bell towers, the garland passes from the seniors to the juniors.

The association of flora with spring femininity and fertility remained intact. Inspired by Vassar's daisy chain, Christian College (the oldest women's college west of the Mississippi River) instituted the ivy chain after 1900 (Hale 1968, 131). In 1964, students changed the name of their yearbook from the *College Widow* to the *Ivy Chain*. The ivy combines Christian lore of the immortality of the soul and a more general association with femininity and fertility. The rose also carries special meaning for Christian College students because seniors carry loving roses on Class Day and write "rose notes" to favorite juniors.

Some traditions featuring natural symbols have been started anew. Since 1993, graduates at Connecticut College have been presented with eastern white pine saplings, which they carry as they march at commencement. The sapling

Fig. 10.3. Vassar sophomores present the daisy chain, 1928. (Author's collection)

represents the tree on the college seal and each student's "growing" connection to the college after he or she graduates. The saplings are wrapped in ribbons of the school colors, blue and white, and green to symbolize the earth. Additionally, the college commencement still includes ritual use of the laurel chain, used in ceremonies since the first Class Day in 1919. Junior class women dressed in white carry chains of laurel through which the graduating seniors march. The laurel is touted as a symbol of honor and fame.

At Mount Holyoke College, located in South Hadley, Massachusetts, the laurel chain tradition is given an activist ring with songs and colors. Linked by the laurel chain, students on the morning of commencement weave around the iron fence surrounding the grave of college founder Mary Lyon. The students sing "Bread and Roses," the anthem of textile workers who struck the Lawrence, Massachusetts, mills in 1912. Participants dress in white as a sign of solidarity and to evoke the attire of women suffragists.

Ivy chains were also used at the University of Nebraska and Eastern Michigan University (Manley 1969, 283). Still relying on the symbolism of ivy is a graduation tradition today of ivy planting at Williams College and ivy cutting at Spring Arbor College. The Vassar daisy chain also inspired the University of Texas's bluebonnet chain used on Class Day until 1963 (Berry 1983, 73–76; 1980, 293). A bluebonnet chain ceremony reserved for women was part of "Senior Swing-Out," during which seniors passed a sophomore-arranged chain of bluebonnets, the state flower of Texas, to new junior leaders. Then the senior women marched out through the protecting bluebonnet chain into the "out-side world." The juniors honored the seniors with a bluebonnet chain song: "We gather, dear seniors, to bid you goodbye, And wish you good luck in each task you shall try, Remember dear Varsity and we who remain, Are bound to you now by the Bluebonnet Chain" (Berry 1983, 74–76).

The Big Day

One difficulty with holding these multiclass events around commencement and after finals is that today underclassmen, and often faculty, want to leave campus as soon as they can. To keep the student body around for a show of community, some schools hold commencement before finals, from which the seniors are excused. At Oregon State University, the benefit of the free week for seniors beginning in the 1930s was that the registrar's office had time to tally final grades and prepare personalized diplomas for the graduates. The benefit for students, as one explained, was having "time to talk to professors, say goodbye to friends, find out where they were going to work" (Krause 1989, 12). But all that changed in 1989, when a Faculty Senate edict to prevent seniors from slacking off required them to take spring finals along with everyone else. "The ceremony this year will take place on a campus that's not very vibrant," warned the senior class president (Krause 1989, 12). Students collected more than 1,000 signatures calling for the retention of traditional commencement, but the university president stood behind the break with tradition.

Before commencement, many colleges recognize the special presence of seniors' families with strawberry (or sometimes champagne) breakfasts in the dining halls. Representing the auspiciousness of the day's graduation, the rich fruit is topped with chocolate, cream, and sugar to ensure a sweet future. The event can carry sentimental meaning, because, as a student from Hood explained to me, "It is the last time you eat at Hood as a student." As part of the day's events, seniors may say their fond farewells to the college by making pilgrimages to favored college spots, occasionally requesting the presence of popular professors (Dundes 1968, 32). Faculty members are also part of a pre-graduation "garden party," a family affair on the campus lawn at Bryn Mawr. With the help of a "garden party girl," an undergraduate who ropes off a circle of chairs for the family and fetches professors the seniors would like her parents to meet, the graduating senior, often, along with her mother, decked out in flowers, invites faculty to join her family. To mark the end of her academic career, the senior may also enlist the garden party girl to help her to ring the college bell, a task that takes ingenuity since the building is often locked (Briscoe 1981a, 69–72).

At large universities, seniors typically divide by school, residence complex, or even department for an intimate morning ceremony honoring class leaders and offering brief orations before the massive commencement during the afternoon. At many colleges, the commencement procession often takes a symbolic route. At the College of William and Mary, students dramatically move from the "old" campus across a bridge to the "new" campus to mark their change in status. At the University of Findlay, the Griffith Memorial Arch serves as the formal gateway to the campus. As freshmen, the students marched in through the arch, greeted by a row of faculty on each side of the wide sidewalk leading to historic Old Main. Graduating seniors take their last walk out through the arch, again past rows of faculty and administrators who bid them farewell (Kern 1984, 342).

Similarly, at Brown University, the elaborate Van Wickle Gates are opened only twice a year: inward, toward the campus, on the day of opening convocation, and outward, on the day of commencement. At Wofford College, seniors make a graduation journey "past the posts" into the outside world. The commencement line forms at Main, and then the students march through campus and through the Church Street gate to the city auditorium. Westminster College has venerated classical columns on campus. Students pass through the columns in front of Westminster Hall only twice in their academic careers: once during orientation week and again during graduation.

After processions are over, the stage is set for the big event. Sometimes number magic is invoked for the setup. At Colgate, lore dictates that thirteen men with $13 and thirteen prayers founded the college in 1819. "Live true to the memory of those thirteen men of yore" is a line from a song sung at most programs by the Thirteen, a male singing group at the college. Among the thirteen traditions observed today at Colgate is the placement of thirteen chairs on the chapel platform for major convocations. Colgate is not alone in its fondness for the number thirteen. The ceremonial mace used at the University of Nevada at Reno has thirteen silver coins symbolizing the thirteen years of minting silver in Carson City.

Many outdoor commencement settings are like Emory's—in the main quadrangle, emphasizing four sides, with a commencement platform on the steps of the administration building. Pointing out the symmetry of the setting, the commencement program notes that spectators are seated facing west between the two oldest buildings on the Atlanta campus. To the east are the physics and history buildings, constructed in the same style. Looking across the quadrangle from the administration building is the other unifying academic symbol, the library.

Most students gather at commencement in black robes and tasseled mortarboard. The dress has its roots in medieval Europe when monastic orders oversaw higher learning. The monk's tippet became the "hood" worn by master's and doctoral students. When caps came into fashion in the fifteenth century, wearers draped hoods down and back and ornamented them with silk or velvet linings and edgings. Master's students received a cap with a tuft at the center. The tassel used today on American mortarboards derives from the use of the tuft. The mortarboard style follows Oxford University custom in which master's students wear the flat-topped cap. In the modern spirit of being environmentally responsible, countering an image of college students as wasteful consumers, an increasing number of universities tout "green" commencements. This usually does not mean wearing green robes, with the exception of Michigan State University (MSU), whose school colors happen to be green and white. Each MSU student dons a cap and gown made from over a dozen recycled plastic bottles. The sum total of recyclables in an average commencement was over 58,000. The new material had a matte finish instead of the old, shiny, petroleum-based polyester finish, and officials estimated that 16,500 yards of fabric were saved. At the end of the ceremony, students can toss their gowns into recycling bins. The "sheepskin," as diplomas students received were once known (Hall 1968, 421–22), are made from recycled paper, as are commencement programs printed with soy-based ink, although students were not about to stuff the certificates of their degrees into the receptacles with the gowns.

The wearing of academic dress in America dates to 1754 when George II chartered King's College, now Columbia University, and transferred academic regulations from Oxford and Cambridge. Colonial colleges rejected the scarlet robes of the English institutions for the somber black preferred by Puritan clergy. In 1895, a commission of American educators adopted black as the standard color for academic robes and established a hierarchy of robe design, from the unadorned undergraduate robe to the ornamented full robes for the doctoral graduate. With revisions to the code in 1935 and 1960 allowing for variation, many universities have adopted colorful robes. Harvard's students sport striking crimson gowns, Rutgers's attract attention in scarlet, and Yale's parade their blues. The University of Texas introduced robes for doctoral students in 2001 of custom-dyed burnt orange, explaining that "many universities have found that distinctive doctoral robes foster greater identity and esprit de corps among graduates" ("UT Austin" 2001). Satin linings in hoods given for master's and doctoral students typically use school colors, and soft six- and eight-cornered caps can be worn. Trimming around the edge of the hood varies in color and designates the degree holder's realm of study.

A ceremonial mace leads most graduation processions. The use of the mace comes from the first royal mace presented by Queen Elizabeth I to Oxford University in 1589. Not about to be outdone, Cambridge received the royal mace from King Charles II in 1629, and thereafter the mace has been a fixture at academic convocations (Heckscher 1970, 9–10).

American universities adopted the mace during the nineteenth century when ceremonies became more elaborate in imitation of European convention. Representing masculine strength as well as regal authority, the mace usually has a finial at the bottom with a shaft capped by an ornamented head. As a sign of command, the mace at many institutions contains the names of former presidents. Commencement programs will also refer to its symbolism of passing on tradition because of its hand-crafted construction. Western New England University's mace crafted by master wood sculptor Dimitrios Klitas in 1997, for example, was touted for being made from a solid piece of walnut. According to the school's publicity, "The carving at the base of its shaft resembles spirals representing the spiraling knowledge to be gained through education. The upper portion of the mace features four petals under the round seal of Western New England University. The base, created as a stand for the mace, also includes four petals. They represent the Schools and depict their firm position and strength as a resting place for this institutional symbol of authority" (Western New England 2012). At Penn State Harrisburg, the top is a crown engraved with the school mascot, the Nittany Lion. The bottom takes the shape of a flame. The most senior faculty member authoritatively carries the mace into commencement with the head up, and flame up on the way out to recognize the light of knowledge acquired. At Sonoma State University, the honor of service as bearer of the mace is accorded the chair of the faculty. At Bethany College, the president of the senior class serves as mace bearer, and commencement concludes with the transfer of the mace to the president of the incoming senior class.

Inviting comment is Emory's mace, which includes a relief rendering of a human skeleton lovingly dubbed "Dooley." This "Dooley-chosen" lord of misrule has Emory's spring carnival named after him, and has class-ending powers. Bedecked in top hat, cane, and cape, the spirit of Emory has been known to enter classrooms during his special week and announce "class dismissed!" Beginning humbly as a teaching aid in the biology department at the turn of the twentieth century, the caped cadaver regularly took part in campus pranks and later contributed to student publications.

Baylor University celebrates Sam Houston, its famous neighbor and friend from the past, with a gold-headed walking stick as one of four elements of the university's mace (Keeth 1985, 41). Variations on the mace are Georgia's sword and Berkeley's baton. The ceremonial scepters often have symbols and legends attached to them. The University of California at Berkeley's baton is said to be made from the wood taken from Old North Hall (Dundes 1968, 27).

An additional symbol of authority worn by the mace bearer or the university president in a commencement procession is the "chain of office" with a university medallion worn about the neck. The University of Colorado's chain of office is typical in carrying many references to the quest for knowledge. Created in 1980, it has three suspended pendants. The top pendant in the front is the university seal surmounted by an arch set with diamonds and topaz, signifying the link between the search for knowledge and its practical application to the world beyond the university. An art professor created James Madison University's chain of office in sterling silver and two gems—a golden citrine and a purple amethyst—representing the university's school colors. The university medallion that hangs from the chain is more than three inches in diameter, and, like many official medallions, it contains the seal of the university and a founding date.

Banners or gonfalons (flags, often with streamers, hanging from a crosspiece on an upright staff) representing the university's divisions or schools often give the commencement procession the look of a medieval festival. At Emory, gonfalons for the arts and sciences show lamps of knowledge; nursing has a globe and red cross against an apricot background; and business administration luxuriously carries Medici bezants (representations of coins) on sapphire.

The traditional uniformity of robes marks the graduates as initiates ready for a special community. Since the 1960s, however, one sees personalized messages pasted onto mortarboards. "Thanks Mom and Dad," "It's Over," "$." Asking students why they add their personal touch to the uniform dress, a campus reporter at Penn State heard "I've been here for four years. I want to be noticed in this crowd"; "I definitely want to do something to say 'Look Mom and Dad'"; and "We want to tell the world the essence of our senior year" (Repcheck 1988, 5). Looking to quantify the trend, four psychologists found that women were more likely to be adorned than were men, and bachelor of arts candidates more likely than bachelor of science candidates (Harrison et al. 1986, 863–74). Women, they offered, "are more likely than men to distinguish themselves and attract attention through individualization of attire" (Harrison et al. 1986, 872). Bachelor of arts students, priding themselves on their imagination and expressiveness, were more willing than bachelor of science seniors to trumpet their individual creativity. The messages also convert the attire prescribed by authority to one controlled by students, especially as adolescents today are more likely to express themselves through secular rather than ritual clothing (Harrison et al. 1986, 873). Overall, the number of expressive gestures is small (12 percent in their sample), and if the psychologists are right, the number increases during times of social and economic unrest.

Besides the caps, robes receive special treatment from students. Hawaiian graduates sport floral leis on their robes. Other students wear shorts and other sportswear underneath the robe. "I need a job" and other signs can occasionally be sighted pinned to robes. Bottles of champagne have been known to be carried in under robes and popped during long commencement speeches (Toelken 1986, 527). Colorful balloons fly up from under robes into the air, sometimes carrying students' messages (Repcheck 1988, 5).

Color is also added to the traditionally black robes with the addition of honor fabric cords given to members of honor societies and students earning collegewide honors. At the University of California campuses, baccalaureate graduates who have received campuswide Latin honors (summa cum laude, magna cum laude, cum laude) wear gold cords, and those who have earned academic unit awards and prizes, or who have been elected to honor societies, wear blue cords. Particular honor societies often have their own colors; civil engineering students who are members of the subject area's honor society Chi Epsilon don purple and white cords at many locations. The twist in the cord has a traditional reference, because of the popular belief that twisting was a sign of good fortune, supposedly because the tangle confused evil forces looking to accost promising young people. The cords are distinguished by a knot in the middle to hold them together. Variations of the cords given as accolades are sashes, stoles, and medallions. Alpha Chi National College Honor Society (or AX) members representing the top 10 percent of an institution's juniors, seniors, and graduate students, for example, don a white stole with a blue monogram.

Commencement may attract cynicism because, at many large institutions, it is hardly an engaging ritual. Graduates are recognized simply by quickly standing together in the midst of a huge arena. Students may also question the significance of commencement for them, when the proceedings often involve political speeches and awards to celebrities and donors. Stephens College seniors answer with a mock ceremony kicking off commencement week. The event includes "Commencement Bingo," which calls for class members to listen for graduation jargon such as "beginning," "challenging," "opportunity," and "future" to fill out their cards. This parodying of commencement is hardly new, although during the nineteenth century it was more a sign of class rivalry than jaded attitudes. Sophomore and junior "exhibitions" showcased mock commencement orations, and broadsides called "burlesques" or "slubs" parodied the official commencement program (Brubaker 1987, 220–22; Dundes 1968, 20–21; Moffatt 1985b, 5, 23; Stadtman 1970, 164–65; Hall 1968, 46, 344–45). The implication of the parodies is that other kinds of rituals in response to the anxiety of separation, less administratively controlled or more socially significant,

Fig. 10.4. Graduate moves his tassel from the right side to the left after proceeding on the stage from right to left to receive his diploma at Penn State Harrisburg. He has put his initials on his mortarboard to be noticed by his family from the arena stands. (Photo by Simon Bronner)

are necessary to mark the transition from the adolescent, socially conscious, idyllic college to the harsh real world where students take on burdensome adult individuality. Or else some of the parodies suggest that commencement is overdone because the boundary between the real world and campus life is not that great, especially in commuter institutions.

Small colleges boast that students receive personal attention, reflected in the handing out of diplomas to students walking on the commencement stage as their names are called out. The walk on stage is a transitional passage to the new status of graduate. The student receives the diploma and shakes hands with administrators. Following the descent from the platform, every student has his or her picture taken with diploma in hand. At Hood and Stephens Colleges, the chief administrator might receive a "secret gift" in return. Hood's president has been known to receive a plastic Lego block, pennies, marbles, pieces of a jigsaw puzzle, and goldfish in plastic bags. At Stephens, the president received birthday candles and shoelaces (she was a jogger). The students connect the tradition to their "Secret Santa" custom, which values tokens of affection. The president of Hood found that the "secret gift" tradition has a therapeutic value for students. "I haven't had to shake a clammy hand in four years," she explained. "It helps them relax" (Torok 1989, 3).

Graduates of Smith College do not receive their own diploma when they walk across the platform. Instead, they participate in a tradition known originally as the "Great Ring" in 1911, then the "Magic Circle" followed by the "Diploma Circle." Students march from the commencement ceremony to Laura

Scales/Franklin King Terrace and form a large ring, several circles deep. Diplomas are passed around each circle, with graduates leaving the circle as soon as they receive their own diploma. Gradually, only one circle remains. The Diploma Circle takes several minutes before each new alumna has her diploma and joins her family to celebrate graduation from Smith.

Administrators chide commencement audiences to keep religiously silent after students receive their diploma at commencement to preserve the decorum of the sober event. Yet the trend is to announce joy by applause and shouts from family members. Occasionally, an air horn and loud whistling resound through the audience section. During the long procession, audience members do not seem to mind the commotion because it provides some comic relief. At a Penn State Harrisburg commencement I witnessed, the house came down when one student's brother bellowed, "Get a job!"

Cheering and gestural displays are especially conspicuous at the service academies. Here is a description of the 1989 graduation at Annapolis: "Clad in their formal white uniforms, midshipmen punched their fists in the air, danced across the stage and held their diplomas aloft as they accepted their degrees. Their families and friends competed to be the loudest cheering section" (Robertson 1989b, 2). If receiving the degree is the postseparation stage in the transition, the preincorporation ritual is moving the tassel from the right to the left on the mortarboard. Placement on the left in American society is considered an odd, but select location. Thus graduates announce entrance into an esoteric community. Despite the air of restraint on stage, some students additionally hoist their diploma and jump for joy.

Advanced degree students receive their hoods in addition to diplomas. By tradition, the student carries the hood to the stage or has it placed on a platform there. In the ceremony, a dean places the hood over the student. Law school graduates at the University of Texas have the unusual distinction of also receiving sunflowers. The custom has its origin in a university-wide student meeting in 1900 to approve the wearing of caps and gowns to graduation. The organizers neglected to invite the law students, and, in protest, the law students wore silk hats and sunflowers pinned on their lapels. Students probably chose the flowers because they grew in abundance near the campus. But later, creative pronouncements about their symbolism emerged. One account held that the sunflower belongs to a family with worldwide distribution, and so do lawyers. Another opined that "as the sunflower always keeps its face turned to the sun, the lawyer turns to the light of justice" (Berry 1983, 122). Today the "Sunflower Ceremony," attended by law graduates and their relatives, occurs on commencement day. The associate dean pins a sunflower on each graduate, and the graduates in turn present sunflowers to relatives and friends (Berry 1980, 301).

At mega-universities, administrators deal with the problem of making the ritual meaningful for large numbers of graduates by decentralizing ceremonies into constituent colleges. Universities also recognize cultural diversity with ceremonies and celebrations devoted to ethnic backgrounds. Cal State–Chico holds separate celebrations for Latino/a and African American students. At the University of Arizona (UA), cultural centers for students of Native American, Asian-Pacific American, Chicano/Hispano, and African American background organize additional graduation convocations. The campus newspaper explains their significance this way: "Surrounded by tens of thousands of their peers, graduating seniors can get lost in the crowd—but the UA's cultural centers give students a special ceremony" (Woodberry 2010, B12). Many of the convocations have cultural features such as the performance of African dance at the African American convocation and Mexican food at the Chicano/Hispano event. At the African American ceremony, students receive either green, blue, or black stoles, depending on whether they are graduate or undergraduate students. Green stoles symbolize growth; blue represents harmony, peace, and love; black stoles for the graduate students stand for spiritual potency and maturity (Woodberry 2010, B12). Many of the ethnic convocations allow students to personalize the event by bringing pictures and messages to display.

A number of campuses also stage "Lavender Graduations" usually hosted by a gay/lesbian/bisexual/transgender organization. The idea is traced to an innovative Lavender Graduation at the University of Michigan in 1995. Four years later, eighteen campuses held Lavender events named for a combination of the pink triangle that gay men were forced to wear in concentration camps and the black triangle designating lesbians as political prisoners in Nazi Germany (Sanlo 2000). By 2004, forty-three colleges reported holding Lavender commencement events (Sanlo 2005). Penn State's evening ceremony opened with musical entertainment by the Harrisburg Men's and Central Pennsylvania Womyn's choruses. On a platform framed by a giant rainbow balloon arch, each senior chose a "significant other," who could be a partner, professor, or friend, and acknowledged him or her with a lavender flower and a speech about how that person affected his or her life. The ceremony closed with rolls of streamers in rainbow colors passed to graduates and their guests. Everyone in the room held a streamer as a symbol of unity (Ingeno 2010). Gay and lesbian students may also announce their identity by wearing rainbow-colored tassels.

Many colleges have devised additional ceremonies after commencement to instill a localized sense of tradition. Adrian College has held an outdoor cane ceremony every year since 1921. Seniors use this opportunity to symbolically transfer leadership for the college to the juniors, and this next class to graduate affixes its colors to the "shepherd's crook." The ribbons on the cane represent

Fig. 10.5. Hat tossing after graduation from the U.S. Naval Academy in Annapolis, Maryland. (Author's collection)

the colors of every graduating class in all the shades of the rainbow. The old cane carries the date 1887 and the words *Non Sine Labote*, or "climb without falling." The cane—and the custom of affixing class colors—dates to 1887, when it was a trophy of the "cane rush" war between the classes. Today, as a crook, it carries a peaceful message in a ceremony by the college tower. At Wofford College, graduating seniors, nearly 300 of them, receive Bibles personally autographed by each member of the faculty and staff in a ceremony.

Often adding to the image of continuity or tradition at commencement is the participation of alumni classes. Brown University includes the holding of five-year reunions coinciding with commencement weekend. The commencement procession on Sunday morning is led by the chief marshal, a member of the fifty-year reunion class. This person is followed by a color guard and alumni aides and marshals from various reunion classes with the faculty, thousands of alumni, and graduating seniors. At one point in the parade, the festive procession stops and forms an inversion to allow each marcher to pass by all the others to mutual applause. A material symbol of continuity is the solid oak cane carried by the president of the Brown Alumni Association in the procession. It is made of wood taken from University Hall, the first and oldest building on campus, when the edifice was reconstructed during the 1880s.

Amid graduation celebrations are occasionally somber commemorations for students who passed away. At Penn State, the event meant to facilitate reflection is called "Day of Remembrance" held at the campus's spiritual center.

Photographs of deceased students, most from auto accidents, are displayed on an altar, and visitors light candles and engage in silent prayer (Stern 2010). At other universities, commencement is also a time for class reunions that include remembrance ceremonies for fallen colleagues. The reflective event at the University of Texas is called "UT Remembers," held on a Friday before commencement. Flags on the Main Mall are lowered to half-staff for the day, and UT Tower lights are darkened from dusk to dawn. Speakers read the names of students, faculty, and staff who have died in the preceding year, and the tower bell tolls in tribute (Meckel 2008).

Probably the largest remembrance ceremony is Texas A&M's "Aggie Muster." In keeping with the military heritage of the school (although now a small part of the curriculum), the name derives from army slang for a gathering, roll call, or retirement of a soldier. As captured in recitation of a poem titled "Roll Call for the Absent" (originally composed as "Heroes' Roll Call" by John Ashton of the school's department of rural sociology and modified a number of times after its introduction in 1943), a central component of the ceremony is the roll call referred to in the closing verse from the poem:

> Softly call the muster,
> Let comrade answer, "here!"
> Their spirits hover round us:
> As if to bring us cheer!
> Mark them "present" in our hearts,
> We'll meet some other day.
> There is no Death but Life Eterne
> For heroes such as they! (Adams 1994)

Held annually on April 21 (coinciding with San Jacinto Day, an official state holiday in Texas commemorating the final battle of the Texas Revolution), the event also includes the reunion of the fiftieth-year class. Aggie groups organize Muster ceremonies worldwide in hundreds of locations, with the biggest staged on the A&M campus in Reed Arena holding over 12,000 participants. In addition to the "Roll Call for the Absent" for those alumni who died in the past year (family members answer "here" when the name of the deceased is called), the solemn ceremony typically includes the lighting of memorial candles, Reflections Display (exhibit of letters, pictures, and senior boots belonging to the honored fallen), a keynote speech, reciting of poems (including "The Last Corps Trip" written by P. H. "Buddy" DuVal Jr., class of 1951, about Judgment Day, when cadets and other Aggies are welcomed into heaven), and Camaraderie Barbecue (or fish fry) (Huffman 2008; Smith 2011). At Reed Arena, a military procession of the Ross Volunteers gives a twenty-one-gun salute, and buglers play "Silver Taps" in farewell. Rhetoric at the event intones much about character, unity, and fellowship—and fidelity to tradition.

The history of Muster dates to 1883, when former A&M students gathered informally to fondly reminisce about their college experience and honor their fallen comrades. With American entrance in World War I taking many lives, the ceremonies took on more poignancy and solemnity. A&M clubs formalized the Muster tradition during the 1920s and expanded the roll call beyond military deaths to deceased alumni. As participation widened, a separate organization emerged to coordinate the Muster on campus sponsored by the Association of Former Students and the Brazos County A&M Club. Students believe that the Muster is different, much like the school, and the tradition serves to validate the special bond of Aggies. According to alum John A. Adams Jr., the Muster tradition's impact lies in the view that "Texas A&M has always been unique. From the earliest days of its opening in October, 1876, its students and former students were influenced and molded by the history of the state of Texas as well as by their surroundings and the sense of camaraderie that only challenging times dictate" (1994, 4). Like most students, Adams recognizes a number of distinctive, time-honored traditions at A&M, and expresses the belief that the campus contains more traditions than any other, but he declares that none is "more important or more universally observed than Aggie Muster" (1994, xvii). In its end-of-year ritualization of a shared bond and hardy character among all A&M students, Muster as a climactic tradition encapsulates the prominent values of loyalty, integrity, and service believed to mark a lifelong Aggie identity ("Core Values" 2011).

At academies devoted to military service, the end of commencement is a hat-raising event. Instead of wearing black robes and mortarboards, cadets don military dress uniforms and white front-brimmed caps emblazoned with the official branch insignia. Traditionally, the graduates toss their hats high in the air accompanied by rousing cheers and animated fist pumps in the air (Robertson 1989b, 1–2). Less honored by tradition are tossing antics at Harvard. When ceremoniously recognized, students in some fields throw a symbolic item up in the air. Business students throw dollar bills while liberal arts students toss their caps. Students at the University of Minnesota learn about the "shoe tree" near the southwest corner of the Washington Avenue bridge, where graduates tossed their footgear to celebrate the completion of their degrees.

After the graduates proceed out of commencement, they join up with their onlookers, drawing hugs and dinners from family—signs of incorporation. The graduation is thus a beginning of a new status, a new venture—in short, a rebirth into society. In the old-time college, this symbolism was more manifest because the college acted as a parent during the student's four years. With this role reduced and the size of graduating classes so much larger, commencement has arguably lost its ritualized meaning of passage. To be sure, it still marks completion, and there is often a rhetorical reference in speeches to "commencement" of one's independent journey into the future.

A sign of completion in traditional festivities is a celebratory communal meal, but the growth of graduating classes and the cost of feeding the masses have made this ritual difficult to stage. Harvard's dinner of thanksgiving became established as a special commencement tradition in the seventeenth century. In a show of communal ties, the dinner featured "the pleasant old ceremony of handing around the loving cup, or grace cup, as it was then called" (Hightower 2010). The old feasting tradition is remembered at annual "tree spread" luncheons in Harvard Yard into the twenty-first century. Bennington College also hosts an annual commencement dinner on its "Commons Lawn" under a tent, followed by speeches and then a late-night "senior party" for the graduates and their families. At Cottey College, first-year students take charge of the dinner during commencement weekend for seniors and present them honors from the newest to the oldest members of the college.

While commencement once marked the culmination of a week full of activities, most graduation ceremonies now are restricted to the day of commencement and involve only the seniors. Some of the changes in commencement can be attributed to loss of cohesiveness in student bodies. Students now divide into a wide spectrum of majors, interests, ages, and cultural backgrounds. No wonder that the most elaborate and traditional ceremonies in my survey occurred at small, relatively homogeneous women's colleges or religious schools. They tend to retain the social function of commencement as a final passage of transition, rather than as a public-relations "pep rally," as some critics have asserted about public university graduations (Hedges 1989, 32).

Still another factor in the deritualization of commencement is the possible devaluation of the degree itself, as more and more Americans treat a college education less as a special status marking learning than a necessary license to practice. Some calls for restoring meaning to graduation suggest shifting emphasis to ceremonies run by smaller units with which the student is affiliated, such as departments or residence complexes; encouraging rather than restraining the celebratory performances of graduates and their audiences; and having the ceremonies become more student-centered rather than administrator-managed (Hedges 1989, 32).

College Sense

Questions of the college degree's value after graduation come up in a good bit of folk humor. Many of the older anecdotes concern the farm boy transformed by college. In one such story, a farmer asks a fellow farmer and father of a recent graduate, "Well, since Tom has a college degree, can you see any change in the way he plows?" "No, he plows the same, but he talks different," was the reply. "How do you mean," the first farmer pressed. "Well, when he gets to the end of a row, instead of saying 'Whoa, Gee, or Haw,' he says, 'Halt, Rebecca, pivot and proceed'" (Mitchell 1976, 347).

A farmer questioning his son at the dinner table about what he learned in college is told "the study of logic." Asked to demonstrate, the son vows to prove that three chickens lie on the plate when it appears that only two are there. The son sticks his fork in one and says, "Here's one, right?" "Yes," says the collegian's dad. Poking the other one, the graduate says, "And this is two?" "All right," the father follows. "Well, don't one and two make three?" the degree-holder beams. "Tell you what," says the old man. "I'll give Mom one of the chickens to eat and I'll take the other, and you can have the third. How's that?" (Copeland and Copeland 1940, 408).

West Virginia–born celebrity raconteur Billy Edd Wheeler tells the traditional joke about a farmer from West Virginia who sends his son off to college:

As soon as the boy came home after graduation the farmer couldn't wait to take him down to the country store and show him off. The boy was a little embarrassed by it all, but he loved his dad and was grateful to him for helping finance his education. So he went along with it. As soon as they got to the store, the farmer proudly exclaimed, "Here's my son, fellers, home from college with a degree in algebra!" He turned to his son and said, "Well, don't be bashful, boy, say something to them in algebra." The son blushed and said, "Okay . . . pi-r-square." The farmer got very flustered at that, blushed himself, and said, "Don't be silly, boy! Pie are round. *Cornbread* are square!" (Jones and Wheeler 1987, 54–55)

The joke also appears as an Aggie joke about the A&M grad who worked himself up to the position of personnel manager of a company and interviewed his first job applicant, who was from Baylor. "What was your major at Baylor?" he asks. "Mathematics," the applicant answers. "Well, say something in Mathematics," the Aggie demands. "Pi-r-square," he offers. "Wrong," says the Aggie, "Pie are round, cornbread are square" (Wassell 1973, 8).

An ethnically styled joke is about the University of Texas grad who has a former Baylor student and several Aggie alums working for him. The Baylor grad stands on a table with his right arm raised, saying, "I'm a light bulb." The Texas boss, figuring he is insane, fires him. Later that day, all the Aggies start walking out. "Where are you going?" asks the Texas grad. "You don't expect us to work in the dark, do you?" replies one of the Aggies (*Best* 1976, 114; cf. Clements 1969b, type E3.6).

The honor of college women comes up in a widely circulating, and variable, joke about the salesman who makes his pitch in, say, Arkansas, when the subject of the University of Alabama comes up. "The only people who go to Alabama are whores and football players," he triumphantly declares. His client coolly informs him that his wife went to Alabama. "Oh," he sputters, "what position did she play?" (cf. Dundes and Pagter 1987, 156; *Best* 1976, 25).

A great deal of humor surrounding graduation concerns the status of a college degree when masses of students attending universities suggest the lowering of standards and narrowing of knowledge. At West Virginia, students walk around in T-shirts emblazoned with the message "I are a college graduate" (Birnbach 1984, 423). This display sometimes leads to the comment suggesting a belief legend that academic success in college does not ensure prosperity in life, and that in fact, those who fail at school often come back as millionaires (Hand et al. 1981, 143). From Wisconsin, for example, comes the story of the math major who graduated only by the skin of his teeth and the charity of his teachers. At his class's twenty-fifth reunion, he drove up in a Cadillac, wore expensive clothes, and showed all the trappings of wealth. When amazed classmates asked him about his secret to success, he explained that he had invented a little gadget, which he manufactured in his own plant. "It cost only $2 to make," this former math major said, "I sold it for $4, and with that 2 percent profit, I built a great business" (Wyman 1979, 82).

Engineers, accused of pursuing profitable careers despite a lack of imagination and literacy, are the most frequent butts of humor passed by photocopiers and email. One sheet shows an overgrown oaf holding a diploma in one hand and a slide rule in the other. The caption reads, "Golly, six weeks ago I could not even spell 'Enjanear'—NOW I ARE ONE!" Another caricature of an engineer shows an ugly nerd, affluently dressed and carrying a rolled diploma under one arm. In a crude hand, the caption announces: "Six munce ugo I cutnt evn spel injuneer—an now I are one" (Dundes and Pagter 1987, 212–14).

Related to this theme is the joke about college graduates registering for rooms at a hotel. The first signs "L.B." after his name. "What does the L.B. stand for?" the clerk asks. He eloquently explains, "I am a law school graduate and the initials indicate that I have earned my degree as a Bachelor of Law." The second man put "B.J." next to his name, and when the clerk asked him about the initials, he answers that he received a bachelor of journalism degree. The third fellow signs his name with an "S.I." "What on earth does S.I. mean?" the clerk inquires. "Hey, I got my degree in civil engineering," the fellow beams (*Best* 1976, 12).

Satirical readings of collegiate initialisms often stereotype campuses as social types and give reality checks to institutional conventions. "ISU" turns into "Inebriated State University"; "LSAT" and "MCAT," exams taken by many graduating seniors, change into "Legally Sadistic Admissions Test" and "Most Costly Aptitude Test" (Howe 1989, 176–77; cf. "Feedback" 1984–85, 261–62). In addition to the humor framing another way for students to assert control of formal institutional symbols, the joking characterizations are also a commentary on the modern proliferation of bureaucratic doublespeak peppered with acronyms that robotic "organization men and women" take for granted (see Howe 1989, 171–82; Bronner 1986b, 116; Lowe 1982, 131–39). In students' humorous turnaround of collegiate initials, the university is exposed as more corporate than the pastoral, premodern image of a campus implies.

Freely using wordplay, the "Master's Degree in Drinking" is offered in various forms around the country. The bogus diploma is bestowed on the student who has excelled in fractions, particularly fifths. T-shirts announce wearers as holders of a M.B.A.: Master of Beer Acquisition. Some wisecracks about degrees target women. One hears about coeds getting the MRS. degree, and about women who earn the Ph.T., or "Pushing Him Through," for supporting a man pursuing his degree (Copeland and Copeland 1940, 407; Egan 1985, 130, 132; Birnbach 1984, 104, 141; "Going" 1986). Uppity female doctoral degree holders are sarcastically called "P.H. Divas." Scatological symbolism is evident in the joke told about the M.S. being more B.S., and the Ph.D. is the same thing, "piled higher and deeper." Another piece of humor referring to the three degrees together comments on the glut of graduates with B.A., M.A., and Ph.D. degrees. The punch-line is "Unfortunately, they don't have a J.O.B."

Making fun of academic wisdom, students also spout parodies of sage proverbs and quotations. "I have never let schooling interfere with my education" can frequently be heard as a retort to why a student cut class (cf. Doyle, Mieder, and Shapiro 2012, 223). "You can lead a boy to college, but you can't make him think" and "See what he learned with his degree?" are traditional remarks after a degree-holder makes a bonehead mistake. Or doing menial work may lead a college grad to self-effacingly say, "See what you can do with a college degree!"

More than mere adolescent irreverence, this humor and the deritualization of graduation speak to the distance between the expansive university and the student seeking a culturally compassionate community. The message emanating from performances of humor is that the distended mega-university has moved over to the dark side of the cold, corporate world. This outlook has probably informed the revival of many customs that offer students a sense of belonging. Even so, reports regularly surface of a woeful number of students wandering directionless in the maze of the massive university (Arum and Roksa 2011; Bloom 1987; Boyer 1987; Hacker and Dreifus 2010).

Campus Traditions and Cultural Passage

Students seek to strengthen their social identity, value system, and emotional growth, but find that the academic setting once noted for assisting this cultural passage has alienated rather than involved them. Increasingly, students turn to one another for support, but struggle to create group harmony in a mass society stressing the uprooted, competitive individual. Collegians speak of this new "self" as taking so many roles that confusion about who "one really is" results. They want a clear identity and yet are often fearful of commitment. They hesitate to turn to the bureaucratic institution for social guidance and prefer cultural outlets to both question and express their coming-of-age. As a result, student lore in the age when the mega-university appears to be the norm is often more privately and spontaneously generated, rather than publicly and predictably shared.

In the heritage of the old-time college, custom conveyed a social and cultural consistency. It was facilitated by, if not promoted in, the institution. Contemporary university lore can seem highly variable and even contradictory (Albas and Albas 1989, 603–13). That makes sense, as today's colleges are a diverse lot often touting their differences to make an impact on the market. Unlike the old popular stereotype of the rah-rah college man decked out in raccoon coat and waving a college banner, today's students are harder to caricature. Sweatshirt-clad couch potatoes share the stage with blazer-attired dream-chasers and geeky lab rats. Students feel the burden of undertaking the serious business of being in school, while realizing that it is not considered a "real job." Surveying an ever-widening curriculum, collegians share anxieties about professional advancement, about grades, about "making it." But more than ever, they belong to any number of permeable student "worlds" divided by major or profession, social and political interest, and racial and ethnic affiliation, among other groupings (Horowitz 1987). In the absence of publicly shared ritual for arrival in adulthood, privatized folklore often serves to culturally identify the connections within these hazy social worlds.

The widening representation of different age groups at many universities is particularly striking. By the mid-twenty-first century, many pundits predict, part-time adult learners on metropolitan campuses will either predominate or need to be reached to sustain universities in the marketplace (Newman, Couturier, and Scurry 2004; Stokes 2006). Will that mean that college campuses will take on even less a role as cultural passage between adolescence and adulthood than they do now in their corporate, nonparental position? And with online degrees earned from the privacy, or isolation, of one's living room and for-profit degree-granting businesses, will the customary physical campus traditionally populated by young residents still have an effective social role?

With coming-of-age and acquisition of identities still uncertain in modern American society, many traditionally aged students will seek cultural passage in small separated groups that promote social ritual and lore within a rising culture of diversity. Fraternities, sororities, teams, dorms, clubs, and ethnic and religious organizations are reporting upswings in student involvement amid talk of creating identity in college. In the information age of the twenty-first century, students are more worldly, more mobile, and more confidently wired than ever before, but they also might be said to be unsure of themselves. The urge to be engaged socially while staying independent creates a renewed tension, however, between the call for an open, tolerant society based on the volition of the unyoked individual and the need for social support from a distinctive community that culturally instills values and offers a feeling of human control (see Bellah et al. 1985; Putnam 2000; Wenger, McDermott, and Snyder 2002). Many universities have introduced courses and recommended guidebooks, often in the first year, to socially navigate the bloated campus, and students dutifully take notes, but their path of self-discovery will probably take them to cultural locations outside the classroom in frames that many administrators and parents may consider risky rather than expressive.

With widening access to higher education in demand by American society, being an alumnus of a college is a significant identity to be shared with a broad network or to be compared with others in a profession or region. Many colleges offer an association to grads who look to the publicly visible institution as a tie that binds. And when grads get together, they often perpetuate lore based on their reminiscences if they were socially engaged on campus. Yet much has been made in the twenty-first century of the increased marginality of collegiate life to the student's total experience and later loyalties, especially at behemoth campuses (Andreatta 2012). One has to wonder about the intellectual and social processes that are supposed to occur during the so-called college years as the attitude spreads that pursuing higher education is a matter of occupational certification rather than of human development.

Campuses may pack so much lore and attract so much criticism precisely because they are expected to bring out the best in our increasingly complex society and in ourselves, although they are rarely equipped for the task. Places of intense work and play, discovery and routine, colleges intensify many of the organizational pressures and uncertainties found generally in modern life stressing being on one's own. Students call on socially significant tradition to provide cultural outlets for imagining, and imaging, the workings of life "out there." In their customs and narratives, students anticipate the mobility, independence, and responsibility of adult life, while also expressing their apprehension. They use their folkloric occasions to relate to one another and share their private fears, joys, and hopes, often at the expense of the organizational giant. The problems dealt with in student traditions are not just the college student's to bear, they are society's. Beyond the statistics and surveys chronicling student attitudes, folklore gives a very human profile of college, and modern, life. It reminds us of the meanings embedded in traditions that collegians inherit and create for the culture in which they will live and work.

REFERENCES

A & A International Education. 2008. "Whether to Study at Home or Abroad for Undergraduate Courses?" *A&A Column*. http://www.aaliuxue.com/en/approaching/whether.asp.

Aarne, Antti. 1964. *The Types of the Folktale: A Classification and Bibliography*. Translated and enlarged by Stith Thompson. 2nd revision. Helsinki: Folklore Fellows Communications, no. 184.

Abrahams, Roger D., ed. 1969. *Jump-Rope Rhymes: A Dictionary*. Austin: University of Texas Press.

———. 1970. *Deep Down in the Jungle: Negro Narrative Folklore from the Streets of Philadelphia*. Chicago: Aldine.

———. 1977. "Toward an Enactment-Centered Theory of Folklore." In *Frontiers of Folklore*, ed. William Bascom, 79–120. Boulder, Colo.: Westview Press.

———. 2005. *Everyday Life: A Poetics of Vernacular Practices*. Philadelphia: University of Pennsylvania Press.

Acheson, Susan. 1987. "'Scoping': Modern Folklore." Danielle Roemer Papers, Northern Kentucky University.

Acri, Kimberly. 1989. "The Folklore of the TKE Little Sisters [St. Francis College]." Penn State Harrisburg Folklore Archives.

Adams, Cecil. 1984. "Do Frank Lloyd Wright's Buildings Have Low Ceilings Because He Was Short?" *Straight Dope* (November 16). http://www.straightdope.com/columns/read/867/do-frank-lloyd-wrights-buildings-have-low-ceilings-because-he-was-short.

Adams, David Wallace. 2001. "More Than a Game: The Carlisle Indians Take to the Gridiron, 1893–1917." *Western Historical Quarterly* 32:25–53.

Adams, John A., Jr. 1994. *Softly Call the Muster: The Evolution of a Texas Aggie Tradition*. College Station: Texas A&M University Press.

———. 2000. *We Are the Aggies: The Texas A&M University Association of Former Students*. College Station: Texas A&M University Press.

Adams, Kylie. 2004. *Ex-Girlfriends*. New York: Kensington.

Adams, Virginia, Katie Armitage, Donna Butler, Carol Shankel, and Barbara Watkins, comps. 1983. *On the Hill: A Photographic History of the University of Kansas*. Lawrence: University Press of Kansas.

"Agony, Then Ecstasy: End of Senior Theses." 1989. *New York Times*, March 26 (sec. 1, part 2), 31.

Albas, Daniel, and Cheryl Albas. 1989. "Modern Magic: The Case of Examinations." *Sociological Quarterly* 30:603–13.

Allison, C. H. 1905. "Pushball, a Strenuous New Game." *National Magazine* 23 (October): 47–49.

Alter, Jonathan. 1983. "Nightmare in California." *Newsweek*, June 20, 28.

Altick, Richard D. 1937. "Pranks and Punishment in an Old Pennsylvania College." *Pennsylvania History* 4:241–47.

Aman, Reinhold. 1984–85. "Queries." *Maledicta* 8:281–84.

———. 1986–87. "Bawdy Books. *Maledicta* 9:141–42.

———. 1988–89. "Kakologia: A Chronicle of Ribald Riddles and Wicked Wordplays." *Maledicta* 10:247–316.

American College Health Association. 2009. "American College Health Association— National College Health Assessment Spring 2008 Reference Group Data Report (Abridged)." *Journal of American College Health* 57:477–88.

Amick, Blair. 1980. "Parking Legends." Indiana University Folklore Archives.

Amidon, Jim. 2007. "A Tradition of Change and Innovation." *Wabash Blogs*, January 28. _of_change_and_inno.html.

Am01337. 2009. Post on "Michael Jackson Jokes." redd.it.com, January 26. http://www .reddit.com/r/funny/comments/8vwon/michael-jackson-jokes.

Anderson, Kelly. 1987. "Steppin' Out: Black Greek Pledges Show Unity in 26-year Tradition." *State News* (Michigan State University, East Lansing), April 13, 1.

Anderson, Olive San Louie. 1878. *An American Girl and Her Four Years in a Boys' College*. New York: D. Appleton.

Anderson, Roslyn. 2009. "JSU Suspends 45 Band Members Amid Hazing Allegations." WLBT.com (Jackson, Miss.), September 22. http:www.wlbt.com/story/11180330/ jsu-suspends-45-band-members-amid-hazing-allegations.

Anderson, William A. 1977. "The Social Organization and Social Control of a Fad." *Urban Life* 6:221–40.

Andreatta, Britt. 2012. *Navigating the Research University: A Guide for First Year Students*. 3rd ed. Boston: Wadsworth.

Andrews, Gigi Babinec. 1988. "Reflections on Brenau 'Tradition.'" *Brenau Magazine* 2(1): n.p.

"Another 'Rush.'" 1884. *New York Times*, March 14, 4.

Anthony, Ted. 1989. "A Vexing Mystery: 20 Years Later, Pattee Stabbing Still Perplexes the State Police." *Daily Collegian* (Pennsylvania State University, University Park), November 28, 1, 4.

Applebaum, Ben, Ryan McNally, and Derrick Pittman. 2006. *Class Dismissed: 75 Outrageous, Mind-Expanding College Exploits (and Lessons That Won't Be on the Final)*. New York: Villard Books.

Arum, Richard, and Josipa Roksa. 2011. *Academically Adrift: Limited Learning on College Campuses*. Chicago: University of Chicago Press.

Badhshah, Billoo. 2003. *The Unofficial Joke Book of Australia*. New Delhi, India: Fusion Books.

———. 2004. *The Unofficial Joke Book of Mexico*. New Delhi, India: Fusion Books.

Bailey, Beth. 1998. "From Panty Raids to Revolution: Youth and Authority, 1950–1970." In *Generations of Youth: Youth Cultures and History in Twentieth-Century America*, ed. Joe Austin and Michael Nevin Willard, 187–204. New York: New York University Press.

Bailey, F. G. 1977. *Morality and Expediency: The Folklore of Academic Politics*. Chicago: Aldine.

Baker, Michael B. 2003. "Naval Reactors Aptitude Test: Practice Test Questions." Etnews .org. http://www.etnews.org/docs/nrat.pdf.

Baker, Ronald L. 1978. "The Phone in the Mausoleum: A Local Legend." *Midwestern Journal of Language and Folklore* 4:70–76.

———. 1982. *Hoosier Folk Legends.* Bloomington: Indiana University Press.

———. 1983. "The Folklore of Students." In *Handbook of American Folklore*, ed. Richard M. Dorson, 106–14. Bloomington: Indiana University Press.

———. 1986. *Jokelore: Humorous Folktales from Indiana.* Bloomington: Indiana University Press.

Bakhtin, Mikhail. 1984. *Rabelais and His World.* Trans. Hélène Iswolsky. Bloomington: Indiana University Press.

Barbieri, Pierpaolo. 2007. "Symbolic Traditions." *Harvard Crimson*, January 17. http://www .thecrimson.com/article/2007/1/17/notes-on-primal-harvard-span-stylefont-weight/.

Barefoot, Daniel W. 2004. *Haunted Halls of Ivy: Ghosts of Southern Colleges and Universities.* Winston-Salem, N.C.: John F. Blair.

Barlow, Sharon. 1989. "The Ghosts of Wesleyan." *Wesleyan Pharos* (West Virginia Wesleyan College), April 14, 4.

Barnes, Daniel R. 1966. "Some Functional Horror Stories on the Kansas University Campus." *Southern Folklore Quarterly* 30:305–12.

Barnes, Earl Bryant. 1898. "The Grind." *Triangle* (New York University) 5:125–26.

Barra, Allan. 2004. *Big Play: Barra on Football.* Washington, D.C.: Potomac Books.

Barrett, Frank J. 2002. "Gender Strategies of Women Professionals: The Case of the U.S. Navy." In *Managing Professional Identities: Knowledge, Performativity and the "New" Professional*, ed. Mike Dent and Stephen Whitehead, 157–73. New York: Routledge.

Barrick, Mac E. 1974. "The Growth of Graffiti." *Folklore Forum* 7:273–75.

Bart, Peter. 1983. "Prigging Out." *Rolling Stone*, April 14, 88–92, 94–95.

Bateson, Gregory. 1955. "A Theory of Play and Fantasy: A Report on Theoretical Aspects of the Project for the Study of the Role of Paradoxes of Abstraction in Communication." In *Approaches to the Study of Human Personality.* American Psychiatric Association. Psychiatric Research Reports, no. 2: 39–51.

———. 1956. "The Message 'This Is Play.'" In *Group Processes: Transactions of the Second Conference*, ed. Bertram Schaffner, 145–242. New York: Josiah Macy, Jr., Foundation.

———. 2000 [1972]. *Steps to an Ecology of Mind.* Chicago: University of Chicago Press.

Battle, Ashley L. 2007. "For Some Fraternities, Body Branding Is a Symbol of Devotion." *Columbia News Service*, March 27. http://jscms.jrn.columbia.edu/cns/2007-03-27/ battle-branding.html.

Battreall, Greg. 1987. "The Michael A. Frang Legend." Indiana University Folklore Archives.

Baughman, Ernest. 1945a "The Cadaver Arm." *Hoosier Folklore Bulletin* 4:30–32.

———. 1945b. "The Fatal Initiation " *Hoosier Folklore Bulletin* 4:49–55.

———. 1966. *Type and Motif-Index of the Folktales of England and North America.* The Hague: Mouton.

Baum, R. Bruce. 2010. *The Almost Wet Your Pants Book of Humor.* Bloomington, Ind.: Author House.

Baum, S. V. 1958. "Legend-Makers on the Campus." *American Speech* 33:292–93.

Beatty, Roger Dean. 1976. "Computerlore: The Bit Bucket." *New York Folklore* 2:223–24.

Becker, Jane S. 1998. *Selling Tradition: Appalachia and the Construction of an American Folk, 1930–1940.* Chapel Hill: University of North Carolina Press.

Beckwith, Martha Warren. 1923. "Signs and Superstitions Collected from American College Girls." *Journal of American Folklore* 36:1–15.

Beezley, William H. 1980. "Locker Rumors: Folklore and Football." *Journal of the Folklore Institute* 17:196–221.

———. 1981. "Better Ag Than Fag! And Other North Carolina Jokes." *North Carolina Folklore Journal* 29:112–19.

———. 1985. "Counterimages of the Student Athlete in Football Folklore." In *American Sport Culture: The Humanistic Dimensions*, ed. Wiley Lee Umphlett, 212–25. Lewisburg, Pa.: Bucknell University Press.

———. 1988. "'Nice Girls Don't Sweat': Women in American Sport." In *The Sporting Image: Readings in American Sport History*, ed. Paul J. Zingg, 337–52. Lanham, Md.: University Press of America.

Belanger, Greg. 1988. "Chuck and His Brothers." *Washington Monthly* 20(10): 42–43.

Bellah, Robert N., Richard Madsen, William M. Sullivan, Ann Swidler, and Steven M. Tipton. 1985. *Habits of the Heart: Individualism and Commitment in American Life.* New York: Harper and Row.

Bennett, Gillian. 1998. "The Vanishing Hitchhiker at Fifty-Five." *Western Folklore* 57:1–17.

Bennett, Gillian, and Paul Smith, eds. 2007. *Urban Legends: A Collection of International Tall Tales and Terrors.* Westport, Conn.: Greenwood Press.

Bennett, Paul. 2001. *The Campus Guide: University of Cincinnati.* New York: Princeton Architectural Press.

Berberoglu, Linda, and David Hilliard. 1986. "Halloween Scare Fits Description of 'Modern Legend.'" *Daily Item* (Sunbury, Pa.), October 30, 1.

Berger, Joseph. 1988. "Honor Code: Rewards and Pitfalls of an Ideal." *New York Times*, March 9 (sec. B), 9.

Berger, Peter, and Richard John Neuhaus. 1977. *To Empower People: The Role of Mediating Structures in Public Policy.* Washington, D.C.: American Enterprise Institute for Public Policy Research.

Bergera, Gary James, and Ronald Priddis. 1985. *Brigham Young University: A House of Faith.* Salt Lake City: Signature.

Berry, Chad. 2003. "'Rammer Jammer . . .': Bama Cheers Have a History of Their Own." *Tuscaloosa News*, September 6. http://www.tuscaloosanews.com/article/20030906/NEWS/309060304.

Berry, Margaret C. 1980. *The University of Texas: A Pictorial Account of Its First Century.* Austin: University of Texas Press.

———. 1983. *UT Austin Traditions and Nostalgia.* Rev. ed. Austin, Tex.: Eakins Press.

The Best of 606 Aggie Jokes. 1976. Dallas: Gigem Press.

Beta Theta Pi. n.d. *Beta Tunes: The Songs of Beta Theta Pi.* http://www.docstoc.com/docs/4856701/Songs-of-Beta-Theta-Pi-Fraternity-Beta-Tunes-SONG.

Betterton, Don. 1988. *Alma Mater: Unusual Stories and Little-Known Facts from America's College Campuses.* Princeton, N.J.: Peterson's Guides.

Bevis, Teresa Brawner, and Christopher J. Lucas. 2007. *International Students in American Colleges and Universities: A History.* New York: Palgrave/Macmillan.

Beyer, Janice M., and Harrison M. Trice. 1988. "The Communication of Power Relations in Organizations through Cultural Rites." In *Inside Organizations: Understanding the Human Dimension*, ed. Michael Owen Jones, Michael Dane Moore, and Richard Christopher Snyder, 141–57. Newbury Park, Calif.: Sage.

Bird, S. Elizabeth. 1994. "Playing with Fear: Interpreting the Adolescent Legend Trip." *Western Folklore* 53:191–209.

Birnbach, Lisa. 1984. *Lisa Birnbach's College Book.* New York: Ballantine Books.

Bishop, Morris. 1962. *A History of Cornell.* Ithaca, N.Y.: Cornell University Press.

Blank, Trevor. 2009. "Moonwalking in the Digital Graveyard: Diversions in Oral and Electronic Humor Regarding the Death of Michael Jackson." *Midwestern Folklore* 35:75–90.

———. 2010. "Cheeky Behavior: The Meaning and Function of 'Fartlore' in Childhood and Adolescence." *Children's Folklore Review* 32:61–85.

———. 2011. "Posthum(or)ous: The Folk Response to Mass-Mediated Disasters in the Digital Age." Ph.D. diss., Pennsylvania State University–Harrisburg.

Blankman, Edward J., and Thurlow O. Cannon. 1987. *The Scarlet and the Brown: A History of St. Lawrence University.* Ed. Neal S. Burdick. Canton, N.Y.: St. Lawrence University.

Bledstein, Burton. 1976. *The Culture of Professionalism: The Middle Class and the Development of Higher Education in America.* New York: W. W. Norton.

"Blinded by the Light." 2007. Snopes.com: Rumor Has It. http://www.snopes.com/horrors/drugs/lsdsun.asp.

Bloch, Arthur. 2003. *Murphy's Law: The 26th Anniversary Edition.* New York: Perigee.

Bloom, Allan. 1987. *The Closing of the American Mind: How Higher Education Has Failed Democracy and Impoverished the Souls of Today's Students.* New York: Simon and Schuster.

Blum, Ernst. 1926. "The Psychology of Study and Examinations." *International Journal of Psycho-Analysis* 7:457–69.

Blumenfeld, Amir, Jeff Rubin, Sarah Schneider, Streeter Seidell, Ethan Trex, and Ricky Van Veen. 2006. *The College Humor Guide to College.* New York: Dutton.

Boas, Louise. 1971 [1935]. *Woman's Education Begins: The Rise of the Women's Colleges.* New York: Arno.

Boettcher, Alexandra. 1980. "Initiation Rites Common at MSU." *State News* (Michigan State University, East Lansing), May 27, 1–2.

Boewe, Charles, 1987. "Who's Buried in Rafinesque's Tomb?" *Pennsylvania Magazine of History and Biography* 111:213–35.

Boney, F. N. 1984. *A Pictorial History of the University of Georgia.* Athens: University of Georgia Press.

Boone, Lalia Phipps. 1959. "Gator (University of Florida) Slang." *American Speech* 34:153–57.

Boorstin, Daniel J. 1965. *The Americans: The National Experience.* New York: Vintage Books.

Boswell, George W. 1976. "Ole Miss Jokes and Anecdotes." *Tennessee Folklore Society Bulletin* 42:72–82.

———. 1979. "Irony in Campus Speech." *Tennessee Folklore Society Bulletin* 45:154–60.

Botkin, B. A., and William G. Tyrrell. 1962. "Upstate, Downstate." *New York Folklore Quarterly* 18:304–14.

Bowlby, Mary Stratton, and Mary Kathleen Gannon. 1944. *The Story of Purdue's Traditions.* Lafayette, Ind.: Purdue University.

Boyd, J. D. 2011. "Kentucky Bass Boat Winner." *Ohio Outdoors.* Forum post, July 5. http://www.theohiooutdoors.com/showthread.php73792-Kentucky-bass-boat-winner.

Boyer, Ernest L. 1987. *College: The Undergraduate Experience in America*. New York: Harper and Row.

Brackett, Frank Parkhurst. 1944. *Granite and Sagebrush: Reminiscences of the First Fifty Years of Pomona College*. Los Angeles: Ward Ritchie Press.

Bradley, Charlotte, Ruth Coleman, and Anita Peck, comps. 1925. *Barnard College Song Book*. New York: A. S. Barnes.

Brady, Jane D. 2005. *The Brigham Young University Folklore of Hugh Winder Nibley: Gifted Scholar, Eccentric Professor and LDS Spiritual Guide*. Privately printed version of 1996 M.A. thesis, Brigham Young University.

Bragg, Rick. 2011. "Come One, Come Y'all: Tailgaiting Is Serious Business at Ole Miss." *Parade*, October 16, 10–12, 15, 20, 27.

Brandes, Stanley H. 1985. *Forty: The Age and the Symbol*. Knoxville: University of Tennessee Press.

Bratcher, James T. 1972. "The Professor Who Didn't Get His Grades In: A Traveling Anecdote." In *Diamond Bessie and the Shepherds*, ed. William M. Hudson, 121–23. Publications of the Texas Folklore Society, no. 36. Austin, Tex.: Encino Press.

"Brawn over Brains: Frosh, Sophs Battled 4 or 5 times Yearly." 1955. *Daily Collegian* (Pennsylvania State University, University Park), February 22, 38.

Brenneis, Donald. "'Turkey,' 'Wienie,' 'Animal,' 'Stud': Intragroup Variation in Folk Speech." *Western Folklore* 36:238–46.

Brenner, Robin E. 2007. *Understanding Manga and Anime*. Westport, Conn.: Libraries Unlimited.

Briscoe, Virginia Wolf. 1981a. "Bryn Mawr College Traditions: Women's Rituals as Expressive Behavior." Ph.D. diss., University of Pennsylvania.

———. 1981b. "Readin', Ritin', and Ritual." *Center for Southern Folklore Magazine* 4(1): 11.

Britton, Ruth. 1987. "The Folklore of College Students at Penn State." Penn State Harrisburg Folklore Archives.

Brod, Harry. 1995. "Pornography and the Alienation of Male Sexuality." In *Rethinking Masculinity: Philosophical Explorations in Light of Feminism*, ed. Larry May and Robert A. Strikwerda, 237–54. Lanham, Md.: Littlefield.

Bronner, Simon J. 1984. "Folklore in the Bureaucracy." In *Tools for Management*, ed. Frederick Richmond and Kathy Nazar, 45–57. Harrisburg, Pa.: PEN Publications.

———. 1985. "'What's Grosser Than Gross?': New Sick Joke Cycles." *Midwestern Journal of Language and Folklore* 11:39–49.

———. 1986a. *Grasping Things: Folk Material Culture and Mass Society in America*. Lexington: University Press of Kentucky.

———. 1986b. *American Folklore Studies: An Intellectual History*. Lawrence: University Press of Kansas.

———. 1989. *American Children's Folklore*, annotated edition. Little Rock, Ark.: August House.

———. 1990. *Piled Higher and Deeper: The Folklore of Campus Life*. Little Rock, Ark.: August House.

———. 1995. *Piled Higher and Deeper: The Folklore of Student Life*. Little Rock, Ark.: August House.

———. 2005. "Menfolk." In *Manly Traditions: The Folk Roots of American Masculinities*, ed. Simon J. Bronner, 1–58. Bloomington: Indiana University Press.

———. 2007. "The Analytics of Alan Dundes." In *The Meaning of Folklore: The Analytical Essays of Alan Dundes*, ed. Simon J. Bronner, 1–50. Logan: Utah State University Press.

———. 2009. "Digitizing and Virtualizing Folklore." In *Folklore and the Internet: Vernacular Expression in a Digital World*, ed. Trevor J. Blank, 21–66. Logan: Utah State University Press.

———. 2010. "Framing Folklore: An Introduction." *Western Folklore* 69:275–97.

———. 2011a. *Explaining Traditions*. Lexington: University Press of Kentucky.

———. 2011b. "The Rise and Fall–and Return–of the Class Rush: A Study of a Contested Tradition." *Western Folklore* 70:5–67.

Bronson, John. 1968a. "Pranks, Customs Alive in Past." *Daily Collegian* (Pennsylvania State University, University Park), May 10, 1.

———. 1968b. "Extensive Class Rivalry Part of University History." *Daily Collegian* (Pennsylvania State University, University Park), May 15, 1, 4.

Brown, Ryan. 2011. "What's Your Major? Probably Not One of These." *Chronicle of Higher Education*, July 29, A19.

Brown, Waln K. 1973. "Cognitive Ambiguity and the 'Pretended Obscene Riddle.'" *Keystone Folklore* 18:89–102.

Browning, Peter. 2003. *Working for Wages: On the Road in the Fifties*. Lafayette, Calif.: Great West Books.

"Brown University: Traditions." 2005. *Spiritus-Temporis Web Ring Community*. http://www.spiritus-temporis.com/brown-university/traditions.html.

Brubaker, John H., III. 1987. *Hullabaloo Nevonia: An Anecdotal History of Student Life at Franklin and Marshall College*. Lancaster, Pa.: Franklin and Marshall College.

Bruce, Alexander M. 2003. *The Folklore of Florida Southern College*. Chula Vista, Calif.: Aventine Press.

Brunvand, Erik. 2000. "The Heroic Hacker: Legends of the Computer Age." In Jan Harold Brunvand, *The Truth Never Stands in the Way of a Good Story*, 170–98. Urbana: University of Illinois Press.

Brunvand, Jan Harold. 1960. "Sex in the Classroom." *Journal of American Folklore* 73:250–51.

———. 1962. "Further Notes on Sex in the Classroom." *Journal of American Folklore* 75:62.

———. 1981. *The Vanishing Hitchhiker: American Urban Legends and Their Meanings*. New York: W. W. Norton.

———. 1984. *The Choking Doberman and Other "New" Urban Legends*. New York: W. W. Norton.

———. 1986. *The Mexican Pet: More "New" Urban Legends and Some Old Favorites*. New York: W. W. Norton.

———. 1989. *Curses! Broiled Again! The Hottest Urban Legends Going*. New York: W. W. Norton.

———. 1990. "Dorson and the Urban Legend." *Folklore Historian* 7:16–22.

———. 1993. *The Baby Train, and Other Lusty Urban Legends*. New York: W. W. Norton.

———. 1998. *The Study of American Folklore: An Introduction*. 4th ed. New York: W. W. Norton.

———. 1999. *Too Good to Be True: The Colossal Book of Urban Legends*. New York. W. W. Norton.

———. 2001. *Encyclopedia of Urban Legends*. Santa Barbara, Calif.: ABC-CLIO.

———. 2002. "Folklore in the News (And, Incidentally, on the Net)." *Western Folklore* 60:47–66.

Bryan, W. F. 1954. "A Modern Ballad." *North Carolina Folklore* 2(1): 8–9.

Bryant, Howard. 2011. "Penn State's Failure of Power." ESPN.com, November 11. http://espn.go.com/espn/commentary/story/_/id/7208029/penn-state-joe-paterno-failure-power?eleven-twelve.

Buehler, Richard Edward. 1964. "An Annotated Collection of Contemporary Obscene Humor from the Bloomington Campus of Indiana University." M.A. thesis, Indiana University.

Buell, Ryan, and Stefan Petrucha. 2010. *Paranormal State: My Journey into the Unknown.* New York: HarperCollins.

Buntz, Samuel. 2007. "Anti-Sexism Posters Turn Heads." *Dartmouth*, November 2. http://thedartmouth.com/2007/11/02/news/daughtersofdartmouth/.

Burgess, Adam, Pamela Donovan, and Sarah E. H. Moore. 2009. "Embodying Uncertainty? Understanding Heightened Risk Perception of Drink 'Spiking.'" *British Journal of Criminology* 49:848–62.

Burns, Thomas A., with Inger H. Burns. 1976. *Doing the Wash: An Expressive Culture and Personality Study of a Joke and Its Teller.* Norwood, Pa.: Norwood Editions.

Burson, Anne C. 1980. "Model and Text in Folk Drama." *Journal of American Folklore* 93:305–16.

———. 1982. "Pomp and Circumcision: A Parodic Skit in a Medical Community." *Keystone Folklore*, n.s., 1:28–40.

Calaprice, Alice, and Trevor Lipscombe. 2005. *Albert Einstein: A Biography.* Westport, Conn.: Greenwood Press.

Calkin, Nancy, and William Randel. 1945. "Campus Slang at Minnesota." *American Speech* 20:233–34.

Camp, Walter. 1909a. *The Substitute: A Football Story.* New York: D. Appleton

———. 1909b. *Jack Hall at Yale.* New York: D. Appleton.

———. 1910. *The Book of Foot-ball.* New York: Century.

———. 1911. *Old Ryerson.* New York: D. Appleton.

———. 1914. *Frank Armstrong at College.* New York: A. L. Burt.

———. 1915. *Danny the Freshman.* New York: D. Appleton.

"Campus Comedy." 1962. *Reader's Digest*, October, 180.

"Campus Comedy." 1963. *Reader's Digest*, June, 217–18.

"Campus Comedy." 1966. *Reader's Digest*, October, 56.

"Campus Halloween Murders." 2007. Snopes.com: Rumor Has It. http://www.snopes.com/horrors/madmen/campus.asp.

Canfield, Dorothy. 1922. *Rough-Hewn.* New York: Harcourt, Brace.

Cannon, Anthon S., collector. 1984. *Popular Beliefs and Superstitions from Utah*, ed. Wayland D. Hand and Jeannine E. Talley. Salt Lake City: University of Utah Press.

Cantwell, Robert. 1991. "Conjuring Culture: Ideology and Magic in the Festival of American Folklife." *Journal of American Folklore* 104:148–63.

Capps, John, and Donald Capps. 2009. *You've Got to Be Kidding! How Jokes Can Help You Think.* Malden, Mass.: Wiley-Blackwell.

Capri, Anton Z. 2007. *From Quanta to Quarks: More Anecdotal History of Physics.* Hackensack, N.J.: World Scientific Publishing.

Caprio, Mike. 2011. "The Great Grout-Fiti Mystery." B-Line, blog post March 18. http://theb-line.tumbler.com/post/3944698707/the-great-grout-fiti-mystery.

Carey, George G. 1971. *Maryland Folk Legends and Folk Songs.* Cambridge, Md.: Tidewater Publishers.

———. 1988. "Mysteries, Legends, and Tall Tales." *Five College Magazine*, Fall, 6–9.

Carlinsky, Dan, ed. 1971. *A Century of College Humor*. New York: Random House.

Carnegie Foundation for the Advancement of Teaching. 1987. *A Classification of Institutions of Higher Education*. Princeton, N.J.: Carnegie Foundation.

Carol, Robin. 2007. "Myths, Rumors Surround Traditional Naked Run at Tufts U." *Minaret*, December 29. http://theminaretonline.com/2007/12/29/article2030.

Carroll, Jon. 1994. "Will This Be on the Final?" *San Francisco Chronicle*, April 4, E10.

Carroll, Michael P. 1987. "Praying the Rosary: The Anal-Erotic Origins of a Popular Catholic Devotion." *Journal for the Scientific Study of Religion* 26:486–98.

Carter, Virginia. 1930–31. "University of Missouri Slang." *American Speech* 6:203–6.

Caso, Daniela. 2009. "Don't Rock the Boat." *Mirror* (Fairfield University), April 14. http://fairfieldmirror.com/2009/04/14/dontrocktheboat/.

Cataldi, Emily Forrest, Caitlin Green, Robin Henke, Terry Lew, Jennie Woo, Bryan Shepherd, and Peter Siegel. 2011. *2008–09 Baccalaureate and Beyond Longitudinal Study (B&B: 08/09): First Look*. Washington, D.C.: National Center for Education Statistics.

Cattermole-Tally, Frances. 1990. "Male Fantasy or Female Revenge? A Look at Some Modern Rape Legends." In *A Nest of Vipers: Perspectives on Contemporary Legend*, Vol. 5, ed. Gillian Bennett and Paul Smith, 41–48. Sheffield, U.K.: Sheffield Academic Press.

Cerf, Bennett. 1945. "Trade Winds." *Saturday Review of Literature*, March 24, 16.

———. 1959. *The Laugh's on Me*. New York: Doubleday.

Chambers, E. O. 1983. "The Mona Lisa Legend of City Park, New Orleans." *Louisiana Folklore Miscellany* 5(3): 31–39.

Champney, Lizzie W. 1885. "Professor Sarcophagus." *Harper's New Monthly Magazine* 70 (February): 366–70.

Chatikavanij, Vasant. 2012. "Clean Wholesome Stories No. 901-20." http://www.jokes.in.th.

Chea, Terence. 2010. "College Enrollments Rise, but Budge Cuts Cap Enrollment." *USA Today*. http://www.usatoday.com/news/education/2010-01014-college-admissions-N.htm.

Chesworth, Jo. 1976. "Shapeless in the Hands of Fate." *Penn Stater* (Pennsylvania State University, University Park) 62(4): 1–5.

———. 1980. "Swampy's Son Revives a Legend." *Penn Stater* (Pennsylvania State University, University Park) 67(1): 8–9.

Chinery, David. 1987. "Snooping for Snipes: America's Favorite Wild Goose Chase." *Children's Folklore Newsletter* 10 (Spring): 3–4 and 10 (Fall): 3–4.

Chopra, Vidhu Vinod, screenwriter. 2009. *3 Idiots*. Mumbai: Vinod Chopra Productions.

Choron, Sandra, and Harry Choron. 2004. *College in a Can*. New York: Houghton Mifflin.

Christiansen, Reidar Th. 1946. *The Dead and the Living*. Oslo: H. Aschehoug.

Christner, Becky. 1967. "A Collection of Songs and Traditions of Alpha Chi Omega Sorority at UCLA." Wayne State University Folklore Archive.

Chronicle of Higher Education. 1989. *Almanac of Higher Education*. Washington, D.C.: Chronicle of Higher Education.

———. 2010. *Almanac of Higher Education*. Washington, D.C.: Chronicle of Higher Education.

———. 2011. *Almanac of Higher Education*. Washington, D.C.: Chronicle of Higher Education.

Clarke, Malea. 1987. "Determination of the Caloric Equivalent of a Single M&M and Evidence of a Population Control Strategy." *Journal of Irreproducible Results* 32(5): 28–29.

"A Class in Itself? Mastering the Art of the 'Gut' Course." 1989. *New York Times*, March 5 (sec. 1, part 2), 52.

Clawges, Patricia. 1989. "The Folklore of Law Students: Coping with Impersonality and Intimidation." Penn State Harrisburg Folklore Archives.

Clements, Jesse, Ingrid Sheaffer, and Jessica Smith. 2003. "Theatre Ghost." *BSC Folklore* (Birmingham-Southern College). http://www.bsc.edu/folklore/oral/ghost.htm.

Clements, William M. 1969a. "The Chain." *Indiana Folklore* 2:90–96.

———. 1969b. *The Types of the Polack Joke.* Folklore Forum Bibliographic and Special Series, no. 3.

———. 1980. "The Walking Coffin." In *Indiana Folklore: A Reader*, ed. Linda Dégh, 279–86. Bloomington: Indiana University Press.

———. "Tongue Twister." In *Folklore: An Encyclopedia of Beliefs, Customs, Tales, Music, and Art*, ed. Thomas A. Green, 793-94. Santa Barbara, Calif.: ABC-CHD.

Clerval, Henry. 1986–87. "Clap Books." *Maledicta* 9:139–41.

Closson, David L. 1977. "The Onomastics of the Rabble." *Maledicta* 1:215–33.

Cnytr. 2005. Blog Archives, May 9. http://cnytr.blogspot.com/2005_05_01_archive.html.

Cochran, Carolyn. 1981. "Candlelights on the Indiana University Campus." Indiana University Folklore Archives.

Cohen, Hennig. 1951. "Going to See the Widow." *Journal of American Folklore* 64:223.

Cohen, Hennig, and Tristam Potter Coffin, eds. 1987. *The Folklore of American Holidays.* Detroit: Gale.

"College Heights Herald Poll: What Was Your Favorite Greek Week Event?" 2008. *College Heights Herald* (Western Kentucky University), May 1. http://www.wkuherald.com/poll/index.cfm?event=displayPollResults&poll_question_id=37788.

"College Holidays." 1856. *Williams Quarterly* (Williams College) 3:378–80.

Collins, Hently. 1988. "Fraternity Rites Stir Sexual Violence, Conference Told." *Philadelphia Inquirer*, October 29, B3.

Collison, Michele. 1990. "8 Major Black Fraternities and Sororities Agree to End the Practice of Pledging." *Chronicle of Higher Education*, February 28, A31.

"Committee Report." 1904. *State Collegian* (Pennsylvania State University), October 20, 3–5.

"Computer Geek Jokes." 2010. *SiteReviver*, September 7. -jokes–4386.html.

Conan, Noel. 2011. "Brutal Incidents Shine Light on Band Hazing Culture." npr.org, December 21. http://www.npr.org/2011/12/21/144077864/brutal- incidents-shine -light-on-band-hazing-culture.

"Confucius Say Jokes." 2011. MustShareJokes.com. http://www.mustsharejokes.com/page/Confucius+Say+Jokes.

Conkin, Paul, assisted by Henry Lee Swint and Patricia S. Mile. 1985. *Gone with the Ivy: A Biography of Vanderbilt University.* Knoxville: University of Tennessee Press.

Consider the Years: 1883–1983, Houghton College. 1982. Houghton, N.Y.: Houghton College.

Cook, Theodore Andrea. 1898. "Pushball." In *The Encyclopedia of Sport*, ed. The Earl of Suffolk and Berkshire, Hedley Peek, and F. G. Aflalo, 2:168–69. London: Lawrence and Bullen.

Copeland, Larry, and Yamiche Alcindor. 2011. "Hazing Culture Mars Marching Bands' Glamour." *USA Today*, December 16. http://www.usatoday.com/news/nation/story/2011-12-19/florida-am-famu-band-hazing-georgia/51972882/1.

Copeland, Lewis, and Faye Copeland, eds. 1940. *10,000 Jokes, Toasts, and Stories*. Garden City, N.Y.: Garden City Books.

"Core Values." 2011. *We Are the Aggie Network*. http://www.aggienetwork.com/theasso ciation/corevalues.aspx.

Costner, Sharon. 1975. "'State' Jokes on the Carolina Campus." *North Carolina Folklore Journal* 23:107–11.

Cottom, Daniel. 1989. *Text and Culture: The Politics of Interpretation*. Minneapolis: University of Minnesota Press.

Cowan, Helen. 1989. "The Worst Way to Get a 4.0 at College: A College Legend." Angus Gillespie Papers, Rutgers, Douglass College, New Brunswick, N.J.

Cowie, A. P., R. Mackin, and I. R. McCaig. 1983. *Oxford Dictionary of Current Idiomatic English*, 2 vols. Oxford: Oxford University Press.

Cowley, W. H., and Glenn A. Reed. "Academics Are Human." 1977. *Change* 9(8): 33–38.

Craig, Allen. 1974. "Songs of Pi Kappa Alpha Fraternity." Wayne State University Folklore Archive.

Cramer, C. H. 1976. *Case Western Reserve: A History of the University, 1826–1976*. Boston: Little, Brown.

Crane, Beverly. 1977. "The Structure of Value in 'The Roommate's Death': A Methodology for Interpretive Analysis of Folk Legends." *Journal of the Folklore Institute* 14:133–49.

Crawford, Michael L. 1974. "Legends from St. Mary-of-the-Woods College." *Indiana Folklore* 7:53–75.

"Craziest College Traditions, The." 2011. OnlineUniversities.com, January 25. http:// www.onlineuniversities.com/blog/2011/01/the-25-craziest-college-traditions/.

Cross, Gary. 2004. *The Cute and the Cool: Wondrous Innocence and Modern American Children's Culture*. New York: Oxford University Press.

Curley, Stephen. 2005. *Aggies by the Sea: Texas A&M University at Galveston*. College Station: Texas A&M University Press.

Dalkoff, Breena. 1974. "Rituals of a Fraternity House." Indiana University Folklore Archives.

Daniels, Cora Linn, and C. M. Stevans, eds. 1903. *Encyclopaedia of Superstitions, Folklore, and the Occult Sciences of the World*. Milwaukee, Wis.: J. H. Yewdale & Sons.

Danielson, Larry. 1979. "Folklore and Film: Some Thoughts on Baughman Z500–599." *Western Folklore* 38:209–19.

Dargan, Amanda, and Steven Zeitlin. 2009. "American Talkers: Expressive Styles and Occupational Choice." *Journal of American Folklore* 96:3–33.

Daughrity, Kenneth L. 1930–31. "Handed-Down Campus Expressions." *American Speech* 6:129–30.

Davidson, Levette Jay. 1943. "Moron Stories." *Southern Folklore Quarterly* 7:101–4.

Davie, James S., and A. Paul Hare. 1974. "Button-Down Collar Culture: A Study of Undergraduate Life at a Men's College." In *Anthropology and American Life*, ed. Joseph Jorgensen and Marcello Truzzi, 262–81. Englewood Cliffs, N.J.: Prentice-Hall.

Davies, Christie. 2011. *Jokes and Targets*. Bloomington: Indiana University Press.

Davis, Eddie. 1956. *Campus Joke Book*. New York: Ace.

Dawson, Jim. 1971. "Ed Diddle Stories." Western Kentucky Folklore Archive.

Dean, Ellee. 2006. "Schoolhouse Sex: It Rocks." *Boston Phoenix*, August 30. http://the phoenix.com/boston/life/21262-schoolhouse-sex-it-rocks/.

de Caro, F. A., and Richard Lunt. 1968. "The Face on the Tombstone." *Indiana Folklore* 1(1): 34–41.

Deford, Frank. 2011a. "For Some Marching Bands, Hazing Means Brutality." npr.org, December 7. arching-bands-hazing-means-brutality.

Dégh, Linda. 1968a. "The Hook." *Indiana Folklore* 1(1): 92–100.

———. 1968b. "The Boy Friend's Death." *Indiana Folklore* 1(1): 101–6.

———. 1969a. "The Haunted Bridges near Avon and Danville and Their Role in Legend Formation." *Indiana Folklore* 2(1): 54–89.

———. 1969b. "The Roommate's Death and Related Dormitory Stories in Formation." *Indiana Folklore* 2(2): 55–74.

———. 1971. "The 'Belief Legend' in Modern Society: Form, Function, and Relationship to Other Genres." In *American Folk Legend: A Symposium*, ed. Wayland D. Hand, 55–68. Berkeley: University of California Press.

———. 2001. *Legend and Belief*. Bloomington: Indiana University Press.

Dégh, Linda, and Andrew Vázsonyi. 1978. "The Crack on the Red Goblet or Truth and the Modern Legend." In *Folklore in the Modern World*, ed. Richard M. Dorson, 253–72. The Hague: Mouton.

———. 2011b. "Sweetness and Light: Is Football Culture the Core of the Problem?" npr.org, November 16. http://www.npr.org/2011/11/16/142355144/is-football-the-core-of-the-problem.

Dekok, David. 2008a. "A Grad Student's Fatal Stabbing: A Mystery for Almost 40 Years." *Sunday Patriot-News* (Harrisburg, Pa.), December 7, A12–14.

———. 2008b. "A 39-year Slaying Investigation: No Motive, No Arrest, No Closure." *Patriot-News* (Harrisburg, Pa.), December 8, A6–7.

DeParle, Jason. 1988. "About Men." *Washington Monthly* 20(10): 38–46, 48.

DeSantis, Alan D. 2007. *Inside Greek U.: Fraternities, Sororities, and the Pursuit of Pleasure, Power, and Prestige*. Lexington: University Press of Kentucky.

Deters, Anna. 2003. "Campus Haunts: Tales of the Supernatural Have Enthralled Generations of IWU Students." *Illinois Wesleyan University Magazine*, Winter. http://www.iwu.edu/iwunews/magazine/pastissues/Winter_2003/ghost.shtml.

Dickey, Eleanor. 1997. "Forms of Address and Terms of Reference." *Journal of Linguistics* 33:255–74.

Dickinson, M. B. 1951. "Words from the Diaries of North Carolina Students." *American Speech* 26:181–84.

Dike, Catherine. 1994. *Canes in the United States: Illustrated Mementoes of American History, 1607–1953*. Ladue, Mo.: Cane Curiosa Press.

Dober, Richard P. 1996. *Campus Architecture: Building in the Groves of Academe*. New York: McGraw-Hill.

Dodge, Willard A., Jr., Reuben B. Moulton, Harrison W. Sigworth, and Adrian C. Smith Jr. 1982. *Legends of Caltech*. Pasadena: Alumni Association, California Institute of Technology.

Dolan, John Patrick, and Dale Irvin. 2008. *The Lawyer's Joke Book*. Charleston, S.C.: Advantage.

Domowitz, Susan. 1979. "Foreign Matter in Food: A Legend Type." *Indiana Folklore* 12:86–95.

Donovan, Dan. 1989. "Mass Murder Rumors on American Campuses." *Foaftale News*, no. 12: 1–2.

Dorson, Richard M. 1949. "The Folklore of Colleges." *American Mercury* 68:671–77.

———. 1959. *American Folklore*. Chicago: University of Chicago Press.

———. 1967. *American Negro Folktales*. Greenwich, Conn.: Fawcett Publications.

Dougherty, Barry, and H. Aaron Cohl, comps. 2009. *The Friars Club Encyclopedia of Jokes.* New York: Black Dog & Leventhal.

Douglas, Paul. 1987. "Bizz-Buzz, Turtles, Quarters, and the One Horse Club: The Role of Drinking Games among High School and College Students." *Alcohol Health and Research World* 11 (Summer): 54–57, 92.

Doyle, Charles Clay. 1973. "Title-Author Jokes, Now and Long Ago." *Journal of American Folklore* 86:52–54.

Doyle, Charles Clay, Wolfgang Mieder, and Fred R. Shapiro, comps. 2001. *The Dictionary of Modern Proverbs.* New Haven, Conn.: Yale University Press.

D'Pnymph, Sue. 1988. *Eat Beans, They Make You Astute.* Research notes by James Withers. Little Rock, Ark.: privately printed.

Dresser, Norine, and Theodor Schuchat. 1980. "In Search of the Perforated Page." *Western Folklore* 39:300–306.

Ducati. 2011. Post on Syracuse.com, November 29. gebasketball/2011/11/in-the-after math-of-assistant.html.

Duda, Ambrose. 1987. "Drinking Games of Male Students Attending Western Oregon State College." Western Oregon State Folklore Archives.

Dunaway, Wayland Fuller. 1946. *History of the Pennsylvania State College.* State College: Pennsylvania State College.

Dundes, Alan. 1961. "Mnemonic Devices." *Midwest Folklore* 11:139–47.

———. 1964. "Here I Sit—A Study of American Latrinalia." *Kroeber Anthropological Society Papers*, no. 34 (Spring): 91–105.

———. 1966. "Metafolklore and Oral Literary Criticism." *Monist* 50:505–16.

———. 1968. "One Hundred Years of California Traditions." *California Monthly* 78(5): 19–32.

———. 1971. "On the Psychology of Legend." In *American Folk Legend: A Symposium*, ed. Wayland D. Hand, 21–36. Berkeley: University of California Press.

———. 1976. "Projection in Folklore: A Plea for Psychoanalytic Semiotics." *MLN* 91:1500–1533.

———. 1978. "Into the Endzone for a Touchdown: A Psychoanalytic Consideration of American Football." *Western Folklore* 37:75–88.

———. 1980. *Interpreting Folklore.* Bloomington: Indiana University Press.

———. 1981. "Many Hands Make Light Work or Caught in the Act of Screwing in Light Bulbs." *Western Folklore* 40:261–66.

———. 1987a. *Cracking Jokes: Studies of Sick Humor Cycles and Stereotypes.* Berkeley, Calif.: Ten Speed Press.

———. 1987b. *Parsing through Customs: Essays by a Freudian Folklorist.* Madison: University of Wisconsin Press.

———. 1990. *Folklore Matters.* Knoxville: University of Tennessee Press.

———. 1994a. "Gallus as Phallus: A Psychoanalytic Cross-Cultural Consideration of the Cockfight as Fowl Play." In *The Cockfight: A Casebook*, ed. Alan Dundes, 241–84. Madison: University of Wisconsin Press.

———. 1994b. "Towards a Metaphorical Reading of 'Break a Leg': A Note on the Folklore of the Stage." *Western Folklore* 53:85–89.

———. 1996. "Two Applications for Admission to U$¢." *Western Folklore* 55:155–62.

———. 1997. *From Game to War, and Other Psychoanalytic Essays on Folklore.* Lexington: University Press of Kentucky.

———. 1998. "Bloody Mary in the Mirror: A Ritual Reflection of Pre-Pubescent Anxiety." *Western Folklore* 57:119–35.

———. 2007 [1966]. "Here I Sit: A Study of American Latrinalia." In *The Meaning of Folklore: The Analytical Essays of Alan Dundes*, ed. Simon J. Bronner, 360–74. Logan: Utah State University Press.

Dundes, Alan, and Lauren Dundes. 2002. "The Elephant Walk and Other Amazing Hazing: Male Fraternity Initiation through Infantilization and Feminization." In *Bloody Mary in the Mirror: Essays in Psychoanalytic Folkloristics*, by Alan Dundes, 95–121. Jackson: University Press of Mississippi.

Dundes, Alan, and Robert A. Georges. 1962. "Some Minor Genres of Obscene Folklore." *Journal of American Folklore* 75:221–26.

Dundes, Alan, and Carl R. Pagter. 1975. "Bar Dice in the San Francisco Bay Area." *Kroeber Anthropological Society Papers*, nos. 51–52 (Spring–Fall): 1–18.

———. 1978 [1975]. *Work Hard and You Shall Be Rewarded: Urban Folklore from the Paperwork Empire*. Bloomington: Indiana University Press.

———. 1987. *When You're Up to Your Ass in Alligators: More Urban Folklore from the Paperwork Empire*. Detroit: Wayne State University Press.

———. 1991. *Never Teach a Pig to Sing: Still More Urban Folklore from the Paperwork Empire*. Detroit: Wayne State University Press.

———. 1996. *Sometimes the Dragon Wins: Yet More Urban Folklore from the Paperwork Empire*. Syracuse, N.Y.: Syracuse University Press.

Dundes, Alan, and C. Fayne Porter. 1963. "American Indian Student Slang." *American Speech* 38:270–77.

Dundes, Alan, and Manuel R. Schonhorn. 1963. "Kansas University Slang: A New Generation." *American Speech* 38:163–77.

Dunn, Herbert. 2003. "Horizontal Violence among Nurses in the Operating Room." *AORN Journal* 78:977–88.

Dunn, Tom. 1973. "Class Scraps Begat Bruises and Arnica." *Penn Stater* (Pennsylvania State University, University Park) 59(5): 8–9.

Earley, James. 1987. *On the Frontier of Leadership*. Tacoma, Wash.: University of Puget Sound, 1987.

Eble, Connie. 1996. *Slang & Sociability: In-Group Language among College Students*. Chapel Hill: University of North Carolina Press.

Editors of Guinness. 1982. *Guinness Book of College Records and Facts*. New York: Sterling.

Egan, Robert. 1985. *From Here to Fraternity*. New York: Bantam.

Eikel, Fred, Jr. 1946. "An Aggie Vocabulary of Slang." *American Speech* 21:29–36.

Eisiminger, Sterling. 1978. "Acronyms and Folk Etymology." *Journal of American Folklore* 91:582–84.

Eliade, Mircea. 1958. *Rites and Symbols of Initiation: The Mysteries of Birth and Rebirth*. Trans. Willard R. Trask. New York: Harper & Row.

Eliason, Eric. 2006. "Mormon Culture Region." In *Encyclopedia of American Folklife*, ed. Simon J. Bronner, 825–29. Armonk, N.Y.: M. E. Sharpe.

Eliot, Charles William. 1969 [1923]. *Harvard Memories*. Freeport, N.Y.: Books for Libraries Press.

Ellis, Bill. 1983. "Legend-Tripping in Ohio: A Behavioral Survey." *Papers in Comparative Studies* 2:61–73.

———. 1990. "Gay Roommates and Unethical Dentists." *Foaftale News*, no. 18: 7.

———. 1991. "Nostradamus and Massacres." *Foaftale News*, no. 24: 8–10.

———. 1994. "'The Hook' Reconsidered: Problems in Classifying and Interpreting Adolescent Horror Legends." *Folklore* 105:61–75.

———. 1995. "Good-Times Cathy Computer Virus." *Foaftale News*, no. 36: 4–5.

———. 2000. *Raising the Devil: Satanism, New Religions, and the Media.* Lexington: University Press of Kentucky.

———. 2001. *Aliens, Ghosts, and Cults: Legends We Live.* Jackson: University Press of Mississippi.

———. 2004. *Lucifer Ascending: The Occult in Folklore and Popular Culture.* Lexington: University Press of Kentucky.

Ellis, Bill, and Alan Mays. 1992. "AIDS." *Foaftale News*, no. 27: 8–9.

Ellis, Junius. 1987. "At Witty Caltech, Pranks Aren't Purely a Laughing Matter." *Smithsonian* 18(6): 100–102, 104, 106–8, 110, 112–13.

Emery, David. 2010a. "Flunk Me If You Can." About.com: Urban Legends. http://urban legends.about.com/od/college/a/flunk_me.htm.

———. 2010b. "Psychic Predicts Halloween Campus Massacre." About.com: Urban Legends. http://urbanlegends.about.com/od/horrors/a/campus_massacre.htm.

———. 2010c. "Return of the 'Blue Star' LSD Tattoo: An Urban Legend." About.com: Urban Legends. 198.htm.

Emmanuel, Greg. 2004. *The 100-Yard War: Inside the 100-Year-Old Michigan–Ohio State Football Rivalry.* Hoboken, N.J.: John Wiley & Sons.

Emrich, Duncan. 1972. *Folklore on the American Land.* Boston: Little, Brown.

English, Cynthia. 2011. "Most Americans See College as Essential to Getting a Good Job." *Gallup*, August 18. http://www.gallup.com/poll/149045/Americans-College-Essential -Getting-Good-Job.aspx.

eNotes.com. 2011. "University of Illinois: Traditions." *eNotes: Study Smarter.* http://www .enotes.com/university-of-llinois-guide/traditions.

Ernstberger, Mary J. 1983. "Little Bo Peep." Indiana University Folklore Archives.

Eschholz, Paul A., and Alfred F. Rosa. 1970. "Course Names: Another Aspect of College Slang." *American Speech* 45:85–90.

Everett, Edward. 1852. "Harvard Alumni Festival." *To-Day: A Boston Literary Journal* 2 (July 31): 65–68.

"Everybody into the Water Even at 50 Degrees." 1989. *New York Times*, May 7 (sec. 1, part 2), 54.

Fagan, Susan Martin. 1981. "Ten Words for a Dollar—A New Campus Custom." *Western Folklore* 40:337–43.

Falk, Gerhard. 2005. *Football and American Identity.* Binghamton, N.Y.: Haworth Press.

"Famous Toasts and Sentiments." 1888. *American Notes and Queries* 1 (October 27): 301–8.

Fantz, Christy. 2009. "'Humans vs. Zombies' on at CU-Boulder, Minus Nerf Guns." ColoradoDaily.com, December 2. http://www.coloradodaily.com/ ci_13911286#axzzolwb2prci.

Farha, Bryan, and Gary Steward Jr. 2006. "Paranormal Beliefs: An Analysis of College Students." *Skeptical Inquirer* 30 (January/February 2006): 37–40.

Farrell, David. 2004. "Berkeley: Traditions." *University of California History Digital Archives.* http://sunsite.berkeley.edu/~ucalhist/general_history/campuses/ucb/tradi tions.html.

"Feedback." 1984–85. *Maledicta* 8:257–67.

Fenichel, Otto. 1953. *The Collected Papers of Otto Fenichel: First Series*. New York: W. W. Norton.

Fidler, Isaac. 1833. *Observations on Professions, Literature, Manners and Emigration in the United States and Canada Made During a Residence There in 1832*. London: Whittaker, Treacher.

Fine, Elizabeth C. 2003. *Soulstepping: African American Step Shows*. Urbana: University of Illinois Press.

Fine, Gary Alan. 1979. "Cokelore and Coke Law: Urban Belief Tales and the Problem of Multiple Origins." *Journal of American Folklore* 92:477–84.

———. 1983. *Shared Fantasy: Role Playing Games as Social Worlds*. Chicago: University of Chicago Press.

———. 1987. "Welcome to the World of AIDS: Fantasies of Female Revenge." *Western Folklore* 46:192–97.

———. 1992. *Manufacturing Tales: Sex and Money in Contemporary Legends*. Knoxville: University of Tennessee Press.

Fine, Gary Alan, and Bruce Noel Johnson. 1980. "The Promiscuous Cheerleader: An Adolescent Male Belief Legend." *Western Folklore* 39:120–29.

Fischer, Paul. 1982. "Fetishes of the American College Fraternity." In *Objects of Special Devotion: Fetishes and Fetishism in American Popular Culture*, ed. Ray B. Browne, 205–14. Bowling Green, Ohio: Bowling Green University Popular Press.

Fish, Lydia. 1972. "The Old Wife in the Dormitory: Sexual Folklore and Magical Practices from State University College." *New York Folklore Quarterly* 28:30–36.

Fitton, Mary Louise. 1941. "Hanover College Has Hoosier Folklore Background." *Yearbook of the Society of Indiana Pioneers*, 17–26.

———. 1942. "College Folklore." *Hoosier Folklore Bulletin* 1(2): 40–41.

———. 2010. "The Florida State Seminoles: A Tradition of Tribute." *Florida State University*. l.

Flanagan, Caitlin. 2012. "Hysteria and the Teenage Girl." *New York Times*, January 24, SR4.

Fleece, Jeffery A. 1946. "Words in-FU." *American Speech* 21:70–72.

Flippo, Chet. 1975. "Near to the Maddening Crowd." *Texas Monthly*, February, 48–54.

Flower, John A. 2003. *Downstairs, Upstairs: The Changed Spirit and Face of College Life in America*. Akron, Ohio: University of Akron Press.

Flugel, J. C. 1939. "The Examination as Initiation Rite and Anxiety Situation." *International Journal of Psycho-Analysis* 20:275–86.

Flynn2Doucet. 2011. "ITT: We All Go to Hell." IGN.com, November 11. http://boards.I'gn .com/college_football/68546/z06733918/r206738914/.

Flynt, Larry C., ed. 2006. *Hustler's Dirtiest Jokes 2*. New York: Citadel Press.

Folb, Edith A. 1980. *Runnin' Down Some Lines: The Language and Culture of Black Teenagers*. Cambridge, Mass.: Harvard University Press.

Fonarow, Wendy. 2006. *Empire of Dirt: The Aesthetics and Rituals of British Indie Music*. Middletown, Conn.: Wesleyan University Press.

Ford, Willa. 2003. *A Toast to Men (F**k the Men)*. CD Single. Burbank, Calif.: Lava.

Forrest, Rex. 1940. "Ranking the Professors." *American Speech* 15:445.

Foster, Michael Dylan. 2009. *Pandemonium and Parade: Japanese Monsters and the Culture of Yôkai*. Berkeley: University of California Press.

Fox, Dov. 2004. *The Truth About Harvard: A Behind-the-Scenes Look at Admissions and Life on Campus*. New York: Princeton Review Publishing.

Fox, William S. 1983. "Computerized Creation and Diffusion of Folkloric Materials." *Folklore Forum* 16:5–20.

———. 1990. "The Roommate's Suicide and the 4.0." In *A Nest of Vipers: Perspectives on Contemporary Legend*, Vol. 5, ed. Gillian Bennett and Paul Smith, 69–76. Sheffield, U.K.: Sheffield Academic Press.

Frank, Russell. 2011. *Newslore: Contemporary Folklore on the Internet.* Jackson: University Press of Mississippi.

Franks, Ray. 1982. *What's in a Nickname? Exploring the Jungle of College Athletic Mascots.* Amarillo, Tex.: Ray Franks Publishing Ranch.

Frantz, Jeff. 2012. "Facing the Heat." *Patriot-News* (Harrisburg, Pa.), January 12, A1, 16.

"Fraternity Pledges Are 'On Line' in Rite of Passage." 1989. *New York Times*, April 9 (sec. 1, part 2), 39.

"Fraternity Policies." 2009. *Kappa Kappa Psi-Gamma Pi.* January 26. http://www.purdue kkpsi.org/chapter/policies.

Free, James. 1982. "Fraternity Jokes, Pranks, and Bore-Asses." Indiana University Folklore Archives.

Freedman, Mervin B. 1967. *The College Experience.* San Francisco: Jossey-Bass.

Freud, Anna. 1966. *The Ego and the Mechanisms of Defense.* New York: International Universities Press.

Freud, Sigmund. 1930. *Civilization and Its Discontents.* Trans. James Strachey. New York: W. W. Norton.

———. 1959 [1922]. *Group Psychology and the Analysis of the Ego.* Trans. James Strachey. New York: W. W. Norton.

———. 1960 [1905]. *Jokes and Their Relation to the Unconscious.* Trans. James Strachey. New York: W. W. Norton.

———. 1964 [1932]. "The Acquisition and Control of Fire." In *The Standard Edition of the Complete Psychological Works of Sigmund Freud*, Vol. 22, trans. and ed. James Strachey, 185–93. London: Hogarth Press.

———. 1989. "Character and Anal Erotism." In *The Freud Reader*, ed. Peter Gay, 293–96. New York: W. W. Norton.

———. 2003 [1901]. *The Psychopathology of Everyday Life.* Trans. Anthea Bell. New York: Penguin.

Frothingham, Andrew. 2002. *Great Toasts: From Births to Weddings to Retirement Parties—and Everything in Between.* Franklin Lakes, N.J.: Career Press.

"Fummer's Guide to the Universe, A." 1988. *F&M Today* (Franklin and Marshall College) 18(1): 36.

Furr, Joel. 1995. "Stalking Chicken Little: Myth, Reality, and Absurdity in Alt.Folklore." *Internet World* 6(2): 86–89.

Gach, Vicki. 1973. "Graffiti." *College English* 35:285–87.

Gaddis, Colleen. 2009. "Powder Puff Football Teams Compete for Championship Thursday." *University Star* (Texas State University), October 26. http://star.txstate.edu/node/1238.

Gadson, A. Denita. 1989. "Greek Power: African-American Greek-Letter Organizations Wield Massive Influence after School Days." *Black Collegian* 20(1): 34–36, 136–37.

Gaither, Carl C., and Alma E. Cavazos-Gaither. 1999. *Medically Speaking: A Dictionary of Quotations on Dentistry, Medicine and Nursing.* London: Institute of Physics.

Galanter, Marc. 2005. *Lowering the Bar: Lawyer Jokes and Legal Culture.* Madison: University of Wisconsin Press.

Gammage, Jeff. 1989. "Groups Keep in Step with Tradition." *Philadelphia Inquirer*, July 9, B2.

Gardner, Robert G. 1972. *On the Hill: The Story of Shorter College*. Rome, Ga.: Shorter College, 1972.

Garfinkel, David. 1986. "High Jinks at Cal Tech." *Business Week Careers* 4(4): 52–54.

Gasso, Jordi. 2010. "Stolen Gnome Back at Home." *Yale Daily News*, April 22. http://www .yaledailynews.com/news/university-news/2010/04/22/stolen-gnome-back-home/.

Gates, Charlene. 1976. "Graffiti and the Environment of the Folk Group: University Music Majors." *Folklore Forum* 9:35–42.

"Geek Jokes: Engineers and Lawyers." 2002. JokesAround.com. http://www.jokesaround .com/j/3497.html.

Geertz, Clifford. 1972. "Deep Play: Notes on the Balinese Cockfight." *Daedalus* 101:1–37.

Geeslin, Ned, and S. Avery Brown. 1989. "With a Campus Legend in Peril, Members of a Fraternity Vow to Save the Endangered M.I.T. Smoot." *People Weekly*, April 24, 93–95.

Gelfand, H. Michael. 2006. *Sea Change at Annapolis: The United States Naval Academy, 1949–2000*. Chapel Hill: University of North Carolina Press.

Genge, N. E. 2000. *Urban Legends: The As-Complete-As-One-Could-Be Guide to Modern Myths*. New York: Three Rivers Press.

Genovese, Eugene D. 1989. *The Political Economy of Slavery: Studies in the Economy and Society of the Slave South*. 2nd ed. Middletown, Conn.: Wesleyan University Press.

George, Nelson. 1999. *Elevating the Game: Black Men and Basketball*. Lincoln: University of Nebraska Press.

German, Richard H. 2010. *Surgeon: The Man Behind the Mask*. Indianapolis, Ind.: Dog Ear.

Gilkey, Carolyn F. 1990. "The Physicist, the Mathematician and the Engineer: Scientists and the Professional Slur." *Western Folklore* 49:215–20.

Girdler, Lew. 1970. "The Legend of the Second Blue Book." *Western Folklore* 29:111–17.

Glass, Robert L. 1991. *Software Folklore*. State College, Pa.: Computing Trends.

Glavan, Joyce. 1968. "Sorority Tradition and Song." *Journal of the Ohio Folklore Society* 3:192–98.

Glazer, Mark. 1987. "The Cultural Adaptation of a Rumour Legend: 'The Boyfriend's Death' in South Texas." In *Perspectives on Contemporary Legend*, Vol. 2, ed. Gillian Bennett, Paul Smith, and J. D. A. Widdowson, 93–108. Sheffield, U.K.: Sheffield Academic Press.

Glimm, James York. 1983. *Flatlanders and Ridgerunners: Folktales from the Mountains of Northern Pennsylvania*. Pittsburgh: University of Pittsburgh Press.

Glowka, Wayne, and Brenda K. Lester. 1997. "Among the New Words." *American Speech* 72:289–313.

Glowka, Wayne, Katherine A. Bonner, and Brenda K. Lester. 1999. "Among the New Words." *American Speech* 74:71–94.

Glowka Wayne, Debra Dent, Megan Melançon, David K. Barnhart, and Grant Barrett. 2006. "Among the New Words." *American Speech* 81:297–311.

Glowka, Wayne, Brenda K. Lester, Hope Blume, Charles Farmer, Keith Hendrix, Mary Nolan Joiner, Deidra Lines, Randall Lastinger, Denzil R. Pugh, Nicholas Roberts, and Barry Popik. 1999. "Among the New Words." *American Speech* 74:298–323.

Gluck, Michael. 1989. "Coin Ingesting Complicating a Tavern Game." *Western Journal of Medicine* 150:343–44.

Goffman, Erving. 1974. *Frame Analysis: An Essay on the Organization of Experience*. Cambridge, Mass.: Harvard University Press.

"Going Back in Time." 1986. *F&M Today* (Franklin and Marshall College) 15(2): n.p.

Golden, Gail D. 1974. "Contemporary Bathroom Graffiti." Wayne State University Folklore Archive.

Goldsmith, Fred I. 1929. *Purdue University Alumni Record and Campus Encyclopedia*. Lafayette, Ind.: Purdue University.

Goldstein, Diane E. 1992. "Welcome to the Mainland, Welcome to the World of AIDS: Cultural Viability, Localization and Contemporary Legend." *Contemporary Legend* 2:23–40.

———. 2004. *Once Upon a Virus: AIDS Legends and Vernacular Risk Perception*. Logan: Utah State University Press.

Gonzales, Susan. 2002. "Senior Class Day." *Yale Bulletin & Calendar*, June 7. http://www .yale.edu/opa/arc-ybc/v30.n31/story104.html.

Goodman, Norman, and Kenneth A. Feldman. 1975. "Expectations, Ideals, and Reality: Youth Enters College." In *Adolescence in the Life Cycle: Psychological Change and Social Context*, ed. Sigmund E. Dragastin and Glen H. Elder, 147–69. Washington, D.C.: Hemisphere Publishing.

Gordon, Beverly. 2003. "Embodiment, Community Building, and Aesthetic Saturation in 'Restroom World,' a Backstage Women's Space." *Journal of American Folklore* 116:444–64.

Gordon, Larry. 2010. "UC San Diego Condemns Student Party Mocking Black History Month." *Los Angeles Times*, February 18. http://articles.latimes.com/2010/feb/18/ local/la-me-ucsd18-2010feb18.

Gore, Willard C. 1895. "Student Slang." *Contributions to Rhetorical Theory* 2:1–29.

Goss, Michael. 1984. *The Evidence for Phantom Hitch-hikers*. Wellingborough, U.K.: Aquarian Press.

Graber, Tom. 2011. "Twitter Archetypes." *Pistachio Media*. http://www.pistachiomedia .org/social-media/twitter/twitter-archetypes/.

Graham, Joe S. 1985. "Old Army Went to Hell in 1958: Aggie War Stories from the Corps of Cadets." In *Sonovagun Stew: A Folklore Miscellany*, ed. Francis Edward Abernethy, 105–21. Publication of the Texas Folklore Society, no. 46. Dallas: Southern Methodist University Press.

"Grave of Nellie L. Vaughn." 2002. *Quahog.org*. http://www.quahog.org/attractions/ index.php?id=66.

Graves, Oliver Finley. 1979. "Folklore in Academe: The Anecdote of the Professor and the Transom." *Indiana Folklore* 12:142–45.

Gray, Joseph M. 1969–70. "The Folk Tradition of the Sweetheart Tree." *Pennsylvania Folklife* 19(2): 14–17.

Green, Jonathon. 2010. *Green's Dictionary of Slang*. 3 vols. London: Chambers.

Green, Thomas A., ed. 2006. *The Greenwood Library of American Folktales*. 4 vols. Westport, Conn.: Greenwood Press.

Greenberg, Andrea. 1973. "Drugged and Seduced: A Contemporary Legend." *New York Folklore Quarterly* 29:131–58.

Greenfield, Jeff. 1999 [1975]. "The Black and White Truth About Basketball." In *Signifyin(g), Sanctifyin', and Slam Dunking: A Reader in African American Expressive Culture*, ed. Gena Dagel Caponi, 373–79. Amherst: University of Massachusetts Press.

Greenspan, Aaron. 2010. "The Legend of Mark Zuckerberg." *Huffington Post*, September 21. http://www.huffingtonpost.com/aaron-greenspan/the-legend-of-mark-zucker_b_732625.html.

Gregerson, Royce. 2006. "Wabash College Freshmen Bringing Back the Pots." *Bachelor* (Wabash College), September 14. http://www.wabash.edu/alumni/news.cfm?news_ID=3810.

Gregory, Jackson, ed. 1905. *The Nineteen Hundred and Six Blue & Gold of the University of California*. Berkeley, Calif.: Junior Class.

Grider, Sylvia. 1973. "Dormitory Legend-Telling Progress: Fall, 1971–Winter, 1973." *Indiana Folklore* 6:1–32.

———. 1980. "The Hatchet Man." In *Indiana Folklore: A Reader*, ed. Linda Dégh, 147–78. Bloomington: Indiana University Press.

———. 2000. "The Archaeology of Grief: Texas A&M's Bonfire Tragedy Is a Sad Study in Modern Mourning." *Discovering Archaeology* 2:68–74.

Griffin, Walter. 2007. "The College Tug-of-War." *Daily Princetonian*, February 23. http://www.dailyprincetonian.com/2007/02/23/17445/.

Griscom, Andy, Ben Rand, and Scott Johnson. 1984. *The Complete Book of Beer Drinking Games*. New Haven, Conn.: RJ Publications.

Griscom, Andy, Ben Rand, Scott Johnson, and Michael Balay. 1986. *Beer Games II: The Exploitative Sequel*. New Haven, Conn.: Mustang Publishing.

Gross, Dan. 1961. "Folklore of the Theater." *Western Folklore* 20:257–63.

Grossman, Lev. 2010. "Person of the Year 2010: Mark Zuckerberg." *Time*, December 15. http://www.time.com/time/specials/packages/article/0,28804,2036683_2037183_2037185-2,00.html.

Grotegut, Eugene K. 1955. "Going to See the O'Reilly Sisters." *Western Folklore* 14:51–52.

Guardia, Juan R., and Nancy J. Evans. 2008. "Factors Influencing the Ethnic Identity Development of Latino Fraternity Members at a Hispanic Serving Institution." *Journal of College Student Development* 49:163–81.

Gutierrez, Lezlee. 2008. "Sadies Encourages Ladies to Enjoy Free Fun." *Optimist* (Abilene Christian University), November 19, 1, 4.

Guynn, Jessica. 2010. "Facebook's Zuckerberg Friends 'The Simpsons.'" *Los Angeles Times*, October 4. http://latimesblogs.latimes.com/technology/2010/10/facebooks-zuckerberg-friends-the-simpsons.html.

Hacker, Andrew, and Claudia Dreifus. 2010. *Higher Education? How Colleges Are Wasting Our Money and Failing Our Kids and What We Can Do About It*. New York: Times Books.

Hafferty, Frederic W. 1988. "Cadaver Stories and the Emotional Socialization of Medical Students." *Journal of Health and Social Behavior* 29:344–56.

Haglund, Elizabeth, ed. 1981. *Remembering: The University of Utah*. Salt Lake City: University of Utah Press.

Hale, Allean Lemmon. 1968. *Petticoat Pioneer: The Story of Christian College, Oldest College for Women West of the Mississippi*. Rev. ed. St. Paul, Minn.: North Central Publishing.

Hall, Benjamin Homer. 1968 [1851]. *A Collection of College Words and Customs*. Detroit: Gale.

Hall, Gary. 1973. "The Big Tunnel: Legends and Legend-Telling." *Indiana Folklore* 6:139–73.

Hall, Ronald E. 2001. "The Ball Curve: Calculated Racism and the Stereotype of African American Men." *Journal of Black Studies* 32:104–19.

Hamilton, Thomas. 1833. *Men and Manners in America*. 2 vols. Edinburgh: William Blackwood.

Hancock, Elsie. 1988. "Zoos, Tunes, and Gweeps: A Dictionary of Campus Slang." *F&M Today* (Franklin and Marshall College) 18(1): 12–16.

Hand, Wayland D. 1958. "Going to See the Widow." *Western Folklore* 17:275–76.

———, ed. 1961. *The Frank C. Brown Collection of North Carolina Folklore*. Vol. 6, *Popular Beliefs and Superstitions from North Carolina*. Durham, N.C.: Duke University Press.

Hand, Wayland D., Anna Casetta, and Sondra B. Thiederman, eds. 1981. *Popular Beliefs and Superstitions: A Compendium of American Folklore from the Ohio Collection of Newbell Niles Puckett*. 3 vols. Boston: G. K. Hall.

Handler, Richard, and Jocelyn Linnekin. 1984. "Tradition: Genuine or Spurious." *Journal of American Folklore* 97:273–90.

Hankey, Rosalie. 1944. "Campus Folklore and California's 'Pedro!'" *California Folklore Quarterly* 3:29–35.

Hansche, Susan, John Berti, and Chris Hare. 2004. *Official (ISC)² Guide to the CISSP Exam*. Boca Raton, Fla.: Auerbach.

Hansen, William B., and Irwin Altman. 1976. "Decorating Personal Places: A Descriptive Analysis." *Environment and Behavior* 8:491–504.

Hansen, William F. 2002. *Ariadne's Thread: A Guide to International Tales Found in Classical Literature*. Ithaca, N.Y.: Cornell University Press.

Harlow, Doug. 2006. "Graduation Celebration Gets Out of Hand." *Morning Sentinel* (Waterville, Me.), May 13. http://findarticles.com/p/news-articles/morning-sentinel-waterville-me/mi_8150/is_20060513/graduation-celebration/ai_n50589596/.

Harlow, Ilana. 2003. "Creating Situations: Practical Jokes and the Revival of the Dead in Irish Tradition." In *Of Corpse: Death and Humor in Folklore and Popular Culture*, ed. Peter Narváez, 83–112. Logan: Utah State University Press.

Harris, Brent. 2006. "Freshmen Show Early Success at Football Camp." *Wabash College*, August 16. http://www.wabash.edu/sports/home.cfm?pages_id=62&news_ID=3719.

Harris-Lopez, Trudier. 2003. "Genre." In *Eight Words for the Study of Expressive Culture*, ed. Burt Feintuch, 99–120. Urbana: University of Illinois Press.

Harrison, Albert A., Robert Sommer, Margaret H. Rucker, and Michael Moore. 1986. "Standing Out from the Crowd: Personalization of Graduation Attire." *Adolescence* 21:863–74.

Harrison, Keith C., and Suzanne Malia Lawrence. 2004. "College Students' Perceptions, Myths, and Stereotypes about African American Athleticism: A Qualitative Investigation." *Sport, Education and Society* 9:33–52.

Hartikka, H. D. 1946. "Tales Collected from Indiana University Students." *Hoosier Folklore* 5:71–82.

Haven, Kendall, and Donna Clark. 1999. *100 Most Popular Scientists for Young Adults: Biographical Sketches and Professional Paths*. Englewood, Colo.: Libraries Unlimited.

Hayden, Robert. 1996. "The Code of the Geeks v3.12." *The Geek Code*. www.geekcode.com/geek.html.

Haynes, Casandra. 2009. "Historic Building in Denton Is Recognized for Its Significance to Community." *Pegasus News* (Dallas/Fort Worth, Tex.), November 3. http://www.pegasusnews.com/news/2009/nov/03/historic-building-gets-recognition-various-places/?refscroll=245.

Healey, Phil, and Rick Glanvill. 1996. *Now! That's What I Call Urban Myths: The Best of Urban Myths*. London: Virgin.

Healy, Dorothy. 1972. "Footnote for Just Before Christmas Exams." *Mirror* (Westbrook College) 12(1): 21.

Heckscher, William S. 1970. *Maces: An Exhibition of American Ceremonial Academic Scepters in Honor of the Inauguration of President Terry Sanford, October 18, 1970.* Durham, N.C.: Duke University Museum of Art.

Hedges, James L. 1989. "It's Time for a Change: The Commencement Ceremony Has Lost Much of Its Historical Value and Power." *Chronicle of Higher Education*, June 28, A32.

Henderson, Al. 2006. "Picnics." In *Encyclopedia of American Folklife*, ed. Simon J. Bronner, 958–61. Armonk, N.Y.: M. E. Sharpe.

Hendricks, George D. 1959. "Folk Process on the Campus." *Sing Out!* 9 (Fall): 25–26.

Henricks, J. Edwin. 1994. "Pearson, Charles Chilton." In *Dictionary of North Carolina Biography*. Vol. 5, *P–S,* ed. William S. Powell, 46. Chapel Hill: University of North Carolina Press.

Hickerson, Joseph. 1958. "College Songs in the Indiana University Folklore Archives." *Folklore and Folk Music Archivist* 1(2): 2.

———. 1963. "The Indiana University Folklore Archives Song Index." *Folklore and Folk Music Archivist* 6(1): 3–6.

Hightower, Marvin. 2010. "The Spirit and Spectacle of Harvard Commencement." *Commencement 2010* (Harvard University). http://www.commencement.harvard.edu/background/spirit.html.

Hindman, Darwin Alexander. 1951. *Handbook of Active Games.* New York. Prentice-Hall.

Hindmarch, Ian, and Rudiger Brinkmann. 1999. "Trends in the Use of Alcohol and Other Drugs in Cases of Sexual Assault." *Human Psychopharmacology* 14:225–31.

Hine, Thomas. 1980. "Penn's Art and Architecture Reflect the History of the Cityscape." *Philadelphia Inquirer*, February 24, I1.

Hobbs, Alexander. 1973. "Downie's Slaughter." *Aberdeen University Review* 45:183–91.

Hobsbawm, Eric. 1983. "Introduction: Inventing Traditions." In *The Invention of Tradition*, ed. Eric Hobsbawm and Terence Ranger, 1–14. Cambridge, U.K.: Cambridge University Press.

Hodson, Daniel. 2000. "99 Crazy/Creative Date Ideas." *Universe* (Brigham Young University), February 8. http://newsnet.byu.edu/story.cfm/7709.

Hoffman, Frank A. 1962. "The Daisy Chain." *Journal of American Folklore* 75:264–65.

Holden, Reuben A. 1967. *Yale: A Pictorial History.* New Haven, Conn.: Yale University Press.

Holland, C. C. 2008. "5 Classic Computer Pranks." *BNET*. Blog. http://blogs.bnet.com/teamwork/?p=254.

"Homicide on the Campus." 1966. *Time*, May 13, 70.

Honeck, Richard P. 1997. *A Proverb in Mind: The Cognitive Science of Proverbial Wit and Wisdom.* Mahwah, N.J.: Lawrence Erlbaum.

Hong, Peter Y. 2004. "Money Top Goal of College Freshmen." *Los Angeles Times*, January 26. http://articles.latimes.com/2004/jan/26/local/me-survey26.

"Hoop-de-doo." 1989. *Sun* (Baltimore), April 17, A3.

Hornbein, George, and Kenneth A. Thigpen Jr. 1982. *Salamanders: A Night at the Phi Delt House.* 16 mm film. State College, Pa.: Documentary Resource Center and Filmspace.

Horowitz, Helen Lefkowitz. 1984. *Alma Mater: Design and Experience in the Women's Colleges from Their Nineteenth Century Beginnings to the 1930s.* New York: Alfred A. Knopf.

———. 1987. *Campus Life: Undergraduate Cultures from the End of the Eighteenth Century to the Present*. New York: Alfred A. Knopf.

Howe, Nicholas. 1989. "Rewriting Initialisms: Folk Derivations and Linguistic Riddles." *Journal of American Folklore* 102:171–82.

Hoy, Jim, and Tom Isern. 1987. *Plains Folk: A Commonplace of the Great Plains*. Norman: University of Oklahoma Press.

Hruby, Patrick. 2011. "What the Catholic Church Can Teach Us About the Penn State Scandal." *Atlantic*, November 16. 011/11/what-the-catholic-church-can-teach-us-about-the-penn-state-scandal/248588.

Hubbard, Elbert. 1904. *Little Journeys to the Homes of Great Philosophers*. Vol. 14. Aurora, N.Y.: Roycrofters.

Huffman, Holly. 2008. "Got a Story for You, Ags." Theeagle.com (Bryan–College Station, Tex.), October 15. http://www.theeagle.com/am/Got-a-story-for-you—Ags.

Hufford, David. 1989. "Customary Observances in Modern Medicine." *Western Folklore* 48:129–43.

Hughey, Matthew W. 2008. "Brotherhood or Brothers in the 'Hood'? Debunking the 'Educated Gang' Thesis as Black Fraternity and Sorority Slander." *Race, Ethnicity, and Education* 11:443–63.

———. 2011. "'You Make the Letters. The Letters Don't Make You': The Construction of Memory and Identity in *Stomp the Yard*." In *Black Greek-Letter Organizations 2.0: New Directions in the Study of African American Fraternities and Sororities*, ed. Matthew W. Hughey and Gregory S. Parks, 191–209. Jackson: University Press of Mississippi.

Huguenin, Charles A. 1961. "Burial of Calculus at Syracuse." *New York Folklore Quarterly* 17:256–62.

———. 1962. "A Prayer for Examinations." *New York Folklore Quarterly* 18:145–48.

Hummon, David. M. 1994. "College Slang Revisited: Language, Culture, and Undergraduate Life." *Journal of Higher Education* 65:75–98.

Hunter, Carolyn. 1977. "Folklore on the Prudish Campus, or Watch Out for the Dean of Women." *Southwest Folklore* 1:11–29.

Hunter, Edwin R., and Bernice E. Gaines. 1938. "Verbal Taboo in a College Community." *American Speech* 13:97–107.

"If M.I.T. Frosh Ted Larkin Knows His Studies Cold, He Can Credit a Textbook Case of Pranksterism." *People Weekly*, February 28, 34–35.

IHTFP Gallery. 2009. *Interesting Hacks to Fascinate People: The MIT Gallery of Hacks*. http://hacks.mit.edu/Hacks/.

"ILoo." 2007. Snopes.com: Rumor Has It. http://www.snopes.com/computer/internet/iloo.asp.

Ingeno, Lauren. 2010. "LGBT Graduation Displays Campus Climate." *Daily Collegian* (Pennsylvania State University), April 26, 1–2.

Institute Archives and Special Collections, Rensselaer Libraries, Rensselaer Polytechnic Institute. 2009. "R.P.I. Student Traditions." http://www.lib.rpi.edu/Archives/traditions/rushes/cane_rush.html.

"It's Funny Business at Business School." 1989. *Wall Street Journal*, February 10, B1.

"It's Newtonian, but with Eggs This Time Around." 1989. *New York Times*, April 23, 43.

Jachimiak, Pam. 1978. "Graffiti from Women's Restrooms." Indiana University Folklore Archives.

Jackson, Bruce. 1972. "'The Greatest Mathematician in the World': Norbert Wiener Stories." *Western Folklore* 31:1–22.

Jackson, Steve. 1992. *Killer: The Game of Assassination*. Austin, Tex.: Steve Jackson Games.

Jacob, Philip E. 1957. *Changing Values in College: An Exploratory Study of the Impact of College Teaching*. New York: Harper and Row.

Jacoby, Jack. 2008. *The Biggest Joke Book Ever*. Victoria, B.C.: Trafford.

Jarnagin, Bert, and Fred Eikel Jr. 1948. "North Texas Agricultural College Slang." *American Speech* 23:248–50.

Jayson, Sharon. 2008. "Students Mark 21st Birthdays with 'Extreme' Drinking." *USA Today*, August 28, 1.

J.C. 1871. "'Rushing.'" *Chronicle* (University of Michigan) 3 (October 21), 28–29.

Jeakle, Bill, and Ed Wyatt. 1989. *How to College in the 90s*. New York: New American Library.

Jennings, Karla. 1986. "Computer Folklore." *American Way*, November 1, 16.

———. 1990. *The Devouring Fungus: Tales of the Computer Age*. New York: W. W. Norton.

Johnnyzip84. 2007. "Army Game." *ZipsNation.org*. Message board post, August 31. http://zipsnation.org/forums//lofiversion/index.php?t6438.html.

Johnson, Jerah. 1960. "Professor Einstein and the Chorus Girl." *Journal of American Folklore* 73:248–49.

Johnson, John William. 1980. "Killer: An American Campus Folk Game." *Indiana Folklore* 13:81–101.

Johnson, W. Brad, and Gregory P. Harper. 2005. *Becoming a Leader the Annapolis Way: 12 Combat Lessons from the Navy's Leadership Laboratory*. New York: McGraw-Hill.

Jokes4U. 2008. "Dumb Jock." *Jokes.Net Sports Jokes: Football Jokes*. http://www.jokes.net/dumbjock.htm.

Jones, Ernest. 1961 [1912]. *Papers on Psycho-Analysis*. Boston: Beacon Press.

Jones, Harold Emery. 1904. "The Original of Sherlock Holmes." *Collier's Weekly* 32 (January 9), 14–15, 20.

Jones, Loyal. 2008. *Country Music Humor and Comedians*. Urbana: University of Illinois Press.

Jones, Loyal, and Billy Edd Wheeler. 1987. *Laughter in Appalachia: A Festival of Southern Mountain Humor*. Little Rock, Ark.: August House.

Jones, Michael Owen. 1991. "Why Folklore and Organization(s)?" *Western Folklore* 50:29–41.

Jones, Michael Owen, Michael Dane Moore, and Richard Christopher Snyder, eds. 1988. *Inside Organizations: Understanding the Human Dimension*. Newbury Park, Calif.: Sage.

Jones, Ricky L. 2004. *Black Haze: Violence, Sacrifice, and Manhood in Black Greek Letter Fraternities*. Albany: State University of New York.

Jones, Suzi. 1977. *Oregon Folklore*. Eugene: University of Oregon and the Oregon Arts Commission.

Jordan. 2011. "Fountain Run." University of Southern California Folklore Archives.

Judge, Roy. 1986. "May Morning and Magdalen College, Oxford." *Folklore* 97:15–40.

Kadison, Richard, and Theresa Foy DiGeronimo. 2004. *College of the Overwhelmed: The Campus Mental Health Crisis and What to Do About It*. Hoboken, N.J.: Jossey-Bass.

Kahn, E. J., Jr. 1969. *Harvard: Through Change and Through Storm*. New York: W. W. Norton.

Kandolf, Cindy. 1991. "Easy Grader." Post (May 17). rec.humor newsgroup.

Kannerstein, Gregory. 1967. "Slang at a Negro College: 'Home Boy.'" *American Speech* 42:238–39.

Kaplin, William A., and Barbara A. Lee. 2006. *The Law of Higher Education: A Comprehensive Guide to Legal Implications of Administrative Decision Making.* 4th ed. San Francisco: John Wiley & Sons.

Kaylor, Earl C., Jr. 1976. *Truth Sets Free: Juniata Independent College in Pennsylvania, Founded by the Brethren, 1876: A Centennial History.* South Brunswick, N.J.: A. S. Barnes.

Keeth, Kent, with Harry Marsh. 1985. *Looking Back at Baylor: A Collection of Historical Vignettes.* Waco, Tex.: Baylor University.

Kelley, Charles Greg. 1992. "Joseph E. Brown Hall: A Case Study of One University Legend." *Contemporary Legend* 2:137–53.

Kelley, Janet Agnes. 1949. *College Life and Mores.* New York: Bureau of Publications, Teachers College, Columbia University.

Kennedy, Robert, and Tania Zamuner. 2006. "Nicknames and the Lexicon of Sports." *American Speech* 81:387–422.

Kenwill, Margaret. 1886. "Home and Social Life." *Southern Workman* 15 (June): 70.

Kern, Richard, 1984. *Findlay College: The First Hundred Years.* Nappannee, Ind.: Evangel Press.

Keseling, Peter C., and John Kinney, eds. 1956. *Summa Cum Laughter: The Best Cartoons and Jokes from College Humor Magazines.* New York: Waldorf Publishing.

Kett, Joseph. 1977. *Rites of Passage: Adolescence in America, 1790 to the Present.* New York: Basic Books.

Keyes, Ralph. 2006. *The Quote Verifier: Who Said What, Where, and When.* New York: St. Martin's Press.

"Kicking Post, The." 2011. *Roanoke College: Traditions.* http://roanoke.edu/about_roa noke/traditions/kicking_post.htm.

Kilde, Jeanne Halgren. 2010. *Nature and Revelation: A History of Macalester College.* Minneapolis: University of Minnesota Press.

Kinder, Franz, and Boaz the Clown, eds. 1989. *Metafolkloristica: An Informal Anthology of Folklorists' Humor.* Salt Lake City: Franz Kinder and Boaz the Clown.

King, Laura. 1993. "Local Pizza Delivery Business Fights Rumors." *Arkansas Traveler* (University of Arkansas), August 4, 1.

Klein, Alan M. 1993. *Little Big Men: Bodybuilding Subculture and Gender Construction.* Albany: State University of New York Press.

———. 2000. "Anti-Semitism and Anti-Somatism: Seeking the Elusive Sporting Jew." *Sociology of Sport Journal* 17:213–28.

Klein, Robert. 1975. "Fraternity Folklore: A Study of the Pledge and Rush Traditions of Theta Chi Fraternity at the University of Michigan." Wayne State University Folklore Archive.

Kline, William, and Marion Newell. 1964. "An Ineradicable Bloodstain." *Keystone Folklore Quarterly* 9:30–31.

Knapp, Mary, and Herbert Knapp. 1976. *One Potato, Two Potato . . . The Secret Education of American Children.* New York: W. W. Norton.

Knott, Blanche. 1982. *Truly Tasteless Jokes.* New York: Ballantine.

Kokesh, Jessica. 2011. "Two Arrested for Campus Vandalism." *Volante* (University of South Dakota), April 14. http://www.volanteonline.com/news/two-arrested-for-campus-vandalism–1.2543230?MMode=true.

Konagaya, Hideyo. 2005. "Performing Manliness: Resistance and Harmony in Japanese American *Taiko*." In *Manly Traditions: The Folk Roots of American Masculinities*, ed. Simon J. Bronner, 134–56. Bloomington: Indiana University Press.

Kopay, David, and Perry Deane Young. 1977. *The David Kopay Story*. Los Angeles: Advocate.

Koppe, Richard, William Irvine, and John Burns, comps. and eds. 1950. *A Treasury of College Humor*. New York: William Penn Publishing.

Korab, Holly. 2011. "A Nose Waiting to Be Rubbed." *LASNews*, Winter. http://www.las .illinois.edu/alumni/magazine/articles/2011/bust/.

Koven, Mikel. 2008. *Film, Folklore, and Urban Legends*. Lanham, Md.: Scarecrow Press.

Krattenmaker, Tom. 1989. "'Animal House' May Be Getting a Den Mother." *Sunday News* (Lancaster, Pa.), April 9 (sec. AA), 9, 12.

Kratz, Henry. 1964. "What Is College Slang?" *American Speech* 39:188–95.

Krause, Betsy. 1989. "Traditions." *Oregon Stater*, June, 9–12.

Kraut, Alan M. 1994. *Silent Travelers: Germs, Genes, and the "Immigrant Menace."* New York: Harper Collins.

Kreston, Rosemary. 1973. "Folklore in the Helen Newberry Joy Residence for Women." Wayne State University Folklore Archive.

Krout, John Allen. 1929. *Annals of American Sport*. New Haven, Conn.: Yale University Press.

Kubie, Lawrence S. 1937. "The Fantasy of Dirt." *Psychoanalytical Quarterly* 6:388–425.

Kuethe, J. Louis. 1931–32. "Johns Hopkins Jargon." *American Speech* 7:327–38.

Kurian, George Thomas, ed. 2001. *The Illustrated Book of World Rankings*. 5th ed. Armonk, N.Y.: M. E. Sharpe.

La Barre, Weston. 1979. "Academic Graffiti." *Maledicta* 3:275–76.

LaDousa, Chaise. 2011. *House Signs and Collegiate Fun: Sex, Race, and Faith in a College Town*. Bloomington: Indiana University Press.

Laing, E. Blair. 2008. "Behind the Scenes of Gaieties." *Stanford Daily*, November 14. http://www.stanforddaily.com/2008/11/14/behind-the-scenes-of-gaieties/.

Lampe, Nelson. 2008. "UNL Calls Dorm's 'Assassin' Game Inappropriate and Bans It." *Boston Globe*, February 21. http://www.boston.com/news/local/maine/ articles/2008/02/21/unl_calls_dorms_assassin_game_inappropriate_and_bans_it/.

Lampkin, Danielle. 2008. "Greek Week 2008: Students Compete in Tug of War." *Campus Times* (University of La Verne), May 2. http://www.ulv.edu/ctimes/050208/life_sto ries/tugowar.htm.

Langlois, Janet. 1978. "'Mary Whales, I Believe in You': Myth and Ritual Subdued." *Indiana Folklore* 11:5–33.

———. 1991. "'Hold the Mayo': Purity and Danger in an AIDS Legend." *Contemporary Legend* 1:153–72.

Langway, Lynn, and Janet Huck. 1980. "An Outbreak of Campus KAOS." *Newsweek*, June 9, 103.

Lasch, Christopher. 1979. *The Culture of Narcissism: American Life in an Age of Diminishing Expectations*. New York: W. W. Norton.

Lau, Kimberly J. 1998. "On the Rhetorical Use of Legend: U.C. Berkeley Campus Lore as a Strategy for Coded Protest." *Contemporary Legend*, n.s. 1:1–20.

Lavin, J. A. 1962. "The Clerk of Oxenford in Oral Tradition." *New York Folklore Quarterly* 18:61–64.

Lawrence University. 1988. *Time and Traditions*. Appleton, Wis.: Lawrence University.

Leacock, Stephen. 1935. *Humor: Its Theory and Technique*. New York: Dodd, Mead.

Lears, T. J. Jackson. 1981. *No Place of Grace: Antimodernism and the Transformation of American Culture, 1880–1920*. New York: Pantheon.

Leary, James P. 1978. "The Notre Dame Man: Christian Athlete or Dirtball?" *Journal of the Folklore Institute* 15:133–45.

———. 1982. "A Trickster in Everyday Life." In *The Paradoxes of Play*, ed. John W. Loy, 57–64. West Point, N.Y.: Leisure Press.

Lebman, Marvin. 2004. *A Collection of Jokes and Funny Stories from the Internet! (Not Appropriate for Children)*. Victoria, B.C.: Trafford.

Lecocq, James Gary. 1980. "The Ghost of the Doctor and a Vacant Fraternity House." In *Indiana Folklore: A Reader*, ed. Linda Dégh 265–78. Bloomington: Indiana University Press.

Leddy, Betty. 1948. "La Llorona in Southern Arizona." *Western Folklore* 7:272–77.

Lee, Dorothy Sara, ed. 1981. *Franklin County Folklore*. Chambersburg, Pa.: Wilson College.

Legman, Gershon. 1964. *The Horn Book: Studies in Erotic Folklore and Bibliography*. New Hyde Park, N.Y.: University Books.

———. 1968. *Rationale of the Dirty Joke: An Analysis of Sexual Humor, First Series*. New York: Grove Press.

———. 1975. *Rationale of the Dirty Joke: An Analysis of Sexual Humor, Second Series*. New York: Breaking Point.

Leibowitz, Brian M. 1990. *The Journal of the Institute for Hacks, Tomfoolery, and Pranks at MIT*. Cambridge, Mass.: MIT Museum.

LeMaster, Megan. 2005. *Georgetown College*. Charleston, S.C.: Arcadia.

Leonard, Wendy. 2010. "University of Utah Seniors Say Goodbye with Vulgar Send Off in the Chronicle." *Deseret News* (Salt Lake City), May 6. http://www.deseretnews.com/article/700030268/University-of-Utah-seniors-say-goodbye-with-vulgar-send-off-in-the-Chronicle.html?pg=2.

Letcher, Nick. 2010. "Our House Song." GreekChat.com (forum post on April 26). http://www.greekchat.com/gcforums/showthread.php?t=86393.

Leventhal, Nancy C., and Ed Cray. 1963. "Depth Collecting from a Sixth-Grade Class." *Western Folklore* 22:159–63.

Levine, Peter. 1992. *Ellis Island to Ebbets Field: Sport and the American Jewish Experience*. New York: Oxford University Press.

Levine, Robert. 1987. "Waiting Is a Power Game." *Psychology Today*, April, 24–33.

Levitt, Paul Michael, ed. 2002. *Vaudeville Humor: The Collected Jokes, Routines, and Skits of Ed Lowry*. Carbondale: Southern Illinois University Press.

Lewis, Margaret Jane. 1970. "Some Nicknames and Their Derivations." *Mississippi Folklore Register* 4:52–57.

Li, Aileen. 2007. "Tech's Favorite Legend Lives On: Burdell Website Launches." *Technique* (Georgia Tech University), April 6, 15.

Lighter, J. E. 1997. *Random House Historical Dictionary of American Slang*. Vol. 2. New York: Random House.

Ligotti, Gregory S. 1987. "Blue Book Legends." Wayne State University Folklore Archive.

Lim, Kevin. 2007. "What Skype's Outage Reminds Us Of . . . " *Theory.isthereason*. Blog post, August 21. http://theory.isthereason.com/?p=1813.

Lindquist, Danille Christensen. 2006. "'Locating' the Nation: Football Game Day and American Dreams in Central Ohio." *Journal of American Folklore* 119:444–88.

Linker, Andy. 1980. "Only a Rumor: Horoscope Writer Denies Predicting Murder in Brumbaugh." *Daily Collegian* (Pennsylvania State University, University Park), October 22, 3.

"List of Chat Acronyms & Text Message Shorthand." *Netlingo*. http://www.netlingo.com/emailsh.cfm.

Little Sisters of the Poor. 2011. "Last Word on Football: We Really Do Exist." *Little Sisters of the Poor*. http://www.littlesistersofthepoor.org.

"Locals." 1890. *Free Lance* (Pennsylvania State College), October 1, 61–64.

Lockwood, Sheree. 1978. "Desk-Top Graffiti at UVM." Folklore and Oral History Collection, University of Vermont Library.

Long, George. 1977 [1930]. *The Folklore Calendar*. London: E. P. Publishing.

Longenecker, Gregory J. 1977. "Sequential Parody Graffiti." *Western Folklore* 36:354–64.

Longley, Kyle. 2008. *Grunts: The American Combat Soldier in Vietnam*. Armonk, N.Y.: M. E. Sharpe.

Longo, Joy. 2007. "Horizontal Violence among Nursing Students." *Archives of Psychiatric Nursing* 21:177–78.

Lopresti, Mike. 2011. "Poisoning of Auburn Trees Is Sign of Times in College Sports." *USA Today*, February 17. http://www.usatoday.com/sports/columnist/lopresti/2011–02–17-auburn-tree-poisoning_N.htm.

Lost Lettermen. 2010. "Top 100 College Football Traditions: #56: Get Pumped Prior to Game Day at Notre Dame's Pep Rallies." *Lost Lettermen*. http://www.lostlettermen.com/top-100-college-football-traditions-56-get-pumped-prior-to-game-day-at-notre-dames-pep-rallies/.

Lowe, Donald M. 1982. *History of Bourgeois Perception*. Chicago: University of Chicago Press.

Lu, Xin-An, and David W. Graf Jr., eds. 2004. *A Concise Collection of College Students' Slang*. New York: iUniverse.

Lucien, John. 2011. *Hear No Evil: How the Sandusky Sex Abuse Scandal Rocked Penn State, Toppled Joe Paterno, and Stunned a Nation*. Harrisburg, Pa.: Patriot-News.

Lundgren, Terry D. 1994. "Computer Virus Folklore." *Journal of End User Computing* 6(2): 19–23.

Lutz, Philip, Jr. 1911. "Humanity in the Schools." *American Educational Review* 32:423–27.

Lycan, Gilbert L. 1983. *Stetson University: The First 100 Years*. DeLand, Fla.: Stetson University Press.

Mackey Mitchell Associates. 2001. *Collegiate Gothic: An Architectural Overview*. St. Louis: Mackey Mitchell.

MacLeod, Wendy. 2007. "The Haunted Kenyon Tour." *Kenyon College Alumni Bulletin* 30 (Fall). http://bulletin.kenyon.edu/x2521.xml.

Major, Claire Howell, and Nathaniel Bray. 2008. "Exam Scams and Classroom Flim-flams: Urban Legends as an Alternative Lens for Viewing the College Classroom Experience." *Innovative Higher Education* 32:237–50.

Manley, Robert N. 1969. *Centennial History of the University of Nebraska*. Vol. 1, *Frontier University (1869–1919)*. Lincoln: University of Nebraska Press.

Manning, Kathleen. 2000. *Rituals, Ceremonies, and Cultural Meaning in Higher Education*. Westport, Conn.: Bergin & Harvey.

"Marching Band Suspension." 2008. nbc15.com (Madison, Wis.), November 24. http://www.nbc15.com/home/headlines/30397789.html.

Marcus, Jasmine. 2010. "In the Sack, Or in the Stacks: The Thrills and Consequences of Sex in the Library." *Cornell Daily Sun*, February 11. http://cornellsun.com/node/40697.

Margaret. 2011. "Dead Cow Lecture at Vet School." *The World as I See It: A Life Filled with Ms, Moments, & Memories*. Blog (posted April 13). http://www.theworldasiseeitbloganddesigns.com/2011/04/dead-cow-lecture-at-vet-school.html.

"Marlboro Greens! Fact or Fiction." Grasscity.com: The Best Counter-Culture Community. http://forum.grasscity.com/recreational-marijuana-use/307384-marlboro-greens-fact-fiction.html.

Martin, William. 1990. "Greek Pledging Process: Hardly 'Ritualistic.'" *Chronicle of Higher Education*, January 10, B3.

Mason, Melissa Caswell. 1977. "Sorority Serenading: Its Pretext and Defense." *Folklore and Mythology Studies* 1:51–52.

Matthews, Gail. 1986. "Mercedes Benzene: The Elite Folklife of Physical Chemists." *Folklore Forum* 19:153–74.

Maurer, Marilyn. 1976. "College Folksongs." Indiana University Folklore Archives.

Maxwell, Kimera. 1987. "Traditions, Myths, and Legends Live On." *Spotlight* (Emporia State University, Emporia, Kans.), December, 11.

"May Day Queen Leona Crowns Virgin's Statue." 1939. *Mount Mary Times* 8 (May): 1.

Mays, Alan E. 1980. "'The Shithouse Poet Strikes Again': A Collection of Latrinalia from Men's Rest Rooms at the Pennsylvania State University, October–November, 1980." Penn State–University Park Folklore Archives.

McCallum, John Dennis, and Charles H. Pearson. 1971. *College Football, U.S.A., 1869–1971*. Greenwich, Conn.: Hall of Fame Pub.

McCarl, Robert. 1986. "Occupational Folklore." In *Folk Groups and Folklore Genres: An Introduction*, ed. Elliott Oring, 71–89. Logan: Utah State University Press.

McCarthy, Barbara. 1975. "Traditions." In *Wellesley College, 1875–1975: A Century of Women*, ed. Jean Glasscock, 235–64. Wellesley, Mass.: Wellesley College.

McCosh, Sandra. 1979. *Children's Humour*. London: Granada Publishing.

McCulloch, Gordon. 1987. "Suicidal Sculptors: Scottish Versions of a Migratory Legend." In *Perspectives on Contemporary Legend*, Vol. 2, ed. Gillian Bennett, Paul Smith, and J. D. A. Widdowson, 109–16. Sheffield, U.K.: Sheffield Academic Press.

McDowell, John. 2008. *Folklore of Student Life*. http://www.indiana.edu/~f351jmcd/index.html.

McGeachy, John A., III. 1978. "Student Nicknames for College Faculty." *Western Folklore* 37:281–96.

McKenna, Brian G., Naumai A. Smith, Suzette J. Poole, and John H. Coverdale. 2003. "Horizontal Violence: Experiences of Registered Nurses in Their First Year of Practice." *Journal of Advanced Nursing* 42:90–96.

McNeil, W. K., ed. 1985. *Ghost Stories from the American South*. Little Rock, Ark.: August House.

McPhee, M. C. 1927–28. "College Slang." *American Speech* 3:131–33.

Meakes, Daryl. 2004. *Drunkcow Landmines*. West Conshohocken, Pa.: Infinity.

Mechling, Jay. 1980. "The Magic of the Boy Scout Campfire." *Journal of American Folklore* 93:35–56.

———. 1983. "Mind, Messages, and Madness: Gregory Bateson Makes a Paradigm for American Culture Studies." In *Prospects 8: An Annual Review of American Cultural Studies*, ed. Jack Salzman, 11–30. New York: Cambridge University Press.

———. 1986. "Children's Folklore." In *Folk Groups and Folklore Genres: An Introduction*, ed. Elliott Oring, 91–120. Logan: Utah State University Press.

———. 1988. "On the Relation between Creativity and Cutting Corners." *Adolescent Psychiatry* 15:346–66.

———. 1989. "Mediating Structures and the Significance of University Folk." In *Folk Groups and Folklore Genres: A Reader*, ed. Elliot Oring, 287–95. Logan: Utah State University Press.

———. 2001. *On My Honor: Boy Scouts and the Making of American Youth*. Chicago: University of Chicago Press.

———. 2004. "'Cheaters Never Prosper' and Other Lies Adults Tell Kids: Proverbs and the Culture Wars Over Character." In *What Goes Around Comes Around: The Circulation of Proverbs in Contemporary Life*, ed. Kimberly J. Lau, Peter Tokofsky, and Stephen D. Winick, 86–106. Logan: Utah State University Press.

———. 2005. "Abu Ghraib and the Folk Culture of Male Hazing." Joseph S. Schick Lecture in Language, Literature, and Lexicography, Indiana State University, Hoosier Folklore Society, November 10.

———. 2008a. "Gun Play." *American Journal of Play* 1:192–209.

———. 2008b. "Paddling and the Repression of the Feminine in Male Hazing." *Thymos: Journal of Boyhood Studies* 2:60–75.

———. 2009. "Is Hazing Play?" In *Transactions at Play*, ed. Cindy Dell Clark, 45–62. Lanham, Md.: University Press of America.

Mechling, Jay, and David Scofield Wilson. 1988. "Organizational Festivals and the Uses of Ambiguity: The Case of Picnic Day at Davis." In *Inside Organizations: Understanding the Human Dimension*, ed. Michael Owen Jones, Michael Dane Moore, and Richard Christopher Snyder, 303–17. Newbury Park, Calif.: Sage.

Meckel, Rob. 2008. "University Hosts Annual Day of Remembrance." *Know* (University of Texas at Austin), May 1. http://www.utexas.edu/know/2008/05/01/utremembers-feature/.

Meley, Patricia. 1990. "Adolescent Legend Trips as Teenage Cultural Response: A Study of Lore in Context." M.A. thesis, Pennsylvania State University–Harrisburg.

———. 1991. "Adolescent Legend Trips as Teenage Cultural Response: A Study of Lore in Context." *Children's Folklore Review* 14:5–24.

Mendelsohn, Daniel. 2011. "Secret Dread at Penn State." *New York Times*, November 19, SR4.

Meredith College. 2010. "Meredith Commencement Weekend Traditions." *Meredith College*. http://www.meredith.edu/commencement/traditions.htm.

Metler, Beverly. 1979. "Wells Plans May Day Mirth." *Syracuse Herald-Journal*, April 30.

Mieder, Wolfgang, and Anna Tóthné Litovkina. 2002. *Twisted Wisdom: Modern Anti-Proverbs*. Hobart, Australia: DeProverbio.

Mieder, Wolfgang, Stewart Kingsbury, and Kelsie B. Harder, eds. 1992. *A Dictionary of American Proverbs*. New York: Oxford University Press.

Mikkelson, Barbara. 2006. "Bubble Buoyed." Snopes.com: Rumor Has It. http://snopes.com/college/exam/scantron.asp.

———. 2007a. "The Saltpeter Principle." Snopes.com: Rumor Has It. http://www.snopes.com/military/saltpeter.asp.

———. 2007b. "Statue Cue." Snopes.com: Rumor Has It. http://www.snopes.com/college/halls/virgin.asp.

———. 2008. "Playboy's Party Schools." Snopes.com: Rumor Has It. http://www.snopes
.com/college/admin/playboy.asp.

———. 2009. "The Going Concern." Snopes.com: Rumor Has It. http://www.snopes.com/
college/admin/laxative.asp.

Mikkelson, Barbara, and David P. Mikkelson. 2010. "Urine For a Surprise." Snopes.com:
Rumor Has It. http://www.snopes.com/college/medical/urine.asp.

———. 2011a. "Brevity, the Soul of Twit." Snopes.com: Rumor Has It. http://www.snopes
.com/college/exam/brevity.asp.

———. 2011b. "God Gets an 'A.'" Snopes.com: Rumor Has It. http://www.snopes.com/
college/exam/godknows.asp.

———. 2011c. "Lead by the Nose." Snopes.com: Rumor Has It. http://www.snopes.com/
college/exam/pencils.asp.

———. 2011d. "Tire Sum Excuse." Snopes.com: Rumor Has It. http://www.snopes.com/
college/exam/flattire.asp.

———. 2011e. "The Unsolvable Math Problem." Snopes.com: Rumor Has It. http://www
.snopes.com/college/homework/unsolvable.asp.

Miller, Laura. 2001. "Women and Children First: Gender and the Settling of the Electronic Frontier." In *Reading Digital Culture*, ed. David Trend, 214–20. Malden, Mass.:
Blackwell.

Miller, Russell E. 1966. *Light on the Hill: A History of Tufts College, 1852–1952*. Boston:
Beacon Press.

Miller, Toby. 2005. "A Metrosexual Eye on Queer Guy." *GLQ: A Journal of Lesbian and
Gay Studies* 11:112–17.

Mills, Randolph V. 1951. "Oregon's Pigger: A College Tradition." *Western Folklore*
10:298–309.

Mills Memorial Center and Peace Monument. 2011. Rollins College website. http://www
.rollins.edu/tour/mills.html.

Minot, John Clair, and Donald Francis Snow. 1901. *Tales of Bowdoin*. Augusta, Me.: Press
of Kennebec.

Minter, Meredith. 2008. "Traditions at Randolph-Macon Woman's College: Bury the
Hatchet." Francis E. Webb, Libscomb Library. http://faculty.randolphcollege.edu/
fwebb/traditions/hatchet.html.

Miss Tech. 2007. "Top 10 Geek Jokes." TheTop10Everything.com, November 15. http://
www.thetop10everything.com/top-10-geek-jokes.

Mitchell, Carol Ann. 1976. "The Differences Between Male and Female Joke Telling as
Exemplified in a College Community." Ph.D. diss., Indiana University.

———. 1985. "Some Differences in Male and Female Joke-Telling." In *Women's Folklore,
Women's Culture*, ed. Rosan A. Jordan and Susan J. Kalcik, 163–86. Philadelphia:
University of Pennsylvania Press.

Mitchell, Roger E. 1982. "Campus Drug Lore and the Sociology of Rumor." *Midwestern
Journal of Language and Folklore* 8:89–108.

Moffatt, Michael. 1985a. "Inventing the 'Time-Honored Traditions' of 'Old Rutgers': Rutgers Student Culture, 1858–1900." *Journal of the Rutgers University Libraries* 47:1–11.

———. 1985b. *The Rutgers Picture Book: An Illustrated History of Student Life in the
Changing College and University*. New Brunswick, N.J.: Rutgers University Press.

———. 1986. "The Discourse of the Dorm: Race, Friendship, and 'Culture' among College
Youth." In *Symbolizing America*, ed. Herve Varenne, 158–77. Lincoln: University of
Nebraska Press.

——. 1989. *Coming of Age in New Jersey: College and American Culture*. New Brunswick, N.J.: Rutgers University Press.

Mohler, Owen. 1977. "Purdue University . . . Tradition." *Purdue Exponent*, June 14, 8B.

Monteiro, George. 1964. "Parodies of Scripture, Prayer, and Hymn." *Journal of American Folklore* 77:45–52.

——. 1976. "Religious and Scriptural Parodies." *New York Folklore* 2:150–66.

Montell, William Lynwood. 1975. *Ghosts along the Cumberland: Deathlore in the Kentucky Foothills*. Knoxville: University of Tennessee Press.

Mook, Maurice A. 1959. "Tongue Tanglers from Central Pennsylvania." *Journal of American Folklore* 72:291–96.

——. 1961. "Quaker Campus Lore." *New York Folklore Quarterly* 17:243–52.

Moore, Alexis. 1989. "Getting into 'Step.'" *Philadelphia Inquirer*, July 8 (sec. D), 1, 5.

Moore, Danny W. 1974. "The Deductive Riddle: An Adaptation to Modern Society." *North Carolina Folklore Journal* 22:119–25.

Moore, Jack B. 1961. "Go Ahead, Ma'm: Washington and Lee Student Lore." *North Carolina Folklore* 9(2): 32–34.

Moore, Michael Dane. 1979. "Linguistic Aggression and Literary Allusion." *Western Folklore* 38:259–66.

Morain, David. 2001. "The 'Ten Commandments' of College Life." *Clarkson Integrator* (Clarkson University), April 1. http://media.www.clarksonintegrator.com/media/storage/paper280/news/2001/04/01/Features/The-8220ten.Commandments8221.Of.College.Life-62681.shtml.

Morgan, Hal, and Kerry Tucker. 1987. *More Rumor!* New York: Penguin.

Morris, Robert S. 1969. "The Lemon Squeezer Legend, 1857–1969." *Trinity Alumni Magazine*, Summer, 13–17.

Morse, Brick. 1930. "Early California Traditions and the Axe Capture." In *The Stanford Axe*, ed. Robert Grant O'Neil. Stanford, Calif.: Stanford University Press. http://www.stanford.edu/group/axecomm/axebook/early.html.

Morton, Kathryn. 2002. "Sorority Jell-O Tug-of-War Planned." *Pine Log* (Stephen F. Austin State University), September 30. http://media.www.thepinelog.com/media/storage/paper954/news/2002/09/30/Inside/Sorority.JellO.TugOfWar.Planned-2661443.shtml.

Moser, Bob. 2002. "Jock Privilege." *Teaching Tolerance: A Project of the Southern Poverty Law Center*. http://www.tolerance.org/supplement/jock-privilege.

Mould, Tom. 2005. "'Running the Yard': The Negotiation of Masculinities in African American Stepping." In *Manly Traditions: The Folk Roots of American Masculinities*, ed. Simon J. Bronner, 77–115. Bloomington: Indiana University Press.

Mr. "J." 1981. *Still More of the World's Best Dirty Jokes*. New York: Ballantine Books.

Mullen, Patrick B. 1997. "Belief, Folk." In *Folklore: An Encyclopedia of Beliefs, Customs, Tales, Music, and Art*, ed. Thomas A. Green, 89–97. Santa Barbara, Calif.: ABC-CLIO.

Muller, Eli. 2001. "Bladderball: 30 Years of Zany Antics, Dangerous Fun." *Yale Daily News*, February 28. http://www.yaledailynews.com/articles/view/374.

Murthi, R. K. 2004. *Rib-Tickling Jokes: Laugh Your Way to Long Life*. New Delhi, India: Pustak Mahal.

Myerhoff, Barbara. 1982. "Rites of Passage: Process and Paradox." In *Celebration: Studies in Festivity and Ritual*, ed. Victor Turner, 109–35. Washington, D.C.: Smithsonian Institution Press.

Mythbusters. 2009. "Middle School Main Explosion!" *Mythbusters*. Message board post, July 7. Discovery Channel. http://community.discovery.com/eve/forums/a/tpc/f/9701967776/m/10119310201.

Naismith, James. 1909. "Interclass Contests." *American Physical Education Review* 14:125–31.

Narváez, Peter. 1994. "'Tricks and Fun': Subversive Pleasures at Newfoundland Wakes." *Western Folklore* 53:263–93.

National Commission on Excellence in Education. 1983. *A Nation at Risk: The Imperative for Educational Reform*. Washington, D.C.: U.S. Government Printing Office.

New Anecdota Americana, The. 1944. New York: Grayson.

Newchurch, Karen. 1985. "The Georgia Tech Legacy." *Georgia Tech Alumni Magazine* 60(2): 12–14.

Newman, Frank, Lara Couturier, and Jamie Scurry. 2004. *The Future of Higher Education: Rhetoric, Reality, and the Risks of the Market*. San Francisco: Jossey-Boss.

Nichols, Raymond. 1983. "Foreword." In *On the Hill: A Photographic History of the University of Kansas*, comp. Virginia Adams, Katie Armitage, Donna Butler, and Carol Shankel. Lawrence: University Press of Kansas.

Nilsen, Don L. F. 1981. "Sigma Epsilon Xi: Sex in the Typical University Classroom." *Maledicta* 5:79–91.

Ninth Generation of 101 Aggie Jokes. Vol. 9. Dallas: Gigem Press.

Nist-Olejnik, Sherrie, and Jodi Patrick Holschuh. 2007. *College Rules! How to Study, Survive, and Succeed in College*. 2nd ed. Berkeley, Calif.: Ten Speed Press.

Nomani, Asra Q. 1989. "Steeped in Tradition, 'Step Dance' Unites Blacks on Campus." *Wall Street Journal*, July 10 (sec. A), 1, 4.

Norlander, Matt. 2010. "Taylor University's Terrific Tradition." *College Hoops Journal*, December 12. http://www.collegehoopsjournal.com/2010/12/12/taylor-universitys-terrific-tradition/.

Nosek, Stan, and Fred Wood. 2008. Open letter to students, University of California at Davis, May 22. http://daviswiki.org/Epic_Quad_Battle?action=Files&do=view&target=bureaucratic_asshattery.pdf.

Nuckols, Ben. 2008. "At Colleges Across U.S., Humans Take on Zombies." *Sunday Patriot-News* (Harrisburg, Pa.), December 7, A19.

"'Nuff Nerf! Zombie Game Locks Down Alfred University Campus with Scare." *Wellsville (N.Y.) Daily Reporter*, April 9. 0.

Nunn, Richard. 2007. *Just Joking Off*. Raleigh, N.C.: Lulu.

Nuwer, Hank. 1990. *Broken Pledges: The Deadly Rite of Hazing*. Athens, Ga.: Longstreet Press.

———. 1999. *Wrongs of Passage: Fraternities, Sororities, Hazing, and Binge Drinking*. Bloomington: Indiana University Press.

———, ed. 2004. *The Hazing Reader*. Bloomington: Indiana University Press.

N.W.B. 1900. "The Flag-Scrap at State." *Free Lance* 13(9) (March): 296–99.

"N.Y.U. Rush Lands Two in Court, Injures One." 1925. *New York Times*, October 7, 28.

Oates, Bob. 1999. *Football in America: Game of the Century*. Coal Valley, Ill.: Quality Sports.

O'Brien, David. 2007. "KSU Dispels Killer Rumor Psychic Predicts Mass Murder on Halloween." Recordpub.com, October 13. http://www.recordpub.com/news/article/2695131.

O'Bryon, Jim. 2008. *"I Fail to Miss Your Point": A Personal Collection of Quips, Quotes, Inspirational Stories and Other Stuff.* Longwood, Fla.: Xulon Press.

Ochs, Steve. 2006. *National Lampoon, Jokes Jokes Jokes: The Collegiate Edition.* Los Angeles: National Lampoon.

Ockerlander, Lynda. 1975. "Methods of Cheating." Indiana University Folklore Archives.

"Of Queens, Courts, Music, and Verse." 2004. *Wells Express* (Winter). http://minerva .wells.edu/pdfs/winter2004-41.pdf.

"Ohio State President Atones for Little Sisters Joke." 2011. SI.com, August 17. http:// sportsillustrated.cnn.com/2011/football/ncaa/08/17/ohio-state-gee-little-sisters.ap/ index.html.

Ohlidal, Susan. 1981. "The Ghost of Norland Hall." In *Franklin County Folklore*, ed. Dorothy Sara Lee, n.p. Chambersburg, Pa.: Wilson College.

"Old Man and the 'C,' The." 2007. Snopes.com: Rumor Has It. http://snopes.com/college/ homework/profpaper.asp.

Olesen, Virginia, and Elvi Whittaker. 1968. "Conditions under Which College Students Borrow, Use, and Alter Slang." *American Speech* 43:222–28.

Olgers, Greg. 2009. "An Enduring Tradition." *News from Hope College.* http://www.hope .edu/pr/pull/tradition.html.

Oliphant, J. Orin. 1965. *The Rise of Bucknell University.* New York: Appleton-Century-Crofts.

"On the Campus." 1909. *Sigma Phi Epsilon Journal* 7:74–80.

"Opening of the Colleges, The." 1899. *Harper's Weekly*, October 21, 1065–66.

Opie, Iona, and Peter Opie. 1985. *The Singing Game.* Oxford: Oxford University Press.

Oriard, Michael. 1998. *Reading Football: How the Popular Press Created an American Spectacle.* Chapel Hill: University of North Carolina Press.

Oring, Elliott. 2003. *Engaging Humor.* Urbana: University of Illinois Press.

———. 2008. "Legendry and the Rhetoric of Truth." *Journal of American Folklore* 121:127–66.

Orr, Cathy M., and Michael J. Preston, eds. 1976. *Urban Folklore from Colorado: Typescript Broadsides.* Ann Arbor, Mich.: University Microfilms.

Ortner, Sherry B. 1974. "Is Female to Male as Nature Is to Culture?" In *Women, Culture and Society*, ed. Michelle Zimbalist Rosaldo and Louise Lamphere, 67–87. Stanford, Calif.: Stanford University Press.

O'Toole, Thomas. 2002. "'Celebratory Riots': Creating Crisis on Campus." *USA Today*, April 9. http://www.usatoday.com/sports/other/2002-04-09-fan-violence.htm.

Pankake, Marcia, and John Pankake. 1988. *A Prairie Home Companion Folk Song Book.* New York: Viking.

Paolantonio, Sal. 2008. *How Football Explains America.* Chicago: Triumph Books.

Parini, Jay. 1989. "The More They Write, the More They Write." *New York Times Book Review*, July 30, 1, 24.

Park, Roberta J. 1984. "Boys into Men—State into Nation: *Rites de Passage* in Student Life and College Athletics, 1890–1905." In *Masks of Play*, ed. Brian Sutton-Smith and Diana Kelly-Byrne, 51–62. New York: Leisure Press.

Parker, Garland G. 1971. *The Enrollment Explosion: A Half-Century of Attendance in U.S. Colleges and Universities.* New York: School and Society Books.

Parker, Samesia. 2003. "'Barfing Barb' Is Kept Alive as ISU Legends Are Passed Down." *Indiana Statesman* (Indiana State University), April 11. http://www.indianastatesman .com/2.3918/barfing-barb-is-kept-alive-as-isu-legends-are-passed-down-1.468787.

Parler, Mary Celestia. 1984. "Folklore from the Campus." In *The Charm Is Broken: Readings in Arkansas and Missouri Folklore*, ed. W. K. McNeil, 25–29. Little Rock, Ark.: August House.

Parochetti, JoAnn Stephens. 1965. "Scary Stories from Purdue." *Keystone Folklore Quarterly* 10:49–57.

Parsons, James J. 1988. "Hillside Letters in the Western Landscape." *Landscape* 30(1): 15–23.

Partridge, Eric. 1986. *A Dictionary of Catch Phrases from the Sixteenth Century to the Present Day*, 2nd ed., ed. Paul Beale. Oxon, U.K.: Routledge.

Pattee, Fred Lewis. 1928. "Penn State Traditions." *Old Main Bell* (Pennsylvania State College) 5(1): 3–7.

———. 1953. *Penn State Yankee: The Autobiography of Fred Lewis Pattee*. State College: Pennsylvania State College.

PCWorld.com Downloads Team. 2001. "Top PC Pranks for April Fool's Day: Wreak Some Havoc on a Friend or a Good-Natured Co-Worker." *PCWorld*, March 25. http://www.pcworld.com/article/45270/top_pc_pranks_for_april_fools_day.html.

Pederson, Daniel. 1986. "10 Minutes of Madness." *Newsweek*, September 1, 18–19.

Pekkanen, John. 1988. *M.D.: Doctors Talk About Themselves*. New York: Delacorte Press.

"Peletiah Gove; Or, the Unfortunate Grind." 1885. *Harvard Advocate* 38: 5–6.

Penn State Alumni Association. 2006. "Spring Week." *Alumni Library Online*. http://alumni.libraries.psu.edu/springweek.html.

Peril, Lynn. 2006. *College Girls: Bluestockings, Sex Kittens, and Coeds, Then and Now*. New York: W. W. Norton.

Peterson, T. F. 2003. *Nightwork: A History of Hacks and Pranks at MIT*. Cambridge, Mass.: MIT Press.

Peterson, Walter F. 1964. "Downer's Rite of Spring: The Hat Hunt." *Historical Messenger* (Milwaukee County Historical Society) 20(2): 31–36.

Pew Research Center. 2011. "Demographics of Internet Users." *Pew Internet & American Life Project*. http://www.pewinternet.org/Trend-Data/Whos-Online.aspx.

"Physical Education." 2010. *Uncyclopedia*. ion.

Pickerall, Albert G., and May Dornin. 1968. *The University of California: A Pictorial History*. Berkeley: University of California Press.

Piehler, G. Kurt. 1988. "Phi Beta Kappa: The Invention of an Academic Tradition." *History of Education Quarterly* 28:207–29.

Pike, Sarah M. 2004. *New Age and Neopagan Religions in America*. New York: Columbia University Press.

Pimple, Kenneth D. 1986. "The Inmates of Eigenmann: A Look at Door Decoration in a Graduate Dormitory." *Folklore Forum* 19:5–35.

Pingry, Carl, and Vance Randolph. 1927–28. "Kansas University Slang." *American Speech* 3:218–21.

Platinum Press, ed. 2005. *Filthy Dirty Jokes*. New York: Pocket Books.

Plowman, Gisela J. 1944. "Pedroing at California." *California Folklore Quarterly* 3:277–83.

Polk, Andrew. 2010. "Flunk Day Friars: Who Are They? What Do They Do? *Knox Student*, April 15. http://www.theknoxstudent.com/newsroom/article/flunk-day-friars-who-are-they-what-do-they-do-/.

Posen, I. Sheldon. 1974. "Pranks and Practical Jokes at Children's Summer Camps." *Southern Folklore Quarterly* 38:299–309.

Posey, Sandra Mizumoto. 2004. "Burning Messages: Interpreting African American Fraternity Brands and Their Bearers." *Voices: The Journal of New York Folklore* 30:42–44.

Post, Julie. 2004. "Yale Traditions: Doing It Old School since 1701." *Yale Daily News*, March 26. http://www.yaledailynews.com/articles/view/10496.

Poston, Lawrence, III. 1964. "Some Problems in the Study of Campus Slang." *American Speech* 39:114–23.

———. 1965. "On the Persistence of Some Older Student Slang Terms." *American Speech* 40:77–78.

Poston, Lawrence, III, and Francis J. Stillman. 1965. "Notes on Campus Vocabulary, 1964." *American Speech* 40:193–95.

Potter, Carrie. 2008. "Young Marriage of College Students Becoming a Trend." *Globe* (Point Park University), March 26. http://www.pointparkglobe.com/2.7418/young-marriage-of-college-students-becoming-a-trend-1.1041353.

Potter, Phyllis. 1979. "St. Peter Jokes." *Southwest Folklore* 3(2): 38–58.

Preston, Michael J. 1973. "The Traditional Ringing at Temple Buell College." *Western Folklore* 32:271–74.

———. 1982. "The English Literal Rebus and the Graphic Riddle Tradition." *Western Folklore* 41:104–21.

Price, Charles Edwin. 1999. *More Haunted Tennessee*. Johnson City, Tenn.: Overmountain Press.

Primiano, Leonard. 1976. "Student Life at a Pennsylvania Dutch College." *Pennsylvania Folklife* 26(1): 34–38.

"Princeton Student Dies in Class Rush." 1915. *New York Times*, September 25, 1.

Procter, Harvey T., Jr. 1966. "Collection of Good Luck Charms and Tales during Final Exam Week from Six College Students." Wayne State University Folklore Archive.

Proctor, Samuel, and Wright Langley. 1986. *Gator History: A Pictorial History of the University of Florida*. Gainesville, Fla.: South Star Publishing.

"Progesterex and Cons." Snopes.com: Rumor Has It. http://www.snopes.com/medical/drugs/progesterex.asp.

Prosser, William L. 1957. "Needlemann on Mortgages." *Journal of Legal Education* 9:489–94.

"Proving That Slime Is on Their Side, Santa Cruz Students Make the Slug Their Mascot." 1986. *People Weekly*, June 16, 85.

Pryor, John H., Sylvia Hurtado, Jaime Saenz, Jose Luise Santos, and Victor B. Saenz. 2007. *The American Freshman: Forty Year Trends 1966–2006*. Los Angeles: Higher Education Research Institute at UCLA.

"PubClub.com's Top 10 College Party Schools: 'Win or Lose, We Booze!'" 2010. PubClub.com: Where the World Goes to Party. http://www.pubclub.com/collegefootball/.

Purnhagen, Mara. 2011. *One Hundred Candles*. New York: Harlequin.

Pursell, Caroll. 2007. *The Machine in America: A Social History of Technology*. Baltimore: Johns Hopkins University Press.

Putnam, Robert D. 2000. *Bowling Alone: The Collapse and Revival of American Community*. New York: Simon & Schuster.

Quarentelli, E. L., and Dennis Wenger. 1973. "A Voice from the Thirteenth Century: The Characteristics and Conditions for the Emergence of a Ouija Board Cult." *Urban Life and Culture* 1:379–400.

Quigley, Christine. 1996. *The Corpse: A History*. Jefferson, N.C.: McFarland.

Quinto, Louis B. 1989. "Pledgeship: Who Needs It?" *Shield and Diamond* [*of Pi Kappa Alpha*] 100(4): 27–28.

Rader, Benjamin G. 1983. *American Sports, from the Age of Folk Games to the Age of Spectators*. Englewood Cliffs, N.J.: Prentice-Hall.

Raftery, Kathleen. 1989. "Vomit Is a Five Letter Word." Elizabeth Tucker Papers, SUNY Binghamton.

Raiks. 2005. "Groutfiti." *Urban Dictionary*, post, March 17. http://www.urbandictionary.com/define.php?term=Groutfiti.

Raines, Howell. 1986. "A Mentor's Presence." *New York Times Magazine*, July 20, 46.

Randolph, Vance. 1928. "A Survival of Phallic Superstition in Kansas." *Psychoanalytic Review* 15:242–44.

———. 1951. *We Always Lie to Strangers: Tall Tales from the Ozarks*. New York: Columbia University Press.

———. 1957. *The Talking Turtle and Other Ozark Folk Tales*. Notes by Herbert Halpert. New York: Columbia University Press.

Ranney, Dave. 2004. "Haskell Storytellers Recall Campus Haunted Legends." *Lawrence (Kans.) Journal-World & News*, September 18. http://www2.ljworld.com/news/2004/sep/18/haskell_storytellers_recall/.

Raphael, Ray. 1988. *The Men from the Boys: Rites of Passage in Male America*. Lincoln: University of Nebraska Press.

Read, Allen Walker. 1935. *Lexical Evidence from Folk Epigraphy in Western North America: A Glossarial Study of the Low Element in the English Vocabulary*. Paris: privately printed.

Reis, Ronald A. 2005. *Eugenie Clark: Marine Biologist*. New York: Facts on File.

Repcheck, Diane. 1988. "Zaniness Abounds at Commencement." *Daily Collegian* (Pennsylvania State University, University Park), April 29, 5.

Renard, Jean-Bruno. 1991. "LSD Tattoo Transfers: Rumor from North America to France." *Folklore Forum* 24:3–26.

Renteln, Paul, and Alan Dundes. 2005. "Foolproof: A Sampling of Mathematical Folk Humor." *Notices of the American Mathematical Society* 52:24–34.

Reuss, Richard A. 1965. "An Annotated Field Collection of Songs from the American College Student Oral Tradition." M.A. thesis, Indiana University.

———. 1974. "'That Can't Be Alan Dundes! Alan Dundes Is Taller Than That!': The Folklore of Folklorists." *Journal of American Folklore* 87:303–17.

Reynolds, Neil B. 1961. "Lore from Union and Princeton." *New York Folklore Quarterly* 17:253–56.

Rich, George W., and David F. Jacobs. 1973. "Saltpeter: A Folkloric Adjustment to Acculturation Stress." *Western Folklore* 32:164–79.

Riesman, David, and Reuel Denney. 1951. "Football in America: A Study in Cultural Diffusion." *American Quarterly* 3:309–25.

Robacabras. 2007. "Hey Navy . . . Missing Anything?" *YouTube*. http://www.youtube.com/watch?v=CgAcXTzf-8s&feature=mfu_in_order&list=UL.

Robbins, Alexandra. 2002. *Secrets of the Tomb: Skull and Bones, the Ivy League, and the Hidden Paths of Power*. Boston: Back Bay Books.

———. 2004. *Pledged: The Secret Life of Sororities*. New York: Hyperion.

Robertson, James Oliver. 1980. *American Myth, American Reality*. New York: Hill and Wang.

Robertson, Lynda. 1989a. "6-Foot-8 Navy Plebe Ends Year's Agony with Long Reach." *Sun* (Baltimore), May 27 (sec. A), 1, 8.

———. 1989b. "Naval Academy's Class of '89 Embarks for Military Life." *Sun* (Baltimore), June 1 (sec. B), 1, 2.

Robertson, Oscar. 2011. "Don't Treat Players Like Gladiators." *Chronicle of Higher Education*, December 16, A8–9.

Roemer, Danielle. 1971. "Scary Story Legends." *Folklore Annual of the University Folklore Association* 3:1–16.

Roeper, Richard. 1999. *Urban Legends: The Truth Behind All Those Deliciously Entertaining Myths That Are Absolutely, Positively, 100% Not True!* Franklin Lakes, N.J.: Career Press.

Rogers, James. 1970. "The Folklore of Faculty Nicknames at the Academy." *Keystone Folklore Quarterly* 15:74–80.

Rogers, Timothy B. 1987. "Hearing the 'Un-Saids': An Essay on the Role of Folkloristics in Metapsychology." In *The Analysis of Psychological Theory: Metapsychological Perspectives*, ed. Hendrikus J. Stam, Timothy B. Rogers, and Kenneth J. Gergen, 193–210. Washington, D.C.: Hemisphere Publishing.

Róheim, Géza. 1945. *The Eternal Ones of the Dream: A Psychoanalytic Interpretation of Australian Myth and Ritual*. New York: International Universities Press.

Rojstaczer, Stuart. 1999. *Gone for Good: Tales of University Life after the Golden Age*. New York: Oxford University Press.

Rollins, Alfred B., Jr. 1961. "College Folklore." *New York Folklore Quarterly* 17:163–73.

"Roll Inverted and Pull." 2010. *Airline Pilot Forum*. Posted February 12. http://www.airlinepilotforums.com/archive/index.php/t–48126.html.

Rosemeyer, Cathy. 1976. "Stories of 625 North Jordan." Indiana University Folklore Archives.

Roskin, David. 1988. "Elmo: The Ghost of Mitchell Hall." University of Delaware Folklore Archives.

Rosnow, Ralph L., and Gary Alan Fine. 1976. *Rumor and Gossip: The Social Psychology of Hearsay*. New York: Elsevier.

Ross, Lawrence C., Jr. 2000. *The Divine Nine: The History of African American Fraternities and Sororities*. New York: Kensington Books.

Rossie, William A. 1993. *The Sex Life of the Foot and Shoe*. Malabar: Krieger.

Roth, Philip. 1988. *The Facts: A Novelist's Autobiography*. New York: Farrar, Straus, and Giroux.

Rountree, Pam. 1985. "Ramblin' Wreck." *Georgia Tech Alumni Magazine* 60(2): 16–18.

Rovin, Jeff. 1987. *1,001 Great Jokes*. New York: New American Library.

Rubinstein, Marv. 2000. *Net-Wit.com*. Rockville, Md.: Vinmar Press.

Rudolph, Frederick. 1962. *The American College and University: A History*. New York: Vintage Books/Random House.

"Rules for Push Ball Scrap." 1912. *Penn State Collegian*, September 12, 3.

Russell, Jason Almus. 1929–30. "Colgate University Slang." *American Speech* 5:238–39.

Russo, John. 1990. "'Reel' vs. Real Violence." *Newsweek*, February 19, 10.

"Rutgers Bans Class Rushes Following Student's Drowning." 1929. *New York Times*, May 25, 8.

Sackett, S. J. 1964. "Student Slang in Hays, Kansas." *American Speech* 39:235.

Safire, William. 1982. *What's the Good Word?* New York: Times Books.

Sailes, Gary A. 1993. "An Investigation of Campus Stereotypes: The Myth of Black Athletic Superiority and the Dumb Jock Stereotype." *Sociology of Sport Journal* 10:88–97.

Salmon, Mike. 1983. "The Banging of the Doors: An Analysis of a Folkloric Event [Purdue University]." Danielle Roemer Papers, Northern Kentucky University.

Saluja, Kuldeep. 2005. *The Unofficial Joke Book of Sydney*. Noida, India: Book Factory.

Sampson, Anthony, and Sally Sampson, comps. 1985. *The Oxford Book of Ages*. New York: Oxford University Press.

Samuelson, Sue. 1979. "The White Witch: An Analysis of an Adolescent Legend." *Indiana Folklore* 12:18–37.

Sanders, Katie. 2011. "FAMU Student Death Prompts Probe of Hazing Practices." *Miami Herald*, November 24. http://www.miamiherald.com/2011/11/24/v-print/2517394/famu-student-death-prompts-probe.html.

Sanderson, Stewart. 1969. "The Folklore of the Motor-Car." *Folklore* 80:241–52.

Sanlo, Ronnie. 2000. "Lavender Graduation: Acknowledging the Lives and Achievements of Lesbian, Gay, Bisexual, and Transgender College Students." *Journal of College Student Development* 41:643–46.

———. 2005. "Is There a Model for a 'Lavender Graduation' Ceremony That We Can Follow or Adapt?" *National Consortium of Directors of LGBT Resources in Higher Education*. http://www.lgbtcampus.org/old_faq/lavender_graduation.html.

Santino, Jack. 1994. "Introduction: Festivals of Death and Life." In *Halloween and Other Festivals of Death and Life*, ed. Jack Santino, xi–xxviii. Knoxville: University of Tennessee Press.

Sanua, Marianne R. 2003. *Going Greek: Jewish College Fraternities in the United States, 1895–1945*. Detroit: Wayne State University Press.

Sauve, Jeff. 2008. "'Frosh' Beanies: A 20th Century Tradition." *St. Olaf Magazine*, Fall, 52.

"Scatological Lore on Campus." 1962. *Journal of American Folklore* 75:260–62.

Schaeper, Thomas J., Jonathan D. Merrill, and John Hutchison. 1987. *The St. Bonaventure University Trivia Book*. St. Bonaventure, N.Y.: St. Bonaventure University.

Schechter, Harold. 1988. *The Bosom Serpent: Folklore and Popular Art*. Iowa City: University of Iowa Press.

Schlereth, Thomas. 1991. *A Dome of Learning: The University of Notre Dame's Main Building*. Notre Dame, Ind.: University of Notre Dame Alumni Association.

Schoeller, Martin. 2010. "Life Inside Facebook's Headquarters: Cubicle Culture in the Social-Networking Site's Silicon Valley Offices." *Time*, December 15. http://www.time.com/time/photogallery/0,29307,2036832_2218560,00.html.

"School Rivalry Jokes Needed." 2006. Snopes.com. Message board. http://msgboard.snopes.com/cgi-bin/ultimatebb.cgi?ubb=get_topic;f=52;t=004262;p=1.

Schultz, William Eben. 1929–30. "College Abbreviations." *American Speech* 5:240–44.

Schwab, John. 1999. *The Little 500: The Story of the World's Greatest College Weekend*. Bloomington: Indiana University Press.

Scott, Dwayne J. 2011. "Factors That Contribute to Hazing Practices by Collegiate Black Greek-Letter Fraternities during Membership Intake Activities." In *Black Greek-Letter Organizations 2.0: New Directions in the Study of African American Fraternities and Sororities*, ed. Matthew W. Hughey and Gregory S. Parks, 235–50. Jackson: University Press of Mississippi.

Scott, John F. 1965. "The American College Sorority: Its Role in Class and Endogamy." *American Sociological Review* 30:514–27.

Sebastian, Hugh. 1934. "Negro Slang in Lincoln University." *American Speech* 9:287–90.

———. 1936. "Agricultural College Slang in South Dakota." *American Speech* 11:279–80.

Sebba, Anne. 1979. *Samplers: Five Centuries of a Gentle Craft*. New York: Thames and Hudson.

Sechrest, Lee, and A. Kenneth Olson. 1971. "Graffiti in Four Types of Institutions of Higher Learning." *Journal of Sex Research* 7:62–71.

"Secret Sauce." 2007. Snopes.com: Rumor Has It. .

Sedor, Michael. 2009. "'We Are Penn State' Slogan Began as a Response to Segregation." February 25. http://blog.pennlive.com/pasports/2009/02/we-are-penn-state-slogan-began.html.

Seidell, Streeter. 2004. "The Ten Commandments of College." *CollegeHumor Classic*, April 5. http://www.collegehumor.com/article:247200.

Senn, Mary C. 1983. "Mona Lisa, Is That You?" *Louisiana Folklore Miscellany* 5(3): 27–30.

Sennett, Richard. 1977. *The Fall of Public Man: On the Social Psychology of Capitalism*. New York: Vintage.

Sentman, Ron. 1972. "Logic Problems of College Students." Indiana University Folklore Archives.

Seuss, Dr. 1950. *If I Ran the Zoo*. New York: Random House.

Seventh Generation of 101 Aggie Jokes. 1988. Dallas: Gigem Press.

Sheldon, Henry D. 1901. *Student Life and Customs*. New York: D. Appleton.

Sherman, Constance D. 1962. "Oberlin Lore." *New York Folklore Quarterly* 18:58–60.

Sherman, Josepha, and T. K. F. Weisskopf. 1995. *Greasy Grimy Gopher Guts: The Subversive Folklore of Children*. Little Rock, Ark.: August House.

Sherzer, Joel. 2002. *Speech Play and Verbal Art*. Austin: University of Texas Press.

Shidler, John Ashton. 1931–32. "More Stanford Expressions." *American Speech* 7:434–37.

Shidler, John Ashton, and R. M. Clarke Jr. 1931–32. "Stanfordiana." *American Speech* 7:232–33.

Shoemaker, Henry W. 1950. "The Ghost of the Buckhorn." *New York Folklore Quarterly* 6:82–84.

Shubnell, Thomas F. 2008. *Greatest Jokes of the Century: Book 1*. Charleston, S.C.: CreateSpace.

Shulman, Max, ed. 1955. *Max Shulman's Guided Tour of Campus Humor: The Best Stories, Articles, Poems, Jokes, and Nonsense from Over Sixty-Five College Humor Magazines*. Garden City, N.Y.: Hanover House.

Shutan, Lynn. 1972. "The Folklore of Stephens College." Indiana University Folklore Archives.

Sibley, Robert. 1928. *The Romance of the University of California*. Berkeley: University of California Alumni Association.

Sigler, Scott. 1988. "Does Olivet Need Ghostbusters?" *Echo* (Olivet College), October 27, 1.

Simmons, Donald G. 1967. "Some Special Terms Used in a University of Connecticut Men's Dormitory." *American Speech* 42:227–30.

Sims, Dunny. 1944. "Moron Jokes." In *From Hell to Breakfast*, ed. Mody C. Boatright and Donald Day, 155–61. Publications of the Texas Folklore Society, no. 19. Dallas: Southern Methodist University Press.

Singh, Joginder. 2004. *Jokes of Joginder Singh*. New Delhi, India: Fusion Books.

Slattery, Patrick. 2006. "Deconstructing Racism One Statue at a Time: Visual Culture Wars at Texas A&M University and the University of Texas at Austin." *Visual Arts Research* 32:28–31.

Sloan, John J., III, and Bonnie S. Fisher. 2011. *The Dark Side of the Ivory Tower: Campus Crime as a Social Problem*. New York: Cambridge University Press.

Slosson, Edwin E. 1910. *Great American Universities*. New York: Macmillan.

Smith, Gloria Walker. 2011. "Aggie Alum Turn Out for Annual Muster." Yourpasadena news.com, April 28. http://www.yourhoustonnews.com/pasadena/news/article _5751bc13–781e–501c–8d08–8d1521ead88o.html.

Smith, Grace P. 1937. "'Rushing' in the Sixties?" *American Speech* 12:156–57.

Smith, Henry Nash. 1950. *Virgin Land: The American West as Symbol and Myth*. Cambridge, Mass.: Harvard University Press.

Smith, Johana H. 1957. "In the Bag: A Study of Snipe Hunting." *Western Folklore* 16:107–10.

Smith, Paul. 1984. *The Complete Book of Office Mis-Practice*. London: Routledge & Kegan Paul.

———. 1986. *Reproduction Is Fun: A Second Book of Photocopy Joke Sheets*. London: Routledge & Kegan Paul.

———. 1990. "'AIDS: Don't Die of Ignorance': Exploring the Cultural Complex." In *A Nest of Vipers: Perspectives on Contemporary Legend*, Vol. 5, ed. Gillian Bennett and Paul Smith, 113–42. Sheffield, U.K.: Sheffield Academic Press.

———. 1991. "The Joke Machine: Communicating Traditional Humour Using Computers." In *Spoken in Jest*, ed. Gillian Bennett, 257–78. Sheffield, U.K.: Sheffield Academic Press.

Smith, Warren Hunting. 1972. *Hobart and William Smith: The History of Two Colleges*. Geneva, N.Y.: Hobart and William Smith Colleges.

Snyder, Henry L. 1949. *Our College Colors*. Nashville, Tenn.: Southern Publishing.

Sobel, Eli. 1951. "'Going to See the Widow' Again." *Journal of American Folklore* 64:420–21.

Solove, Daniel. 2010. "A Guide to Grading Exams." *Concurring Opinions*. http://www .concurringopinions.com/archives/2006/12/a_guide_to_grad.html.

Sonenklar, Carol. 2006. *We Are a Strong, Articulate Voice: A History of Women at Penn State*. University Park: Pennsylvania State University Press.

"Songs/Chants???" 2000. GreekChat.com Forums. http://www.greekchat.com/gcforums /archive/index.php/t–5139.html.

"Sophs Will Revive Poverty Day Today." 1953. *Daily Collegian* (Pennsylvania State University), March 20, 1.

South Carolina Delta Chapter. 2011. "Paddy Murphy." *Sigma Alpha Epsilon South Carolina Delta Chapter*. http://www.saeusc.com/paddy-murphy.

Sparks, Linda, and Bruce Emerton, comps. 1988. *American College Regalia: A Handbook*. New York: Greenwood Press.

Spectorsky, A. C., ed. 1958. *The College Years*. New York: Hawthorn Books.

SpikedMath. 2011. "Sex Math Jokes." *Spiked Math Forums*. Message board, post, April 12. http://spikedmath.com/forum/viewtopic.php?f=12&t=112.

"Spirit Club." 2007–9. *Hillsdale College Student Life*. http://www.hillsdale.edu/studentlife /organizations/clubs/spirit.asp.

Spivey, Sara. 2004. "Urban Legends Roam Campus: Death Myth Has Circulated for Twenty Years." *Spartan Daily* (San Jose State University), October 29. http://media .www.thespartandaily.com/media/storage/paper852/news/2004/10/29/Campus News/Urban.Legends.Roam.Campus–1499810.shtml.

Spradley, James P., and Brenda J. Mann. 1975. *The Cocktail Waitress: Woman's Work in a Man's World*. New York: John Wiley and Sons.

Stadtman, Verne A. 1970. *The University of California, 1868–1968*. New York: McGraw-Hill.

Stalker, Heather Dawkins. 2011. "Legendary Landmarks: A Spine-Tingling Tour of College Campuses." *Sandlapper Magazine*. http://www.sandlapper.org/education/sandlapper_magazine_lesson_plans/grade_8_college_legends/.

Starr, Mrs. Morton H. 1954. "Wisconsin Pastimes." *Journal of American Folklore* 67:184.

Steach, Kristen. 2011. "USC Seniors Gear Up for Annual Fountain Run." *ATVN: Annenberg TV News*, April 21. http://www.atvn.org/news/2011/06/usc-seniors-gear-annual-fountain-run.

Stec, Kathleen. 1985. "The Folklore of College Students: Cheating." Mac Barrick Memorial Folklore Archives, Shippensburg University.

Steinberg, Neil. 1992. *If at All Possible, Involve a Cow: The Book of College Pranks*. New York: St. Martin's Press.

Stephanoff, Alexander. 1970. "College Interviews as a Folklore Genre." *Keystone Folklore Quarterly* 15:106–13.

"Steps Can Be Taken to Save the Undie Run." 2008. *Daily Bruin* (UCLA), September 30. http://www.dailybruin.com/articles/2008/9/30/emsteps-can-be-taken-save-undie-runem/.

Stern, Laurie. 2010. "Day Helps Students Reflect." *Daily Collegian* (Pennsylvania State University, University Park), April 26, 4.

Stokes, Peter J. 2006. "Hidden in Plain Sight: Adult Learners Forge a New Tradition in Higher Education." Issue Paper 11. *A National Dialogue: The Secretary of Education's Commission on the Future of Higher Education*. http://ed.gov/about/bdscomm/list/hiedfuture/reports/stokes.pdf.

Strum, Philippa. 2002. *Women in the Barracks: The VMI Case and Equal Rights*. Lawrence: University Press of Kansas.

"Student Activities." 2011. St. Andrews Presbyterian College website. http://www.sapc.edu/studentlife/StudentActivities.php.

"Students Examined on Death of Mount." 1923. *New York Times*, May 4, 3.

Stuller, Jay. 1987. "Fight, Fight, Fight, Fight, Banana Slugs, Banana Slugs." *Audubon* 89(2): 128–30, 132–35.

Suffern, Betty. 1959. "'Pedro' at California." *Western Folklore* 18:326.

Súilleabháin, Seán Ó. 1967. *Irish Wake Amusements*. Cork, Ireland: Mercier.

Sutton-Smith, Brian. 1960. "'Shut Up and Keep Digging': The Cruel Joke Series." *Midwest Folklore* 10:11–22.

Swanger, Serena. 2009. "The Scariest Locations in Ventura County." *Student Voice* (Ventura, Oxnard, and Moorpark Colleges). October 27. http://www.studentvoiceonline.com/student-life/the-scariest-locations-in-ventura-county–1.2041474.

Swayne, M. L. 2011. *Haunted Valley . . . The Ghosts of Penn State*. Lexington, Ky.: Campus Ghost Tour.

Swift, Beth. 2009. "Senior Bench." *Wabash College*. http://www2.wabash.edu/blog/dear_old_wabash/2009/03/senior_bench.html.

Sykes, Charles J. 1988. *ProfScam: Professors and the Demise of Higher Education*. New York: St. Martin's Press.

"Symbols of Campus Community." 1989. *Educational Record* 70(3–4): 36–38.

Syrett, Nicholas L. 2009. *The Company He Keeps: A History of White College Fraternities*. Chapel Hill: University of North Carolina Press.

T., M. 1976. "Fraternity Lore." Folklore Collection, University Archives, Pennsylvania State University Libraries.

————. 1979. "The Pattee Murder." Folklore Collection, University Archives, Pennsylvania State University Libraries.

Taboada, Margaret. 1967. "The Sorority Song Tradition [UCLA]." Wayne State Folklore Archive.

Taft, Michael. 1984. *Inside These Greystone Walls: An Anecdotal History of the University of Saskatchewan*. Saskatoon: University of Saskatchewan.

Tangherlini, Timothy R. 1998. *Talking Trauma: Paramedics and Their Stories*. Jackson: University Press of Mississippi.

Taylor, Archer. 1945. "Still More about the Ineradicable Bloodstain." *Hoosier Folklore Bulletin* 4:32.

————. 1947a. "Pedro!" *Western Folklore* 6:85–86.

————. 1947b. "'Pedro! Pedro!'" *Western Folklore* 6:228–31.

Taylor, Troy. 2000. "Black Aggie: The Haunted History of One of America's Most Mysterious Graveyard Monuments." *Ghosts of the Prairie: Haunted Maryland*. http://www.prairieghosts.com/druidridge.html.

Tenth Generation of 101 Aggie Jokes. 1988. Dallas: Gigem Press.

Theroux, Alexander. 1986. "Nerd U.: What Is It about MIT, Anyway?" *New England Monthly*, October, 60–65.

————. 1987. "Caution: Geniuses at Work and Play." *Reader's Digest*, October, 215–18, 220.

Theta Epsilon Omicron Iota Fraternity Pledge Manual. N.d. Typescript, private collection.

Thigpen, Kenneth A., Jr. 1971. "Adolescent Legends in Brown County: A Survey." *Indiana Folklore* 4:141–215.

Thobaden, Marshelle. 2007. "Horizontal Workplace Violence." *Home Health Care Management Practice* 20:82–83.

Thomas, Jeannie B. 1991. "Pain, Pleasure, and the Spectral: The Barfing Ghost of Burford Hall." *Folklore Forum* 24:27–38.

Thomas, Mark, collector. 2011. "Fountain Run." Posted May 11. University of Southern California Folklore Archives.

Thomas, Susanne Sara. 1995. "'Cinderella' and the Phallic Foot: The Symbolic Significance of the Tale's Slipper Motif." *Southern Folklore* 52:19–31.

Thompson, Stith. 1975. *Motif-Index of Folk-Literature*. Rev. ed. 6 vols. Bloomington: Indiana University Press.

Thompson, Tyler. 2007. "Opinions: Real Sports Have Bikinis." *Web@Devil* (Arizona State University), April 5. http://asuwebdevilarchive.asu.edu/issues/2007/04/05/opinions/700633.

"Thousands Attend Dedication of A&M Bonfire Memorial." 2004. KWTX.com (Waco, Temple, Killeen, Tex.), November 18. http://www.kwtx.com/home/headlines/1201326.html.

"Three Students Charged in FAMU Hazing." 2011. ESPN.com, December 13. http://espn.go.com/college-football/story/_/id/7347459/tallahassee-police-charge-3-florida-rattlers-band-hazing.

Thripshaw, E. Henry. 2010. *The Mammoth Book of Tasteless Jokes*. London: Constable & Robinson.

Thurman, Lindsey. 2004. "Phi Delts, Phi Mu Pull Off Tug Wins." *College Heights Herald* (Western Kentucky University), April 27. http://media.www.wkuherald.com/media/storage/paper603/news/2004/04/27/News/Phi-Delts.Phi.Mu.Pull.Off.Tug.Wins-672342.shtml.

Thwing, Charles Franklin. 1914. *The American College: What It Is and What It May Become*. New York: Platt & Peck.

Tiger, Lionel. 1969. *Men in Groups*. New York: Vintage Books.

Till, Gerry Marie. 1976. "The Murder at Franklin College." *Indiana Folklore* 9:187–95.

Tillson, William. 1961. "How the Boilermakers Did Not Get Their Name." *Midwest Folklore* 11:105–14.

———. 1962. "Purdue Classroom Recollection." *New York Folklore Quarterly* 18:55–57.

Toelken, Barre. 1986. "The Folklore of Academe." In *The Study of American Folklore: An Introduction*, by Jan Harold Brunvand, 502–28. 3rd ed. New York: W. W. Norton.

———. 1995. "Academe, Folklore of." In *American Folklore: An Encyclopedia*, ed. Jan Harold Brunvand, 1–3. New York: Garland.

Tolley, William Pearson. 1989. *At the Fountain of Youth: Memories of a College President*. Syracuse, N.Y.: Syracuse University Press.

Topping, Robert W. 1988. *A Century and Beyond: The History of Purdue University*. West Lafayette, Ind.: Purdue University Press.

"Top Ten GC Traditions." 2011. *Georgetown College*. http://wordpress.georgetowncollege .edu/admissions/traditions/.

Torok, Tom. 1989. "You've Got to Hand It to Her." *Philadelphia Inquirer*, May 27 (sec. A), 3.

Torry, Jack. 2010. "Woody Hayes: The Man, the Legend." *Columbus Monthly*, October. http://www.columbusmonthly.com/October-2010/Woody-Hayes-The-Man-The-Legend.

Townsend, Malcolm. 1895. "A Cane Rush." In *The Book of Athletics and Out-of-Door Sports*, ed. Norman W. Bingham, 225–37. Boston: Lothrop.

Trachtenberg, Alan. 1982. *The Incorporation of America: Culture and Society in the Gilded Age*. New York: Hill and Wang.

"Tradition Crumbles, Students Grumble." 1989. *New York Times*, July 23 (sec. 1, part 2), 35.

"Tradition Is Basis of May Day Contests." 1935. *Lamron* (Western Oregon State College) 12 (April 27): 1.

"Traditions: Here's the Rub." *Dartmouth University*. http://parents.dartmouth.edu/ news_and_events/news_articles/bentley.html.

Traditions Cluster of the New Dimensions in Total Teaching Program. 1981. *Traditions: Roanoke College Yesterday and Today*. [Salem, Va.]: Roanoke College.

Travelpunk. 2003. "Drinking Toasts?" !Travelpunk.com. Message board post, September 18. http://www.travelpunk.com/boards/world-food-drink/502-drinking-toasts.html.

Tucker, Elizabeth. 1977. "Tradition and Creativity in the Storytelling of Pre-Adolescent Girls." Ph.D. diss., Indiana University.

———. 1978. "The Seven-Day Wonder Diet: Magic and Ritual in Diet Folklore." *Indiana Folklore* 6:141–50.

———. 2005. *Campus Legends: A Handbook*. Westport, Conn.: Greenwood Press.

———. 2006. "Legend Quests." *Voices: The Journal of New York Folklore* 32:34–38.

———. 2007. *Haunted Halls: Ghostlore of American College Campuses*. Jackson: University Press of Mississippi.

Tufekci, Zeynep. 2008. "Can You See Me Now? Audience and Disclosure Regulation in Online Social Network Sites." *Bulletin of Science, Technology & Society* 28:20–36.

Tumulty, Karen. 2008. "Can Obama Shred the Rumors?" *Time*, June 23, 40–41.

Turk, Diana B. 2004. *Bound by a Mighty Vow: Sisterhood and Women's Fraternities, 1870–1920*. New York: New York University Press.

Turner, Patricia A. 1993. *I Heard It through the Grapevine: Rumor in African-American Culture*. Berkeley: University of California Press.

Turner, Paul Venable. 1987. *Campus: An American Planning Tradition*. Cambridge, Mass.: MIT Press.

Turner, Victor. 1967. *The Forest of Symbols: Aspects of Nedembu Ritual*. Ithaca, N.Y.: Cornell University Press.

———. 1969. *The Ritual Process: Structure and Anti-Structure*. Chicago: Aldine.

Turrell, William. 1961. "Editor's Page." *New York Folklore Quarterly* 17:162, 237, 242, 309–11.

"2012: The Year the Internet Ends." 2008. ScrewAttack.com. http://wwww.screwattack .com/node/4003.

UC Photographers. 2011. "Architecture." *UC Magazine*. http://magazine.uc.edu/media/ gallery/architecture.html.

"Underclass Regulations." 1905. *State Collegian* (Pennsylvania State College), September 28, 3, 10.

Underwood, Gary N. 1975. "Razorback Slang." *American Speech* 50:50–69.

———. 1976. "Some Characteristics of Slang Used at the University of Arkansas at Fayetteville." *Mid-South Folklore* 4:49–54.

University of Illinois. 2011. "David Kinley, 1920–1930." *History of the University*. http:// www.uillinois.edu/president/history/kinley.cfm.

University of Maryland Archives. 2010. *MAC to Millennium*. http://www.lib.umd.edu/ ARCV/macmil/testudo.html.

"University of Wisconsin Basketball Prospects 1988." 1986–87. *Maledicta* 9:37–38.

University Statement on Investigation of Fraternity. 2006. News release, Office of News and Information, Johns Hopkins University, October 30. .

U.S. News Staff. 2011. "The Most Popular Universities." *U.S. News & World Report*, January 29. http://www.usnews.com/education/articles/2011/01/25/the-most-popular-universities.

"UT Austin Enhances and Creates New Commencement Traditions with New Doctoral Robe Design Prototype." 2001. University of Texas Office of Public Affairs, May 15. http://www.utexas.edu/news/2001/05/15/nr_robe/.

Uther, Hans-Jörg. 2004. *The Types of International Folktales: A Classification and Bibliography*. 3 vols. Helsinki: Academia Scientiarum Fennica.

Utt, Walter C. 1968. *A Mountain, a Pickax, a College*. Angwin, Calif.: Alumni Association, Pacific Union College.

Van Gennep, Arnold. 1960. *The Rites of Passage*. Trans. Monika B. Vizedom and Gabrielle L. Caffee. Chicago: University of Chicago Press.

Vargas, Jose Antonio. 2010. "The Face of Facebook." *New Yorker*, September 20. http:// www.newyorker.com/reporting/2010/09/20/100920fa_fact_vargas.

Varounis, Athena. 2009. *Franklin County Ghosts of Pennsylvania*. Atlgen, Pa.: Schiffer.

Vassar Historian. 2004. "Daisy Chain." *Vassar Encyclopedia*. http://vcencyclopedia.vas sar.edu/traditions/daisy-chain.html.

Vasvári, Louise O. 1998. "Fowl Play in My Lady's Chamber: Textual Harassment of a Middle English Pornithological Riddle and Visual Pun." In *Cheating, Social Control and Artistic Creation in the European Middle Ages*, ed. Jan M. Ziolkowski, 108–35. Leiden, The Netherlands: Brill.

Veblen, Thorstein. 2007 [1918]. *The Higher Learning in America*. New York: Cosimo.

"Violent Hazing at Times in College Band Repertoire." 2009. *USA Today*, May 16. http:// www.usatoday.com/news/education/2009-05-16-band-hazing-N.htm.

Virginia Delta. 2010. "The Legend of Paddy Murphy." *Sigma Alpha Epsilon—Virginia Delta of George Mason University.* http://www.gmu.edu/org/sae/paddy/paddy.php.

Vizedom, Monika. 1976. *Rites and Relationships: Rites of Passage and Contemporary Anthropology.* Beverly Hills, Calif.: Sage.

"V.M.I.'s 'Brother Rats' May Get Some Sisters." 1989. *New York Times,* June 4 (sec. 1, part 2), 47.

Von Hoffman, Nicholas. 1966. *The Multiversity: A Personal Report on What Happens to Today's Students at American Universities.* New York: Holt, Rinehart and Winston.

Vosgerchian, Jessica. 2009. "Boys, Girls and Bathroom Graffiti." *Michigan Daily* (December 8). http://www.michigandaily.com/content/boys-girls-and-bathroom-graffiti?page=0,1.

Wadler, Joyce. 1983. "Mary in the Lavender Pumps." *Rolling Stone,* April 14, 25–28, 33, 36, 113, 116–17.

Walden, Keith. 1987. "Respectable Hooligans: Male Toronto College Students Celebrate Hallowe'en, 1884–1910." *Canadian Historical Review* 68:1–34.

Walton, Sally, and Faye Wilkinson. 1977. *We're Number 1: Purdue-Indiana Jokes.* Vicksburg, Miss.: Mortgage Row Press.

———. 1980. *Ole Miss-State Jokes.* Brandon, Miss.: Quail Ridge Press.

———. 1981. *Alabama-Auburn Jokes.* Brandon, Miss.: Quail Ridge Press.

Warrick, Bryan. 2010a. "'Humans vs. Zombies' Provides Much-Needed Break from Class." *BG News* (Bowling Green State University), March 26. http://bgnews.com/opinion/humans-vs-zombies-provides-much-needed-break-from-class/.

———. 2010b. "'Humans' Use Weapon Upgrades, Prepare for Battle Against 'Zombies.'" *BG News* (Bowling Green State University), April 1. http://bgnews.com/campus/humans-use-weapon-upgrades-prepare-for-battle-against-zombies/.

Washburn, B. E. 1955. "College Folklore at Chapel Hill in the Early 1900's." *North Carolina Folklore* 3(2): 27–30.

Washburn, Jane. 1976. "Changes in Alpha Mu Chapter Customs." Indiana University Folklore Archives.

Wassell, Gayle. 1973. "Aggie Jokes and Riddles." Special Collections, University of Arkansas Libraries.

Watkins, Martin A. 1968. "Some Notes on Flunk Notes." *American Speech* 43:76–77.

Waymire, Susan. 1978. "Myths and Legends of Indiana University." Indiana University Folklore Archives.

Weales, Gerald. 1957. "Ritual in Georgia." *Southern Folklore Quarterly* 21:104–9.

Webley, Kayla. 2011. "Cornell Fraternity Sued for Allegedly Hazing a Student to Death." *Time,* June 29. http://newsfeed.time.com/2011/06/29/cornell-fraternity-sued-for-allegedly-hazing-a-student-to-death/.

Weitz, Rose. 2004. *Rapunzel's Daughters: What Women's Hair Tells Us About Women's Lives.* New York: Farrar, Straus, and Giroux.

Welch, Kelley. 1982. "Dirty Sorority Folksongs." Indiana University Folklore Archives.

Wenger, Etienne, Richard McDermott, and William N. Snyder. 2002. *Cultivating Communities of Practice: A Guide to Managing Knowledge.* Boston: Harvard Business School Press.

Wenger, Kaimi. 2005. "The Wackiness of Mormon Teen Dating Rituals." *Times and Seasons,* January 5. http://timesandseasons.org/index.php/2005/01/the-wackiness-of-mormon-teen-dating-rituals/.

Wenke, Christie. 2010. "Candle Lightings." *BSC Folklore* (Birmingham-Southern College). http://www.bsc.edu/folklore/customary/candle.htm.

Western New England University. 2012. "Academic Regalia." *Western New England University*. http://www1.wne.edu/commencement/index.cfm?selection=doc.3772.

Wexler, Laura. 2008. "Commando Performance." *Washington Post*, April 13, W16.

Whatley, Marianne H., and Elissa R. Henken. 2000. *Did You Hear about the Girl Who . . . ? Contemporary Legends, Folklore & Human Sexuality*. New York: New York University Press.

White, William. 1943. "Whitman College Slang." *American Speech* 18:153–55.

———. 1955. "Wayne University Slang." *American Speech* 30:301–5.

Whiting, Bartlett Jerre. 1977. *Early American Proverbs and Proverbial Phrases*. Cambridge, Mass.: Belknap Press of Harvard University Press.

Whitney, Gertrude Churchill. 1962. "Frogs and Their Imitators." *New York Folklore Quarterly* 18:141–44.

Wibeto, Lara. 2010. *Your Personal Tool Kit for Life: Facing a Major Life Renovation and Constructing the Best Life Possible*. Minneapolis, Minn.: Mill City Press.

Wilgus, D. K. 1970. "The Girl in the Window." *Western Folklore* 29:251–56.

———. 1972. "More Norbert Wiener Stories." *Western Folklore* 31:23–25.

Wilkinson, Jeff. 2004. "Assorted Jokes from Physics, Engineering, Math, Etc." *Wilkinson Family Home Site*. http://wilk4.com/humor/humore30.htm.

Willard, Sidney. 1855. *Memories of Youth and Manhood*. Cambridge, Mass.: John Bartlett.

Williams, B. D. 1999. "Classroom Jokes." BDWilliams.com. http://www.bdwilliams.com/jokes/class.html.

Williams, Clover Nolan. 1994. "The Bachelor's Transgression: Identity and Difference in the Bachelor Party." *Journal of American Folklore* 107:106–20.

Williams, Stewart (writer). 2007. "Way to Go." *Urban Legends*. Television series, Season 1, Episode 6. Aired July 28. Newark, N.J.: Biography Channel.

Williams, Yona. 2007. "Exploring the Haunted University of North Alabama." *Unexplainable.Net: Watching the World Change*, April 5. http://www.unexplainable.net/artman/publish/article_6565.shtml.

Wilson, David. 2010. "Parodies of College Football Fight Songs." http://homepages.cae.wisc.edu/~dwilson/rfsc/fightsongsII.txt.

Wilson, F. P. 1970. *The Oxford Dictionary of English Proverbs*. 3rd ed. London: Oxford University Press.

Wilson, Frank R. 1999. *The Hand: How Its Use Shapes the Brain, Language, and Human Culture*. New York: Vintage.

Wilson, Michael. 1998. "'The Boyfriend's Death' and 'The Mad Axeman.'" *Folklore* 109:89–95.

Wilson, Robin. 1990. "Worried about 'Anything Goes' Moral Code, Colleges Are Stepping In to Help Students Shape Values." *Chronicle of Higher Education*, January 3, A1, A28.

Windham, Kathryn Tucker, and Margaret Gillis Figh. 1969. *13 Alabama Ghosts and Jeffrey*. Huntsville, Ala.: Strode.

Winger, Matt. 1975. "Methods of Cheating." Indiana University Folklore Archives.

Wise, James. 1977. "Tugging on Superman's Cape: The Making of a College Legend." *Western Folklore* 36:227–38.

Wiseman, Richard. 2007. *Quirkology: How We Discover the Big Truths in Small Things*. New York: Basic.

WKU [Western Kentucky University] Greek Affairs. 2009. "2009 Greek Week Schedule." http://www.wkugreeks.com/page.php?page_id=103314.

Wolcott, Maggie. 2003. "Truman's Ghost Stories." *Truman State University Index*, April 29. http://media.www.trumanindex.com/media/storage/paper607/news/2003/10/30/Trulife/Trumans.Ghost.Stories-542776.shtml.

Wolfe, Suzanne Rau. 1983. *The University of Alabama: A Pictorial History*. University: University of Alabama Press.

Wolfenstein, Martha. 1978 [1954]. *Children's Humor: A Psychological Analysis*. Bloomington: Indiana University Press.

Wolverton, Brad. 2011. "An Icon Falls and a President with Him." *Chronicle of Higher Education*, November 18, A1, 3–6.

Woodberry, Jazmine. 2010. "Campus Cultural Centers Celebrate Commencement." *Arizona Daily Wildcat*, May 12, B12, B14.

Woodside, Jane Harris. 2009. "Womanless Weddings." In *The New Encyclopedia of Southern Culture*. Vol. 14, *Folklife*, ed. Glenn Hinson and William Ferris, 379–82. Chapel Hill: University of North Carolina Press.

Woodward, Kenneth L. 1984. "The Lessons of the Master." *Notre Dame Magazine* (Notre Dame, Ind.) 13(2): 14–21.

Worthington, Chesley. 1965. "From the Folklore of Brown University." *Brown Alumni Monthly* (Brown University) 65(8): 52–57.

Wright, Lili. 2002. *Learning to Float: The Journey of a Woman, a Dog, and Just Enough Men*. New York: Broadway Books.

Wylie, Jeanne Porter. 1933. "Student Customs in the University of Arkansas." M.S. thesis, University of Arkansas.

Wyman, Walker D. 1979. "Academic or Campus Folklore." In *Wisconsin Folklore*, 81–91. River Falls: University of Wisconsin–Extension Department of Arts Development.

Xavier, G. F. Francis. 2004. *The World's Best Thought-Provoking Jokes*. New Delhi, India: Pustak Mahal.

Yale Daily News Staff. 1990. *The Insider's Guide to the Colleges*. New York: St. Martin's Press.

———. *Insider's Guide to the Colleges 2011: Students on Campus Tell You What You Really Want to Know*. New Haven, Conn.: Yale Daily News.

Yasinsac, Rob. 2000. "Briarcliff Lodge and King's College." HudsonValleyRuins.Org. http://www.hudsonvalleyruins.org/yasinsac/kingscollege/kingscollege.html.

Yeung, King-To, and Mindy Stombler. 2000. "Gay and Greek: The Identity Paradox of Gay Fraternities." *Social Problems* 47:134–52.

Yohe, Charles. 1950. "Observations on an Adolescent Folkway." *Psychoanalytic Review* 37:79–81.

Young, Frank W. 1962. "The Function of Male Initiation Ceremonies: A Cross-Cultural Test of an Alternative Hypothesis." *American Journal of Sociology* 67:379–96.

Young, Kristi A. 2005. "Now That I've Kissed the Ground You Walked On: A Look at Gender in Creative Date Invitations." *Marriage & Families* (Brigham Young University), March, 10–17.

Young, Paul. 2002. *L.A. Exposed: Strange Myths and Curious Legends in the City of Angels*. New York: St. Martin's Press.

Zekas, Joe. 2007. Post in response to "Law Professors and Knitting" by Christine Hurt. *Conglomerate*, April 23. http://www.theconglomerate.org/2007/04/law_professors_.html#c67404350.

INDEX